APPLIED C:
THE IBM®
MICROCOMPUTERS

APPLIED C:
THE IBM®
MICROCOMPUTERS

J. TERRY GODFREY

The MITRE Corporation
McLean, Virginia

and

The Johns Hopkins University
Continuing Professional Programs
GWC Whiting School of Engineering
Baltimore, Maryland

PRENTICE HALL, Englewood Cliffs, New Jersey 07632

Library of Congress Cataloging-in-Publication Data

Godfrey, J. Terry
    Applied C : the IBM microcomputers / J. Terry Godfrey
        p.   cm.
    Bibliography: p.
    Includes index.
    ISBN 0-13-039686-9 :
    1. IBM microcomputers--Programming. 2. C (Computer program
language)   I. Title.
QA76.8.I1015G62 1990
005.265--dc19   88-31642
                                                                 CIP

Editorial/production supervision and
  interior design: Kathleen Schiaparelli
Cover design: Wanda Lubelska
Manufacturing buyer: Mary Noonan

 © 1990 by Prentice-Hall, Inc.
A Division of Simon & Schuster
Englewood Cliffs, New Jersey 07632

TRADEMARK INFORMATION

IBM Personal Computer, DOS, OS/2, XT, AT, XT286, PC, Personal System/2 Model 30, Personal System/2 Model 50, Personal System/2 Model 60, Personal System/2 Model 80, PS/2, and Operating System/2 are trademarks and IBM is a registered trademark of International Business Machines Corporation.

Intel is a registered trademark of the Intel Corporation.

VEDIT is a trademark of Compuview Products, Inc.

Microsoft Windows, CodeView, and SYMDEB are trademarks and Microsoft is a registered trademark of the Microsoft Corporation.

Lattice is a registered trademark of Lattice, Inc.

Printed in the United States of America

10 9 8 7 6 5 4 3 2 1

ISBN 0-13-039686-9

Prentice-Hall International (UK) Limited, *London*
Prentice-Hall of Australia Pty. Limited, *Sydney*
Prentice-Hall Canada Inc., *Toronto*
Prentice-Hall Hispanoamericana, S.A., *Mexico*
Prentice-Hall of India Private Limited, *New Delhi*
Prentice-Hall of Japan, Inc., *Tokyo*
Simon & Schuster Asia Pte. Ltd., *Singapore*
Editora Prentice-Hall do Brasil, Ltda., *Rio de Janeiro*

To Judy

Contents

PREFACE   *xiii*

Part I Introductory C Programming

  1 INTRODUCTION   **1**

    1.1   The IBM Microcomputer Family   1
          1.1.1 PC and XT (8088), 3
          1.1.2 The Personal System/2 Model 30 (8086), 4
          1.1.3 XT286 and AT (80286), 4
          1.1.4 The Personal System/2 Models 50 and 60 (80286), 4
          1.1.5 The Personal System/2 Models 70 and 80 (80386), 5
          1.1.6 Microcomputer Hardware Features, 5

    1.2   The IBM C Programming Environment   7
          1.2.1 A Beginning C Program, 11
          1.2.2 Symbolic Debugging, 14
          1.2.3 The Equivalent Assembler Listing, 18
          1.2.4 QuickC and the MAKE Utility, 20
          1.2.5 Graphics: Versions 4.0 and 5.0, 21

    1.3   A Brief Review of C
          1.3.1 C Language Syntax, 22
          1.3.2 Functions, Structures, and Unions, 34

          Summary   42

          References   42

          Problems   43

2 PROGRAMMING EXAMPLES   50

2.1   Introduction   50

2.2   Beginning Program Examples   51
        2.2.1   Introductory Programs, 51
        2.2.2   Dow Jones Behavior, 63
        2.2.3   FM Spectra, 77
        2.2.4   Gaussian Random Numbers, 84

        Summary   95

        References   96

        Problems   96

3 SOFTWARE DESIGN AND C   98

3.1   Introduction   99
        3.1.1   Parameter Passing and the Stack, 99
        3.1.2   I/O Control and Architecture Structures, 102
        3.1.3   Size versus Complexity, 103
        3.1.4   Type Definitions, 104
        3.1.5   Iterative and Recursive Programming, 106
        3.1.6   Bitwise Operators, 107

3.2   Optimizing the C Design Process   110
        3.2.1   Top-down Design, 110
        3.2.2   Modular Programming, 114
        3.2.3   Structured Code, 117

3.3   Structured Techniques with C   119
        3.3.1   Module Exit Conditions, 119
        3.3.2   Templates, Style, and Form, 120
        3.3.3   Algorithm Development, 123
        3.3.4   Data Structures, 124

3.4   Software Testing and Debugging   125
        3.4.1   Complexity Metrics, 125
        3.4.2   Module Size, 126
        3.4.3   Software Drivers, 127
        3.4.4   Hierarchy of Modules, 127

3.5   Higher-level Design Concepts   127
        3.5.1   Abstraction and Information Hiding, 127
        3.5.2   Data Structure-oriented Design, 128
        3.5.3   Object-oriented Design, 128

        Summary   129

        References   129

        Problems   130

4   DOS, BIOS, AND LIBRARY SERVICES   134

4.1   DOS and BIOS Service Routines   135
   4.1.1   BIOS Interrupts, 138
   4.1.2   Interrupt 21H: DOS Function Calls, 139
   4.1.3   IBM Microcomputer Port Definition, 143

4.2   Interrupts and Services for the PS/2 Computers   145
   4.2.1   Model 30 BIOS Service, 146
   4.2.2   Model 50/60 BIOS Service, 146

4.3   Representative Programs   147
   4.3.1   Global Motion: The Bouncing Ball, 147
   4.3.2   Screen Buffer DMA and Sound, 160
   4.3.3   An Interval Timer, 169
   4.3.4   Time of Day, Date, and Memory Size, 170

4.4   The C Library   175
   4.4.1   Include Functions, 175
   4.4.2   Library Files, 177
   4.4.3   Three-dimensional Motion: The Rotating Cube, 185

Summary   197

References   198

Problems   199

Part II   Advanced Topics

5   C AND ASSEMBLY LANGUAGE   201

5.1   Programming in Assembly Language   202
   5.1.1   Segments, Offsets, and Program Structure, 202
   5.1.2   Addressing, Instructions, and Pseudo-ops, 207
   5.1.3   The Coprocessor, 226

5.2   Interfacing C and Assembly Language   235
   5.2.1   Passing Parameters, 235
   5.2.2   The Assembler Template, 236
   5.2.3   C Compiler Optimization, 238

5.3   C and Assembler   240

5.4   Memory Models   261

Summary   262

References   262

Problems   263

Contents

6 REAL-TIME PROGRAMMING WITH C   *266*

6.1   General Real-time Processing   267
        6.1.1   Hardware and Software Considerations, 268
        6.1.2   Implementation and Testing, 269
        6.1.3   Uniprocessor and Multitasking Systems, 270

6.2   The IBM Microprocessor Communications
        Interface   271
        6.2.1   IBM Adapter Hardware, 271
        6.2.2   Software for Communications, 277
        *6.2.3   A Typical Communications Driver: Hayes
                 Smartmodem 1200, 280*

6.3   An Extended Example: Analog-to-Digital (A/D)
        Conversion   289
        6.3.1   IBM Microcomputer A/D Adapters, 290
        6.3.2   Driver Software: Data Translation DT2828, 291

        Summary   304

        References   304

        Problems   305

Part III   Higher Levels of Abstraction

**7 COMPILER ENHANCEMENTS AND IBM
DISPLAY MODES**   *306*

7.1   Microsoft C Compiler Version 5.0
        Enhancements   307
        7.1.1   Syntax Changes, 307
        7.1.2   Invoking the Compiler and Linker, 308
        7.1.3   DOS and BIOS Additions, 309
        7.1.4   Graphic Primitives, 309
        7.1.5   Other Functions, 310

7.2   PS/2 Display Support   312

7.3   Additional Graphic Examples   312
        7.3.1   EGA Mode, 313
        7.3.2   VGA Mode, 315
        7.3.3   Structures Revisited, 317
        7.3.4   More on Modularity, 322
        7.3.5   Correlation Functions, 326
        7.3.6   Stock Market Forecasting, 336

7.4   Three-dimensional Surfaces   340
        7.4.1   Functions of Two Variables, 340
        7.4.2   A Simple Mathematical Example, 348

Summary   354

References   354

Problems   355

8   WINDOWS: AN INTEGRATED C ENVIRONMENT   **356**

8.1   Introduction to the Windows Software Development Kit
        (SDK)   356
        8.1.1   The Windows Template, 357
        8.1.2   Simple Beginning Examples, 359
        *8.1.3   Executing with the MS-DOS Presentation
                Manager: Windows 2.0, 377*

8.2   Windows SDK Program Architecture   378
        8.2.1   Windows as a Dynamic Framework, 378
        *8.2.2   Windows SDK Defined Functions: An Operational
                Protocol, 379*
        8.2.3   Implications of Multitasking, 379
        8.2.4   Initialization and Termination, 380

8.3   Windows SDK Program Components   380
        8.3.1   Window Functions, 381
        8.3.2   Graphics Device Interface (GDI) Functions, 386
        8.3.3   Windows Data Types and Superstructures, 390
        8.3.4   Messages, 394
        8.3.5   The Remaining Components, 394

8.4   Additional Windows Examples   395
        8.4.1   A Menu Program, 395
        8.4.2   Three-D Graphics, 400

        Summary   420

        References   420

        Problems   421

9   WINDOWS: A STRUCTURED METHODOLOGY   **423**

9.1   Windows I/O   423

9.2   Data Passing: The Clipboard   440

9.3   Text I/O   451

9.4   Printing with Windows   458

        Summary   473

        References   473

        Problems   474

Contents   **xi**

Part IV OS/2

10 THE OS/2 ENVIRONMENT 476

10.1 Architecture Considerations 476
  10.1.1 DOS Compatibility Mode and Protected Mode, 477
  10.1.2 Hardware Characteristics, 478
  10.1.3 Threads, Processes, and Protection, 482
  10.1.4 The Application Program Interface (API), 482
  10.1.5 Dynamic Linking, 483
  10.1.6 Debugging: CodeView, 489

10.2 Introductory Assembly Language Programming for OS/2, 489
  10.2.1 Creating, Assembling, and Linking, 490
  10.2.2 Function-calling Conventions, 490
  10.2.3 Getting Started, 492
  10.2.4 Protected Mode Screen Graphics, 494
  10.2.5 Multitasking, 499

10.3 Protected Mode and C Programming 510
  10.3.1 Protected Mode C Compiler, 511
  10.3.2 Simple Protected Mode C Programs, 512

  Summary 526

  References 526

  Problems 527

A THE FAST FOURIER TRANSFORM AND SPECTRAL ANALYSIS 529

B A SUMMARY OF C LANGUAGE SYNTAX 552

C PROGRAMS USED IN THIS TEXT 559

D SYSTEMS PROGRAMMING AND C 568

ANSWERS TO SELECTED ODD-NUMBERED PROBLEMS 580

INDEX 597

Preface

The goal of this book is to teach programming techniques rather than demonstrate operational software. Hence, the emphasis is on using systems-oriented programs (compilers, operating system calls, debuggers, linkers, and Windows) instead of applications such as spreadsheets or database managers. The material is of an advanced nature and is suitable for a course in C programming that assumes a basic familiarity with the language. It is also ideally suited to complement a beginning text with specific examples of the richness available to the C programmer.

Many of the graphics techniques are developed at a low level in the first seven chapters. This reflects the capability of earlier compilers (Microsoft Version 4.0). In addition, it provides the programmer with a grasp of the needed register interfaces to achieve graphics display handling. In Chapter 8, the Microsoft C Optimizing Compiler Version 5.0 enhancements are discussed. These enhancements illustrate examples using higher abstraction, when contrasted with the Version 4.0 code. In actuality, the graphics provided with the Version 5.0 primitives represent only slight simplifications of the routines developed using earlier techniques. Chapter 10 addresses the Microsoft C Optimizing Compiler Version 5.1 in an OS/2 context.

It is hoped that the reader will rapidly develop a grasp of the C language. At the same time, the needed interfaces in the IBM microcomputer environment are illustrated in order to achieve desirable special-purpose applications, such as the graphics display presentation and communications. The result of this effort is the generation of a set of mixed programs: some portable and some special purpose. Sufficient depth is presented in both cases to allow the reader to discern between portability and code with special-purpose structures. This is characteristic, for example, of the programming needed to achieve interfacing for microcomputer hardware, as we move into the fifth generation of computer systems.

How did this situation come about? With the advent of fourth-generation (1980–1990) computer technology, the dynamic growth in hardware capability outstripped software development. A great deal of variability entered the marketplace and hardware interfaces became fragmented. The search for an ultimate standardized language became more impractical. Development strategies altered, and the advent of serious artificial intelligence (AI) applications resulted in new directions for underlying concepts, such as compilers and operating systems.

C has been widely recognized as a very useful and elegant implementation within the microcomputer community. Certainly, it has many desirable features, not the least of which is its portability. Within C the user has access to virtually all levels of programming, from low-level I/O to high-level abstract mathematics. The language is quite flexible and, for example, permits operations at the bit level with simple instruction syntax. C also is a structured language, and this facilitates understanding and maintenance, as well as efficiency during the planning and development stages.

With the advent of IBM microcomputers, an effort was made to separate I/O services from other system software entities (the Basic Input Output System or BIOS code). OS/2 has further extended a form of standardization within the IBM environment by making newer (normally nonstandard) I/O accessible without requiring that special-purpose routines be developed by the programmer. Hence, the burden for many peripheral interfaces is shifting to the operating system. It is to be expected that increased standardization of system services will take place as operating systems become more universal. This, then, is the picture faced by programmers as we enter the 1990s. C can be expected to maintain a prominent place with more portability as special-purpose interfaces become standardized across the industry.

Outside the IBM microcomputer community, C is widely connected with the UNIX operating system developed at Bell Laboratories. IBM's chosen operating system for its microcomputers is OS/2 with DOS as a fall-back. IBM has based its product line on Intel microprocessors (the 8088, 8086, 80286, and 80386). An alternative class of microprocessors developed by Motorola, the 68000 family, and centered around the VME bus architecture has evolved. These systems have moved toward UNIX as the preferred operating system and also have standard as well as special-purpose C libraries. It is likely that both groups of microcomputers will exist for some time, and C code will only be portable in a general sense across these machines. (The special-purpose routines needed for graphics and other nonstandard hardware functions must be rewritten when code is ported from one class to another.)

With these thoughts in mind on the C language and its usefulness in the IBM microcomputer environment, consider the topics addressed in this book (with regard to the hardware and software discussed and illustrated). Table I presents these topics and their compatibility across the various modes available through the Intel microprocessors. Chapters 8, 9, and 10 deal with programming in the confines of Windows and OS/2. The basic C programming concepts are independent of operating system mode.

As discussed, there is a mix of code, emphasizing both the portable and nonportable, but extremely useful, aspects of programming C in the IBM microcomputer

TABLE I SOFTWARE AND HARDWARE TREATED IN THIS BOOK VERSUS MICROPROCESSOR MODE

Topic	Hardware/ Software	80286/80386 Only		Compatibility Mode Programming	Normal 8086 Mode
		Real Address Mode Programming	Protected Mode Programming		
PC/XT	H	—	—	—	×
XT286/AT	H	×	×	×	×
PS/2 Model 25	H	×	—	—	×
PS/2 Model 30	H	×	—	—	×
PS/2 Model 50/60	H	×	×	×	×
PS/2 Model 80	H	×	×	×	×
Microsoft C Compiler					
Version 4.0	S	×	—	×	×
Version 5.0	S	×	—	×	×
Version 5.1	S	×	×	×	×
Microsoft CodeView	S	×	—	×	×
Version 1.00	S	×	—	×	×
Version 2.10	S	×	×	×	×
IBM Macro Assembler					
Version 1.0	S	×	—	×	×
Version 2.0	S	×	—	×	×
Version /2	S	×	×	×	×
IBM DOS 3.x	S	×	—	—	×
IBM OS/2 Standard Edition (1.02)	S	×	×	×	×
Microsoft Windows Software Development Kit					
Version 1.03	S	×	—	×	—
Version 2.03	S	×	—	×	×
Microsoft Windows Presentation Manager					
Version 2.03	S	×	×	×	×
Microsoft Mouse (Inport)	H	×	×	×	×
Graphics Adapters					
Text (IBM)	H	×	×	×	×
CGA (Emulex IBM)	H	×	×	×	×
EGA (IBM)	H	×	×	×	—
VGA (IBM)	H	×	×	×	—
Displays					
Amdek 300G	H	×	×	×	×
Princeton Graphics (MAX-12)	H	×	×	×	×
IBM 8514 (PS/2) Other	H	×	×	×	×
Printers					
Epson MX-80 (F/T)	H	×	×	×	×
Epson FX-85	H	×	×	×	×
IBM (Other)	H	×	×	×	×

TABLE I *(Concluded)*

Topic	Hardware/ Software	80286/80386 Only		Compatibility Mode Programming	Normal 8086 Mode
		Real Address Mode Programming	Protected Mode Programming		
Data Translation (A/D)					
DT2828	H	×	—	×	×
DT707	H	×	—	×	×
Microsoft Symdeb					
Windows SDK	S	×	—	×	×
Support Software					
OS/2 Toolkit	S	×	×	×	×
WYSE Terminal					
Model 50	H	×	×	×	×
Intel					
AboveBoard 286 (2M)	H	×	×	×	×

environment. It is hoped that the C programmer using this book will acquire a good understanding of the IBM microcomputer interfaces. Within the IBM microcomputer world, a certain amount of ''special-purpose standardization'' exists through such include files as dos.h. The text presents this material in a fashion that readily demonstrates the connection between IBM hardware and requisite C code functions.

Throughout the book, there is an emphasis on modularity and, of course, structured code. Top-down design is highlighted and flow charts used as appropriate. It is intended that the serious student will grasp the importance of these techniques from both a theoretical and practical design viewpoint. The actual programming examples follow normal programming practice. From a style perspective, the variable definition tends to be slightly cryptic. Every effort has been made to make code easy to understand and follow. Compactness has only been implemented where time-sensitive programming is called for.

Within the text, graphics have been emphasized because visual output of information is becoming more important as microcomputer usage proliferates. This book presents most of the graphic output using the Color Graphics Adapter (CGA) mode 320 × 200. In Chapter 8, the Enhanced Graphics Adapter (EGA) mode 640 × 350 and the Video Graphics Adapter (VGA) mode 640 × 480 are discussed. Screen graphics are developed for the EGA and VGA modes and graphic output for the EGA mode is presented. In general, C is not taught as a course in most colleges and universities. This textbook is suited for an advanced formal course, self-help, or a supplement to an introductory course. Finally, the text is designed to provide insight into large-scale programming techniques (particularly modular approaches). Although the user would probably implement a Program Design language (PDL) treatment for design in the large-scale environment, flow charts are used as a substitute in this book because they are compact and the examples small scale, and they illustrate dynamic program behavior. The applications include some assembly language to illustrate how and when such interfaces can be used.

ACKNOWLEDGMENTS

During the course of writing this textbook, many people provided inputs to the writing process either through direct participation or indirect (and usually casual) asides. It is beyond the scope of these comments to recognize them all, however, we list a few who certainly provided major assistance. First, my wife, Judy, did all typing and a great deal of the editing. Second, Marcia Horton, Senior Editor at Prentice-Hall, was always available for questions and commentary, and Kathleen Schiaparelli did a superb job during the production phases. Steve Pequigney and Melissa Montgomery at Data Translation were very helpful in providing a DT2828 for the section on A/D converters. Nancy Bernhard provided the line drawings used throughout the text. Finally, thanks to the reviewers who helped mold the text into its present focus through their thoughtful remarks: Frank T. Gergelyi, Metropolitan Technical Institute and New Jersey Institute of Technology and Alan Filipski, GTX Corporation, Tempe, Arizona.

PART I
Introductory C Programming

1

Introduction

This is a text about programming with the C language in the IBM microcomputer environment. C is usually implemented as a high-level language independent from hardware considerations. In practice, however, each implementation includes special-purpose system routines that provide for the manipulation of a fixed class of computer peripheral hardware, such as the IBM microcomputer display graphics mode. These routines extend beyond the normal standard C modules, common to all C libraries. In this text we address both standard C library functions and special-purpose C modules unique to the IBM microcomputer circumstances. Hence, we include references to both the C language and IBM microcomputers in topical discussions about the book.

We generally assume some familiarity with C programming. The emphasis of the text is to implement C techniques for a broad class of problems. These problems are developed in the IBM microcomputer context. Part I encompasses introductory programming using the Microsoft C Compiler Version 4.0. Part II addresses mixed-language programming with assembler and real-time programming. Part III presents C environments with a more abstract or high-level flavor: the Microsoft C 5.0 Optimizing Compiler and Microsoft Windows. Finally, Part IV focuses on C in the context of IBM's Operating System/2.

1.1 THE IBM MICROCOMPUTER FAMILY

IBM has developed a set of microcomputers based on the Intel Corporation 8088, 8086, 80286, and 80386 microprocessor integrated circuits [1–6]. The 8088, 8086, and 80286 are 16-bit microprocessors and the 80386 is a 32-bit microprocessor. (The size of a microprocessor is determined by the length of its internal registers, as will be discussed shortly.) Associated with these microprocessors are coprocessor chips, which provide a high-speed floating point capability: the 8087, associated with the 8088 and 8086 [1, 2], the 80287, associated with the 80286 [3, 4], and the 80387, associated with the 80386 [7].

The 80286 is programmed in one of two modes: Real Address Mode or Protected Virtual Address Mode (Protected Mode, for short). In the Real Address Mode all source code developed for the 8088 and 8086 will execute. We should point out that this reference is to assembly language source code because C source code will be compiled independent of mode (since this dependency is principally an operating system function). All 80286 Real Address Mode source code is downward compatible to the 8088 and 8086 with minor exceptions. Clearly, C code operating in a Real Address Mode can be compiled to run on either an 8088/8086 or 80286-based system using, for example, the Microsoft C Compiler Version 4.0. The impact of the hardware mode will be transparent to the user. Within the confines of IBM Operating System/2 (OS/2), the Protected Mode will allow multitasking and requires modification to the compiled object code to accommodate such a configuration. C source code intended for the OS/2 Compatibility Mode is portable and will look the same as earlier Real Address Mode programming. Also, the 80286 has some additional assembly language instructions not found in the 8088/8086 world. The 80386 Real Mode is compatible with the Real Address Mode for the 80286. In addition, the 80386 has a Virtual 8086 Mode for running 8088/8086 code and, finally, the 80386 has its own Protected Mode which runs 80286 Protected Mode software as a subset.

Intel developed microprocessors (the 80286 and 80386) capable of operating in the Protected Mode primarily to facilitate multitasking operations. (Multitasking consists of operations that encompass more than one task or user simultaneously. It has individual task execution regulated under a set of priority constraints that are dynamic.) Prior to the development of these microprocessors, the 8088 and 8086 (all part of the 8086 Family) served as the basis for the Intel microcomputer microprocessor family. IBM developed its microcomputers around this Intel family of microprocessors and has historically offered the following systems:

IBM Personal Computer (8088): no longer available

IBM Personal Computer XT (8088): no longer available

IBM Personal Computer AT (80286): no longer available

IBM Personal Computer XT286 (80286): no longer available

IBM Personal Computer Jr. (8088): no longer available

IBM Personal Portable Computer (8088): no longer available

IBM Personal System/2 Model 25 (8086)

IBM Personal System/2 Model 30 (8086)

IBM Personal System/2 Model 50 (80286)

IBM Personal System/2 Model 60 (80286)

IBM Personal System/2 Model 80 (80386)

The purpose of the following subsections is to discuss briefly these systems in order to provide the reader with a framework from which to consider the IBM hardware. IBM has made their microcomputers downward compatible from a software viewpoint. Hence, this hardware discussion is only intended to illustrate the IBM system differences, not their performance differences.

1.1.1 PC and XT (8088)

These two systems were the first microcomputers offered by IBM [8]. Their system boards are similar. Each board contains (in addition to normal decoding logic and memory/memory logic), the following integrated circuits (ICs):

1. 8088: central processor unit (CPU)
2. 8087: coprocessor (if populated)
3. 8259A: programmable interrupt controller (PIC)
4. 8255A: programmable peripheral interface (PPI)
5. 8237A: direct memory access (DMA) controller
6. 8253: interval timer

These are all Intel chips. The 8259A is a chip that can be programmed to cause software to stop and save a program state and then "vector" to another routine in the code to perform an ancillary task (before resuming execution of the original task). Such shifting in program execution, or interrupting, is controlled by either hardware input signals or software calls. The 8255A allows the CPU to off-load tasks associated with interfacing peripheral equipment to the system and the 8237A provides a capability for direct memory-to-memory data transfers (or memory-to-I/O port transfers, and vice versa). These transfers are performed at high speed and facilitate moving large blocks of data around in memory. One very useful application is the transfer of data between memory and the display buffer. (The term buffer refers to local aggregates of small amounts of memory used to store variable amounts of data on an intermediate basis.) Finally, the 8253 is an on-board timer used to keep track of events in process during program execution.

The IBM PC and XT had several display modes available: a 25 × 80 line alphanumeric mode and two graphics modes, a 320 × 200 pel raster mode and a 640 × 200 pel raster mode. Both monochrome and color displays are supported. Aside from the monochrome adapter, which uses the alphanumeric mode, a color graphics adapter (CGA) board can be installed to provide graphics in color format (this generic CGA board also has an alphanumeric mode). Following the release of later systems an enhanced graphics adapter (EGA) standard developed that provided increased vertical resolution in the graphics display (640 × 350).

Many hardware adapters for the PC and XT contain hardware formats (such as addresses) that are compatible with later IBM microcomputer systems. We will find, on occasion, that it is useful to refer to PC, XT, and AT hardware architecture to illustrate in example fashion how various functions are achieved. IBM has provided extensive documentation on the PC, XT, and AT, and such illustrations can be presented with authority. These references serve as a basis for tying the hardware implementations to software.

1.1.2 The Personal System/2 Model 30 (8086)

The Model 30 replaces the PC and XT as IBM's low-end commercial microcomputer offering and is based on the 8086 processor (which has a 16-bit data bus instead of an 8-bit data bus, as found in the 8088 CPU) [9]. Both the 8086 and 8088 have 16-bit address buses. The PS/2 Model 30 runs under DOS 3.x and supports three graphics modes, as well as the usual text mode (8 × 16 character box): a graphics mode with 320 × 200 pixels and a mode with 640 × 200 pixels (the CGA modes) and a 640 × 480 pixel mode (pixel and pel refer to dot size on the screen and are used interchangeably). A new integrated graphics controller, the Multi Color Graphics Array (MCGA), is used to provide screen control. The Model 30 I/O bus supports six levels of interrupt, DMA, and memory refresh among other features. All software designed to run on the PC and XT will run on the Model 30 under DOS 3.x. The video subsystem is resident on the system board and the MCGA controller is a custom IC. Since the Model 30 does not support the concept of a Protected Mode, software employing physical address specification can be executed. The MCGA is more complex in format than the CGA subsystem. Disk I/O under program control has several new features over the PC and XT systems. The Model 30 has provision for a 20-Megabyte hard disk and controller.

The IBM microcomputer systems are equipped with a Basic Input Output System (BIOS), which resides in read only memory (ROM) and contains most of the low-level I/O service routines, which are callable based on software interrupts. The BIOS available in the Model 30 is compatible with the earlier IBM microcomputer systems. Some of these services, however, have additional features beyond the normal IBM PC/XT/AT subset.

1.1.3 XT286 and AT (80286)

The IBM PC AT system board uses some upgraded ICs for intelligent support (over those found on the PC and XT) [10]. The real-time clock is an Intel 88284, and the coprocessor is the 80287, a complement to the 80286 CPU. Two 8259As are employed, yielding 16 levels of interrupt. This system is also discontinued but can execute the OS/2 Protected Mode software because of its 80286 microprocessor and AT bus architecture. The XT286 is a cross between the XT (8088) and the AT (80286).

1.1.4 The Personal System/2 Models 50 and 60 (80286)

The Model 50 is a table-top system and the Model 60 is floor mounted [11]. Both employ the 80286 CPU. Each supports 16 levels of interrupt and multitasking via control bus arbitration. I/O is carried out on a new bus architecture: the Micro Channel I/O Bus. Display capability is provided by the new Video Graphics Array (VGA) standard with the following new modes:

1. 640 × 480 graphics
2. 720 × 400 alphanumeric

3. 360 × 400 16-color alphanumeric

4. 320 × 200 graphics with 256 colors

In addition, all modes on the IBM Monochrome, CGA, and IBM Enhanced Graphics Adapter (EGA) are supported. Unlike the earlier IBM systems with graphics adapters built around the Motorola 6845 Controller, the VGA display uses special-purpose IBM ICs to achieve a high-speed display interface based on digital-to-analog (DAC) conversion of the final video signal. The display update rate is significantly faster than in earlier systems. The VGA has four major components: a CRT (cathode ray tube) controller, a sequencer, the graphics controller, and an attribute controller.

The CRT controller generates horizontal and vertical synchronization, refresh, and timing signals. The sequencer regulates timing for video memory transfers. The graphics controller is the interface between the screen buffer (video memory) and the attribute controller, and this latter device generates the digital output to the DAC for display. Both systems support fixed disk operation with the Model 60 capable of 44-, 70-, or 115-megabyte disk operation.

1.1.5 The Personal System/2 Models 70 and 80 (80386)

The IBM PS/2 Models 70 and 80 employ the Intel 80386 microprocessor for their CPU. The Model 80 is floor mounted in a chassis similar to the Model 60. The 80386 is a 32-bit processor with most 32-bit registers divided into two 16-bit halves, enabling 16-bit 80286 software to run on the 80386. The Model 70 and 80 will run both DOS 3.3 and OS/2. They run 8088 and 8086 software under DOS 3.3 or the Compatibility Mode of OS/2.

1.1.6 Microcomputer Hardware Features

For the most part in C programming the user will not need to worry about low-level arithmetic such as the binary interpretation of an operation. Both integer and floating point arithmetic is performed transparently. During program debugging, however, the programmer will need to access variables in a variety of formats, and a hexadecimal representation frequently facilitates the bit-level examination of values. Also, an understanding of register value manipulation is essential to any assembly language correspondence.

Each intelligent chip in a microcomputer makes use of one or more registers to manipulate and hold data and address values. (For the time being the reader can assume an address value specifies a physical location in the computer.) Registers are simply storage devices internal to these chips and consist of transistor circuits ganged together to represent bytes (8 bits) and words (16 or 32 bits). In the 8088, 8086, and 80286, there are essentially 14 application registers (the 80286 has some additional registers for address specification): 12 general purpose, an instruction pointer, and a flags register. These registers have a specific Intel nomenclature, as follows:

AX (AH,AL)   Accumulator
BX (BH,BL)   Base

CX (CH,CL)	Count
DX (DH,DL)	Data
SP	Stack pointer
BP	Base pointer
SI	Source index
DI	Destination index
CS	Code segment
DS	Data segment
SS	Stack segment
ES	Extra segment
IP	Instruction pointer
SF	Status flags

When we address interfacing assembly language to C, we will be particularly concerned with these registers. Also, it is possible to directly access these registers from C, as will be illustrated later. At that time the reader will need to have developed an appreciation for these CPU registers. Basically, symbolic manipulation of these registers results in a direct manipulation of the hardware.

We have pointed out that C is a portable language and, consequently, brings a powerful tool to the microcomputer world. There are, however, aspects of microcomputer programming still best performed by using the basic register building blocks of the hardware. C is not portable with regard to this programming, and philosophically such programming should be minimized because it requires special knowledge beyond a general-purpose language understanding. Both maintenance and portability are strong considerations in this regard. Throughout this book both portable code (code that conceptually runs on any C compiler) and special-purpose code are mixed (code that only runs on IBM microcomputers). This is unfortunate but necessary, and Appendix C delineates some of the limitations of the various functions used.

Associated with any given microcomputer implementation are one or more bus structures. These structures consist of interconnecting wires that pass bits in parallel fashion. For example, wire A0 would carry the signal associated with bit 0 of the address word, wire A1 the signal associated with bit 1 of the address word, and so forth. In the IBM PC and XT, then, an address bus can be expected to consist of 20 parallel wires (for the 20 bits in the physical address, to be discussed shortly). Similarly, in the 80286-based systems, such as the AT with a 16-megabyte address capability, the address bus consists of 24 parallel wires. Since the PC and XT utilize 8-bit data structures, these microcomputers can be expected to have an eight-line data bus. The AT has a larger data bus because it manipulates data 16 bits at a time. The control bus is more fragmented.

Bits are grouped into bytes, 8 bits at a time. Memory is usually specified in bytes. Here 1024 bytes is usually specified as 1K byte and multiples of this are specified in K bytes. Each memory location is characterized by two parameters, a physical location or address and a value stored at that address. Hence, the need for an address bus and a data bus. In practice, signals on the address bus simply activate or select a given location and allow the contents of that location to be placed or latched onto the data bus.

Intel has structured its CPU chip internal address architecture to combine two quantities in order to obtain the final physical address in the 8088 and 8086. These quantities are the segment address and offset address and have their analog in the 80286 (and 80386) segment selector and offset. Each quantity is a 16-bit number, hence, offsets can specify up to a 64K block associated with a given segment. The final 8088 (or 8086) physical address is obtained by shifting the segment address left 4 bits, or one nibble, and adding this (with a zero in the least significant nibble) to the offset:

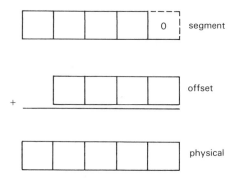

This, then illustrates the purpose of the segment registers: they hold the segment address value for data, code, stack, and extra segment areas.

In the 80286 and 80386, segments play a similar role, except descriptor tables have been added. The mapping of segment and offset addresses is no longer directly to physical locations in memory because a new dimension, time, is present with the multitasking capability. Hence, the operating system is left to resolve physical locations. Programs that specify actual physical locations, such as some of the screen direct memory access (DMA) routines used in this book must be rewritten to run under the 80286 Protected Mode where descriptor table registers reference such virtual memory locations.

In the C programming language, data values are specified through the usual type casting variable assignments. Address values can be manipulated symbolically through an artifact known as a pointer. Basically, a pointer has a value that specifies or points to an address. Throughout the Intel family, addresses can be thought of as specified by a segment and an offset; hence, compatibility exists for all IBM microcomputer addressing. The physical locations in memory can vary.

THE IBM C PROGRAMMING ENVIRONMENT

This book describes C. Associated with C programming are programs for generating machine instructions from the C source code: C compilers. We use the Microsoft C Compiler versions 4.0 and 5.0 [12–17] throughout this book. The version of C used as a basis for the Microsoft compilers is that of Kernighan and Ritchie [18]. This evolved from BCL, an earlier language [19]. To facilitate independent generation of separate modules, each source code module can be compiled, and the final totality of all resulting object modules (the compiled output) can be linked together using a program called a linker. We use Microsoft's linker throughout this text (this linker comes with the C compiler). At compile time, routines called but not present in a given module are treated as external and designated accordingly. The linker checks to make sure all these external modules are available at link time. Finally, debugging of code can be greatly facilitated through debugging programs. Some debuggers access software at the address level, DEBUG.EXE, while others use a more symbolic approach. Microsoft supplies such a symbolic debugger with its C compiler: CodeView.

Aside from the needed compilers, linkers, and debuggers, C programming requires an external operating system to serve as the framework for run-time implementation. We address two such operating systems appropriate to IBM microcomputers: Disk Operating System (DOS) 3.x (where x = 1, 2, or 3) and Operating System/2 (OS/2). DOS is the initial IBM offering and has a wide base of acceptance with the PC/XT/XT286/AT systems. OS/2 will run on the XT286/AT/(PS/2) families. Also, DOS 3.x will run on the PS/2 family. It is generally anticipated that both systems will be used for some years to come.

DOS executes in Real Address Mode on the 80286- and 80386-based microcomputers. It executes in native 8086 Mode on 8088- and 8086-based microcomputers. The multitasking feature enabled by the 80286 and 80386 Protected Modes can only be accessed via OS/2. OS/2 also has a Compatibility Mode intended to run 8088- or 8086-based programs or 80286 Real Address Mode programs, in lieu of the Protected Mode. Generally, switching modes requires that new compilers, linkers, and debuggers be implemented. While the generic C source code remains the same the language handling routines must change to accommodate operating system changes. Much of the programming illustrated in the book has been developed under DOS 3.3 and is fully compatible with this operating system concept.

The development of C source code is most easily accomplished using a programming editor. IBM provides such an editor, called EDLIN, with its DOS operating system [20]. This editor is referred to as a line editor because modifications must be made to an entire line at a time. Line editors are usually suited to languages that have short instructions such as an assembler. C, on the other hand, has a more involved instruction architecture, and it is desirable to be able to modify portions of the instruction line without redoing an entire line of code. Use of a screen editor is recommended in this case (screen editors are usually preferred over line editors because of their flexibility). A suitable screen editor, for example, is VEDIT, which has been developed by CompuView Products, Incorporated [21], and is the editor used to develop the programs in this book.

C compilers are characterized by support routines that are contained in include files or library files. Table 1.1 illustrates the include and library files that come with the Microsoft C compiler. As mentioned, many of these routines go by the standard C naming convention. The include files all have an extension .h and derive their name from the fact that they are attached to a program through the use of an instruction (which appears in the preprocessor) of the form

```
#include <....>
```

TABLE 1.1   MICROSOFT C COMPILER INCLUDE/LIBRARY FILES

File	Discussion
assert.h	Used to define assert (macro) to test (true/false) an expression.
conio.h	Contains function declarations for console/port I/O.
ctype.h	Defines macros, constants, manifest constants, and a global array used in character classification. Bit masks are defined for use with characters.
direct.h	Contains function declarations for directory control functions.
dos.h	Contains macros, function declarations, and type definitions for the DOS/BIOS interface and interrupt service routines.
errno.h	Defines the values returned by errno.
fcntl.h	Defines flags used by open( ) and sopen( ).
float.h	Has definitions of constants that specify ranges of floating point data types.
io.h	Function declarations for low-level I/O.
limits.h	Specifies ranges of integer and character data types.
malloc.h	Declares memory allocation functions.
math.h	Declares all floating point math functions.
memory.h	Contains function declarations for buffer-manipulation routines.
process.h	Declares all process control functions except signal( ).
search.h	Declares bsearch( ), lsearch( ), lfind( ), and qsort( ). These special-purpose functions are used in list manipulation.
setjump.h	Declares setjump( ) and longjmp( ) functions for manipulating the stack.
share.h	Defines flags used in sopen( ) to set the sharing mode of a file.
signal.h	Declares signal( ), which is used to control direction of program execution following interrupt or exception processing.
stdarg.h	Defines macros that provide for access to functions with variable-length argument lists.
stddef.h	Contains definitions for NULL, errno, ptrdiff_t and size_t.
stdio.h	Contains definitions of constants, macros, and types, plus the functions themselves for stream I/O. This includes ''standard'' I/O quantities.
stdlib.h	Contains function declarations for 29 special-purpose functions and declarations for a number of global variables.
string.h	Declares the string manipulation functions.
sys\locking.h	Contains definitions of flags used in calls to locking( ). Controls locking (the ability to read and write) of all or portions of a file.
sys\stat.h	Defines the structure type returned by fstat( ) and stat( ). These functions obtain information about file status (date last modification and the like).
sys\timeb.h	Defines timeb structure type and declares ftime( ). This function gets the current time.
sys\types.h	Defines types used by system-level calls to return file status and time information.
sys\utime.h	Defines the utimbuf structure and declares utim( ). Sets the modification time for a file.
time.h	Declares the time functions.

TABLE 1.1 *(Concluded)*

File	Discussion
varargs.h	Defines macros for accessing arguments in functions with variable-length argument lists.
v2tov3.h	Allows users with version 2.03 and earlier of the Microsoft C compiler to use existing library calls in their earlier source code.
SLIBC.LIB	Small-model standard C library
SLIBFP.LIB	Small-model floating point math library
SLIBFA.LIB	Small-model alternate math library
MLIBC.LIB	Medium-model standard C library
MLIBFP.LIB	Medium-model floating point math library
MLIBFA.LIB	Medium-model alternate math library
CLIBC.LIB	Compact-model standard C library
CLIBFP.LIB	Compact-model floating point math library
CLIBFA.LIB	Compact-model alternate math library
LIBH.LIB	Model-independent code-helper library
LLIBC.LIB	Large-model standard C library
LLIBFP.LIB	Large-model floating point math library
LLIBFA.LIB	Large-model alternate math library
EM.LIB	Model-independent emulator floating point library
87.LIB	Model-independent 8087/80287 floating point library

To include the standard I/O handling routines, for example, it is necessary to have the following statement in the preprocessor:

```
#include <stdio.h>
```

In addition to the include and library files, the Microsoft C compiler comes with a number of executable files. These encompass the compiler control programs and a symbolic debugger called CodeView. The compiler files employ the standard

TABLE 1.2 MICROSOFT C COMPILER EXECUTABLE FILES

File	Discussion
msc.exe	Compiler control program.
c1.exe	Compiler preprocessor and language parser used in pass 1.
c2.exe	Compiler code generator used in pass 2.
c3.exe	Compiler optimizer, link text emitter, and assembly-listing generator used in pass 3.
cv.exe	Microsoft CodeView window-oriented symbolic debugger
exemod.exe	Microsoft EXE file header utility
exepack.exe	Microsoft EXE file compression utility
lib.exe	Microsoft library manager
make.exe	Microsoft program maintenance utility
setenv.exe	Microsoft environment expansion utility
link.exe	Microsoft overlay linker
cl.exe	Alternate control program for the compiler

TABLE 1.3 DIFFERENCES AMONG MEMORY MODELS

Model	Number of Allowed Segments
Small	1 Code, 1 data, 1 stack
Medium	1 Code per module, 1 data, 1 stack
Compact	1 Code, 1 default data,[a] 1 stack
Large	1 Code per module, 1 default data,[a] 1 stack
Huge	1 Code per module, 1 default data,[a] 1 stack

[a] Additional data segments may be defined depending on program requirements.

C nomenclature, and the debugger is a special separate entity intended for use with linked C code. Table 1.2 illustrates these files. Also illustrated in Table 1.2 are some additional object modules that can be used for optimizing program execution. As the table descriptions indicate, files have been developed for several programming options based on the size of available memory. The compiler has support routines tailored to small, compact, medium, large, and huge memory allocations. Table 1.3 illustrates some of the differences among these models.

1.2.1 A Beginning C Program

It was suggested earlier that it is appropriate to introduce the subject of C programming with an example. This will provide a basis for illustrating the mechanics of how one goes about preparing a C program in the IBM environment. Figure 1.1a presents a listing of the program firstc.c (the first C program appearing in this book), which is located in directory C. There are 13 nonblank lines of code appearing in this program. The first nonblank line is simply a comment that describes the purpose of the program. Comments are delineated as follows in C programs:

```
/* . . . */
```

In this expression, the construct /* is used to set off the beginning of the comment, and */ indicates the termination of the comment. Next comes the preprocessor area, which contains all the include and define statements appearing in this program. Following the preprocessor area, is the actual executable code, which consists of a single function, main(). The C language always requires a function with the name main as the very first executable routine. Returning to the preprocessor, the first statement is simply the include described previously (this statement attaches the standard I/O library). Next are three define statements. The first two statements define constant identifiers. The format of these statements is

```
#define IDENTIFIER value
```

Here IDENTIFIER has been capitalized to indicate that it represents a working constant. The capitalization makes identification easy in the subsequent code. In the example, two define statements have initialized the constant identifiers MESSAGE1 and MESSAGE2 to be character strings by using quotation marks. These strings are used in the program as messages to be printed to the screen. The system I/O function, printf(), is executed for this purpose.

```
/* This program reads and calculates the cube of "x" */

#include <stdio.h>
#define MESSAGE1 "Input integer value magnitude less than 32"
#define MESSAGE2 "Cube = "
#define CUBE(x) (x * x * x)                    /* MACRO. Cube of "x" */

main()
        {

        int x;

        printf("%s\n",MESSAGE1);        /* Print request message */
        scanf("%d",&x);                 /* Input integer value */
        x = CUBE(x);                    /* Calculate cube of x */
        printf("%s %d\n",MESSAGE2,x);   /* Output cube value*/


        }
```

Figure 1.1a   Program firstc.c that calculates the cube of an input quantity.

```
msc \c\firstc.c/Zi
Microsoft (R) C Compiler  Version 4.00
Copyright (C) Microsoft Corp 1984, 1985, 1986.  All rights reserved.

Object filename[firstc.OBJ]:
Source listing [NUL.LST]:
Object listing [NUL.COD]: firstc

<C:\>link firstc/CO
Microsoft (R) Overlay Linker  Version 3.51
Copyright (C) Microsoft Corp 1983, 1984, 1985, 1986.  All rights reserved.

Run File [FIRSTC.EXE]:
List File [NUL.MAP]:
Libraries [.LIB]:

<C:\>firstc
Input integer value magnitude less than 32
30
Cube =  27000

<C:\>firstc
Input integer value magnitude less than 32
5
Cube =  125
```

Figure 1.1b   Interactive session illustrating compiling, linking, and execution for firstc.c.

The last define statement is slightly more complex. This statement assigns an operation to an identifier with a parameter list. The form of this statement is as follows:

```
#define IDENTIFIER(parameter-list) text
```

In the program example, the IDENTIFIER is CUBE (for computing the cube) and the parameter-list is merely x. Here x is the symbol for the value that will be cubed. This statement uses ((x)*(x)*(x)) for "text," which symbolically calculates the cube of x using the multiplication operation denoted by the operator *. When CUBE appears in the subsequent code, it will be replaced by the text at compile time. This statement defines the *macro* CUBE(x). Here macro denotes an IDENTIFIER that is used to replace or expand code at compile time by substituting the actual text directly into the source code during pass 1 of the compiler.

Following the preprocessor area is the function main( ), mentioned earlier. All C functions are characterized by a name and a set of opening and closing parentheses, which may or may not contain parameters. In the example, the function is main( ), which is the only function encountered. The function code is delimited by script braces of the form { . . . }:

```
main( )
{

    . . .

}
```

The ellipsis contains the actual function code. In Figure 1.1a, the function main prints a message to the screen, which requests the user to input an integer number less than 32. The program accomplishes this by using the output routine, printf( ). The arguments appearing in this function use the identifier %s to indicate a string is to be output. The escape sequence, \n, indicates that a new line should be generated following output of the string. The fact that these items are enclosed in quotation marks indicates that they comprise a character string and should be treated as such by the compiler. Hence the sequence

```
"%s\n"
```

indicates that a string is to be output followed by a carriage return and line feed. The actual string to be output is MESSAGE1, which has been specified earlier in the preprocessor directives.

Next the reply from the user is read from the keyboard using the input function, scanf( ). In the program, scanf( ) has the argument list

```
"%d",&x
```

Here the character string (in quotations) indicates that a decimal integer will be read in. It will be stored at the *address of* x as indicated by the ampersand, &. Basically, each variable has a value and an address. The scanf( ) function requires that the input quantity be stored in a variable whose address must be specified, not the variable itself. The printf( ) function differed from this in that the variable name was specified rather than the address of the variable. The address operator & returns the address of a variable when allowed to operate on this variable. For example, the quantity

```
&x_value
```

returns the address of the variable x_value. This address always corresponds to the starting byte for the variable. If the variable is an integer, it consists of 2 bytes of data and the first byte of storage is the address specified by the & operator. (In the IBM microcomputers, integer data are stored in reverse order, least significant byte first, hence the address operator specifies the position of this least significant byte.)

Once the input quantity is read in it is then cubed using the macro CUBE. Finally, the cubed value is output using the printf() function again. In this second call of printf( ), two identifiers are used in the character string, indicating that two variables will be output: in this case, a message and the cubed input value. As part of the input request, the integer was specified to be less than 32. This is because x was defined as being of type int. Since this integer is signed, it can never exceed a magnitude of 32,767 (one less than 2 raised to the 15 power). The cube root of 32,767 rounded to the nearest integer is 32; thus, a limit of 32 was placed on the input values. Later we will consider other types of variables and larger ranges will be appropriate. The very first statement appearing in the function main() was the type specifier for x:

```
int x
```

Figure 1.1b illustrates the steps necessary to compile, link, and execute the program firstc. The Microsoft C compiler is executed using the MSC command followed by a filename. Had the filename been omitted, the compiler would have prompted the user for a source file. In the figure, the file input to the compiler is firstc.c, which is located on the C drive. The Zi option is specified for this compiler, and this causes the object file to be produced with full symbolic debugging information for use by the Microsoft CodeView symbolic debugger. We will consider symbolic debugging in the next section. Following the MSC command, the compiler indicates the default object file, source listing file, and object listing file. These can be changed by specifying an alternate name after each prompt. The NUL filename indicates that no file is to be generated.

Once the file is compiled, it must be linked. The Microsoft linker is called in much the same fashion as the compiler. The CO option indicates that the linked output file will be in a format for use by CodeView. The linker assumes as input the object file, in this case firstc.obj. It creates a run file with extension exe and a list file with extension MAP. Any routines that exist in the user's libraries and are needed by the object module must be included at the Libraries prompt. The default extension for these libraries is LIB; however, the user can have other library extensions provided these extensions are specified at link time. Finally, the figure illustrates an example of execution of the file firstc.exe. In this case, the value 3 was input to the prompt and its cube calculated.

1.2.2 Symbolic Debugging

Microsoft has a symbolic debugger called CodeView [14], as previously mentioned. A symbolic debugger can be used to execute a program under test and watch the variables and parameters of the program change at each stage of execution. Also, many other features of the program can be observed during execution of each line of code. CodeView has an option that will allow the user to change from C code to the actual assembled instructions used to replace the C instructions. These assembler instructions can be further executed a line at a time as in a normal debug operation using IBM's debugger, DEBUG. The term symbolic refers to the fact that symbols such as variable names can be specified to CodeView and the program will, for example, report the value of these symbolic quantities at each point during the debug execution. Those readers familiar with conventional debuggers, such as DE-BUG, will recall that variables must be monitored using their address in memory, rather than symbolically following the variable by simply specifying its name. Perhaps the easiest approach to understanding a symbolic debugger is to consider an example.

Figure 1.2a and b illustrates the execution of CodeView for the program firstc.exe. In Figure 1.2b, the screen output is also illustrated. This output demonstrates that the call to CodeView is

```
cv firstc.EXE
```

Once executed, CodeView loads the exe file and positions the line pointer at the end of the overhead code and prior to the actual compiled program code. The output illustrates the display window and the dialog window. The former contains the displayed source code, and the latter is located below this window and used for inputting commands to CodeView. In Figure 1.2a, the display window contains the entire program firstc.exe. By implementing the Watch function, the Watch window can be defined as in Figure 1.2b. Here the variable x has its value returned in the Watch window. By now the advantage of a symbolic debugger is probably becoming clear. In the case of CodeView, the user can toggle between CodeView screens and the output screen using one of the function keys. Another function key causes the program to execute a line at a time. In Figure 1.2b, the first executable statement in firstc.exe has been executed, and the debugger is positioned at the input statement, which uses scanf( ). Note that the value of x is 25. This value has no meaning in terms of the program because x has not been initialized.

Figure 1.3a illustrates execution of the next statement. Here the integer 3 has been input to the program. Also, the value of x displayed in the Watch window is now in agreement with the input value. Figure 1.3b presents the equivalent assembler code that applies at this point in the execution. This assembler display can be reached by toggling a function key. Superimposed on the assembler is the C source code from which the assembler has been derived. In Figure 1.4, the cubed value and output message have been executed, and the line pointer is at the bottom of the program. The output screen indicates that the squared value and output message have been displayed.

CodeView is a very useful symbolic debugger, as the reader has no doubt decided. We will rely heavily on the use of symbolic debugging to validate programs during development. These debuggers greatly enhance the capability to find and correct errors during the program development process. Each manufacturer has a recommended symbolic debug package that goes with the corresponding compiler. It is necessary that the reader obtain the debugger appropriate to his or her compiler.

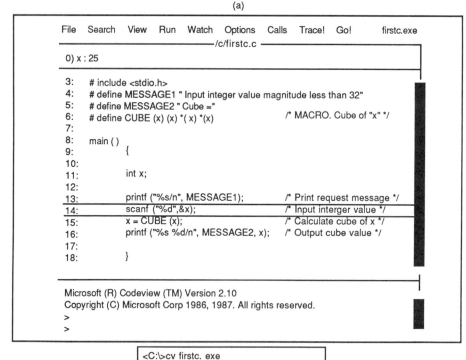

Figure 1.2 Use of CodeView with firstc.c illustrating (a) initialization and (b) execution of the first output message. (Courtesy of the Microsoft Corporation.)

```
File    Search   View   Run   Watch   Options   Calls   Trace!   Go!        firstc.exe
                              ─────── /c/firstc.c ───────
 0) x : 25

   3:    # include <stdio.h>
   4:    # define MESSAGE1 " Input integer value magnitude less than 32"
   5:    # define MESSAGE2 " Cube ="
   6:    # define CUBE (x) (x) *( x ) *(x)          /* MACRO. Cube of "x" */
   7:
   8:    main ( )
   9:            {
  10:
  11:            int x;
  12:
  13:            printf ("%s/n", MESSAGE1);          /* Print request message */
  14:            scanf ("%d",&x);                    /* Input interger value */
  15:            x = CUBE (x);                       /* Calculate cube of x */
  16:            printf ("%s %d/n", MESSAGE2, x);    /* Output cube value */
  17:
  18:            }


 Microsoft (R) Codeview (TM) Version 2.10
 Copyright (C) Microsoft Corp 1986, 1987. All rights reserved.
 >
 >
```

(a)

```
File    Search   View   Run   Watch   Options   Calls   Trace!   Go!        firstc.exe
                              ─────── /c/firstc.c ───────
 0) x : 3

  15:              x= = CUBE (x);                   /* Calculate cube of x */
  4324:0035 8B46FE             MOV   AX, Word Ptr [x]
  4324:0038 F7E8               IMUL  AX
  4324:003A F76EFE             IMUL  Word Ptr [x]
  4324:003D 8946FE             MOV   Word Ptr [x], AX
  16:              printf ("%s %d/n", MESSAGE2,x);  /* Output cube value*/
  4324:0040 50                 PUSH  AX
  4324:0041 B86800             MOV   AX,0068
  4324:0044 50                 PUSH  AX
  4324:0045 B87000             MOV   AX,0070
  4324:0048 50                 PUSH  AX
  4324:0049 F8C700             CALL  _printf (0113)
  4324:004C 83C406             ADD   SP,+06
  18:              }
  4324:004F 8BE5               MOV   SP, BP
  4324:0051 5D                 POP   BP


 Microsoft (R) Codeview (TM) Version 2.10
 Copyright (C) Microsoft Corp 1986, 1987. All rights reserved.
 >
 >
```

(b)

Figure 1.3. CodeView execution (a) illustrating an input of 3 in the Watch Window and (b) the assembly code for generating the cube activity. (Courtesy of the Microsoft Corporation.)

```
 File   Search   View   Run   Watch   Options   Calls   Trace!   Go!        firstc.exe
                              ────────/c/firstc.c ────────────────────────────────┐
 0) x : Unknown symbol                                                             │
                                                                                   │
   3:     # include <stdio.h>                                                      │
   4:     # define MESSAGE1 " Input integer value magnitude less than 32"
   5:     # define MESSAGE2 " Cube ="
   6:     # define CUBE (x) (x) *(x) *(x)              /* MACRO. Cube of "x" */
   7:
   8:     main ( )
   9:              {
  10:
  11:              int x;
  12:
  13:              printf ("%s/n", MESSAGE1);          /* Print request message */
  14:              scanf ("%d",&x);                    /* Input interger value */
  15:              x = CUBE (x);                       /* Calculate cube of x */
  16:              printf ("%s %d/n", MESSAGE2, x);    /* Output cube value */
  17:
  18:              }
  ────────────────────────────────────────────────────────────────────────────
 Microsoft (R) Codeview (TM) Version 2.10
 Copyright (C) Microsoft Corp 1986, 1987. All rights reserved.
 >
 >
```

```
<C:\>cv firstc. exe
Input integer value magnitude less than 32
3
Cube = 27
```

Figure 1.4 CodeView completion illustrating the output screen. (Courtesy of the Microsoft Corporation.)

1.2.3 The Equivalent Assembler Listing

In Figure 1.1a, an output listing file was specified with extension COD. This listing contains the equivalent assembler code for the program firstc.c. The presence of an asterisk in the title of this section indicates that this discussion depends to some degree on an understanding of assembly language for the IBM microcomputers [22]. We will explore assembler in more detail in Chapter 5; however, this material is not necessary for an understanding of the C language and is primarily included for the benefit of those readers with an assembler background. Also, the assembler equivalent of the C source code is illuminating with regard to how the code actually executes on the IBM microcomputers. Figure 1.5 illustrates this file.

One of the first pseudo-ops that is encountered in this routine is the 80287 coprocessor pseudo-op, .287. This tells the compiler that an 80287 coprocessor is installed in the host computer (in this case an IBM AT). The code segment in the small model, which is being used for these examples, is denoted by the label __TEXT. Similarly, the data segment is denoted by __DATA. These segments are the only ones of their type that appear in the small model programs, and the code segment, for example, never exceeds 64K; hence no need exists to add additional segments to the assembled code. In the larger models, multiple code segments are

```
;       Static Name Aliases
;
        TITLE    firstc
;       NAME     \c\firstc.c

        .287
_TEXT   SEGMENT  BYTE PUBLIC 'CODE'
_TEXT   ENDS
_DATA   SEGMENT  WORD PUBLIC 'DATA'
_DATA   ENDS
CONST   SEGMENT  WORD PUBLIC 'CONST'
CONST   ENDS
_BSS    SEGMENT  WORD PUBLIC 'BSS'
_BSS    ENDS
$$SYMBOLS        SEGMENT  BYTE PUBLIC 'DEBSYM'
$$SYMBOLS        ENDS
$$TYPES SEGMENT  BYTE PUBLIC 'DEBTYP'
$$TYPES ENDS
DGROUP  GROUP    CONST, _BSS, _DATA
        ASSUME   CS: _TEXT, DS: DGROUP, SS: DGROUP, ES: DGROUP
EXTRN   __chkstk:NEAR
EXTRN   _printf:NEAR
EXTRN   _scanf:NEAR
_DATA      SEGMENT
$SG62   DB       'Input integer value magnitude less than 32', 00H
$SG63   DB       '%s', 0aH, 00H
$SG64   DB       '%d', 00H
$SG65   DB       'Cube = ', 00H
$SG66   DB       '%s %d', 0aH, 00H
_DATA      ENDS
_TEXT      SEGMENT
; Line 9
        PUBLIC  _main
_main   PROC NEAR
        *** 000000   55                      push     bp
        *** 000001   8b ec                   mov      bp,sp
        *** 000003   b8 02 00                mov      ax,2
        *** 000006   e8 00 00                call     __chkstk
;       x = -2
; Line 13
        *** 000009   b8 00 00                mov      ax,OFFSET DGROUP:$SG62
        *** 00000c   50                      push     ax
        *** 00000d   b8 2b 00                mov      ax,OFFSET DGROUP:$SG63
        *** 000010   50                      push     ax
        *** 000011   e8 00 00                call     _printf
        *** 000014   83 c4 04                add      sp,4
; Line 14
        *** 000017   8d 46 fe                lea      ax,[bp-2]        ;x
        *** 00001a   50                      push     ax
        *** 00001b   b8 2f 00                mov      ax,OFFSET DGROUP:$SG64
        *** 00001e   50                      push     ax
        *** 00001f   e8 00 00                call     _scanf
        *** 000022   83 c4 04                add      sp,4
; Line 15
        *** 000025   8b 46 fe                mov      ax,[bp-2]        ;x
        *** 000028   f7 e8                   imul     ax
        *** 00002a   f7 6e fe                imul     WORD PTR [bp-2]  ;x
        *** 00002d   89 46 fe                mov      [bp-2],ax        ;x
; Line 16
        *** 000030   50                      push     ax
        *** 000031   b8 32 00                mov      ax,OFFSET DGROUP:$SG65
        *** 000034   50                      push     ax
        *** 000035   b8 3a 00                mov      ax,OFFSET DGROUP:$SG66.
        *** 000038   50                      push     ax
        *** 000039   e8 00 00                call     _printf
        *** 00003c   83 c4 06                add      sp,6
; Line 18
        *** 00003f   8b e5                   mov      sp,bp
        *** 000041   5d                      pop      bp
        *** 000042   c3                      ret

_main   ENDP
_TEXT   ENDS
END
```

Figure 1.5 Assembly language equivalent file firstc.cod.

allowed, and the 64K limit no longer applies to program size. The external library routines __chkstk, __printf, and __scanf are all called from __TEXT and are, consequently, NEAR calls. The Microsoft C compiler collects the segments __BSS, CONST, and __DATA as part of the group DGROUP. This group is referenced from the overhead code, and DGROUP serves as the starting address label for this group.

In the data segment, each character string is specified in single quotation marks, the assembler delimiters for character strings. All new-line characters are replaced by the byte 0AH, which is the ASCII equivalent to the line feed character (the carriage return is automatically put in by each call to printf or scanf). Finally, all data values are terminated by the null character, 00H.

The function main( ) is represented as a NEAR procedure, which is PUBLIC with the name __main. The library routines mentioned previously must be set up using the AX register. As indicated in the assembler instructions for source code lines 9, 13, and 14, the appropriate messages and data variables are specified in terms of their addresses and then pushed onto the stack, prior to calling each of the system routines. The actual cubing operation occurs with the instructions

```
mov ax,[bp-2]
imul ax
imul WORD PTR[bp-2]
mov [bp-2],ax
```

Here the variable value stored at address [bp-2] is loaded into ax and an integer multiply of ax with itself performed. The result is then stored and multiplied again. The reader should not be concerned at this time with the significance of the address specified by the base pointer, bp. We will describe in detail how the compiler passes parameters via the stack in Chapter 3. In describing the register convention, we will generally use capital letters to denote register names, such as AX and BX. Since the compiler uses lowercase letters, it will be assumed that this convention applies to specific examples of code (where ax is used, for example, to refer to the AX register).

In Figure 1.5, the final code appearing after the cubing operation simply sets up and calls the __printf procedure. The entry base pointer value is reloaded into bp and the return call made. This bp value is used to obtain an offset for the NEAR return to DOS. By now it is also clear that the compiler adds the underline, __, to the beginning of function names when turning these functions into procedures. Care should be used when naming functions because the underline character at the beginning of a procedure can result in a possible conflict with some library routines that employ a double underline.

1.2.4 QuickC and the MAKE Utility

As part of the Version 5.0 enhancements, Microsoft has provided a user-friendly C compiler and linker environment called QuickC. This environment has its own editor, debugger, compiler, and linker, which are menu driven and respond rapidly to user input. We do not intend to discuss the features of QuickC in detail but merely point to this implementation as very easy to use. It displays all the attributes of the larger more professional compiler/linkers embodied in Versions 4.0 and 5.0.

All the Microsoft compilers come with a system utility called MAKE. This utility receives as input a source file in batch format, which contains combinations of compiler directives, followed by source files to be compiled, and link directives, which are followed by object files to be linked. Depending on whether the Version 4.0 or Version 5.0 compiler is used, for example, the compile options will vary. The link option, however, will remain the same across both compilers. In Appendix C, the content of the MAKE files for each program in this book is indicated. These files indicate the link option only, in most cases.

1.2.5 Graphics: Versions 4.0 and 5.0

The definition of system software is quite dynamic in the microcomputer area. During the writing of much of this text an emphasis on the Microsoft C Compiler Version 4.0 has been assumed. Several graphics functions are developed to accomplish primitive graphics operations:

SCRCL( )	Clear screen
SC320( )	Set 320 × 200 CGA mode
SC80( )	Set text mode
WRDOT( )	Write dot at (x,y)

Routines for generating lines and curves based on these functions are then developed. Each of these functions is based on the use of a low-level call to INT 10H, the video control interrupt, which is accessible using the C library function, int86( ). Hence, a clear understanding of how screen graphics are generated in the IBM environment is possible. These arguments illustrate system-level programming considerations in the IBM framework.

With the advent of Version 5.0, Microsoft has provided an additional graphics library with the include file, graph.h. This file contains a number of graphics primitives that accomplish composite screen operations. For example, the function __lineto( ) can be used to generate a straight line. The parallel between a low-level formulation and the more abstract implementation of Version 5.0 is clear. Hence, in Chapter 8 the high-level syntax equivalence is adopted for the graphic routines developed earlier (in low-level form). Functionally, these routines are equivalent and this approach provides the reader with a grasp of the low-level implementation.

1.3 A BRIEF REVIEW OF C

We have implicitly assumed that the reader of this book has an elementary grasp of the C language. Also, we assume he or she is interested in learning about more advanced concepts (as discussed earlier) in the IBM microcomputer environment. That is not to say, however, that the novice cannot understand the material being presented here. Languages are like most other disciplines; exposure and persistence frequently pay off in the form of new ideas and insights. Hence, the beginner who has a rudimentary grasp of C syntax will see many applications of potential interest here. We encourage such individuals to examine the programming examples with regard to modularity and other aspects of program development (see, for example, the concepts presented in Chapter 2).

With these thoughts in mind, it is appropriate to review briefly the conventional C syntax and program architecture constraints. In the next two sections, each of these topics is addressed. The emphasis is on review, not a deeper discourse.

1.3.1 C Language Syntax

Both syntax and logic will be covered in this section. The logic associated with conditional structures and loops serves as the basis for implementing structured coding concepts, while the subdivision of code into functions leads to modular programming. Throughout this book, these aspects of programming will be emphasized. C is a language that makes structured code and modular programming easily feasible, and this promotes program development from a top-down approach.

Data types and operators. C is a typed language, and all variables and constants belong to one of several categories:

int	signed int, signed short int, signed long int, unsigned int, unsigned short int, unsigned long int
char	signed char, unsigned char
float	long float (also denoted as double)
other	void

Table 1.4 illustrates each of the basic data types and their length.

So far we have not actually defined how the type declaration is inserted in source code statements. The placement of a type declaration must precede actual use of the typed variable. Generally, it is useful and considered good form to put all type definitions at the beginning of the program module or routine (function). This localizes the variable declarations and ensures correct declaration. A typical set of declarations might be

```
. . .
int n,m1,NN,count;
float xarray[],alpha,beta,gamma;
. . .
```

Here the variables n, m1, NN, and count have been declared of type integer. Similarly, alpha, beta, and gamma are declared of type float, and an array of variables, xarray[], has also been declared of type float. Arrays are specified blocks of consecutive memory locations that can be addressed using indexes. For example,

```
xarray[0]
```

is the first element of the array and

```
xarray[i]
```

TABLE 1.4 THE C DATA TYPES

Data types	Characteristic	Discussion	Structure
int	Integer	This data type is 16-bit with 2's complement arithmetic used to represent negative numbers. If the first numeral of an integer constant is 0, it is octal. An integer beginning with ''0x'' is hexadecimal. Range: ($-32,768$ to $32,767$)	(16-bit field, bits 15 … 0)
short	Integer	This data type is identical to int for the IBM microcomputers.	(16-bit field, bits 15 … 0)
long	Integer	This data type is the same as int except it spans 4 bytes and has an approximate range of -2.14×10^9 to 2.15×10^9.	(32-bit field, bits 31 … 0)
unsigned	Integer	This data type is used as a modifier to int, short, or long to indicate that the most significant bit (MSB) should not be treated as a sign bit. The ranges are: Unsigned int (0 to 65,535) Unsigned short (0 to 65,535) Unsigned long (0 to 4.29×10^9)	See previous integer types
char	Integer	This data type is used as an ASCII equivalent integer to represent members of the standard (in this case IBM) character set. Each character is represented by a byte quantity; hence there can only be 256 characters per set.	(8-bit field, bits 7 … 0)
float	Floating point	This data type is 32-bit (4 bytes) and can be used to represent decimal values. The range of numbers if approximately -10^{38} to 10^{38}. In the structure, E7 to E0 denote the normalized exponent (value must have 129 subtracted from it). S is set for neg numbers and $f1 = 2^{-1}$, $f2 = 2^{-2}, \ldots, f23 = 2^{-23}$ with this mantissa referenced to 1.0.	bits 31 … 24 (E7 … E0, S), bits 23 … 0 (f1 f2 … f23)
double	Floating point	The double data type is the same as float except that the structure is based on a 64-bit quantity. In this case, the exponent is 11 bits and the mantissa is 52 bits. The exponent normalization is about 513.	bits 63 … 53 (E10 … E0, S), bits 52 … 0 (f1 f2 … f52)

is the (i + 1)th element. Arrays must initially be specified as to length so that during link no ambiguity about the array size exists. We will discuss this initialization shortly. Finally, in the type declaration, variables can be initialized such as

```
int n,m1=33,NN=16,count;
```

Operators are used to link variables and constants. Table 1.5 illustrates the arithmetic operators available in the C language. Tables 1.6 through 1.10 present the complex assignment, relational, logical, address, and size and conditional operators, respectively. The use of these operators is fairly self-explanatory.

TABLE 1.5 THE C ARITHMETIC OPERATORS

Operator	Activity	Precedence
( )	Delimit	1
+ +	Increment	2
− −	Decrement	2
− (unary)	Negate	3
*	Multiply	4
/	Divide	4
+	Add	5
− (subtract)	Subtract	5
= (assignment)	Equate	6
% (integer only)	Modulus	Recommended usage with ( )

TABLE 1.6 COMPLEX ASSIGNMENT OPERATORS

Operator	Function
+ =	Adds the right-hand quantity to the left-hand variable: x + = 3 is equal to x = x + 3.
− =	Subtracts the right-hand quantity from the left-hand variable: x − = 3 is equal to x = x − 3.
* =	Multiplies the left-hand variable by the right-hand quantity: x * = 3 is equal to x = 3 * x.
/=	Divides the left-hand variable by the right-hand quantity: x /= 3 is equal to x = x/3.
% =	Yields the remainder from dividing the left-hand quantity by the right-hand quantity: x %= 3 is equal to x = x % 3.

Pointers and Arrays.   Essentially, a pointer locates or points to a variable in memory. This is apparent in Table 1.9. A pointer defines the associated address of a variable. The ampersand is used to define a pointer, as in

```
ptr1 = &alpha1;
```

Here ptr1 contains the address of alpha1, not its value. Declaring pointers must take place in such a fashion that the type of variable, whose address is represented

TABLE 1.7 RELATIONAL OPERATORS

Operator	Function
<	Less than. For example, x < y is true if x is less than y.
< =	Less than or equal. x < = is true if x is less than or equal y.
= =	Equal to. x = = y is true if x equals y. *x is left unchanged.* The expression x = y changes x to equal y.
> =	Greater than or equal to. x > = y is true if x is greater than or equal to y.
>	Greater than. x > y is true if x is greater than y.
! =	*Not equal.* x ! = y is true if x is not equal to y.

TABLE 1.8 LOGICAL OPERATORS

Operator	Function
&&	AND; this operator yields the following truth table for x && y:

x	y	
T	T	T
T	F	F
F	T	F
F	F	F

| ¦ ¦ | OR; this operator yields the following truth table for x ¦ ¦ y: |

x	y	
T	T	T
T	F	T
F	T	T
F	F	F

| ! | NOT; this operator yields |

x	
T	F
F	T

for !x.

TABLE 1.9 ADDRESS OPERATORS

Operator	Function
&	This operator returns the address of a variable. In y = &x, the address of x is returned in y.
*	This operator is the indirection operator. It returns the value of a pointer. For y = &x, the pointer, y, assigns the value of x to z in z = *y;

by the pointer (alpha1 here), is apparent in the pointer definition. To accomplish this in C, the indirection operator is used. If, for example, alpha1 is an integer, then the type declaration for ptr1 is

```
int *ptr1;
```

TABLE 1.10 SIZE AND CONDITIONAL OPERATORS

Operator	Function

sizeof	This operator yields the size in bytes of the operand. For example the sequence
	
	 `int x,y;`
	
	 `. . .`
	
	 `y = sizeof (x);`
	
	 assigns the value 2 to y.

?:	The conditional operator has the form `expression1 ? expression2: expression3` This operation has the value of expression2 if expression1 is true; otherwise, it has the value of expression3.

Note that this statement literally declares the value pointed to by ptr1 as type integer. The compiler interprets this statement as a pointer declaration for ptr1.

Arrays occupy space on the stack if declared locally within a function. (We will discuss functions in the next section, but the reader can assume, for now, that a function is a localized block of code performing a fixed activity. Furthermore, a function is easily callable and returns a single value.) The stack is a dynamic area used to pass variables among functions. Normally, the maximum stack size is fixed at compile time, and it is useful to minimize stack size because of the subsequent bookkeeping needed to track stack parameters dynamically (the PUSH and POP operations of assembly language).

Most C implementations provide for minimizing stack size in the presence of large arrays by defining a global area within the preprocessor. The C preprocessor consists of language extensions that provide for the definition and inclusion of additional instructions. Typically, a statement of the form

```
#include <stdio.h>
```

causes the file stdio.h to be included at that point in the program. Similarly,

```
#define CUBE(x) ((x)*(x)*(x))
```

causes every subsequent occurrence of CUBE(z), for example, to be replaced with the cube of z. In the preprocessor area located with the first module, global declarations are possible. For the Microsoft C Compiler, variables defined in this area are located in a special segment accessible from all other modules (see Chapter 3). Hence, the storage of these variables does not reside on the stack and they are truly global. It is usual to declare and initialize arrays in this area. To declare an array of 1024 elements (floating point), the following statement would reside in the preprocessor:

```
float xarray[1024],yvalue;
```

Here we have also made yvalue a global variable.

Input/output. An extremely important aspect of any programming environment is the facility for input/output (I/O) of information during program execution. Generally, at an assembler level this requires a direct interface, with hardware driver routines, to peripheral equipment. In most higher-level languages, provision is made to call standard I/O instructions, which are machine independent. C is no exception, and use of the include files previously mentioned provides the link with machine-dependent drivers. In the C programming environment, three types of I/O exist:

1. Console/port I/O
2. Stream I/O
3. Low-level I/O

Table 1.11 contains the major functions available to the C programmer for achieving I/O within the confines of Microsoft's C Compiler Version 4.0. In Chapter 6, we examine the Version 5.0 enhancements.

Console I/O is simply input/output directed between the computer and the keyboard or display. Port I/O similarly accepts formatted (structured) inputs from specified port addresses. Standard I/O is a form of console/port I/O that requires format specifiers. Stream I/O consists of input/output, which occurs until a specified delimiter occurs, the end of the I/O list is reached, or a fixed number of bytes is transferred. The stream is a conceptual entity that corresponds to the information passing across the interface. Typically, in the C library the standard I/O module has several standard streams associated with it:

STREAM	INTERFACE
stdin	Keyboard
stdout	Display
stdaux	Asynchronous port 1
stdprn	Printer 1

These functions have corresponding pointers that are predefined in a library-controlled C structure, FILE. Reference to pointers (streams) associated with I/O must include, for example, the following:

```
...
#include<stdio.h>
...
FILE *infile,*outfile;
...
```

where infile and outfile represent pointers that can be used to refer to desired streams for I/O purposes.

Low-level I/O involves the use of functions that provide maximum control in the C environment. Essentially, these functions form the basis from which more tailored high-level I/O functions (such as the standard I/O routines) are generated.

TABLE 1.11 C FUNCTIONS FOR PERFORMING I/O

Function	Type	Library	Comments
cgets(str)	Console/port	conio.h	Reads a string from the keyboard. str 0 = maximum buffer length, str 1 = actual string length, and str 2 points to character buffer.
cprintf(format-str,arg...)	Console/port	conio.h	Formats and prints a series of characters and values to the display.
cputs(str)	Console/port	conio.h	Writes the null-terminated string pointed to by str in the display.
cscanf(format-str,arg...)	Console/port	conio.h	Reads data directly from the keyboard into arguments (pointer to corresponding variables).
getch()	Console/port	conio.h	Reads a single character from the keyboard (no echo).
getche()	Console/port	conio.h	Reads a single character from the keyboard (echo).
inp(port)	Console/port	conio.h	Reads a single byte from the port specified by port.
kbhit()	Console/port	conio.h	Checks keyboard for a keystroke.
outp(port)	Console/port	conio.h	Outputs a byte to port.
putch(c)	Console/port	conio.h	Writes the character c to the display.
ungetch(c)	Console/port	conio.h	Pushes the character c back to the keyboard, causing it to be the next character input.
clearerr(stream)	Stream	stdio.h	Resets the error and end-of-file indictor for stream.
fclose(stream)	Stream	stdio.h	Closes the stream.
fcloseall()	Stream	stdio.h	Closes all streams.
fdopen(handle,type)	Stream	stdio.h	Associates a stream with the file identified by handle, thus allowing a low-level I/O file to be buffered and formatted. Type: r (read only), w (write em- ploy file), a (write at end of file), r+ (both read/ write), w+ (empty for read/write), a+ (open for reading and appending).
feof(stream)	Stream	stdio.h	Tests for end of file on stream.
ferror(stream)	Stream	stdio.h	Tests for read/write error on stream.
fflush(stream)	Stream	stdio.h	Clears the contents of the associated stream buffer following a write to stream.
fgetc(stream)	Stream	stdio.h	Reads a single character from stream and advances the pointer.

`fgetchar()`	Stream	stdio.h	Equivalent to fgetc(stdin).
`fgets(str,n,stream)`	Stream	stdio.h	Reads a string and stores it in str, Characters are read until (1) a newline or (2) n − 1 characters have been input (the input is from stream).
`fileno(stream)`	Stream	stdio.h	Returns stream's file handle.
`flushall()`	Stream	stdio.h	Flushes all stream buffers.
`fopen(pathname,type)`	Stream	stdio.h	Opens the file specified by pathname. Type is the same as specified with fdopen( ).
`fprintf(stream,format-str,arg,...)`	Stream	stdio.h	Formats and prints a series of characters and values to stream.
`fputc(c,stream)`	Stream	stdio.h	Writes the character c to stream.
`fputchar(c)`	Stream	stdio.h	Equivalent to fputc(c,stdout).
`fputs(str,stream)`	Stream	stdio.h	Outputs the string, str, to stream until terminated by a null.
`fread(buf,size,ct,stream)`	Stream	stdio.h	Reads as many as ct items of size "size" from stream and stores them in the buffer, "buf".
`freopen(pathname,type,stream)`	Stream	stdio.h	Closes the current stream file and reassigns stream to pathname. Type is the same as specified with fdopen( ).
`fscanf(stream,format-str,arg,...)`	Stream	stdio.h	Reads data from stream into arguments as formatted. Args are pointers.
`fseek(stream,offset,origin)`	Stream	stdio.h	Moves the file pointer associated with stream an amount of offset from origin.
`ftell(stream)`	Stream	stdio.h	Gets the position of the file pointer associated with stream.
`fwrite(buf,size,ct,stream)`	Stream	stdio.h	Writes as many as ct items of size "size" from buffer "buf", to stream.
`getc(stream)`	Stream	stdio.h	Reads a single character from stream and advances the position.
`getchar()`	Stream	stdio.h	Equivalent to getc(stdin).
`gets(buffer)`	Stream	stdio.h	Reads a string up to the newline from stdin and stores it in buffer.
`getw(stream)`	Stream	stdio.h	Reads the next two bytes of type int from stream.
`printf(format-str,arg,...)`	Stream	stdio.h	Formats and prints a series of characters and values to stdout (the display).
`putc(c,stream)`	Stream	stdio.h	Writes a single character, c, to stream.

TABLE 1.11 (Concluded)

Function	Type	Library	Comments
putchar(c)	Stream	stdio.h	Same as putc(c,stdout).
puts(str)	Stream	stdio.h	Writes str to stdout, replacing the termination null with a newline.
putw(binint,stream)	Stream	stdio.h	Writes a binary value of type int to stream.
rewind(stream)	Stream	stdio.h	Repositions stream's file pointer to the file beginning.
rmtmp()	Stream	stdio.h	Removes temporary files created by tmpfile().
scanf(format-str,arg...)	Stream	stdio.h	Reads data from keyboard into variables pointed to by args and according to specified format.
setbuf(stream,buffer)	Stream	stdio.h	Allows stream to associate with a buffer, which is a specified character array.
setvbuf(stream,buf,type,size)	Stream	stdio.h	Allows control of buffering (as in setbuf) and buffer size. "Size" is used as the size of the buffer. Type: _IONBUF (in buffer), _IOFBF (full buffer), and _IOLBF (same as _IOFBF).
sprintf(buf,format-str,arg...)	Stream	stdio.h	Formats and stores a series of characters/values in buffer.
sscanf(buf,format-str arg...)	Stream	stdio.h	Reads data from buffer (buf) into locations pointed to by args and as specified (format).
tempnam(dir,prefix)	Stream	stdio.h	Creates a temporary file in the directory, dir; prefix is the prefix to the filename.
tmpfile()	Stream	stdio.h	Creates a temporary file and returns a pointer.
tmpnam(str)	Stream	stdio.h	Generates a temporary filename stored in string.
ungetc(c,stream)	Stream	stdio.h	Pushes a character, c, back onto an *input* stream.
rfprintf(stream,format-str,arg-ptr)	Stream	stdio.h	Formats and outputs data to stream. Arg-ptr is a variable argument list pointer.
rprintf(format-str,arg-ptr)	Stream	stdio.h	Same as rfprintf(stdout,format-str,arg-ptr).
rsprintf(buf,format-str,arg-ptr)	Stream	stdio.h	Same as rfprintf except output to buffer file, buffer.
close(handle)	Low level	io.h	Closes file associated with handle.
creat(pathname,Pmode)	Low level	sys types.h	Creates new file (or opens existing file). Pmode: S_IWRITE (writing permitted), S_IREAD

30

Function	Category	Header files	Description
		sys stat.h	(reading permitted), and S_IREAD S_IWRITE (both permitted).
dup(handle)	Low level	io.h	Used as a function to assign a second file handle to "handle."
dup2(handle1,handle2)	Low level	io.h	Forces handle2 to refer to same file as handle1.
eof(handle)	Low level	io.h	Determines whether end of file has been reached for file associated with handle.
lseek(handle,offset,origin)	Low level	io.h	Moves pointer associated with handle an offset number of bytes from origin. Origin must be a manifest constant: SEEK_SET (beginning of file), SEEK_CUR(current position), or SEEK_END (eof).
open(panthname,oflag,pmode)	Low level	io.h fcutl.h sys types.h sys stat.h	Opens the file specified by pathname and prepares the file for I/O according to oflag. O_APPEND (reposition to eof before every write), O_CREAT (create), O_EXCEL (return error if file exists), O_WRONLY (write), O_BINARY (binary mode), and O_TEXT (text mode). The parameter pmode is used with O_CREAT and can be: S_WRITE (write permission), S_IREAD (read permission, S_IREAD S_IWRITE (both).
read.(handle,buf,count)	Low level	io.h	Attempts to read count bytes from file associated with handle into buffer.
sopen(pathname,oflag,shflag,pmode)	Low level	io.h fentl.h sys types.h sys stat.h share.h	Opens the file and prepares it for shared reading and writing. oflag and pmode are the same as for open( ). shflag satisfies SH_DENYWR (deny write access), SH_DENYRD (deny read access), SH_DENYNO (permit read/write).
tell(handle)	Low level	io.h	Gets current position of pointer associated with handle.
write(handle,buffer,count)	Low level	io.h	Writes count bytes from file associated with handle into buffer.

I/O involves text-type transfers. In text-type transfers, numerical equivalences for numbers and letters are passed back and forth based on the American Standard Code for Information Interchange (ASCII). Information is transferred a byte (character) at a time, and the ASCII equivalences for the first 128 characters (out of a possible 256) are indicated in Table 1.12. Clearly, the text-type convention based on ASCII coding is useful for information using letters or numbers or both.

TABLE 1.12 ASCII Character Set (First 128 Characters)

Character	Hex	Character	Hex	Character	Hex
Null	00	+	2B	V	56
Open face	01	,	2C	W	57
Closed face	02	-	2D	X	58
Heart	03	.	2E	Y	59
Diamond	04	/	2F	Z	5A
Club	05	0	30	L. brack.	5B
Spade	06	1	31	L. slash	5C
Beep	07	2	32	R. brack.	5D
White dot	08	3	33	Up sign	5E
Black circle	09	4	34	—	5F
White circle	0A	5	35	Apostrophe	60
Male	0B	6	36	a	61
Female	0C	7	37	b	62
Note	0D	8	38	c	63
Note	0E	9	39	d	64
Sun	0F	:	3A	e	65
R. arrow	10	;	3B	f	66
L. arrow	11	L.T.	3C	g	67
V. arrow	12	=	3D	h	68
Double excl.	13	G.T.	3E	i	69
Paragraph	14	?	3F	j	6A
Circle "S"	15	@	40	k	6B
Full bar	16	A	41	l	6C
V. arrow/line	17	B	42	m	6D
Up arrow	18	C	43	n	6E
Down arrow	19	D	44	o	6F
R. arrow	1A	E	45	p	70
L. arrow	1B	F	46	q	71
Bracket	1C	G	47	r	72
Hor. arrow	1D	H	48	s	73
Up triangle	1E	I	49	t	74
Down triangle	1F	J	4A	u	75
Blank	20	K	4B	v	76
Exclamation	21	L	4C	w	77
Quote	22	M	4D	x	78
#	23	N	4E	y	79
$	24	O	4F	z	7A
%	25	P	50	L. brack.	7B
&	26	Q	51	Bold colon	7C
ℓ	27	R	52	R. brack.	7D
(	28	S	53	Approximate	7E
)	29	T	54	Opn. triang.	7F
*	2A	U	55		

Introduction   Chap. 1

From an I/O viewpoint, either text or binary files (or mixed) can be generated, depending on which I/O function is employed. For specifying standard formats, the following identifiers are appropriate:

IDENTIFIER	INPUT/OUTPUT TYPE
%f	Floating point number (decimal)
%e	Floating point number (exponential)
%d	Integer number (decimal)
%u	Unsigned decimal integer
%o	Unsigned octal integer
%x	Unsigned hexadecimal integer
%c	Character
%s	String

A key question is how string variables are delimited. In C, a string is assumed to terminate when white-space characters are encountered. These characters are defined in the following manner:

CHARACTER(S)	HEX	IDENTIFICATION
(space)	20	Space
\t	09	Tab
(LF)	0A	Line feed
\r	0D	Carriage return
\f	—	Form feed
\v	—	Vertical tab
\n	—	New line

A more general classification of special character combinations that includes white-space sequences and associated nongraphic characters is escape sequences. An escape sequence consists of a backslash followed by a letter or combination of digits. In addition to the previous white-space characters, the following sequences are included in this category:

CHARACTER(S)	IDENTIFICATION
\t	Horizontal tab
\b	Backspace
\a	Bell
\'	Single quote
\"	Double quote
\\	Backslash
\ddd	ASCII character in octal
\xdd	ASCII character in hexadecimal

The backslash character also serves as a continuation character in strings and preprocessor definitions.

Control logic. Control logic allows the programmer to achieve conditional execution of selected code in response to changes in the state of program variables. The logic provides for iterative or conditional selection of program statements (to be executed) in response to a changing variable, such as an index, a numerical value, or a Boolean quantity. Table 1.13 presents the logic available with the standard C syntax.

1.3.2 Functions, Structures, and Unions

Earlier we saw the use of a function main(). This function is at the root of any C hierarchy of functions called within a particular program architecture. We also saw reference to two C library functions: scanf() and printf(). In true mathematical analogy, a C function can only return a single value. A typical call of a function that returns a value is

```
...
x=__lineto(x,y);
...
```

Here x assumes the value returned by __lineto(). The two parameters x and y are formal parameters and are used to pass data to the function. Consider the following code fragment:

```
...
#include <stdio.h>
float xx[10];
main()
    {
    int n;
    extern float xx[];
    float x,y;
    for(n=1;n<3;n++)
        {
        xx[n]=CUBE(n);
        printf("%f",xx[n]);
        }
    }
CUBE(m)
    int m;                      /*integer parameter*/
    {
    float x;
    x=(float)(m);
    x=x*x*x;
    return(x);
    }
```

This simple program illustrates the use of a function CUBE. The variable m is a formal parameter declared outside the body of CUBE and x is defined locally within

TABLE 1.13 C CONTROL LOGIC

Expression	Comments
`if(exp)` `    statement:`	When exp is true, statement executes.

`if(exp)`
`    statement1;`
`else`
`    statement2;`
	When exp is true, statement1 executes. Statement2 executes for all other situations.

`exp1?exp2:exp3`	When expl is true, the conditional expression assumes the value of exp2. Otherwise, the expression assumes the value of exp3.

`switch(exp)`
`{`
`case expl:`
`    statement1;`
`case exp2:`
`    statement2;`
`...`
`case expn:`
`    statementn;`
`(default:`
`    statement;)`
`}`
	This logic examines exp for each case assignment: expl, exp2, . . . , expn. When a match is achieved, all remaining statements [statementm, statement(m + 1), . . . , statementn, statement] are executed. If no match is achieved, then only the default statement is executed.

`switch(exp)`
`{`
`case expl:`
`    statement1;`
`    break;`
`case exp2:`
`    statement2;`
`    break;`
`...`
`case expn:`
`    statementn;`
`    break;`
`(default:`
`    statement;)`
`}`
	The addition of the break mechanism causes the preceeding statement to execute, followed by a jump to the end of the switch. This structure is the familiar CASE-type logic.

`while(exp)` `    statement;`	This loop executes statement iteratively when exp is true. Clearly, exp must modify in statement after the iteration process begins.

`do`
`{`
`  statement;`
`}while(exp)`
	This loop executes in a fashion similar to the while loop, except the while test is at the trailing end of the loop.

`for(init-exp;cond-exp;\` `loop-exp) statement;`	This loop initializes a set of conditions for exp, provides a conditional test on exp, and indicates the incremental variation for exp each time statement is executed. (The \ is used for continuation only.)

TABLE 1.13 (*Concluded*)

Expression	Comments
| ```
loop-structure
   {
   statement1;
      continue;
   statement2;
   }
``` | When the continue is encountered in a loop structure, control passes to the end of the loop. |
| ```
...
goto label;
...
label:
   statement;
...
``` | The goto passes control to the goto statement associated with label. When used, gotos are usually encountered as the result of a conditional process because of their unconditional nature. |

each function [as is y within main( )]. The array xx[ ] is global. Note how the brackets are used to delimit code blocks. The declaration

```
extern float xx[];
```

indicates to the compiler that the array xx[] resides in the special global segment. Technically, this statement is not needed because the global definition (preprocessor) and the use of the variable occur in the same module. If global variables are referenced in separately compiled modules, however, the extern declaration must reside in the user functions.

It is probably clear that C intends the user to return one value from a function. This is an ideal notion, and in practice the user frequently wants to return more than one value (we will avoid discussion of redefining code to conform to a single return value by restructuring) for convenience. This can be accomplished using global variables that are accessible within all program functions. Problems arise with this technique when programmers proliferate the variables and cross referencing becomes difficult. A second technique for returning small numbers of variables is to pass pointers. Consider the following structure:

```
...
#include <math.h>
#include <stdio.h>
#define pi 3.141592654
main()
   {
   float x1,y1;
   x1=pi;
   y1=pi;
   CSINE(&x1,&y1);
   printf("cosine=%f sine=%f",x1,y1);
   }
CSINE(m,n)
   float *m,*n;
   {
```

```
double a,b;
a= (double)(*m);
b= (double)(*n);
a= cos(a);
b= sin(b);
*m= (float)(a);
*n= (float)(b);
}
```
...

Here x1 and y1 contain the returned cosine and sine values.

The C programming language possesses a special data type called a structure, which can be composed of groups of other data types including other structures. The following format is used to define a structure:

```
struct(tag)
    {
    member-declaration-list
    }(declarator(,declarator));
```

Here the items in parentheses are optional; however, at least the tag or one declarator must be specified. The brackets contain the list of structure members in declaration fashion. A typical example would be

```
struct account
    {
    int number;
    float balance;
    }
```

Here a structure template has been defined with the tag account. It contains one integer value and one floating point value. This definition does not associate a variable name with the structure, and this must be accomplished using a second call, for example,

```
struct account Judy, Terry, Mike;
```

This call sets up three structures with the variables Judy, Terry, and Mike. To reference the account number, for example, for Judy we might have

```
...
x = Judy.number;
...
```

Here the period is used as the structure member operator.

One difficulty with structures is that they cannot be passed as variables to a function. It is possible, however, to pass pointers to structures. To do this, two steps are involved, aside from the initial structure definition: the pointer must be defined and then assigned to a structure variable. Consider the following example:

```
...
struct ID
    {
    char name[81];
    long ssum;
    }
struct member__char
    {
    struct ID specification;
    float income;
    };
main()
{
static struct member__char MJT=
    {
        {"MJTompkins",364111111L},
        53786.00
        };
    ...
    struct member__char *member;      /*ptr defined */
    ...
    member=&MJT;                      /*ptr assigned */
    ...
    printf("member income=%f",member--> income);
    ...
    }
```

Here the pointer to the general structure template is defined and then assigned the address of the structure variable MJT. To access members of the structure the operator --> is used. Note that this is a new operator. For example,

```
ptr --> member == (*ptr).member
```

are equivalent ways to specify structure pointer variables when referencing the members of a structure. The type identifier static will be discussed shortly.

Unions are defined with the following syntax:

```
union(tag)
    {
    member-declaration-list
    }(declarator(,declarator));
```

which is identical to the syntax for a structure. Union members are referenced in a fashion identical to similar references for structures. How then do unions differ? Unions must be considered as common storage declarations. The largest member declared in a union becomes the storage size for the union. For example, consider the union JKG of type data:

```
union data
    {
    int num1;
    float num2;
    char num3;
    double num4;
    }JKG;
```

The largest data type for this union is type double with 8 bytes of storage. Hence, the union type data will yield unions that have 8 bytes of common storage.

An excellent example of structures and unions in a practical setting is the definition of structure and union types used to hold the microprocessor CPU register variables defined as keywords in the macro assembler (AX, BX, CX, DX, SI, DI, SP, BP, ES, DS, CS, SS, and CF). Figure 1.6 illustrates the relevant code from the dos.h include file. Note that three structures and one union are illustrated. The structure type WORDREGS contains space for the general-purpose registers, pointer registers, and flags register. It should be pointed out that the entities appearing in Figure 1.6 are structure and union templates. The user must associate an actual structure or union variable with each. The structure BYTEREGS simply contains the 1-byte upper and lower general-purpose registers. The structure SREGS contains the segment registers. Finally, the union REGS provides common storage between WORDREGS (structure) and BYTEREGS (structure). Note that, even though the union can only have a single member defined at one time, in this case each member is a structure. Thus, the full complement of included member registers can be defined within the structure definition (within the union definition).

We have not explicitly described how to use these 8088 (8086) or 80286 registers because that will follow throughout the remainder of the book. (When we describe programming in the context of OS/2, these registers will be less important, but for BIOS and DOS applications they are essential.) A brief discussion will make their use more understandable.

Access to BIOS and DOS service routines is accomplished using interrupts. Within C, the function int86() can be used to call a DOS (or BIOS) interrupt, and the call has the syntax

```
int86(intno, &inregs, &outregs);
```

where a definition of the form

```
union REGS inregs;
union REGS outregs;
```

or, for example,

```
union REGS regs;
```

is assumed. (We can actually use inregs==outregs, because one set of variables is the same as the other. We distinguish, however, between input and output values in the first example.) The parameter intno is the interrupt number.

```
/* word registers */

struct WORDREGS {
        unsigned int ax;
        unsigned int bx;
        unsigned int cx;
        unsigned int dx;
        unsigned int si;
        unsigned int di;
        unsigned int cflag;
        };

/* byte registers */

struct BYTEREGS {
        unsigned char al, ah;
        unsigned char bl, bh;
        unsigned char cl, ch;
        unsigned char dl, dh;
        };

/* general purpose registers union - overlays the corresponding word and
 * byte registers.
 */

union REGS {
        struct WORDREGS x;
        struct BYTEREGS h;
        };

/* segment registers */

struct SREGS {
        unsigned int es;
        unsigned int cs;
        unsigned int ss;
        unsigned int ds;
        };

/* dosexterror struct */

struct DOSERROR {
        int exterror;
        char class;
        char action;
        char locus;
        };
```

Figure 1.6 Representative dos.h structures and unions.

By specifying the needed register values and calling the appropriate interrupt, the user can accomplish a system operation such as clearing the screen. Obviously, we need to know what these system calls are, and this constitutes the subject of Chapter 4. By way of introduction we illustrate the code for a simple screen clear, to be used shortly:

```
SCRCL()
  {
  union REGS regs;
  regs.h.ah=6;                  /*Scroll active page up*/
  regs.h.al=0;                  /*Blanks entire page*/
  regs.h.ch=0;                  /*row-0*/
  regs.h.cl=0;                  /*col=0*/
```

```
regs.h.dh=23;              /*row lower right*/
regs.h.dl=79;              /*col lower right*/
regs.h.bh=7;               /*Blank attribute*/
int86(0x10,&regs,&regs);
}
```

The actual register functions are indicated in the comments and will be presented in tabular form in the next section. Setting ah = 6, for example, puts the screen in a mode where the display scrolls upward. It scrolls from the position of the cursor (in this case the 23rd row and 79th column, dh = 23 and dl = 79). When calling int86, the interrupt number is 10H (hexadecimal) or 0 × 10 or 16. Under the Version 5.0 compiler, for example, the function _clearscreen (_GCLEARSCREEN) defined in graph.h accomplishes the same action. Note how the structure members were employed in this example. Only the union variable was actually defined with the reference backward to BYTEREGS (h) and then the actual members (al, ah, ch...).

We saw how extern variables must be declared in the modules, which use them but do not declare them. This is an example of a storage class (extern). Table 1.14 presents the various storage classes available under the C language. Locally defined variables that are only associated with a given function are automatic. Static variables are also locally defined but retain their value after successive calls to the defining function are made, as defined during each call to the function. Register variables are assigned by the compiler. If the CPU registers are free, they will be associated with a register variable. External static variables are declared ahead of the using function. This declaration allows a variable to be used by more than one function as an external variable, provided the functions follow the declaration and lie in the same module.

TABLE 1.14 SUMMARY OF STORAGE CLASS RELATIONSHIPS

Class	Range	Keyword	Comments
Automatic	Local	`auto`	Variables exist locally within defining function and value is lost upon exit from function.
External	Global	`extern`	Variables exist across all functions and modules and retain their values unless explicitly changed.
Static	Local	`static`	Variables exist locally within defining function and the value is saved and passed forward for successive calls.
Register	Local	`register`	Variable is associated with a CPU register, if possible, during compilation. If not possible, the variable is treated as an automatic variable.
External static	Global (single module)	`static`	Variable is treated as an external variable within the defining module and only for functions following the static declaration in a preprocessor area.

Sec. 1.3   A Brief Review of C

SUMMARY

This chapter has introduced the IBM microcomputer family in the context of the Intel CPU chips associated with each system. The nature of the CPU registers has been discussed, and the importance of these registers in programming has been emphasized. The Intel use of segments and offsets in addressing memory was described.

Next a representative C environment was presented: the Microsoft C Compiler Version 4.0. We started with a beginning program and illustrated its execution using CodeView, Microsoft's symbolic debugger. The .COD output from the compiler was examined for the equivalent assembly language representation. QuickC and the MAKE utility were mentioned briefly, with the reader referred to Appendix C for a listing of the MAKE files (link only) for the programs in this book. Graphics usage was discussed for both Versions 4.0 and 5.0. This discussion focused on the compiler library routine differences.

Finally, the C language was quickly reviewed. This review included both syntax and program architecture. The review was intended to be used by a reader who already has some exposure to the C programming language.

REFERENCES

1. *iAPX 86/88, 186/188 User's Manual: Hardware Reference,* Intel Corporation, Intel Literature Distribution, MS SC6-714, 3065 Bowers Avenue, Santa Clara, CA (1985).
2. *iAPX 86/88, 186/188 User's Manual: Programmer's Reference,* Intel Corporation, Intel Literature Distribution, MS SC6-714, 3065 Bowers Avenue, Santa Clara, CA (1986).
3. *iAPX 286 Hardware Reference Manual,* Intel Corporation, Intel Literature Distribution, MS SC6-714, 3065 Bowers Avenue, Santa Clara, CA (1983).
4. *iAPX 286 Programmer's Reference Manual,* Intel Corporation, Intel Literature Distribution, MS SC6-714, 3065 Bowers Avenue, Santa Clara, CA (1985).
5. *80386 Hardware Reference Manual,* Intel Corporation, Intel Literature Distribution, MS SC6-714, 3065 Bowers Avenue, Santa Clara, CA (1986).
6. *80386 Programmer's Reference Manual,* Intel Corporation, Intel Literature Distribution, MS SC6-714, 3065 Bowers Avenue, Santa Clara, CA (1986).
7. *80387 Programmer's Reference Manual,* Intel Corporation, Intel Literature Distribution, MS SC6-714, 3065 Bowers Avenue, Santa Clara, CA (1987).
8. *IBM Technical Reference,* Personal Computer Hardware Reference Library, IBM Corporation, P. O. Box 1328, Boca Raton, FL (1981), 6025008.
9. *IBM Personal System/2 Model 30 Technical Reference,* IBM Corporation, P. O. Box 1328, Boca Raton, FL (1987), 80X0661.
10. *IBM Technical Reference Personal Computer AT,* IBM Corporation, P. O. Box 1328, Boca Raton, FL (1984), 1502494.
11. *IBM Personal System/2 Model 50 and 60 Technical Reference,* IBM Corporation, P. O. Box 1328, Boca Raton, FL (1987), 80X0902
12. *Microsoft C Compiler for the MS-DOS Operating System: User's Guide,* Microsoft Corporation, P. O. Box 97017, Redmond, WA (1986).
13. *Microsoft C Compiler for the MS-DOS Operating System: Run-Time Library Reference,* Microsoft Corporation, P. O. Box 97017, Redmond, WA (1986).

14. *Microsoft CodeView Window Oriented Debugger for the MS-DOS Operating System,* Microsoft Corporation, P. O. Box 97017, Redmond, WA (1986).
15. *Microsoft C 5.0 Optimizing Compiler: User's Guide and Mixed Language Programming Guide,* Microsoft Corporation, P. O. Box 97017, Redmond, WA (1987).
16. *Microsoft C 5.0 Optimizing Compiler: Run-Time Library References,* Microsoft Corporation, P. O. Box 97017, Redmond, WA (1987).
17. *Microsoft C 5.0 Optimizing Compiler: Language Reference, Microsoft CodeView, and Utilities,* Microsoft Corporation, P. O. Box 97017, Redmond, WA (1987).
18. Kernighan, B. W., and Ritchie, D. M., *The C Programming Language,* Prentice-Hall, Inc., Englewood Cliffs, NJ (1978).
19. Editors of Dr. Dobb's Journal, *Dr. Dobb's Toolbook of C,* A Brady Book, Prentice Hall Press, New York (1986).
20. *Disk Operating System Version 3.30 Reference,* IBM Corporation, Personal Computer, P. O. Box 1328-C, Boca Raton, FL 33432 (1987).
21. *VEDIT PLUS: Multiple File Editor Word Processor,* CompuView Products, Inc., Ann Arbor, MI 48103 (1986).
22. Godfrey, J. T., *IBM Microcomputer Assembly Language: Beginning to Advanced,* Prentice-Hall, Inc., Englewood Cliffs, NJ (1988).

PROBLEMS

1.1. Using the CS and IP relationship discussed, what is the IBM PC/XT physical address corresponding to a segment value 07F8H and an offset 274AH? A segment value 0FFFA and an offset value FFFFH?

1.2. What are the following decimal quantities in binary (16 bits)? In hexadecimal? (a) 24,783, (b) 10, (c) 111, (d) 1024, (e) 32,767.

1.3. Using an arithmetic that sets bit 16 for sign and maintains the remaining 15 bits in normal binary representation, how would you specify (a) -10,476, (b) -32,765, (c) 5832, (d) -48,521, (e) 528?

1.4. Using an arithmetic that employs two's-complement notation how would you specify the values appearing in Problem 1.3?

1.5. In two's-complement notation what is the difference (subtraction) between (a) 47,252 and 48,243, (b) 718 and 2844, (c) 13,941 and 12,788, (d) 10 and 20, and (e) 70,111 and 72,110?

1.6. What value will cause a 32-bit register to overflow if the arithmetic is signed? Unsigned?

1.7. Why is the 8088 not a "full" 16-bit CPU, unlike the 80286?

1.8. How many hexadecimal digits are needed to describe a byte? A word?

1.9. Explain why communications programs will not run properly under the normal Protected Mode architecture (without special hardware enhancements).

1.10. Why is the Model 80 particularly suited for real-time applications? What would be the expected real-time limitations of the Model 80?

1.11. What general library file is required for port I/O?

1.12. Is it possible to define a macro that generates the square root of a variable? Is it possible to define a macro that raises a variable to the tenth power? To an arbitrary power?

1.13. What is incorrect in the following program?

```
char array [100];
main()
    {
    int n;
    for (n=0; n<=100;n++)
        array[n]='a';
    }
```

1.14. Illustrate I/O-oriented decision logic by writing a program that looks for a Y (for yes) or N (for no) as input from the keyboard and prints a 1 or 0, respectively, to the display.

1.15. What is incorrect in each of the following statements?

(a) `for (n=10; n<=9; n++)`

(b)
```
char alpha;
...
scanf("%^c",alpha);
...
```

(c)
```
...
int int1;
FILE input;
...
fscanf(input,"%d",int1);
...
```

(d)
```
...
int n;
...
n=5;
while (n<7)
    printf("%d=",n);
n++;
...
```

(e)
```
...
char n;
...
for (n=1;n<=10;n++)
printf("%d",n);
...
```

1.16. Write a program that reads in two floating point numbers, compares them, and displays the largest value.

1.17. Write a fragment that uses stream I/O *only* to terminate reading a string when a new line character is read.

1.18. Why is the following logic undesirable?

```
...
switch(a)
    {
    case 1:
        printf(""Branch value is 1\n");
    case 0:
        printf("Branch value is 0\n");
    case -1:
```

```
        printf("Branch value is -1\n");
     }
...
```

Assume a can be any value. Write a more desirable version of this code.

1.19. As an example of the confusion that can result from unrestrained use of gotos, consider

```
...
if (a<b)
     goto a1;
else
     goto a2;
statement3;
a1:
     statement2;
goto a3;
a2:
     statement1;
a3:
     statement4;
```

Rewrite this, with corrections as needed, eliminating the gotos.

1.20. Write a fragment that illustrates how to input a string of characters, that can include blanks, and terminates the read when a new line is encountered.

1.21. Using the Newton–Raphson estimator for square roots based on successive estimation,

$$x_n = 0.5 \, (N/x_{n-1} + x_{n-1})$$

write a routine to calculate the square root of an input integer. Here N is the number to square root and x_{n-1} is the $(n - 1)$th estimate, with x_n the nth estimate for this square root. Calculate this square root to the nearest integer value.

1.22. Reduce the following code, while still accomplishing functionally the equivalent operations:

(a)
```
...
if (x<1)
{
if (y>2)
          xx=0;
     }
else
     {
     if (x<10)
          {
     if (y>10)
          xx=1;
     }
     }
...
```

(b)
```
...
if (x<1)
     xx=0;
     if (y>2)
     xx=0;
```

```
if (x<10)
    xx=1;
if (y>10)
    xx=1;
...
```

1.23. Write a fragment that converts an input voltage value, v, to a decibel power value using

$$p = 20 * \log_{10} v$$

1.24. Write a fragment that calculates the distance squared between two points specified in polar coordinate form: (r1,theta1) and (r2,theta2).

1.25. Modify the fragment in Problem 1.24 to yield the actual distance between the two points in question.

1.26. The problem of using low-level I/O is that only character (byte-oriented) I/O can be accomplished. Clearly, conversion routines are needed to accomplish int, float, and double conversion to char. These routines are in the C library, and a good example is the routine to convert floating point values to character:

```
gcvt(value, ndec, buffer)
```

Here value is a double-precision floating point variable, and buffer is the array (or buffer) containing ndec significant digits in FORTRAN F format (or FORTRAN E format). Write a fragment that outputs a floating point variable to outfile (which is a file on drive B) using low-level I/O.

1.27. What addition could be made to the fragment in Problem 1.26 that permits low-level I/O for integer variables?

1.28. DOS provides a file, ANSI.SYS, that can be used to control cursor movement and screen configuration. This file must be initialized in the *fig.sys* file as

```
device = ansi.sys
```

The sequence

```
ESC [2J
```

can be used to clear the screen. Note that the ESC character can be written as a single character in hexadecimal format as

```
'\x1B'
```

Write a program that clears the screen (call it clear.c) using console/port I/O.

1.29. For the program in Problem 1.28, add an output that beeps the speaker. Note the single-character beep ASCII designation is

```
'\x07'
```

1.30. The accompanying table illustrates some cursor control sequences. Using the hexadecimal single-character representation for ESC ('\x1B'), write a program that positions the cursor at the bottom-left point on the screen.

TABLE OF SOME CURSOR CONTROL SEQUENCES (ANSI.SYS FILE)

Sequence	Function
ESC [# A	Moves the cursor up # rows without changing the column position.
ESC [# B	Moves the cursor down # rows without changing the column position.
ESC [# C	Moves the cursor forward # columns without changing the row position.
ESC [# D	Moves the cursor back # columns without changing the row position.
ESC [# ; # f	Moves the cursor to the row (first #) and column (second #) indicated.
ESC [# ; # R	Reports the cursor position (row then column) on the display.
ESC [s	Save cursor position.
ESC [u	Restore cursor position from save.
ESC [2 J	Erase screen and move cursor to HOME.
ESC [K	Erase from cursor to end of line.

1.31. Write a program that iteratively continues to beep the speaker for an extended period: 1000 loop iterations.

1.32. What is wrong with the following sequence of instructions:

```
. . .
main()
    {
    float x,y;
    . . .
    y=square(x);
    printf("square=%f",y);
    . . .
    }
square(x1)
    float *x1;
    {
    float y1;
    y1=*x1;
    y1=y1*y1;
    *x1=y1;
    }
    . . .
```

1.33. Rewrite the code fragments appearing in Problem 1.32 so that they are correct based on the code implemented in main().

1.34. Rewrite the code fragments appearing in Problem 1.32 so that they are correct based on the code illustrated in the function square (x1).

1.35. What is wrong with the following functions:

```
(a) print1(x)
        {
        printf("Value=%f",x)
        }
```

(b)
```
read1(x)
int *x;
{
scanf("%f",x)
    }
```
(c)
```
square(x)
int x;
{
x=x*x;
}
```
(d)
```
square()
{
float y,x;
y=x*x;
return(y);
}
```

1.36. What is wrong with the following code fragment?

```
...
float x,y,z;
...
main()
   {
   int z1;
        ...
   x=z1;
   y=square();
   printf("Square=%f",y);
        ...
   }
square()
   {
   float x;
   x=x*x;
   return(x);
   }
...
```

1.37. What is wrong with

```
#include <stdio.h>
#define pi=3.141592654

main()
   {
   double a;
   float x;
   printf("Input angle in degrees")'
   scanf("%f",x);
   x=x/180;
   a=(double)(2.*pi*x);
   a=cos(a);
   x=(float)(a);
```

```
        printf("Cosine=%f",x);
        }
```

1.38. What is wrong with the following code fragment:

```
...
main()
    {
    square();
    }
square()
{
float x[4096];

for (n=1;n<=4096;n++)
    x[n]=n*n;
}
```

1.39. Given a union:

```
union ID
    {
    int nam1;
    char num2[3];
    }
```

What is wrong with

```
...
main()
    {
    int a[3];

union ID id;

for(n=1;n<=2;n++)
    a[n]=n;
id.num2[1]=a[1];
id.num2[2]=a[2];
id.num2[3]=a[3];
}
```

2

Programming Examples

This chapter presents programming examples that span the range from introductory low-level programming to moderately complex single-task integrated modules. The goal of the discussion is to provide the reader with a rapid grasp of basic C programming features. Basically, the subject of C programming is taught through example in this book and every effort is made to make these examples useful, if not interesting.

2.1 INTRODUCTION

Example programs by nature reflect many of the design aspects covered in Chapter 3. Fortunately, at this point we can begin to implement some fairly elementary programs based on the architecture and syntax considerations of Chapter 1. This is without a need to explore more subtle programming nuances as discussed in Chapter 3. The reader is cautioned that style is frequently the major impediment to rapid assimilation of programs. A particular programmer's idiosyncrasies will eventually become obvious upon study. In this text the style is brief, not lengthy. Usually, variable names are short and characterized by an acronymlike nature. In most cases the underlying relationships are obvious. Also, we explain algorithm development in the text associated with each example. This prevents unnecessary laboring over mathematical relationships, which are not really the intent of the text. The one exception to this is the Fast Fourier transform, which is developed in Appendix A.

While this is a course in applied C, the focus of the text is on how to implement various techniques in software. The intent is to illustrate how programs are actually converted from basic algorithms to software. This is presented with a broad class of useful examples throughout the book as a means of illustration of generic technique.

As we have emphasized elsewhere, this text is predicated on example. This chapter simply initializes that process with full-length, complete illustrations.

2.2 BEGINNING PROGRAM EXAMPLES

The examples presented in this chapter all constitute beginning examples. This assumes that the algorithms are well understood. A collection of very elementary programs is discussed in Section 2.2.1. Then programs that calculate values and display them on the screen are developed. Frequently, throughout the text we will display results using screen graphics. This feature is readily accessible using the software developed and the basic graphic primitive operations, such as drawing a box or line. This chapter presents techniques for doing this using the Version 4.0 library functions. In Chapter 7, we introduce the Version 5.0 enhancements. Library graphic primitives exist so that the lower-level techniques of Version 4.0 can be circumvented with direct calls to these routines. It is very instructive, however, to understand the nature of these low-level techniques if any sort of systems programming is contemplated. Hence, we devote considerable effort toward explaining the low-level interfaces between C and the IBM system software in the early portion of this book. Also, when mixed-language programming is discussed using assembly language, a low-level appreciation for the system interfaces is extremely valuable.

2.2.1 Introductory Programs

The beginning study of any subject requires a certain amount of memorization to become familiar with concepts and terminology. Typically, the student is faced with lists of topical relations (such as the various tables of operators presented earlier). Once this associative phase has developed, meaningful presentation of examples becomes possible. This section is the start of this process.

Value/time-history database creation. An important programming task is reading and writing to various media (displays, keyboards, disks, and so on). Since extensive use of value/time-history data (such as stock prices versus month-year of occurrence) is made in current analytical projections, it is desirable to develop some simple tools for generating and maintaining databases associated with these entities. This process will serve as an example of several techniques for achieving I/O using standard devices and disk peripherals.

Figure 2.1a illustrates a functional flow chart for a program that creates a time-history/value database (timhist.c). The corresponding C code is presented in Figure 2.1b. The C library routine, stdio.h, is "included" as part of the preprocessor directives. This routine contains all the standard I/O drivers and the definition of the standard stream pointers (stdin, stdout, stdprn, stdaux, and stderr). Next the integer arrays, month and year, are declared, as well as the floating point array, value, and the character array, FN1. These arrays are simultaneously initialized (to 288 elements for month, year, and value and 81 elements for FN1).

The location of the initialization of arrays is very important in C. When functions

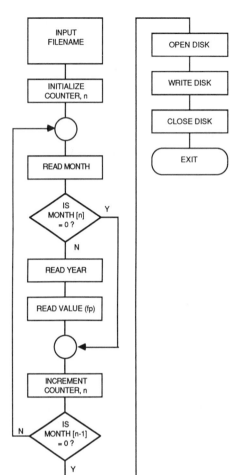

Figure 2.1a Flow chart for the program timhist.c used to create a database.

are employed (to be discussed in Chapter 3), it becomes clear that, as program execution moves from function to function, the calling function's variables are saved in an area called the stack. As progressive calls to higher-nested functions are made, the stack increases in size. The stack must be specified at link time, and it is possible to overflow memory. Hence, the main calling function preprocessor area becomes very useful. This area acts as a common area in that variables declared here may be accessed by all other program modules, whether external or otherwise. Thus, arrays declared in this preprocessor area do not load the stack area. For this reason, all arrays should be declared in the main calling function, main(), preprocessor area. (If arrays are small and do not add appreciably to the stack, it is permissible to declare them locally in the function that uses them.) We will discuss this stack at some length in Chapter 3.

The main calling function, main(), contains two types of additional variables: the integers n, counter, and check, and the FILE structure pointer, outfile. The variable n is simply used as an index, and counter is used to keep track of the number of time-history/value records to be written to the storage media. This integer is the first value output to the media and, consequently, serves as a parameter to

```
/* Routine to create time-history/value database */

#include <stdio.h>                                /* I/O file */

int month[288],year[288];                         /* time arrays */
float value[288];                                 /* quant. interest */
char FN1[81];                                      /* filename array */

main()
       {
       int n,counter,check;                       /* integer var. */
       FILE *outfile;                             /* stream pointer */

       printf("Input database filename \n");
       gets(FN1);                                 /* library routine */
       n = 1;                                     /* initialize index */
       month[0] = 1;                              /* init month not 0 */
       while(month[n-1] != 0)
          {
          printf("Input month as int (0 terminates)\n");
          scanf("%d",&month[n]);
          if(month[n] != 0)
             {
             printf("Input year as 2-digit int\n");
             scanf("%d",&year[n]);
             printf("Input value - floating point\n");
             scanf("%f",&value[n]);
             }
          n++;                                    /* increment index */
          if(n > 288)
             exit(1);                             /* overflow mem */
          }
       counter = n - 2;                           /* fix count */

       if((outfile = fopen(FN1,"w")) == NULL)     /* open out file */
          {
          printf("Output file failure: %s",FN1);
          exit(1);
          }
       fprintf(outfile,"%d ",counter);            /* output count */
       for(n = 1;n <= counter;n++)
          fprintf(outfile,"%d %d %f ",month[n],year[n],value[n]);

       if((check = fclose(outfile)) != 0)         /* close file */
          {
          printf("Error in output file close");
          exit(1);
          }
       }

<C:\>
```

Figure 2.1b   Code for timhist.c.

be read back to a program (indicating the length of the remaining contents of, say, a disk file).

The program initially executes an output to the display using the standard output function printf(). The query asks for the name of the database file to be created. This is read in using the get-string function, gets(). This function reads a line from the standard input stream, stdin, and stores it in the array specified as parameter. This array is referred to as a buffer because it represents a memory area where different input data items can reside prior to final passage to the program. In timhist.c, the gets() buffer is called FN1 and has been dimensioned to 81 characters (the standard input line is 80 characters). The gets() function reads all characters up to and including the new-line character. (It subsequently replaces the new-line with the NULL character.)

Next the index is set equal to 1, the zeroth array element of month is made nonzero, and the while loop is entered. The while test looks at the $(n - 1)$th element of month to make sure it is nonzero before processing the remaining record. In the while loop, the first I/O outputs a message asking for the month and indicating that a zero will terminate the file creation. The standard input function, scanf(), is called to read the month integer value. Both gets() and scanf() have the standard input device associated with their input stream (the keyboard). Note that scanf() reads the input value into a variable by specifying the address of this variable rather than the variable itself.

The value for month[n] is checked, and if nonzero both the associated year and value are input. The index is incremented and checked to ensure it has not exceeded the array dimensions. If it does exceed the array size, a call to exit() is made (which flushes any buffers and closes any open files). The nonzero exit() parameter (in this case 1) causes an error message to appear on the display. If n is less than 288, the while loop continues to input records until month becomes 0. At this point, counter is adjusted to reflect the number of complete records input, and the output file is opened using the function fopen(). The pathname is FN1, and a write only option is selected with ''w.'' Since fopen() can return a value of NULL if an error is encountered, this condition is checked for. The return value of fopen() is a pointer to the open file. This stream has been assigned to the variable outfile. If no error results, the fprintf() function is used to output the number of data records (specified by counter) to outfile. Next all data records are written to this output stream with the for loop. Finally, the file is closed using the function fclose(). As part of this close, the return value is set equal to check and tested to see if an error occurred (in a fashion similar to fopen).

Figure 2.1c illustrates a simple interactive session with timhist. The file IBMHIST.DAT is created on drive B. It contains 5 months of data representing the price of IBM stock for the beginning months of 1983 ($100, $100, $101, $115, and $115 per share) rounded approximately. Figure 2.1d is a check of the contents of the diskette in drive B following this execution of timhist. Finally, we indicate the contents of IBMHIST.DAT using the type command (it clearly agrees with the input).

Reading the value/time-history database. Figure 2.2a illustrates the flow chart for a small program that reads the time-history/value database created by program timhist.c. The code for this program is in Figure 2.2b. This latter program, thistin.c, has the same variable declaration (as timhist) except the FILE structure pointer is now called infile (this pointer is arbitrary). Initially, the program asks for the database filename using the standard output function, printf(). The keyboard input is again read using the function gets(). A file is opened on the appropriate media using fopen() with the read-only option specified by ''r.'' The input stream function, fscanf(), is used to read in the record count first. (Note the value is read into a variable, counter, specified by the address of counter.) The data records are then read using a for loop, which has the counter value to specify the upper index count. In this for loop, fscanf() is used to read the records and an output stream function, fprintf, is used to cause the record values to print on the standard printer device (stdprn). In this case, stdprn is the printer attached to the computer printer port. Finally, the standard output function, printf(), prints the record values on the display. Following this, the file is closed in a fashion similar to that employed for timhist.c. Figure 2.2c illustrates the screen output for execution of thistin, and Figure 2.2d illustrates the printer output.

Mortgage payment. The flow chart for a program that calculates monthly mortgage payments is illustrated in Figure 2.3a. This program also calculates monthly

```
timhist
Input database filename
b:IBMHIST.DAT
Input month as int (0 terminates)
1
Input year as 2-digit int
83
Input value - floating point
100.
Input month as int (0 terminates)
2
Input year as 2-digit int
83
Input value - floating point
100.
Input month as int (0 terminates)
3
Input year as 2-digit int
83
Input value - floating point
101.
Input month as int (0 terminates)
4
Input year as 2-digit int
83
Input value - floating point
115.
Input month as int (0 terminates)
5
Input year as 2-digit int
83
Input value - floating point
115.
Input month as int (0 terminates)
0
```
(c)

```
dir b:

 Volume in drive B has no label
 Directory of  B:\

IBMHIST  DAT       82   7-18-87  12:23p
        1 File(s)     361472 bytes free

<C:\>type b:IBMHIST.DAT
5 1 83 100.000000 2 83 100.000000 3 83 101.000000 4 83 115.000000 5 83 115.00000
0
<C:\>
```
(d)

Figure 2.1c,d (c) Typical interactive session with timhist.exe and (d) the directory for drive B and the output file contents.

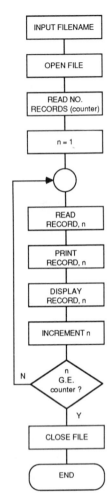

Figure 2.2a Flow chart for thistin.c, a program that reads the time history (value database).

principal and interest portions of the payment. The following formula serves as the basis for this calculation:

$$P = RL \frac{1}{1 - [1/(1 + R)^N]}$$

Here

P = monthly payment
R = monthly interest rate
L = loan amount
N = number months financed

The monthly interest satisfies

$$M_I = P_R R$$

```
/* Routine to read time-history/value from disk */

#include <stdio.h>

int month[288],year[288];                              /* time arrays */
float value[288];                                      /* quantity */
char FN1[81];                                          /* filename array */

main()
       {
       int n,counter,check;                            /* integer var. */
       FILE *infile;                                   /* stream pointer */

       printf("Input database filename\n");
       gets(FN1);                                      /* library routine */
       if((infile = fopen(FN1,"r")) == NULL)
           {
           printf("Input file failure: %s",FN1);
           exit(1);
           }
       fscanf(infile,"%d ",&counter);                  /* no. records */
       for(n = 1;n <= counter;n++)
           {
           fscanf(infile,"%d %d %f ",&month[n],&year[n],&value[n]);
           fprintf(stdprn,"%d %d %f \n",month[n],year[n],value[n]);
           printf("%d %d %f \n",month[n],year[n],value[n]);
           }
       if((check = fclose(infile)) != 0)
           {
           printf("Error in input file close");
           exit(1);
           }
       }
```

(b)

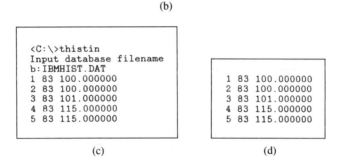

```
<C:\>thistin
Input database filename
b:IBMHIST.DAT
1 83 100.000000
2 83 100.000000
3 83 101.000000
4 83 115.000000
5 83 115.000000
```

```
1 83  100.000000
2 83  100.000000
3 83  101.000000
4 83  115.000000
5 83  115.000000
```

(c)   (d)

Figure 2.2b,c,d (b) Code for thistin.c, (c) an interactive session with the display, and (d) the output at the printer.

and the monthly principal is

$$M_P = P - M_I$$

where P_R is the remaining principal loan amount. The program code for mortgage.c appears in Figure 2.3b. Finally, Figure 2.3c contains a typical interactive session.

The C library file math.h. is "included" in mortgage.c (Figure 2.3b) because this file contains the function pow(x,y), which raises x to the power y. In main(), the variables x, y, and z are declared type double because the function pow() uses double precision arithmetic. After the number of months financed, the annual mortgage rate (%), and the loan amount are input, the payment is calculated according to

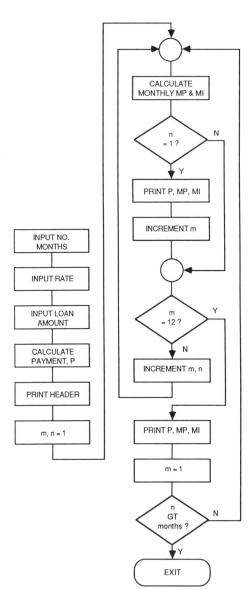

Figure 2.3a Flow chart for mortgage.c, a program that calculates monthly mortgage and principal/interest

the preceding formula. [Note that the scanf() function uses addresses, not values.] The annual rate was converted to a decimal monthly rate.

Next a for loop is set up to generate the first and successive 12- month principal and interest portions of the monthly payment (except the second value is reported for month 11). The conditional if statements are used to generate print values at appropriate points.

Savings appreciation. The next program example is designed to illustrate the effects of inflation on the appreciated value of savings. It has been assumed

```
/* This routine calculates a monthly mortgage payment */

#include <stdio.h>
#include <math.h>                                          /* math library */

main()
        {
        double x,y,z;                                      /* needed by pow() */
        float P,R,L,pr,mp,mi;
        int N,n,m;
                                                           /* mort. parm */
        printf("Input no. months financed (less than 361)\n");
        scanf("%d",&N);
        printf("Input annual mortgage rate (percent)\n");
        scanf("%f",&R);
        R = R/(100. * 12.);                                /* convert decimal */
        printf("Input amount loan (dollars)\n");
        scanf("%f",&L);
                                                           /* calc. mort. pay. */

        y = (double)(N);
        x = (double)(1.0 + R);
        z = pow(x,y);                                      /* (1+R) to the N */
        z = 1.0/(1.0 - (1.0/z));

        P = R * L * ((float)(z));                             /* payment */
        printf("   MONTHLY MORTGAGE PAYMENT = %f \n",P);
        printf("   Month        Principal        Interest \n");

        m = 1;
        pr = L;                                            /* Initial prin. */
        for(n = 1;n <= N;n++)
            {
            mi = pr * R;                                   /* monthly interest */
            mp = P - mi;                                   /* monthly prin. */
            L = L - mp;
            pr = L;                                        /* reduce prin. */
            if(n == 1)
                {
                printf("   %d           %5.2f          %5.2f \n",n,mp,mi);
                m++;
                }                                          /* selective print */
            if(m == 12)
                {
                printf("   %d           %5.2f          %5.2f \n",n,mp,mi);
                m = 1;                                     /* reinitialize */
                }
            else
                m++;
            }
        }
```

Figure 2.3b   Code for mortgage.c.

that the interest appreciation (at annual rate $r1$) is compounded daily. Similarly, it is assumed that inflation detracts from this value daily to yield overall constant dollars. The face value of the appreciated principal satisfies

$$p1 = p\left(1 + \frac{r1}{365}\right)^{n \times 365}$$

Here p is the principal and n is the year in which the appreciated principal is calculated. The factor 365 denotes days in a year and leap year is ignored. The constant dollar value satisfies

```
mortgage
Input no. months financed (less than 361)
360
Input annual mortgage rate (percent)
12.75
Input amount loan (dollars)
98000.
  MONTHLY MORTGAGE PAYMENT = 1064.959359
  Month       Principal        Interest
    1           23.71          1041.25
   11           26.35          1038.61
   23           29.92          1035.04
   35           33.96          1031.00
   47           38.55          1026.41
   59           43.77          1021.19
   71           49.68          1015.27
   83           56.40          1008.56
   95           64.03          1000.93
  107           72.69           992.27
  119           82.52           982.44
  131           93.68           971.28
  143          106.34           958.62
  155          120.72           944.24
  167          137.05           927.91
  179          155.58           909.38
  191          176.62           888.34
  203          200.50           864.46
  215          227.61           837.35
  227          258.39           806.57
  239          293.33           771.63
  251          332.99           731.97
  263          378.02           686.94
  275          429.13           635.83
  287          487.16           577.80
  299          553.04           511.92
  311          627.82           437.14
  323          712.71           352.25
  335          809.09           255.87
  347          918.49           146.47
  359         1042.69            22.27

<C:\>
```

Figure 2.3c Typical interactive session with mortgage.

$$p2 = \frac{p1}{(1 + (r2/365)^{n \times 365}}$$

Here $r2$ is the annual rate of inflation.

Figure 2.4a contains a flow chart for the program savings.c and Figure 2.4b the corresponding code. This program reads the principal (savings), the annual inflation rate (assumed constant), and the savings interest rate. These are converted to daily decimal values and a for loop generated to output the year, face value, and constant-dollar value of the savings, each year for 30 years. Again, the function pow() is used for raising the adjusted rates to the appropriate power. All output is sent to the screen with printf(). Figure 2.4c is a typical interactive session.

Low-level file creation. So far we have used the standard I/O functions that reside in the library stdio.h. Another set of more primitive I/O routines exists in the library io.h (also, the libraries fcntl.h, sys/types.h, and sys/stat.h are needed). What is the difference between these two types of I/O functions? Basically, the low-level I/O routines are byte or character oriented. Usually, a memory array (buffer) is loaded with the appropriate bytes of information to be output. Then, for

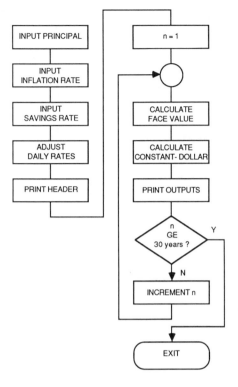

INPUT PRINCIPAL

INPUT
INFLATION RATE

INPUT
SAVINGS RATE

ADJUST
DAILY RATES

PRINT HEADER

n = 1

CALCULATE
FACE VALUE

CALCULATE
CONSTANT- DOLLAR

PRINT OUTPUTS

n
GE
30 years ? Y

N

INCREMENT n

EXIT

Figure 2.4a Flow chart for savings.c a program that determines the appreciated and constant dollar value for a principal amount over 30 years.

example, a call is made to write() to output a fixed count of bytes starting at a specified address.

The specification of integer, floating point, double, or other typed value becomes meaningless in byte-oriented I/O. The user can develop a scheme or convert numbers to ASCII, for example, in byte-oriented I/O, but the normal typed variable declarations are meaningless. In Table 1.11, the major low-level I/O functions are open(), read(), close(), and write(). To illustrate the use of these functions, it will be useful to consider I/O of a character array called buffer that contains ASCII bytes.

Figure 2.5a illustrates a low-level I/O program used to create a file. This program, llcr.c, reads a filename using gets() and reads a character string using cgets(). The routine cgets() loads a string buffer, pointed to by its argument, which has the maximum string size as its first byte and the number of bytes read as its second byte. In llcr.c, buffer is buffer[0], which can act as a pointer to the array buffer. Hence, the statement

```
cgets(buffer);
```

uses buffer as a pointer. Note that numbuf is assigned the length of the input string.

The function open() is used to open the file. Here the pathname (FN1) is the first argument. The second argument consists of *bit-OR'd* manifest constants. This expression is complex. Essentially, the bitwise-OR operator (|) is used to OR (1 bit at a time) the three manifest constants defined in fcntl.h and used as follows:

```
/* This routine calculates savings appreciation/constant-dollar value */

#include <stdio.h>
#include <math.h>                                    /* math library */

main()
        {
        double x1,x2,y,z;                            /* needed by pow */
        float r1,r2,p,p1,p2;
        int n,N;

        printf("Input principal amount \n");
        scanf("%f",&p);
        printf("Input annual inflation rate(percent) \n");
        scanf("%f",&r2);
        printf("Input annual savings rate(percent) \n");
        scanf("%f",&r1);

        r1 = r1/(100. * 365.);                       /* adj daily rate */
        r2 = r2/(100. * 365.);                       /* adj daily rate */
        N = 30;                                      /* max no. years */

        printf("Year   Face Value    CD Value \n");

        x1 = (double)(1.0 + r1);                     /* inflation fact. */
        x2 = (double)(1.0 + r2);                     /* savings factor */
        for(n = 1;n <= N;n++)
            {
            y = (double)(n * 365.);                  /* exponent */
            z = pow(x1,y);
            p1 = (float)(p * z);                     /* Face Value */
            z = pow(x2,y);
            p2 = (float)(p1/z);                      /* CD Value */

            printf(" %d      %7.2f     %7.2f \n",n,p1,p2);
            }
        }
```

Figure 2.4b   Code for savings.c.

O_WRONLY	Open file for writing only
O_TRUNC	Destroy earlier existing contents, if any
O_CREAT	Create and open new file for writing

The third argument is only used with O_CREAT and contains the read/write permission of the file. We use

```
S_IREAD-read
S_IWRITE-write
```

to allow both. The function open() returns a file handle, which is less than 0 for an error condition. The routine perror is called (which uses the library stdlib.h) if such an error occurs. Basically, perror prints the assigned string (in this case "Output file failure") followed by a colon and a hardware-oriented error message.

The write() function has as first argument the file handle. The second argument is the address of the start of the array to be output. Finally, the count of bytes is the third argument. The returned value from write() is integer and if less than zero denotes an error. After the write operation, the file must be closed using close(). Figure 2.5b illustrates an interactive session with llcr.exe. Note that a file LLTXT.DAT is created on drive B and the string "Test ll I/O" written to this file. The test using

```
type b: LLTXT.DAT
```

```
savings
Input principal amount
1000.
Input annual inflation rate(percent)
7.
Input annual savings rate(percent)
10.
Year  Face Value   CD Value
  1     1105.16     1030.45
  2     1221.37     1061.82
  3     1349.80     1094.15
  4     1491.74     1127.47
  5     1648.61     1161.79
  6     1821.97     1197.17
  7     2013.56     1233.62
  8     2225.30     1271.18
  9     2459.30     1309.88
 10     2717.91     1349.76
 11     3003.71     1390.86
 12     3319.57     1433.21
 13     3668.64     1476.85
 14     4054.42     1521.81
 15     4480.77     1568.15
 16     4951.95     1615.89
 17     5472.67     1665.09
 18     6048.16     1715.79
 19     6684.15     1768.03
 20     7387.03     1821.86
 21     8163.82     1877.34
 22     9022.29     1934.50
 23     9971.04     1993.40
 24    11019.55     2054.09
 25    12178.32     2116.63
 26    13458.94     2181.08
 27    14874.23     2247.48
 28    16438.34     2315.91
 29    18166.93     2386.43
 30    20077.29     2459.09

<C:\>
```

Figure 2.4c Typical interactive session with savings.c.

indicates that LLTXT.DAT contains the correctly written string.

Low-level file read.   Figure 2.6a contains the last small program of this chapter, llrd.c. This is another low-level I/O program that opens, reads, and closes a file. The open() function in this program has the manifest constant

O_RDONLY   Open to read only

In this program the read() function is very similar to the write() function. The second argument is the pointer to an array or buffer. In the example, buffer = buffer[0] is a pointer to the array: buffer (we have used the name "buffer" for a buffer). Figure 2.6b illustrates an interactive session where the file LLTXT.DAT (created by llcr.c) is read by llrd.exe. Note that the printf() function outputs the string, which has been correctly read, "Test ll I/O."

2.2.2 Dow Jones Behavior

By way of introduction, it is useful to consider a simple program example in which a time history for the Dow Jones Average is read from disk and displayed graphically on the screen. Figure 2.7a illustrates a structure chart for the program that reads

```
/* Low-level I/O text file creation */

#include <fcntl.h>
#include <sys\types.h>
#include <sys\stat.h>
#include <io.h>
#include <stdio.h>
#include <conio.h>
#include <stdlib.h>                              /* used by perror */

char buffer[82],FN1[81];

main()
        {
        int numbuf,outfile;
        unsigned int bf;

        buffer[0] = 80;                          /* max char */

        printf("Input text-filename \n");
        gets(FN1);
        printf("Input string \n");
        cgets(buffer);                           /* buffered stream */
        numbuf = buffer[1];                      /* length string */

                                                 /* Begin low-level I/O */

        if((outfile = open(FN1,O_WRONLY¦O_TRUNC¦O_CREAT,S_IREAD¦S_IWRITE)) < 0)
            {
            perror("Output file failure");
            exit(1);
            }
        if((bf = write(outfile,&buffer[2],numbuf)) == -1)
            {
            perror("Write file failure");
            exit(1);
            }
        if((bf = close(outfile)) < 0)
            {
            perror("Close file failure");
            exit(1);
            }
        }

<C:\>
```

(a)

```
llcr
Input text-filename
b:LLTXT.DAT
Input string
Test ll I/O
<C:\>type b:LLTXT.DAT
Test ll I/O
<C:\>
```

(b)

Figure 2.5 (a) Low-level I/O file creation program 11cr.c and (b) a typical interactive session illustrating the creation of a file LLTXT.DAT and its contents.

the data and plots the time history. We discuss structure charts in detail in Chapter 3, but as evidenced they present the program architecture in a formal nondynamic way (based on a hierarchical description). In the example considered, the Dow

```
/* Low-level I/O text file read */

#include <fcntl.h>
#include <sys\types.h>
#include <sys\stat.h>
#include <io.h>
#include <stdio.h>
#include <stdlib.h>                                    /* used by perror */

char buffer[82],FN1[81];

main()
        {
        int numbuf = 80,infile,bf;

        printf("Input text filename \n");
        gets(FN1);

        if((infile = open(FN1,O_RDONLY)) < 0)
            {
            perror("Input file failure");
            exit(1);
            }
        if((bf = read(infile,buffer,numbuf)) == -1)
            {
            perror("Read file failure");
            exit(1);
            }
        else
            printf("%s",buffer);
        if((bf = close(infile)) < 0)
            {
            perror("Close file failure");
            exit(1);
            }
        }
```

(a)

```
11rd
Input text filename
b:LLTXT.DAT
Test 11 I/O
<C:\>
```

(b)

Figure 2.6 (a) Low-level I/O file program 11rd.c, and (b) an interactive session reading LLTXT.DAT (Figure 2.10).

Jones Average was obtained from the Value Line reports [1], and a median value for the month was selected, rounded to the nearest five points. The program timhist.c (Figure 2.1b) was used to create a database consisting of 229 values from February 1968 to March 1987. Figure 2.7b illustrates the corresponding flow chart for main().

Figure 2.7c presents the code for the main calling program that reads the disk and generates the plot. A function, read—title(), is used to read the title from the keyboard (this function appears in Figure A.12 and will be used throughout the book to input title material for graphics). Next the code searches the array of data, value[], for a maximum and minimum and sets up the plot scaling accordingly. Finally, a delimiting box and tick marks are drawn and the points plotted.

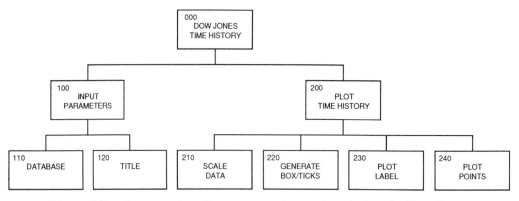

Figure 2.7a Structure chart for a program that reads and plots the Dow Jones time history.

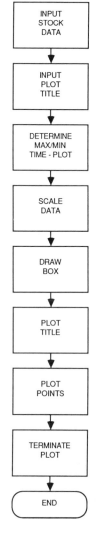

Figure 2.7b Flow chart for the main calling program that plots the Dow Jones Average time history.

66

```
/* Routine to read Dow Jones history */

#include <stdio.h>
#include <dos.h>
#include <math.h>
#include <stdlib.h>

int month[288],year[288];                              /* time arrays */
float value[288];                                      /* quantity */
char FN1[81];                                          /* filename array */
float xx[1024];                                        /* Scratch buffers */
char buffer[90],buffer1[90];

main()
        {
        int n,counter,check,N,i,delta,nmaxs,nmins;     /* integer var. */
        FILE *infile;                                  /* stream pointer */
        double x,y,z;
        float maxt,mint,b,b1;


        printf("Input database filename\n");
        gets(FN1);                                     /* library routine */
        if((infile = fopen(FN1,"r")) == NULL)
            {
            printf("Input file failure: %s",FN1);
            exit(1);
            }
        fscanf(infile,"%d ",&counter);                 /* no. records */
        for(n = 1;n <= counter;n++)
            {
            fscanf(infile,"%d %d %f ",&month[n],&year[n],&value[n]);
            printf("%d %d %f \n",month[n],year[n],value[n]);
            }
        if((check = fclose(infile)) != 0)
            {
            printf("Error in input file close");
            exit(1);
            }

        read_title();

        mint = 1.e4;
        maxt = 0.0;

        N = counter;
        for(i = 1;i <= N;i++)
            {
            if(maxt < value[i])
                maxt = value[i];
            if(mint > value[i])
                mint = value[i];
            }
                                                       /* Set scale */
        delta = maxt - mint;
        delta = delta/10;
        if(delta < 1)
            delta = 1;
        if(delta > 1 && delta < 5)
            delta = 5;
        if(delta > 5 && delta < 10)
            delta = 10;
        if(delta > 10 && delta < 50)
            delta = 50;
```

Figure 2.7c Program code for the Dow Jones time history plot program.

```
if(delta > 50 && delta < 100)
    delta = 100;
if(delta > 100 && delta < 500)
    delta`= 500;
if(delta > 500)
    {
    printf(" delta > 500");
    exit(1);
    }
nmaxs = maxt/delta + 1;
nmins = mint/delta;
maxt = delta*nmaxs;
mint = delta*nmins;
if(mint <= 0)
    mint = mint - delta;

x = mint;
y = fabs(x);
z = (float)(y);
b1 = (z)/((float)(x));
if(maxt > z && b1 < 0)
    mint = -maxt;
else
    {
    if(maxt < z && b1 < 0)
        maxt = z;
    }

b = 150./(maxt - mint);
for(i = 1;i <= N;i++)
    {
    value[i] = 25. + (150. - b*(value[i] - mint));
    xx[i] = 25. + (i - 1)*(256./(float)(N));
    }
box_norm();
for(n = 0;n <= 89;n++)
    buffer[n] = buffer1[n];
PLTBUF(0,0);

for(n = 1;n <= (N-1);n++)
    plotpoint(xx[n],xx[n+1],value[n],value[n+1]);

plotterm();

printf("maxt = %f\n",maxt);
printf("mint = %f\n",mint);

}
```

Figure 2.7c   *(Concluded)*

To understand how the graphics are generated, it is necessary to recall the discussion of Section 1.3 regarding interrupts and 8088 (80286) register values. Examination of Figure 2.7c demonstrates that a function box__norm() is called following scaling of the data. Figure 2.8a illustrates this function. It, in turn, calls the following functions [where the corresponding figures containing the code are indicated and some of these functions are nested, for example WRDOT() is called by bbox(). . .]:

```
bbox()
xtick()
```
(Figure 2.8a)
(Figure 2.8a)

```
/* Function to draw box for normal plot */

#include <stdio.h>

box_norm()
        {
        int xxbeg,xxend,yybeg,yyend;
        int row,col,grid,xxtick,yytick,n;
        int ssxtick,ssytick,eextick,eeytick;
        int x_space = 64;

        printf("Input 1-grid or 0-no grid");
        scanf("%d",&grid);


        xxbeg = 25;                                     /* Box parameters */
        xxend = 281;
        yybeg = 25;
        yyend = 175;

        SCRCL();                                        /* Clear screen */
        SC320();                                        /* 320 x 200 mode */

        bbox(xxbeg,xxend,yybeg,yyend);                  /* Plot box */

        xxtick = 89;                                    /* Draw x-ticks */
        ssxtick = 173;
        eextick = 177;
        for(n = 1;n <= 3;n++)
            {
            xtick(xxtick,ssxtick,eextick);
            xxtick = xxtick + x_space;
            }

        yytick = 100;                                   /* Draw y-tick */
        ssytick = 23;
        eeytick = 27;
        ytick(yytick,ssytick,eeytick);

        if(grid == 1)
            {                                           /* Draw grids */
            linev(xxtick,yybeg,yyend);
            linev(xxtick+x_space,yybeg,yyend);
            linev(xxtick+x_space*2,yybeg,yyend);

                                                        /* Hor. lines */
            lineh(yytick,xxbeg,xxend);
            }
        }
```

Figure 2.8a Program code for the function box_norm( ), which plots a box and tick marks.

ytick()	(Figure 2.8a)
SCRCL()	(Figure 2.8b)
SC320()	(Figure 2.8b)
KEYDEL()	(Figure 2.8b)
SC80()	(Figure 2.8b)
PLTBUF()	(Figure 2.8c)
plotpoint()	(Figure 2.8d)
plotterm()	(Figure 2.8d)
linev()	(Figure 2.8e)

```
/* Function bbox */

bbox(xxbeg,xxend,yybeg,yyend)
        int xxbeg,xxend,yybeg,yyend;
        {
        int row,col;

        row = yybeg;
        col = xxbeg;

        for(row = yybeg;row <= yyend;row++)
            WRDOT(row,col);
        row--;
        for(col = xxbeg;col <= xxend;col++)
            WRDOT(row,col);
        col--;
        for(row = yyend;row >= yybeg;row--)
            WRDOT(row,col);
        row++;
        for(col = xxend;col >= xxbeg;col--)
            WRDOT(row,col);
        col++;
        }

/* x-tick function */

xtick(xpos,ssxtick,eextick)
        int xpos,ssxtick,eextick;
        {
        int row,col;

        col = xpos;
        for(row = ssxtick;row <=eextick;row++)
            WRDOT(row,col);
        }

/* y-tick function */

ytick(ypos,ssytick,eeytick)
        int ypos,ssytick,eeytick;
        {
        int row,col;

        row = ypos;
        for(col = ssytick;col <= eeytick;col++)
            WRDOT(row,col);
        }
```

Figure 2.8a *(Concluded)*

```
lineh()          (Figure 2.8e)
WRDOT()          (Figure 2.8b)
```

The functions indicated are all part of a library called cplotlib.lib, which was generated using the Microsoft library utility, and the contents of this library are illustrated in Figure A.13. Also illustrated in Figure A.13 is a typical session with lib during which the object files, title and pltbuf, are being added to the library. (Throughout this text, libraries will be used to simplify reference to existing routines. The corresponding code will always be referenced by figure number for each routine referenced.)

What do the preceding functions do during their execution? SCRCL() clears the screen and SC320() places the computer in 320×200 graphics mode. These functions call INT 10H and appropriately set registers. The setting of these register values is in accordance with Table 2.1, and they are obtained from the *IBM Technical*

```
/* This file, CPLOT.C, contains plot routines written in C */

#include <dos.h>

SCRCL()                                 /* Function to clear screen */
        {
        union REGS regs;

        regs.h.ah = 6;                  /* Scroll active page up */
        regs.h.al = 0;                  /* Blanks entire page */
        regs.h.ch = 0;                  /* row = 0 upper left */
        regs.h.cl = 0;                  /* column = 0 upper left */
        regs.h.dh = 23;                 /* row lower right */
        regs.h.dl = 79;                 /* col lower right */
        regs.h.bh = 7;                  /* Blank attribute */

        int86(0x10,&regs,&regs);
        }

WRDOT(row,col)                          /* Function to write dot-graphics */
        int row,col;

        {
        union REGS regs;

        regs.x.dx = row;                /* Row value */
        regs.x.cx = col;                /* Column value */
        regs.h.al = 1;                  /* Attribute 1 */
        regs.h.ah = 12;                 /* Write dot */

        int86(0x10,&regs,&regs);
        }

SC320()                                 /* Function to set graphics mode */
        {
        union REGS regs;

        regs.h.ah = 0;                  /* Set mode */
        regs.h.al = 5;                  /* 320 x 200 graphics mode */

        int86(0x10,&regs,&regs);
        }

SC80()                                  /* Function to set alpha mode */
        {
        union REGS regs;

        regs.h.ah = 0;                  /* Set mode */
        regs.h.al = 2;                  /* 80 x 25 BW alpha mode */

        int86(0x10,&regs,&regs);
        }

KEYDEL()                                /* Function set delay */
        {
        union REGS regs;

        regs.h.ah = 0;                  /* Keyboard interrupt */

        int86(0x16,&regs,&regs);        /* Wait for keystroke */
        }
```

Figure 2.8b Functions for controlling screen output for graphics mode.

Reference [2]. This table describes the setting of the ah register to select the video I/O option and the values for the remaining needed registers: ax(ah,al), bx(bh,bl), cx(ch,cl), dx(dh,dl), si, di, sp, bp, and cf. The segment registers, ss, cs, ds, and es, are only used for segment addressing. For example, to output a character in

```
/* Plot graphics char buffer in "buffer". */

#include <dos.h>

PLTBUF(x1,y1)
        int x1,y1;
        {
        extern char buffer[];
        int n;
        union REGS regs;

        regs.h.dh = y1;                                    /* Initialize regs */
        regs.h.dl = x1;
        regs.h.bh = 0;

        for(n = 2;n < (buffer[1]+2);n++)
            {
            regs.h.ah = 2;                                 /* position cursor */
            int86(0x10,&regs,&regs);

            regs.x.cx = 1;                                 /* Single char */
            regs.h.ah = 10;                                /* Write char */
            regs.h.al = buffer[n];
            regs.h.bl = 1;                                 /* Attribute */
            int86(0x10,&regs,&regs);
            regs.h.dl++;                                   /* Inc x-pos */
            }
        }
```

Figure 2.8c Function PLTBUF(), which writes a string of characters from buffer to the display in graphics mode.

```
/* This routine plots a connecting line*/

plotpoint (x1,x2,y1,y2)
        float x1,x2,y1,y2;

        {
        float m;
        int row;
        int col;

        if (x1 == x2)
                m = 1000;                        /*Upper limit on slope*/

        else
                m = (y2 - y1)/(x2 - x1);

        for (col = x1; col <= x2; col++)
                {
                row = y1 + m*(col - x1);
                WRDOT(row,col);
                }
        }
/*Assembler calls to return to 80 x 25 mode with delay*/

plotterm()
        {
        KEYDEL();
        SC80();
        }
```

Figure 2.8d Functions to generate a connecting line between plotted points and terminate plot.

```
/* This routine plots a vertical line */

linev(x,y1,y2)
        int x,y1,y2;

        {
        int ncount,col,row,n;

        if(y1 > y2)
            {
            ncount = y1 - y2;
            col = x;
            row = y2;
            for(n = 0;n <= ncount; n++)
                {
                WRDOT(row,col);
                row++;
                }
            }
        else
            {
            ncount = y2 - y1;
            col = x;
            row = y1;
            for(n = 0;n <= ncount; n++)
                {
                WRDOT(row,col);
                row++;
                }
            }
        }
/* Function to plot horizontal line */

lineh(y,x1,x2)
        int y,x1,x2;
        {
        int ncount,col,row,n;

        if(x1 > x2)
            {
            ncount = x1 - x2;
            row = y;
            col = x2;
            for(n = 0;n <= ncount;n++)
                {
                WRDOT(row,col);
                col++;
                }
            }
        else
            {
            ncount = x2 - x1;
            row = y;
            col = x1;
            for(n = 0;n <= ncount;n++)
                {
                WRDOT(row,col);
                col++;
                }
            }
        }
```

Figure 2.8e Functions linev() and lineh(), which plot vertical and horizontal lines.

graphics mode, the character value must reside at the address pointed to by ds:dx. In all references, lowercase letters are used in the programs, but frequently tabular data employ both upper- and lowercase. The two letter cases are to be used interchangeably in the IBM environment with AX=ax, BX=bx, ...

The remaining functions generate the box, *x*-axis tick marks, and *y*-axis tick

TABLE 2.1 THE 8088 (80286) REGISTER SETTINGS FOR VIDEO I/O

AH	Purpose	Description
0	Mode	The AL register contains the mode value: 0, 40 × 25 pixel black/white; 1, 40 × 25 pixel color; 2, 80 × 25 pixel black/white; 3, 80 × 25 pixel color; 4, 320 × 200 pixel color; 5, 320 × 200 pixel black/white; and 6, 640 × 200 pixel black/white.
1	Set cursor type	This option uses CH and CL: CH, (bits 4 to 0) start line for cursor; CL, (bits 4 to 0) end line for cursor. All other bits should be set to zero to avoid erratic behavior.
2	Set cursor position	(DH, DL) = (row, column) cursor. Upper left is (0, 0). BH = page number (0 for graphics).
3	Read cursor position	(DH, DL) = (row, column) cursor on exit. (CH, CL) = cursor mode.
4	Read light pen position	See *IBM Technical Reference Manual*.
5	Select active display page	This allows the user to scroll pages in video memory for the 40 × 25 and 80 × 25 displays, where more than one page can be stored. AL = 0 to 7 for 40 × 25 and AL = 0 to 3 for 80 × 25.
6	Scroll active page up	AL = number of lines. Lines are blanked at the bottom and 0 blanks the entire screen. (CH, CL) = (row, column) upper left corner, (DH, DL) = (row, column) lower right corner, and BH = attribute used on blank lines.
7	Scroll active page down	Same as 6 except lines blanked from top down.
8	Read attribute/ character at cursor	BH = display page, AL = character, and AH = attribute. 40 x 25 and 80 x 25 displays only.
9	Write attribute/ character at cursor	BH = display page, CX = character count, AL = character to write, and BL = attribute of character.
10	Write character at cursor	Same as 9 with no attribute.
11	Set color palette	Sets the color palette. User should experiment with this option. See *IBM Technical Reference Manual* for register settings.
12	Write dot	DX = row number, CX = column number, AL = color value (for high-resolution displays, this varies the intensity).
13	Read dot	DX = row number, CX = column number, and AL = dot read.
14	Graphics/alpha character write	AL = character, BL = foreground color in graphics mode, BH = display page in alpha mode.
15	Current video state	AL = mode, AH = number columns on screen, and BH = active display page.

marks, and draw grid lines as needed. To do this, the routines all call WRDOT(), a function that writes a single dot or pel to the screen at a row and column position. Most of the graphics in this book are generated using WRDOT() as the basic unit for drawing. By repeatedly calling WRDOT() and moving the location of the dot each time, complex graphics can be generated. In Figure 2.8b, the code for writing a dot, WRDOT(), is quite simple and based on the INT 10H and register values indicated in Table 2.1. Returning to Figure 2.7c, we see that PLTBUF() (Figure 2.8c) is called to output the character buffer that contains the title. This buffer must be output one character at a time using INT 10H with register values set as indicated in Table 2.1.

Next the actual Dow Jones data contained in value[] are plotted using the routine plotpoint(). To understand how plotpoint operates, consider two disjoint points on the screen at coordinates (x_1, y_1) and (x_2, y_2), respectively. (Assume x corresponds to a column value [1, 320] and y corresponds to a row value [1, 200].) If we are plotting a dot at these points, it is desirable perhaps to link the two points with a line to show connectivity. Since there may exist pels on the screen between these two points, a program could fill in these pels and the screen would appear to have a line connecting the two points. To do this, we use the equation for a straight line:

$$y = y_0 + m(x - x_0) \qquad (2.1)$$

Here

$$m = \frac{y_2 - y_1}{x_2 - x_1} \qquad (2.2)$$

This connecting line is simply a vector between the points in question.

Unfortunately, the density of dots available on the IBM Color Graphics Adapter (CGA) screen is at most 320×200 or 640×200. While this seems like a lot of points, the screen is large and frequently the connecting lines appear jagged. This is because the slope is effectively quantized. To understand this, consider two points with slope 0.1 between them. Recognizing that y, y_0, x, and x_0 are all integers in Equation (2.1), it follows that

$$y = y_0 + (0.1)(x - x_0) \qquad (2.3)$$

Clearly, for y to increase by one pel on the screen, $x - x_0$ must change by 11 pels in the horizontal direction. Thus, the lines appear broken.

In the plot of the Dow Jones, however, we will be providing 229 values in a space that has room for 256 values. Hence, almost all points will appear as independent of each other. There will be essentially no possibility for implementing a connecting line. Later in this section the effects of connecting line graphics will become apparent.

The function plotterm() calls the functions KEYDEL() and SC80(). The latter simply invokes INT 10H to return the screen to normal 80×25 alphanumeric mode (Table 2.1). KEYDEL() calls INT 16H, which stops the program until an external keyboard interrupt (implemented by pressing a key) occurs. This function simply freezes the graphics on the screen and then returns to the normal alphanumeric mode when a key is struck.

DJ AVERAGE (FEB 1968 — MAR 1987)

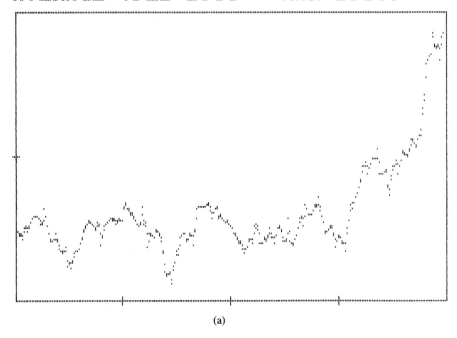

(a)

DJ AVERAGE (FEB 1968 — MAR 1987)

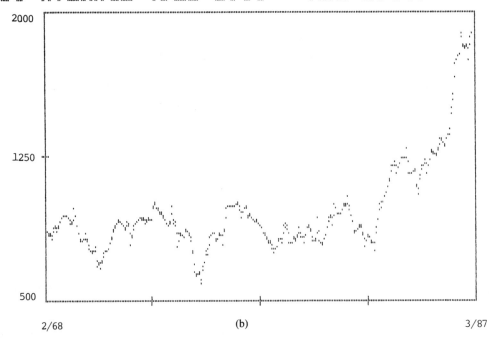

2/68   (b)   3/87

Figure 2.9   Graph of the Dow Jones Average from February 1968 to March 1987:
(a) normal output and (b) annotated output.

Figure 2.9a illustrates the output for this program. The title, DJ AVERAGE (FEB 1968-MAR 1987), was input at the keyboard in response to the prompt. The program is called dja.c and the box generator is called boxnorm.c. The link sequence is as follows:

```
link dja + boxnorm
Microsoft(R) Overlay Linker Version 3.51
Copyright (c) Microsoft Corp. 1983, 1984, 1985, 1986. All
rights reserved.

Run File [DJA.EXE]:
List File [NUL.MAP]:
Libraries [.LIB]: cplotlib
```

Figure 2.9b is a second illustration of the same figure presenting labels on the graph for clarification. This latter, annotated version of graphics will always be the form we will present in future examples. The last two print statements in the program appearing in Figure 2.7c were used to obtain the vertical scale of the output. The horizontal scale was known from the input data.

2.2.3 FM Spectra

We have set this section off with an asterisk because it assumes some knowledge of advanced mathematical techniques in the form of the Fourier transform. Although it is not absolutely necessary that the reader be familiar with the Fourier transform to complete the programming of this section, such an understanding does facilitate an appreciation for the results obtained. [The reader can use the functions FFT() and hanwt() from Appendix A with test drivers to validate this code, without a knowledge of the Fourier transform itself.]

With these thoughts in mind, the focus of this section is to illustrate frequency modulation (FM) waveforms and their resulting spectra. First a brief digression into FM waves. Normal amplitude modulation (AM) involves the amplitude variation of a sinusoidal wave. Typically,

$$x(t) = a(t) \cos(2\pi ft) + jb(t) \sin(2\pi ft) \tag{2.4}$$

is a complex sinusoid of frequency f. Here $j = \sqrt{-1}$. The information content of such a signal is contained in $a(t)$ and $b(t)$. The frequency is *fixed*. If one considers a wave

$$x(t) = \cos[2 (ft + a(t))] + j \sin[2\pi(ft + a(t))] \tag{2.5}$$

the phase of the wave and, consequently, the instantaneous frequency vary with time. This wave is representative of a class known as frequency modulated waves. For purposes of illustration, it is convenient to consider a linear FM pulse defined by

$$x(t) = \begin{cases} \cos\left(2\pi\dfrac{ft + at^2}{2}\right) + j \sin\left(2\pi\dfrac{ft + at^2}{2}\right), & (0 < t < 32 \ \mu s) \\ 0 & \text{elsewhere} \end{cases} \tag{2.6}$$

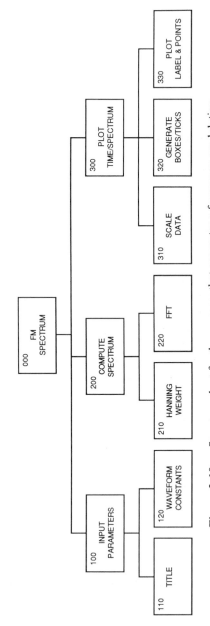

Figure 2.10a Structure chart for the program that generates a frequency modulation (FM) waveform and associated spectrum.

Here

$$a = \frac{B}{T} \qquad (2.7)$$

where B is the bandwidth of the pulse and T the dispersion.

If we quantize the time in sample intervals of width dt, it is possible to define the discrete Fourier transform of $x(t)$ as

$$X(mdf) = \frac{1}{N} \sum_{n-N/2}^{N/2} x(n\ dt) e^{j2\pi mn/N} \qquad (2.8)$$

The frequency $f_m = mdf$ and the time $t_n = ndt$. The total number of intervals defined across 32 microseconds is N, where we have assumed that the transform can be periodically extended.

The spectrum at frequency f_m is given by

$$S(f_m) = |X(mdf)|^2 \qquad (2.9)$$

Figure 2.10a presents a structure chart for the program that generates a linear FM pulse based on input parameters, calculates the resulting spectrum using the fast fourier transform of Appendix A, and plots both the spectrum and input time series. Figure 2.10b contains the flow chart for main().

Figure 2.10c illustrates the main calling program, main(). A center frequency, bandwidth, and dispersion are read into the program as input data. Next, 128 values for the time series are calculated spaced at normalized sample units of 0.25. All frequency units are assumed to be in megahertz (MHz), and time units are assumed in microseconds (μs). The sample interval is assumed to correspond to 0.25 μs, which yields a total time span of 32 μs for the truncated 128 samples. Both real and imaginary terms are calculated as in Equation (2.6). The input real-time series

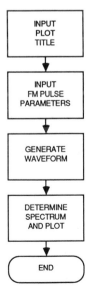

Figure 2.10b Flow chart for the main calling program that plots the FM waveform and associated spectra.

```
/* Function to display FM spectrum */

#include <stdio.h>
#include <dos.h>
#include <math.h>
#include <stdlib.h>

float areal[1024],aimag[1024],ssignal[1024];        /* FFT array-input */
float xx[1024],xx1[1024];                            /* Scrat
ch buffer */
char buffer[90],buffer1[90];                         /* title buffers */
char FN1[81];                                        /* title array */

main()
        {
        float B,T,t,dt,a,f0,pi = 3.141592654;
        int m,N,n;
        double x,y;

        read_title();
        printf("Input center frequency (MHz)\n");
        scanf("%f",&f0);
        printf("Input bandwidth (MHz)\n");
        scanf("%f",&B);
        printf("Input time delay (microseconds)\n");
        scanf("%f",&T);

        m = 7;                                       /* Order FFT */
        N = 128;                                     /* Number points */
        t = 0.0;                                     /* Start time */
        dt = 1./4.;                                  /* Time spacing */
        a = B/T;                                     /* phase constant */

        for(n = 1;n <= N;n++)
            {
            x = 2. * pi * (f0*t + a*t*t/2.);
            y = cos(x);
            areal[n] = (float)(y);
            ssignal[n] = areal[n];
            aimag[n] = (float)(y);
            t = t + dt;
            }

        spectrum2(m);
        }
```

Figure 2.10c   Code for the FM waveform and associated spectra program.

is saved in the array ssignal[] for eventual display. The function spectrum2(), whose flow chart appears in Figure 2.11a, is called to calculate the power spectrum of the pulse. The code for spectrum2() is contained in Figure 2.11b.

In spectrum2() the following functions are called:

hanwt()	(Figure A.2b)
FFT()	(Figure A.2b)
box_spect()	(Figure A.10)
PLTBUF()	(Figure 2.8c)
plotpoint()	(Figure 2.8d)
plotterm()	(Figure 2.8d)

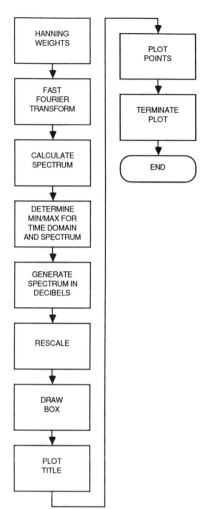

Figure 2.11a Flow chart for the function spectrum2( ).

These in turn call the other graphics input/output (I/O) functions of Figure 2.8b. The function hanwt() simply weights the time series input to the fast Fourier tranform routine, FFT(). This routine calculates the transform of Equation (2.8).

After the power spectra are generated, appropriate scaling for the time domain and frequency domain is obtained. Then the input time series is plotted as well as the output spectrum. Figure 2.12a, b, and c illustrates typical plots. The title input for each of these figures was FM WAVEFORM. In Figure 2.12a the bandwidth was assumed equal to 0 MHz, hence the time series is a simple sinusoid. The frequency of the sinusoid was chosen equal to 100 kilohertz (kHz). It is clear that the peak in the spectrum is at 0.1 MHz.

The maximum resolvable frequency in the FFT output is given by the Nyquist value [3] of

$$F_{max} = \frac{1}{2dt} \tag{2.10}$$

```
/* This routine generates a power spectrum and plots it */

#include <stdio.h>
#include <math.h>
#include <stdlib.h>

spectrum2(m)
        int m;                                          /* FFT order */
        {
        extern float areal[],aimag[],ssignal[],xx[],xx1[];
        extern buffer[],buffer1[],buffer2[];

        double x,y,z;
        float maxt,mint,maxs,mins,b,b1;
        int N,n,i;
        int delta,nmaxs,nmins;


        x = 2.;
        y = m;
        z = pow(x,y);
        N = z;


        hanwt(m);                                       /* Hanning wt */
        FFT(m,1);                                       /* FFT */

                                                        /* Calc spectra */
        for(i = 1;i <= N;i++)
            {
            areal[i] = areal[i]*areal[i]+aimag[i]*aimag[i];
            areal[i] = .5*sqrt(areal[i]);
            }


        mins = 1.e4;
        maxs = 0.0;
        mint = 1.e4;
        maxt = 0.0;

        for(i = 1;i <= N;i++)                           /* max/min */
            {
            if(maxt < ssignal[i])
                maxt = ssignal[i];
            if(mint > ssignal[i])
                mint = ssignal[i];
            if(maxs < areal[i])
                maxs = areal[i];
            if(mins > areal[i])
                mins = areal[i];
            }
                                                        /* Log plot */
        for(i = 1;i <= N;i++)
            {
            aimag[i] = areal[i]/maxs;
            x = areal[i];
            y = log10(x);
            areal[i] = 20. * y;
            }

                                                        /* Rescale */
        maxs = 0.0;
        mins = 1.e4;
```

Figure 2.11b The program code for the function spectrum2( ), which computes the power spectrum of an input time series and plots the one-sided spectrum.

```
for(n = 1;n <= N;n++)
    {
    if(maxs < areal[n])
        maxs = areal[n];
    if(mins > areal[n])
        mins = areal[n];
    }

delta = maxs - mins;
delta = delta/10;
if(delta < 10)
    delta = 10;
if(delta > 10 && delta < 20)
    delta = 20;
if(delta > 20 && delta < 50)
    delta = 50;
if(delta > 50 && delta < 100)
    delta = 100;
if(delta > 100 && delta < 500)
    delta = 500;
if(delta > 500 && delta < 1000)
    delta = 1000;
if(delta > 1000)
    exit(1);
nmaxs = maxs/delta+1;
nmins = mins/delta;
maxs = delta*nmaxs;
mins = delta*nmins;
if(mins <= 0)
    mins = mins - delta;

delta = maxt - mint;
delta = delta/10;
if(delta < 1)
    delta = 1;
if(delta > 1 && delta < 5)
    delta = 5;
if(delta > 5 && delta < 10)
    delta = 10;
if(delta > 10 && delta < 50)
    delta = 50;
if(delta > 50 && delta < 100)
    delta = 100;
if(delta > 100 && delta < 500)
    delta = 500;
if(delta > 500)
    exit(1);
nmaxs = maxt/delta+1;
nmins = mint/delta;
maxt = delta*nmaxs;
mint = delta*nmins;
if(mint <= 0)
    mint = mint - delta;

x = mint;
y = fabs(x);
z = (float)(y);
b1 = (z)/((float)(x));
if(maxt > z && b1 < 0)
    mint = - maxt;
else
    {
    if(maxt < z && b1 < 0)
        maxt = z;
    }
```

Figure 2.11b (*Continued*)

```
/* Scale -- time domain fit between 75 and 25 on CRT and spectra fit
** between 175 and 95 on CRT */
        b = 50./(maxt - mint);
        b1 = 80./(maxs - mins);
        for(i = 1;i <= N;i++)
            {
            ssignal[i] = 25 + (50 - b*(ssignal[i] - mint));
            areal[i] = 95 + (80 - b1*(areal[i] - mins));
            xx[i] = 25 +(i - 1)* (256/N);
            xx1[i] = 25 + 2*(i - 1)*(256/N);
            }

                                                        /* Plot */
        box_spect();
                                                        /* Labels */

        for(n = 0;n <= 89;n++)
            buffer[n] = buffer1[n];
        PLTBUF(0,0);

        for(n = 1;n <= (N-1);n++)
            plotpoint(xx[n],xx[n+1],ssignal[n],ssignal[n+1]);
        for(n = 1;n <= N/2;n++)
            plotpoint(xx1[n],xx1[n+1],areal[n],areal[n+1]);

        plotterm();

        printf(" maxs = %f\n",maxs);
        printf(" mins = %f\n",mins);
        printf(" maxt = %f\n",maxt);
        printf(" mint = %f\n",mint);
        }
```

Figure 2.11b *(Concluded)*

For the spacing of 0.25 μs, this corresponds to a frequency of 2 MHz. Using $N = 128$, however, means that a range of 4 MHz is output from the FFT. One-half of these values are redundant due to symmetry. Hence, in the FFT output (such as the spectra of Figure 2.12) only half of the output will be presented.

Figure 2.12b illustrates a true linear FM pulse. The frequency variation with time is readily apparent. Here the frequency is 0.1 MHz again, but the bandwidth (B) is now nonzero at 0.01 MHz. A dispersive delay (T) of 1 μs has been assumed. The pulse spectrum is significantly broadened, with bandwidth of roughly 0.01 MHz at roughly 3 decibels (dB) below the peak. Note that all spectra magnitudes are expressed in decibels according to

$$S_{dB}(f) = 20 \log_{10}[S(f)] \qquad (2.11)$$

Finally, Figure 2.12c presents a second linear FM waveform and spectrum for another 0.1-MHz center frequency example. In this case, however, the linear FM bandwidth is double that for Figure 2.12b (.02 MHz) and the dispersion is chosen the same.

2.2.4 Gaussian Random Numbers

This discussion centers on the definition of Gaussian random numbers and their display on the screen. It is possible to generate two independent Gaussian random numbers, y_1 and y_2, using the following expressions:

FM WAVEFORM

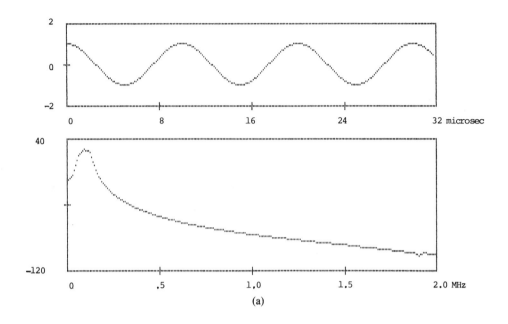

(a)

FM WAVEFORM

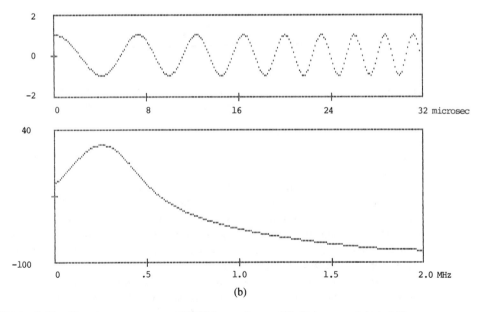

(b)

Figure 2.12 Time/spectrum outputs for FM waveforms with (frequency, bandwidth, dispersion) equal to (a) (0.1 MHz, 0.0 MHz, 1 μs) (b) (0.1 MHz, 0.01 MHz, 1 μs) and (c) (0.1 MHz, 0.02 MHz, 1 μs).

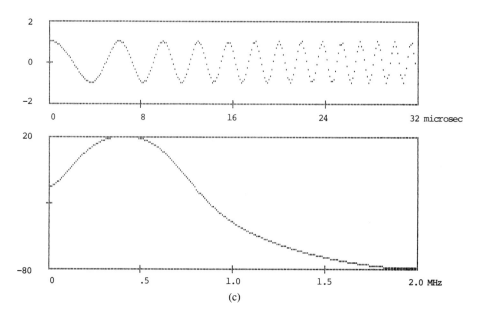

(c)

Figure 2.12   *(Concluded)*

$$y_1 = \sqrt{-2 \ln(x_1)} \, \cos(2\pi x_2) \tag{2.12a}$$

$$y_2 = \sqrt{-2 \ln(x_1)} \, \sin(2\pi x_2) \tag{2.12b}$$

Here x_1 and x_2 are two uniformly distributed random numbers in the range 0 to 1.

Figure 2.13a presents the structure chart for a program that generates and plots Gaussian random numbers. Figure 2.13b is the flow chart for the main calling module, main(). Figure 2.13c illustrates the function main() that calls four functions: box(), grand(), plotpoint(), and plotterm(). This program is designed to generate 100 Gaussian random numbers and plot the 50 of these numbers associated with num1, the sine term appearing in Equation (2.12b). First the function box() is called, which draws a box on the screen. Next the function grand() is called, which returns the Gaussian random numbers. These numbers are scaled to lie between 25 and 175. Note that the exact association for the Gaussian random numbers is not explicitly stated (25 corresponds to num1 = 10. and 175 corresponds to num = -10.), but follows from Figure 2.13a.

The function plotpoint() actually plots the points on the display. Plotterm() terminates the plot and waits for a keyboard input to return the display to the normal alphanumeric mode, as discussed previously. Figure 2.13d illustrates the display output.

Figure 2.14 illustrates the functions box() and tick() used to develop the outlying

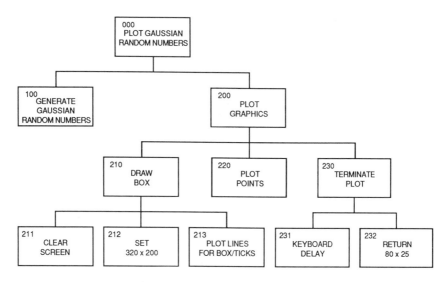

Figure 2.13a Structure chart for program that generates and plots Gaussian random numbers.

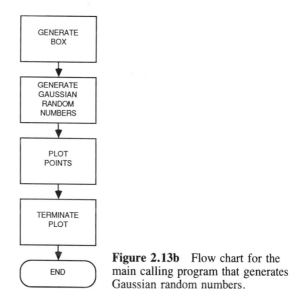

Figure 2.13b Flow chart for the main calling program that generates Gaussian random numbers.

box on the graphics display that contains the graph material (and the associated tick marks). The reader should note that beginning and ending coordinates, x and y, are passed to this module via extern declarations. [In Figure 2.13c, these variables are defined and initialized as global variables in the preprocessor area for main().] Both box() and tick() call another function WRDOT() used to write a dot at the selected row and column value. The function box() calls SCRCL() to clear the screen and SC320() to put the screen in 320 × 200 graphics mode.

In Figure 2.15, the function grand() is presented. This function calls the random

```
/*Gaussian random number calling plot program*/

#include <stdio.h>

int xbeg = 25, xend = 275, ybeg = 25, yend = 175;
int sytick = 23, eytick = 27, sxtick = 173, extick = 177;
int xcount = 4, ycount =1;
int xvalue[4] = {75,125,175,225};
int yvalue[1] = {100};
float xx[51];
float yy[51];
int n;
float num1,num2;

main()
        {
        box();
        for (n = 0; n <= 50; n++)
                {
                xx[n] = (n*5.)+25.;
                grand();
                yy[n] = 100. - (num1*75./10.0);
                }
        for (n = 0; n <= 49; n++)
                plotpoint(xx[n],xx[n+1],yy[n],yy[n+1]);
        plotterm();
        }
```

(c)

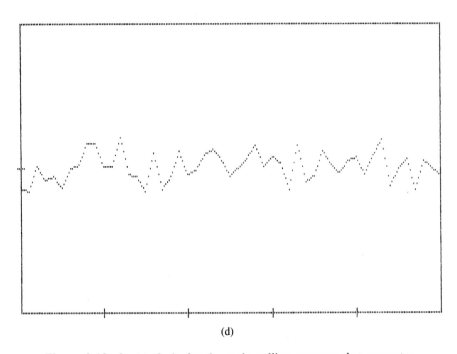

(d)

Figure 2.13c,d (c) Code for the main calling program that generates Gaussian random numbers and (d) the plotted output.

```
/* This routine draws a box and generates tick marks */

box()
        {
        int row;
        int col;

        extern int xbeg;           /*Beginning x*/
        extern int xend;           /*Ending x*/
        extern int ybeg;           /*Beginning y*/
        extern int yend;           /*Ending y*/

        row = ybeg;                /*Initialize row*/
        col = xbeg;                /*Initialize col*/

        SCRCL();                   /* Screen clear */
        SC320();                   /* 320 x 200 mode */
                                   /*Draw left vertical line*/
        for (row = ybeg; row <= yend; row++)
                WRDOT(row,col);
        row = row - 1;
                                   /*Draw bottom horizontal line*/
        for (col = xbeg; col <= xend; col++)
                WRDOT(row,col);
        col = col - 1;
                                   /*Draw right vertical line*/
        for (row = yend; row >= ybeg; row--)
                WRDOT(row,col);
        row = row + 1;
                                   /*Draw top horizontal line*/
        for (col = xend; col >= xbeg; col--)
                WRDOT(row,col);
        col = col + 1;
                                   /*Draw ticks*/
        tick();



}
tick()
        {
        extern int sxtick;
        extern int extick;
        extern int sytick;
        extern int eytick;
        extern int xvalue[],yvalue[],xcount,ycount;
        int n,row,col;

        for (n = 0; n <= (xcount-1); n++)
                {
                col = xvalue[n];
                for (row = sxtick; row <= extick; row++)
                        WRDOT(row,col);
                }
        for (n = 0; n <= (ycount-1); n++)
                {
                row = yvalue[n];
                for (col = sytick; col <= eytick; col++)
                        WRDOT(row,col);
                }
        }
```

Figure 2.14 Functions to generate box and tick marks on display.

```
/*Gaussian random number pair*/

#include <stdlib.h>
#include <math.h>

grand()
        {
        extern float num1,num2;
        double pi = 3.141592654,arg1,arg2,x,y;
        double z,w;
        int x1,x2;
        float y1,y2;

        x1 = rand();
        x2 = rand();
        y1 = (float)(x1)/32767.;
        y2 = (float)(x2)/32767.;

        y = y1;
        x = -2.*log(y);
        arg1 = sqrt(x);
        z = 2.*pi*y2;
        arg2 = sin(z);
        num1 = arg1*arg2;
        w = z;
        arg2 = cos(w);
        num2 = arg1*arg2;

        }
```

Figure 2.15 Function to generate Gaussian random number.

number library function, rand(), that generates a random number between 0 and 32767. Observe that two calls are made to rand() and the result is set equal to x_1 and x_2, respectively. Since these variables are locally defined, there is no global conflict with their use in plotpoint(), where they are also local. The remainder of grand() is a simple implementation of Equation (2.12a) and (2.12b).

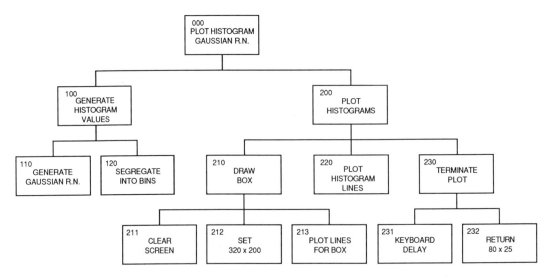

Figure 2.16a Structure chart for program that plots histograms for Gaussian random numbers, illustrating normal distribution.

Gaussian random numbers constitute values that are normally distributed about zero. A convenient mechanism to illustrate this normal or bell-shaped distribution is to compute a histogram for many values of Gaussian random numbers. Since an appreciation of these variables requires defining proportions over various intervals (such as the one, two, three, ... sigma points), we will only examine the distribution with regard to its general bell-shaped characteristic. This examination will be in the form of a visual inspection of the histogram as presented on the display.

Figure 2.16a is a structure chart for a program that generates Gaussian random numbers, by calling grand(), and plots a normalized graph of the resulting histogram. Figure 2.16b contains the corresponding flow chart. The bins in the histogram are spaced at unit intervals across the screen between 0 and 250, with the mean value of the Gaussian random variable at 125. The program appearing in Figure 2.16c calls a function linev() to generate the vertical line for each histogram bin. Figure 2.8e illustrates this function, which appears in the library cplotlib.lib, and it is clear that it in turn calls WRDOT() to plot the actual points.

Figure 2.17(a) through (e) presents the histogram output for 1000, 5000, 10,000, 20,000, and 40,000 samples, respectively. Examination of these figures demonstrates

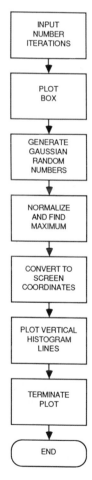

Figure 2.16b Flow chart for the main calling program that generates the Gaussian random number histogram.

```
/* Gaussian r.n. histogram */

#include <stdio.h>

int xvalue[4] = {75,125,175,225};
int yvalue[1] = {100};
float xx[250],yy[250],num1,num2,array[251];
int num_iterations,nx11;
int xbeg = 25, xend = 275, ybeg = 25, yend = 175;
int sxtick = 173, extick = 177, sytick = 23, eytick = 27;
int xcount = 4, ycount = 1;

main()
       {
       int n,xx1,yy1,yy2;
       float maxarray = 0.0;

       printf("Input number of iterations.");
       scanf("%d",&num_iterations);

       box();                                         /* Box on screen */


       for(n = 0;n <= 250; n++)
            array[n] = 0.0;                           /* Initialize array */
       for(n = 0;n <= num_iterations;n++)
            {
            grand();                                  /* Gaussian r.n. */
            nx11 = (int)((num1 * 100.)/4.0);
            if((nx11 < 125) && (nx11 > -125))
                 array[nx11 + 125]++;                 /* Hist. count #1 */
            nx11 = (int)((num2 * 100.)/4.0);
            if((nx11 < 125) && (nx11 > -125))
                 array[nx11 + 125]++;                 /* Hist. count #2 */
            }

       array[125] = array[125]/2.;                    /* Normalize zero */

       for(n = 0;n <= 250;n++)                         /* Find maximum */
            {
            if(maxarray < array[n])
                 maxarray = array[n];
            }
       for(n = 0;n <= 250;n++)
            {
            array[n] = array[n]/maxarray;             /* Normalize array */
            yy[n] = 25. + (150. * (1. -array[n]));     /* Convt screen cord*/
            xx[n] = n + 25.;                           /* Screen cord.*/
            }
       for(n = 1;n <= 250;n++)
            {
            xx1 = xx[n];
            yy1 = yy[n];
            yy2 = yend;
            linev(xx1,yy1,yy2);                        /* Vert. graph ln */
            }
       plotterm();                                    /* Terminate plot */
       }
```

Figure 2.16c Main calling program for generating the histogram of Gaussian random numbers (gauhist.c).

a fairly uniform convergence to the normal distribution, and the bell-shaped characteristic shape is clearly delineated. The functions called by the main calling routine for Gaussian random numbers (Figure 2.13c) are

```
box()
```
        (Figure 2.14)
```
grand()
```
        (Figure 2.15)

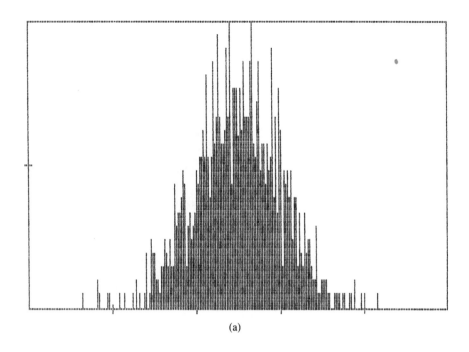

(a)

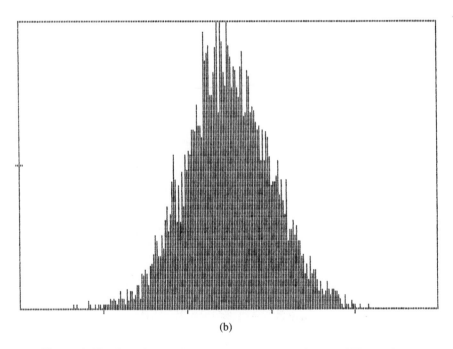

(b)

Figure 2.17 Gaussian random number histograms for (a) 1000 samples, (b) 5000 samples, (c) 10,000 samples, (d) 20,000 samples, and (e) 40,000 samples.

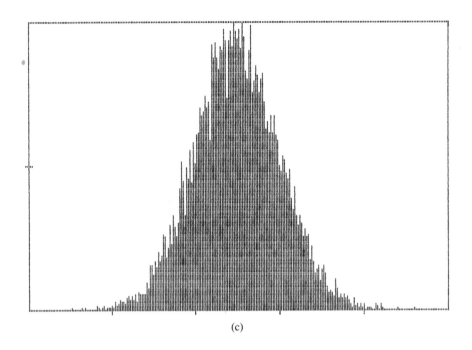

(c)

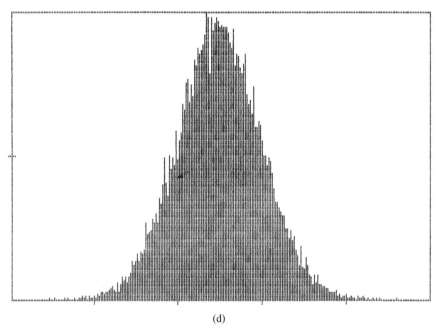

(d)

Figure 2.17 (*Continued*)

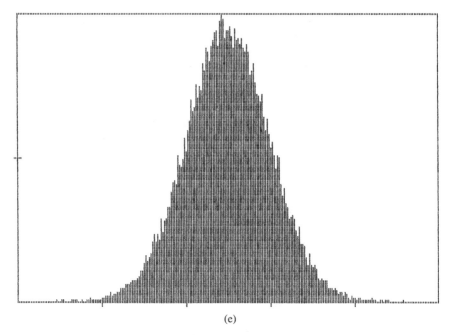

(e)

Figure 2.17 (*Concluded*)

```
plotPoint()      (Figure 2.8d)
plotterm()       (Figure 2.8d)
```

Aside from the graphics I/O routines, box() calls

```
tick()      (Figure 2.14)
```

The main calling program for the Gaussian random number histograms (Figure 2.16b) uses the following functions:

```
linev()      (Figure 2.8e)
box()        (Figure 2.14)
grand()      (Figure 2.15)
```

SUMMARY

This chapter has developed a number of beginning program examples. We started with some very elementary programs for creating and reading simple databases. Next a program for generating mortgage payments was derived and a program that illustrates the effect of inflation on savings. Finally, low-level file I/O was considered.

Following this discussion three beginning examples of a more advanced nature were employed: a program that plots the Dow Jones average, a program that generates frequency modulation waveforms, and programs that calculate Gaussian random numbers and plot their histograms. These examples were selected for their diversity and ability to draw on key programming features of the C language. Also, the display interface using Version 4.0 low-level techniques was delineated.

REFERENCES

1. *The Value Line Investment Summary*, Value Line, Inc., 711 Third Ave., New York, NY 10017 (1986).
2. *IBM Technical Reference*, Personal Computer Hardware Reference Library, IBM Corporation, P. O. Box 1328, Boca Raton, FL (1981), 6025008.
3. Papoulis, A., *Probability*, *Random Variables*, *and Stochastic Processes*, McGraw-Hill Book Co., New York (1965).

PROBLEMS

2.1. Rewrite the routine to blank the screen using scroll down for INT 10H.

2.2. The associated table indicates the value from January 1968 to December 1986 for the Dow Jones Average. These values were derived from the Value Line data as follows: An estimate for the mean value was made for each month and rounded to the nearest 5 points. Using these data, generate a data file on disk and write a program that reads these data and smooths these by performing a moving average across 5-month intervals.

2.3. Write a function that writes two floating point arrays, x[] and y[], to a disk file based on a formal parameter NCOUNT that contains the number of array elements to be output.

2.4. Write a function that reads the two floating point arrays x[] and y[], of Problem 2.3. The function should print these arrays as a check on the input. The array length should be returned as an integer variable.

2.5. In the program code for box__norm(), the vertical grid lines occur at columns 89, 153, and 217. Is this valid? Explain.

2.6. Assuming the library cplotlib.lib exists as in Figure A.13 and each module has the name of the first function appearing in it, what is the link sequence for the FM spectrum program? (Use fmwave.obj for the main calling function.)

2.7. In the program that generates Gaussian random numbers (Figure 2.13c), what are the maximum and minimum values allowed by theory? What does this mean in terms of the program that plots these numbers?

2.8. In the program that plots the Gaussian random number histogram (Figure 2.16c), what is the purpose of the statement that normalizes zero:

```
array[125] = array[125]/2
```

Dow Jones Average Data for Problem 2.2

1	68	875	1	72	895	1	76	910	1	80	830	1	84	1240
2	68	850	2	72	905	2	76	980	2	80	870	2	84	1160
3	68	840	3	72	915	3	76	990	3	80	800	3	84	1160
4	68	840	4	72	925	4	76	990	4	80	790	4	84	1160
5	68	835	5	72	920	5	76	990	5	80	815	5	84	1170
6	68	875	6	72	920	6	76	990	6	80	845	6	84	1080
7	68	880	7	72	905	7	76	995	7	80	890	7	84	1070
8	68	875	8	72	920	8	76	990	8	80	925	8	84	1160
9	68	905	9	72	920	9	76	960	9	80	930	9	84	1200
10	68	930	10	72	915	10	76	950	10	80	920	10	84	1200
11	68	935	11	72	985	11	76	980	11	80	975	11	84	1210
12	68	935	12	72	1000	12	76	980	12	80	945	12	84	1190
1	69	930	1	73	970	1	77	925	1	81	945	1	85	1230
2	69	920	2	73	965	2	77	935	2	81	950	2	85	1270
3	69	905	3	73	945	3	77	920	3	81	975	3	85	1260
4	69	915	4	73	940	4	77	910	4	81	995	4	85	1260
5	69	935	5	73	915	5	77	905	5	81	990	5	85	1260
6	69	885	6	73	900	6	77	900	6	81	995	6	85	1300
7	69	840	7	73	885	7	77	885	7	81	940	7	85	1330
8	69	810	8	73	910	8	77	870	8	81	905	8	85	1320
9	69	810	9	73	960	9	77	840	9	81	850	9	85	1300
10	69	820	10	73	890	9	77	835	9	81	860	10	85	1340
11	69	820	11	73	870	11	77	810	10	81	870	11	85	1360
12	69	785	12	73	800	12	77	795	12	81	880	12	85	1400
1	70	760	1	74	840	1	78	790	1	82	860	1	86	1530
2	70	750	2	74	835	2	78	765	2	82	820	2	86	1610
3	70	755	3	74	825	3	78	760	3	82	800	3	86	1740
4	70	755	4	74	865	4	78	780	4	82	830	4	86	1760
5	70	680	5	74	845	5	78	815	5	82	825	5	86	1780
6	70	695	6	74	825	6	78	820	6	82	800	6	86	1880
7	70	690	7	74	785	7	78	820	7	82	800	7	86	1810
8	70	725	8	74	705	8	78	880	8	82	800	8	86	1810
9	70	750	9	74	640	9	78	875	9	82	900	9	86	1815
10	70	760	10	74	630	10	78	850	10	82	950	10	86	1795
11	70	770	11	74	640	11	78	800	11	82	1000	11	86	1880
12	70	805	12	74	600	12	78	800	12	82	1005	12	86	1900
1	71	830	1	75	680	1	79	820	1	83	1040			
2	71	870	2	75	710	2	79	810	2	83	1060			
3	71	890	3	75	760	3	79	840	3	83	1100			
4	71	900	4	75	770	4	79	860	4	83	1140			
5	71	905	5	75	830	5	79	830	5	83	1200			
6	71	890	6	75	840	6	79	830	6	83	1200			
7	71	880	7	75	845	7	79	830	7	83	1200			
8	71	870	8	75	810	8	79	875	8	83	1180			
9	71	895	9	75	820	9	79	880	9	83	1210			
10	71	870	10	75	840	10	79	850	10	83	1240			
11	71	810	11	75	835	11	79	805	11	83	1240			
12	71	860	12	75	830	12	79	810	12	83	1240			

3

Software Design and C

The past two chapters have devoted considerable effort toward defining the syntax and rules of usage for the C language. C is a portable language, which means that, in most cases, the source code generated for a particular application will execute across many machines using different C compilers. Associated with each C compiler are include files that provide interfacing to standard C input/output (I/O), for example, and the Microsoft Version 4.0 compiler used in this book (Chapters 1 to 6) comes with such files. An additional feature of the Microsoft compiler is access to the IBM microcomputer service routines and particularly the graphics capability. We have used this in the examples in Chapter 2. This graphics usage constitutes nonstandard C programming; however, it is very useful for illustrating the I/O capabilities of the IBM microcomputers.

Clearly, with any implementation of the C language nonstandard features exist that are desirable for the programmer to use when developing code. The user must decide the best way to employ such aspects of his or her compiler's capability. In this book we are primarily concerned with C programming, in a conventional sense, but the code is to be applied in the IBM microcomputer context where special-purpose requirements exist (such as the screen graphics modes) that are desirable from an I/O viewpoint. IBM developed interfaces for handling hardware, which can be accessed via the special library function int86(). This requires that the library files dos.h be employed to set 8086 and 8088 (or 80286) register values to access these DOS and BIOS services. [In OS/2 we achieve access to the IBM services through the Application Program Interface (API), as discussed later.] Through the use of this nonstandard file, dos.h, the C programmer in the IBM microcomputer environment has access directly to the IBM-generated services. We used dos.h to access the graphics mode through such functions as SCRCL(), SC320(), and WRDOT().

To summarize this discussion it is useful to note that, while C is a portable language, and we emphasize its portability when developing source code, it has desirable programming features that can only be accessed within the confines of the system within which it is implemented. To access the system hardware directly requires special-purpose routines for the particular machine in question, except for standard I/O. In the IBM microcomputer environment with DOS, this access is achieved using the file dos.h and interrupt calling function int86(). Since this is also a book about IBM microcomputers we include the usage of these special-purpose calls as part of the discussion.

The purpose of this chapter is to address concepts related to programming practice in a philosophical sense. We have now developed a basic understanding of C syntax and usage and are in a position to begin to think about the optimal methods for employing this syntax. To some extent, the methodology for programming presented in this chapter has already been alluded to in the foregoing discussion. We now extend this discussion in a more formal sense.

3.1 INTRODUCTION

This section deals with implementations, within the C programming language, that help shape the underlying aspects of the language. For example, ambiguities with variable typing have been eliminated in C. We will explore why this is desirable and what impact it has on C structure. The C language used in the mid-to-late 1980s is an evolution of languages starting with the early BCPL [1]. This evolution is most commonly associated with the Kernighan and Ritchie [2] architecture. It is this version of the language that we discuss with regard to conceptual architecture and practical configuration. Throughout this chapter, we present aspects of the language in a generalized context that we hope will broaden the reader's understanding of why particular implementations were chosen.

3.1.1 Parameter Passing and the Stack

In Chapter 2 we saw examples of using functions in C programs. Variable information was passed back and forth between functions using the following techniques:

1. Formal parameter variable arguments, which pass variable quantities in the forward direction only
2. Formal parameter pointer arguments, which can be used to pass variable quantities in both directions (to and from the called function)
3. External variables, which can be used to pass values in both directions
4. Returned variables, using return(), that define a function with a returned value

Corresponding to the use of variables in functions and techniques for passing values to and from a called function is the notion of local and global variables discussed in Chapter 1. Local variables are defined only within the confines of the function declaration either as formal parameters or type declarations within the function brackets. The amount or size of local data storage for a particular function definition is of particular concern in C function calls because these local variables are stored on the stack. This memory area is a last-in, first-out (LIFO) buffer with default value of 2K (2048) bytes. To understand fully the definition of stack storage, we resort to the modular memory allocation used in assembly language descriptions, the segment. At the assembler level, four segment registers exist, which define up to four segments at any one time: the code segment (CS register), the data segment (DS register), the stack segment (SS register), and the extra segment (another data segment usually, with the ES register). The stack address is specified by one of these segment registers, and in C function calls this buffer contains new local variable values that are pushed downward in the stack memory area as they are defined, and at the conclusion of the function call the stack pops upward until all local variables have been removed.

Clearly, as function calls nest, stack variables progressively build up in the LIFO buffer. Because of this nature of the stack, it is apparent that large arrays must be defined as other than local data items (the 2K limit precludes default stack storage for more than a moderate amount of data). Figure 3.1 presents an illustration of typical memory mapping for the C linker. Table 3.1 defines each of these segments as they are used by the linker. Note that uninitialized global data resides in c_ common. Since all these segments can contain up to 64K bytes of storage, ample opportunity exists to employ large arrays during program development. The stack is a special segment in that it is arbitrarily fixed in size by the compiler, while the other data-bearing segments simply occupy the memory needed to contain the variables specified with type indicated in Table 3.1. In other words, the stack is dynamic in its usage during program execution, while the other data segments are always fixed. Since we must specify a fixed storage size at link time, an upper bound of 2K is selected for the stack.

Based on this discussion of the stack, it is now convenient to return to the indicated techniques for passing parameters between functions. Consider the first technique: passing variables using formal parameters. In this case a copy of the parameter is placed on the stack and is locally accessible when the function is called. The function can change the value of the parameter without affecting the original value from which the copy was taken. This value appears in one of the defining data segments. In the second situation, the parameter is passed by reference. Here an actual address is passed to the called function. If the function is expected to change the actual value of a variable as a method for returning a result, then the call by reference must be chosen with pointer values passed. Based on the function

High Memory	(heap)
	STACK
	_BSS and c_common
	CONST
	_DATA
	NULL
	(Data Segments)
Low Memory	_TEXT

Figure 3.1 Typical memory mapping for the C linker.

Software Design and C Chap. 3

TABLE 3.1 MEMORY MAP DEFINITIONS FOR THE C LINKER

Segment	Definition
(heap)	An area of unallocated memory available for dynamic allocation by the program using variable scratch buffer requirements.
STACK	A segment used for all local data storage.
_BSS	A segment that contains all uninitialized static data items except *far* and *huge* items.
c_common	A segment that contains all uninitialized global data storage.
_DATA	This is the default data segment. Initialized global and static data reside in this segment.
NULL	This special-purpose segment contains the copyright notice and is read before and after execution. An error indicates a memory fault.
overwrite, (Data Segments)	Initialized static and global data items with *far* attribute area contained in these segments.
_TEXT	This is the code segment. In small and compact models, this is the only code segment. In other models, each module has its code segment defined as the module name plus __TEXT as a suffix.

definition, the compiler recognizes that pointer arguments pass addresses and variable arguments pass values. Global variables with uninitialized values reside in c_common. These variables constitute a second technique for returning a value from a function. Unlike local variables, these variables are preserved in memory based on preprocessor definitions. Finally, the return() instruction can be used to return a value from a function. Consider the following definition:

```
float cube(x)
    float x;
    {
    float y;
    y = x*x*x;
    return(y);
    }
```

This example illustrates the description of a function that returns the cube of an input value, x. A call of the form

```
z = cube(x1);
```

returns the cube of x1 in z.

Before concluding this section, it is instructive to examine global variables. Structured programming, as discussed in Section 3.2.3, attempts to minimize the ways in which values can be input to functions and output from these same functions, in addition to providing other control mechanisms. This is an effort to clarify the intent and execution of the code in question. When global variables are used, the programmer and person maintaining the code can have difficulty in remembering how and when a particular global variable was defined. We recommend that arrays and variables requiring initialization be treated as global. Also, multiple variables that must be returned or passed from a single function qualify for consideration as global quantities. Although not optimum, deviations from this are permissible when the code can be measurably improved both as to clarity and compactness (generally smaller programs). In examining the structured programming concept, minimized usage of global variables will be treated as the least confining requirement.

3.1.2 I/O Control and Architecture Structures

At the very lowest level, input/output (I/O) can be achieved using the DOS and BIOS service calls. This involves defining buffers and using pointer variables to transfer data back and forth with the interrupt function int86(). Such I/O is tedious and unnecessary since C has many routines designed to support keyboard input, writing to the display, and writing to a printer. In addition, output to a communications port is also possible with these standard I/O operations. Should the user desire to implement I/O at a lower level, again C has a number of byte- or character-oriented I/O functions that can be used for such low-level I/O. The disadvantage of using these lower-level I/O functions is that all numerical values must be converted to ASCII for proper handling by the user-written I/O routines. In the standard I/O routines, this conversion is automatic.

A major advantage of standardized I/O is the portability of code from machine to machine. The routines contained in stdio.h., io.h, and conio.h all interface to conventional C code in reproducible and predictable fashion. Hence, portability is achieved even though the underlying module is tailored to the specific computer system in question, the raw include file itself.

The stream functions allow the passing of data to nonstandard devices by using device-name specifiers in the filename contained in the stream definition. Strictly speaking, this is an artifact that is generic to the IBM DOS. For example, some other computer system would be at a loss as to what to do with

```
b: filename.ext
```

Such a system, however, would have its own naming convention, and stream definition would follow this convention. Hence, C I/O as implemented is quite portable as long as provision is made for appropriate stream definition.

Architecture structures are the structures intrinsic to the architecture for the language: for, while, if, do while, and others. These syntactical entities limit the freedom of the programmer in defining his or her algorithm. The branching possible in assembly language (using conditional and unconditional jumps) and such languages as FORTRAN is no longer possible with the C architecture structures. Generally, program execution is sequentially downward through the code. This is probably most difficult to comprehend in the case of a transformation where a loop is being executed, such as

```
for (n=1; n<=N;n++)
    y[n]=array1[n]*n;
```

Here it is clear that even though an apparent backward motion exists at each iteration the general momentum is forward. The statements

```
y[1]=0.;
for (n=Z;n,=N;n++)
    {
    y[n]=array1[n]*n;
    y[n]=2.+y[n]*y[n-1];
    }
```

constitute a slightly more difficult example. Again, the general understanding is of a forward momentum. We will return to architecture structures in Section 3.2.3.

3.1.3 Size versus Complexity

A major and somewhat intangible issue is module size. Central to this issue is the question of module complexity. This can be measured a number of ways, and the variety and difficulty of methods for testing a module certainly point toward a measure of its complexity. Rules, such as a module should be no longer than two pages of output or 100 lines, have tended to proliferate in programming circles. The truth is probably closer to a mixture between intuition and rigorous calculation based on deterministic aspects of the underlying algorithm.

Requirements on the reproducibility of a complexity metric, when defined in a similar context, suggest an analytical approach to establishing such a measure. Results based on graph theory, for example, have led to reasonable yet reproducible predictions for the complexity of modules and overall program content [3]. It is unlikely that a programmer will set out to achieve a given complexity measure when code is developed initially. However, as a result of the development process over an extended period, module size should achieve a balance between difficulty in understanding and efficiency in execution. Such an optimum state tends to be subjective, hence the desirability of analytical measures.

As a rule of thumb, the programmer should stress clarity over efficiency in all but the most time critical applications. A great deal of programming time is spent in maintenance or rewriting code to accomplish the same task in a different language, for example. The designer's task is greatly simplified if the initial code is easy to follow.

Although we indicated an aversion to stating module size based on lines of code, addressing this topic is a suitable way to conclude this section because there is some merit in providing such a guideline. First, due to the architecture structures inherent in C, the language tends to be reasonably straightforward to understand in the context of moderately sized modules. That is not to say C cannot become obtuse. Consider the following code

```
if((check=fopen(FN1,"r"))==NULL)
    exit(1);
```

This is not a particularly clear statement. A slightly clearer form would be

```
check=fopen(FN1,"r");
if (check==NULL)
    exit(1);
```

It is in this fashion that C can become obtuse. Although the programmer saves a line of source code, the actual assembly language translation is roughly the same. In all fairness, we use both approaches indicated here, where it is felt that experience will cause the reader to become familiar with either code sequence. But clearly one code sequence requires more thought than the other. Again, as a rule of thumb, clarity over efficiency should always be preferred except in applications that are time critical.

Experience has tended, and this is a purely heuristic assertion, to favor moderately sized modules. Martin and McClure [4] address the issue of module size directly in lines of code. They indicate a size range of from 10 to 100 instructions, with more than 100 instructions as being too difficult to test and fewer than 10 as being inefficient. (Reference 4 also addresses a number of complexity metrics that are easy to implement based on source code listings.) This guideline will be followed throughout the text, with 100 lines of executable code serving as an approximate upper bound to module size.

3.1.4 Type Definitions

Some earlier implementations of languages tend to be word oriented. For example, on older Control Data Corporation mainframes (6400, . . .), the 60-bit word was not an uncommon unit for the measure of computational quantization. With the advent of recent trends in packaging digital hardware (and earlier theoretical optimization), the byte has come to represent a basic unit of measure in computing systems. Hence, it is no small surprise that the basic building block for variable size is 1 byte in the C language. This 8-bit quantity corresponds to the character type denoted by char.

Many machine architectures specify addresses at the word level, and the programmer loses the ability to access individual bytes. The existence of the char type in C avoids this problem. With a judicious use of the cast operator and bitwise operators (Section 3.1.6), it is possible to reduce most variables to their character equivalent. Care must be exercised in such demotions when the original value is greater than 256. Suitable bookkeeping, such as decimal-to-ASCII conversion, must be implemented before the demotion takes place.

We have seen (in Chapter 1) the basic C types: int (2 bytes), float (4 bytes), double (8 bytes), long (4 bytes), short (2 bytes), and unsigned (2 bytes). Pointers

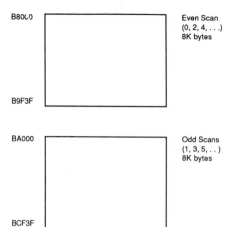

B80C0 — Even Scan (0, 2, 4, . . .) 8K bytes

B9F3F

BA000 — Odd Scans (1, 3, 5, . .) 8K bytes

BCF3F

Figure 3.2 Screen buffer addressing for medium graphics mode with the IBM PC/XT/AT.

are a special class being 2 bytes in length. Pointers essentially indicate an offset (up to 64K) from the start of the data area in question. How, for example, does one access a specific address in memory? First, one might ask why would the need arise to access a specific address in memory? After all, the linker takes care of all those relocatable addresses. Consider the screen memory area for the IBM microcomputers. This buffer is defined as in Figure 3.2. To access individual screen buffer locations, which effectively turns the pels on or off via direct memory access (DMA), the programmer must write to specific addresses in memory.

With this need established for access to actual memory locations, how is it accomplished? The data segment register DS must be loaded with the correct segment value. To access even scans, for example, DS must be loaded with B800H. Then the pointer offsets defined in the program can be used to generate even scan results. In this example, the reader should recognize that a particular byte actually contains attribute information associated with 4 pels as specified by

BIT:

7	6	5	4	3	2	1	0
C_1	C_0	C_1	C_0	C_1	C_0	C_1	C_0

where

C_1	C_0	
0	0	Pel takes on background color
0	1	First color preset value
1	0	Second color preset value
1	1	Third color preset value

Here the color values are defined in the *IBM Technical Reference* [5].

To summarize this section, typing is a convenient mechanism for defining and accessing the components of a variable. The basic building block for many computer systems is the byte (this is particularly true in the microcomputer world). With the cast and bitwise operators, it is possible to access any variable in known fashion. One last area, which will be discussed in Section 3.3.2, is the question of style. Ledgard [6] examines the issue of type definition with regard to naming conventions. Type names should accurately reflect an attribute of the variable in question. In this text we tend to define variables in somewhat cryptic fashion, more like acronyms than actual natural language syntax. This is a carry-over from earlier programming style when the user was limited as to how many characters could be used to specify a variable (usually seven or less). The reader should feel free to develop his or her own style within the constraint that clarity and ease of understanding are desirable goals for program code development.

3.1.5 Iterative and Recursive Programming

This section is included primarily to provide the reader with a glimpse of the theoretical background behind much of programming technique as it is used today. Consider the following code fragment:

```
y1=.05;
y=.6,
x=.5,
ERROR=1.;
while (ERROR>1.e-5)
   {
   x=y*x;                      /*x less 1*/
   y=x
z=y-y1;
   ERROR=(float)(fabs(z));
   y1=x;
   }
   ...
```

This code fragment is an example of iterative programming. Iterative programming involves the use of the assignment instruction, which results in a change of state of a variable [7]. The assignment

```
x=y*x;
```

replaces x with a new value. The old value for x is *not* preserved. Such behavior is impulsive and characterized by no traceable time history.

The iterative solution of a problem has in basis the loop instruction, which is formally invariant. (The code contained within the preceding while loop does not change dynamically.) This formal invariance is characterized by a procedure used to define the loop. First, a recurrence hypothesis is developed, which consists of invariant code. Next, checks are evolved that serve as the basis for loop termination. When no termination results, the loop must continue while maintaining the recurrence hypothesis. The process must be appropriately initialized in agreement with the hypothesis.

Consider a second code fragment:

```
...
n=1;
ERROR=1;
x[0]=.5;
y1=.05;
y=.5;
while (ERROR>1.e-5&&n<2500)
    {
    x[n]=y*x[n-1];
    y=x[n];
    z=y-y1;
    ERROR=(float)(fabs(z));
    y1=x[n];
    n++;
    }
...
```

This fragment is recursive. Basically, it has a time history associated with x, and no assignment occurs that involves a change of state for x[n]. The variable x[n] is never defined in terms of itself. The assignments for y, y1, and z are based on replacement, not recursion.

Conceptually, what is the significance of iterative versus recursive programming? As seen in both fragments, the number of calculations done depends on the speed with which the test parameter converges to the terminating condition. The iterative program simply continues to replace the recurrent variable through transformation. Here the overhead is low, but no time history is preserved. The recursive fragment requires a stack, or buffer area, that contains the complete time history for the variable. For applications of a causal nature, this time history can be useful.

In general, the value of iterative versus recursive programming is not clearly defined. When the depth of recursion is small, the time history is small, as well as the stack. Additional overhead associated with iterative calls can take time, and iterative forms are more difficult to generate and test than recursive forms. Hence, both these programming techniques constitute viable approaches, and the programmer must develop skill with each.

3.1.6 Bitwise Operators

C possesses a remarkable degree of flexibility when handling variables. We have seen how type definitions clearly delineate the span of a variable in terms of the basic memory unit, the byte. What about smaller subunits such as bits? Can C manipulate values at the bit level? The answer is yes, using bitwise operators. These operators are illustrated in Table 3.2. Suppose we wish to check whether or not the sign bit in an integer is set (bit 16). The following code can be used to accomplish this task using bitwise operators (note that bit 16 is the sign bit only in unsigned arithmetic, where this bit has been chosen to designate negative integers when set):

```
...
unsigned int x,y,z;
...
x=0x8000;
if((x&y)==0)
    z=0;                    /*ysign=0*/
else
    z=1;                    /*ysign=1*/
    ...
```

The mask, 0x8000, is used to check the status of the 16th bit only.

Another application for bitwise operators is in checking the status of various service functions. We will address this topic in some detail in Chapter 4, but for

TABLE 3.2 THE BITWISE OPERATORS

Bitwise operator	Designation	Comments
~	COMPLEMENT	This operator changes all the 1s to 0s and 0s to 1s. The type must be int.
¦	OR	This operator generates bit combinations on a bit-by-bit basis between two integers according to

C1	C2	
0	0	0
1	0	1
0	1	1
1	1	1

&	AND	This operator generates bit combinations on a bit-by-bit basis between two integers according to

C1	C2	
0	0	0
1	0	0
0	1	0
1	1	1

^	EXCLUSIVE OR	This operator generates bit combinations on a bit-by-bit basis between two integers according to

C1	C2	
0	0	0
1	0	1
0	1	1
1	1	0

TABLE 3.2 (*Concluded*)

Bitwise operator	Designation	Comments
<<	LEFT SHIFT	This operator shifts the bit pattern of an integer to the left with zero fill to the right. The expression $$x << 2$$ shifts the bits of x two places to the left.
>>	RIGHT SHIFT	This operator performs the reverse of the LEFT SHIFT.

now it is useful to consider the return value from checking the status of the communications port. Calling INT 14H with AH=3 returns the following values:

AH: **BIT**

     7   Timeout

     6   Transmit shift register empty

     5   Transmit holding register empty

     4   Break detect

     3   Framing error

     2   Parity error

     1   Overrun error

     0   Data ready

AL: **BIT**

     7   Received line signal detect

     6   Ring indicator

     5   Data set ready

     4   Clear to send

     3   Delta receive line signal detect

     2   Trailing edge ring detector

     1   Delta data set ready

     0   Delta clear to send

Many of these values can be appreciated only by examining the National Semiconductor data sheet on the 8250 ACE [8], which explains the particular hardware meaning. It is clear, however, that error conditions can be readily understood based on bits 3, 2, and 1 of AH, and an acceptable communication results in bit 0 being set. The following code is designed to flag these conditions:

```
...
int86(0x14,&reg,&reg);
if((reg.h.ah & 0x0008)!=0)
    {
    printf("Framing error");
    exit(1);
    }
if((reg.h.ah & 0x0004)!=0)
    {
    printf("Parity error");
    exit(1);
    }
if((reg.h.ah & 0x0002)!=0)
    {
    printf("Overrun error");
    exit(1);
    }
if((reg.h.ah & 0x0001)!=0)
    printf("Data ready");
    ...
```

The sign bit is set with the following code:

```
...
unsigned int x;
x = x | 0x8000;
...
```

The bitwise operators are, in general, very useful for accessing encoded bytes that are used to pass information to and from service routines. This facility is similar to the flexibility available to the assembly language programmer, and it is no surprise that these operators are most useful when interfacing to assembly language routines.

3.2 OPTIMIZING THE C DESIGN PROCESS

Most modern texts address the topics of structured programming, modular code, and top-down design. These techniques have come to embody an organized approach to program development that is repeatable in an optimal sense. This approach is predictable and meaningful in that programmers of differing backgrounds will approach algorithm development in the same fashion when these tools are used. In the following discussion we explore each of these topics, starting with top-down design because it represents the start of the design process.

3.2.1 Top-down Design

Top-down design is an informal strategy for starting with a global problem statement and then subdividing the development into smaller and smaller modules until each module accomplishes a singular task. Such a systematic approach to design leads to the modular techniques, described in the next section, that develop and link program elements together to solve the overall task.

A convenient starting point for the top-down approach is to define the functional structure for the program under consideration. This functional structure has been reflected in the structure charts of the earlier programming examples. These charts illustrate a hierarchy of importance for the components of the program.

Structure charts are established by associating with level 0 an overall functional statement of the programming problem. This occupies a single box at the top of the hierarchy. Next, at the level 1 position, categories associated with variable I/O and algorithm computation are indicated at a reasonably high level. Below this level, successive reduction of the problem into multiple smaller pieces occurs with the relationships clearly defined. Through this process the program architecture is defined in terms of hierarchy. The structure chart does not, however, illustrate the dynamic interrelationship among modular components. Also, it does not illustrate at the module level the flow of execution for the program. To achieve this, the top-down design process needs an additional mechanism for describing program activity. This mechanism can take one of two forms: the flow chart or pseudo code, which describes the program activity in natural language syntax. In this text we employ flow charts for describing programs dynamically. (The reader can just as conveniently approach program design using pseudo code, but it is generally less compact than flow charts. Hence, we use the latter technique.)

In Chapter 2 we developed programs based on structure charts and flow charts. It should be clear that the approach simplifies design because it simplifies understanding of the program and the underlying architecture. Part of the design process is a specification of data structures. As we have seen, it is fortunate that C has recordlike entities called structures that facilitate this design. We saw several examples of how structures can be used in programs in Chapter 2. In general, some thought about the organization of the data may lead to commonality, which can be reflected in the overall database by using the C structures and unions.

Figure 3.3a illustrates the structure chart for a program that reads a time history (month, year, and value) from disk and segregates the values into brackets

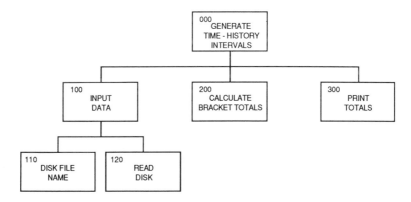

Figure 3.3a Structure chart for the program that reads a data file and determines bracket intervals for the values input.

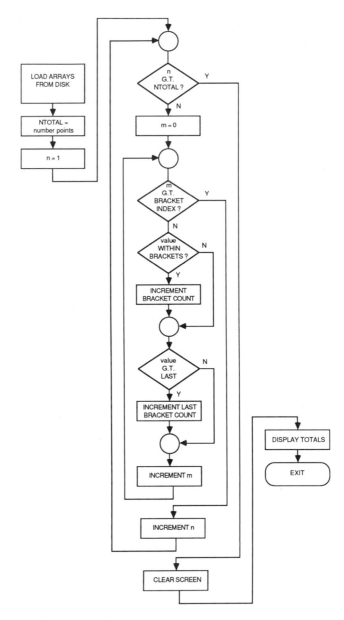

Figure 3.3b Main calling routine for the program that reads a data file and determines bracket intervals for the values input.

or groups. The flow chart for the main calling program is illustrated in Figure 3.3b, and Figure 3.3c contains the flow chart for the disk read module. Figure 3.4a, b, and c contains the code for the main calling module, printed output, and the code for the disk read functions, respectively. This latter code is essentially the same as found in Figure 2.7c except in the form of a function. The example illustrated in Figure 3.4b is from the Dow Jones data of Problem 2.2.

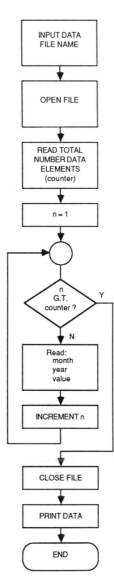

Figure 3.3c Module that contains the function diskrd( ) that reads the time-history data.

In general, the procedure illustrated for this example is a reasonable approach to program design. The structure chart reflects the high-level functionalism, and the flow charts illustrate the more detailed dynamics at the module level. The data structures are simple enough in this example that they do not need to be separately delineated on the flow chart. While the common basis of reference for month, year, and value exists and suggests possibly a structure mechanism, the added complexity of passing arguments to and from functions implies an unnecessary step in describing these data elements if these elements were grouped in a structure. As program size increases, however, such bookkeeping may become desirable.

Top-down design is informal and, consequently, most useful for small-scale design tasks. When faced with larger design problems, the programmer must resort to additional techniques to supplement the guidance obtained from the top-down methodology. We will consider two additional tools, as discussed earlier: modular programming and structured code.

3.2.2 Modular Programming

The reader will note by now that there is a tendency to relegate many of the tasks in programs appearing in this text to smaller functions and modules. This suggests the notion of modular programming. Modular programming concepts have been established over a long period of time during which theoretical methods evolved for designing programs [9,10]. The principal requirement on smaller program units or modules is that they be independently testable and can be integrated to accomplish the overall program objective.

```
/* Function to allocate time-history values into brackets */

#include <stdio.h>

int month[288],year[288],talley[5] = {0,0,0,0,0};
float value[288],bbrak[5] = {0.,500.,1000.,1500.,2000.};

main()
        {
        int n,m,NTOTAL;

        NTOTAL = diskrd();                              /* Input data */

        for(n = 1;n <= NTOTAL;n++)
            {
            for(m = 0;m <= 3;m++)
                {
                if((value[n] > bbrak[m]) && (value[n] <= bbrak[m+1]))
                    talley[m]++;
                if(value[n] > bbrak[4])                 /* check upper */
                    talley[4]++;
                }
            }

        SCRCL();                                        /* Screen clear */

        for(n = 0;n <= 4;n++)
            printf("Bracket = %d has Total = %d \n",n,talley[n]);
        }
```

(a)

```
Bracket = 0 has Total = 0
Bracket = 1 has Total = 179
Bracket = 2 has Total = 37
Bracket = 3 has Total = 12
Bracket = 4 has Total = 0
```

(b)

Figure 3.4 (a) Main calling program code for the routine that reads a data file and determines bracket intervals and (b) program output for the Dow Jones data from Problem 3.10.

```
/* Function to read arrays month, year, & value from disk */

#include <stdio.h>

diskrd()
        {
        int n,check,counter;
        extern int month[],year[];
        extern float value[];
        FILE *infile;
        char FN2[81];

        printf("Input read database filename \n");
        gets(FN2);

        if((infile = fopen(FN2,"r")) == NULL)
           {
           printf("Input file failure ");
           exit(1);
           }
        fscanf(infile,"%d ",&counter);
        for(n = 1;n <= counter;n++)
           fscanf(infile,"%d %d %f ",&month[n],&year[n],&value[n]);
        if((check = fclose(infile)) != 0)
           {
           printf("Error in input file close ");
           exit(1);
           }
        for(n = 1;n <= counter;n++)
           printf("%d %d %f \n",month[n],year[n],value[n]);
        return(counter);
        }
```

(c)

Figure 3.4c   Code for the function diskrd().

Modules are generally defined, in the context of C programming, in terms of one or more related functions. Each function should perform a single independent task and be self-contained with one exit and entry point. This suggests a single thread to program execution, which is the manner in which most modern computers execute code. [We bypass consideration of distributed processing in this book since we are concerned with the concept of centralized processing and the central processor unit (CPU).] Module execution in the world of the CPU is sequential. With this architecture in mind, it becomes straightforward to accept the one-entry and one-exit feature associated with functions, at least theoretically.

We discussed global variables as a mechanism for returning more than one value from a function. When is this likely to become most necessary? One situation is the generation of an array of similar values. Here a single function might be used to compute a time series, for example, and each computation would generate an array element in recursive fashion. Obviously, the function should be self-contained and all array values generated at once. Consider the following function:

```
filter (N)
   int N;
   {
   extern float y[], x[];        /*x=time element*/
   float b, c;
int n;
```

```
y[0]=0;                        /*Initialize*/
b=.01;
c=.001;

   for (n=1; n<=N; n++)
      y[n]=c*y[n-1]+b*x[n];
   }
```

This low-pass filter generates a smoothing of the time series x[n]. The array y[n] is generated in its entirety with the simple one-statement for loop. It would be highly undesirable to fail to return the complete array from this function, hence, the use of global variables is appropriate. This use does not detract from the modular nature of the function. Thus, even though a module (or function) has one entry and one exit point, multiple values can be returned.

In Section 3.1.3, we considered the implications of size and complexity on module definition. Size was handled by accepting a general guideline that modules contain between 10 and 100 lines of code. This was suggested as a rule of thumb, and if, for example, the code were written in APL, 100 lines would be very tiresome to debug. For C, however, the guideline seems appropriate, as evidenced by the modules in this text [see, for example, the function spectrum2() appearing in Figure 2.11b as a candidate for a large module].

A more rigorous enforcement of size must resort to quantitative measures such as complexity and complexity metrics. Consider the metric [11]

$$N = N_1 + N_2 \tag{3.1}$$

where

N_1 = total number of operators in a module
N_2 = total number of operands in a module

Returning to the function filter, the following counts apply:

OPERATOR	COUNT	OPERAND	COUNT	
=	6	y[0]	2	
for	1	b	3	
<	1	c	3	
++	1	0	1	
*	2	y[]	3	
		x[]	2	
		n	7	
		N	3	(variable)
	11		24	

Here N is 35 (from Equation 3.1). What does this mean? To interpret N, a body of statistical data must evolve based on complex interactions between programmers and code. It is clear from this example that $N = 35$ is a reasonably simple program.

In reference 4, a similar example with $N = 28$ is illustrated. Again, this metric value indicates a relatively small and understandable module.

The programmer is unlikely to apply a complexity metric during program development. It is, nonetheless, useful to allow complexity to guide program development, particularly when modules begin to approach the difficult (for the programmer developing the code). To summarize some general guidelines on module development *in C*:

1. Restrict modules to between 10 and 100 lines of code.
2. Within the module concept, allow one entry and one exit (exception handling can call for multiple exits, but this is an abortive condition and the error state should be flagged before the exit).
3. Arrays should be treated globally.
4. Modules returning a single value should do so formally with return().
5. Modules returning multiple but small numbers of variables should do so with pointers (pointers are complex, so the trade-off here is how many pointers are involved).
6. Modules returning large numbers of variables, other than arrays, should be rewritten.
7. Modules returning an intermediate number of variables can do so with global declarations.
8. A module should perform one self-contained task.
9. Finally, allow for exceptions to these guidelines when the code can be made easier to understand and it is not time critical.

An example of point 9 would be where very simple bookkeeping is involved in a module for clarity and maintenance purposes. Also, the use of globals does not appreciably increase the level of difficulty of a *small program*, but can reduce the size of variable handling code significantly (particularly when pointers are used as an alternative).

3.2.3 Structured Code

The major difficulty with software development is ensuring that a given program actually generates the output it was intended to generate, not determining how to make the computer function to execute a program. The emphasis here is on software integrity, with the presumption made that the programmer will learn the mechanics of programming within a particular language. To simplify program design and development, structured programming techniques evolved. Dijkstra [12] defined the initial concept, and structured programming is now a well-established discipline that has greatly affected the C architecture. The notion of structured programming in the broadest sense encompasses top-down design and modular programming. At a more localized level, structured programming focuses on coding techniques intended to simplify program understanding and facilitate program use (such as program modification and maintenance). In this section we focus on this latter area: structured code.

The most desirable structure concept is sequentially defined code. In this instance, instructions are executed as they are encountered. C provides for two deviations from this approach: conditional execution and iterative loops. We have seen examples of both of these conditions in earlier chapters. Conditional execution included use of the forms (Chapter 1)

```
1. if...
2. if...else
3. the conditional operator
4. switch...case...break
```

Similarly, iterative loops utilize the forms (Chapter 1)

```
1. while...
2. do...while
3. for...
```

These two groups of statements are the most important control mechanisms in the C language. They form the basis of C structured coding techniques. Although C allows the goto . . . statement, it is discouraged and only appropriate in very extenuating circumstances. It should be forcefully argued that any code segment using a goto can be rewritten to avoid this statement. The major difficulty with goto statements, as pointed out by Dijkstra, is that unrestrained branching within a module can take place. This can lead to difficulty in understanding the intent of the code.

Structured code begins with a hierarchical description in the structure chart. This artifact illustrates what functional activities are subordinate to other activities. At a glance, the user can glean overall functional program relationships from the program structure chart. This entity should be developed as the first component of program design. Next the execution flow must be developed. The functional flow chart serves as a convenient vehicle for accomplishing this.

Briefly, there are a number of types of flow charts. They vary from more functionally oriented descriptions of program behavior, in which generalized activity is interconnected, to very detailed descriptions where each line of code literally occupies a place in the overall flow chart. In this text we favor the functional approach because it is a good compromise: it gives the user a sense of the program execution and does not require pages of description.

As an alternative to the flow chart, pseudo-code can be used. Pseudo-code has the advantage that it is very close to the actual program mechanics and is natural language in structure. With pseudo-code, the uninitiated can grasp a feel for the program execution while not fully comprehending the language syntax in which the program is written. A number of authors of high-level languages are developing program design languages (PDL) that are essentially pseudo-code. The PDL approach to program design is particularly appropriate for very large scale program development that may require significant development time. In this case a need exists to have an easily understood design document that can be made available to new programming team members. For most microcomputer applications, however, the flow chart is suitable.

Actual module implementation within the confines of structured code employs the sequential and control statements discussed previously. The module should have one entry and one exit path (with exception control handled so as to delineate the error condition). Finally, each module should be documented to explain its function and what data structures exist, where needed. The relationship of one module to another can be delineated in special cases where it is not explained in an associated flow chart or structure chart.

3.3 STRUCTURED TECHNIQUES WITH C

The purpose of this short section is to reemphasize the importance of structured programming in the C language by briefly illustrating several features of the language. Also, we discuss some philosophical implications for structured code.

We begin with the one-entry and one-exit precept applied to module definition. This control mechanism can be extended backward to the architectural structures mentioned in the previous section. That is the subject of Section 3.3.1. Next we discuss the implications of style and form in Section 3.3.2. (Also, a brief look at templates is treated as part of style.) Finally, a general look at algorithm development is used to round out the discussion (Section 3.3.3). Also, data structures are treated (Section 3.3.4).

3.3.1 Module Exit Conditions

The control and loop structures used in the C language are designed to provide one entry and one exit to modules. This ensures that control flow is linear through the structure (if, if . . . else . . . , while, do . . . while . . .). Also, exit conditions are clearly made available to the user during execution. With regard to iterative structures such as loops, it is clear that multiple exits can be disastrous because the user may never learn about the state of the system that causes the exit condition. To jump outside a loop that is undergoing normal execution is highly undesirable. With conditional structures, the use of exception handling must be clarified. Consider the if . . . statement in the following form:

```
. . .
if(check==0)
   {
   printf ("Denominator zero");
   exit(1);
   }
. . .
```

Here the if statement specifically looks for an error condition and prints the message explaining this condition prior to exit. The exception handling is part of the if purpose. A sequence of the form

```
...
for (n=1; n<=N; n++
    {
    x=x+a;
    if (x==NTOTAL)
        {
        printf ("x max exceeded");
        exit(1);
        }
    a=a+b;
    }
```

is less desirable because the causative factors (a, b, and x too large) are unclear at time of the exit. In general, we use the unconditional exit only [exit(1)], and we only use this exit when it is absolutely clear as to the complete nature of the error condition. Also, it is used subject to the constraints indicated previously. A typical use would be

```
...
if ((check=fopen (FN1,"r"))==NULL)
    {
    printf ("Error on read file open");
    exit(1);
    }
...
```

To some extent this discussion is semantic. Exits from within loops should not occur. Since C does not allow branching or jumps (as in assembler, FORTRAN, and other languages), there is really no way to exit a loop except with an exception handler or a goto. We have virtually ruled out goto statements, so only exception handling remains. This latter exit should be avoided within a loop structure. Flag the condition and upon exit from the loop report *all* relevant parameter data prior to exit. This latter exit should be accomplished using a conditional structure that specifically tests the exception status.

3.3.2 Templates, Style, and Form

Style is a somewhat elusive feature of programming, and it reflects individual thought patterns as much as any organized approach to program development. Consider, for example, the problem of variable definition as mentioned earlier. The following is easily understood:

```
mortgage_int = loan_principal * interest_rate.
```

What about

```
Instantaneous_amp = exp(-time/delay_factor)*
/        cos(2. * pi * frequency * time)
```

For knowledgeable persons, the following is much easier

```
A = exp(-t/tau) * cos(2, * pi * f * t)
```

(Those persons unknowledgeable probably will not care about such details at any rate.)

Programmers with a background in FORTRAN, ALGOL, or original BASIC are familiar with restrictions on the length of a variable name. They tend to be more cryptic than programmers of more recent vintage, who are used to 32-character limits. This is decidedly a learned style feature. More importantly is the need to clarify variable meaning. If the programmer provides a design document, which is essential for a clear understanding of the program, each variable should be delineated in an unambiguous fashion. In cumbersome assignments, spelling out each variable name in a wordy fashion can often obscure the meaning of the underlying relationship. Similarly, by being too cryptic or obscure, the meaning of the equality can escape the reader.

An additional feature of style is the nature of actual code reduction. In other words, is the code compact or can each relationship be followed in easily readable form? While

```
if(((x1==c1) | (x2==c2)) & ((x3==c3) | (x4==c4)))
    A1;
```

is compact, the following is slightly easier to follow

```
if((x1==c1) | (x2==c2))
    {
    if((x3==c3) | (x4==c4))
        {
        A1;
        }
    }
```

(If the reader has doubts as to which is easier, try assigning values and working out the truth table.)

As part of style, we need to consider templates. This topic is meant to cover the overall program structure. A general template is as follows:

Module 1 (main())

Documentation (Comment describing module)
Preprocessor (Include files, define directions, globals)

```
main() (function definition)
```

Module 2 (function1(), . . . functionN())

Documentation (Comment describing functions)
Preprocessor (Optional)

```
        function1()
...

        functionN()
```

Module 3 (function(N+1)(), . . . , functionM())

Documentation (Comment describing functions)
Preprocessor (Optional)

```
        function(N+1)()
...
        fucntionM()

...
```

Module L (functionQ(), . . . functionR())

Documentation (Comment describing functions)
Preprocessor (Optional)

```
        functionQ()
...
        functionR()
```

Here $1 < N < N + 1 < \cdots < M < \cdots < Q < \cdots < R$ and $2 < 3 < \cdots < L$.

Finally, we consider form. Good form consists of defining the optimum methodology for implementing an algorithm. Unfortunately, most algorithms are sufficiently complex that it is difficult to decide what the best way to implement the algorithm might be. The issue of form must be addressed in a somewhat simplistic fashion. Consider the following code fragment:

```
...
for (n=1;n<=N;n++)
    {
    for (m=1;m<=M;m++)
        {
        v[n]=v[n]*v[n];
        if(((v[n]>q[m]) & (v[n]<q[m+1]))
            increment++;
        }
    }
    ...
```

Now consider the alternative:

```
...
for (n=1;n<=N;n++)
    {
    v[n]=v[n]*v[n]
    for (m=1;m<=M;m++)
        {
```

```
      if(((v[n]>q[m]) & (v[n]<q[m+1])))
        increment++;
    }
  }
}
```

The second form is admittedly more cumbersome although easier to understand. What about time criticality? In the first fragment, the expression

```
v[n] = v[n]*v[n]
```

is executed NM times, while in the second fragment it only executes N times. The latter program fragment ensures an optimum time-critical compiled result. While this example may appear academic, it is representative of the decisions regarding form that must be made.

3.3.3 Algorithm Development

The topic of this section is algorithms. Algorithms are structured approaches to mathematically solving particular problems amenable to such solutions. A more general definition would encompass most programming efforts. We have examined iterative and recursive programming, and it was clear that a fundamental technique in designing efficient solutions was the recursive method because this approach builds on an earlier solution. Table 3.3 illustrates some typical algorithms as discussed by Sedgewick [13].

We have already seen examples of some of these algorithm techniques (arithmetic, random numbers, interpolation, line intersection, closest point, and FFT). In general, we will not address the complete class of problems covered by Table 3.3, and the interested reader is referred to reference 13 for a complete discussion. It is important, however, to recognize that algorithms are what computer programs are

TABLE 3.3 SOME TYPICAL ALGORITHMS

Type	Comments
Mathematical	Arithmetic, random numbers, interpolation, simultaneous equations, integration
Sorting	Exchange, bubble, quicksort, radix, priority queues, selection/merging
Searching	Sequential, binary, tree, hashing
String processing	Pattern matching, parsing, file compression
Geometric	Polygons, line intersection, convex surfaces, grids, closest point
Graph	Connectivity, mazes, shortest path, topological sorting, networks
Advanced	Systolic arrays, FFT, dynamic programming, linear programming

Based on Reference 13.

all about. Problems amenable to algorithmic solution can be easily tailored to computers.

3.3.4 Data Structures

We briefly consider the subject of data structures [14] (as opposed to file structures [15]). Table 3.4 illustrates some well-known data structures that are used in small- and large-scale program development. We have already seen arrays used as a basic element of the C language. Using the bitwise operators, it is possible to enter or extract information from data elements at the bit level. Databases tend to be more

TABLE 3.4 SOME REPRESENTATIVE DATA STRUCTURES

Type	Comments
Arrays	These structures consist of concatenated variables stored in a block and accessible via one or more indexes.
Bit strings	These structures constitute the basic building blocks of any language and are accessible in C by using the bitwise operators.
Bit maps	This is a mapping of a set of variables and their associated parameters onto a set of bits, which constitutes a smaller set of storage. All attributes of the variables are not represented in this fashion, and the mapping must be attribute specific.
Databases	Databases are complex data structures consisting of data items or fields collected into records that are accessible either sequentially, randomly, or directly via indexes or keys.
Hashing	This is a structure technique in which an algorithm or function is used to generate an address of a data element from a key. Typical associated structures would be a hash list.
Heaps	Heaps are most easily described as binary tree structures possessing *order* and *shape*. Order, for example, might specify that the value at any node is less than or equal to the value at the children. Shape suggests the tree architecture.
Linked lists	These data structures are used as indexes to other structures and have an associated pointer index that points to a relative record in the primary list.
Priority queues	This is a set of elements arranged according to priority. When an element is added or deleted, it is done so in accordance with assigned priority or associated rules.
Sparse arrays	These are data structures with many zero elements. They can be reduced significantly to smaller storage by using additional indexing arrays with an appropriate indexing algorithm.

complex, and we saw a simple example of database structure usage in Chapter 2 with the programs of Figure 2.6b and Figure 2.7b.

More complex data structures, such as hashed lists, heaps, linked lists, and priority queues, are specialized algorithms for handling large data organizations that require speed of access of optimized storage. Similarly, sparse array techniques minimize the amount of storage needed for multidimensional data.

All these techniques are used in developing the area of data structures and database design. The interested reader is referred to reference 14 for specific details of large-scale implementations. In this text, we will confine most of the discussion to the primitive structures listed in the beginning of Table 3.4.

3.4 SOFTWARE TESTING AND DEBUGGING

The subject of this section is software testing and debugging. What is the difference between these two aspects of the design process? Debugging is used to refer to syntactical correction and the elimination of catastrophic run-time errors. Testing is used to denote those fine-tuning aspects of programming wherein the program output is examined to determine whether or not the output is valid. Consider, for example, a program that generates a Bessel function value in response to an input argument. Debugging is the art of making the program execute and generate an output, while testing is the extension that looks for the correct Bessel function result in response to argument input. One process is action, while the other is validation.

3.4.1 Complexity Metrics

A good measure of the complexity of a module is the degree of difficulty needed to write a software driver for testing the module. Consider the code

```
...
square(x)
    float x;
    {
    x=x*x;
    return(x);
    }
...
```

To test this module, the following code is sufficient:

```
#include<stdio.h>
main()
    {
    float x=2,y;
    y=square(x);
    printf("square should be 4;=%f",y);
    }
```

This is fairly simple code. The function square() has complexity $N = 9$ (based on the Halstead metric described earlier). The test routine has complexity $N = 13$. The function

```
...
distance2(x,y)
    float x,y;
    {
    x=x*x;
    y=y*y;
    x=x+y;
    return(y);
    }
...
```

requires a test module

```
#include<stdio.h>
main()
{
float x=2,y=3 z;
z=square(x,y);
printf("Distance 2 should be 13;=%f",z);
```

Note that $N = 20$ for the function and $N = 16$ for the test routine. Clearly, testing is more difficult as complexity increases. The complexity of the testing routine directly reflects the complexity of the tested module.

3.4.2 Module Size

The normal testing procedure is to select a set of input test data, determine the expected output, run the program, and analyze the results. This process is quite ad hoc, and no formal approaches actually exist to testing. Some heuristic rules have evolved based on practical experience:

1. Test each statement.
2. Test each program path.
3. Test modules individually.
4. Predict the test results prior to execution.

What is the impact of module size? Basically, by confining modules to between 10 and 100 lines of code so that each module performs a *single* task, the module functionalism can be readily tested. Central to this discussion is the need to ensure that a module performs only one task. With this restriction, the causal nature of module execution can be readily traced. Such testing is sometimes referred to as unit testing. In C, the nature of the function simplifies unit testing because each function, if properly structured, should return only one answer or one class of answers (an array global).

Module size is, consequently, very important from a testing viewpoint. We emphasize that size used here is oriented toward the module activity, which translates into effective lines of code in an abstract sense. The requirement for ensuring single task execution is of paramount importance from the viewpoint of simplified testing.

3.4.3 Software Drivers

In Appendix A, we check the adequacy of the FFT() and hanning() functions using the drivers ckfft (Figure 3.3a) and ckffti (Figure A.3c). These programs are examples of software drivers used to validate modules. Software drivers are required for the testing process. Just as modular development of code is needed to simplify program development, modular testing is needed to simplify program validation.

3.4.4 Hierarchy of Modules

The definition of relationships among modules is essential in order to complete testing of the overall program. McCabe talks about "battleplans" and "essential complexity" for programs. The basic goal for these entities is to define program complexity, including the relationships modules have to each other. If, for example, modularity is fragmented to the point that many modules are intricately interconnected, then complexity increases even though each module is simple. The overall complexity can become very large. As a consequence, a trade-off must exist between module simplicity and the complexity of the module linkages. This is reflected in the hierarchy of modules.

3.5 HIGHER-LEVEL DESIGN CONCEPTS

C is a moderately low level language in spite of its recognition as being among the high-level family. With C, we can access memory, addresses, and I/O at the bit level. This translates to a very powerful tool in the hands of systems programmers. For more pedestrian applications, however, the need for low-level access is minimal, and we focus on high-level features.

3.5.1 Abstraction and Information Hiding

In Appendix D, we discuss the notion of a process that can be thought of as an information transformation. Basically, a process is a function that receives inputs and generates an output. During an executable period, the information appears to flow into and out of functions in a dynamic fashion that is fully interfaced to ensure continuity. The separation or layering of information and functional activity is known as *abstraction*. This procedure ensures that the information used by the system is treated as an isolated group of entities that is divorced from the actual process used to manipulate the data.

A very similar notion is that of information hiding. This approach to system design is based on the premise that data information and functional activity not needed at one level of modularity are not made available to that level. Both abstraction and information hiding are techniques used in the Windows environment (discussed in Chapter 8). We also use these approaches to a large extent in the modular code generated in this text. One impediment to abstraction and information hiding is use of global areas. The trade-off that must be made in this regard is whether or not modules remain truly functional in a mathematical context. For example, we will see examples where it is useful to access large arrays of data and incrementally modify the contents of these arrays or pass multiple parameters back and forth between functions with modification. In these cases, global variable usage is particularly convenient, but abstraction and information hiding disappear because the data entities become part of the process in question (since they represent various stages of the overall transformation). The user must determine how best to implement these tools depending on whether he or she is in a small programming environment (as represented by the programs in this book) or a large programming environment (as represented by the potential of a Windows-like application).

3.5.2 Data Structure-oriented Design

The structure of information, referred to as the data structure, has a significant impact on the complexity and efficiency of algorithms designed to process this information. It goes without saying that a strategy for developing programs based on the underlying data structures could be developed. Such approaches to program architecture are in fact a reality and are known as data structure-oriented programs. Pressman [16] describes these approaches in some depth. Their applications are typically in the areas where well-defined, hierarchical structures of information exist, such as examples with distinct I/O structures, tabular processing such as database management, and computer-aided design. The latter area includes extensive manipulation of organized data to portray items of interest in the screen buffer.

In general, we will not address data structure-oriented programming because it requires highly structured data entities beyond the scope of this text. We do, however, address object-oriented programming through the Windows environment in Chapters 8 and 9. It has been said that in many respects data structure-oriented programming is actually a subset of object-oriented program development. Finally, there is a third methodology referred to as data flow-oriented design, which is based on the perception that data can be characterized by their transformation during execution. This latter approach is an obvious interpretation between data structure-oriented and object-oriented programming.

3.5.3 Object-oriented Design

Object-oriented programming assumes program entities can be treated as self-contained objects capable of being manipulated during execution to achieve desired output configurations. For example, it is possible to divide each object into a data structure, a set of operations for this structure, and an interface between this object and the other objects in the associated environment. Messages are sent across the interfaces, which cause various activities to take place on each object. Information hiding is represented by the messages crossing the interfaces where only commands to and from objects are visible in a dynamic sense. The objects themselves are intrinsically modular.

We have mentioned the Windows environment as being object oriented. Here the Windows executive passes messages to the window procedure, and the programmer is never actually aware of the executive object other than as a generator of messages. Clearly, this is an excellent example of information hiding. Also, each function represents an object in the Windows hierarchy. The overall program implementation is very structured and reflects an object-oriented approach to design.

SUMMARY

This chapter has dealt with the subject of software design. Particular emphasis has been placed on the disciplines of top-down design, modular programming, and structured code. In addition to these design techniques, a number of C features were examined in Section 3.1 that enhance the development process. Both algorithms and data structures were briefly considered in a general context. References to examples in the text were included. The emphasis in this text is on mathematical and advanced algorithms. Most of the data structures we use in the text are simple entities. The reader is appraised, however, of the additional areas in algorithm development and data st•uctures.

Finally, testing and debugging are briefly examined. Modular approaches to testing are emphasized, and reference to illustrations of this technique are provided. The same caveats that apply to modular programming also apply to the testing process.

REFERENCES

1. Richards, M., "BCPL: A Tool for Compiler Writing and Systems Programming," *Proceedings AFIPS SJCC*, No. 34, pp. 557–566 (1969).
2. Kernighan, B. W., and Ritchie, D. M., *The C Programming Language*, Prentice-Hall, Inc., Englewood Cliffs, NJ (1978).
3. McCabe, T. J., "Automating the Testing Process through Complexity Metrics," McCabe and Associates, Inc., 5501 Twin Knolls Road, Suite 111, Columbia, MD 21045 (1987).
4. Martin, J., and McClure, C., *Structured Techniques for Computing*, Prentice-Hall, Inc., Englewood Cliffs, NJ, p. 70 (1985).
5. *IBM Technical Reference*, IBM Corporation, Boca Raton, FL 33432, pp. 2–52 to 2–53 (1981).
6. Ledgard, H., *Professional Software Programming Practice*, Addison-Wesley Publishing Co., Reading, MA, p. 123 (1987).
7. Arsac, J., *Foundations of Programming*, Academic Press, New York, p. 2 (1985).
8. "NS16450/INS8250A/NS16C450/INS82C50A Asynchronous Communications Element," National Semiconductor Corporation, 2900 Semiconductor Dr., Santa Clara, CA 95052 (1985).

9. LaBudde, K., *Structured Programming Concepts*, McGraw-Hill Book Co., New York, p. 26 (1987).

10. Parnas, D., "Information Distribution Aspects of Design Methodology," Carnegie-Mellon University Technical Report, Carnegie-Mellon University, Pittsburgh, PA (1971).

11. Fitzsimmons, A., and Love, T., "A Review and Evaluation of Software Science," ACM Computing Surveys, Vol. 10, No. 1, pp. 3–18 (1978).

12. Dijkstra, E., "Structured Programming," *Software Engineering 1969*, NATO Scientific Affairs Division, Brussels, Belgium (1969).

13. Sedgewick, R., *Algorithms*, Addison-Wesley Publishing Co., Inc., Reading, MA (1984).

14. Bentley, J., *Programming Pearls*, Addison-Wesley Publishing Co., Inc., Reading, MA (1986).

15. Folk, M. J., and Zoellick, B., *File Structures*, Addison-Wesley Publishing Co., Inc., Reading, MA (1987).

16. Pressman, R. S., *Software Engineering: A Practitioner's Approach*, McGraw-Hill Book Company, New York, p. 293 (1987).

PROBLEMS

3.1. Define a function rread() that uses two formal parameters to pass addresses for x and y to a call to scanf that reads these floating point variables.

3.2. The figures for this problem illustrate a very simple do-nothing program and the associated assembler listing. This program is intended to address global variable allocation in memory. How and where are the variables array[] and a allocated?

3.3. What is wrong with the following code using the default compiler:

```
/* Do-nothing test program */
main()
    {
    printa();
    }
printa()
    {
    int n,a[2048];
    for (n=1;n=100;n++);
        {
        a[n]=n;
        printf("for n=%d  a=%d",n,a[n]);
        }
    }
```

3.4. Write a routine that accepts a positive integer value less than 64K and converts it to an ASCII array of characters.

3.5. Write a routine that accepts a five character ASCII string in array[] and converts it to an integer. Assume the string represents a positive integer less than 64K.

```
/* Function to check memory allocation */

int array[2048];
int array1[3] = {1,1,4};
int a = 2;

main()
        {
        a = 3;
        array[1] = 10;
        }
```

(a)

```
;          Static Name Aliases
;
           TITLE    prb4ck
;          NAME     \c\prb4ck.c

           .287
_TEXT      SEGMENT  BYTE PUBLIC 'CODE'
_TEXT      ENDS
_DATA      SEGMENT  WORD PUBLIC 'DATA'
_DATA      ENDS
CONST      SEGMENT  WORD PUBLIC 'CONST'
CONST      ENDS
_BSS       SEGMENT  WORD PUBLIC 'BSS'
_BSS       ENDS
DGROUP     GROUP    CONST, _BSS, _DATA
           ASSUME   CS: _TEXT, DS: DGROUP, SS: DGROUP, ES: DGROUP
PUBLIC     _array1
PUBLIC     _a
EXTRN      __chkstk:NEAR
EXTRN      _array:BYTE
_DATA        SEGMENT
           PUBLIC   _array1
_array1 DW          01H
           DW       01H
           DW       04H
           PUBLIC   _a
_a      DW          02H
;          .comm _array,01000H
_DATA        ENDS
_TEXT        SEGMENT
; Line 8
           PUBLIC   _main
_main      PROC NEAR
           *** 000000      55                      push    bp
           *** 000001      8b ec                   mov     bp,sp
           *** 000003      33 c0                   xor     ax,ax
           *** 000005      e8 00 00                call    __chkstk
; Line 9
           *** 000008      c7 06 06 00 03 00       mov     _a,3
; Line 10
           *** 00000e      c7 06 02 00 0a 00       mov     WORD PTR _array+2,10
; Line 11
           *** 000014      8b e5                   mov     sp,bp
           *** 000016      5d                      pop     bp
           *** 000017      c3                      ret

_main      ENDP
_TEXT      ENDS
END
```

(b)

Figure for Problem 3.2: (a) Program code and (b) assembler output, .COD.

3.6. Given the program

```
/* printx */

main()
    {
    int x;

    printf("Input x-value (integer less than 64K)");
    scanf("%d",&x);
    printa(x);
    }
printa(x)
    int x;
    {
    printf("Output value=%d",x);
    }
```

discuss the implications of module size.

3.7. Write a program that turns on the first four pels of the display. Have the program first clear the screen and then set the graphics mode. The screen buffer should be loaded directly. Do not use interrupts.

3.8. Indicate which of the following is iterative and recursive:

(a) ...
```
while(n<N)
    {
    x[n]=a*x[n-1];
    n++;
    }
...
```

(b) ...
```
while(n<N)
    {
    x[n]=a*x[n];
    n++;
    }
...
```

(c) ...
```
for(n=1;n<=N;n++)
    {
    y=x;[n];
    x[n]=a*y;
    }
...
```

(d) ...
```
for(n=1;n<=N;n++)
    {
    y=x[n-1];
    x[n]=a*y+b*x[n-2];
    }
...
```

3.9. What is the value of x when $y = 0 \times 55$ and $z = 0 \times 11$ (x,y, and z are type char):
(a) x = ~y

(b) x = y | z

(c) x = y & z

(d) x = y ^ z

3.10. Communications is established through handshaking with a Universal Asynchronous Receiver Transmitter (UART), such as the 8250 ACE. Indicate the control logic needed to check the UART and either load the character buffer, through a call to buffer_ service(), or initiate a retry, through retry_data(). This code fragment should reflect a check for the appropriate UART status. Assume INT 14H is needed with AH=3 as input to the status check.

3.11. Correct the form in the bracketed program appearing in Figure 3.4.

3.12. What is wrong with the following code:

```
...
filter()
    {
    extern float x[],y[];
    float a,b;
    int n;
    a=.1;
    b=.2;

    for (n=0;n<=32;n++)
        {
        y[n]=a*y[n-1]+b*x[n-1];
        if (y[n]<1.e-15)
            {
            printf("Underflow in filter");
            exit(1);
            }
        }
    ...
```

3.13. In the function

```
distance2()
    {
    extern x[],y[],z[];
    int n;

    for (n=1;n<=1000;n++)
        z[n]=x[n]*x[n]+y[n]*y[n];
    }
```

what is the complexity in terms of the metric N appearing in Equation (4.1)?

4

DOS, BIOS,
and Library Services

The purpose of this chapter is to discuss and illustrate service routines available to the C programmer in the IBM microcomputer environment. We have already seen examples of some of these services in the program illustrations that use the library file dos.h. and call BIOS and DOS interrupts using the library function int86(). We will now discuss in some depth the available DOS, BIOS, and Microsoft C library services.

Several comments are in order about the usefulness of these services for future IBM applications. First, the services described in this chapter will always run under DOS 3.x, whether using an IBM AT, XT286, or PS/2 Model 25, 30, 50, 60, or 80. In addition, these services will run on the IBM PC and XT. What about OS/2? OS/2 has a compatibility mode that runs DOS 3.x. All the DOS and BIOS services used in this book are documented and run under OS/2 compatibility mode [1], with one exception. This exception is represented by the programs related to exercising the 8253 timer. In general, the programs will run but count intervals will vary. If, for example, the timer is used to generate a tone on the speaker, the frequency will vary depending on machine and OS/2 operation. In Part IV of the text we discuss the implications for programming with C in the OS/2 environment. At that time the Protected Mode services under the Application Program Interface (API) will be explored.

What is an interrupt? Basically, this is an event in which the current processing by the CPU is switched to a new section of code, this code is executed, and the earlier processing resumed. Interrupts may be initiated by hardware inputs, such as depressing specific keys on the keyboard, or called from software using int86(). In the IBM microcomputers using DOS and BIOS, the interrupt service code for a number of BIOS interrupts is contained in programmable read only memory (PROM).

The DOS interrupts are software driven. Section 4.1 deals with these interrupts. Section 4.2 briefly describes the operation of these interrupts for the PS/2 computers. Section 4.3 presents some representative programs, and Section 4.4 describes the Microsoft C library files.

4.1 DOS AND BIOS SERVICE ROUTINES

Within the DOS environment or OS/2 compatibility mode, a number of interrupt services are available to the C programmer. Table 4.1 illustrates the available DOS and BIOS services that are callable using int86() [2–7]. The form of this function is

```
int86(intno, inregs, outregs);
```

where

$$intno = \text{interrupt number}$$
$$inregs = \text{input register values}$$
$$outregs = \text{output register values}$$

The function returns a value in AX. Here the registers are the 8086, 8088, or 80286 registers discussed in Chapter 1.

A similar function is int86x() defined by

```
int86x(intno, inregs, outregs, segregs);
```

which has the same parameter definitions as int86(), but

$$segregs = \text{called segment registers}$$

Finally, specific DOS functions may be accessed using

```
intdos(inregs, outregs);
intdosx(inregs, outregs, segregs);
```

These calls all access interrupt 21H and call the appropriate function depending on inregs. In intdosx(), segregs allows intersegment calls.

We briefly discuss the BIOS interrupts in Section 4.1.1. Then the DOS functions corresponding to interrupt 21H are discussed in Section 4.1.2. Section 4.1.3 presents the I/O port addresses that are common to the IBM family of microcomputers. These ports are dependent on how the hardware chips are wired together and, consequently, reflect the hardware architecture. Later, in Section 4.3.2 when the speaker is discussed, an example is presented of how hardware port configuration is translated to addresses.

TABLE 4.1 INTEL, BIOS, AND DOS INTERRUPTS

Interrupt	Type	Purpose	Description
0	Intel	Divide overflow	This interrupt occurs when a divide overflow takes place. The interrupt vector varies with the DOS version.
1	Intel	Single step	This interrupt simulates single-step execution. IBM uses the Trace command in DEBUG to accomplish this task.
2	BIOS	Nonmaskable interrupt	This interrupt cannot be prevented. It calls the BIOS NEAR procedure NMI__INT and results from memory errors on the system board ("PARITY CHECK 1") or add-on boards ("PARITY CHECK 2").
3	Intel	Set breakpoint	This interrupt stops the processing at a particular address.
4	Intel	Interrupt if overflow	This interrupt activates an INTO instruction return (IRET).
5	BIOS	Print screen	This interrupt prints the screen under program control. The FAR procedure called is PRINT__SCREEN and the address 0050:0000 contains the status.
6	—	—	Not used.
7	—	—	Not used.
8	BIOS	Timer interrupt	This routine handles the timer interrupt from channel 0 of the 8253 timer. There are approximately 18.2 interrupts/second. This handler maintains a count of the number of times it was called since power up. The FAR procedure is TIMER__INT and it calls an interrupt 1C H, in turn, which can contain a user routine.
9	BIOS	Keyboard interrupt	This routine is FAR procedure KB__INT. It continues to address F000:EC32 and constitutes the keyboard interrupt. INT 16H is the keyboard I/O routine and is much more flexible.
A	—	—	Not used.
B	—	—	Not used.
C	—	—	Not used.
D	—	—	Not used.
E	BIOS	Floppy diskette	This FAR procedure, DISK__INT, handles the diskette interrupt.
F	DOS	INTO	This interrupt activates the same call as TYPE 4.

TABLE 4.1   (Continued)

Interrupt	Type	Purpose	Description
10	BIOS	Video interface	This set of routines contained in the NEAR procedure VIDEO__10 provides the CRT interface.
11	BIOS	Equipment	This procedure looks for the number of printers, any game I/O, the number of RS-232C cards, number of diskette drives, video mode, and RAM size.
12	BIOS	Memory size	Determines the memory size from data.
13	BIOS	Diskette I/O	This procedure calls a series of routines that accomplish diskette I/O. Since a number of parameters are involved, this routine will be discussed separately.
14	BIOS	Communications adapter	This procedure lets the user Input/output data from the RS-232C communications port.
15	BIOS	Cassette I/O	This interrupt is used to control cassette I/O.
16	BIOS	Keyboard I/O	This interrupt manipulates AX to read the keyboard. It will be discussed separately.
17	BIOS	Printer I/O	This routine provides communication with the printer. It uses the AX and DX registers to set up parameters. We will discuss it later.
18	BIOS	Cassette BASIC	This interrupt calls cassette BASIC.
19	BIOS	Bootstrap	Track 0 sector 1 of drive A is read into the boot location. Control is transferred there.
1A	BIOS	Time of day	This routine allows the clock to be set/read. CX contains the high portion of the count and DX the low portion.
1B	DOS	Control break	This interrupt results when a keyboard interrupt is used.
1C	BIOS	Dummy return	This interrupt simply calls an IRET instruction.
1D	BIOS	Video parameters	This is simply a table of byte values and routines for setting up various graphics parameters.
1E	DOS	Floppy table	
1F	DOS	Graphics table	Used with DOS 3.0.
20	DOS	Program terminate	This interrupt is issued by DOS to exit from a program. It is the first address in the Program Segment Prefix area.

TABLE 4.1 *(Concluded)*

Interrupt	Type	Purpose	Description
21	DOS	Function request	This interrupt has many options and will be discussed later.
22	DOS	Terminate address	Control transfers to the address specified at this interrupt location when the program terminates. Do not issue this address directly.
23	DOS	Control break exit address	This interrupt is issued in response to a control from the standard input.
24	DOS	Critical error handler vector	This interrupt is called when a critical error occurs within DOS such as a disk error.
25	DOS	Absolute disk read	This interrupt transfers control to the device driver for a read.
26	DOS	Absolute disk write	This interrupt transfers control to the device driver for a write.
27	DOS	Terminate but stay resident	This vector is used by programs to remain resident after DOS regains control.
28-2E		Reserved for DOS	
2F	DOS	Multiplex interrupt	This interrupt defines a general interface between two processes. Each handler is assigned a specific number in AH and the function of the handler in AL.
30-3F		Reserved for DOS	

4.1.1 BIOS Interrupts

The interrupts appearing in Table 4.1 are called with the int86() or int86x() function. There are three types: Intel, BIOS, and DOS. In this section we concentrate on the BIOS services. The Intel interrupts tend to be hardware specific and not usually callable. The DOS interrupts, with the exception of 21H, are system oriented and also not likely to be useful.

Interrupts 0 to 0FH. Interrupts 0 to 4 are clearly hardware oriented and will not be discussed further. Interrupt 5 is used to print the screen contents under program control. Interrupt 8 is the timer interrupt and returns a time count in specified locations not easily accessible to the C programmer. (For timer functions, the programmer should use interrupt 1CH.) Interrupt 9 activates when keys are pressed or released and simply stops the processing. A more useful interrupt of the same type is interrupt 16H, which served as the basis for KEYDEL() appearing in Figure 2.8b. Interrupts 0AH to 0FH tend to be either unused or system oriented.

Interrupts 10H to 15H. Interrupt 10H is the video I/O interrupt. We have already made extensive use of this service routine. Table 2.1 illustrates the register settings needed to specify various options under interrupt 10H. Interrupt 11H returns a summary of what options are attached to the basic system unit. This summary is returned in AX as specified in the appropriate technical reference. Interrupt 12H returns the amount of installed random access memory (RAM) in blocks of 1024 bytes. Interrupt 13H is a low-level disk and diskette I/O interrupt. This interrupt uses file control blocks (FCBs) for disk I/O, and since file handles are preferred, the interrupt 21H functions are more useful. Interrupt 14H is used for RS-232C communications via the communications adapter. Interrupt 15H is the cassette I/O routine and will not be discussed further.

Interrupts 16H to 20H. Interrupt 16H freezes the processor until a keystroke (depression or release) occurs. Interrupt 17H is used to communicate with the printer attached to the system. The options are as follows:

AH=0   Prints the ASCII character in AL
AH=1   Initializes the printer
AH=2   Returns printer status byte in AH

DX should be set to zero for one printer (BIOS supports up to three printers). With the AH=0 option, carriage control is achieved with the following ASCII characters:

08H   Backspace
0AH   Line feed
0CH   Form feed
0DH   Carriage return

Interrupt 18H is used to load cassette BASIC. Interrupt 19H reinitializes DOS from disk. Interrupt 1AH allows the time to be set (AH=1), where CX = high count and DX = low count. AL is nonzero if 24 hours have elapsed since the last call to this interrupt. When AH=0, the clock is read and the count returned in CX and DX.

Interrupt 1BH activates for a control-break. Interrupt 1CH points to a return instruction and can be used to point to a user routine. Interrupt 1EH points to a table of parameters needed for diskette operation, and 1FH points to a table of extended characters. Interrupt 20H causes a program termination.

Remaining DOS interrupts. Interrupts greater than 20H are DOS interrupts. Only 21H will be considered further. This interrupt is the basis for the DOS function calls discussed in Section 4.1.2. The other interrupts are for the most part low level and system oriented.

4.1.2 Interrupt 21H: DOS Function Calls

Interrupt 21H has many options depending on how AH is specified. Table 4.2 lists these DOS function calls and provides a brief description of each. Much of the

TABLE 4.2 DOS FUNCTION CALLS: INT 21H

AH	Purpose	Type	Description
0	Program terminate	Control	Terminates the execution of a program.
1	Keyboard input	Keyboard	Waits for keyboard input, displays it, and returns it in AL.
2	Display output	Display	Displays the character in DL.
3	Auxiliary input	Misc.	Waits for a character from the COM port and puts it in AL.
4	Auxiliary output	Misc.	Outputs the character in DL to the COM port.
5	Printer output	Printer	Outputs the character in DL to the printer.
6	Direct console I/O	Keyboard	Waits for a character from the keyboard (no control-break check).
7	Direct console input/no echo	Keyboard	Waits for a character from the keyboard and puts it in AL.
8	Console input without echo	Keyboard	Waits for a character from the keyboard, returns it in AL, and executes an interrupt for control-break.
9	Print string	Display	Outputs the string to the display. String must end with "$."
A	Buffered keyboard input	Keyboard	Reads characters from the keyboard into a buffer. DS:DX points to buffer, 1st byte = max characters, and 2nd byte = number characters read.
B	Check standard input status	Keyboard	Checks to see if a character is available from the keyboard.
C	Clear keyboard buffer/invoke keyboard function	Keyboard	Clears the keyboard buffer and executes the function call in AL (onlt 01H, 06H, 07H, 08H, or 0AH).
D	Disk reset	Disk	All files not closed are lost.
E	Select disk	Disk	Selects the drive in DL as default (0 = A, 1 = B, etc.).
F	Open file	File	Searches the directory for the file pointed to in DS:DX. AL = FFH (not found) or 00H (found). If found, the FCB is filled.
10	Close file	File	Closes the file after a write. DS:DX points to FCB.
11	Search for first entry	Disk	Searches the directory for the first matching filename. AL = FFH if none found.
12	Search for next entry	Disk	After a filename has been found, this call searches for the next occurrence.
13	Delete file	File	Deletes all directory entries that match DS:DX pointer.
14	Sequential read	Disk	Loads the record addressed by the current block and record at the DTA and increments the record address.
15	Sequential write	Disk	Opposite 14H.
16	Create file	File	Searches the directory for a matching entry; if found, it is reused; if not found, opens a file.

TABLE 4.2 (*Continued*)

AH	Purpose	Type	Description
17	Rename file	File	Changes the filename at DS:DX to the filename at DS:DX + 11.
19	Current disk	Disk	Determines the default drive and returns it in AL.
1A	Set disk DTA	Disk	Sets the disk transfer address to DS:DX.
1B	Allocation table information	Disk	Returns DS:BX = pointer to media descriptor byte, DX = number allocation units, AL = numbersectors/allocation unit, and CX = size physical sector.
1C	Allocation table info for drive	Disk	DL = drive number; this function returns the same parameters as 1CH.
21	Random read	Disk	Reads the record addressed by the current block and record fields into memory at the DTA.
22	Random write	Disk	Opposite 21H.
23	File size	File	Searches the directory for entry matching DS:DX and sets the FCB random record field equal to the number records in file.
24	Set relative record field	File	Sets the random record field to the same address as the current block and record fields.
25	Set interrupt vector	Misc.	The interrupt vector in AL is set to address DS:DX.
26	Create new program segment	Misc.	This call should not be used.
27	Random block read	Disk	Reads the number of records in CX from DS:DX into DTA.
28	Random block write	Disk	Opposite 27H.
29	Parse filename	File	See *DOS Technical Reference* manual.
2A	Get date	Misc.	Returns AL = day of week, CX = year, DH = month, and DL = day of month.
2B	Set date	Misc.	Reverse 2AH.
2C	Get time	Misc.	Returns CH = hour, CL = minutes, DH = seconds, and DL = hundredths of a second.
2D	Set time	Misc.	Reverse 2CH.
2E	Set/reset verify switch	Misc.	When set, DOS performs a verify operation for each disk write. AL = 0 (off) and AL = 1 (on).
2F	Get DTA	Disk	Returns the disk transfer address in ES:BX.
30	Get DOS version no.	Misc.	Returns DOS major version number (AL) and minor version (AH).
31	Terminate process/ remain resident	Control	See *DOS Technical Reference* manual.
33	Control break check	Control	Requests/sets BREAK, AL = 0(request) or 1(set) and DL = 0(off) or 1(on).
35	Get vector	Misc.	For interrupt number in AL, it returns the pointer in ES:BX.

TABLE 4.2 (*Continued*)

AH	Purpose	Type	Description
36	Get disk free space	Disk	Returns for DL (drive) the available clusters (BX), clusters/drive (DX), bytes/sector (CX), and sectors/cluster (AX).
38	Country dependent information	Misc.	See *DOS Technical Reference* manual.
39	Create subdirectory	Disk	Generates the MKDIR function with DS:DX pointing to an ASCIIZ string containing drive and directory path names.
3A	Remove subdirectory	Disk	RMDIR function; DS:DX points to string containing drive and path names.
3B	Change current directory	Disk	CHDIR function; DS:DX points to string containing drive and path names.
3C	Create file	File	CREATE function; if file pointed to in DS:DX does not exist, the file is opened.
3D	Open file	File	DS:DX points to file; AL = 0 (read only), 1 (write only), or 2(read/write) (see *DOS Technical Reference* manual).
3E	Close file handle	File	BX contains file handle; file closed, directory updated, and internal file buffers removed.
3F	Read from file/device	File	BX = file handle, CX = number bytes to read, DS:DX buffer to be loaded. After call, AX = number bytes read.
40	Write to file/device	File	Inverse of 3F.
41	Delete file from directory	File	Removes a directory entry associated with the filename pointed to in DS:DX.
42	Move file read/write pointer	File	See *DOS Technical Reference* manual.
43	Change file mode	File	See *DOS Technical Reference* manual.
44	I/O control for devices	I/O	See *DOS Technical Reference* manual.
45	Duplicate file handle	File	On entry BX = handle, on exit AX = duplicate.
46	Force duplicate file handle	File	Forces the handle in CX to refer to the same file at the same position as the handle in BX.
47	Get current directory	Disk	DL = drive number; DS:SI = pointer to 64-byte user area to contain directory; and AX returns error codes.
48	Allocate memory	Memory	BX = number paragraphs and AXL0000 points to the allocated blocks.
49	Free allocated memory	Memory	Frees the memory allocated with 48H.
4A	Modify allocated memory blocks	Memory	Modifies blocks to contain new block size. ES = block segment and BX = new block size in paragraphs.
4B	Load/execute program	Control	Provides for overlaying. DS:DX points to program and ES:BX points to parameter block for load.
4C	Terminate process	Control	Exits to invoking process.

TABLE 4.2 (*Concluded*)

AH	Purpose	Type	Description
4D	Get return code	Misc.	See *DOS Technical Reference* manual.
4E	Find first matching file	File	Finds the first filename that matches the file pointed to in DS:DX. CX = attribute used in search.
4F	Find next matching file	File	Same as 4E except finds second match. The DTA contains information from 4EH or previous 4FH.
54	Get verify setting	Misc.	Returns the value of verify set with 2EH in AL.
56	Rename file	File	Renames the file in DS:DX with ES:DI.
57	Get/set file date and time	Misc.	On entry: AL = 0(get) or 1(set), BX = file handle, CX = time, and DX = date.
59	Get extended error (DOS 3.00 and 3.10)	Error	Returns additional error information (see *DOS Technical Reference* manual).
5A	Create unique file (DOS 3.00 and 3.10)	File	Generates file pointed to by DS:DX (path ends with /) and CX = attribute.
5B	Create new file (DOS 3.00 and 3.10)	File	Creates new file pointed to by DS:DX with attribute in CX.
5C	Lock/unlock file access (DOS 3.00 and 3.10)	File	AL = 0(lock) or 1(unlock), BX = file handle, CX = byte offset high, DX = byte offset low, SI = length high, and DI = length low.
5E00	Get machine name (DOS 3.10)	Misc.	DS:DX points to location where computer name returned.
5E02	Set printer setup (DOS 3.10)	Network	BX = redirection list index, CX = length string, and DS:SI points to string to be put in front of all print files.
5E03	Get printer setup	Network	Reverse 5E02.
5F02	Get redirection list entry (DOS 3.10)	Network	Returns nonlocal network assignments.
5F03	Redirect device (DOS 3.10)	Network	Principally for networking.
5F04	Cancel redirection	Network	Principally for networking.
62	Get PSP (DOS 3.00 and 3.10)	Misc.	Returns the program segment prefix in BX.

functionalism available through interrupt 21H is file related, and C has an extensive library of functions for this purpose. It is only the special-purpose options, such as setting the time, that we will be interested in examining.

4.1.3 IBM Microcomputer Port Definition

Associated with the microcomputer hardware processing is a collection of parallel lines used to carry signals corresponding to each bit in the address word. This address bus connects to various chips on the system board and can be used to

TABLE 4.3 PORT ADDRESSES FOR THE IBM PC/XT/AT

PC Port No. (Hex)	PC Device	XT Port No. (Hex)	XT Device	AT Port No. (Hex)	AT Device
00-0F	DMA controller 8237	00-0F	DMA controller 8237	00-0F	DMA controller 1, 8237
20-21	Programmable interrupt controller 8259A	20-21	Programmable interrupt controller 8259A	20-3F	PIC 1, 8259A, master
40-43	Timer 8253	40-43	Timer 8253	40-5F	Timer 8254
60-63	Programmable peripheral interface 8253A	60-63	Programmable peripheral interface 8255	60-6F	Keyboard 8042
80-83	DMA page registers	80-83	DMA page registers	80-9F	DMA page registers
3F8-3FF	RS-232-C adapter	200-20F	Game I/O adapter	200-207	Game I/O adapter
3F0-3F7	Floppy disk drive adapter	210-217	Expansion unit	300-31F	Prototype card
2F8-2FF	Reserved	2F8-2FF	RS-232-C adapter (secondary)	378-37F	Printer 1
378-37F	Parallel printer port	300-31F	Prototype card	3A0-3AF	Binary synchronous communications 1
300-3DF	Color/graphics adapter	320-32F	Fixed disk	3B0-3BF	Monochrome/printer adapter
278-27F	Reserved	378-37F	Printer	3D0-3DF	Color graphics adapter
200-20F	Game I/O adapter	380-389	RS-232-C adapter (primary)	3F0-3F7	Diskette controller
3B0-3BF	Monochrome/printer adapter	390-393	Cluster	3F8-3FF	Serial port 1
		3A0-3A9	Binary synchronous communications (primary)	70-7F	Real-time clock
		3B0-3BF	Monochrome/printer adapter	A0-BF	PIC 2, 8259A, slave
		3D0-3DF	Color graphics adapter	C0-DF	DMA controller 2, 8237
		3F0-3F7	Floppy disk drive adapter	F0	Clear coprocessor busy 80287
		3F8-3FF	RS-232-C-adapter (primary)	F1	Reset 80287
				F8-FF	80287 coprocessor
				1F0-1F8	Fixed disk
				278-27F	Parallel printer port 2
				2F8-2FF	Serial port 2
				360-36F	Reserved
				3C0-3CF	Reserved

activate these chips depending on whether or not the chip address is present on the bus. In Section 4.3.2, we will see an example of this translation from software address to chip activation. For now, however, it is only necessary to recognize that each chip has a fixed address (set) associated with it based on how it is wired in the system. In Table 4.3, we present these port addresses for the major port activities used in the IBM PC/XT/AT. The PS/2 computers have similar addresses.

4.2 INTERRUPTS AND SERVICES FOR THE PS/2 COMPUTERS

The interrupts and services for the PS/2 computers are essentially identical to the PC/XT/AT under DOS 3.x. There are some added routines. Table 4.4 presents typical differences for the BIOS associated with the PS/2 Model 30.

TABLE 4.4 PS/2 MODEL 30 BIOS FUNCTION DIFFERENCES

Interrupt	Purpose	Comment
0	Divide overflow	Same
1	Single step	Same
2	NMI	Same
3	Breakpoint	Same
4	Overflow	Same
5	Print screen	Same
6	Reserved	—
7	Reserved	—
8	Timer	Same
9	Keyboard	Same
A	Reserved	—
B	Communications	Added from PC, XT
C	Communications	Added from PC, XT
D	Fixed disk	Added from PC
E	Floppy diskette	Same
F	Printer	Added in place of INTO
10	Video BIOS	Same (modified service)
11	Equipment	Same
12	Memory site	Same
13	Diskette/disk I/O	Same
14	Communications	Same
15	System services	Added in place of cassette I/O
16	Keyboard	Same
17	Printer	Same
18	Resident BASIC	Same function
19	Bootstrap	Same
1A	Time of day	Same
1B	Keyboard break	Same
1C	Timer tick	New
1D	Video	Same

TABLE 4.4 *(Concluded)*

Interrupt	Purpose	Comment
1E	Diskette parameter	Same
1F	Video graphics character	Same
40	DTA fixed disk	New
41	Fixed disk parameter	New
42	Video	New
43	Character graphics table	New
46	Extended disk parameter	New
4A	Real-time clock alarm	New
60–67	Reserved for user programs	New

4.2.1 Model 30 BIOS Service

The Model 30 BIOS is almost completely entry point compatible with the BIOS for the earlier PC, XT, XT286, and AT. The only difference will exist for software that is time critical during execution. This software will not run the same between the Model 30 and the earlier machines because the Model 30 is faster (8-MHz clock versus 4.77 MHz on the PC). Table 4.4 illustrates many of the changes and additions for the Model 30 BIOS interrupt structure. In the PS/2 computers, IBM has added significant new capabilities for graphics presentation and alpha mode screen display. While these video calls are still accessed via INT 10H, the meaning of the register options (specified with AH, AL, CH, CL, BH, BL, DH, and DL) reflects the MCGA format. The MCGA graphics modes, for example, are 320 × 200 (AL = 4, 5, or 13), 640 × 200 (AL = 6), and 640 × 480 (AL = 11). Here AH = 00H.

In Table 4.4, several new meanings are attached to video processing, such as masking to achieve gray shading. Also, the option of obtaining functionalism and video state information from a table pointed to by DI is possible using AH = 1BH. These are but a few of the different options needed and available with the improved graphics. We will not dwell on the PS/2 interrupts because the interested user should obtain a copy of the appropriate technical reference. The interrupt calls for the PS/2 computers will be almost identical to those presented earlier in this chapter. This allows the portability of code that exists across the IBM family.

As might be expected, these PS/2 interrupts are called from the PS/2 BIOS. Unlike the earlier technical reference descriptions, the PS/2 technical references do not contain code listings; hence, we cannot consider the interrupt structure in as much detail.

4.2.2 Model 50/60 BIOS Service

As mentioned previously the PS/2 BIOS routines are almost completely compatible with the BIOS interrupt calls from the earlier IBM microcomputers. The advanced 16-bit BIOS comes in two versions: a compatibility BIOS, CBIOS, and an advanced

BIOS, ABIOS. The former is intended for stand-alone applications, while the latter is used for multitasking applications.

4.3 REPRESENTATIVE PROGRAMS

The purpose of this section is to apply the preceding discussion to specific programming applications. In Section 4.3.1, a problem of general interest is treated: motion using interrupt 10H. While we have already seen examples of this interrupt, this is the first instance in which motion is simulated on the screen. Section 4.3.2 is a modification to the screen motion illustration in which interrupt 10H is not used for the display generation and direct memory access (DMA) of the screen buffer is used with screen buffer address access achieved using movedata(), a C library function. Also, in this section sound is employed by properly exercising the speaker using the 8253 interval timer (to set tone frequencies) and the 8255A programmable peripheral interface. This requires an understanding of port usage in the IBM microcomputer context. Sections 4.3.3 and 4.3.4 illustrate additional interrupt calls and the resulting actions.

It is worthwhile pointing out that DMA activity is easily possible using DOS; however, under OS/2 the memory maps change. Since OS/2 software must map to physical addresses in a many-to-one fashion, it is not always clear how the linker will achieve this mapping. Hence, DMA becomes difficult, if not impossible, under direct program control. (The screen buffer is not guaranteed to be at B800 segment address.) This means that interrupt 10H is the preferred method for screen access with OS/2. For time-critical applications, this can present problems, and the user may need to resort to assembly language routines to achieve suitable response. We discuss the assembly language interface in Chapter 5 and in Part IV, when OS/2 is discussed. Even assembly language may be insufficient for some applications.

In the example of the next section, we generate the motion of a ball confined in a boxlike structure. As the program runs using interrupt 10H, certain segments must be repetitively executed. The time needed to execute these segments, between successive displays of the ball, is a measure of the update rate. We have assumed an update rate of 0.05 second in the calculations of the ball's position. With scaling, this will be approximately correct if the time needed to execute this code is in reality 0.05 second. As the reader will see, it is very close to this value. In Section 4.3.2, when DMA is used, the refresh rate of the screen is much faster than using interrupt 10H. Here a delay must be specified by the user. By varying this delay, the user can begin to get a feel for the importance of real-time considerations in time-critical applications.

4.3.1 Global Motion: The Bouncing Ball

This example is of particular interest to those readers intending to develop programs requiring motion, such as video-game applications. We consider the topic of motion and how one goes about realistically simulating the movement of simple shapes: in this case a ball bouncing under the influence of gravity.

The title of this section uses the term global. In this context, we mean to

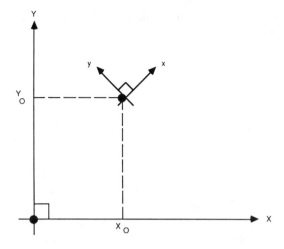

Figure 4.1 Local and global coordinate systems.

refer to a coordinate system within which the motion is described, such as the "world" coordinate system. Attached to the moving object, however, is a local coordinate system. This local system moves along with the object in question (within the larger, fixed, global coordinate system). The local system would have its origin and orientation described relative to the global system and could be used for relative motion, such as a description of the ball as it rotates. Figure 4.1 illustrates a local coordinate system (x, y) and its larger global coordinate system (X, Y). Here only two dimensions are presented and the local coordinate system has its origin $(0, 0)$ at the global coordinate (X_0, Y_0).

In the example of the bouncing ball, we will describe the ball by a fixed

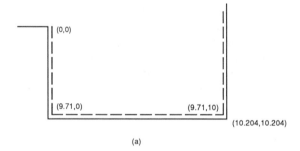

(a)

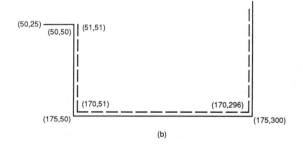

(b)

Figure 4.2 Geometry used for bouncing ball illustrating outer-box (solid) and motion box (dashed): (a) the physical motion coordinates and (b) the screen coordinates.

local representation using a shape table [8]. Then we will replicate this shape at various points along the ball's trajectory. The coordinates of the ball will be calculated to match its theoretical position. This theoretical position will be determined from physics equations that describe object motion under the influence of gravity. As a starting point, consider the structure to contain the ball. This boxlike structure is illustrated in Figure 4.2a, where the real-world coordinates have been specified. Similarly, in Figure 4.2b the same structure is illustrated with screen coordinates (assuming the 320 × 200 graphics mode).

In Figure 4.2b, the right-side coordinates show a gap of 4 pels between the motion box (dashed line) and the actual displayed box. (The motion box ends at column 296, while the displayed box is at column 300.) This is because the ball coordinate (global) is referenced 4 pels to the left of the actual ball structure. Similarly, since the ball global coordinate occurs at the leftmost edge of the ball shape, only one unit spacing between the motion box and structure box is needed on the left side (column 51 versus column 50).

All motion in two dimensions can be described using two orthogonal coordinate systems. We use the Cartesian or x-y system of Figure 4.3. Illustrated in the figure are the x-displacement, s_x, and y-displacement, s_y. We will assume that the ball starts at coordinate (0, 0) in the physical system. All dimensions in the physical system (Figure 4.2a) are in meters. The initial velocity of the ball is v_x (x-direction only). Hence, neglecting friction losses, the equation of motion in the x-direction is

$$s_x = s_{x0} + v_x t \qquad (4.1)$$

where t is the elapsed time. We will assume a discrete time interval of $dt = 0.05$ second for the update rate. The actual time is fixed by the time needed to execute the intervening code between position updates. Denoting this time spacing by dt, it is possible to consider discrete intervals, with the nth interval given by

$$t_n = n\,dt \qquad (n = 0, 1, 2, \ldots) \qquad (4.2)$$

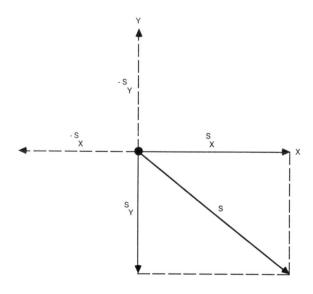

Figure 4.3 Decomposition of distance vector s into x and y components.

The change in s_x between two intervals is then

$$ds_x = s_x(n + 1) - s_x(n) = [s_{x0} + (n - 1)v_x \, dt] - [s_{x0} + (n)v_x \, dt]$$

$$= v_x \, dt$$

(4.3)

Thus

$$s_x(n) = s_x(n - 1) + v_x \, dt \qquad (4.4)$$

Here $s_x(n)$ is the current value and $s_x(n - 1)$ is the previous value. Note that

$$s_x(0) = s_{x0}$$

$$= 0$$

(4.5)

where the last equation follows from Figure 4.2a. Also, when the ball strikes a vertical wall, we assume it reverses direction and loses speed (reduced to 95% of its current value) because of friction.

The vertical motion is slightly more complicated since the acceleration of gravity exists. The equation of motion in the y-direction satisfies

$$s_y = s_{y0} + v_y t + 0.5gt^2 \qquad (4.6)$$

Using Equation (4.2),

$$s_y(n) = s_{y0} + v_y(n) \, dt + 0.5g(n)^2 \, dt^2 \qquad (4.7)$$

Generating another difference equation,

$$ds_y = s_y(n + 1) - s_y(n)$$

$$= v_y \, dt + 0.5g \, dt^2[(n^2 + 2n + 1) - n^2]$$

$$= v_y \, dt + gn \, dt^2 + 0(1)$$

(4.8)

We will ignore the term of order unity. Equation (4.8) yields

$$s_y(n) = s_y(n - 1) + v_y \, dt + gn \, dt^2 \qquad (4.9)$$

as the present y-position. Again, when the ball bounces at the bottom of the box, we assume its velocity reverses, and a slight change in the x-velocity occurs due to sliding friction (this velocity becomes 0.99 its previous value).

Figure 4.4a contains the structure chart for a bouncing ball program, and Figure 4.4b the flow chart for the calling module. Figure 4.4c illustrates the code for the main calling program for this bouncing ball illustration. The user must input an x-velocity in meters/second. Finally, a change in the gravitational constant from 9.81181 meters/sec/sec is allowed. Following initialization of distance parameters, the box coordinate parameters are set up. The x-scaling is by a factor of 24.5, and the y-scaling by a factor of 12.25. This yields motion that is somewhat uniform in both dimensions. The function setup() is called that clears the screen, puts the screen in 320×200 graphics mode, and draws the box used to represent the physical barrier. A while loop is used to create the motion: first the function balshp0() is called to clear the existing ball position; then the x-y coordinates are calculated for the updated positions, and the new position is filled with a ball shape. An if statement checks to see if the ball x-velocity is close to zero and, if so,

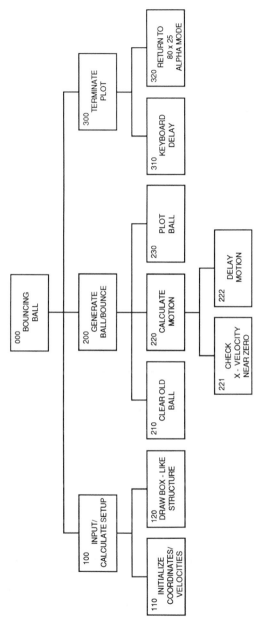

Figure 4.4a Structure chart for the bouncing ball program.

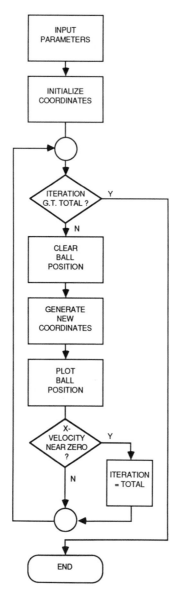

INPUT
PARAMETERS

INITIALIZE
COORDINATES

ITERATION
G.T. TOTAL ?   Y

N

CLEAR
BALL
POSITION

GENERATE
NEW
COORDINATES

PLOT
BALL
POSITION

X-
VELOCITY
NEAR ZERO
?   Y

N

ITERATION
= TOTAL

END

Figure 4.4b Flow chart for the main calling program for the bouncing ball.

terminates the motion. Finally, plotterm() returns the display to 80 × 25 alpha mode.

Figure 4.5 presents the two motion functions, xmotion() and ymotion(), which are the heart of the program. In xmotion(), Equation (4.4) is implemented where $s_{x_0} = s_x(n - 1)$. A check on the x-motion occurs at each side of the box. In ymotion(), Equation (4.9) is implemented with checks on the bounce and peak. In all cases, when the ball strikes an edge, the velocity is reversed and a friction effect introduced.

```
/* Program to generate bouncing ball */

#include <stdio.h>
#include <dos.h>

float sy0,g,a11,a22;
float sx0,vx,a1,a2;
float dt = 0.05;                                        /* interval */
int N,NN;                                               /* Iteration */

main()
        {
        int x,y,NTOTAL;
        int cc;

        printf("Input ball velocity\n");
        scanf("%f",&vx);
        printf("Input total iterations\n");
        scanf("%d",&NTOTAL);
        printf("Do you wish to change gravitational constant (Y/N)\n");
        cc = getchar();                                 /* Read terminator */
        cc = getchar();                                 /* Read character */
        if(cc == 'Y')
            {
            printf("Input new constant\n");
            scanf("%f",&g);
            }
        else
            g = 9.81181;                                /* m/sec2 */

                                                        /* Initialization */
        sy0 = 0.0;
        sx0 = 0.0;

        a1 = 51/24.5;                                   /* x-minimum */
        a2 = 296/24.5;                                  /* x-maximum */
        a11 = 51/12.25;                                 /* y-minimum */
        a22 = 170/12.25;                                /* y-maximum */

        N = 1;                                          /* Reset Interval */
        NN = 0;                                         /* Iteration */
        setup();

        x = 0;
        y = 0;

        while(NN < NTOTAL)
            {
            balshp0(x,y);                               /* Old clear */
            x = xmotion();                              /* x-position */
            y = ymotion();                              /* y-position */
            balshp1(x,y);

            if((vx < .01) && (vx > -.01))
                NN = NTOTAL;

            N++;                                        /* Inc interval */
            NN++;
            }
        plotterm();
        }
```

Figure 4.4c Main calling program that generates the bouncing ball.

```
/* Function to generate x-motion */
 xmotion()
        {
        extern float sx0,dt,vx,a1,a2;
        float sx,sxx,yxx,scalex = 24.5,frictionx = .95;
        int x;

        sx = sx0 + vx*dt;                            /* Distance */
        sxx = sx + a1;

        if(sxx > a2)
           {
           yxx = sxx - a2;                           /* Overshoot */
           sxx = a2 - yxx;                           /* bounce back */
           vx = -frictionx*vx;
           if(sxx < a1)
              exit(1);                               /* Oscillation */
           }
        if(sxx < a1)
           {
           yxx = a1 - sxx;                           /* Undershoot */
           sxx = yxx + a1;                           /* bounce back */
           vx = -frictionx*vx;
           if(sxx > a2)
              exit(1);                               /* Oscillation */
           }
        sx0 = sxx - a1;
        x = sxx*scalex;
        return(x);
        }
/* Function to generate y-motion */

#include <math.h>

ymotion()
        {
        extern int N;                                /* Interval no. */
        extern float sy0,dt,g,vx,a11,a22;
        float sy,vy,syy,yyy,scaley = 12.25,slidfricx = .99;
        int y;

        sy = sy0 + vy*dt + N*g*dt*dt;
        syy = sy + a11;

        if(syy > a22)
           {
           yyy = syy - a22;                          /* Bounce */
           syy = a22 - yyy;                          /* Approximation */
           vy = - vy;                                /* reverse velocity */
           vx = slidfricx*vx;                        /* sliding friction */
           N = 1;                                    /* start over */
           if(syy < a11)
              exit(1);                               /* Oscillation */
           }
        if(syy < a11)
           {
           yyy = a11 - syy;                          /* reach peak */
           syy = yyy + a11;                          /* Approximation */
           vy = -vy;
           N = 1;
           if(syy > a22)
              exit(1);                               /* Oscillation */
           }
        vy = vy + g*dt;                              /* Adjust velocity */
        sy0 = syy -a11;
        y = syy*scaley;
        return(y);
        }
```

Figure 4.5 Functions xmotion() and ymotion() that produce the position for the ball in screen coordinates based on elapsed time.

```
/* Function to write ball shape */

balshp1(col,row)
        int col,row;
        {
        int n;

        for(n = 1;n <= 2;n++)
            WRDOT(row - 1,col + n);                    /* Top */
        for(n = 0;n <= 3;n++)
            WRDOT(row,col + n);                        /* 1st middle */
        for(n = 0;n <= 3;n++)
            WRDOT(row + 1,col + n);                    /* 2nd middle */
        for(n = 0;n <= 3;n++)
            WRDOT(row + 2,col + n);                    /* 3rd middle */
        for(n = 1;n <= 2;n++)
            WRDOT(row + 3,col + n);                    /* bottom */
        }
/* Function to clear ball shape */

balshp0(col,row)
        int col,row;
        {
        int n;

        for(n = 1;n <= 2;n++)
            WRDOT0(row - 1,col + n);                   /* top */
        for(n = 0;n <= 3;n++)
            WRDOT0(row,col + n);                       /* 1st middle */
        for(n = 0;n <= 3;n++)
            WRDOT0(row +1,col + n);                    /* 2nd middle */
        for(n = 0;n <= 3;n++)
            WRDOT0(row + 2,col + n);                   /* 3rd middle */
        for(n = 1;n <= 2;n++)
            WRDOT0(row + 3,col + n);                   /* bottom */
        }
```

Figure 4.6. Functions balshpl() and balshp0() that write and clear the ball image.

Figure 4.6 illustrates the two functions balshp1() and balshp0(). The former writes a ball structure at the row and column specified. The ball shape is

```
x x
y x x x
x x x x
x x x x
  x x
```

where each x stands for a pel and the y denotes the pel that corresponds to the coordinate (col,row). Note that in balshp1() the routine WRDOT() is called. This routine generates a dot (the attribute = 1). In balshp0(), the routine WRDOT0() is called. This routine clears the pel using attribute = 0. Figure 4.7 presents setup() and WRDOT0().

It is useful to list the nonlibrary functions (and where they appear) that are used in this program:

```
main():
    setup()        (Figure 4.7)
    balshp0()      (Figure 4.6)
```

balshp1()	(Figure 4.6)
xmotion()	(Figure 4.5)
ymotion()	(Figure 4.5)
plotterm()	(Figure 2.8d)
balshp1():	
WRDOT()	(Figure 2.8b)
balshp0():	
WRDOT0()	(Figure 4.7)
setup():	
SCRCL()	(Figure 2.8b)
SC320()	(Figure 2.8b)
lineh()	(Figure 2.8e)
linev()	(Figure 2.8e)

Figure 4.8 presents the bouncing ball display for six periods: $n = 6, 20, 30, 35, 40,$ and 50, respectively. There is no substitute for actually watching the motion on the display, but the reader can begin to get a feel for this motion from the figure. The initial x-velocity in this figure was 10 meters/second.

```
/* Function to setup bouncing ball screen */

#include <dos.h>

setup()
        {
        SCRCL();                          /* Clear screen */
        SC320();                          /* 320 x 200 mode */

        lineh(50,25,50);
        lineh(175,50,300);
        linev(50,50,175);
        linev(300,25,175);
        }


/* Function to "clear" dor */

#include <dos.h>

WRDOT0(row,col)
        int row,col;
        {
        union REGS regs;

        regs.x.dx = row;                  /* Row value */
        regs.x.cx = col;                  /* Column value */
        regs.h.al = 0;                    /* Clear dot */
        regs.h.ah = 12;                   /* Write dot */

        int86(0x10,&regs,&regs);
        }
```

Figure 4.7 Functions setup(), which defines the boxlike structure, and WRDO-TO(), which clears the ball image.

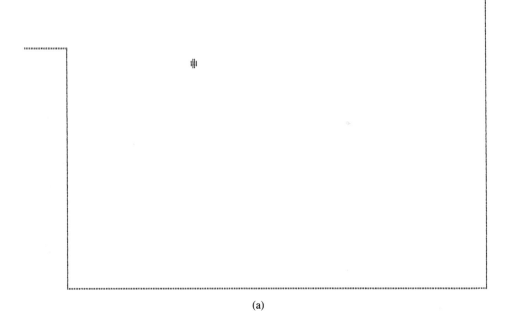

(a)

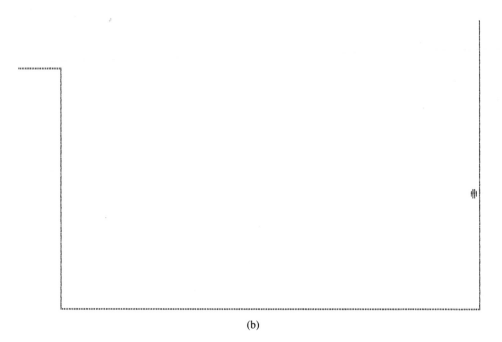

(b)

Figure 4.8 Ball motion for delays (a) 6, (b) 20,

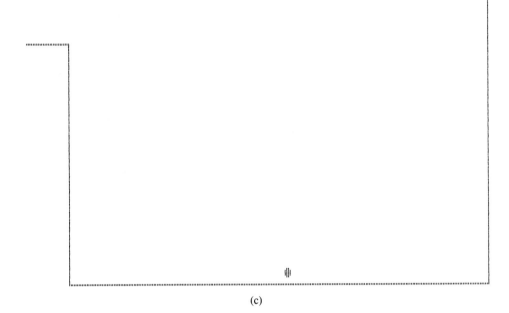

(c)

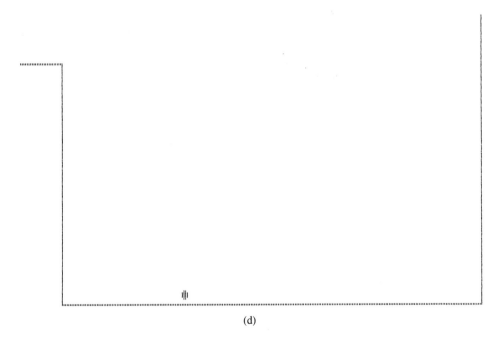

(d)

Figure 4.8 (*Continued*)   (c) 30, (d) 35,

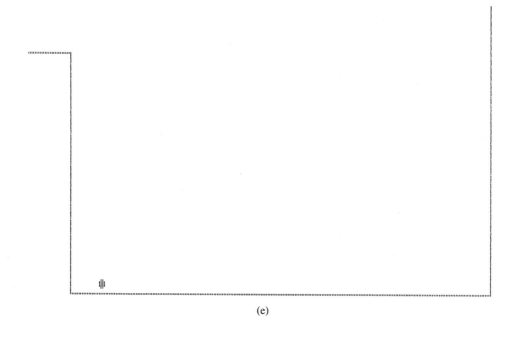

(e)

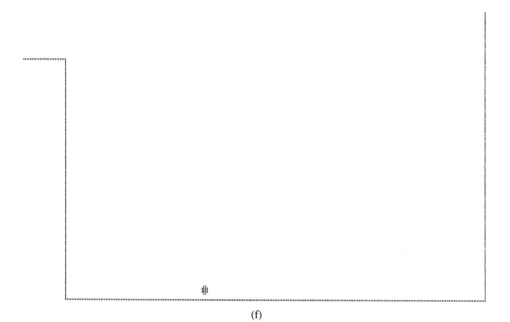

(f)

Figure 4.8 (*Concluded*)   (e) 40, and (f) 50. The *x* velocity is initially
10 meters/second.

4.3.2 Screen Buffer DMA and Sound

This section reconsiders the program for generating the bouncing ball. Two additional features are presented: sound and direct memory access of the screen. To implement sound, it is necessary to consider the operation of the chips themselves. Since each IBM microcomputer will perform in a compatible fashion, we examine the IBM PC implementation by way of example. The reader should recognize that, in addition to specifying the correct port addressing using address lines XA9 to XA5 and XA0 and XA1, the proper control bytes must be sent to the chip internal registers via these ports. (Address line XA0 corresponds to address bit 0, XA1 to address bit 1, ...) The specification of these internal register control words must depend on the chip manufacturer requirements. This is discussed later when the speaker is considered. In this discussion, the chip interconnection is illustrated in Figure 4.9, where negative or LOW active chip signals are denoted by a small circle on each chip. As with the address bus, data bus signals have an X prefix (XD0-XD7).

The DMA action is based on the screen buffer memory map appearing in Chapter 4. Here pels for rows 0, 2, 4, . . . , 198 occur starting at address B8000H

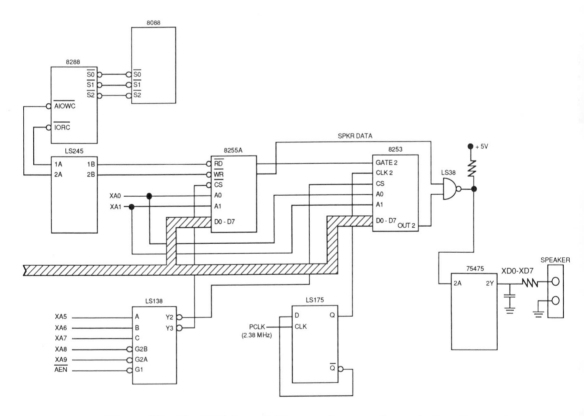

Figure 4.9 The 8253 Interval Timer environment for controlling the speaker. (Reprinted by permission from the *Technical Reference*; copyright 1981 by International Business Machines Corporation.)

and for rows 1, 3, 5, . . . , 199 starting at address BA000H. Since these are physical addresses, they map directly using movedata() under DOS.

The speaker.   To obtain a glimpse of how microcomputer hardware functions, it is useful to consider the speaker operation as it occurs in the IBM microcomputers. Specifically, the discussion will focus on the IBM PC as an example, and the rationale behind port addressing and control word structure will become clear for this case. Since all the IBM microcomputers are downward compatible with this model, it serves as a good example. The starting point for this discussion is Figure 4.9. Here we illustrate the interconnections for the various chips needed to drive the speaker. These chips are as follows:

1. Intel 8088, IBM PC/XT control processor unit
2. Intel 8288, bus controller for 8086/8088
3. Intel 8255A, programmable peripheral interface
4. Intel 8253, programmable interval timer
5. LS138, decoder/demultiplexer
6. LS175, quad D flip-flop
7. LS245, octal transceiver
8. 75475, inverter

Clearly a detailed discussion of these chips is beyond the scope of this text, and the interested reader is referred to the literature [9, 10]. We will, however, discuss these chips in sufficient detail to understand how one goes about generating sound from the speaker.

In Section 4.1.3, we saw that the port addresses for the 8253 and 8255A were, respectively, ports 40 to 43 and 60 to 63 hexadecimal. It is possible to see how this selection takes place by considering the addressing represented in Figure 4.9. The signals marked XA0, XA1, XA2, . . . , XA9 correspond to bits 0 through 9 of the address appearing on the address bus (parallel lines, one for each bit in the address). Hence, when an output from the 8088 corresponding to port address 60H occurs, the following address lines are set (for the first ten lines):

	XA9	XA8	XA7	XA6	XA5	XA4	XA3	XA2	XA1	XA0
· · ·	0	0	0	1	1	0	0	0	0	0
					6				0	

If one looks at the LS138 decoder/demultiplexer, it is clear that Y3 should go LOW. A LOW state on this pin would cause CS* to go LOW and activate the 8255A. (The chip select signal is indicated as active LOW by an asterisk in the text and an overbar in the figure. This signal effectively selects or turns the chip on.) To see the effect of this address on the LS138, consider the truth table for this state (for the LS138) [11]:

G1	G2A	G2B	A	B	C	Y0	Y1	Y2	Y3	Y4	Y5	Y6	Y7
1	0	0	1	1	0	1	1	1	0	1	1	1	1

But

G1	G2A	G2B	A	B	C
AEN*	XA9	XA8	XA7	XA6	XA5

Hence, since port address 60H sets XA5 and XA6 HIGH, this mapping is valid and Y3 goes LOW to select the 8255A. Note that address lines XA4 to XA0 do not affect chip selection (hence addresses 60H to 63H all select the same chip).

A similar mapping for port address 40H yields the following

XA9	XA8	XA7	XA6	XA5	XA4	XA3	XA2	XA1	XA0
0	0	0	1	0	0	0	0	0	0

$$\cdots \qquad \underbrace{\qquad}_{4} \qquad \underbrace{\qquad}_{0}$$

The LS138 truth table for this case is

G1	G2A	G2B	A	B	C	Y0	Y1	Y2	Y3	Y4	Y5	Y6	Y7
1	0	0	0	1	0	1	1	0	1	1	1	1	1

This clearly sets Y2 LOW and selects the 8253. Again, the *chip select* is independent of addresses XA4 to XA0.

Turning to the speaker operation (right side of Figure 4.9), it is necessary to generate a LOW signal out of the LS38 NAND gate to turn on the speaker. This requires that SPKR DATA (PB1 on the 8255A) and OUT2 on the 8253 both be HIGH. We first consider the 8253. It will be convenient to use this timer to turn the speaker on, count down some predetermined time interval, and turn off the speaker. This is accomplished by providing a gate signal to GATE2 (gating the output on) and a clock signal that varies periodically to generate a periodic output at OUT2. This periodic output will then yield a tone at the speaker. We use the third counter, counter 2, in the 8253. This counter can be programmed to generate an on–off state periodically by counting down from a faster clock. The countdown interval must be programmed into the 8253 via the data lines D0 to D7 after an appropriate MODE selection takes place. Internal to the 8253 are four registers selected by A0 to A1. When A0 to A1 are both 1, this control word register is selected for loading data via D0 to D7. Hence, port address 43H causes data appearing on the data bus to be loaded into the 8253 control word register. Similarly, the 8253 counters are selected according to

A0	A1	Counter
0	0	0
1	0	1
0	1	2

We use counter 2 (remember OUT2 is selected); hence port 42H will be the input for the clock divisor.

```
/* Program to generate bouncing ball */

#include <stdio.h>
#include <dos.h>

float sy0,g,a11,a22;
float sx0,vx,a1,a2;
float dt = 0.05;                                          /* Time interval */
int N,NN,NDELAY;                                          /* Iteration */

main()
        {
        int x,y,NTOTAL;
        char cc;

        printf("Input number DELAY iterations\n");
        scanf("%d",&NDELAY);
        printf("Input ball velocity\n");
        scanf("%f",&vx);
        printf("Input total iterations\n");
        scanf("%d",&NTOTAL);
        printf("Do you wish to change gravitational constant (Y/N)\n");
        cc = getchar();                                  /* Read terminator */
        cc = getchar();                                  /* Read character */
        if(cc == 'Y')
            {
            printf("Input new constant\n");
            scanf("%f",&g);
            }
        else
            g = 9.81181;                                 /* m/sec2 */

                                                         /* Initialization */
        sy0 = 0.0;
        sx0 = 0.0;

        a1 = 53/24.5;                                    /* x-minimum */
        a2 = 292/24.5;                                   /* x-maximum */
        a11 = 51/12.25;                                  /* y-minimum */
        a22 = 169/12.25;                                 /* y-maximum */

        N = 1;                                           /* Interval */
        NN = 0;                                          /* Delay count */
        setup();

        x = xmotion();
        y = ymotion();
        bbalsp1(x,y);

        while(NN < NTOTAL)
            {
            bbalsp0(x,y);                                /* Old clear */
            x = xmotion();                               /* x-position */
            y = ymotion();                               /* y-position */
            bbalsp1(x,y);

            if((vx < .05) && (vx > -.05))
                NN = NTOTAL;

                DELAY();                                 /* Delay interval */

            N++;                                         /* Inc interval */
            NN++;
            }
        plotterm();
        }
```

Figure 4.11 Main calling program for generating the bouncing ball with direct memory access (DMA) of the screen in graphics mode.

```
/* Function to generate x-motion */
  xmotion()
        {
        extern float sx0,dt,vx,a1,a2;
        float sx,sxx,yxx,scalex = 24.5,frictionx = .95;
        int x;

        sx = sx0 + vx*dt;                       /* Distance */
        sxx = sx + a1;

        if(sxx > a2)
            {
            BEEP();
            yxx = sxx - a2;                     /* Overshoot */
            sxx = a2 - yxx;                     /* bounce back */
            vx = -frictionx*vx;
            if(sxx < a1)
                exit(1);                        /* Oscillation */
            }
        if(sxx < a1)
            {
            BEEP();
            yxx = a1 - sxx;                     /* Undershoot */
            sxx = yxx + a1;                     /* bounce back */
            vx = -frictionx*vx;
            if(sxx > a2)
                exit(1);                        /* Oscillation */
            }
        sx0 = sxx - a1;
        x = sxx*scalex;
        return(x);
        }
```

Figure 4.12 Modified function xmotion( ), which sounds the speaker at each sidewall collision using BEEP( ).

The variable src is the same as src[0], which is a pointer to the array or its address (offset). Hence the offset of src is simply given by src. The C library function movedata() has the form

```
movedata (srcseg, srcoff, destseg, destoff, nbytes);
```

where

srcseg	Source segment address
srcoff	Source offset
destseg	Destination segment address
destoff	Destination offset
nbytes	Number bytes transferred

This function transfers nbytes starting with srcseg:srcoff to destseg:destoff, where a far move is assumed.

Clearly, to complete the specification of data to be moved for the ball example, a destination must be specified (since we will move 1 byte at a time, nbytes = 1). In specifying a pel, a row and column value are needed. Thus, for the first row, bytes (0, 79) are possible offsets from B800H segment. These 80 bytes correspond to 4 pels per byte out of a total of 320 pels for the first row. Since offsets from

B800H (less than 2000) correspond to even rows, each row is a multiple of 2 (even), and any given group of 4 pels is specified by

```
row * 40 + col/4
```

(Since the rows are specified 0, 2, 3, . . . 198, this actually jumps in groups of 80 bytes per change in row.) A similar formula applies to odd rows, except the segment locator is BA00H, and the offsets are calculated identically, except the input row value is subtracted from 1. To see this, note that row 1 must actually become row 0 at address BA004.

This approach is used in both bbalsp1() and bbalsp0(). For bbalsp0(), the 4-pel attribute is simply 0x00. For the first and last row of the ball in bbalsp1(), only the middle-odd bits should be active (0x14) and the three middle rows require all 4 pels active (0x55). An alternate scheme will be presented in Section 4.4.3.

Figure 4.14 illustrates the delay specification introduced between DMA updates. This function, DELAY(), uses an external variable NDELAY to specify the limit

```
/* Function to write to screen directly */

#include <dos.h>
#include <memory.h>
#include <string.h>

bbalsp1(col,row)
        int col,row;
        {
        unsigned int evenadd = 0xB800,oddadd = 0xBA00;
        unsigned char src[1];
        int row1;
        struct SREGS reg;

        segread(&reg);

        if((row % 2) == 0)
            {
            src[0] = 0x14;                              /* Even row */
            movedata(reg.ds,src,evenadd,row*40+col/4,1);
            movedata(reg.ds,src,evenadd,(row+4)*40+col/4,1);
            src[0] = 0x55;
            movedata(reg.ds,src,oddadd,row*40+col/4,1);
            movedata(reg.ds,src,evenadd,(row+2)*40+col/4,1);
            movedata(reg.ds,src,oddadd,(row+2)*40+col/4,1);
            }
        else
            {
            row1 = row - 1;
            src[0] = 0x14;                              /* Odd row */
            movedata(reg.ds,src,oddadd,row1*40+col/4,1);
            movedata(reg.ds,src,oddadd,(row1+4)*40+col/4,1);
            src[0] = 0x55;
            movedata(reg.ds,src,evenadd,row1*40+col/4,1);
            movedata(reg.ds,src,oddadd,(row1+2)*40+col/4,1);
            movedata(reg.ds,src,evenadd,(row1+2)*40+col/4,1);
            }
        }
```

(a)

Figure 4.13a Function bbalspl(), which generates the ball shape using DMA output at the (row, column) position.

```
/* Function to clear shape on screen directly */

#include <dos.h>
#include <memory.h>
#include <string.h>

bbalsp0(col,row)
        int col,row;
        {
        unsigned int evenadd = 0xB800,oddadd = 0xBA00;
        unsigned char src[1];
        int row1;
        struct SREGS reg;

        segread(&reg);

        src[0] = 0x00;

        if((row % 2) == 0)
          {
                                                        /* Even row */
          movedata(reg.ds,src,evenadd,row*40+col/4,1);
          movedata(reg.ds,src,evenadd,(row+4)*40+col/4,1);
          movedata(reg.ds,src,oddadd,row*40+col/4,1);
          movedata(reg.ds,src,evenadd,(row+2)*40+col/4,1);
          movedata(reg.ds,src,oddadd,(row+2)*40+col/4,1);
          }
        else
          {
          row1 = row - 1;
                                                        /* Odd row */
          movedata(reg.ds,src,oddadd,row1*40+col/4,1);
          movedata(reg.ds,src,oddadd,(row1+4)*40+col/4,1);
          movedata(reg.ds,src,evenadd,row1*40+col/4,1);
          movedata(reg.ds,src,oddadd,(row1+2)*40+col/4,1);
          movedata(reg.ds,src,evenadd,(row1+2)*40+col/4,1);
          }
        }
```

(b)

Figure 4.13b Function bbalsp0( ), which erases the ball shape using DMA output at the (row, column) position.

```
/* Function to delay -- this routine is somewhat arbitrary */

DELAY()
        {
        int n,nop;
        extern int NDELAY;

        for(n = 1;n <= NDELAY;n++)
           nop = 0;
        }
```

Figure 4.14 Function DELAY( ), which introduces a time delay between screen updates during DMA output.

on the number of loop iterations needed to delay motion. For a value of NDELAY = 100 the behavior of Figure 4.8 is approximated.

4.3.3 An Interval Timer

The DOS interrupt 0x21 allows a number of functions to be called (specified by the value in AH). Functions 0x2C and 0x2D get time and set time, respectively, with register values specified by

CH = hours
CL = minutes
DH = seconds
DL = hundredths

Figure 4.15 illustrates a main calling program that sets up an interval for timing and displays the time at each second. At the conclusion of the interval, a short tone sounds. This program calls three functions: zero_tm(), which sets the

```
/* Function to generate interval timer */
#include <stdio.h>
char h,m,s;                                     /* hour,min,sec */

main()
        {
        int hour,hour1,hour2,min,min1,min2,sec,sec1,sec2;

        printf("Input hours \n");
        scanf("%d",&hour);
        printf("Input minutes \n");
        scanf("%d",&min);
        printf("Input seconds \n");
        scanf("%d",&sec);

        zero_tm();                              /* Clear timer */
        SCRCL();                                /* Clear screen */
        rd_tm();
        hour1 = (int)(h);
        min1 = (int)(m);
        sec1 = (int)(s);

        while((hour1 != hour) || (min1 != min) || (sec1 != sec))
            {
            rd_tm();
            hour2 = (int)(h);
            min2 = (int)(m);
            sec2 = (int)(s);
            if((sec1 < sec2) || ((sec2 == 0) && (sec1 > 0)))
                {
                printf(" %d:%d:%d \n",hour2,min2,sec2);
                }
            hour1 = hour2;
            min1 = min2;
            sec1 = sec2;
            }
        TONE();                                 /* sound at end */
        }
```

Figure 4.15 Main calling program for the interval timer.

time to zero, SCRCL(), which clears the screen, and rd__tm(), which reads the time. Figure 4.16 presents zero__tm() and rd__tm() and illustrates how the function calls are implemented. Figure 4.17 is the function TONE(), which is identical to BEEP() except the sound lasts longer. Finally, Figure 4.18 is a typical interactive session output for a 10-second interval.

4.3.4 Time of Day, Date, and Memory Size

Figure 4.19 illustrates a program that can be used to set the time. This program is conceptually similar to the program in Figure 4.15, except it calls the function set__tm() if it is desired to set the time. This function appears in Figure 4.20 and is very similar to zero__tm(), except register values are actually fixed at values other than zero. Figure 4.21 represents an interactive session with ttime, the linked program of Figure 4.19. We have periodically used the system routine, time, as a check.

```
/* Function to zero time */

#include <dos.h>

zero_tm( )
        {
        union REGS regs;

        regs.h.ah = 0x2D;                    /* Set time */
        regs.h.ch = 0;                       /* hours (0-23) */
        regs.h.cl = 0;                       /* min (0-59) */
        regs.h.dh = 0;                       /* sec (0-59) */
        regs.h.dl = 0;                       /* hundredths (0-99)*/

        int86(0x21,&regs,&regs);
        }




/* Function to read time */

#include <dos.h>

rd_tm( )
        {
        extern char h,m,s;
        union REGS regs;

        regs.h.ah = 0x2C;                    /* Get time */
        int86(0x21,&regs,&regs);

        h = regs.h.ch;                       /* hour as char */
        m = regs.h.cl;                       /* min as char */
        s = regs.h.dh;                       /* sec as char */
        }
```

Figure 4.16 Functions to zero the time value, zero_tm( ), and read the time value, rd_tm( ).

```
/* Function to beep speaker */

#include <conio.h>
#define TCTLP 0x43                                    /* Timer cntl port */
#define TIM2P 0x42                                    /* Timer 2 port */
#define PPIP 0x61                                     /* PPI port */
#define MODEV 0xB6                                    /* Timer mode cntl */
#define TIMLSV 0x33                                   /* LS timer byte */
#define TIMMSV 0x05                                   /* MS timer byte */

TONE()
        {
        int n,nop;
        char result,result1;

        outp(TCTLP,MODEV);                            /* Ctr 2,LS 1st,bin */

        outp(TIM2P,TIMLSV);                           /* Divider 0x533 */
        outp(TIM2P,TIMMSV);

        result = inp(PPIP);                           /* Save PPI status */
        result1 = result;
        result1 = (result1 | 3);                      /* Set bits 0,1 */
        outp(PPIP,result1);                           /* turn on spkr */

        for(n = 1;n <= 5000;n++)
           nop = 0;                                   /* No operation */
        outp(PPIP,result);                            /* turn off spkr */
        }
```

Figure 4.17 Function TONE() used to generate an extended tone.

As with time, the date can be set using the interrupt 0x21 functions get date (AH=2A) and set date (AH=2B). Figure 4.22 represents a main calling program for checking and setting the date. This program calls set__date() and get__date(), which appear in Figure 4.23. Figure 4.24 illustrates a typical interactive session with ddate, the linked program of Figure 4.22. Also, in this figure the system routine date is called as a check.

Finally, Figure 4.25 illustrates a program to check memory size. This program uses the BIOS interrupt 0x12 and returns the size in increments of 1024 bytes (K). Figure 4.26 illustrates the result for the IBM AT used in writing this book.

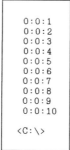

Figure 4.18 Typical display output from the interval timer program. The program also sounds a tone at the end of the interval period. Here 10 seconds is the assumed interval.

```
/* Function to read-set time */

#include <stdio.h>
char h,m,s;                                              /* hour,min,sec */

main()
        {
        int ch;
        int hour,min,sec;

        printf("Do you wish to set time (Y/N)? \n");
        if((ch = getch()) == 'Y')
           {
           printf("Input hour \n");
           scanf("%d",&hour);
           printf("Input minutes \n");
           scanf("%d",&min);
           printf("Input seconds \n");
           scanf("%d",&sec);

           h = (char)(hour);
           m = (char)(min);
           s = (char)(sec);

           set_tm();
           }
        rd_tm();

        hour = (int)(h);
        min = (int)(m);
        sec = (int)(s);

        printf("%d:%d:%d \n",hour,min,sec);
        }
```

Figure 4.19 Main calling program to read and set the time-of-day clock.

```
/* Function to set time */

#include <dos.h>

set_tm()
        {
        extern char h,m,s;
        union REGS regs;

        regs.h.ah = 0x2D;                                /* Set time */
        regs.h.ch = h;                                   /* hours */
        regs.h.cl = m;                                   /* min */
        regs.h.dh = s;                                   /* secs */
        regs.h.dl = 0;

        int86(0x21,&regs,&regs);
        }
```

Figure 4.20 Function to set the time.

```
time
Current time is 21:10:18.18
Enter new time:

<C:\>ttime
Do you wish to set time (Y/N)?
Input hour
22
Input minutes
11
Input seconds
30
22:11:29

<C:\>time
Current time is 22:11:34.51
Enter new time:

<C:\>
```

Figure 4.21 Typical interactive session used in displaying and setting the clock. Also indicated are checks with the system routine, time.

```
/* Function to check-set date */

#include <stdio.h>

int y;                                          /* year */
char m,d;                                        /* month,day */

main()
        {
        int ch;                                  /* character */
        int year,month,day;

        printf("Do you wish to set date (Y/N)? \n");
        if((ch = getch()) == 'Y')
            {
            printf("Input year \n");
            scanf("%d",&y);
            printf("Input month \n");
            scanf("%d",&month);
            printf("Input day \n");
            scanf("%d",&day);

            m = (char)(month);
            d = (char)(day);

            set_date();
            }
        get_date();
        year = y;
        month = (int)(m);
        day = (int)(d);

        printf("%d/%d/%d \n",month,day,year);
        }
```

Figure 4.22 Main calling program to check and set the date.

```
/* Set date */

#include <dos.h>

set_date()
        {
        extern int y;
        extern char m,d;
        union REGS regs;

        regs.h.ah = 0x2B;                              /* Set date */
        regs.x.cx = y;                                 /* year - int */
        regs.h.dh = m;                                 /* month */
        regs.h.dl = d;                                 /* day */

        int86(0x21,&regs,&regs);
        }

/* Get date */

get_date()
        {
        extern int y;
        extern char m,d;
        union REGS regs;

        regs.h.ah = 0x2A;                              /* Get date */
        int86(0x21,&regs,&regs);
        y = regs.x.cx;                                 /* year - int */
        m = regs.h.dh;                                 /* month */
        d = regs.h.dl;                                 /* day */
        }
```

Figure 4.23 Functions used for obtaining the date, get_date( ), and setting the date, set_date( ).

```
ddate
Do you wish to set date (Y/N)?
Input year
1988
Input month
9
Input day
18
9/18/1988

<C:\>ddate
Do you wish to set date (Y/N)?
9/18/1988

<C:\>date
Current date is Sun  9-18-1988
Enter new date (mm-dd-yy):

<C:\>ddate
Do you wish to set date (Y/N)?
Input year
1987
Input month
9
Input day
17
9/17/1987

<C:\>date
Current date is Thu  9-17-1987
Enter new date (mm-dd-yy):

<C:\>
```

Figure 4.24 Typical interactive session with the program that checks and sets the date, ddate. Also indicated are checks with the system routine, date.

```
/* Function to read memory size (K) */

#include <stdio.h>
#include <dos.h>

main()
        {
        int AX;
        union REGS regs;

        int86(0x12,&regs,&regs);

        AX = regs.x.ax;
        printf("Memory size (K) = %d",AX);
        }
```

Figure 4.25 Program to read memory size.

```
memory
Memory size (K) = 640
<C:\>
<C:\>
```

Figure 4.26 Typical memory size results for memory, the program appearing in Figure 4.25 (and the computer system used in the book, 640K).

4.4 THE C LIBRARY

Most of this book uses the Microsoft Version 4.0 C compiler [12–14]. Many of the include functions and library routines constitute standard entities that have been implemented for the IBM microcomputers. The topic of this section is the C library services (covering the include files). A discussion is presented for both the include functions and associated library files. We close the section with an example that illustrates three-dimensional motion: a rotating cube.

4.4.1 Include Functions

Table 4.5 lists the various include file functions available with the Version 4.0 compiler. As can be seen, this table is quite extensive and the routines are listed in alphabetical order. A functional grouping is as follows:

Buffer manipulation:

memccpy, memchr, memcmp, memcpy, memicmp, memset, movedata

Character classification and conversion:

isalnum, isalpha, isascii, iscntrl, isdigit, isgraph, islower,
isprint, ispunct, isspace, isupper, isxdigit, toascii, tolower,
toupper, _tolower, _toupper

Sec. 4.4   The C Library   **175**
```
```

Data conversion:

atof, atoi, atol, ecvt, fcvt, gcvt, itoa, ltoa, strtod, strtol, ultoa

Directory control:

chdir, getcwd, mkdir, rmdir

File handling:

access, chmod, chsize, filelength, fstat, isatty, locking, mktemp, remove, rename, setmode, stat, umask, unlink

Stream:

clearerr, fclose, fcloseall, fdopen, feof, ferror, fflush, fgetc, fgetchar, fgets, fileno, flushall, fopen, fprintf, fputc, fputchar, fputs, fread, freopen, fscanf, fseek, ftell, fwrite, getc, getchar, gets, getw, printf, putc, putchar, puts, putw, rewind, rmtmp, scanf, setbuf, setrbuf, sprintf, sscanf, tempnam, tmpfile, tmpram, ungetc, vfprintf, vprintf, vsprintf

Low level:

close, creat, dup, dup2, eof, lseek, open, read, sopen, tell, write

Console and port I/O:

cgets, cprintf, cputs, cscanf, getch, getche, inp, kbhit, outp, putch, ungetch

Math:

acos, asin, atan, atan2, bessel, cabs, reil, _clear87, _control87, cos, cosh, dieeetomsbin, dmsbintoieee, exp, fabs, fieeetomsbin, floor, fmod, fmsbintoieee, _fpreset, fvexp, hypot, ldexp, log, log10, matherr, modf, pow, sin, sinh, sqrt, _status87, tan fanh

Memory:

alloca, calloc, _expand, _ffree, _fmalloc, free, _freect, _fmsize, halloc, hfree, malloc, _memarl, _msize, _nfree, _nmalloc, _nmsize, realloc, sbrk, stackavail

DOS interface:

bdos, dosexterr, FP_OFF, FP_SEG, int86, int86x, intdos, intdosx, segread

Process control:

```
abort, execl, execle, execlp, execlpe, execu, execue, execup,
execupe, exit, _exit, getpid, oneexit, signal, spawnl, spawnle,
spawnlp, spawnlpe, spawnu, spawnue, spawnup, spawnupe, system
```

Search/sort:

```
bsearch, lfind, lsearch, qsort
```

String:

```
strcat, strchr, strcmp, strcmpi, strcpy, strcspn, strdup,
strerror, stricmp, strlen, strlwr, strncat, strncmp, strncpy,
strnicmp, strnset, strpbrk, strrchr, strrev, strset, strspn,
strstr, strtok, strupr
```

Time:

```
asctime, ctime, difftime, ftime, gmtime, localtime, time, tzset,
utime
```

Variable length argument:

```
va_arg, va_end, va_start
```

Miscellaneous:

```
abs, assert, getenv, labs, longjmp, perror, putenv, rand, setjmp,
srand, swab
```

It is very important that the reader become familiar with these routines (hence the need to consider them functionally as well as specifically), because they form the core of any ability to implement utilities in C. The reader is referred to the appropriate reference manual for his or her system to obtain a full explanation on how to call these functions (for the Microsoft C compiler this is reference 12).

It is beyond the scope of this text to consider these routines in detail. There are simply too many of them and most are too specialized. We have already used a number of them in examples and will continue to explore their features throughout the remainder of the book.

4.4.2 Library Files

Many of the include functions simply set up the actual function code for access and calling by the application programs. The actual execution code, which implements the function call, is contained in one of a number of compiler library files. For the Microsoft C compiler, these library files are defined as in Table 4.6. As can be seen from the descriptions in Table 4.6 each memory model (except huge) has its own associated library files. This brief look at library files completes the discussion of available services under DOS for the Microsoft C Compiler Version 4.0. In the section, we consider a final example for this chapter.

TABLE 4.5 C COMPILER INCLUDE FILE FUNCTIONS

Function	Discussion
`abort`	Terminates the program.
`abs(n)`	Returns the absolute value of the integer n.
`access(pathname,mode)`	Determines the access mode for a file, pathname. Mode satisfies: 06, read/write permission; 04, read only; 02, write only; and 00, existence only. A return value 0 is TRUE.
`acos(x)`	Returns the arc cosine of x.
`alloca(size)`	Allocates size bytes on the stack. Returns a character pointer to the allocated space.
`asctime(time)`	Converts a time [stored as a structure from gmtime() or localtime()] to a character string. The return value is a pointer to the string.
`asin(x)`	Returns to the arc sine of x.
`assert(expression)`	Prints a diagnostic message if expression is FALSE.
`atan(x), atan2(x)`	Returns the arc tangent of x (atan in the range -90, 90 and atan2 in the range -180, 180).
`atof(string), atoi(string),` `and atol(string)`	Converts a character string to a double-precision floating point value (atof), an integer (atoi), or a long integer (atol).
`bdos(dosfn,dosdx,dosal)`	Invokes the DOS function, dosfn, after setting AL = dosal and DX = dosdx.
`bessel: j0(x),j1(x),jn(x),y0(x),` `y1(x), and yn(x)`	Returns the Bessel functions of the first and second kinds for x.
`bsearch(key,base,num,width,compare)`	Performs a binary search of an array of num elements, each of width bytes, with base as a pointer to the array and key the value being sought.

`cabs(x)`	Calculates the absolute value of a number with structure type complex:
	
	`struct complex`
	`    double x,y;`
	`    ;`

`calloc(n,size)`	Allocates storage for an array of n elements each of length size. Returns a pointer to the array.
`ceil(x)`	Returns a double value that is the smallest integer greater than or equal to x.
`cgets(string)`	Reads a string of characters from STDIN and stores the string and its length at the location pointed to by string. The first element is the maximum allowed length and the second value is the actual length.
`chdir(pathname)`	Changes the current working directory to pathname.
`chmod(pathname,pmode)`	Changes the permission of a file specified by pathname to pmode.
`chsize(handle,size)`	Extends or truncates the file associated with handle to size.

Function	Description
`_clear87`	Clears the floating point status word for the coprocessor.
`clearerr(stream)`	Resets the error indicator for the indicated stream.
`close(handle)`	Closes the file associated with handle.
`_control87(new,mask)`	Gets/updates the control word in the coprocessor.
`cos(x), cosh(x)`	Returns the cosine or hyperbolic cosine of x.
`cprintf(format-string (,arguments))`	Formats and prints a series of characters and values to the console.
`cputs(str)`	Writes the string pointed to by str to the console.
`create(pathname,pmode)`	Creates a file described by pathname in mode pmode. .
`cscanf(format-string (,arguments))`	Reads data from the console into arguments.
`ctime(time)`	Converts a time stored as a long value to a character string.
`dieeetomsbin(src,dst) and dmsbintoieee(src,dst)`	Converts a double-precision number in IEEE format to Microsoft binary format and vice versa.
`difftime(time2,time1)`	Computes time2 − time1.
`dosexterr(buffer)`	Obtains the register values returned by DOS function call 59H.
`dup(handle), dup2(handle1,handle2)`	Duplicates a file handle.
`ecvt(value,ndigits,decptr,signptr)`	Converts a floating point number to a character string. Value is the number, ndigits of value are converted, decptr is the position of the decimal, and signptr the sign.
`eof(handle)`	Determines whether an end of file has been reached for the file associated with handle.
`The excel funcitons`	These functions load and execute new child processes.
`exit(status) and _exit(status)`	Terminate the calling process.
`exp(x)`	Returns the exponential of x.
`_expand(ptr,size)`	Changes the size of a block pointed to by ptr.
`fabs(x)`	Returns the absolute value of a floating point variable, x.
`fclose(stream) and fcloseall`	Closes the stream or all streams.
`fcvt(value,ndec,decptr,signptr)`	Converts a floating point number to a character in the manner of ecvt.
`fdopen(handle,type)`	Associates a stream with the file identified by handle. Type specifies the access: "r," read, "w," write, "a," appending, "r+," both, "w+," open an empty file for both, and "a+," open for reading and appending.
`feof(stream)`	Determines if EOF for stream has been reached.
`ferror(stream)`	Tests for an error on stream.
`fflush(stream)`	Causes the contents of the associated buffer (with stream) to be written to the file.
`_free(ptr)`	Deallocates the memory block pointed to by ptr.
`fgetc(stream) and fgetchar()`	Gets a single character from the input stream. The stream is STDIN for fgetchar.
`fgets(string,n,stream)`	Reads a string from a stream and stores n characters.

TABLE 4.5 (*Continued*)

Function	Discussion
`fieeetomsbin(src,dst)` and `fmsbintoieee(src,dst)`	Converts a floating point number in IEEE format to Microsoft binary and vice versa.
`filelength(handle)`	Returns the length in bytes of the file associated with handle.
`fileno(stream)`	Returns the file handle associated with stream.
`floor(x)`	Returns the largest integer less than x.
`flushall`	Causes the contents of all output streams to be written to their associated files.
`_fmalloc(size)`	Returns a far pointer to a block that is allocated of size bytes outside the default segment.
`fmod(x,y)`	Calculates the remainder of x/y.
`_fmsize(ptr)`	Returns the size in bytes of a block allocated by __fmalloc.
`fopen(pathname,type)`	Opens a file associated with pathname of type.
`FP_OFF(longptr)`	Returns the offset of longptr.
`FP_SEG(longptr)`	Returns the segment address of longptr.
`_fpreset`	Reinitializes the floating point math package.
`fprintf(stream,format-string (,arguments))`	Formats and prints a series of characters and values to stream.
`fputc(c,stream)` and `fputchar(c)`	Writes the character c to the output stream (for fputchar this is STDOUT).
`fputs(string,stream)`	Copies string to stream.
`fread(buffer,size,count,stream)`	Reads count items of length size from stream to buffer.
`free(ptr)`	Deallocates the memory block pointed to by ptr.
`_freect(size)`	Returns a number representing the approximate number of times a call to malloc can be made to allocate a memory block of length size.
`freopen(pathname,type,stream)`	Reassigns the file specified by pathname to stream with type characteristic.
`frexp(x,expptr)`	Returns the mantissa of a floating point number, x, with associated exponent expptr.
`fscanf(stream,format-string (,arguments))`	Reads data from stream as indicated by format string and stores these data in argument.
`fseek(stream,offset,orgin)`	Moves the pointer associated with stream an offset from origin.
`fstat(handle,buffer)`	Obtains information about the file associated with handle and stores it in the structure pointed to by buffer.
`ftell(stream)`	Gets the current position of the file pointer associated with stream.
`ftime(timeptr)`	Gets the current time and stores it in the structure pointed to by timeptr.
`fwrite(buffer,size,count,stream)`	Writes count items of length size from buffer to stream.
`gcvt(value,ndec,buffer)`	Converts a floating point value to a character string in buffer with ndec digits.

Function	Description
`getc(stream) and getchar()`	Reads a character from stream (STDIN for getchar).
`getch()`	Reads without echoing a character from the console.
`getche()`	Reads a character from the console and echos it.
`getcwd(pathbuf,n)`	Gets the full path name for the current working directory and stores it in pathbuf. The name must be less than n characters.
`getenv(varname)`	Searches the list of environment variables for varname.
`getpid()`	Returns the process ID, an integer that uniquely specifies the calling process.
`gets(buffer)`	Reads a line from STDIN and stores it in buffer.
`getw(stream)`	Reads the next value of type int from stream and increases the pointer.
`gmtime(time)`	Converts a time stored as a long to a structure.
`halloc(n,size)`	Allocates storage for a huge array of n elements of length size.
`hfree(ptr)`	Deallocates a memory block.
`hypot(x,y)`	Calculates the hypotenuse of a right triangle of sides x and y.
`inp(port)`	Reads a byte from port.
`int86(intno,inregs,outregs)`	Executes the interrupt intno with registers specified as in inregs and returned as in outregs.
`int86x(intno,inregs,outregs,segregs)`	Executes the same as int86() except allows specification of far call through segregs.
`intdos(inregs,outregs)`	Performs a DOS function call with values specified in inregs and returned in outregs.
`intdosx(inregs,outregs,segregs)`	Performs a far function call using segregs.
`isalnum(c), isalpha(c), and isascii(c)`	Test c for alphanumeric, letter, ASCII character and return nonzero value if successful.
`isatty(handle)`	Determines whether handle is associated with character device.
`The iscntrl family`	These functions perform various tests on integers.
`itoa(value,string,radix)`	This function converts value of base radix to characters in string.
`kbhit()`	Checks the console for a recent keystroke.
`labs(n)`	Produces the absolute value of the long integer, n.
`ldexp(x,exp)`	Calculates the value of x times 2 to the power exp.
`The lfind family`	These functions perform a linear search for key in an array.
`localtime(time)`	Converts time stored as a long to a structure.
`locking(handle,mode,nbyte)`	Locks/unlocks a file associated with handle depending on mode. Locking is for nbytes.
`log(x) and log10(x)`	Calculates the natural and base 10 logarithm of x.
`logjmp(env,value)`	Restores a stock environment previously saved in env by setjmp. The value returned must be nonzero.
`lseek(handle,offset,orgin)`	Moves the file pointer associated with handle an offset from origin.

TABLE 4.5 (*Continued*)

Function	Discussion
`ltoa(value,string,radix)`	Converts the digits of base radix in value to characters in string.
`malloc(size)`	Returns a pointer to an allocated block of memory made to be of length size.
`matherr(x)`	Processes errors generated by the math library.
`_memavl`	Returns the approximate size of available memory for dynamic allocation.
`memcpy(dest,src,c,cnt)`	Copies cnt bytes of src to dest including the first copy oc c.
`memchr(buf,c,cnt)`	Returns a pointer to the location of the first occurrence of c in buf within cnt bytes.
`memcmp(buf1,buf2,cnt)`	Compares the first cnt bytes of buf1 and buf2 and returns a value representing agreement.
`memcpy(dest,src,cnt)`	Copies cnt bytes from sarc to dest.
`memicmp(buf1,buf2,cnt)`	Compares the first cnt bytes of buf1 and buf2 without regard to case.
`memset(dest,c,cnt)`	Sets the first cnt bytes of the dest to c.
`mkdir(pathname)`	Creates a new directory with specified pathname.
`mktemp(template)`	Returns a pointer to a unique filename by modifying template.
`modf(x,intptr)`	Breaks down the floating point value, x, into fractional and integer parts.
`movedate(srcseg,srcoff,destseg,destoff, nbytes)`	Moves far data from src to dest for a total of nbytes.
`_msize(ptr)`	Returns the size in bytes of the memory block pointed to by ptr.
`_nfree(ptr)`	Deallocates the memory block pointed to by ptr.
`_nmalloc(size)`	Allocates a memory block of length size bytes.
`_nmsize(ptr)`	Returns the size in bytes of a block allocated by __nmalloc.
`onexit(func)`	This function is passed the address of a function (func) to be executed upon normal termination.
`open(pathname,oflag (,Pmode))`	Opens the file specified by pathname as defined by oflag. Pmode is the read/write status.
`outp(port,value)`	This function outputs a value to port.
`perror(string)`	Prints an error message in string to STDERR.
`pow(x,y)`	Returns x raised to the power y.
`printf(format-string (,argument))`	Prints on STDOUT the arguments according to format string.
`putc(c,stream) and putchar(c)`	Writes the character c to the output stream.
`putch(c)`	Writes the character c to the console.
`putenv(envstring)`	Changes environment variables.
`puts(string)`	Writes the string to STDOUT.

Function	Description
`putw(binint,stream)`	Writes a binary value to stream.
`qsort(base,num,width,compare)`	Implements a quick sort on num elements each of width bytes in size. The array is pointed to by base.
`rand()`	Returns a random number between 0 and 32767.
`read(handle,buffer,count)`	Reads count bytes from the file associated with handle into buffer.
`realloc(ptr,size)`	Changes the size of the block pointed to by ptr to size.
`remove(pathname)`	Deletes the file specified by pathname.
`rename(old,new)`	Changes the name of old to new.
`rewind(stream)`	Repositions the file pointer associated with stream to the beginning of file.
`rmdir(pathname)`	Deletes the directory specified by pathname.
`rmtmp`	Removes files created by tmpfile.
`sbrk(incr)`	Resets the break value of a calling process.
`scanf(format-string (,arguments))`	Reads from STDIN data according to format string into arguments.
`segread(segregs)`	Obtains the segment register values.
`setbuf(stream,buffer)`	Controls buffering for stream based on buffer.
`setjmp(env)`	Saves the stack environment pointed to by env.
`setmode(handle,mode)`	Sets the mode of a file given by handle to mode where mode can be TEXT or BINARY.
`setvbuf(stream,buf,type,size)`	Sets buffering for stream with array pointed to by buf of type and length size.
`The signal function`	This function is used to fix the way interrupt signals can be handled.
`sin(x) and sinh(x)`	Returns the sine and hyperbolic sine of x.
`sopen(pathname,oflag,shflag (,pmode))`	Opens the file specified by pathname as defined by oflag and shflag with read/write permission as in pmode.
`The spawnl family`	This group of functions creates and executes child processes.
`sprintf(buffer,format-string (,arguments))`	Formats and stores a series of characters and values in buffer based on format string from arguments.
`sqrt(x)`	Returns the square root of x.
`srand(seed)`	Sets the starting point for a series of random integers (pseudorandom).
`sscanf(buffer,format-string (,arguments))`	Reads data from buffer into arguments according to format string.
`stackavail()`	Returns the approximate size in bytes of the available stack space.
`stat(pathname,buffer)`	Obtains information about the file pointed to by pathname and stores it in the structure pointed to by buffer.
`_status87()`	Gets the coprocessor status work.
`The strcat family`	These functions manipulate strings.
`strerror(string)`	Returns a message describing user error message, colon, space, and system error message.

TABLE 4.5 (*Concluded*)

Function	Discussion
`strlen(string)`	Returns the length in bytes of string.
`strlwr(string)`	Converts uppercase letters in string to lowercase.
The `strncat` family	More string manipulation functions.
`strpbrk(str1,str2)`	Finds the first occurrence in str1 of any character from str2.
`strrchr(string,c)`	Finds the last occurrence of c in string and returns a pointer to this location.
`strrev(string)`	Reverses the order of the characters in string.
`strset(string,c)`	Sets all characters in string to c.
`strspn(str1,str2)`	Returns an integer specifying the position of the first character in str1 not in str2.
`strstr(str1,str2)`	Returns a pointer to the first occurrence of str1 in str2.
`strtod(nptr,endptr)` and `strtol(nptr,endptr,base)`	Convert a character string to a double-precision value or a long-integer value.
`strtok(str1,str2)`	This function uses the character (groups) in string 2 (str2) to act as delimiters for the intervals or tokens in str1. Each call returns a successive token.
`strupr(string)`	Converts the characters that are lowercase in string to uppercase.
`swab(src,dest,n)`	Copies n bytes from src to dest and swaps pairs of adjacent bytes.
`system(string)`	Executes string as a DOS command.
`tan(x)` and `tanh(x)`	Returns the tangent and hyperbolic tangent of x.
`tell(handle)`	Gets the current position of the file pointer associated with handle.
`tmpnam(string)` and `tempnam(dir,prefix)`	Generates a temporary filename that is usable as a temporary file.
`time(ptr)`	Returns the time elapsed in seconds since 00:00:00.
`tmpfile()`	Returns a stream pointer to a temporary file.
The `toascii` family	These functions manipulate upper- and lowercase.
`tzset()`	Sets environment variables on daylight, time zone, etc.
`ultoa(value,string,radix)`	Converts the digits of value to a character string. The digits are assumed of base radix.
`umask(pmode)`	Sets the file permission mask of the current process to pmode.
`ungetc(c,stream)`	Pushes the character c back onto stream.
`ungetch(c)`	Pushes the character c back onto the console.
`unlink(pathname)`	Deletes the file specified by pathname.
`utime(pathname,times)`	Sets the modification time to the file specified by the pathname.
The `va_arg` family	Used with functions of variable arguments.
`vfprintf(stream,format-string,arg-ptr)`, `vprintf(format-string,arg-ptr)`, and `vsprintf(buffer,format-string,arg-ptr)`	These functions of format and output data to stream, STDOUT, or buffer. They accept a pointer to a list of arguments rather than arguments themselves.
`write(handle,buffer,count)`	Writes count bytes from buffer into the file associated with handle.

184

TABLE 4.6 C COMPILER LIBRARY FILES

Filename	Description
SLIBC.LIB	Small-model standard C library
SLIBFP.LIB	Small-model floating point library
SLIBFA.LIB	Alternate small-model math library (8087)
MLIBC.LIB	Medium-model standard C library
MLIBFP.LIB	Medium-model floating point library
MLIBFA.LIB	Alternate medium-model math library (8087)
CLIBC.LIB	Compact-model standard C library
CLIBFP.LIB	Compact-model floating point library
CLIBFA.LIB	Alternate compact-model math library (8087)
LIBH.LIB	Model-independent code-helper library
LLIBC.LIB	Large-model standard C library
LLIBFP.LIB	Large-model floating point library
LLIBFA.LIB	Alternate large-model math library (8087)
EM.LIB	Model-independent emulator floating point library
87.LIB	Model-independent 8087/80287 floating point library

4.4.3 Three-dimensional Motion: The Rotating Cube

Throughout this book we have used library functions as a means for accomplishing ancillary tasks needed to complete the programming. We will continue to call on these functions when needed. It is convenient to provide, as the final illustration in this chapter, an example of three-dimensional graphics: the cube. Furthermore, we will rotate the cube using some of the techniques employed in the bouncing ball example. This illustration uses some of the library functions that we have already seen and employs DMA as a method for addressing the screen. It is a true DOS program and because of the DMA access to memory will not run under OS/2 in the compatibility mode. The user must have access to physical addresses. Clearly, a compatibility mode can be developed using interrupt 0x10, but this version will run slower than the existing DMA version. The reader should note that this program is a good illustration of the implications for real-time programming: the cube rotation increments in quantized steps, not as a smooth motion. This limitation is a function of the IBM PC/XT/AT or PS/2 computer (will not happen on the Model 80) and reflects the service time for each update.

In Chapter 6 we discuss real-time programming. At that time, the inherent speed of processors will become an issue. Many PC applications require high-speed accelerators for enhancing execution or special-purpose boards with additional processors running at higher clock speeds. The reader should note the performance of the rotating cube on his or her computer and develop an awareness for speed versus what a relatively small amount of intervening code can do to slow this speed down. With these thoughts in mind, we begin the discussion of the rotating cube.

Consider two-dimensional (2D) space represented by the conventional Cartesian x-y axes. Furthermore, consider a point $(x_1, y_1$ in this space that is rotated through some angle, alpha, to a second position (x_2, y_2). Figure 4.27 illustrates this situation. Here, the angles satisfy

$$\text{alpha} = \text{alpha2} - \text{alpha1} \qquad (4.10)$$

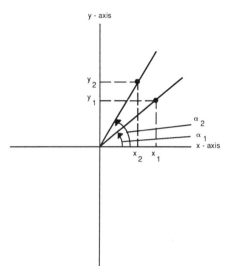

y - axis

x - axis

Figure 4.27 Two-dimensional co-ordinate system illustrating rotated point.

If the radius from the origin to each point is r, then

$$x_1 = r \cos (\text{alpha1}) \qquad (4.11a)$$

$$y_1 = r \sin (\text{alpha1}) \qquad (4.11b)$$

$$x_2 = r \cos (\text{alpha2}) \qquad (4.11c)$$

$$y_2 = r \sin (\text{alpha2}) \qquad (4.11d)$$

In terms of

$$\text{alpha2} = \text{alpha} + \text{alpha1}$$

we have the rotated point as

$$\binom{x_2}{y_2} = \binom{r \cos (\text{alpha} + \text{alpha1})}{r \sin (\text{alpha} + \text{alpha1})} \qquad (4.12)$$

Using the formula for the addition of angles [15],

$$\cos(a + b) = \cos a \cos b - \sin a \sin b \qquad (4.13a)$$

$$\sin(a + b) = \sin a \cos b + \cos a \sin b \qquad (4.13b)$$

it follows that

$$\binom{x_2}{y_2} = r \binom{\cos(\text{alpha}) \cos(\text{alpha1}) - \sin(\text{alpha}) \sin(\text{alpha1})}{\sin(\text{alpha}) \cos(\text{alpha}) + \cos(\text{alpha}) \sin(\text{alpha1})}$$

$$= \binom{x_1 \cos(\text{alpha}) - y_1 \sin(\text{alpha})}{x_1 \sin(\text{alpha}) + y_1 \cos(\text{alpha})} \qquad (4.14)$$

or

$$\begin{pmatrix} x_2 \\ y_2 \end{pmatrix} = \begin{pmatrix} \cos(\text{alpha}) & -\sin(\text{alpha}) \\ \sin(\text{alpha}) & +\cos(\text{alpha}) \end{pmatrix} \begin{pmatrix} x_1 \\ y_1 \end{pmatrix} \qquad (4.15)$$

Extending this rotation to three dimensions (3D), where

alpha: Rotation angle about x-axis

beta: Rotation angle about y-axis

gamma: Rotation angle about z-axis

we obtain the rotation matrices (**A, B,** and **C,** respectively) appearing in Table 4.7. Choosing an order to the rotation, we generate an overall 3D rotation given by the matrix

$$\mathbf{R = CBA} \qquad (4.16)$$

This matrix is indicated in Table 4.7 and will serve as the basis for rotation of the cube. Note that the three rotations in Equation (4.16) are not orthogonal. We would need to select a different set of rotation angles to ensure orthogonality.

If we have a point on the cube (such as a vertex) given by (x, y, z), it is possible to define a rotated point based on R using

$$\begin{bmatrix} x_1 \\ y_1 \\ z_1 \end{bmatrix} = \mathbf{R} \begin{bmatrix} x \\ y \\ z \end{bmatrix} \qquad (4.17)$$

In this example the cube appearing in Figure 4.28 will be used and rotated using **R.**

Figure 4.29 is the main calling program, which reads in the three angular rates of rotation (in radians/second), a scale increase from unity, and the number of iterations as well as a delay interval. Each iteration assumes an effective time increment of $dt = 0.05$ unit. Increasing the delay further slows the rotation rate from an already slow-motion condition; hence, we usually select the delay input to be 1. This calling program calls rot_CUBE(), the function appearing in Figure 4.30.

TABLE 4.7 ROTATION MATRICES FOR 3D MOVEMENT

$$\mathbf{A} = \begin{bmatrix} 1 & 0 & 0 \\ 0 & \cos\alpha & -\sin\alpha \\ 0 & \sin\alpha & \cos\alpha \end{bmatrix} \qquad \mathbf{B} = \begin{bmatrix} \cos\beta & 0 & \sin\beta \\ 0 & 1 & 0 \\ -\sin\beta & & \cos\beta \end{bmatrix}$$

$$\mathbf{C} = \begin{bmatrix} \cos\gamma & -\sin\gamma & 0 \\ \sin\gamma & \cos\gamma & 0 \\ 0 & 0 & 1 \end{bmatrix}$$

$$\mathbf{R = CBA} = \begin{bmatrix} \cos\beta\cos\gamma & \sin\alpha\sin\beta\cos\gamma - \cos\alpha\sin\gamma & \cos\alpha\sin\beta\cos\gamma + \sin\alpha\sin\gamma \\ \cos\beta\sin\gamma & \sin\alpha\sin\beta\sin\gamma + \cos\alpha\cos\gamma & \cos\alpha\sin\beta\sin\gamma - \sin\alpha\cos\gamma \\ -\sin\beta & \sin\alpha\cos\beta & \cos\alpha\cos\beta \end{bmatrix}$$

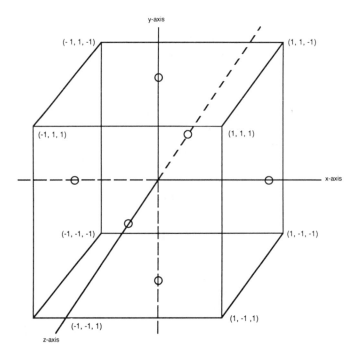

Figure 4.28 Three-dimensional coordinate system used in rotating cube example.

The function rot__CUBE() calls the plotting routines to either erase a line [uDMApoin()] or plot a line [DMApoint()]. Since we visualize the cube as a two-dimensional display, its z-coordinates must be collapsed when presenting the cube graphically on the screen (we simply set these coordinates to zero). Hence, rot__CUBE() connects the vertices of the cube using straight lines with the z-coordinates collapsed to zero. The connecting lines used to represent the cube are the 12 illustrated in Figure 4.28.

Two functions are called by rot__CUBE(): rot__mat() and rot__point(). The first, rot__mat(), simply generates a new rotation matrix **R** [see Equation (4.16)] from the input angles. The second function, rot__point(), calculates the rotated point coordinates using Equation (4.17). Figures 4.31 and 4.32 illustrate rot__mat() and rot__point(), respectively. Note that the **R** matrix is represented by an array, a[ ], in the code appearing in these figures.

The functions DMApoint() and uDMApoin() (Figure 4.33a and b) plot and erase connecting lines by calling dot() and udot(), respectively. Note that unlike plotpoint() (Figure 2.8d) the functions that plot connecting lines in this example are general and do not assume $x[n + 1] > x[n]$. The functions dot() and udot() generate a DMA point or ''unpoint'' on the screen at a fixed row and column position in the 320×200 graphics mode. Again, unlike the earlier DMA screen point generators bbalsp1() and bbalsp0() (Figure 4.13), dot() and udot() are very efficient but somewhat convoluted. First, they assume a base address of B800H for the segment value. Since each memory byte represents 4 pels, a 320-pel line is represented

DOS, BIOS, and Library Services   Chap. 4

```
/* Program to generate rotating cube */

#include <stdio.h>

float XX[9] = {0.,1.,1.,1.,1.,-1.,-1.,-1.,-1.};          /* Cube */
float YY[9] = {0.,1.,1.,-1.,-1.,1.,1.,-1.,-1.};          /* Cube */
float ZZ[9] = {0.,1.,-1.,1.,-1.,1.,-1.,1.,-1.};          /* Cube */
float x,y,z;                                             /* point */
float scale;                                            /* Cube size /2 */
float a[10];                                            /* rotation matrix */
float xx1[9],yy1[9];                                    /* dynamic cube */
float xxx1[9],yyy1[9];                                  /* undo array */
float dt = 0.05;                                        /* time interval */
int NDELAY;                                             /* delay limit */

main()
      {
      float alpha,beta,gamma,alpha0,beta0,gamma0;        /* angular data */
      int NTOTAL,n;

      printf("Input x-rotation rad/sec \n");
      scanf("%f",&alpha0);
      printf("Input y-rotation rad/sec \n");
      scanf("%f",&beta0);
      printf("Input z-rotation rad/sec \n");
      scanf("%f",&gamma0);
      printf("Input scale \n");
      scanf("%f",&scale);
      printf("Input no. iterations \n");
      scanf("%d",&NTOTAL);
      printf("Input delay \n");
      scanf("%d",&NDELAY);

      alpha = 0.0;
      beta = 0.0;
      gamma = 0.0;

      SCRCL();                                           /* Clear screen */
      SC320();                                           /* Plot mode */

      for(n = 1;n <= NTOTAL;n++)
          {
          DELAY();                                       /* Delay screen */

          alpha = alpha + alpha0*dt;
          beta = beta + beta0*dt;
          gamma = gamma + gamma0*dt;

          rot_CUBE(alpha,beta,gamma,n-1);
          }
      plotterm();                                        /* Freeze screen */
      }
```

Figure 4.29   Main calling program for rotating cube.

by 80 bytes. Thus, each row is described in groups of 4 pels for each byte. Furthermore, the even rows (0, 2, 4, . . . , 198) start at addresses B8000H, B8050H, B80A80H, . . . , B9FB0H. Similarly, the odd rows (1, 3, 5, . . . , 199) start at addresses BA000H, BA050H, BA0A0H, . . . , BBFB0H.

To differentiate even- from odd-row memory, the following segment addresses were used:

```
0xB800   (even)
0xBA00   (odd)
```

```
/* Function to rotate cube with DMA */

rot_CUBE(alpha,beta,gamma,N)
        float alpha,beta,gamma;                            /* angles */
        int N;
        {
        extern float XX[],YY[],ZZ[];                       /* Cube points */
        extern float x,y,z;                                /* point */
        extern float scale;                                /* scaling */
        extern float xx1[],yy1[];                          /* dynamic cube */
        extern float xxx1[],yyy1[];                        /* undo array */

        int n;

        rot_mat(alpha,beta,gamma);                         /* load rotate */

        for(n = 1;n <= 8;n++)
            {
            x = XX[n];
            y = YY[n];
            z = ZZ[n];
            rot_point();                                   /* rotate point */
        xx1[n] = x*scale + 150.;
        yy1[n] = y*scale + 100.;
        }

        if(N > 0)
            {
            uDMApoin(xxx1[1],xxx1[2],yyy1[1],yyy1[2]);                  /* Clear cube */
            uDMApoin(xxx1[1],xxx1[3],yyy1[1],yyy1[3]);
            uDMApoin(xxx1[1],xxx1[5],yyy1[1],yyy1[5]);
            uDMApoin(xxx1[2],xxx1[6],yyy1[2],yyy1[6]);
            uDMApoin(xxx1[2],xxx1[4],yyy1[2],yyy1[4]);
            uDMApoin(xxx1[3],xxx1[7],yyy1[3],yyy1[7]);
            uDMApoin(xxx1[3],xxx1[4],yyy1[3],yyy1[4]);
            uDMApoin(xxx1[4],xxx1[8],yyy1[4],yyy1[8]);
            uDMApoin(xxx1[5],xxx1[6],yyy1[5],yyy1[6]);
            uDMApoin(xxx1[5],xxx1[7],yyy1[5],yyy1[7]);
            uDMApoin(xxx1[6],xxx1[8],yyy1[6],yyy1[8]);
            uDMApoin(xxx1[7],xxx1[8],yyy1[7],yyy1[8]);
            }

        DMApoint(xx1[1],xx1[2],yy1[1],yy1[2]);             /* Rotated cube */
        DMApoint(xx1[1],xx1[3],yy1[1],yy1[3]);
        DMApoint(xx1[1],xx1[5],yy1[1],yy1[5]);
        DMApoint(xx1[2],xx1[6],yy1[2],yy1[6]);
        DMApoint(xx1[2],xx1[4],yy1[2],yy1[4]);
        DMApoint(xx1[3],xx1[7],yy1[3],yy1[7]);
        DMApoint(xx1[3],xx1[4],yy1[3],yy1[4]);
        DMApoint(xx1[4],xx1[8],yy1[4],yy1[8]);
        DMApoint(xx1[5],xx1[6],yy1[5],yy1[6]);
        DMApoint(xx1[5],xx1[7],yy1[5],yy1[7]);
        DMApoint(xx1[6],xx1[8],yy1[6],yy1[8]);
        DMApoint(xx1[7],xx1[8],yy1[7],yy1[8]);

        for(n = 1;n <= 8;n++)
            {
            xxx1[n] = xx1[n];
            yyy1[n] = yy1[n];
            }
        }
```

Figure 4.30 Function rot_CUBE( ), which rotates the cube point, clears the screen, and displays the updated cube.

```
/* Function to calculate rotation matrix */

#include <math.h>

rot_mat(alpha,beta,gamma)
        float alpha,beta,gamma;                          /* angles */
        {
        extern float a[];                                /* rotation matrix */
        double a1,CA,CB,CG,SA,SB,SG;

        a1 = (double)(alpha);                            /* Sines & cosines */
        CA = cos(a1);
        SA = sin(a1);
        a1 = (double)(beta);
        CB = cos(a1);
        SB = sin(a1);
        a1 = (double)(gamma);
        CG = cos(a1);
        SG = sin(a1);

        a[1] = (float)(CB*CG);                           /* Matrix elements */
        a[2] = (float)(SA*SB*CG - CA*SG);
        a[3] = (float)(CA*SB*CG + SA*SG);
        a[4] = (float)(CB*SG);
        a[5] = (float)(SA*SB*SG + CA*CG);
        a[6] = (float)(CA*SB*SG - SA*CG);
        a[7] = (float)(-SB);
        a[8] = (float)(SA*CB);
        a[9] = (float)(CA*CB);
        }
```

Figure 4.31 Function rot_mat(), which generates the rotation matrix for 3D rotations.

A row was checked to see whether it is odd using

```
if (row & 0x01)
```

If this logical operation yields a TRUE value, the row is odd, and an offset 0x200 was added to 0xB800 for the segment address value.

```
/* Function to generate rotated point */

rot_point()
        {
        extern float x,y,z;                              /* point */
        extern float a[];                                /* rotation matrix */
        float x1,y1,z1;                                  /* intermediate */

        x1 = a[1]*x + a[2]*y + a[3]*z;
        y1 = a[4]*x + a[5]*y + a[6]*z;
        z1 = a[7]*x + a[8]*y + a[9]*z;

        x = x1;
        y = y1;
        z = z1;
        }
```

Figure 4.32 Function rot_point() that actually generates the rotated point coordinates using the rotation matrix and old coordinates.

```
/* This routine plots a connecting line using DMA */

DMApoint (x1,x2,y1,y2)
        float x1,x2,y1,y2;
        {
        float m;
        int row;
        int col;

        if (x1 == x2)
                m = 1000;                       /*Upper limit on slope*/
        else
                m = (y2 - y1)/(x2 - x1);
        if(x2 > x1)
                {
                for (col =(int)(x1)+1; col <= (int)(x2); col++)
                        {
                        row = (int)(y1 + m*(col - x1));
                        dot(row,col);
                        }
                }
        else
                {
                if(x2 < x1)
                        {
                        for(col =(int)(x2)+1;col <= (int)(x1); col++)
                                {
                                row = (int)(y2 + m*(col - x2));
                                dot(row,col);
                                }
                        }
                else
                        {
                        col = (int)(x1);                        /* Vertical line */
                        if(y1 > y2)
                                {
                                for(row = (int)(y2)+1;row <= (int)(y1);row++)
                                        dot(row,col);
                                }
                        else
                                {
                                for(row = (int)(y1)+1;row <= (int)(y2);row++)
                                        dot(row,col);
                                }
                        }
                }
        }

/* Function to generate high speed dot -- DMA */

#include <math.h>
#include <dos.h>
#include <memory.h>
#include <string.h>
#define MASK 0x01
#define OFFSET 0x200

dot(row,col)
        int row,col;
        {
        unsigned int address = 0xB800;
        unsigned char src[1];

        struct SREGS reg;
        segread(&reg);

        if(row & 0x01)
                address += OFFSET;                      /* Add odd offset */
                                                        /* Calculate pel */
        src[0] = (MASK << (2*(3 - col % 4)));
                                                        /* write screen */
        movedata(reg.ds,src,address,(80*(row >> 1) + (col >> 2)),1);
        }
```

Figure 4.33a Functions DMApoint( ) and dot( ) used for generating a line between two points based on DMA output.

```
/* This routine removes a connecting line using DMA */

uDMApoin(x1,x2,y1,y2)
        float x1,x2,y1,y2;
        {
        float m;
        int row;
        int col;

        if (x1 == x2)
                m = 1000;                       /*Upper limit on slope*/
        else
                m = (y2 - y1)/(x2 - x1);
        if(x2 > x1)
            {
            for (col =(int)(x1)+1; col <= (int)(x2); col++)
                {
                row = (int)(y1 + m*(col - x1));
                udot(row,col);
                }
            }
        else
            {
            if(x2 < x1)
                {
                for(col =(int)(x2)+1;col <= (int)(x1); col++)
                    {
                    row = (int)(y2 + m*(col - x2));
                    udot(row,col);
                    }
                }
            else
                {
                col = (int)(x1);                        /* Vertical line */
                if(y1 > y2)
                    {
                    for(row = (int)(y2)+1;row <= (int)(y1);row++)
                        udot(row,col);
                    }
                else
                    {
                    for(row = (int)(y1)+1;row <= (int)(y2);row++)
                        udot(row,col);
                    }
                }
            }
        }

/* Function to generate high speed dot removal-- DMA */

#include <math.h>
#include <dos.h>
#include <memory.h>
#include <string.h>
#define MASK0 0x00                                      /* Remove dot */
#define OFFSET 0x200

udot(row,col)
        int row,col;
        {
        unsigned int address = 0xB800;
        unsigned char src[1];

        struct SREGS reg;
        segread(&reg);

        if(row & 0x01)
            address += OFFSET;                          /* Add odd offset */
                                                        /* Calculate pel */
        src[0] = (MASK0 << (2*(3 - col % 4)));
                                                        /* write screen */
        movedata(reg.ds,src,address,(80*(row >> 1) + (col >> 2)),1);
        }
```

Figure 4.33b Functions uDMApoin( ) and udot( ) used for erasing a line between two points based on DMA output.

To locate the correct (row, col) byte in screen buffer memory, it must be remembered that the even-row value starts at location

```
80 * (row/2)
```

offset from 0xB8000. Similarly, recognizing that integer division truncates (3/2 becomes 1, . . .), the same expression serves to locate an odd-row relative to 0xBA000. Since there are 80 bytes for 320 columns, we need to locate

```
col/4
```

Hence, using the shift operators, the offset location of a given byte in terms of (row, col) is given by

```
80*(row>>1) + (col>>2)
```

as discussed by Prata [16].

To identify an individual pel within a byte, we note that the LSB and LSB + 1 correspond to the attribute positions for the fourth pel, (LSB + 2, LSB + 3) correspond to the attribute positions for the third pel, and so forth. Hence

BIT:	7	6	5	4	3	2	1	0
PEL:	#1	#1	#2	#2	#3	#3	#4	#4

We will simply turn the pel on and off using masks 1 and 0, respectively. Dividing col by 4 generates a remainder (0, 1, 2, 3), which is in reverse order to the pel number (assuming we now start numbering the pels 0, 1, 2, 3). Hence

```
3 - col % 4
```

indicates the actual pel position within the (row, col) byte. Starting with

```
0  0  0  0  0  0  0  1
```

it is clear that a shift

```
2 * (3-col % 4)
```

will place 1 in bits 6, 4, 2 or 0 as needed to specify the pel attribute. These operations are, in fact, what dot( ) and udot( ) accomplish. The only difference betweeen the two functions is that MASK = 0x00 in udot( ) and MASK = 0x01 in dot( ).

The functions used in these routines are summarized as follows:

```
main:
    SCRCL()          (Figure 2.8b)
    SC320()          (Figure 2.8b)
    DELAY()          (Figure 4.14)
    rot_CUBE()       (Figure 4.30)
    plotterm()       (Figure 2.8d)

rot_CUBE:
    rot_mat()        (Figure 4.31)
    rot_point()      (Figure 4.32)
    uDMApoin()       (Figure 4.33b)
    DMApoint()       (Figure 4.33a)

    dot()            (Figure 4.33a)
    udot()           (Figure 4.33b)
```

Figure 4.34 illustrates representative results for the rotating cube display. In each case, all angular rates were fixed at 0.5 radian/second and scaling set at 60. The display freezes after the fixed amount of iterations are complete and these were chosen to be (a) 25, (b) 100, (c) 110, and (d) 200. For the actual motion, a delay of 1 was selected. Since the number of points plotted affects the speed with

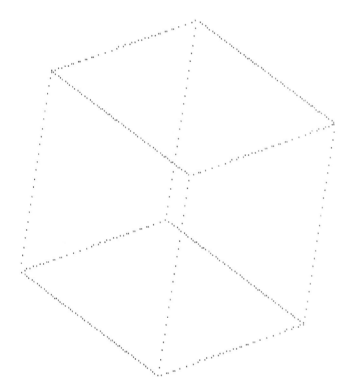

Figure 4.34a Rotated cube with angular rates = 0.5 rad/s after 25 iterations. Scaling is 60.

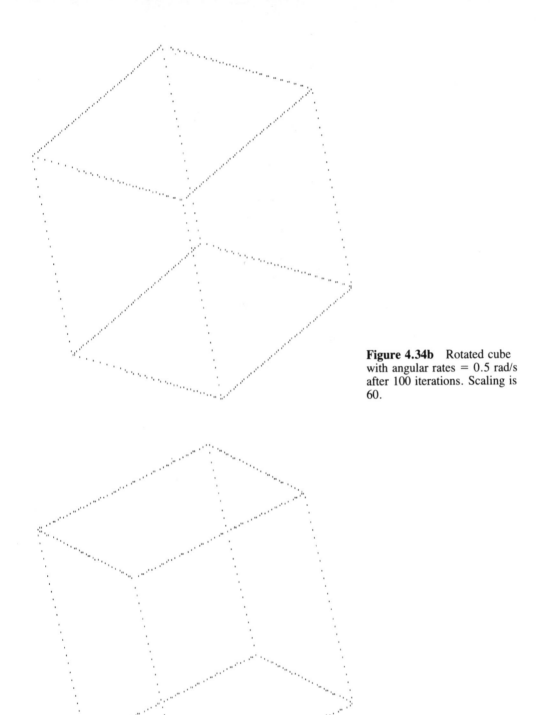

Figure 4.34b Rotated cube with angular rates = 0.5 rad/s after 100 iterations. Scaling is 60.

Figure 4.34c Rotated cube with angular rates = 0.5 rad/s after 110 iterations. Scaling is 60.

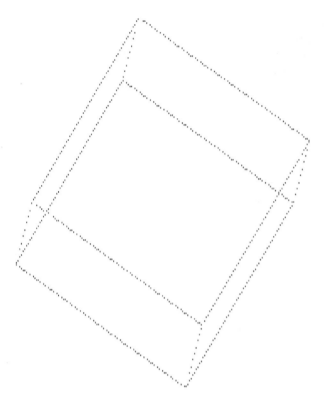

Figure 4.34d Rotated cube with angular rates = 0.5 rad/s after 200 iterations. Scaling is 60.

which the motion is generated, as previously discussed, small-scale values will yields fairly continuous motion. The graphics used in this book correspond to the color graphics adapter (CGA) resolution. As users implement the enhanced graphics adapter (EGA), a significant improvement in image quality is possible for the higher-resolution mode. Similarly, the MultiColor Graphics Array (MCGA) used with the PS/2 Model 30 and the Video Graphics Array (VGA) used with the remaining PS/2 microcomputers provide a significant enhancement over the illustrations appearing in Figure 4.34. This program is a good illustration of the performance of the IBM microcomputers (excluding the Model 80) versus such high-end processors as graphics workstations where 3D motion is essentially continuous. The user should recognize that this program uses DMA and, consequently, must be run under DOS 3.x. The real-time nature of the screen updates requires access to the physical addresses of the screen buffer. Under OS/2, the motion must be described with a call to interrupt 10H (compatibility box) and a subsequent reduction in efficiency or use of the Applications Program Interface (API).

SUMMARY

This chapter has delineated the DOS, BIOS, and library services available with the Microsoft C compiler and the IBM microcomputers. While the discussion does not cover every feature available, it is extensive and is intended to serve as a mechanism for motivating the reader to become familiar with the tabulated services. Actual implementation of a given routine must be accomplished based on user initiative, but this chapter itemizes and summarizes most of the available services. The reader is encouraged to periodically review the tables of this chapter in order to develop an awareness of the utility services available.

REFERENCES

1. Gillman, J., "OS/2 DOS Environment: Compatibility and Transition for MS-DOS Programs," *Microsoft Systems Journal*, Vol. 2, No. 2, p. 19 (1987).

2. *IBM Technical Reference Personal Computer*, Personal Computer Hardware Reference Library, IBM Corporation, P. O. Box 1328, Boca Raton, FL 33432 (1981), 6025008.

3. *IBM Technical Reference Personal Computer XT*, Personal Computer Hardware Reference Library, IBM Corporation, P. O. Box 1328, Boca Raton, FL 33432 (1983).

4. *IBM Technical Reference Personal Computer AT*, Personal Computer Hardware Reference Library, IBM Corporation, P. O. Box 1328, Boca Raton, FL 33432 (1984), 1502494.

5. *IBM Personal System/2 Model 30 Technical Reference*, IBM Corporation, P. O. Box 1328, Boca Raton, FL 33432 (1987), 80X0661.

6. *IBM Personal System/2 Model 50 and 60 Technical Reference*, IBM Corporation, P. O. Box 1328, Boca Raton, FL 33432 (1987), 80X0902.

7. *Disk Operating System Technical Reference*, IBM Corporation, P. O. Box 1328, Boca Raton, FL 33432 (1987), 80X0945.

8. Scanlon, L. J., *IBM PC and XT Assembly Language: A Guide for Programmers*, Brady Communications Company, Inc., Simon and Schuster Publishing Co., New York, p. 266 (1985).

9. *Microsystem Components Handbook: Microprocessors and Peripherals*, Volume I, Intel Corporation, 3065 Bowers Avenue, Santa Clara, CA 95051 (1985).

10. *Microsystem Components Handbook: Microprocessors and Peripherals*, Volume II, Intel Corporation, 3065 Bowers Avenue, Santa Clara, CA 95051 (1985).

11. *TTL Data Manual*, Signetics Corporation, 811 East Arques Avenue, Sunnyvale, CA 94088-3409 (1984).

12. *Microsoft C Compiler Run-time Library Reference*, version 4.0, Microsoft Corp., Redmond, WA 98073 (1986).

13. *Microsoft F Compiler Language Reference and Code View*, version 4.0, Microsoft Corp., Redmond, WA 98073 (1986).

14. *Microsoft C Compiler User's Guide*, version 4.0, Microsoft Corp., Redmond, WA 98073 (1986).

15. Burington, R. S., *Handbook of Mathematical Tables and Formulas*, McGraw-Hill Book Co., New York, p. 18 (1962).

16. Prata, S., *Advanced C Primer + +*, Howard W. Sams and Co., Indianapolis, IN, p. 344 (1986).

PROBLEMS

4.1. Interrupt 14H has four options:

AH = 0 Initialization
AH = 1 Send the character in AL
AH = 2 Receive the character into AL
AH = 3 Return the comm port status

For initialization, the byte in AL satisfies

Bit: 7, 6, 5 (baud)	4, 3 (parity)	2 (stopbit)	1, 0 (word)
000– 110	X0, none	0–1	10, 7 bits
001– 150	01, odd	1–2	11, 8 bits
010– 300	11, even		
011– 600			
100–1200			
101–2400			
110–4800			
111–9600			

Write a code fragment that initializes the comm port for 1200 baud, no parity, 1 stopbit, and 8 bit words. Use a port address of 3FBH for the 8250 ACE control register. Also, write a routine based on int86( ).

4.2. Write a code fragment that initializes the printer. Use the fact that internal to the interrupt service the initialization port is 3BEH and during initialization a value of 8 is output to this port (holds the STROBE* line LOW, thereby allowing receipt of data). Also, write a service fragment based on int86( ).

4.3. Write a code fragment that sets the Model 30 screen into 640 × 480 graphics mode.

4.4. What modification is needed to the main calling program for the bouncing ball (Figure 4.4c) if the program is to yield approximately the same performance for MCGA or VGA mode 640 × 480?

4.5. Y4 is selected for the LS138 when the following signals are present:

G1	G2A	G2B	A	B	C	Y0	Y1	Y3	Y4	Y5	Y6	Y7
1	0	0	0	0	1	1	1	1	0	1	1	1

For the LS138 in Figure 4.9, what address would be required to select Y4?

4.6. Write a code fragment that reads a string input from the keyboard in floating point numerical form and converts this ASCII number to internal decimal format.

4.7. Write a code fragment that converts a floating point number to an ASCII character string and outputs the number using putchar( ). Assume the number has ten digits of significance.

4.8. Write a fragment that efficiently reads memory size in K and prints out the actual number of bytes.

4.9. In the main calling program for the rotating cube (Figure 4.29), what deletion is possible with minimal effect on the outcome?

4.10. Write a general code fragment that illustrates a calling sequence and a code fragment for vector-matrix multiplication. Assume a matrix of maximum length of ten elements on a side and vectors of ten elements.

4.11. Write a general code fragment that illustrates a calling sequence and code fragment for two-dimensional matrix multiplication. Assume matrices of maximum length of ten elements.

4.12. In Table 4.6 a number of memory model library files are described. How does the user ensure that he or she is using the correct memory file at compilation?

4.13. The functions dot( ) and udot( ) employ screen buffer DMA to write and erase a dot, respectively. These functions appear in Figure 4.33a and b, respectively, and use the library routine movedata( ) to perform the actual FAR replacement. It is possible to use a FAR pointer to accomplish the same replacement without resorting to use of movedata( ). A FAR pointer is a 32-bit entity defined such that the 16 most significant bits correspond to the segment address and the 16 least significant bits correspond to the offset address. For example,

```
...
char far * address;
...
address = (char far *) 0 x B8002000;
```

defines the start address for the odd-row screen buffer memory 0xBA000000. Rewrite dot( ) and udot( ) using FAR pointers to accomplish screen buffer DMA. Does this appear to increase the speed with which the rotating cube is generated when used with this program?

5

C and Assembly Language

There are two reasons why the C programmer should be interested in assembly languages: first, assembly language constructs provide an understanding about both the underlying software architecture for a given microprocessor and the needed chip interfaces for a given microcomputer; and, second, situations can arise where C code is inadequate for achieving optimized performance. The former becomes important in understanding how to use such library functions as movedata( ) or generate a tone on the speaker. Here the basic fabric of memory organization and hardware manipulation is best illustrated within the assembly language context where simple operations are possible. Programming the microprocessor must eventually be understood in terms of the manufacturer's (in this case Intel) instruction set, the basis for the assembly language, if a fundamental grasp of the hardware interfaces is to be acquired.

If the C code is inadequate to achieve the required performance, then it usually executes too slowly. Such code, when compiled (even with an optimizing compiler), usually has a number of instruction references based on memory addressing. These references are intrinsically slower than instructions that employ the microprocessor registers directly. Hence, by developing routines that are based on register manipulation exclusively, the code can be optimized with regard to execution time.

The purpose of this chapter is to present the IBM microcomputer Macro Assembler (for Versions 1.0 and 2.0) in an abbreviated but highlighted fashion. The goal is not to develop an extensive assembler programming background, but to develop the capability for writing simple yet needed assembly language routines. Furthermore, the reader will understand how to interface these routines to C code and, as a by-product, what the Microsoft C compiler assembler representation is and means for C source code input to this compiler. The assumption is made that assembler programs will not be employed in a stand-alone fashion, but as functions to be called from a

C routine. This constraint minimizes the depth to which assembly language programming must be covered. It is decidedly a parochial focus for the treatment of assembly language, but one appropriate to understanding the C language interface and, at the same time, treating this topic secondarily to the overall intent of the text. The interested reader is referred to one of several books [1–6] for a full discussion of assembler in the IBM microcomputer context.

5.1 PROGRAMMING IN ASSEMBLY LANGUAGE

Chapter 1 introduced the idea of memory segmentation. This subject, plus offsets and program architecture, is the topic of Section 5.1.1. Next, an extended discussion including addressing modes and the Macro Assembler instructions is presented. Finally, the first section ends with programming the coprocessor. This material is presented in an abbreviated fashion with the key aspects emphasized.

Basic to developing Macro Assembler routines is the assembler itself: IBM has a small assembler, ASM, and the standard assembler, MASM [7, 8]. The small assembler is designed to use only 64K RAM for program development, while the MASM requires a minimum of 96K. To invoke the assembler, the user simply types MASM(ASM), and the assembler will initiate a series of queries to the screen. First a source file, the .ASM file, is asked for. Next, a name for the output object file, the .OBJ file, is solicited. Finally, a listing filename and cross-reference filename, the .LST and .CRF files, are prompted. The .OBJ file contains the machine code, which is used by the linker to generate the run file, with extension .EXE. We will see the needed format for .ASM files in Section 5.2 for use with C functions. This format is prescribed by the program structure used with the Microsoft C Compiler.

5.1.1 Segments, Offsets, and Program Structure

The next section describes the Macro Assembler instruction set. These instructions represent the active instruments in the language and usually act on one or more operands. In addition to the instructions, however, the assembler has a class of statements that provide the assembler information about the program environment. These statements do not result in machine code (but are needed to inform the assembler about the operational program) and are referred to as pseudo-operations or pseudo-ops for short. Typical of the pseudo-ops is the SEGMENT directive, which is used to demarcate the various segment definitions within the source code. This pseudo-op has the form

```
segname SEGMENT align-type combine-type 'class'
```

where segname is the name of the segment, align-type indicates how the segment begins in memory [PARA: paragraph boundary (address divisible by 16); BYTE; WORD; or PAGE: last 8 bits of address are zero], and combine-type indicates how the segment is to be linked (PUBLIC: all public segments with the same name are linked; COMMON: all segments with the same name overlap; AT(exp): segment located at nearest paragraph to "exp"; STACK: stack segment; and MEMORY:

higher addresses than other segments). The designator 'class' refers to a collection of segments with the same class name. Each segment must end with the following statement:

```
segname ENDS
```

It is clear that the segment address discussed earlier (in Chapter 1, for example) denotes the beginning address of a segment as defined by the assembler using the SEGMENT pseudo-op. Within a segment are data variable definitions, instructions and operands, other pseudo-ops, and assorted language entities (such as comments and macros).

A convenient point for discussion is the function illustrated in Figure 5.1a. This C function is familiar and simply accepts an input integer, x, and returns its cube. We know from previous discussion that the Microsoft C compiler returns a .COD file that represents a listing of the equivalent assembler code for the input C source code, as generated using the compiler. Figure 5.1b presents this .COD output for the CUBE() function of Figure 5.1a. In Figure 5.1b we see a number of uses of the SEGMENT pseudo-op, as discussed previously.

Initially, some descriptive information is provided preceded by a semicolon. (In the Macro Assembler, semicolons are used to indicate that a comment follows on the same line.) Next a title is presented using the TITLE pseudo-op. In this case the title is equal to the input C source file name, chap61. The pseudo-op .287 tells the assembler that an 80287 coprocessor is resident. The next eight lines of code are used to define four segments with the SEGMENT pseudo-op. The first segment is __TEXT and is of align-type BYTE, combine-type PUBLIC, and class CODE. The second segment is __DATA, defined as indicated. The third is CONST and the fourth __BSS. We considered these segments in Chapter 3. Each segment is empty at this juncture and terminated with the ENDS pseudo-op.

Following the segment definitions, the GROUP pseudo-op is used to collect three of the segments under one name, DGROUP, so they are all within a 64K physical segment (small compiler). The form of this pseudo-op is

```
name GROUP seg-name(,...)
```

Up to this point the segments have not been defined with regard to type (the 'class' specification is only a category). To define segment type, the ASSUME pseudo-op is used to associate a name with a segment register:

```
ASSUME CS:seg-name, SS:seg-name[,DS:seg-name[,ES:seg-name]]
```

Here CS and SS are required, with DS and ES optionally specified. In Figure 5.1b, the code segment is __TEXT and all remaining segments fall under the name DGROUP.

Next, the pseudo-op EXTRN is used to declare the system function __chkstk external. During this declaration, __chkstk is specified to have distance attribute NEAR. What does this mean? We saw in Chapter 4 that when the screen DMA was implemented both a new segment address and new offset address were required

```
/* Function to illustrate assembler code equivalent */

CUBE(x)
        int x;
        {
        x = x*x*x;                                          /* cube operation */
        return(x);
        }
```

(a)

```
;       Static Name Aliases
;
        TITLE    chap61
;       NAME     \c\chap61.c

        .287
_TEXT   SEGMENT  BYTE PUBLIC 'CODE'
_TEXT   ENDS
_DATA   SEGMENT  WORD PUBLIC 'DATA'
_DATA   ENDS
CONST   SEGMENT  WORD PUBLIC 'CONST'
CONST   ENDS
_BSS    SEGMENT  WORD PUBLIC 'BSS'
_BSS    ENDS
DGROUP  GROUP    CONST, _BSS, _DATA
        ASSUME   CS: _TEXT, DS: DGROUP, SS: DGROUP, ES: DGROUP
EXTRN   __chkstk:NEAR
_TEXT       SEGMENT
; Line 4
        PUBLIC  _CUBE
_CUBE   PROC NEAR
        *** 000000      55                      push    bp
        *** 000001      8b ec                   mov     bp,sp
        *** 000003      33 c0                   xor     ax,ax
        *** 000005      e8 00 00                call    __chkstk
; Line 5
;       x = 4
; Line 6
        *** 000008      8b 46 04                mov     ax,[bp+4]       ;x
        *** 00000b      f7 e8                   imul    ax
        *** 00000d      f7 6e 04                imul    WORD PTR [bp+4] ;x
        *** 000010      89 46 04                mov     [bp+4],ax       ;x
; Line 7
        *** 000013      8b e5                   mov     sp,bp
        *** 000015      5d                      pop     bp
        *** 000016      c3                      ret

_CUBE   ENDP
_TEXT   ENDS
END
```

(b)

Figure 5.1 Program to generate (a) cube function and (b) .COD file.

for the arguments of movedata() or the screen buffer pointer. This was due to the fact that the data segment associated with the calling routine was different from the data segment containing the screen buffer addresses. Such a reference is referred to as a FAR reference, and it requires that both a segment and an offset address be used. For the case of the function __chkstk, however, the NEAR attribute indicates that it is defined within the segment __TEXT specified in another module (it is external). Once the modules are linked, calls to __chkstk will only involve saving an offset on the stack (for the calling program) upon entry to __chkstk. When the return to the calling program is made (following execution of a RET instruction in __chkstk), a single offset address will be recovered from the stack. (The routine __chkstk checks and sets up the stack at each call.)

Following the external declaration for __chkstk, the __TEXT segment for the C function CUBE() is established. Referring to Figure 5.1a, line numbers can be defined starting with CUBE(x). The compiler adds a line, so this defining statement becomes line 4 in the .COD reference (note the comment). In the Microsoft C compiler, the function CUBE() is referenced by the label __CUBE and is declared to be public by the PUBLIC pseudo-op. This declaration makes __CUBE accessible by other programs. Next, __CUBE is defined to be a procedure with the procedure pseudo-op PROC. This pseudo-op identifies a block of code used to perform a function. This block of code has the form

```
Procedure-name  PROC  FAR
            o r
Procedure-name  PROC  (NEAR)
      • • •
      RET
      • • •
Procedure-name  ENDP
```

In Figure 5.1b the procedure is NEAR and is delimited by the __CUBE ENDP statement.

Within the body of the procedure __CUBE are contained the equivalent assembly language instructions needed to generate the statements

```
x = x*x*x;
return(x);
```

As part of this assembler code, appropriate instructions are included for preserving formal parameters and setting up the stack pointer to properly point to these parameters. These parameters (in this case x) are placed on the stack as part of the overhead code generated by the linker.

Without attempting to address all the overhead code, we will simply examine the cube statement, line 6 of the reference in Figure 5.1b. The four lines that follow the comment line, ";Line 6", contain a number of fields. Each begins with three asterisks and a six digit-number corresponding to the byte offset of the instruction (which follows) from the beginning of the segment. Next, the machine code equivalence of the assembly language instruction is presented. This machine code is the actual byte order placed in memory by the assembler for execution by the processor. Finally, the assembly language instruction and operands are indicated and any comments. We concentrate on the four assembly language instructions used to define the cube operation:

```
mov ax,[bp+4]
imul ax
imul WORD PTR [bp+4]
mov [bp+4],ax
```

In the first instruction the reader no doubt recognizes the accumulator register ax and the base pointer register bp. The expression [bp + 4] is a form of address reference, which indicates that the value located at the address pointed to by the contents of the base pointer register plus 4 is to be used. The instruction indicates that this value should be moved into ax. Earlier the base pointer register was loaded with a pointer value corresponding to the top of the stack:

```
mov bp,sp
```

By now the reader probably, correctly, suspects that the stack has been loaded locally with parameters to be passed from the calling module. Why is the quantity 4 (bytes) added to bp? First, the calling program base pointer value has been saved on the stack earlier (this is 2 bytes). Second, prior to this the return address to the calling module was also saved on the stack. For NEAR calls this is merely an offset (2 bytes). Hence, the location of x in CUBE( ) is 5 bytes below the stack top.

Remember, we are going to generate the cube of x, where x is now loaded into ax. The second instruction performs an integer multiply (imul) of ax with itself. To understand this instruction, the reader should note that this is a one-operand instruction. Before considering this form, we need to examine the general form for an instruction:

```
[label] instruction-mneumonic [operand(s)] [;comment]
```

The label field is optional and only used to indicate entry points. The instruction-mneumonic represents the instruction name or code (such as mov or imul), and this is followed by zero, one, or two operands depending on the form of the instruction. Finally, comments preceded by a semicolon are permitted.

In

```
imul ax
```

an implicit operand, the destination operand, is multiplied by ax, the source operand. When an implicit operand is used, it is almost always the accumulator, ax; hence the programmer must determine the correct form for an instruction based on the Macro Assembler reference [7]. It is clear that the form of the preceding instruction leaves the accumulator with the value x*x. The value specified by [bp + 4] references a byte quantity on the stack. In the MOV instruction that loaded ax, the assembler automatically assumed a word quantity was to be loaded (2 consecutive bytes starting at [bp + 4]) because of the reference to ax. Now that a second multiply is needed to complete the cube operation and the single operand instruction imul will again be used, the assembler needs to know whether a byte or a word multiply is to take place. (The assembler needs to know whether AL or AX should be implicitly assumed in the imul operation.) To achieve this, a length attribute override is used with the pointer operator (PTR). Here the instruction

```
imul WORD PTR [bp+4]
```

overrides the BYTE type characteristic of [bp + 4] and indicates a WORD quantity is to be used in the multiply (the 2 consecutive bytes starting at [bp + 4]). At the completion of this instruction, ax is loaded with the cube of the integer x.

The next instruction loads the location corresponding to x (on the stack) with the computed value of the cube of x, now residing in ax. For purposes of this program module, this is an unnecessary instruction. To understand this, we need only be aware that, when a value is returned from a function using the small compiler, this value is always resident in the accumulator (if it is an integer). Hence, the return(x) statement in Figure 5.1a ensures that the accumulator will contain the cube of x upon exit from CUBE(). The compiler must reference locations in standardized form, and since the C source code was recurrent, x had to be replaced following the cube operation (the compiler does not know that x will not be further referenced later in the module).

This brief illustration of how assembly language is implemented provides some insight into how hardware designers think. For example, the first mov instruction inherently involved a word move from the stack because of the destination operand ax. If the instruction had been

```
mov al, [bp+4]
```

the assembler would automatically move a byte quantity into al. Similarly, the type attribute override in

```
imul WORD PTR[bp+4]
```

is automatically interpreted to mean that the instruction references word quantities (hence, ax), rather than byte quantities (or al). These are all translated to hardware operations by the assembler and indicate the operation at the hardware level.

In the next section we examine the basic syntax of the Macro Assembler. Here, the reader will be exposed to all the essential constructs of the language. Code fragments will be used briefly to illustrate selected examples. The information is presented in tabular form to expedite coverage, and the remainder of the chapter serves as a basis for further (more detailed) examination of this syntax.

5.1.2 Addressing, Instructions, and Pseudo-ops

Associated with each value referenced in a program is an address where this value is stored in memory. The pointer arithmetic in C source code provided a mechanism for accessing these addresses. In assembly language there are seven ways an address can be referenced: immediate, register, direct, register indirect, base relative, direct indexed, and based indexed. Table 5.1 presents these addressing modes with suitable

TABLE 5.1 MACRO ASSEMBLER ADDRESSING MODES

Mode	Comment
Immediate	A byte or word constant in the source operand is loaded into a register operand. Example: mov ax,18.
Register	Register destination operands are loaded from register source operands. Example: mov ds,ax.
Direct	A register destination operand is loaded with the *value* of a location specified by its offset added to DS. Example: mov ax,dddw, where dddw is a variable in the data segment (addressed by DS).
Register indirect	The effective address (segment offset) is contained in BX, BP, SI, or DI, and this is used to load a register. Example:

```
mov bx, OFFSET dddw
mov ax,[bx]
```

Here the brackets indicate bx contains an address.

Base relative	The effective address for the source is obtained by adding a displacement to BX or BP, which are assumed to contain an offset, Example:

```
mov bp,OFFSET dddw
mov ax,[bp+4]
```

Direct indexed	Here the effective source address is the sum of an index register (SI or DI) and an offset. Example:

```
mov si,4
mov ax,dddw [si]
```

This loads ax with the same value as loaded in the base relative example.

Base indexed	Typically, the effective source address is the sum of a base register (BX or BP), an index register (SI or DI), and a displacement. Example:

```
mov bx,OFFSET dddw
mov si,4
mov ax,[bx][si+2]
```

descriptions, and it is noted that the earlier reference [bp + 4] is of base relative mode. In Table 5.1, reference is made to two-operand instructions with the mov instruction used as an illustration. The general form of this instruction is

```
mov destination,source
```

In the table some examples employ the OFFSET operator, which returns the offset address of a variable.

Instructions. Table 5.2 illustrates the core set of Macro Assembler instructions. This table has the instructions grouped by functional category: arithmetic,

TABLE 5.2 MACRO ASSEMBLER INSTRUCTIONS (8086 CONVENTION)

Instruction	Purpose	Comments
Arithmetic		
ADC dest,src	Add with carry	Performs an addition of the two operands and adds one if CF is set.
ADD dest,src	Addition	Adds the two operands.
DIV src	Unsigned divide	Divides the numerand (AL and AH for byte division and AX and DX for word division) by src. The result is returned in AL (byte) or AX (word).
IDIV src	Signed integer division	Signed division using the registers of DIV.
IMUL src	Signed integer multiply	Multiplies AL or AX times src.
MUL src	Unsigned multiply	Same as IMUL.
SBB dest,src	Subtract with borrow	Subtracts the two operands and subtracts one if CF is set.
SUB dest,src	Subtract	Subtracts the two operands.
Logical		
AND dest,src	Logical AND	Performs the bit conjunction of the two operands: the result is zero except when both bits are set.
NEG dest	Two's complement	Forms the two's complement of dest.
NOT dest	Logical NOT	Inverts dest bit by bit.
OR dest,src	Logical inclusive OR	Performs the bit logical inclusive disjunction of the two operands: returns a one except when both bits are zero.
TEST dest,src	Logical compare	Performs the bit conjunction of the two operands with only the flags affected.
XOR dest,src	Exclusive OR	Performs the bit logical exclusive disjunction of the two operands: returns a one when one operand is zero.
Move		

MOV dest,src	Move	Moves:
		1. To memory from AX (AL)
		2. To AX (AL) from memory
		3. To seg-reg from memory/reg
		4. To reg from seg-reg
		5. To reg from reg
		   To reg from memory
		   To memory from reg
		6. To reg from immediate
		7. To memory from immediate

MOVS dest-str, src-str	Move byte or word string	Transfers a byte or word string from src, addressed by SI, to dest, addressed by DI.
Load		
LODS src-str	Load byte or word string	Transfers a byte (word) from src, addressed by SI, to AL (AX) and adjusts SI.

TABLE 5.2 *(Continued)*

Instruction	Purpose	Comments
LAHF	Load AH from flags	Transfers the flags to AH.
LDS dest,src	Load data segment register	Loads a 32-bit address into DS and dest (offset).
LEA dest,src	Load effective address	Transfers the offset of src to dest.
LES dest,src	Load extra segment register	Loads a 32-bit address into ES and dest (offset).
Loop		
LOOP short-label	Loop until count complete	Control is transferred to short-label if CX $\neq$ 0 and CX is decremented.
LOOPE short-label	Loop if equal	Same as LOOP but control transfers if ZF = 1, as an additional requirement.
LOOPNE short-label	Loop if not equal	Same as LOOPE except ZF must equal 0.
Stack		
POP dest	Pop word off the stack	Transfers a word from the stack (pointed to by SP) to dest.
POPF	Pop flags off the stack	Transfers the word from the stack top to the flags register.
PUSH src	Push word onto the stack	src is placed on the stack top.
PUSHF	Push flags onto the stack	The flags register is loaded onto the top of the stack.
Count		
DEC dest	Decrement	Subtract one from dest.
INC dest.	Increment	Add one to dest.
Flags		
CLC	Clear carry flag	Sets Cf = 0.
CLD	Clear direction flag	Sets DF = 0.
CLI	Clear interrupt flag	Sets IF = 0.
CMC	Complement carry flag	Changes setting of CF.
STC	Set carry flag	Sets CF = 1.
STD	Set direction flag	Sets DF = 1.
STI	Sets interrupt flag	Sets IF = 1.
Shift		
SAL dest,cnt	Shift arithmetic left	Shifts dest cnt bits left. CL contains cnt.
SHL dest,cnt	Shift logical left	Same as SAL.
SAR dest,cnt	Shift arithmetic right	Same as SAL except shift if to the right.
SHR dest,cnt	Shift logical right	Same as SAR.
Rotate		
RCL dest,cnt	Rotate left through carry	Rotates dest left in wrap-around fashion cnt bits where cnt is in CL.

TABLE 5.2 (*Continued*)

Instruction	Purpose	Comments
RCR dest,cnt	Rotate right through carry	Rotates dest right in wrap-around fashion cnt bits where cnt is in CL.
ROL dest,cnt	Rotate left	Same as RCL except the high-order bit rotates into CF as well as the low-order bit.
ROR dest,cnt	Rotate right	Same as ROL except to the right.
Store		
STOS dest-str	Store byte or word string	Transfers a byte (word) from AL (AX) to the location pointed to by DI.
SAHF	Store AH in flags	Transfers the value in AH to the flags register.
String		
REP	Repeat string operation	Causes the string operation that follows to repeat until CX = 0, ZF = 1.
REPNE	Repeat string operation	Same as REP except ZF = 0.
SCAS dest-str	Scan byte or word string	Subtracts the dest-str from AL (AX) one byte at a time and affects the flags.
Convert		
CWD	Convert word to doubleword	Sign extends AX into DX.
CBW	Convert byte to word	Sign extends AL into AX.
Control		
CALL target	Calls a procedure	Calls a procedure (target).
RET	Return from a procedure	Returns control to the calling routine.
ESC ext-opcode, src	Escape	Initiates the ext-opcode with operand src.
LOCK	Lock bus	Closes the bus to access.
NOP	No operation	A do-nothing operation.
WAIT	Wait	A bus cycle state used for synchronization.
ASCII		
AAA	ASCII adjust for addition	Adjusts the sum for an ASCII numerical value following addition.
AAD	ASCII adjust for division	Adjusts the quotient for ASCII numerical value following division.
AAH	ASCII adjust for multiply	Adjusts the product for ASCII numerical value following multiplication.
AAS	ASCII adjust for subtraction	Adjusts the difference for an ASCII numerical value following subtraction.
Decimal		
DAA	Decimal add adjust	Adjust for decimal addition.

TABLE 5.2   (*Concluded*)

Instruction	Purpose	Comments
DAS	Decimal subtract adjust	Adjust for decimal subtraction.
I/O		
IN acc, port	Input byte/word	The byte/word contents of port are loaded into AL/AX.
OUT port, acc	Output byte/word	The contents of the accumulator are sent to port output.
Miscellaneous		
XCHG dest,src	Exchange	Exchanges the source (src) with dest.
XLAT src-table	Translate	BX is loaded with a table address. AL contains a location number (byte) in the table and this byte is replaced in AL.

logical, move, load, and so on. We will briefly indicate typical usage for selected instructions in the following discussion.

Arithmetic

Addition:
```
mov ax ,18
add ax ,dddw            ;add 18 to dddw,leave in ax
```

Subtraction:
```
mov ax ,18
sub ax ,dddw            ;subtract dddw from 18
```

Multiply:
```
mov dx ,0               ;clear upper register
mov bx ,2
mov ax ,dddw
mul bx                  ;multiply dddw by 2
```

Divide:
```
mov dx ,0               ;clear upper register
mov bx ,2
mov ax ,dddw
div bx                  ;divide dddw by 2
```

Logical

And:
```
mov ah ,80H
mov bh ,FFH
and bh ,ah              ;bh=ah=80H
```

Or:
```
mov ah ,80H
mov bh ,FFH
or bh , ah              ;bh=FFH
```

Xor:
```
mov ah ,80H
mov bh ,FFH
xor bh , ah             ;bh=7FH
```

Move.   The examples in this subsection *all* use the move instruction.

Load

Load byte:
```
cld                      ;clears DF(increment)
mov si,OFFSET ddw        ;pointer to dddw byte-string
lods dddw                ;al=dddw[0],si=si+1
```

Load word:
```
std                      ;sets DF (decrement)
mov si,OFFSET ddw        ;pointer to dddw,now
                         ;word-string
lods dddw                ;ax=dddw,si=si-2
```

Loop
```
mov ax,0
```
Loop:
```
mov cx,100               ;loop count=100
sl:                      ;loop label
add ax,1
loop sl
                         ;ax=100
```

Stack
```
mov ax,0
```
Pop/push:
```
mov cx,dddw              ;load cx
push cx                  ;preserve dddw
mov cx,100               ;loop count=100
sl:                      ;loop label
add ax,1
loop sl                  ;ax=100
pop cx                   ;cx=dddw
```

Count
Inc:
```
mov ax,0
mov cx,100               ;loop count=100
sl:                      ;loop label
inc ax
loop sl
                         ;ax=100
```

Flags. The flags instructions have no operands and are basically self-explanatory.

Shift

Shift left:
```
mov cl,8
mov ax,1
sal ax,cl                ;ax=10H
```

Shift right:
```
mov cl,8
mov ax,10H
sar ax,cl                ;ax=1
```

Rotate

Rotate left:
```
mov cl,17
mov ax,1
rcl ax,cl                    ;ax=2
```

Store

Store byte:
```
mov di,OFFSET dddw
mov al,18
stosb                        ;stores 18 in dddw[0]
```

String

Repeat:
```
mov cx,80                    ;length string
mov si,OFFSET dddw           ;byte operand-source
mov di,OFFSET dddz           ;byte operand-destination
cld                          ;increment
rep movsb                    ;transfer dddw to dddz
```

Convert These instructions are self-explanatory.

Control

Call:
```
          ...
mov ax,3
call cube                    ;ax=27
          ...
cube   proc near
mov bx,ax                    ;multiplicand
mov dx,0                     ;clear upper reg
mul bx                       ;square
mul bx                       ;cube
ret                          ;ax=cube input
```

ASCII and Decimal. These instructions are used to adjust the outcome of operations for ASCII arithmetic and packed decimal. We will not consider either of these features in this text. The interested reader is referred to references 1 through 6.

I/O

Input:
```
mov cx,43H                   ;8253 cntl port
mov al,B6H                   ;ctr 2,1,s,1st,bin
out dx,al
```

Miscellaneous

Exchange:
```
xchg ax,bx                   ;register with accumulator
xchg dh,alpha                ;memory with register
```

So far we have seen most of the 8086 family application instructions and how a selected subset is programmed (in conjunction with the mov instruction). One group of instructions that was not included determines conditional and unconditional branching within the program.

Control instructions. Table 5.3 presents the jump instructions. Virtually all of these instructions are used in conjunction with an instruction that changes the flags (usually by comparing or testing two operands). The compare instructions are illustrated in Table 5.4. The reference to short-label means that the jump or branch must be to a label within +128/−127 bytes of the instruction. A typical use of the instruction would be the if . . . else construct:

```
        ...
        mov  bx,0
        cmp  ax,bx          ;test
        jne  else1          ;conditional branch
             ...(Process1)  ;executes if ax=bx
        jmp  if1
else1:
             ...(Process2)  ;executes if ax.ne.bx
if1:
        ...
```

TABLE 5.3 JUMP INSTRUCTION GROUP

Instruction	Purpose	Comments
JA short-label (JNBE)	Jump if above/ if not below or equal	This jump is used in conjunction with the carry and zero flags. If either or both are set, no jump occurs. Suppose two operands are compared; then if the destination is greater than the source (above) CF = ZF = 0 and the jump occurs. The jump is within −128 to +127 bytes (short-label) and unsigned operands are used.
JAE short-label (JNB)	Jump if above or equal/if not below	This jump is similar to JA except only the carry flag is examined. If a previous compare, for example, is performed and the destination is greater or equal to the source (above or equal), CF = 0 and the jump occurs. This is a short-label instruction with unsigned operands.
JB short-label (JNAE) (JC)	Jump if below/if not above or equal/if carry	This jump is the opposite of JAE. If the carry flag is set, the jump will occur. Suppose a previous compare is performed and the destination is less than the source (below); CF = 1 and the jump occurs. This is a short label instruction with unsigned operands.
JBE short-label (JNA)	Jump if below or equal/if not above	This jump is the same as JB except it also takes place if the zero flag is set (below or equal). It is short-label with unsigned operands.
JCXZ short-label	Jump if CX is zero	Suppose an instruction sequence causes the count register (CX) to decrement. When CX reaches 0, control would transfer to the short-label after execution of JCXZ. This is a short-label jump.

TABLE 5.3 (*Concluded*)

Instruction	Purpose	Comments
JE short-label (JZ)	Jump if equal/ if zero	If the last operation to change ZF set this flag (gave a result of 0), JE will cause a jump to occur. This is a short-label jump.
JG short-label (JNLE)	Jump if greater/if not less or equal	If ZF = 0 and SF = OF, the JG instruction will cause a jump to short-label. This instruction is used with signed operands.
JGE short-label (JNL)	Jump if greater or equal/if not less	This instruction is the same as JG except ZF is not considered. If SF = OF, the jump occurs. This is a short-label instruction with signed operands.
JL short-label (JNGE)	Jump if less/if not greater or equal	If SF $\neq$ OF, the JL instruction will result in a jump. This instruction is short-label with signed operands.
JLE short-label (JNG)	Jump if less or equal/if not greater	If ZF = 1 or SF $\neq$ OF, the JLE instruction yields a short-label jump. The instruction is used with signed operands.
JMP target	Jump	This is a direct and unconditional jump.
JNC short-label	Jump if no carry	If CF = 0, this instruction yields a short-label jump.
JNE short-label (JNZ)	Jump if not equal/ if not zero	If ZF = 0, this short-label jump will occur.
JNO short-label	Jump if no over-flow	If OF = 0, this short-label jump will occur.
JNB short-label (JPO)	Jump if no parity/ if parity odd	If PF = 0, this short-label jump will occur.
JNS short-label	Jump if no sign/if positive	If SF = 0, this short-label jump will occur.
JO short-label	Jump on overflow	If OF = 1, this short-label jump will occur.
JP short-label (JPE)	Jump on parity/ if parity even	If PF = 1, this short-label jump will occur.
JS short-label	Jump on sign	If SF = 1, this short-label jump will occur.

Here ax is compared with bx(=0), and if they are equal, process1 executes followed by an unconditional branch to if1. If ax is not equal to bx, process2 executes.

It is possible to simulate loop behavior, for example, using conditional jumps:

```
        ...
        mov dx,10000      ;count index
do1:
        ... (process1)
        dec dx            ;subtract 1 from count
        cmp dx,0          ;check count=0
        jne do1           ;loop
        ...
```

TABLE 5.4 THE COMPARE INSTRUCTION GROUP

Instruction	Purpose	Comments
CMP destination, source	Compare two operands	This instruction causes the source to be subtracted from the destination; however, only the flags are affected. The destination remains unchanged.
CMPS destination-str source-str (CMPSB) (CMPSW)	Compare byte or word string	The source string (with DI as an index for the extra segment) is subtracted from the destination string (which uses SI as index). Only the flags are affected and both DI and SI are incremented. A typical sequence of instructions could be

```
                        MOV SI, OFFSET AAA
                        MOV DI, OFFSET BBB
                        CMPS AAA, BBB
```

Other 80286 and 80386 instructions. Tables 5.5, 5.6, and 5.7 illustrate the additional (beyond the 8086) application and systems-oriented instructions for the 80286 and 80386. In some cases, these are of the same form as the corresponding 8086 instruction, but have different meaning in the context of the 80286 or 80386 architecture. We will not dwell on all these instructions because only a subset will be used in the examples and further consideration is left to the reader. A fruitful approach is to become familiar with a small subset of the assembler and then expand as experience develops and more efficiency (and flexibility) is required.

At this point the reader has been exposed to virtually all the 8086 family instructions including those specific to the 80286 and 80386. In Section 5.1.3, we consider the coprocessors for this family (8087, 80287, and 80387), and many of the instructions common to these processors are illustrated. Again, the presentation is brief and the application of these coprocessor instructions is only sketched. In Section 5.4 we will consider the use of various instructions in an ordered fashion through the development of assembly language programs. At that time the reader can expect to become familiar with the approaches and techniques needed to apply the IBM Macro Assembler in a C context.

Operators. Table 5.8 illustrates the various operators available to the Macro Assembler programmer. We have already seen examples of the PTR and OFFSET operators. These operators are all used to affect operands. (In the address specification, [bp + 4], for example, the + operator is employed to generate the final pointer value.)

Pseudo-ops. We have seen examples of several pseudo-ops that are available for generating information to the assembler. Table 5.9 presents a list of application-oriented pseudo-ops for the 8086 family of processors. These pseudo-ops are listed

TABLE 5.5 ADDITIONAL 80286 APPLICATION INSTRUCTIONS

Instruction	Purpose	Comments
BOUND dest,,source	Check array index against bounds	This instruction ensures that an index (destination) is above or equal to the first word in the memory location defined by source. Similarly, it must be below or equal to "source + 2."
ENTER immediate-word, immediate-byte	Make stack frame for procedure parameters	"Immediate-word" specifies how many bytes of storage to be allocated on the stack for the routine being entered. "Immediate-byte" specifies the nesting level of the routine within the high-level source code being entered.
IMUL dest,,immediate	Integer immediate multiply	Does a signed multiplication of destination by an immediate value.
INS/INSB/INSW dest,-string,port	Input from port to string	Transfers a byte or word string from the port numbered by DX to ES:DI. The operand dest.-string determines the type of move: byte or word.
LEAVE	High-level procedure exit	Executes a procedure return for a high-level language.
OUTS/OUTSB/OUTSW port,source-string	Output string to port	Transfers a byte or word string from memory at DS:DI to the port numbered by DX.
POPA	Pop all general registers	Restores the eight general-purpose registers saved on the stack by PUSHA.
PUSH immediate	Push immediate onto stack	This instruction pushes the immediate data onto the stack.
RCL dest,,CL	Rotate left through carry	Same as RCL for 8088 except count can be 31.
RCR dest,,CL	Rotate right through carry	Same as RCR for 8088 except count can be 31.
ROL dest,,CL	Rotate left	Same as ROL for 8088 except count can be 31.
ROR dest,,CL	Rotate right	Same as ROR for 8088 except count can be 31.
SAL/SHL dest,,CL	Shift arithmetic left/ shift logical left	Same as 8088 instructions except count can be 31.
SAR dest,,CL	Shift arithmetic right	Same as 8088 instruction except count can be 31.
SHR dest,,CL	Shift logical right	Same as 8088 instruction except count can be 31.

by category: conditional, listing, mode, data, and macro. Most of the conditional pseudo-ops are used to set up and modify source code during pass 1 of the assembler (the assembler is a two-pass assembler with many of the forward references defined based on pass 1). The listing pseudo-ops are used primarily to structure the printout of the assembler listing, the .LST file. The mode pseudo-op allows specification of hardware-oriented capabilities for the microprocessor. Some of the data pseudo-

TABLE 5.6 ADDITIONAL 80386 APPLICATION INSTRUCTIONS

Instruction	Purpose	Comments
BSF dest,,source	Bit scan forward	The source word (doubleword) is scanned for a set bit and the index value of this bit loaded in destination. Scanning is from right to left.
BSR dest,,source	Bit scan reverse	Scans as in BSF but reverse order.
BT base,offset	Bit test	This instruction loads the bit value from base at offset in the base, into the CF register.
BTC base,offset	Bit test and complement	This instruction loads the bit value from base at offset in the base, into the CF register, and complements the bit in base.
BTR base,offset	Bit test and reset	This instruction loads the bit value from base at offset in the base, into the CF register, and resets the bit to 0.
BTS base,offset	Bit test and set	This instruction is identical to BTR, but the resulting bit is set to 1.
CWDE, CWD	Convert word to doubleword	This instruction converts the signed word in AX to a doubleword in EAX.
CMPSD	Compare doublewords	This instruction compares ES:[EDI] with DS:[ESI].
CDQ	Convert doubleword to quadword	Converts the signed doubleword in EAX to a signed 64-bit integer in the register pair EDX:EAX by extending the sign into EDX.
INSD	Input	Input from port DX to ES:[EDI] (doubleword).
LODSD	Load string operand	Load doubleword DS:[ESI] into EAX.
MOVSD	Move data from string to string	Move doubleword DS:[ESI] to ES:[EDI].
MOVSX	Move with sign-extend	Move byte to word, byte to dword, and word to dword with sign extend.
MOVZX	Move with zero-extend	Move byte to word, byte to dword, and word to dword with 0 extend.
OUTSD	Output	Output dword DS:[ESI] to port in DX.
POPAD	Pop all general registers	Pops the eight 32-bit general registers.
POPFD	Pop stack into EFLAGS	Pops the 32-bit stack top into EFLAGS.
PUSHAD	Push all general registers	Pushes the eight 32-bit general registers onto the stack.
PUSHFD	Push EFLAGS onto stack	Pushes the EFLAGS register onto the stack.
SCASD	Compare string data	Compares dwords EAX and ES:[EDI] and updates. EDI.
SETcc dest,	Byte set on condition	Stores a byte (equal to 1), if cc, the condition, is met (following a compare, for example). Otherwise, a value of 0 is stored at the destination.
SHLD dest,,Count	Double-precision-shift left	The destination is shifted left by count.
SHRD dest,,Count	Double-precision shift right	Same as SHLD but shift is to the right.
STOSD	Store string data	Store EAX in dword ES:[EDI] and update EDI.

TABLE 5.7 SYSTEMS-ORIENTED 80286 AND 80386 INSTRUCTIONS

Instruction	Purpose	Comments
ARPL dest,,source	Adjust RPL field of selector	If the RPL field of the selector (protection bits) in dest. is less than the RPL field of source, ZF = 1 and the RDL field of dest. is set to match source.
CLTS	Clear Task Switched Flag	The Task Switch Flag is in the Machine Status Word and is set each time a task change occurs. This instruction clears that flag.
LAR dest,,source	Load access rights byte	Destination contains a selector. If the associated descriptor is visible at the called protection level, the access rights byte of the descriptor is loaded into the high byte of source (low byte = 0).
LGDT/LIDT m	Load Global/Interrupt Descriptor Table register	m points to 6 bytes of memory used to provide Descriptor Table values (Global and Interrupt). This instruction loads these tables into the appropriate 80286 registers.
LLDT source	Load Local Descriptor Table register	Source is a selector pointing to the Global Descriptor Table. The GDT should, in turn, be a Local Descriptor Table. The LDT register is then loaded with source.
LMSW source	Load Machine Status Word	The Machine Status Word is loaded from source.
LSL dest,,source	Load segment limit	If the Descriptor Table value pointed to by the selector in destination is visible at the current protection level, a limit value specified by source is loaded into this descriptor.
LTR source	Load Task Register	The Task Register is loaded from source.
SGDT/SIDT m	Store Global/Interrupt Descriptor Table register	The contents of the specified Descriptor Table register are copied to 6 bytes of memory pointed to by m.
SLDT dest,	Store Local Descriptor Table register	The Local Descriptor Table register is stored in the word register or memory location specified by destination.
SMSW dest,	Store Machine Status Word	The Machine Status Word is stored in the word register or memory location specified by destination.
VERR/VERW source	Verify a segment for reading or writing	Source is a selector. These instructions determine whether the segment corresponding to this selector is reachable under the current protection level.
STR dest,	Store Task Register	The contents of the Task Register are stored in destination.

TABLE 5.8 IBM MACRO ASSEMBLER OPERATORS

Operator	Type	Description
PTR	Attribute	This operator has the form type PTR expression. It is used to override the type attribute (BYTE, WORD, DWORD, QWORD, or TBYTE) of a variable or the attribute of a label (NEAR or FAR). The expression field is the variable or label that is to be overridden.
Seg-reg, Seg-name	Attribute	The segment override operator changes the segment attribute of a label, variable, or address expression. It has three forms:
Group-name		seg-reg:addr-expression seg-name:addr-expression group-name:addr-expression
SHORT	Attribute	This operator is used when a label follows a JMP instruction and is within 127 bytes of the JMP. It has the form JMP SHORT label and changes the NEAR attribute. A pass 2 NOP instruction is avoided.
THIS	Attribute	The form of this operator is THIS type. The operator produces an operand whose segment attribute is equal to the defining segment, whose offset equals IP, and a type attribute defined by "type." For example, "AAA EQU THIS WORD" yields an AAA with attribute WORD instead of NEAR (if used in the same code segment).
HIGH	Attribute	This operator accepts a number/address argument and returns the high-order byte.
LOW	Attribute	This operator accepts a number/address argument and returns the low-order byte.
SEG	Value returning	This operator returns the segment value of the variable or label.
OFFSET	Value returning	This operator returns the offset value of the variable or label.
TYPE	Value returning	For operand arguments, this operator returns a value equal to the number of bytes of the operand. If a structure name, it returns the number of bytes declared by STRUC. If the operand is a label, it returns 65534 (FAR) and 65535 (NEAR).
SIZE	Value returning	This operator returns the value LENGTH × TYPE.
LENGTH	Value returning	For a DUP entry, LENGTH returns the number of units allocated for the variable. For all others it returns a 1.
SHIFT COUNT	Record specific	This operator is used with the RECORD pseudo-op and is the name of the record field. The format of RECORD is: recordname RECORD field-name:width. The value of fieldname, when used in an expression, is the shift count to move the field to the far right within the byte or word.

TABLE 5.8 (*Concluded*)

Operator	Type	Description
MASK	Record specific	The format of this operator is MASK recfield. It returns a bit mask for the field. The mask has bits set for positions included in the field and 0 for bits not included in the field.
WIDTH	Record specific	The format of this operator is WIDTH recfield. It evaluates to a constant in the range 1 to 16 and returns the width of a record or record field.
+	Arithmetic	Returns the sum of two terms. Form: term1 + term2.
−	Arithmetic	Returns the difference of two terms. Form: term1 − term2.
*	Arithmetic	Returns the product of two terms. Form: term1 * term2.
MOD	Arithmetic	Form: term1 MOD term2. It returns the remainder obtained by dividing term1 by term2.
SHL	Arithmetic	Form: term1 SHL term2. It shifts the bits of term1 left by the amount contained in term2. Zeros are filled in the new bits.
SHR	Arithmetic	Same as SHL except the shift is to the right.
EQ	Relational	Form: term1 EQ term2. Returns a value −1 (TRUE) if term1 equals term2, or 0 (FALSE) otherwise.
NE	Relational	Form: term1 NE term2. Returns a value −1 (TRUE) if term1 does not equal term2, or 0 (FALSE) otherwise.
LT	Relational	Form: term1 LT term2. Returns a value −1 (TRUE) if term1 is less than term2, or 0 (FALSE) otherwise.
LE	Relational	Form: term1 LE term2. Returns a value −1 (TRUE) if term1 is less than or equal to term2, or 0 (FALSE) otherwise.
GT	Relational	Form: term1 GT term2. Returns a value −1 (TRUE) if term1 is greater than term2, or 0 (FALSE) otherwise.
GE	Relational	Form: term1 GE term2. Returns a value −1 (TRUE) if term1 is greater than or equal to term2, or 0 (FALSE) otherwise.
AND, OR, and XOR	Logical	These operators have the form term1 (operator) term2 and return each bit position as follows:
NOT	Logical	Form: NOT term. This operator complements each bit of term.

term1 bit	term2 bit	AND	OR	XOR
1	1	1	1	0
1	0	0	1	1
0	1	0	1	1
0	0	0	0	0

C and Assembly Language   Chap. 5

TABLE 5.9 APPLICATION-ORIENTED PSEUDO-OPS

Pseudo-op	Description
ELSE	This pseudo-op must be used in conjunction with a conditional pseudo-op and serves to provide an alternate path.
ENDIF	This pseudo-op ends the corresponding IFxxx conditional.
IF	Form: IF expression. When the expression is true, the code following this pseudo-op is executed; otherwise it branches to an ELSE entry point or an ENDIF. IF pseudo-ops can be nested.
IFB	Form: IFB <operand>. This is the "if blank" pseudo-op and it is true if the operand has not been specified as in a MACRO call, for example. The code following the IFB is executed when operand is blank. Otherwise, the IP jumps to ENDIF.
IFDEF	Form: IFDEF symbol. If symbol has been defined via the EXTRN pseudo-op, this is true and the code following the pseudo-op is executed.
IFDIF	Form: IFDIF <operand1>, <operand2>. The code following this pseudo-op is executed if the string operand1 is different from the string operand2.
IFE	Form: IFE expression. The code following this pseudo-op is executed if expression = 0.
IFIDN	Form: IFIDN <operand1>, <operand2>. The code following this pseudo-op is executed if the string operand1 is identical to the string operand2.
IFNB	Form: IFNB <operand>. The code following this pseudo-op is executed if the operand is not blank.
IFNDEF	Form: IFNDEF symbol. The code following this pseudo-op is executed if the symbol has not been defined via the EXTRN pseudo-op.
IF1	This pseudo-op is true if the assembler is in pass 1, and it is used to load macros from a macro library (as an example).
IF2	This pseudo-op is true if the assembler is in pass 2, and it can be used to inform the programmer what version of the program is being used (when coupled with appropriate logic and a %OUT).
.286C	This pseudo-op tells the assembler to recognize and assemble 80286 instructions used by the IBM AT.
.8086	This pseudo-op tells the assembler not to recognize and assemble 80286 instructions.
.8087	This pseudo-op tells the assembler to recognize and assemble 8087 coprocessor instructions and data formats.
ASSUME	Form: ASSUME seg-reg:seg-name, ... This pseudo-op tells the assembler which segment register segments belong to.
COMMENT	Form: COMMENT delimiter text delimiter. COMMENT allows the programmer to enter comments without semicolons. It is not recognized by the SALUT program.
DB	Form: [variable] DB [expression]. It is used to initialize byte storage.
DD	DD has the same form as DB except it applies to doubleword quantities.
DQ	DQ has the same form as DB except it applies to four-word quantities.
DT	DT has the same form as DB except it applies to 10-byte packed decimal.
DW	DW has the same form as DB except it applies to word quantities.

TABLE 5.9 (*Continued*)

Pseudo-op	Description
END	Form: END [expression]. END identifies the end of the source program, and the optional expression identifies the name of the entry point.
ENDP	Form: procedure-name ENDP. Designates the end of a procedure.
ENDS	Form: structure-name ENDS or seg-name ENDS. Designates the end of a structure or segment.
EQU	Form: name EQU expression. Assigns the value of expression to name. This value may not be reassigned.
=	Form: label = expression. Assigns the value of expression to label. May be reassigned.
EVEN	EVEN ensures that the code following starts on an even boundary.
EXTRN	Form: EXTRN name:type, ... EXTRN is used to indicate that symbols used in this assembly module are defined in another module.
GROUP	Form: name GROUP seg-name, ... GROUP collects all segments named and places them within a 64K physical segment.
INCLUDE	Form: INCLUDE [drive] [path] filename.ext. INCLUDE assembles source statements from an alternate source file into the current source file.
LABEL	Form: name LABEL type. LABEL defines the attributes of name to be type.
NAME	Form: NAME module-name. NAME gives a module a name. It may be used only once per assembly.
ORG	Form: ORG expression. The location counter is set to the value of expression.
PROC	Form: procedure-name PROC [attribute]. PROC identifies a block of code as a procedure and must end with RET/ENDP. The attribute is NEAR or FAR.
PUBLIC	Form: PUBLIC symbol, ... PUBLIC makes symbols externally available to other linked modules.
.RADIX	Form: .RADIX expression. .RADIX allows the default base (decimal) to be changed to a value between 2 and 16.
RECORD	Form: recordname RECORD fieldname:width [=exp], ... RECORD defines a bit pattern to format bytes and words for bit packing (see text).
SEGMENT	Form: segname SEGMENT [align-type] [combine-type] ['class'] (see Chapter 3 for a discussion of this pseudo-op).
STRUC	Form: structure-name STRUC. STRUC is used to allocate and initialize multibyte variables using DB, DD, DQ, DT, and DW. It must end with ENDS.
.CREF and .XCREF	This listing pseudo-op provides cross-reference information when a filespec is indicated in response to the assembler prompt (CREF). It is the normal default condition. .XCREF results in no output for cross reference when in force.
.LALL, .SALL, and .XALL	.LALL lists the complete macro text for all expansions. .SALL suppresses listing of all text and object code produced by macros. .XALL produces a source line listing only if object code results.

TABLE 5.9 (*Concluded*)

Pseudo-op	Description
.LFCOND	This pseudo-op causes the listing of conditional blocks that evaluate as false.
.LIST and .XLIST	.LIST causes a listing of source and object code in the output assembler list file. .XLIST turns this listing off. These pseudo-ops can be used to selectively list code during the assembly of programs, especially long sequences of instructions.
%OUT	Form: %OUT text. This pseudo-op is used to monitor progress through a long assembly. The argument "text" is displayed, when encountered, during the assembly process.
PAGE	Form: PAGE operand1, operand2. Controls the length (operand1) in lines and the width (operand2) in characters of the assembler list file.
.SFCOND	This pseudo-op suppresses the listing of conditional blocks that evaluate as false.
SUBTTL	Form: SUBTTL text. Generates a subtitle to be listed after each listing of title.
.TFCOND	This pseudo-op changes the listing setting (and default) for false conditionals to the opposite state.
TITLE	Form: TITLE text. This pseudo-op specifies a title to be listed on each page of the assembler listing. It may be used only once.
ENDM	ENDM is the terminator for MACRO, REPT, IRP, and IRPC.
EXITM	EXITM provides an exit to an expansion (REPT, IRP, IRPC, or MACRO) when a test proves that the remaining expansion is not needed.
IRP	Form: IRP dummy, <operandlist>. The number of operands (separated by commas) in operandlist determines the number of times the following code (terminated by ENDM) is repeated. At each repetition, the next item in operandlist is substituted for all occurrences of dummy.
IRPC	Form: IRPC dummy, string. This is the same as IRP except at each repetition the next character in string is substituted for all occurrences of dummy.
LOCAL	Form: LOCAL dummylist. LOCAL is used inside a MACRO structure. The assembler creates a unique symbol for each entry in dummylist during each expansion of the macro. This avoids the problem of a multiply defined label, for example, when multiple expansions of the same macro take place in a program.
MACRO	Form: name MACRO dummylist. The statements following the MACRO definition, before ENDM, are the macro. Dummylist contains the parameters to be replaced when calling the macro during assembly. The form of this call is name parmlist. Parmlist consists of the actual parameters (separated by commas) used in the expansion.
PURGE	Form: PURGE macro-name, ... PURGE deletes the definition of a specified MACRO and allows the space to be used. This is beneficial when including a macro library during assembly but desiring to remove those macros not used during the assembly.

ops have already been used: ASSUME, END, ENDP, ENDS, EXTRN, GROUP, NAME, PROC, PUBLIC, and SEGMENT. Finally, the macro pseudo-ops constitute an important class of pseudo-ops. These pseudo-ops can be used to define insertable blocks of instructions that accomplish specific functions. For example, suppose it is desired that two variables be tested to see if one is greater than the other and, if the test is TRUE, the first variable is to be cubed and returned in x. The following macro accomplishes this task:

```
CUBE        MACRO            X,Y
            LOCAL ELSE1
            MOV AX,X
            MOV BX,Y
            CMP AX,BX            ;check AX>BX
            JLE ELSE1
                MOV BX,AX        ;cube operation
                IMUL BX          ;x*x
                IMUL BX          ;x*x*x
                MOV X,AX
ELSE1:
            EXITM
```

The pseudo-ops, MACRO . . . EXITM, delimit the macro, and it has name, CUBE, with dummylist, X and Y. The LOCAL pseudo-op acts to ensure ELSE1 is replaced by a uniquely defined label at each call of CUBE. In a program, each call to CUBE X,Y would be replaced by the preceding code during Pass1. For example, a typical program sequence might look like

```
. . .
CUBE X1,X2
. . .
CUBE YSTATUS,XSTATUS
. . .
CUBE Z1,Z4
. . .
```

At each instance X and Y would assume the parameter values specified and the code would be placed in the source program appropriately. This is unlike a procedure where a jump to the appropriate code occurs at each calling sequence. A limitation on macro usage is that if macros are large they can cause short-label references (see the jump instructions) to expand beyond $+128/-127$ bytes, and such instruction references are no longer valid.

Finally, in Table 5.10 we have some special purpose operators that can be used with macros. These operators are self-explanatory based on the tables and effectively increase the capability for forward references using macro calls.

5.1.3 The Coprocessor

This integrated circuit family (the 8087, 80287, and 80387) allows the corresponding CPU to perform high-speed computations while maintaining an appreciable amount of numerical significance (beyond that available using the standard CPU registers).

TABLE 5.10 SPECIAL-PURPOSE MACRO OPERATORS

Operator	Description
&	Format: text&text. This operator concatenates text or symbols. An example is

```
TC1     MACRO   X
        LEA DX , CHAR&X
        MOV AH , 9
        INT 21H
        ENDM
```

Here a call TC1 A would load DX with a character start position CHARA.

;;	Format: ;;text. A comment preceded by two semicolons is not produced as part of the expansion when a MACRO or REPT is defined in an assembly.
!	Format: !character. Causes the character to be interpreted as a literal value, not a symbol.
%	Format: %expression. Converts expression to a number. During expansion, the number is substituted for expression. Consider

```
MAC1    MACRO   X
L1      =       X * 1000
        MAC2    %L1 ,X
        ENDM
                        ;
MAC2    MACRO   Y ,X
PROD&X  DB      'Production No, &X = &Y'
        ENDM
```

This yields "PROD5   DB   'Production No. 5 = 5000,' "
when called with MAC1 5.

Internal to the 8087 and 80287 are a number of registers that may be accessed by the assembler programmer: eight stack registers [designated ST(0), ST(1), . . . , ST(7)] with 80 bits of internal significance, a status word register, a control word register, and a tag word register. We will confine this discussion to the 8087 and 80287 and refer the reader to the Intel literature for a discussion of the 80387 registers [9]. The status word is defined as follows:

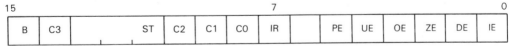

Here B = busy, (C0, C1, C2, and C3) comprise the condition code, ST = stack top pointer [000 = STL(0), . . . , 111 = ST(7)], IR = interrupt request, PE = precision, UE = underflow, OE = overflow, ZE = zero divide, DE = denormalized operand, and IE = invalid operation. An example of the use of the status word would be the evaluation of the compare instruction (8087), which returns its result in C0, C1, C2, and C3. These bits must be examined to determine what operation to implement following the compare operation. (Shortly we will examine the coprocessor instructions.)

The coprocessors are designed to handle both real numbers and integers. Within the context of the Macro Assembler, real numbers are defined in the Microsoft binary format, which has the form (single-precision real):

Here E7, . . . , E0 are exponent bits, S is the sign, and f1, . . . , f23 are the significand bits. Real numbers are stored in normalized form where the significand is assumed to be defined as

$$(1).x_1x_2x_3x_4\cdots$$

Here $x_1x_2x_3x_4$ . . . are represented by the binary equivalence of f1f2 . . . f23, with the 1 to the left of the decimal point suppressed. An example of this would be the single-precision number stored as

00 50 43 91

which loads as

91 43 50 00

and is as follows

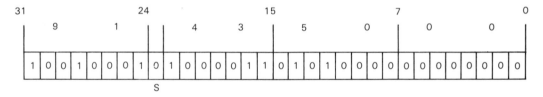

The exponent is biased about 129 for the Microsoft single-precision real format. Here $2^{-1} + 2^{-6} + 2^{-7} + 2^{-9} + 2^{-11} + 1.0 = 1.52588$. Removing the exponential bias $145 - 129 = 16$, we have

$$1.52588 \times 2^{16} = 100,000$$

We have included a representation of the Microsoft single-precision real format by way of illustration of the complex nature for handling real numbers in assembly language. The coprocessor has a similar set of formats for dealing with real numbers, and rather elaborate conversion routines are needed to change Microsoft reals to coprocessor reals. In this book we will not concern ourselves with the real number format. Virtually all the precision we will need can be obtained with the 32-bit integer arithmetic available from long integers. This applies to both values passed to the CPU via function calls to assembly language and values passed from within

C and Assembly Language   Chap. 5

assembly language routines to coprocessor routines. This is not to say that we will not continue using floating point numbers. We merely emphasize that when using assembly language modules the values passed will be integer.

The coprocessor has a slightly different designation for integer types than that represented within the Microsoft C compiler standard interpretation. The C compiler assumes that integer and short (integer) are the same (word length) while long (integer) is doubleword length (32 bits). In the coprocessor, the assumption is word integer (16 bits), short integer (32 bits), and long integer (64 bits), where the most significant bit is a sign bit. It should be recognized that all values input to the coprocessor are converted to an internal temporary real format:

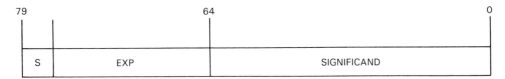

Hence, a great deal of significance is available within the coprocessor itself. Before considering coprocessor I/O further, we address the coprocessor instruction set. It is very useful to consider stack operand references for these instructions:

1. Classical stack, [ST(1), ST(0)]: Here ST(1) is the destination and the source is ST(0) with both operands implicit.
2. Register, ST(i), ST or ST, ST(i): Here the destination is ST(i) and the source is ST [ST(0)], or vice versa.
3. Register pop, ST(i), ST. The destination is ST(i) and the source is ST. The source is popped off the stack following execution.
4. Real memory, (ST) real memory: The destination is ST(0), which is implicit (hence the parentheses), and the source is real memory.
5. Integer memory, (ST) integer memory: The destination is ST(0), which is implicit (hence the parentheses), and the source is integer memory.

In these operand formats, register references enclosed in parentheses are assumed implicit.

By way of illustration, consider the instructions that load an integer into the coprocessor and move an integer from the coprocessor to storage. These instructions take the form, respectively,

    FILD source

and

    FIST destination

Here the implicit operand is ST, the stack top. [Note that ST is the abbreviated referenced for ST(0), the stack top.] The coprocessor instructions should not reference the CPU registers; thus, a data area must be defined in most cases for coprocessor variables. Table 5.11 illustrates the coprocessor instructions that are available under

TABLE 5.11 COPROCESSOR INSTRUCTION SET

Instruction	Purpose	Comments
Data transfer		
FLD source	Load real	Pushes the source data onto the top of the register stack, ST(0).
FST destination	Store real	This instruction copies ST(0) into the indicated destination (real), which can be a memory operand or register.
FSTP destination	Store real/pop	This instruction copies ST(0) into the indicated destination and then pops ST(0) off the stack.
FXCH destination	Exchange ST	This instruction exchanges ST(0) with the indicated destination.
FILD source	Load integer	This instruction pushes the source data (integer) onto the top of the stack, ST(0).
FIST destination	Store integer	This instruction stores ST(0), the stack top, in the indicated destination, which must be an integer memory operand.
FISTP destination	Store integer/ pop	This instruction stores ST(0), the stack top, in the indicated destination, which must be an integer memory operand, and then pops ST(0) off the stack.
FBLD source	Load BCD	This instruction pushes the source, which must be a BCD number, onto the stack at ST(0).
FBSTP destination	Store BCD/pop	This instruction stores ST(0) as a BCD number at the destination and pops ST(0) off the stack.
Addition		
FADD	Real addition	This instruction can be used without operands [assumes ST(1) added to ST(0) with the result in ST(0)], with a real-memory operand added to ST(0), or with explicit reference to ST(0) added to another register.
FADDP destination, source	Real add/pop	The source is ST(0) and the destination must be another stack register. The result is left in the alternate stack register used as the destination.
FIADD integer-memory	Integer addition	The destination, ST(0), is added to the source, integer memory, and the sum returned in ST(0).
Subtraction		
FSUB	Real subtraction	This instruction can be used without operands [assumes ST(1) is the destination and ST(0) is subtracted from it with the result in ST(1)], with a real-memory operand subtracted from ST(0) and the result in ST(0), or with explicit reference to ST(0) and another register (the destination containing the result).
FSUBP destination, source	Real subtract/ pop	The source, ST(0), is subtracted from the destination, another stack register, and the result stored in the destination.

TABLE 5.11 (*Continued*)

Instruction	Purpose	Comments
FISUB source	Integer subtraction	The destination, ST(0), has the source operand, an integer-memory operand, subtracted from it and the result is stored in ST(0).
FSUBR	Real reversed subtract	The destination is subtracted from the source and the result left in the destination. The operand configuration is the same as for FSUB.
FSUBRP	Real reversed subtract/pop	This instruction is the same as FSUBP except the destination is subtracted from the source. ST(0) still serves as the source operand.
FISUBR source	Integer reversed subtract	This instruction is the same as FISUB except the destination is subtracted from the source. The source is still an integer-memory operand.
Multiplication		
FMUL	Real multiply	This instruction multiplies the destination operand by the source and returns the product in the destination. The instruction can be executed with no operands [ST(0) is the implied source and ST(1) the destination], with the source specified as a real-memory operand and ST(0) the destination, and with both destination register and source register [one of which is ST(0)] specified.
FMULP destination, source	Real multiply/ pop	This instruction uses ST(0) as the source operand and another register as the destination. The product is returned in the destination register and the stack top popped.
FIMUL source	Integer multiply	This instruction multiplies the destination by the source and returns the product in the destination. The destination is ST(0) and source is an integer-memory operand.
Division		
FDIV	Real divide	This instruction divides the destination by the source and returns the quotient to the destination. The instruction can be executed with no operands [ST(0) is the implied source and ST(1) the implied destination], with a source specified and ST(0) the implied destination, and with a source [ST(0)] and destination (another register) specified.
FDIVP destination, source	Real divide/pop	This instruction divides the destination by the source and returns the quotient to the destination. It then pops the top of the 8087 stack. The source is the ST(0) register and the destination operand is another stack register.

TABLE 5.11 (Continued)

Instruction	Purpose	Comments
FIDIV source	Integer divide	This instruction divides the destination by the source and returns the quotient to the destination. The destination is ST(0) and the source is an integer-memory operand.
FDIVR	Real reversed divide	This instruction is identical with FDIV except the source is divided by the destination. The quotient is still returned in the destination.
FDIVRP destination, source	Real reversed divide/pop	This instruction is identical to FDIVP except the source is divided by the destination. The quotient is still returned in the destination.
FIDIVR source	Integer divide reversed	This instruction is identical to FIDIV except the source is divided by the destination. The quotient is still returned in the destination.
Miscellaneous		
FSQRT	Square root	This instruction replaces the content of ST(0) with its square root.
FSCALE	Scale	This instruction interprets the value of the number contained in ST(1) as an integer. This value is added to the exponent of the number in ST(0), which is equivalent to multiplying ST(0) by 2 raised to this integer power.
FPREM	Partial remainder	This instruction takes the modulo of ST relative to the number contained in ST(1). The sign is the same as that of ST(0).
FRNDINT	Round to integer	This instruction rounds ST(0) to an integer. The rules for rounding are determined by setting the RC field of the control word. RC = 00 (round to nearest integer), 01 (round downward, 10 (round upward), and 11 (round toward 0).
FXTRACT	Extract exponent/significand	This instruction reduces the number in ST(0) to a significand and an exponent for 80-bit arithmetic.
FABS	Absolute value	This instruction yields the absolute value of ST(0).
FCHS	Change sign	This instruction reverses the sign of ST(0).
Comparison		
FCOM	Real compare	This instruction compares the source operand [which can be specified as a real-memory operand or implicit as ST(1)] and ST(0).
FCOMP	Real compare/ pop	This instruction is identical with FCOM except the stack top, ST(0), is popped following the compare.
FCOMPP	Real compare/ pop twice	This instruction is identical with FCOM except the stack top, ST(0), and ST(1) are popped following the compare.

C and Assembly Language   Chap. 5

TABLE 5.11 (*Continued*)

Instruction	Purpose	Comments
FICOM source	Integer compare	This instruction compares ST(0) to the source operand, which is an integer-memory operand.
FICOMP source	Integer compare/ pop	This instruction is identical to FICOM except the stack top, ST(0), is popped following the compare.
FTST	Test	This instruction tests ST(0) relative to +0.0. The result of the test is returned in the condition code of the status word: (C3, C0) = (0, 0) for ST positive, (0, 1) for ST negative, (1, 0) for ST zero, and (1,1) if ST cannot be compared.
FXAM	Examine	The stack top, ST(0), is examined and the result returned in the condition code field as specified in the Version 2.0 *Macro Assembler Reference* manual.
Transcendental		
FPTAN	Partial tangent	This instruction calculates $Y/X = TAN(z)$. The value z is contained in ST(0) prior to execution. Following execution, Y is contained in ST(1) and X contained in ST(0).
FPATAN	Partial arc tangent	This instruction calculates $z = ARCTAN(Y/X)$, where X is ST(0) and Y is ST(1). The result, z, is returned to ST(0).
F2XM1	$2^x - 1$	This instruction calculates $2^x - 1$, where x is taken from ST(0) and must be in the range (0, 0.5). The result is replaced in ST(0).
FYL2X	$Y * \log_2(X)$	This instruction calculates $Y * \log_2(X)$, where X is ST(0) and Y is ST(1). The stack top is popped and the result returned to the new ST(0).
FYL2XP1	$Y * \log_2 (X + 1)$	This instruction is the same as FYL2X except 1 is added to X. X must be in the range $(0, 1 - \sqrt{2}/2)$.
Constant		
FLDZ	Load zero	This instruction loads +0.0 in ST(0).
FLD1	Load +1.0	This instruction loads +1.0 in ST(0).
FLDP1	Load pi	This instruction loads pi into ST(0).
FLDL2T	Load $\log_2(10)$	This instruction loads $\log_2(10)$ into the stack top, ST(0).
FLDL2E	Load $\log_2(e)$	This instruction loads $\log_2(e)$ into ST(0).
FLDLG2	Load $\log_{10}(2)$	This instruction loads $\log_{10}(2)$ into ST(0).
FLDLN2	Load $\log_e(2)$	This instruction loads $\log_e(2)$ into ST(0).
Control		
FINIT/FNINIT	Initialize processor	This instruction accomplishes a hardware reset of the 8087.
FDISI/FNDISI	Disable interrupts	This instruction prevents the 8087 from issuing an interrupt request.

TABLE 5.11 (*Concluded*)

Instruction	Purpose	Comments
FENI/FNENI	Enable interrupts	This instruction is the reverse of FDISI and clears the interrupt mask in the control word.
FLDCW source	Load control word	This instruction replaces the current control word with the word defined by the source operand.
FSTCW/FNSTCW destination	Store control word	This instruction writes the current control word to the memory location defined by destination.
FSTSW/FNSTSW destination	Store status word	This instruction writes the current status word to the memory location defined by destination.
FCLEX/FNCLEX	Clear exceptions	Clears all exception flags, the interrupt request and busy flag.
FSTENV/FNSTENV destination	Store environment	Writes the basic status and exception pointers to the memory location defined by destination.
FLDENV source	Load environment	Reloads the 8087 environment from the memory area defined by the source.
FSAVE/FNSAVE destination	Save state	Writes the environment and register stack to the memory location specified by the destination operand.
FRSTOR source	Restore state	Reloads the 8087 from the source operand.
FINCSTP	Increment stack pointer	Adds 1 to the stack pointer.
FFREE destination	Free register	Changes the destination's tag to empty.
FDECSTP	Decrement stack pointer	Subtracts 1 from the stack pointer.
FNOP	No operation	Causes no operation.
FWAIT	Wait instruction	Causes the 8088 to wait until the current 8087 instruction is complete before the 8088 executes another instruction.

the IBM Macro Assembler version 2.00. These instructions are self-explanatory based on the table. The compare operation is implicit to C0 and C3 as follows:

C3	C0	Condition
0	0	ST greater than the source
0	1	ST less than the source
1	0	ST equal to the source
1	1	Operands cannot be compared

In Section 5.3, we will consider explicit examples of the Macro Assembler programming, and programming the coprocessor will be treated at that time.

C and Assembly Language   Chap. 5

5.2 INTERFACING C AND ASSEMBLY LANGUAGE

We have previously emphasized that this book only considers assembler programming within the context of an interface to the C language. We do not address the general topic of Macro Assembler programming in a stand-alone environment. There are several advantages to dealing with assembly language at this level. First, any external interfaces to the keyboard, disks, and other peripherals (we exclude the display for illustrative purposes) can be accomplished via C code using standard I/O. Second, computation-intensive code can be implemented using the C language, where a much more symbolic (abstract) approach is possible, unless such code becomes time sensitive.

Why, then, do we bother with assembly language at all? There are two areas of interest that can employ assembly language programming in useful fashion in the C language:

1. Special-purpose hardware adapter interfacing: here the user needs to interface a possibly unique hardware feature,
2. Time-sensitive code: where sequential processing dictates that computations or actions must be performed within a fixed time period before control transfers to a second objective.

Examples of these two areas are presented in Chapter 6. The first case is illustrated with an example that includes the interface of an analog-to-digital (A/D) converter. In this case, the A/D registers are of word length, and C I/O is accomplished via two special-purpose (but simple) assembly language routines that transfer word data (versus byte data) between the adapter and the microcomputer ports. A second example addresses time-sensitive coding.

We illustrate a communications program that handles 1200-baud I/O. This program is written entirely in C, but demonstrates some limitations because of the C implementation. Basically, when communicating at 1200 baud, a problem arises if the CPU must scroll the screen (IBM PC AT). The roughly 2000-character block representing the display map must be shifted prior to output if a scroll operation is to occur. This shift must take place between receipt of consecutive symbols when the bottom of the screen is reached. The solution arrived at in Chapter 7 was proposed by Lafore [10] and simply avoids scrolling, with the continuation occurring by jumping to the top of the screen and "writing over" old text. Clearly, this code is time sensitive, and an appropriately implemented assembly language routine using, for example, direct memory access (DMA) would allow scrolling in this environment.

With these thoughts in mind, we consider the methodology needed to link C programs with assembly language routines. In keeping with a modular approach, the specific assembler entities to be used will be procedures with a NEAR attribute.

5.2.1 Passing Parameters

To receive values from C language functions or to pass values to C functions, the assembly language modules must follow C rules. Arguments are passed to assembly language routines by pushing the value of these arguments onto the stack. The order of the arguments determines where they are located on the stack: the first argument is pushed last, resides on the stack top going into the assembly language routine, and the last argument is pushed first.

The space occupied on the stack is as follows:

1. Word (16 bits): char, short, int, signed char, signed short, signed int, unsigned char, unsigned short, or unsigned int
2. Double word (32 bits): long or unsigned long
3. Quad word (64 bits): float (converted to double) and double

Note that normally the char type arguments are sign extended to int type. (If the /J option in the Microsoft C compiler is used, this extension is zero.) In the small-memory model used in this text, all pointers are passed as word-length variables (16 bit). These pointers are NEAR and only offset values are passed.

The C language return convention applied to the IBM microcomputers is as follows [where the location in the assembler program is specified for the return() operation]:

1. AX: char, short, int, signed char, signed short, signed int, unsigned char, unsigned short, unsigned int, and NEAR pointer
2. High-order word DX; low-order word AX: long and unsigned long
3. Address in AX; value constant or static/global: struct, union, float, or double
4. Segment DX; offset AX: FAR pointer

We will see that when a proper assembler template is set up (next section) the first variable input to an assembly language routine by a calling C function occurs at the fifth byte location from the stack top for a NEAR call, which is the type of call used in this book (the small compiler). Similarly, all return values will be passed via AX or DX and AX.

5.2.2 The Assembler Template

Earlier we saw an example of a C function translated to assembly language (Figure 5.1a and b). The form of this example suggests a basic structure or template:

```
TITLE...
;
; DESCRIPTION...
;
_DATA1     SEGMENT BYTE PUBLIC 'DATA'
           PUBLIC _VAR1,...
_VAR1      ...
_DATA1     ENDS
;
_TEXT      SEGMENT BYTE PUBLIC 'CODE'
           ASSUME CS:_TEXT,DS:_DATA1
           PUBLIC _Function
```

```
_Function PROC    NEAR
          PUSH BP              ;Same caller's frame pointer
          MOV BP,SP            ;frame ptr to old BP
          SUB SP,10            ;allocate lcl var space
          PUSH BX
          PUSH CX
          PUSH DX
          PUSH SI
          PUSH DI
                               ;
          PUSH DS
          MOV AX,SEG DATA1
          MOV DS,AX
          ...
          (main body)
          ...
          MOV AX,...
          POP DS
          POP DI
          POP SI
          POP DX
          POP CX
          POP BX
          MOV SP,BP
          POP BP
          RET
_Function ENDP
_TEXT     ENDS
          END
```

To interpret this template, consider first the segment definitions. Two segments are defined: __TEXT and __DATA1, the code segment and data segment, respectively. The data segment is different than __DATA, which is the default data segment. This is because any assembler routine called by the C compiler will have all its parameters passed via the stack. Hence, there is no need to keep the "old" data segment during execution of the assembly language routine. A new data segment with locally defined variables can be employed, if needed. We have indicated that a variable, __VAR1, is defined PUBLIC in this segment. Note that the underline must precede the name so that the linker recognizes this as a variable quantity.

The code segment __TEXT contains the ASSUME statement, which defines the segment registers. A procedure

```
_Function
```

has been defined and this name is generic. The user should substitute an appropriate procedure name at this point. This function must be PUBLIC so that it can be called externally. Upon entry to the procedure, a return address will be pushed on the stack. This address is an offset (2 bytes) for NEAR calls, hence, for the small model the stack frame initially has 2 bytes on it. After the call, the old calling routine has its frame pointer in the BP register. This pointer comprises the linkage for moving from frame to frame. The template calls for pushing this address on the stack also. Thus, 4 bytes now reside on the stack (NEAR call). The stack pointer now contains the new frame pointer, which is loaded into BP and space allocated on the stack by setting the stack pointer advanced 10 bytes. All these steps are accomplished with the following code

```
PUSH BP
MOV BP,SP
SUB SP,10
```

Next, the BX, CX, DX, SI, and DI registers are pushed on the stack. Finally, the old data segment address is saved on the stack and a new data segment address for __DATA1 loaded into DS.

At this point the parameters passed to the assembly language routine reside *starting* at [BP + 4] because a return address and a frame pointer have been loaded between them and the current position of BP. Assuming all parameters are of type int, they will reference as [BP+4], [BP+6], [BP+8], . . . and so forth. Clearly, other data types will occupy space accordingly.

After the assembly language routine has completed its intermediate function, the return value is loaded into AX (indicated here by the MOV AX, . . . instruction) or DX and AX. Then all registers are popped and the frame pointer to the caller's frame restored.

This then completes the definition of an appropriate assembler template. It will be useful to note that for the compact, large, and huge memory models, FAR calls are accomplished and segment addresses come into play.

5.2.3 C Compiler Optimization

We have already mentioned C compiler optimization, but it is useful to consider this aspect of programming again in light of the intervening discussion. In the example of Figure 5.1b, the parameter x resides on the stack at address [bp + 4]. Consider the two instructions

```
mul ax
imul WORD PTR [bp+4]
```

The former requires 21 clock cycles, while the latter requires 24 clock cycles, an increase of 14.3% in processing time. Compare instructions, for example, increase by 100% when referencing memory rather than registers. Move instructions that involve movement of memory operands to registers, and vice versa, typically increase by 50% over register-to-register moves. These are but a few instruction types, and the others behave in similar fashion; memory operand instructions take longer.

It is clear that in small programs very little savings can be effected. In large programs, however, where local function variables are used repeatedly, many memory operand references can occur for the same operand, and loading this operand in a register with appropriate instruction organization can facilitate execution speed. Another example would be filling the screen using DMA techniques. The access from C would involve, as we have seen, overhead code on each reference to memory. In assembly language, for example, if a stack buffer area were reserved for the screen (text mode) called buffer1, the following minimal instruction sequence would completely fill the screen in roughly 28,000 clock cycles (the number in parentheses indicates the approximate number of clock cycles needed to execute the instruction):

```
        ...
        MOV SI,0                ;Index
        MOV CX,2000             ;Loop count
        MOV AX,B800H            ;Segment address
        MOV ES,AX               ;Extra segment register
LOOP1:
        MOV AL,[BP+N+SI]        ;(5) N=buffer1 stack offset
        MOV ES:[SI],AL          ;(3) Output to screen
        INC SI                  ;(2) Increase index
        LOOP LOOP1              ;(4) Loop using CX
        ...
```

Here the buffer1 address on the stack is assumed to start at [BP+N], where N is known, and the stack buffer1 area is increased to accommodate 2000 characters. For 1200-baud communications, there are roughly 4400 clock cycles at the IBM PC clock rate and roughly 6900 clock cycles at the IBM AT clock rate between symbols. Hence, for the AT, for example, approximately four symbol periods are required to fill the screen using code such as the preceding. Some added logic of the form

```
        ...
        CMP CX,1500             ;1st quarter boundary
        JNE ELSE1
            CALL READ           ;read symbol
ELSE1:
        CMP CX,1000             ;2nd quarter boundary
        JNE ELSE2
            CALL READ           ;read symbol
            JMP CONT1
ELSE2:
        CMP CX,500              ;3rd quarter boundary
        JNE CONT1
            CALL READ           ;read symbol
CONT1:
        ...
```

would allow the screen to be filled at intervals of one-fourth of a buffer, between symbols. Clearly, the procedure READ would need to fill a second buffer (double buffering) simultaneously. These are but a few examples of how accessing assembly language directly, instead of using compiler-generated code, can lead to faster processing and the accomplishment of tasks not ordinarily feasible with C.

5.3 C AND ASSEMBLER

In Chapter 6, a real need for mixed programming is demonstrated with the communications program and scrolling the screen display. Also, the A/D converter example illustrates the need for flexibility in being able to call assembly language routines to provide special-purpose hardware I/O (in this case simple word I/O is desired versus the byte I/O routines provided with the standard C library).

The purpose of this section is to present several examples of the C and assembler interface. These examples are applied to simple illustrations of how such programming is accomplished. We examine a two-dimensional (2D) log plot and then a bar chart. The graphics routines typically call assembly language functions at the lower levels. These routines can be compared with their C language counterparts for ease in understanding the assembly language implementation.

Much of the graphics programming in this textbook is tailored to specific applications, with the plot routines called as part of the overall program implementation. An alternative school of thought suggests that applications should generate general-purpose data files (containing records consisting of an x-value and a y-value, for example) which can then be graphed using an overall general-purpose plot package. Intermediate to the two programs would be storage of the data file on disk, where it can be easily accessed for plotting. This section presents such general-purpose graphics for 2D geometries.

Log plots. It will be useful to illustrate 2D graphics using assembly language routines with a simple logarithmic graph (we have already seen representative 2D graphics for linear plots). Consider the sum

$$1 + x + x^2 + x^3 + \cdots + x^n + \cdots = \frac{1}{1-x} \tag{5.1}$$

This is the usual result for a geometric series summed over all terms with the assumption $x < 1.0$, in order to achieve the closed form solution. Figure 5.2 presents the main calling function for generating values of the geometric sum between 0 and 1.0. The function main() calls geom_series(), which loads the sum into an array, y[ ], for the values x[ ]. This latter function then calls a general-purpose disk write routine, diskwt(), which takes as a parameter the count of array values (in this case the count equals 98). Figure 5.3 contains this general-purpose disk write routine. The routine is similar to diskrd(), contained in Figure 3.4c, except it is a function used to write two arrays to disk and is general purpose.

The program that plots these data is illustrated in Figure 5.4. This program calls two routines: log_plot() and plotterm(). Plotterm() is familiar, and log_plt() is depicted in Figure 5.5. This latter function calls diskrd() [a new general-purpose function used to read a diskwt() file from disk], sets up new scaled minimum and maximum values for y[ ], and plots the result. In the case of the geometric sum, the sum is plotted on log scales when input to log-plot(). Figure 5.6 contains diskrd() and Figure 5.7 the function box_log(), which generates the box and grid lines for the log plot.

So far the reader has been exposed to C programs only. In Figures 5.8 through 5.12, however, low-level assembly language counterparts for the screen I/O routines

```
/* Main calling program for geometric series */

float x[100],y[100];                              /* 2D arrays */

main()
      {
      geom_series();                              /* generate series */
      }

/* Function to generate series */

geom_series()
      {
      extern float x[],y[];
      float inc = .01;
      int n,NCOUNT;

      x[0] = 0;                                   /* start series */
      x[1] = inc;                                 /* 1st iteration */
      for(n = 1;n <= 98;n++)
         {
         y[n] = 1./(1. - x[n]);                   /* summed series */
         x[n+1] = x[n] + inc;                     /* independent var */
         }
      NCOUNT = 98;                                /* limit pts plotted */

      diskwt(NCOUNT);                             /* disk write */
      }
```

Figure 5.2 Main calling program for generating geometric sum.

```
/* This function writes two arrays, x & y, to disk */

#include <stdio.h>

diskwt(NCOUNT)
      int NCOUNT;                                 /* Array length */
      {
      int n,check;
      FILE *outfile;
      char FN1[81];
      extern float x[],y[];                       /* Arrays output */

      printf("Input database filename \n");
      gets(FN1);                                  /* input filename */

      if((outfile = fopen(FN1,"w")) == NULL)
         {
         printf("Output file failure ");
         exit(1);
         }
      fprintf(outfile,"%d ",NCOUNT);
      for(n = 1;n <= NCOUNT;n++)                   /* array start = 1 */
         fprintf(outfile,"%f %f ",x[n],y[n]);      /* output arrays */
      if((check = fclose(outfile)) != 0)
         {
         printf("Error on output file close ");
         exit(1);
         }
      }
```

Figure 5.3 General-purpose disk write routine.

```
/* Function to drive log-plot */

#include <stdio.h>
#include <conio.h>

float x[100],y[100],xx[100],yy[100];              /* data and screen */
char buffer[90];                                  /* plot title */
char *result;

main()
        {
        printf("Input title ");
        *buffer = 90;                             /* 1st element */
        result = cgets(buffer);

        log_plot();
        plotterm();
        }
```

Figure 5.4 Logarithmic plotting function (calling program).

are presented. These routines illustrate in simple fashion the form assembly language routines must take to interface to the C code. [The functions SCRCL(), SC320(), SC80(), KEYDEL(), and WRDOT() are illustrated in assembly language form.] These functions have no added intrinsic value based on an assembly language development because the 2D static graphics I/O presented is neither time critical nor hardware intensive and can just as easily be written in C. They do illustrate, however, the mechanics of the C and assembly language interface. Figure 5.13 indicates the annotated output for the general-purpose log plot routine with the geometric sum data used as input. Functions such as PLTBUF(), linev(), and lineh() are employed in their usual form (see Appendix C).

The routines used in this program are as follows:

main()-generate series	(Figure 5.2)
geom_series()	(Figure 5.2)
diskwt()	(Figure 5.3)
main()-logplot	(Figure 5.4)
log_plot()	(Figure 5.5)
plotterm()	(Figure 2.8d)
diskrd()	(Figure 5.6)
box_log()	(Figure 5.7)
PLTBUF()	(Figure 2.8c)
plotpoint()	(Figure 2.8d)
SCRCL()-asm	(Figure 5.8)
SC320()-asm	(Figure 5.9)
SC80()-asm	(Figure 5.12)
WRDOT()-asm	(Figure 5.10)
KEYDEL()-asm	(Figure 5.11)

```
/* Function to create log plot */

#include <dos.h>
#include <math.h>
#include <stdio.h>
#include <conio.h>

log_plot()
        {
        extern float x[],y[],xx[],yy[];                /* Data arrays */
        int N,n,yy1;
        float min,max,yy11,scale;
        double x1,y1;

        N = diskrd();                                  /* Read data disk */

                                                       /* max/min */
        max = -1.e14;
        min = 1.e14;
        for(n = 1;n <= N;n++)                           /* determine from y */
            {
            if(max < y[n])
                max = y[n];
            if(min > y[n])
                min = y[n];
            }

        printf("max = %f ,min = %f \n",max,min);
        printf("Input adjusted max\n");                /* input new max/min */
        scanf("%f",&max);
        printf("Input adjusted min\n");
        scanf("%f",&min);

        box_log();                                     /* Draw box-grids */
        PLTBUF(0,0);                                   /* Write title */

                                                       /* Scale [0,100] */
        scale = 100/(max - min);
        for(n = 1;n <= N;n++)
            {
            x1 = (double)(scale*y[n]);                 /* start y log */
            if((y[n]>min) && (y[n]<max))
                {
                y1 = log10(x1);                        /* calculate y log */
                yy11 = (float)(y1);
                yy1 = (int)(175. - yy11*75.);          /* scaled for graph */
                }
            else
                yy1 = 0.;                              /* out of range */
            xx[n] = 25. + (n - 1)*(250./N);            /* x scale */
            yy[n] = yy1;
            }

        for(n = 1;n <= (N - 1);n++)                     /* plot in range pts */
            {
            if((y[n]>=min) && (y[n+1]>=min) && (y[n]<=max) && (y[n+1]<=max))
                plotpoint(xx[n],xx[n+1],yy[n],yy[n+1]);
            }
        }
```

Figure 5.5 Logarithmic plotting function (driver).

```
/* Function to read arrays x & y from disk */

#include <stdio.h>

diskrd()
     {
     int n,check,counter;
     FILE *infile;
     char FN2[81];
     extern float x[],y[];                        /* x & y points */

     printf("Input read database filename \n");
     gets(FN2);                                   /* input filename */

     if((infile = fopen(FN2,"r")) == NULL)
          {
          printf("Input file failure ");
          exit(1);
          }
     fscanf(infile,"%d ",&counter);               /* input # points */
     for(n = 1;n <= counter;n++)
          fscanf(infile,"%f %f ",&x[n],&y[n]);    /* input points */
     if((check = fclose(infile)) != 0)
          {
          printf("Error in input file close ");
          exit(1);
          }
     for(n = 1;n <= counter;n++)
          printf("%f %f ",x[n],y[n]);             /* point pairs */
     return(counter);
     }
```

Figure 5.6 General-purpose disk read routine.

```
bbox()                          (Figure A.10)
lineu()                         (Figure 2.8e)
lineh()                         (Figure 2.8e)
```

Bar chart.   In the geometric series example, we saw some relatively simple applications of assembly language in the C environment. The assembler template was delineated and the interface described in terms of the segment names required by the C compiler (Microsoft). Also, the stack organization was defined for parameter passing. The topic to be addressed at this point is plotting bar graphs with the bar generated by a general-purpose assembly language routine. This serves as another illustration of both how to write assembly language routines for use by C programs and the C assembly language interface.

Figure 5.14 is a small calling program that establishes three elements in the array value[]. This array is treated as global, so it loads in the c_common data segment and not on the stack. A variable, N, is used to set the limit for the number of elements of value[] that are to be graphed (each element of value[] that is defined will correspond to a single bar in the bar chart). We see that three bars will be generated for Figure 5.14. The graph setup function is bar_graph(), presented in Figure 5.15, and this is called from main().

In bar_graph(), N is treated as a formal parameter defining the number of bars. First, box limits are defined, a minimum and maximum determined, and the spacing along the x-axis for the bars is determined. Next, the screen is cleared,

```
/* Function to draw log box */

#include <math.h>
#include <dos.h>

box_log()
        {
        int xxbeg,xxend,yybeg,yyend;
        int n,yy1;
        float yy11;
        double x1,y1;

        xxbeg = 25;                                     /* box limits */
        xxend = 275;
        yybeg = 25;
        yyend = 175;

        SCRCL();                                        /* clear screen */
        SC320();                                        /* 320 x 200 mode */

        bbox(xxbeg,xxend,yybeg,yyend);                  /* standard box */

        linev(75,25,175);                               /* Vertical grids */
        linev(125,25,175);
        linev(175,25,175);
        linev(225,25,175);

                                                        /* 2 cycle log */
        for(n = 2;n <= 10;n++)
            {
            x1 = (double)(n);
            y1 = log10(x1);                             /* 1st y-grids */
            yy11 = (float)(y1);
            yy1 = (int)(175. - yy11*75.);               /* scaled point */
            lineh(yy1,25,275);
            }
        for(n = 20;n <= 100;n = n + 10)
            {
            x1 = (double)(n);
            y1 = log10(x1);                             /* 2nd y-grids */
            yy11 = (float)(y1);
            yy1 = (int)(175. - yy11*75.);               /* scaled point */
            lineh(yy1,25,275);
            }
        }
```

Figure 5.7 Routine for drawing box and grid lines on logarithmic plot.

320 × 200 mode set, and the bars plotted using a call to bar(), the assembly
language procedure appearing in Figure 5.16. It was necessary to scale the array
elements for value[] to match the desired screen coordinates. The form of the call
to bar() is

```
bar (xx,yy,xxscale,yyend)
```

where

        xx   start *x*-position for the bar
        yy   maximum *y*-value for the
                 bar

```
xxscale    width of bar
  yyend    minimum y-value for the
           bar
```

The routine appearing in Figure 5.16 generates the bar in the bar graphs. When bar( ) is called in the form shown, the stack is loaded as follows (once BP is set equal to the frame pointer, SP): [BP + 4] = xx-position, and [BP + 10] = yyend-position. A locally defined data segment, __DATA1, is developed for the procedure in Figure 5.16. The reader may wonder what happens to the old data segment __DATA, which is common to all the basic compiler routines via DGROUP. This routine still exists in memory, but the locally defined procedure __BAR does not make use of any variables in __DATA. Hence, this routine [bar( )] can define its own local variables in a separate data segment. The word variables __X, __Y, __XE, __XB, __YE, and __YB are all defined in __DATA1 and are not initialized (the ? symbol is used to indicate this condition).

```
PAGE 40,132
TITLE SCRCL - SCREEN CLEAR FOR CALL FROM "C"
;
;        DESCRIPTION: This routine clears the screen when called
;        from a C program.  The stack is preserved.
;
_TEXT    SEGMENT BYTE PUBLIC 'CODE'
         ASSUME CS:_TEXT
         PUBLIC _SCRCL
_SCRCL   PROC    NEAR

BEGIN1:  PUSH BP                      ;
         MOV BP,SP                    ;save caller's frame pointer
         SUB SP,8                     ;frame pointer to old BP
         PUSH DI                      ;allocate local variable on stack
         PUSH SI
         PUSH AX
         PUSH BX
         PUSH CX
         PUSH DX

         MOV AH,6                     ;
         MOV AL,0                     ;Scroll active page up
         MOV CX,0                     ;Blanks entire page
         MOV DH,23                    ;(CH,CL)=(row,column) up left
         MOV DL,79                    ;Row lower right
         MOV BH,7                     ;Column lower right
         INT 10H                      ;Blank attribute
                                      ;
         POP DX
         POP CX
         POP BX
         POP AX
         POP SI
         POP DI
         MOV SP,BP
         POP BP
                                      ;
         RET
                                      ;
_SCRCL   ENDP
_TEXT    ENDS
         END
```

Figure 5.8. Assembly language procedure to clear screen.

```
PAGE 40,132
TITLE SC320 - ROUTINE TO SET 320 X 200 GRAPHICS MODE
;
;         DESCRIPTION: Sets the 320 x 200 graphics mode
;
_TEXT    SEGMENT BYTE PUBLIC 'CODE'
         ASSUME CS:_TEXT
         PUBLIC _SC320
_SC320   PROC    NEAR
                                          ;
         PUSH BP                          ;save caller's frame pointer
         MOV BP,SP                        ;frame pointer to old BP
         SUB SP,8                         ;allocate local variable space
         PUSH DI
         PUSH SI
         PUSH AX
         PUSH BX
         PUSH CX
         PUSH DX

         MOV AH,0                         ;
         MOV AL,5                         ;Set mode
         INT 10H                          ;320 x 200 graphics mode
                                          ;Interrupt
         POP DX                           ;
         POP CX
         POP BX
         POP AX
         POP SI
         POP DI
         MOV SP,BP
         POP BP
                                          ;
         RET
_SC320   ENDP
_TEXT    ENDS
         END
```

Figure 5.9   Assembly language procedure to set 320 × 200 mode.

Next, __TEXT is presented and the data segment register DS defined using __DATA1. Finally, __BAR is developed. This procedure begins with the usual template assignments and the segment address for __DATA1 loaded into DS. The parameter values are then placed in x-begin (__XB), x-end (__XE), where the bar width is added to __XB, y-begin (__YB), and y-end (__YE). Note that many loads require move instructions of the form

```
MOV general purpose register1, memory-operand1
MOV memory-operand2, general purpose register1
```

As, for example,

```
MOV AX,[BP+4]
MOV _XB,AX
```

This is because

```
MOV _XB,[BP+4]
```

consists of a direct memory-to-memory move, which is not allowed.

```
PAGE 40,132
TITLE WRDOT - ROUTINE TO WRITE DOT
;
;        DESCRIPTION: This routine writes a dot at the row = [BP+4] and
;        column = [BP+6] since the function call is NEAR.
;
_TEXT   SEGMENT BYTE PUBLIC 'CODE'
        ASSUME CS:_TEXT
        PUBLIC _WRDOT
_WRDOT  PROC   NEAR
                                                    ;
        PUSH BP                             ;save caller's frame pointer
        MOV BP,SP                           ;frame pointer to old BP
        SUB SP,8                            ;allocate local variable space
        PUSH DI
        PUSH SI
        PUSH AX
        PUSH BX
        PUSH CX
        PUSH DX
                                                    ;
        MOV DX,[BP+4]                       ;Row value
        MOV CX,[BP+6]                       ;Column value
        MOV AL,1                            ;Attribute 1
        MOV AH,12                           ;Write dot
        INT 10H                             ;Interrupt
                                                    ;
        POP DX
        POP CX
        POP BX
        POP AX
        POP SI
        POP DI
        MOV SP,BP
        POP BP
                                                    ;
        RET
                                                    ;
_WRDOT  ENDP
_TEXT   ENDS
        END
```

Figure 5.10   Assembly language procedure to write dot.

Since the bar already has the bottom horizontal line in place (the box), only a top horizontal line need be drawn. This is accomplished using __LINEHH. The procedure __LINEHH is NEAR and requires a y-start value, __Y. Prior to the call to __LINEHH, __Y must be loaded (in this case with __YB). Similarly, two vertical lines must be drawn to demarcate the bar. One line appears at x-position __XB, and the second at x-position __XE. Both extend from __YB to __YE and are drawn using the procedure __LINEVV. Before calling __LINEVV, the x-start value must be passed as __X. Both __LINEHH and __LINEVV call INT 10H with AH=12, the write dot mode. This write occurs in a loop of the form (for__LINEVV)

```
D02:     ...
         MOV BX,DX
         SUB BX,_YE
         JNE D02
         ...
```

```
PAGE 40,132
TITLE KEYDEL - KEYBOARD DELAY
;
;           DESCRIPTION: This routine waits for a keyboard interrupt
;           to continue the processing.
;
_TEXT    SEGMENT BYTE PUBLIC 'CODE'
         ASSUME CS:_TEXT
         PUBLIC _KEYDEL
_KEYDEL PROC     NEAR

         PUSH BP                         ;
         MOV BP,SP                       ;Save caller's frame pointer
         SUB SP,8                        ;Frame pointer to old BP
         PUSH DI                         ;Allocate local variable space
         PUSH SI
         PUSH AX
         PUSH BX
         PUSH CX
         PUSH DX

         MOV AH,0                        ;
         INT 16H                         ;Keyboard interrupt
                                         ;Wait for keystroke to continue
                                         ;
         POP DX
         POP CX
         POP BX
         POP AX
         POP SI
         POP DI
         MOV SP,BP
         POP BP

         RET                             ;
_KEYDEL ENDP
_TEXT    ENDS
         END
```

Figure 5.11 Assembly language procedure to generate keyboard delay.

Here the subtraction sets the flags, and when __YB, the value in DX, is equal to __YE, the loop terminates. Figure 5.17 presents the annotated output for the program in this example. Note that a maximum and minimum of 500 and 0, respectively, were input following the prompt from bar__graph( ).

Compound interest.   This example is intended to illustrate coprocessor programming. It is somewhat artificial in that it is not necessary (and, in fact, simpler) to program the example directly in C, but it serves to illustrate how such coprocessor programming is accomplished. Furthermore, although it is beyond the scope of this text, an excellent candidate for implementation in assembler, using the coprocessor, is the FFT routine developed in Appendix A. This routine is very computation intensive, and use of time-critical coprocessor assembly language code would greatly enhance the execution speed of this routine.

The function to be calculated is given by

$$A_n = P \left(\frac{1 + R}{Q} \right)^{NQ} \tag{5.2}$$

```
PAGE 40,132
TITLE SC80 - ROUTINE TO SET 80 X 25 ALPHA MODE
;
;        DESCRIPTION: Calls interrupt to set 80 x 25 alpha mode
;
_TEXT    SEGMENT BYTE PUBLIC 'CODE'
         ASSUME CS:_TEXT
         PUBLIC _SC80
_SC80    PROC    NEAR
                                            ;
         PUSH BP                            ;Save caller's frame pointer
         MOV BP,SP                          ;Frame pointer to old BP
         SUB SP,8                           ;Allocate local variable space
         PUSH DI
         PUSH SI
         PUSH AX
         PUSH BX
         PUSH CX
         PUSH DX
                                            ;
         MOV AH,0                           ;Set mode
         MOV AL,2                           ;80 x 24 alpha B/W mode
         INT 10H                            ;Interrupt
                                            ;
         POP DX
         POP CX
         POP BX
         POP AX
         POP SI
         POP DI
         MOV SP,BP
         POP BP
                                            ;
         RET
_SC80    ENDP
_TEXT    ENDS
         END
```

Figure 5.12   Assembly language procedure to set 80×25 alpha mode.

where

R = annual interest rate paid
P = principal
Q = number of times compounded annually
N = total number of years compounded

Figure 5.18 is the main calling program, which illustrates the calculation of A_n, the total accumulated investment. The program generates compounded results assuming an investment length of 5, 10, 15, 20, 25, 30, 35, and 40 years and plots a bar graph of the result. The eight values plotted in this example (M1=8) require a call to POWW() to generate the term in parentheses $(1 + R/Q)$, raised to a power, NQ. This power calculation routine appears in Figure 5.19 and is written in assembly language. The routine has two parameters passed via the stack: [BP + 4] = (1 + R/Q) and [BP + 6] = NQ.

Upon entry to the module POWW.ASM, the .8087 pseudo-op is encountered, which informs the assembler that coprocessor instructions are present in the module. Again, variables local to __POWW are defined in a segment, __DATA1. Several

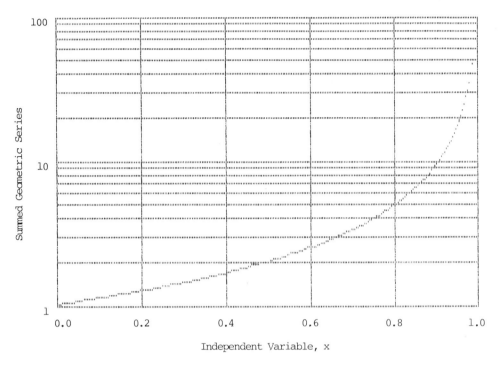

Figure 5.13 Annotated output for geometric sum data.

```
/* Function to check bar graph */

float value[10];

main()
      {
      int N;

      value[1] = 100.;
      value[2] = 200.;
      value[3] = 300.;

      N = 3;                                        /* # points */

      bar_graph(N);
      plotterm();
      }
```

Figure 5.14 Calling program for checking bar chart output.

```
/* Function to create bar graph */

#include <stdio.h>

bar_graph(N)
        int N;                                          /* # bars */
        {
        int xxbeg,xxend,yybeg,yyend;
        int n,NN,xx,yy,xxscale;
        extern float value[];                           /* bar array */
        float max,min,yscale,xscale;
        extern bar();

                                                        /* box limits */
        xxbeg = 25;
        xxend = 275;
        yybeg = 25;
        yyend = 175;

        max = -1.e4;                                    /* purposely out */
        min = 1.e4;

        for(n = 1;n <= N;n++)                            /* determine min/max */
            {
            if(value[n] > max)
                max = value[n];
            if(value[n] < min)
                min = value[n];
            }
                                                        /* New min/max */
        printf("max = %f min = %f \n",max,min);
        printf("Input adjusted max \n");
        scanf("%f",&max);
        printf("Input adjusted min \n");
        scanf("%f",&min);
        yscale = 150./(max-min);                        /* screen scale */

        NN = 2*N + 1;                                   /* x spacing count */
        xscale = (xxend-xxbeg)/(float)(NN);
        xxscale = (int)(xscale);

        SCRCL();                                        /* Screen clear */
        SC320();                                        /* 320 x 200 mode */
        bbox(xxbeg,xxend,yybeg,yyend);                  /* standard box */

        for(n = 1;n <= N;n++)
            {
            yy = (int)(yyend - yscale*value[n]);        /* screen y value */
            xx = (int)(xxbeg + (2*n - 1)*xscale);       /* screen x value */
            bar(xx,yy,xxscale,yyend);                   /* plot bar */
            }
        }
```

Figure 5.15 Bar chart setup function.

of these variables are double word variables (DD), in order to take advantage of the coprocessor accuracy, and these span 4 bytes. Once in __POWW, the usual template operations occur and then the coprocessor is initialized.

Remember that all coprocessor operations occur via the internal stack: ST(0), ST(1), . . . , ST(7). Hence, even though this stack is not explicitly referenced, it is understood to be in place. Following FINIT, for example, the variable __XXX (a word variable) is loaded with the first parameter value, $(1 + R/Q)$. This is then placed on the coprocessor stack using

```
FILD _XXX
```

```
PAGE 50,132
TITLE BAR - ROUTINE TO GENERATE BAR (BAR.ASM)
;
;           DESCRIPTION: This assembly language routine
;           generates a bar for graphics 320 x 200 charts.
;
_DATA1  SEGMENT BYTE PUBLIC 'DATA'
        PUBLIC  _X,_Y,_XE,_XB,_YE,_YB
_X      DW      ?                       ;dummy variable
_Y      DW      ?                       ;dummy variable
_XE     DW      ?                       ;x-end
_XB     DW      ?                       ;x-begin
_YE     DW      ?                       ;y-end
_YB     DW      ?                       ;y-begin
_DATA1  ENDS
;
_TEXT   SEGMENT BYTE PUBLIC 'CODE'
        ASSUME  CS:_TEXT,DS:_DATA1
        PUBLIC  _BAR
_BAR    PROC    NEAR
                                        ;
        PUSH BP                         ;Save caller's frame ptr
        MOV BP,SP                       ;Frame ptr to old BP
        SUB SP,10                       ;Allocate lclvar space
                                        ;
        PUSH BX
        PUSH CX
        PUSH DX
        PUSH SI
        PUSH DI
                                        ;
        PUSH DS                         ;Save old data seg addr
        MOV AX,SEG _DATA1               ;New data seg
        MOV DS,AX
                                        ;
        MOV AX,[BP+4]                   ;xx
        MOV _XB,AX                      ;load x value-begin
        ADD AX,[BP+8]                   ;increment by bar width
        MOV _XE,AX                      ;load 2nd x value-end
        MOV AX,[BP+6]                   ;ymax value
        MOV _YB,AX                      ;load y value-begin
        MOV AX,[BP+10]                  ;lower y value
        MOV _YE,AX                      ;load y value-end

                                        ;Generate bar
                                        ;
                                        ;Horizontal line
        MOV AX,_YB                      ;y axis position
        MOV _Y,AX
        CALL _LINEHH
                                        ;Vertical lines
        MOV AX,_XB                      ;x axis position(1)
        MOV _X,AX
        CALL _LINEVV
        MOV AX,_XE                      ;x axis position(2)
        MOV _X,AX
        CALL _LINEVV
                                        ;
        POP DS
        POP DI
        POP SI
        POP DX
        POP CX
        POP BX
```

Figure 5.16 Assembly language procedure for generating the bar.

```
                MOV SP,BP
                POP BP
                RET
_BAR    ENDP
;
_LINEHH PROC    NEAR
                MOV DX,_Y                       ;y value
                MOV CX,_XB                      ;start x value
DO1:
                MOV AH,12                       ;Write dot
                MOV AL,1                        ;Attribute 1
                INT 10H
                ADD CX,1                        ;Increment x value
                MOV BX,CX                       ;Setup compare
                SUB BX,_XE                      ;Set flags for end
                JNE DO1
                RET
_LINEHH ENDP
 ;
_LINEVV PROC    NEAR
                MOV CX,_X                       ;x value
                MOV DX,_YB                      ;y start value
DO2:
                MOV AH,12                       ;Write dot
                MOV AL,1                        ;Attribute 1
                INT 10H
                ADD DX,1                        ;Increment y value
                MOV BX,DX                       ;Setup compare
                SUB BX,_YE                      ;Set flags for end
                JNE DO2
                RET
_LINEVV ENDP
                                                ;
_TEXT   ENDS
                END
```

Figure 5.16 (*Concluded*)

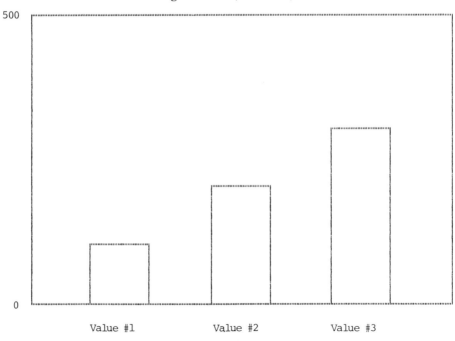

Figure 5.17 Annotated output for bar chart (check program).

254

```
/* Function to generate compound amount 5,10,15,20,25,30,35,40 years */

#include <stdio.h>

float value[10];
int year[10];

main()
    {
    float princp,interest,Q;
    int n,IFACTOR,QQ,power_rate,M1=8;
    extern int POWW();

    year[0] = 0;                                    /* Initialize */
    for(n = 1;n <= M1;n++)                          /* years compounded */
        year[n] = year[n-1] + 5;

    printf("Input principal (dollars) \n");
    scanf("%f",&princp);
    printf("Input annual interest (decimal) \n");
    scanf("%f",&interest);
    printf("Input number times annually compounded \n");
    scanf("%f",&Q);

    IFACTOR = (int)(10000.*(1. + interest/Q));      /* scale and convert */

    for(n = 1;n <= M1;n++)
        {
        QQ = (int)(year[n]*Q);                      /* Exponent */
        power_rate = POWW(IFACTOR,QQ);              /* power */
        value[n] = princp*power_rate/100.;          /* compounded amt */
        }

    bar_graph(M1);                                  /* Bar graph */
    plotterm();                                     /* Terminate plot */
    }
```

Figure 5.18 Main calling program for generating accumulated principal and interest.

Here the value is loaded into ST [ST(0)]. Note that all transfers to the coprocessor stack do not directly involve the 8088 or 80286 registers. Next a doubleword quantity, __XX, is loaded with 10000 and this is in turn placed on the stack at ST [while pushing the previous ST value to ST(1)]. At this point ST(1), which contains $(1 + R/Q)$, is divided by ST. The result then resides in ST(1), but the stack is popped and the result moves to ST. The instruction for doing this is

```
FDIVP ST(1),ST
```

This divide was necessary because the value passed to __POWW was scaled up by 10,000 (IFACTOR) in order to be able to pass an integer value to this procedure. In the example program, this scaling limits the size of $(1 + R/Q)$, the base, that may be considered.

What is the computation to be performed using this routine? Essentially, we will calculate a quantity of the form

$$M^x$$

```
PAGE 50,132
TITLE POWW - COMPOUND INTEREST FACTOR (POWW.ASM)
;
;         DESCRIPTION: This routine calculates (1+r/q)**(nq)
;         where r = annual rate, q = compounding rate, and
;         n = # years.  The input value, 1+r/q, is in [BP+4]
;         and is scaled by 10000.  The result is returned in
;         AX scaled by 100.
;
.8087
_DATA1   SEGMENT BYTE PUBLIC 'DATA'
         PUBLIC _M,_XX,_MM1,_MM2,_MM3,_XX,_OHALF,_TTWO
_M       DD      ?
_XX      DD      ?
_XXX     DW      ?                            ;Parameter dummy
_MM1     DW      ?
_MM2     DW      ?
_MM3     DD      ?
_OHALF   DD      0.5
_TTWO    DD      2
_DATA1   ENDS
;
_TEXT    SEGMENT BYTE PUBLIC 'CODE'
         ASSUME  CS:_TEXT,DS:_DATA1
         PUBLIC  _POWW
_POWW    PROC    NEAR

         PUSH BP                        ;Save caller's frame ptr
         MOV BP,SP                      ;Frame ptr to old BP
         SUB SP,10                      ;Allocate lcl var space
                                        ;
         PUSH BX
         PUSH CX
         PUSH DX
         PUSH SI
         PUSH DI

         PUSH DS                        ;Save old seg addr
         MOV AX,SEG _DATA1              ;New data seg addr
         MOV DS,AX
                                        ;
         FINIT                          ;Initialize 80287
                                        ;
         MOV AX,[BP+4]
         MOV _XXX,AX
         FILD _XXX                      ;Load 1st parameter
         LEA BX,_XX                     ;Location _XX
         MOV AX,10000                   ;Lower divisor
         MOV DS:[BX],AX
         MOV AX,0                       ;Upper divisor
         MOV DS:[BX+2],AX
         FILD _XX                       ;10000 in ST,1st in ST(1)
         FDIVP ST(1),ST                 ;Unscaled base in ST
                                        ;
         FNSTCW _MM1                    ;Store control word
         MOV AX,0400H                   ;RC mask round downward
         OR _MM1,AX                     ;Set bit 10
         MOV AX,0F7FFH                  ;Set RC mask
         AND _MM1,AX                    ;Set bit 11 to 0
         FLDCW _MM1                     ;Reload control word
                                        ;
         MOV AX,[BP+6]
         MOV _XXX,AX
         FILD _XXX                      ;Power in ST,base in ST(1)
         FXCH
         FYL2X                          ;Power*LOG2(base) in ST
         FST ST(1)                      ;ST in ST(1)
```

Figure 5.19 Assembly language procedure for calculating accumulated interest (power calculation). Coprocessor instructions are used.

```
                    FRNDINT                     ;ST truncated to integer
                    FIST _MM3                    ;Save integer
                    FXCH
                    FSUB ST,ST(1)                ;Fraction in ST
                                                 ;
                    FLD _OHALF                   ;ST = .5,ST(1) = fraction
                    FCOM ST(1)                   ;C3C0 = (0,0) ST>ST(1) else set
                    FSTSW _MM2                    ;Load status word
                    MOV AX,4100H                 ;Mask for status word
                    AND _MM2,AX                   ;mask
                    MOV AX,0100H                 ;C3C0 mask
                    CMP _MM2,AX                   ;Compare
                    JNGE ELSE1
                        FSUBP ST(1),ST           ;Fraction in ST
                        F2XM1                    ;2**(ST)-1
                        FLD1                     ;ST = 1.0
                        FADD ST,ST(1)            ;ST = 2**fraction
                        FILD _MM3                ;Integer in ST
                        FXCH
                        FSCALE                   ;2**(fraction+integer) in ST
                        FILD _TTWO               ;ST = 2
                        FSQRT
                        FMUL ST,ST(1)            ;answer
                    JMP SHORT IF1
ELSE1:
                        FXCH                     ;Fraction in ST
                        F2XM1                    ;2**(ST)-1
                        FLD1                     ;ST = 1.0
                        FADD ST,ST(1)            ;ST = 2**fraction
                        FILD _MM3                ;Integer in ST
                        FXCH
                        FSCALE                   ;2**(fraction+integer)
IF1:
                    LEA BX,_XX
                    MOV AX,100                   ;Output scale
                    MOV DS:[BX],AX
                    MOV AX,0
                    MOV DS:[BX+2],AX
                    FILD _XX                     ;ST = 100,ST(1) = answer
                    FMULP ST(1),ST               ;Popped result in ST
                    FIST _M                      ;Save integer result
                                                 ;
                    FWAIT
                    LEA BX,_M
                    MOV AX,DS:[BX]               ;Answer in AX
                                                 ;
                    FINIT
                                                 ;
                    POP DS
                    POP DI
                    POP SI
                    POP DX
                    POP CX
                    POP BX
                                                 ;
                    MOV SP,BP
                    POP BP
                    RET
_POWW           ENDP
_TEXT           ENDS
                    END
```

Figure 5.19 (*Concluded*)

Using

$$2^{x \log_2(M)}$$

if $M = 2^N$, then $\log_2(M) = N$ and

$$\begin{aligned}
2^{x \log_2(M)} &= (2^x)^N \\
&= (2^N)^x \\
&= (M)^x
\end{aligned}$$

Thus

$$M^x = 2^{x \log_2(M)}$$

The instruction FYL2X calculates

$$y \log_2(x)$$

where $y = \text{ST}(1)$ and $x = \text{ST}$. This result is suitable for calculating M^x provided

$$y \log_2(x)$$

is in the range $(0, 0.5)$. The instruction FYL2X1 returns

$$y \log_2(x + 1)$$

Here $x = \text{ST}$, $y = \text{ST}(1)$, and the result is returned in ST following a pop. This result is in the range $[0, 1 - 1/\text{SQRT}(2)]$.

$$\begin{aligned}
x &= M^{\log_M(x)} \\
&= 2^{\log_2(x)}
\end{aligned}$$

it follows

$$\begin{aligned}
\log_2(x) &= \log_2[M^{\log_M(x)}] \\
&= \log_M(x) \log_2(M)
\end{aligned}$$

With these identities in mind, it is possible to use the coprocessor instructions to calculate M^x. We will specifically end up with the form

$$M^x = 2^{x \log_2(M)}$$

Consider the notation

```
base  = M
power = x
```

Now returning to the routine __POWW, it is necessary to implement the coprocessor arithmetic calculations where integer truncation occurs by rounding downward. The next few instructions set up this method for handling truncation. Corresponding to the preceding, we use

```
power = [BP+6]
base  = [BP+4]
```

Thus ST is loaded with power and ST(1) with base and these are exchanged using FXCH. The computation then proceeds as follows:

```
        • • •
        (ST(1) = power)
        (ST = base)
FYL2X
        (ST = power log₂(base))
FST ST(1)
        (ST(1) = ST)
FRNDINT
        (ST = Integer(ST))        - Truncation
FIST _MM3
        (_MM3 = Integer (power  log₂(base)))
FXCH
        (ST = power  log₂(base)))
        (ST(1) = Integer (power  log₂(base)))
FSUB ST,ST(1)
        (ST = Fraction (power  log₂(base)))
FLD _OHALF
        (ST = .5)
        (ST(1) = Fraction (power  log₂(base)))
FCOM ST(1)
        (-compare ST and ST(1) if ST>ST(1) (C3,C0) = (0,0)
            else set)
-Calculate value less than 1/2
    • • •
F2XM1
        (ST = 2^Fraction(power log₂(base)) -1 )
FLD1
        (ST = 1)
        (ST(1) = old ST)
FADD ST,ST(1)
        (ST = 2^Fraction (power log₂(base)) )
FILD _MM3
        (ST = Integer (power  log₂(base)))
        (ST(1) = 2^Fraction(power log₂(base)) )
FXCH
        -exchange ST and ST(1)
FSCALE
        (ST = 2^[Integer(power log₂(base))+Fraction(power log₂(base))]
          = 2^power log₂(base)
        = (base)^power)
```

This, then, completes the computational portion of the program. The return value is scaled up by 100 and saved in __M. Following this, a *very important* instruction, FWAIT, appears. This instruction is needed to synchronize the coprocessor and the CPU. It is needed anytime the coprocessor stores a value in memory followed immediately by an access of that same memory location. We end the procedure by loading AX with the result (the returned register value) and resetting the coprocessor.

The annotated results for two inputs are presented in Figure 5.20a and b. Here an initial principal of 100 units (conveniently dollars) has been input and a 10% annual rate of return assumed. In Figure 5.20a, the accumulated amount was

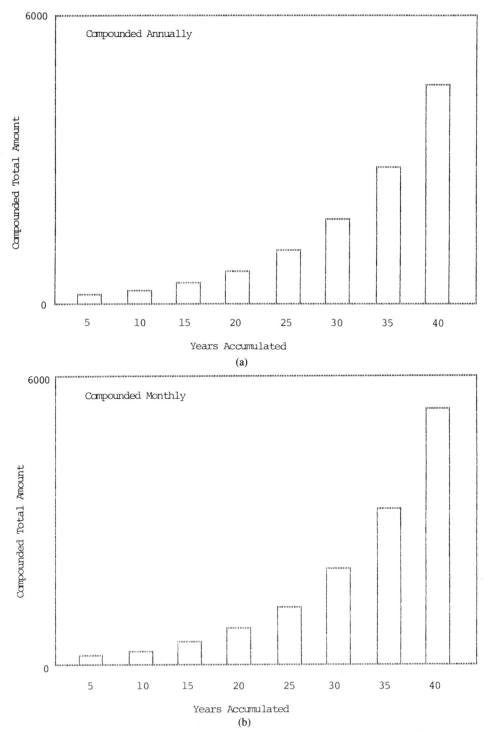

Figure 5.20 Principal and accumulated interest compounded (a) annually and (b) monthly. Principal was equal to 100 units at 10% annual rate.

assumed to only compound once a year, while in Figure 5.20b the compounding was assumed to occur on a monthly basis.

5.4 MEMORY MODELS

The Microsoft C compiler allows the user to specify one of five different memory model environments for program development. These environments have been alluded to earlier, and related parameters are summarized in Table 5.12. In this chapter we have seen the concept of a segment clarified, and it is apparent that in the Intel microprocessor domain segments with a maximum of 64K bytes constitute an upper limit on size (this is because of the 16-bit offset address capability). Each program only requires two segments: a code segment defined using CS and a stack segment defined using SS. In addition, the Microsoft C compiler defines at least one data segment (depending on the model) using DS.

Typically, models with 16-bit pointers can only access a single segment of the pointer type. Models with 32-bit pointers can access multiple segments because changes in the segment register variable can be easily implemented with FAR calls. In Table 5.12, it is clear that the small model has only 16-bit text and data pointers; hence, this model will always compile to the same text and data segment address. The medium model allows compilation of code in excess of 64K, while the compact model allows compilation of data variable space in excess of 64K (although not a single array variable in excess of this amount). Finally, both the large and the huge models allow both text and data segments to be defined on a multiple-segment basis. The preceding reference to arrays means that each array cannot exceed the maximum segment size of 64K bytes. This restriction is removed for the huge model, where the compiler addressing permits a ''huge'' address that allows arrays, for example, to span more than a 64K maximum segment block size.

With these thoughts in mind concerning memory models, we briefly examine the rationale behind such an organization for memory. Why would the program designer need the flexibility afforded by Table 5.12? First, he or she might be faced with system limitations either within the confines of a single microcomputer or OS/2, for example, in a multitasking role. Second, a need might exist to ensure portability of code (for example, the user might want to port code across many machine types). Using the models available in the Microsoft C compiler environment,

TABLE 5.12 MICROSOFT C COMPILER MEMORY MODEL PARAMETERS

	No. of Segments		Pointer/Integer Size			Segment Names	
Model	Text	Data	Data	Text	Int	Text	Data
Small	1	1[a]	16	16	16	_TEXT	_DATA
Medium	1/module	1[a]	16	32	16	mod_TEXT	_DATA
Compact	1	1 default	32	16	16	_TEXT	_DATA
Large	1/module	1 default	32	32	16	mod_TEXT	_DATA
Huge	1/module	1 default	32	32	16	mod_TEXT	_DATA

[a] When using mixed programming, the assembler can be written to interface more segments, as in this text.

memory-independent code is easily generated with the management function assumed by the compiler (based on appropriate switch settings at compile time). As long as special-purpose library functions, which require specific physical address parameters, are not used, code can be ported across systems that, for example, do not use segmented architectures (even though such code is written for the IBM microcomputer family). Clearly, in the IBM environment, assembly language interfaces remove the portability inherent in the memory model architecture, but afford the programmer the flexibility of using additional data segmentation, as we did in the examples illustrated (__DATA1). The programmer must support additional code segmentation under the appropriate memory model of Table 5.12. The use of assembly language routines must be driven by the necessity to achieve speed in executing programmed tasks. Selection of an appropriate memory model can also facilitate task execution if, for example, recurrent programming is called for. Assembly language routines can increase the efficiency with which code is implemented under these circumstances.

5.5 SUMMARY

The subject of assembly language is difficult at best, but has been developed in this chapter to serve as an adjunct to understanding how to program efficiently using the C language. In Chapter 6, we will see specific examples, alluded to earlier, where C code fails to provide enough flexibility and the user must resort to assembly language.

The structure of the chapter has been to present the essential features of IBM Macro Assembler in a compact representation and then apply these features to several simple examples. It is intended that the reader will use the notion of the assembler template as a framework for constructing simple assembly language procedures that can be strategically employed to enhance code execution. This, then, is the primary goal of the chapter. The dominant attribute possessed by the assembly language routine (in the C environment) is efficiency and it is in this circumstance that the techniques developed in this chapter are most useful.

REFERENCES

1. Godfrey, J. T., *IBM Microcomputer Assembly Language: Beginning to Advanced*, Prentice-Hall, Inc., Englewood Cliffs, NJ (1988).
2. Kolzner, S., *Advanced Assembly Language on the IBM PC*, A Brady Book, published by Prentice-Hall Press, New York (1987).
3. Norton, P., and Socha, J., *Peter Norton's Assembly Language Book for the IBM PC*, A Brady Book, published by Prentice-Hall Press, New York (1986).
4. Scanlon, L. J., *IBM PC & XT Assembly Language: A Guide for Programmers*, Brady Communications Company, Inc., New York (1985).
5. Bradley, D. J., *Assembly Language Programming for the IBM Personal Computer*, Prentice-Hall, Inc., Englewood Cliffs, NJ (1984).

6. Abel, P., *IBM PC Assembler Language and Programming*, Prentice-Hall, Inc., Englewood Cliffs, NJ (1987).

7. *Macro Assembler Version 2.00 Reference*, IBM Corp., Personal Computer, P. O. Box 1328-C, Boca Raton, FL 33432 (1984), 6361620.

8. *Macro Assembler Version 2.00*, IBM Corp., Personal Computer, P. O. Box 1328-C, Boca Raton, FL 33432 (1984), 6361612.

9. *80387 Programmer's Reference Manual*, Intel Corporation, Literature Distribution, Mail Stop SC6-59, 3065 Bowers Avenue, Santa Clara, CA 95051 (1987).

10. Lafore, R., *Microsoft C Programming for the IBM*, Howard W. Sams and Co., Indianapolis, IN (1987).

PROBLEMS

5.1. What is wrong with the following references between two modules?
Module 1

```
...
EXTRN      _CCC
_TEXT      SEGMENT BYTE PUBLIC 'CODE'
           ASSUME ...
           PUBLIC _DDD
_DDD       PROC NEAR
           ...
           MOV AX,_CCC
           ...
_DDD       ENDP
_TEXT      ENDS
           END _DDD
```

Module 2

```
...
_TEXT1     SEGMENT BYTE PUBLIC 'CODE'
           ASSUME ...
           PUBLIC _CCC
_CCC       PROC NEAR
           ...
_CCC       ENDP
_TEXT1     ENDS
           END
```

(*Hint:* What models could this code be used with?)

5.2. What is incorrect in the following instructions?
  (a) MOV BH,AX
  (b) MOV DS,MEM1[SI]
  (c) SHL AX,12
  (d) MOV AL,F8H
       ADD AL,08H

Problems   263

5.3. What is incorrect in the following fragments:

(a)
```
                ...
        MOV SI ,0
        MOV CX ,10000
    DO1:
        MOV AX ,0
        MOV ,BX ,TABLE1[SI]
        INC SI
        CMP AX ,1
        JMP DO1
        LOOP DO1
                ...
```

(b)
```
                ...
        MOV CX ,1000
        MOV SI ,0
        MOV DI ,2
    DO1
        MOV AX ,TABLE1[SI]
        MOV TABLE2[DI] ,AX
        ADD SI ,2
        ADD DI ,2
        JNE ELSE1
        LOOP DO1
    ELSE1:
                ...
```

(c)
```
                ...
        CLD
        MOV DI ,OFFSET TABLE1[0]
        MOV AX ,20H              ;Blank
        MOV CX ,72000
        REPE SCASB
        JE ELSE1
        DEC DI
                ...
    ELSE1:
                ...
```

5.4. Macro pseudo-ops were not emphasized in the text, but are extremely useful devices for inserting repetitious or fixed code into programs. Write a simple macro that checks to see if a variable is greater than 10 and returns a 1 if greater or a 0 otherwise. Assume the value is of word size.

5.5. How would the macro of Problem 5.4 be inserted into an operational program?

5.6. Define a macro, CLSCR, to clear the screen.

5.7. Using the concatenation operator, define a macro that reads one of several tables (TABLE1,TABLE2, . . .) and jumps to an error routine if the table value, specified by N, is a blank.

5.8. Write a macro that beeps the speaker.

5.9. Write a macro to initialize the printer, read status, and output a single character.

5.10. Define a macro that puts the screen in 320 × 200 graphics mode (X = 1) or 640 × 200 graphics mode (X = 2) for CGA.

5.11. Define a macro that generates a line feed to the screen, a carriage return, and a line feed and carriage return.

5.12. Illustrate the following numbers in the coprocessor format: (a) 1,500,000, (b) 250,000, (c) 7.4E4, (d) −2.5E5, and (e) 75,000.

5.13. Define the coprocessor instruction sequence that obtains a real-memory operand, X, squares that operand, and returns the squared value to the memory location.

5.14. Given an angle, Z, in radians, define the steps needed to return the tangent of this angle in Z.

5.15. Define the code needed to calculate the area of a circle assuming the radius is initially in a real variable, A.

5.16. Define the code needed to calculate the power dissipated in a 1-ohm resistor when a voltage drop of V is measured across this resistor. Return the power in decibels relative to 1 volt (dBV). Assume 20 is loaded in TWENTY.

6

Real-Time Programming with C

Real-time programming is a descriptive term used to indicate code that is responsive to data I/O that must be handled in an immediate or real-world manner. Perhaps the best way to describe real-time programming is to present a simple example. Consider computer-to-computer communications. Here, one computer initiates a query to the second computer in the form of a message. Clearly, the second computer must receive and process this message in real time, that is, as the message actually occurs on the second computer's input lines. If the second computer fails to process the message immediately, the incoming information will be lost. Hence, the second computer must practice real-time processing [1].

The purpose of this chapter is to expose the reader to real-time programming with C. We will first consider some general aspects of real-time programming and then two very specific examples: communications and analog-to-digital (A/D) conversion. The communications example develops routines for the Hayes Smartmodem 1200 [2], and the A/D example develops routines for the Data Translation DT2828 A/D Adapter for the IBM AT [3]. Both examples are presented in such a fashion that the reader does not need to actually implement the code in order to acquire an understanding of how real-time processing is achieved. The goal of this chapter is to provide a general familiarity with real-time programming concepts and how hardware must be manipulated to achieve real-time processing. Typically, real-time hardware involves the setting and reading of registers resident in the hardware logic. The examples illustrate this process both from the static conceptual viewpoint and the dynamic real-world perspective (the order in which registers are set and read is very important).

266

6.1 GENERAL REAL-TIME PROCESSING

The real-time systems described in this chapter are of two types:

1. Interactive or on line (such as the communications example)
2. Process control (such as the A/D monitoring function)

In the first of these applications, the computer interfaces with the real-world via a serial port (to be discussed in Section 6.2). This special-purpose device allows a form of standardized interface with external peripherals, and both synchronous and asynchronous exchanges are possible depending on the interface. The rates for exchanging information are generally low. All control employs a device known as a Universal Asynchronous Receiver Transmitter (UART) [4] for asynchronous interfacing.

The UART interfaces with a telephone modem that converts digital data (to and from the UART) to information suitable for telephone line transmission. Figure 6.1 schematically illustrates the communication process, where it has been assumed that two computers are involved in the exchange of data. A UART resides in each RS-232C serial adapter.

The A/D adapter interfaces to the IBM AT via the AT I/O bus. This is a direct linkage, which is achieved by plugging the A/D adapter card into one of the AT expansion slots and sampling the analog signal at a high rate based on an on-board pacer clock. The A/D adapter also has the capability to achieve direct memory access (DMA) processing whereby blocks of digitized data are transferred at high speed directly to the AT's memory. The A/D adapter transfers all data in parallel, as opposed to serial fashion whether in DMA mode or the single-conversion mode used in the illustration of Section 6.3.

Several characteristics of real-time systems are probably apparent. First, each system has an associated maximum throughput or bandwidth. For the communications example, this is typically expressed as the baud rate or number of characters per second. In the A/D example, an on-board clock creates samples at a fixed rate, which defines a maximum bandwidth for the sampled process (based on the Nyquist criterion [5]). Second, when data are being input at some fixed maximum rate, the associated processor must accept and utilize these data without allowing it to overflow. Frequently, for asynchronous exchanges a buffer is employed that fills during data bursts and is then serviced in between these bursts. For on-line applications, the data character or symbol rate is usually slow enough that many processor cycles exist between symbols. Hence, upon receipt of a symbol, the processor has ample

Figure 6.1 Functional diagram for computer communications via serial ports.

time to manipulate the symbol in memory in order to extract the desired information from the symbol, prior to receipt of another symbol.

A convenient analogy for real-time processing systems is a pipeline: once the information enters the processing, it moves smoothly along until it is extracted or it overflows. In the two examples to be illustrated, overflow is a serious consideration. For the communications application, information is to be displayed as it is received. If the response of the display is too slow, the incoming symbols will be lost because of the lag in accepting these symbols. At communications rates of 300 baud, this is not a problem, but for 1200 baud, the case considered, overflow in the AT can occur without judicious programming. Similarly, for the A/D adapter example, as the sample rate increases, samples are dropped if intervening code requires more processing time than the sample interval. All these remarks can be put in perspective by considering assembler instruction times [6]. These times are usually indicated in clock cycles. It is very important to recognize that instructions involving memory operands take substantially longer than instructions involving register operands. Since compilers almost always reference memory locations in general code structure, compiled code can be expected to run slower than optimized routines based on register manipulation. Thus, there are some advantages to writing optimized assembly language routines in critical applications where speed is essential.

6.1.1 Hardware and Software Considerations

Real-time microcomputer hardware differs little from other general-purpose computer hardware except at the real-time interface. Here, generally, an analog signal is being converted to digital data and input for processing (for example, a modem/ telephone line or an A/D converter). We focus on the receiving processing because it is usually here that the bottlenecks occur. (There are digital-to-analog converters that change the digital data back to an analog signal.)

The primary real-time microcomputer feature, not absolutely required by general-purpose microcomputer processing, is speed. Real-time hardware must run much faster than the bandwidth of the process to be sampled. As indicated earlier, this allows time to accomplish all the requisite intermediate processing. In the IBM AT (6-MHz clock) with an approximate cycle time of 160 nanoseconds (ns), a 1200-baud communications link allows approximately 5200 cycles between symbols. If the 80286 has an average instruction time of 15 cycles, then 346 instructions can be executed between symbols.

Clearly, central processor unit (CPU) speed is an important requirement for real-time systems. If the CPU is much faster than associated memory, then WAIT states must be introduced that slow the processing down. Virtually all real-time processing is performed on integer values. With the advent of coprocessors, however, such as the 8087 or 80287, it is possible to perform high-speed floating point operations. This increases the flexibility and accuracy of real-time calculations.

Memory is of two types: static random access memory (SRAM) and dynamic random access memory (DRAM). In general, SRAM is faster than DRAM, but considerably more expensive. Hence for data acquisition examples, the slower memory tends to limit throughput in all but very expensive systems (which use SRAM).

Most real-time data handling is via a data register in an associated controller (or UART as an example). Software must be provided to initialize and set up this data register for reading and writing the data. This frequently involves the use of other registers in the real-time processor (controller). In this chapter we will deal with controller registers and the programming of these registers to set up various processing configurations. In the case of the Hayes Smartmodem 1200, the registers are less apparent because a low-level language interface exists between the modem and the IBM microcomputer. This interface is achieved via the RS-232C serial port. Both data and control signals are exchanged via this port. The Data Translation DT2828, however, employs a number of registers that are accessed with different addresses. Each register controls a fixed set of A/D functions and must be set up appropriately in ordered fashion.

Many of the programs presented in this textbook will run under OS/2 Protected Mode as well as DOS 3.x (or they will run in the OS/2 Compatibility Mode). Some notable exceptions are those programs that specify absolute physical addresses, such as the DMA screen functions. Most real-time applications will not run under OS/2 [7] because these programs involve time-critical or time-sensitive software, and in multitasking applications the real-mode environment is suspended when the system switches to a Protected Mode task. Clearly, if the user foregoes multitasking and runs in Compatibility Mode, this problem should be obviated. IBM has an additional real-time operating system under development, and it is likely that this operating system will prevail in applications where DOS 3.x and OS/2 cannot.

6.1.2 Implementation and Testing

This section deals with the debugging and testing of real-time systems in the C environment for IBM microcomputers. The debugging problems faced in a real-time system are significantly different from those encountered in general-purpose software development. Tools such as CodeView are virtually useless against real-time bugs. This is because the CodeView software has too much overhead to allow an accurate picture of the real-time performance. Frequently, interrupts are triggered and such software will not work at all. How, then, can the developer hope to debug an application?

Companies such as Intel have long recognized this problem and have developed numerous tools to help the real-time programmer. Real-time operating systems such as iRMX and development hardware/software such as an In-Circuit Emulator (ICE) all help keep track of registers during real-time debugging. Unfortunately, these tools are not always available to the user and more straightforward techniques must be applied. Software based on assembly language can usually be debugged with tools such as DEBUG.EXE provided by IBM. Here appropriate breakpoints must be set and, following execution to these breakpoints, the registers checked.

For programs employing C compiled software, run-time debugging of real-time code is more difficult. First, anticipated results must be carefully understood. Then strategically located I/O must be used to probe the executing software. Obviously, the I/O routines cannot be allowed to affect operation of the real-time program. This is where the difficulty arises in testing real-time software. Also, frequently in real-time applications the anticipated result yields an untested quantity because the input data values (say, an analog waveform) vary too rapidly to allow prediction.

This constitutes an additional unknown, and the developer can only hope to qualify a result, not predict the actual value, unless a rigid test environment is specified, such as a direct current (dc) voltage into an A/D converter.

We have generally been discussing small-scale real-time development characteristics of the examples in this chapter. The applications are assumed to be intended for the IBM microcomputer environment. Furthermore, this is a book about software and software applications. We will not address hardware development any more than needed to understand the examples. It should be clear, however, that real-time programming is very close to the actual hardware entities. The programmer frequently makes use of input/output directly to hardware registers.

6.1.3 Uniprocessor and Multitasking Systems

Uniprocessor or monoprocessor systems are systems that execute a single task or process at any given point in time. DOS constitutes such an operating system and has at its core a single infinite loop that is subject to interrupts that result in subsequent tasks being performed. A typical loop structure might be

```
...
    while (1)
    {
    activity();
    }
...
```

Here the loop is constantly active unless an interrupt such as the keyboard, for example, causes the system to vector to a service routine and perform some task. In the above fragment the function, activity(), is typically a NOP-type statement.

OS/2 is a multitasking operating system in which a single computer switches among several tasks simultaneously. In this context the control passes freely among tasks, depending on task completion and priority, as well as a task management function. One problem with multitasking operating systems is that when task switching occurs all registers must be saved, as well as task parameters. Furthermore, new instruction code must be "rolled in" and a new process continued. If a real-time activity is being executed, then I/O during the roll-out period is effectively cut off. Consequently, time-critical operation is not possible unless the processor is very fast and capable of many operations between real-time I/O events.

With these thoughts in mind (on real-time processing), we now examine two useful examples of real-time processing for the IBM microcomputer environment. The first example deals with telephone communications via modems. We spend some time discussing the hardware for this application because this is a good illustration of how one interfaces C code to the IBM BIOS interrupt service routines. The second example deals with an analog-to-digital conversion application. We illustrate the programming of the Data Translation DT2828 board mentioned earlier. This latter example is more difficult to implement because it requires a special-purpose adapter (most readers will probably have access to inexpensive Hayes-compatible modems used in the first example). The emphasis in presenting this example, however,

TABLE 6.1 RS-232C PIN SELECTION/SIGNAL IDENTIFICATION

Pin	Signal name	Comments
1	Chassis ground	Grounding
2	Transmitted data (TD)	Output data
3	Received data (RD)	Input data
4	Request to send (RTS)	Defines condition ready to send
5	Clear to send (CTS)	Permits transmission
6	Data set ready (DSR)	Notifies ready status
7	Signal ground	Signal-only ground
8	Data carrier detect (CD)	Carrier present indicator
20	Data terminal ready (DTR)	Signal indicating ready to transmit
21	Ring indicator (RI)	Older "ringing" indicator

is to make it self-contained so that the reader can understand how to program such devices and what pitfalls exist in such programming.

6.2 THE IBM MICROPROCESSOR COMMUNICATIONS INTERFACE

This section addresses communications via telephone lines in which modems are used to convert digital data to tonal data capable of such transmission (see Figure 6.1). Within the standards of the Electronic Industries Association (EIA), a serial adapter configuration known as RS-232C has been developed, and this configuration is the one common to the IBM Asynchronous Communications Adapter. The RS-232C serial port to the communications modem is one form for implementing a communications interface. In the example discussed in this section, an RS-232C serial adapter is provided via an IBM AT expansion slot. This adapter is interfaced via cable to a Hayes Smartmodem 1200. The modem is, in turn, cabled to a wall-mounted telephone connector. Table 6.1 lists the RS-232C pin connections that are active as part of the adapter 25-pin connector (DB-25 type connector); see reference 4.

The digital data that are provided to the serial port are in the form of eight parallel input lines. These are converted to serial data using a counter shift register: eight parallel bits of data load the counter shift register a frame at a time and are serially shifted out a bit at a time at a higher transfer rate. These digital data in serial form consist of ones (MARK) or zeros (SPACE) and can be converted by the modem to one of two tones depending on the MARK/SPACE condition. These tones are suitable for transmission via conditioned telephone lines. This form of modulation (tonal) is applicable for 300-baud operation. At 1200 baud, the Smartmodem employs phase shift keying (PSK) of a carrier with a center frequency of 1200 Hz (instead of the frequency shift keying discussed above). Basically, PSK modulation consists of a phase shift in the carrier of $\pm 180°$, depending on MARK/SPACE condition.

6.2.1 IBM Adapter Hardware

This section addresses the topic of communications hardware as implemented for the IBM microcomputers. It will be useful to consider two facets of this hardware:

TABLE 6.2 THE 8250 INTERNAL REGISTERS. COURTESY OF NATIONAL
SEMICONDUCTOR

Register	Register select			Comments
	A2	A1	A0	
Receiver Buffer Register (RBR)	0	0	0	This is a read-only register with data input. (DLAB = 0)
Transmitter Holding Register (THR)	0	0	0	This is a write-only register with data output. (DLAB = 0)
Interrupt Enable Register (IER)	0	0	1	The first four bits enable received data available, transmitter holding register empty, receiver line status enable, and modem status enable.
Interrupt Identification Register (IIR)	0	1	0	Bit 0 indicates interrupt and bits 1 and 2 the bit set in the IE register.
Line Control Register (LCR)	0	1	1	This register contains the communications protocol: bits 0 and 1 = word length select, bit 2 = # stop bits, bit 3 = parity enable, bit 4 = even parity select, bit 5 = stick parity, bit 6 = spacing output and bit 7 = access to divisor latches of band rate generator.
MODEM Control Register (MCR)	1	0	0	Sets DTR, RTS, and two user-designated output lines which act like ancillary DTR lines.
Line Status Register (LSR)	1	0	1	Errors: Data Ready (DR), Overrun Error (OE), Parity Error (PE), Framing Error (FE), Break Interrupt (BI), THR Empty, Transmit Shift Register Empty.
MODEM Status Register (MSR)	1	1	0	CTS, DSR, RI, Signal Detect, DSR state change, CTS state change, RI state change, Received Line Signal Detect State change.
Divisor Latch (LS) (DLL)	0	0	0	Least significant band rate generator divisor value. Yields output band frequency 16 times desired value (DLAB = 1).
Divisor Latch (MS) (DLM)	0	0	1	Most signficant band rate generator divisor value. (DLAB = 1)

Reprinted with permission National Semiconductor Corp.

the serial port adapter and the National Semiconductor 8250 Asynchronous Communications Element (ACE). The ACE is a UART, as mentioned previously. In this discussion, the adapter for the IBM PC will be considered as an example. While this is somewhat dated, it is well documented and a representative illustration of serial port configurations for the IBM microcomputers; that is, it is current in terms

272

Real Time Programming with C   Chap. 6

of architecture. The principal purpose in discussing the serial port adapter is to illustrate the methodology for obtaining addresses of the ACE registers.

The 8250 ACE. Table 6.2 presents the 8250 internal registers that must be programmed to accomplish various initialization and operational instructions [8]. This UART is the heart of the communications adapter. Figure 6.2 illustrates the pin selection for this element. Pins 1 to 8 contain the I/O signals to be loaded into or read from each internal register. We will briefly consider these bytes shortly. Pin 9 can be tied to pin 16 to generate a receiver clock. Pins 10 and 11 are the serial input and output lines, respectively. Pins 12 to 14 are the chip select lines. When CS0 and CS1 are HIGH and CS2* is LOW, the chip is selected. Pin 15 is then 16 times transmit clock and pins 16 and 17 are the reference oscillator output. Pins 18 and 19 are the data output strobe pins, and these regulate the CPU writes to 8250 internal registers. Pin 20 is GROUND. Pins 21 and 22 are the data input strobe pins, and these regulate the CPU read from the 8250 internal registers. Pin 23 goes LOW to indicate a CPU read. Pin 24 is HIGH for a chip select. Pin 25 is used to load the register select lines, and pins 26 to 28 are the register select lines (they are attached to address lines A0, A1, and A2). Pin 30 indicates a fault and pins 31 and 34 are extra data set ready lines. Pin 32 is a request to send line. Pin 33 is the data terminal ready line, and pin 35 is the master reset. Pin 36 is the clear to send line and pin 37, the data set ready line. Pin 38 is carrier detect, pin 39 ring indicator, and pin 40, high voltage.

Figure 6.3 illustrates the functional block diagram for the 8250 ACE. The parallel I/O portion of this UART contains the data buffer interface (D0 to D7), which is also used to load the internal registers via multiplexing. The internal register structure of the 8250 is functionally indicated in Figure 6.3. For purposes of establishing communications link control with a telephone modem, the most important 8250 registers are:

Line control register (LCR)

Line status register (LSR)

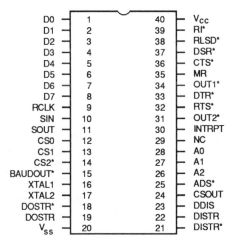

Figure 6.2 The 8250 Asynchronous Communication Element pin description. (Reprinted with permission of National Semiconductor.)

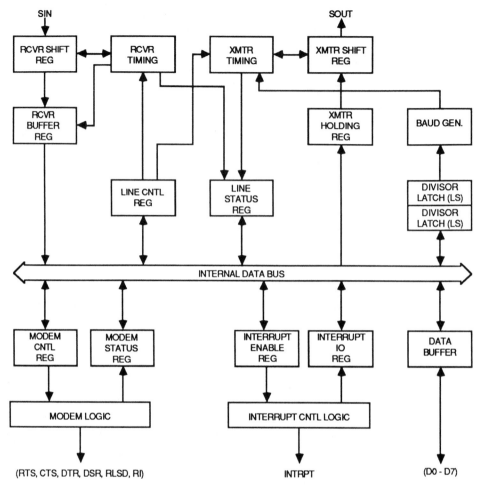

Figure 6.3 Functional block diagram for the INS8250 ACE. (Reprinted with permission of National Semiconductor.)

Model control register (MCR)

Modem status register (MSR)

We will see shortly how the registers are used to control the modem (and serial port) and check status.

IBM asynchronous communications adapter. Figure 6.4 illustrates schematically the asynchronous communications adapter for the IBM PC [9]. As indicated earlier, the heart of this adapter is the National Semiconductor 8250 Asynchronous Communications Element. Based on this figure, it is clear that byte data are input through a transceiver from the multiplexed microcomputer address/data bus lines (AD2 to AD9). These lines can carry either data or address information depending on the multiplexing condition determined by the CPU.

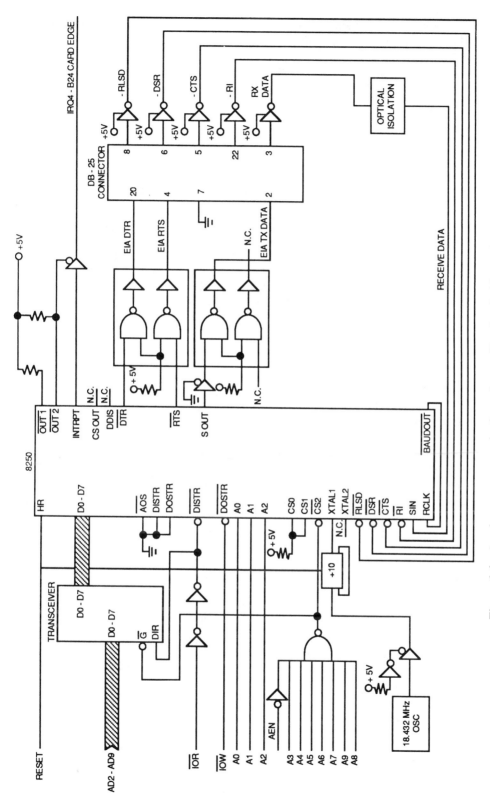

Figure 6.4 Asychronous communications adapter. (Reprinted with permission from the *Technical Reference*; copyright 1981 by International Business Machines Incorporated.)

275

How are port addresses specified for this adapter? Examination of the left side of Figure 6.4 illustrates that address lines A3 to A9 are attached to the 8250 chip select pin (CS2*) through a NAND gate. Hence this pin goes LOW only when all these address lines are HIGH (plus a LOW on AEN). If the address word is examined, it is clear the following condition must exist:

A15	A14	A13	A12	A11	A10	A9	A8	A7	A6	A5	A4	A3	A2	A1	A0
x	x	x	x	0	0	1	1	1	1	1	1	1	x	x	x
X				3				F				(8-F)			

Here the ×'s indicate don't-care conditions. Address bits A11 and A10 are set to zero in IBM convention, although based on Figure 6.4 they could technically be anything. Similarly, bits A12 to A15 are assigned port settings of zero. Hence based on this logic, the asynchronous communications adapter ACE can be addressed through the address range 03F8H to 03FFH. The selection within this range is based on bits A0 to A2 and has the correspondence indicated in Table 6.2. That is, the receiver buffer corresponds to address 03F8H, the transmitter holding register, 03F9H, the line control register, 03FBH, and so forth.

The IBM asynchronous communications adapter service routine has four functions:

1. Initialize (AH = 0)
2. Send a character (AH = 1)
3. Receive a character (AH = 2)
4. Check status (AH = 3)

These functions are clearly illustrated in the BIOS code for interrupt 0 × 14. Here, AH is the upper half of the AX register in the 80286 or other 8086 family CPU. Generally, AH is used to select the communications function, and AL is the active register half. Typically, AL contains the character to be sent or received when AH = 1 or 2, respectively.

For initialization, AL must contain the byte appropriate to Table 6.3. Here the communications parameters must be selected according to the desired communica-

TABLE 6.3 AL BIT SETTINGS VICE PARAMETERS (AH = 0)

Baud Rate	Bit 7	Bit 6	Bit 5	Parity	Bit 4	Bit 3	Stop Bit	Bit 2	Word Length	Bit 1	Bit 0
110	0	0	0	None	×	0	1	6	7	1	0
150	0	0	1	Odd	0	1	2	1	8	1	1
300	0	1	0	Even	1	1					
600	0	1	1								
1200	1	0	0								
2400	1	0	1								
4800	1	1	0								
9600	1	1	1								

tions protocol. The reader should note that the AH and AL correspondence is for CPU AX register specification for INT 14H, not the actual 8250 internal registers. The INT 14H service routine must translate these AL values to appropriate port I/O for the 8250 internal registers. We will see an example of how this is accomplished when an assembly language routine is presented that implements the character receive function. For 1200 baud, no parity, one stop bit, and word length equal to 8 bits, the AL setting for INT 14H with AH = 0 would be 0 × 83.

For checking status, AL contains the following values:

Bit 7   Received line signal detect
Bit 6   Ring indicator
Bit 5   Data set ready
Bit 4   Clear to send
Bit 3   Delta receive line signal detect
Bit 2   Trailing edge ring detector
Bit 1   Delta data set ready
Bit 0   Delta clear to send

In general, we will not be concerned with these status bits. One bit we will check, however, is bit 0 of AH (AH also returns status information when it is set to 3 prior to an INT 14H call). The AH = 3 call to INT 14H returns the following AH values:

Bit 7   Time out
Bit 6   Transmitter shift register empty
Bit 5   Transmitter holding register empty
Bit 4   Break detect
Bit 3   Framing error
Bit 2   Parity error
Bit 1   Overrun error
Bit 0   Data ready

Many of these bits indicate hardware conditions not amenable to programming consideration. We ignore this information. Bit 0 of AH, however, can be checked to see if incoming or received data (a single 8-bit character) are available on port address 0 × 03F8.

6.2.2 Software for Communications

Normally, all the service for communications is performed using the INT 14H service routines resident in the BIOS code. For the most part we will follow this convention. It is useful, however, to consider an assembly language routine that handles the receive character function. This routine is similar to the BIOS service but is slightly faster than a call to INT 14H. It serves to illustrate the programming of the 8250 since it directly addresses this element and has an identical calling format as INT 14H (hence, later we can substitute a C routine for this assembly language function). In Chapter 5, we discussed mixed C and assembly language programming, and the routine, RCVR(), appearing in Figure 6.5 is the receive assembly language routine callable from C code. This routine will be the focal point for discussion in this section. Routines to generate the other communication functions (transmit, status, and initialization) are programmed in similar fashion.

Figure 6.5 contains two segments: a data segment (_DATA) and a code segment (_TEXT). The segment label _TEXT is the default code segment name for the small C compiler. The data segment label _DATA1 must be addressed by the RCVR() code when calling the variable _MES1 to indicate that DSR is never set. This is an error check. Note that this data segment does not conflict with the usual default data segments because no other variables are called by RCVR(). Hence, there is no potential for conflicting calls to the wrong data segment parameters based on the segment address in DS. All operations in RCVR() are register operations (except the output of _MES1).

RCVR() begins with the usual saving of the frame pointer and stack allocation. Next the segment address for _DATA1 is loaded into DS after first pushing the current DS value onto the stack. At this point the RS-232C base address, 03F8H (or 0 × 03F8), is loaded into DX. DX is the active address register for the IN and OUT port operations. The first operation is to check the modem for a receive condition. The modem control register is used for either transmission or reception of data, and it is specified as follows:

BIT:	7	6	5	4	3	2	1	0
	0	0	0	LOOP	OUT 2	OUT 1	RTS	DTR

Only data terminal ready (DTR) is needed for the receive function. Hence, one would like to send 0 × 01 to this register. Using Table 6.2, it is clear that address 03FCH must be used. Following output of this byte, a check is made on the modem status (address 03FEH). This register has the following form:

BIT:	7	6	5	4	3	2	1	0
	RLSD	RI	DSR	CTS	Delta RLSD	TERI	Delta DSR	Delta CTS

We need to check the DSR bit to see if the modem (data set) is ready with a character. The test is performed by ANDing the contents of the modem status register and 20H, using the TEST instruction.

Following a successful qualification of the modem, it is necessary to check the line status register (address 03FDH, as indicated in Table 6.2). This register has the following form:

BIT:								
	7	6	5	4	3	2	1	0
	0	Xmit Shift Reg Empty	Xmit Hold Reg Empty	Break Interrupt	Framing Error	Parity Error	Overrun Error	Data Ready

We test bit 0 to see if data are ready (a character in the receive buffer). If the test is unsuccessful, the routine loops until a data ready condition is achieved (there is

```
PAGE 40,132
TITLE RCVR - RECEIVE/ECHO CHAR FROM SERIAL PORT (RCVR.ASM)
;
;          DESCRIPTION: This routine checks status, receives a character,
;          and echos this character from the UART.  It uses addresses
;
;                         3F8H  -  RS232C Base
;                         3FBH  -  Line Control Register
;                         3FCH  -  Modem Control Register
;                         3FDH  -  Line Status Register
;                         3FEH  -  Modem Status Register
;
;
_DATA1  SEGMENT BYTE PUBLIC 'DATA'                           ;
        PUBLIC _MES1
_MES1   DB      'DSR never ready'
        DB      '$'
                                                            ;
_DATA1  ENDS

_TEXT   SEGMENT BYTE PUBLIC 'CODE'                           ;
        ASSUME  CS:_TEXT,DS:_DATA1
        PUBLIC _RCVR
_RCVR   PROC    NEAR
                                                            ;
        PUSH BP                             ;Save caller's frame pointer
        MOV BP,SP                           ;frame ptr to old BP
        SUB SP,8                            ;allocate local var space
        PUSH DX
        PUSH CX
        PUSH BX

        PUSH DS                             ;
        MOV AX,SEG _DATA1
        MOV DS,AX
                                            ;
        MOV DX,3F8H                         ;load RS232 base
        ADD DX,4                            ;modem control reg
        MOV AL,1
        OUT DX,AL                           ;set DTR
        ADD DX,2                            ;modem status reg
        MOV CX,10000                        ;loop count
DO1:
        IN AL,DX                            ;check modem status
        TEST AL,20H                         ;DSR ?
        JNZ ELSE1
            LOOP DO1                        ;test unsuccessful
            PUSH DX
            LEA DX,_MES1
            MOV AH,9
            INT 21H
            POP DX
            JMP END1                        ;ABORT
ELSE1:
        DEC DX                              ;line status reg
DO2:
        IN AL,DX                            ;line status
        TEST AL,1                           ;receive buffer full?
        JNZ ELSE2
            JMP DO2                         ;test unsuccessful
ELSE2:
        MOV DX,3F8H                         ;reload RS232 base
        IN AL,DX                            ;get character
                                            ;
        MOV AH,0                            ;return AH = 0
END1:
        POP DS
        POP BX
        POP CX
        POP DX
        MOV SP,BP
        POP BP
        RET
_RCVR   ENDP
_TEXT   ENDS
        END
```

Figure 6.5 Assembly language version for RCVR( ), the serial port receive function which is C callable.

a potential to ''hang'' the system at this point if a hardware failure occurs in the communications link). Next, the input status is checked for errors. The base address 03F8H is reloaded and the character read in. Finally, since we do nothing with errors, AH is reset to zero. All pushed registers are popped and a return to the calling C routine is made. Note that any returned value is expected to be in AX (here the returned character is in AL with AH = 0). The function called from the C program should be RCVR(), and this is specified by the procedure label, _RCVR.

This completes the preliminary discussion of communications software. We have looked at how the 8250 is programmed for receiving a character in some detail, and the other three communication functions employ similar techniques. The hardware was considered in Section 6.2.1, and it is now useful to address the more global problem of how to implement an actual communications program that contains all the necessary code to set up a link with another terminal (see Figure 6.1).

6.2.3 A Typical Communications Driver: Hayes Smartmodem 1200

The communications modem must attach to the computer through a single serial port. The other side of the modem then attaches to the telephone line and carries the information exchange. At first it may be puzzling as to how information and control signals are both passed to the modem in this configuration. The Hayes Smartmodem 1200, which is similar to most modems, has two states: on line and off line or local command state. In the on-line state, data are passed directly from the serial port to the communication line. In the local command state, the serial port data are treated as a command string. Clearly, any communications program must be capable of handling both local commands and the on-line traffic.

How does such a program cause the modem to change state? Basically, the modem can be made to go from the local command state to on line only by receiving a carrier from an answering modem after placing a call to that modem. If no carrier is detected after 30 seconds (variable), the phone is hung up. If the carrier is lost, the phone is hung up. Following a hang-up of the phone, the modem is placed in local command state. Last, if an escape code (+++) is sent to the modem in an on-line state, the modem switches to local command state. It is clear, then, that aside from the escape code the modem must be made to change state (under program control) by initiating a call. (There is an answer mode, which we will not discuss.)

Table 6.4 lists the commands that can be used with the Hayes Smartmodem 1200 to cause events to occur (see reference 2). To initialize or reset the modem when it is in the local command state, the following string should be sent:

```
AT Z\r
```

Here the Z command causes the rest. To dial a number, for example, the following is used:

```
AT DT 555-1212\r
```

TABLE 6.4 HAYES SMARTMODEM 1200 COMMAND SYNTAX (PARTIAL)

Command	Comment
AT	Attention command: A sets speed and T sets parameters based on communication port.
\r	Carriage return: causes execution of the preceding command string.
Z	Terminate command: enforced termination of call.
O	Return command: returns to on line following a command. This assumes an escape code has been issued followed by a local command.
D	Dial command: sets up the modem for dialing.
,	Pause command: causes a wait for a second dial tone.
T	Touch-Tone dialing.
P	Pulse dialing.
A/	Repeat last command.
;	Puts the modem back in local command state after dialing.
S6	Length of time Smartmodem 1200 waits for dial tone (default = 2 seconds).
S7	Length of time Smartmodem 1200 waits for carrier before hang-up (default = 30 seconds).
S8	Length of pause time (default = 2 seconds).
S9	Length of time carrier must be present before connection (default = 600 milliseconds).
S10	Time between carrier loss and hang up (default = 700 milliseconds).
S11	Tone spacing (default = 70 milliseconds).
Cn	n = 1 sets carrier on, n = 0 sets carrier off.
En	n = 0 echo off, n = 1 echo on.
Fn	n = 0 half-duplex, n = 1 full duplex.
Hn	n = 0 on hook (hung up), n = 1 off hook (dial tone present).
Mn	n = 0 turns modem speaker off, m = 1 turns speaker on until carrier detected, and n = 2 turns speaker on always.
Qn	n = 0 provides result codes from the modem, n = 1 eliminates result codes from the modem.
Vn	n = 0 has result codes sent as digits, n = 1 has the result codes transmitted as words.

Figure 6.6 illustrates a calling function for a communications program. The called functions are indicated as follows:

SCRCL()	(Figure 3.3b)
INITSP()	(Figure 6.13)
resetmd()	(Figure 6.9)
tele_dial()	(Figure 6.9)
loopio()	(Figure 6.12)

The overall communications program is very simplified. Figure 6.7 is a structure chart for the overall program, and Figure 6.8 is a functional flow chart illustrating the program dynamics.

In Figure 6.9, a number of modem and serial port routines are illustrated. It is useful to consider each in turn. The function modout() is used to send a character string to the modem when it is in local command mode. First, a loop is executed to ensure that any previously transmitted strings have completed processing. Then the XMIT() function is used to send the string, one character at a time. Following each character, the function RCVR() is used to receive the echo from the serial port. If result codes have been requested, modck() can be used to perform a limited check following the carriage return. This function looks for the ASCII value for zero, in byte form, and prints an OK to the screen if present. If the OK status does not occur, an error message is printed. The function reads the carriage return and line feed characters first.

The function resetmd() sets up the modem parameters in local command mode. First, the reset command is sent. At this point, modck() cannot be used because the result codes are in word format. Next, the command

```
AT E1 F0 Q0 V0\r
```

is sent. This causes echo to be turned on, sets full-duplex mode, and requests result codes in digit format. Following this command, modck() is used to check status. The command

```
AT\r
```

clears the command buffer. The function tele_dial() actually dials the desired telephone number. This function first resets the modem and requests the telephone number. Next the number is dialed using the command

```
AT DT
```

followed by the telephone number.

The function modck() calls a function charout(), which prints the character received (from the serial port) to the screen. Since speed is important, it is necessary to minimize the time needed to print the incoming character on the screen. Placement

```
/* main calling program for RS232C modem */

#define SP 0x83                          /* 1200 8-1-N */
int row,col;                             /* global screen */

main()
       {
       SCRCL();                          /* clear screen */
       INITSP(SP);                       /* initialize port */
       resetmd();                        /* reset modem */
       tele_dial();                      /* place call */
       loopio();                         /* accept I/O */
       }
```

Figure 6.6 Main calling routine for the serial port communications program.

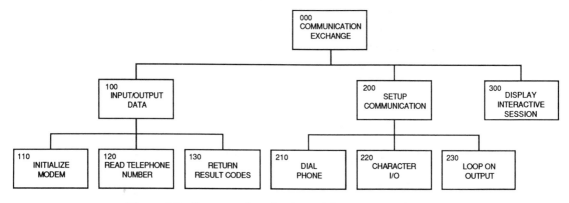

Figure 6.7 Structure chart for the serial port communications program.

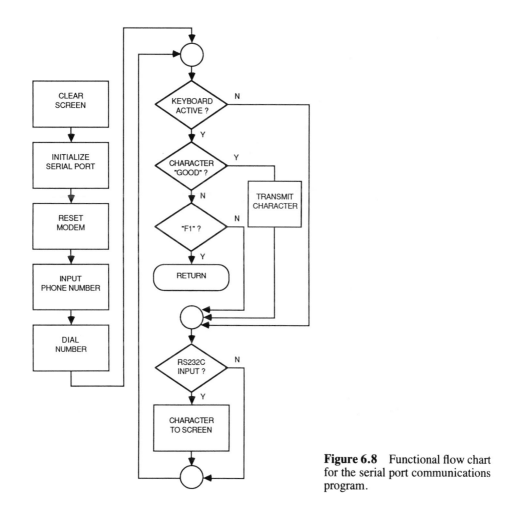

Figure 6.8 Functional flow chart for the serial port communications program.

```
/* Modem control functions */

#include <stdio.h>

/* send output to modem */
modout(str)
        char *str;
        {
        long int n1,n2,N = 1000;
        char ch;
        extern int RCVR();

        n1 = 0;
        while(n1 < 50*N)                                /* wait last cmd */
            n1++;

        for(n1 = 0;(ch = *(str+n1)) != '\0' ;n1++)
            {
            XMIT(ch);                                   /* send RS232C */
            ch = (char)(RCVR());                        /* echo RS232C */
            }
        }

/*check modem status */
modck()
        {
        char ch;
        extern int RCVR();
        long int n1,n2,N = 500;

        ch = (char)(RCVR());                            /* read c.r. */
        ch = (char)(RCVR());
        charout(ch);                                    /* print status */

        if(ch == '\x30')                                /* one-byte '0' */
            printf("\nOK\n");
        else
            printf("\nERROR\n");
        }

/* Reset modem */
resetmd()
        {
        modout("AT Z\r");                               /* reset */
        modout("AT E1 F1 Q0 V0\r");                     /* initialize */
        modck();                                        /* c.r. status */
        modout("AT\r");                                 /* terminate */
        modck();                                        /* c.r. status */
        }

/* Dial telephone number */
tele_dial()
        {
        char number[20];                                /* phone no. */

        resetmd();                                      /* reset modem */
        printf("Input telephone no.:");
        gets(number);                                   /* obtain no. */
        modout("AT DT");                                /* precursor */
        modout(number);                                 /* output no. */
        modout("\r");                                   /* end */
        }
```

Figure 6.9 Functions used for modem control in the local command mode.

```
/* Function to write character to screen -- DMA */

charout(ch)
        char ch;
        {
        int n;
        extern int row,col;
        char far *ptr;

        ptr = (char far *) 0xB8000000;                    /* base address */
        if(ch == 0x0A)                                     /* check c.r. */
           col = 0;
        else
           {
           if(ch == 0x0D)                                  /* check linefeed */
              row++;
           else
              {
              if(ch == 0x08)                               /* check backspace */
                 {
                 if(col > 0)
                    col--;
                 *(ptr + (col<<1) + row*160) = 0x00;       /* blank */
                 *(ptr+1 + (col<<1) + row*160) = 0x07;
                 }
              else
                 *(ptr + (col<<1) + row*160) = ch;
                 *(ptr+1 + (col<<1) + row*160) = 0x07;
              col++;
              }
           }
        if(col >= 80)                                      /* end of line */
           {
           col = 0;
           row++;
           }
        if(row >= 25)                                      /* bottom screen */
           row = 0;
        if(col == 0)
           for(n = 0;n < 80;n++)                           /* clear line */
              *(ptr + (n<<1) + row*160) = 0x00;
              *(ptr+1 + (n<<1) + row*160) = 0x07;

        CURSOR(row,col);
        }

/* Function to position cursor */

#include <dos.h>

CURSOR(row1,col1)
        int row1,col1;
        {
        union REGS regs;

        regs.h.ah = 2;                                     /* set cursor */
        regs.h.dh = (char)(row1);                          /* row */
        regs.h.dl = (char)(col1);                          /* column */
        regs.h.bh = 0;                                     /* page */

        int86(0x10,&regs,&regs);                           /* Interrupt 10H */
        }
```

Figure 6.10 Functions charout() and CURSOR() used for display output with reset to top of screen.

```
/* Function to write character to screen -- DMA */

charout(ch)
        char ch;
        {
        int n;
        extern int row,col;
        char far *ptr;

        ptr = (char far *) 0xB8000000;                  /* base address */
        if(ch == 0x0A)                                  /* check c.r. */
          col = 0;
        else
            {
            if(ch == 0x0D)                              /* check linefeed */
               row++;
            else
                {
                if(ch == 0x08)                          /* check backspace */
                    {
                    if(col > 0)
                        col--;
                    *(ptr + (col<<1) + row*160) = 0x00;    /* blank */
                    *(ptr+1 + (col<<1) + row*160) = 0x07;
                    }
                else
                    *(ptr + (col<<1) + row*160) = ch;
                    *(ptr+1 + (col<<1) + row*160) = 0x07;
                col++;
                }
            }
        if(col >= 80)                                   /* end of line */
            {
            col = 0;
            row++;
            }
        if(row >= 25)                                   /* bottom screen */
            {
            SCROLL();
            row = 24;
            }
        CURSOR(row,col);
        }
/* Function to scroll screen */

#include <dos.h>

SCROLL()
        {
        union REGS regs;

        regs.h.ah = 6;                                  /* scroll option */
        regs.h.al = 1;                                  /* #blank lines */
        regs.x.cx = 0;                                  /* row/col top */
        regs.h.dh = 25;                                 /* row bottom */
        regs.h.dl = 79;                                 /* col bot right */
        regs.h.bh = 7;                                  /* attribute */

        int86(0x10,&regs,&regs);
        }
```

Figure 6.11 Functions charout( ) (modified) and SCROLL( ) used for display output with scrolling.

of a character on the display using INT 10H, for example, is not necessarily that time consuming. It is reasonable to expect that this action could be interleaved between incoming symbols from the serial port at, say, 1200 baud. What happens, however, when the screen is full? Clearly, it must be scrolled or otherwise manipulated to make room for additional characters. Scrolling requires moving all 2000 (approximately) display buffer characters. This is time consuming. Lafore [10] has suggested an alternate approach in which the cursor is moved to the top of the screen and the screen rewritten top to bottom each time it is filled. This approach is used in Figure 6.10 and was found to be quite successful in providing the display/communications port interface. A similar routine based on scrolling is illustrated in Figure 6.11; however, this routine did drop characters as the scrolling interrupt was called. Both these routines use direct memory access and, consequently, are not useful for OS/2 operation. An assembly language interface is needed in practice for this function. (It is important to note that the base screen segment address is $0 \times B800$ not $0 \times B000$, for the color card.)

Figure 6.12 presents the infinite loop (actually this loop can be exited by pressing F1), which is at the core of the communications on-line processing. This loop checks for keyboard activation and either exits the program or displays an incoming character in the absence of keyboard activity. Finally, Figure 6.13 illustrates four C routines that perform the serial port functions described earlier. These functions set up the registers and call interrupt 0×14.

At 1200 baud, it is necessary to write portions of this program in assembly language that would cause the screen, for example, to scroll. We have, however, generated a workable communications program that illustrates the essentials of com-

```
/* Function to loop on I/O */

#include <conio.h>

loopio()
      {
      char ch;
      extern int RCVR(),STATUS();

      SCRCL();                              /* clear screen */
      while(1)                              /* always on */
        {
        if(kbhit())                         /* ck keyboard on */
          {
          if((ch = getch()) != 0)
            XMIT(ch);                       /* transmit char */
          else
            if(getch() == 59)               /* F1 */
              return;
          }
        if(STATUS())
          {
          ch = (char)(RCVR());              /* load character */
          charout(ch);                      /* to screen */
          }
        }
      }
```

Figure 6.12 Function loopio( ), which contains the operational loop in the communications processing.

```
/* Functions to access the communications port */

#include <dos.h>

INITSP(IO)                                       /* Init ser pt */
        char IO;
        {
        union REGS regs;

        regs.h.ah = 0;                           /* initialize */
        regs.x.dx = 0;                           /* port number */
        regs.h.al = IO;                          /* I/O setup */

        int86(0x14,&regs,&regs);                 /* Interrupt 14H-comm*/
        }

XMIT(ch)                                         /* Transmit char */
        char ch;
        {
        union REGS regs;

        regs.h.ah = 1;                           /* transmit */
        regs.x.dx = 0;                           /* port number */
        regs.h.al = ch;                          /* char to send */

        int86(0x14,&regs,&regs);                 /* Interrupt 14H-comm*/
        }

STATUS()
        {
        union REGS regs;

        regs.h.ah = 3;                           /* status */
        regs.x.dx = 0;                           /* port number */

        int86(0x14,&regs,&regs);                 /* Interrupt 14H-comm*/
        return(regs.x.ax & 0x0100);              /* data ready flag */
        }
/* Function to receive comm port data */

#include <dos.h>

RCVR()
        {
        int xx;
        union REGS regs;

        regs.h.ah = 2;                           /* receive */
        regs.x.dx = 0;                           /* port number */

        int86(0x14,&regs,&regs);                 /* Interrupt 14H-comm*/
        xx = (regs.h.al & 0x007F);               /* Mask */
        return(xx);
        }
```

Figure 6.13 Four C routines for serial port initialization, character transmission, status checking, and character reception.

munications in a real-time programming context. The next section further illustrates real-time programming by presenting an A/D converter example. Again, the time-critical nature of such processing will become apparent.

Results were obtained for the program(s) indicated in this section (both the program that rewrites communications output from the top of the screen and one that scrolls the screen). The scrolling program did, in fact, drop characters, as mentioned, while the program that returns to the screen top seemed to work quite well (although it took a short time to get familiar with this format). In practice, the function charout() should be written in assembly language based on a scrolling format, as indicated. This is beyond the scope of this textbook. The example presented contains the essential features of communications programming.

6.3 AN EXTENDED EXAMPLE: ANALOG-TO-DIGITAL (A/D) CONVERSION

This section describes the implementation of analog-to-digital converters in the IBM microcomputer environment as a means for presenting a second example of real-time computer applications. Basically, A/D converters change an analog voltage (usually time varying) into values capable of being stored and manipulated by digital circuitry such as that found in computers. A user, for example, might like to check the response of a particular audio component such as an amplifier. By sending a swept series of tones through the amplifier, digitizing the output, and using an FFT to generate the output spectrum, a spectrum analysis can be performed on the amplifier response. Such an application is easily within the grasp of existing A/D board adapters available for the IBM microcomputers.

Several comments are in order about the actual A/D process. First, the quality of the conversion assumes that no frequency components exist in the input signal higher than the Nyquist frequency for the conversion process. Typically, this frequency is related to the sample time, t_s, by

$$f_{\text{Nyquist}} = \frac{1}{2t_s} \qquad (6.1)$$

This frequency is the highest usable frequency that can be resolved in the digitized output. A convenient method for ensuring that no higher components exist in the incoming analog data is to pass these data through a low-pass filter that removes all higher-frequency components. Second, when actually implementing the software to accomplish the A/D processing, the code between successive A/D operations should be minimized to ensure that samples occur at the true sample rate, t_s, and not some adjusted slower rate. If, for example, intervening operations cause a sample to be lost each update period, then t_s will assume a period twice its actual clock time and f_{Nyquist} will halve. Also, all frequencies in the digitized output will appear at one-half their actual value. A typical frequency component with period $T = mt_s$ is given by

$$f_m = \frac{1}{mt_s} \qquad (6.2)$$

This example requires the acquisition of some ancillary equipment by the user. Since we do not expect that everyone will have access to such equipment, the example is presented in self-contained fashion as an illustration of real-time computing. That is, the reader will be presented with complete information to be able to understand the nature of the processing. He or she should treat the descriptive code as a representative approach for writing driver software (in the context of real-time computing and hardware interfacing).

There are several aspects to capturing the A/D digitized output data. First, the digitized data can be stored in an output register and acquired upon reading the corresponding port. This mode is referred to as the single-conversion mode. It has the disadvantages described above in that intervening code must be minimized between locations where the actual A/D is triggered for successive conversions. This mode should only be considered for low-speed applications, but it is simple and is the form we will consider in this section. A second mode, the direct memory access (DMA) mode, employs a direct transfer of A/D data from the output register to memory in the host computer. This mode should be employed for high-speed applications where sample coherence must be maintained (the relative phase and amplitude relationship between samples).

With these brief thoughts in mind, it is now useful to consider IBM microcomputer A/D adapters with a particular focus on the Data Translation DT2828. Both hardware functionalism and driver programming will be considered.

6.3.1 IBM Microcomputer A/D Adapters

Analog-to-digital conversion is a process normally of interest to engineers and scientists. The mechanism, however, is used as the basis for such commonplace features as game adapters and the digitizing ''mouse'' used to locate the screen cursor. As we have seen, an analog voltage is converted to a referenced digital value capable of being stored and manipulated by the computer. Table 6.5 lists a number of A/D adapters and their manufacturers. All adapters listed accept input voltages in the range ±10 volts. Most yield 12 or 16 bits of resolution and have varying maximum sample rates. Several support DMA transfer of data to memory. This list is representative of the adapters available and should not be taken as complete.

TABLE 6.5 REPRESENTATIVE HIGH-LEVEL IBM MICROCOMPUTER A/D ADAPTERS

Adapter	Manufacturer	Comments
DT2801 series	Data Translation	±10 V, 27.5 kHz; 12/10-bit accuracy, DMA
DT2821 series	Data Translation	±10 V, 159 kHz; 12/16-bit accuracy, DMA
PCI-20002M-1	Burr-Brown	±10 V, 25 kHz; 12-bit resolution, no DMA
PCI-20019M-1	Burr-Brown	±10 V, 65 kHz; 12-bit resolution, no DMA
#INST 51	Cyber Research, Inc.	±10 V, 14.8 kHz max; 12-bit resolution, no DMA
#INST 52	Cyber Research, Inc.	±10 V, 29.5 kHz max; 12-bit resolution, no DMA
ML-16	Industrial Computer Source	±10 V, 100 kHz; 8 bits
AI08-B	Industrial Computer Source	±10 V, 30 kHz; 12 bits, no DMA
AI016-B	Industrial Computer Source	±10 V, 100 kHz, 12 bits, DMA

6.3.2 Driver Software: Data Translation DT2828

The purpose of this subsection is to consider in detail a representative A/D processor (the Data Translation DT2828) set up for single-conversion mode without DMA. As indicated earlier, the goal of this presentation is to illustrate how one goes about programming a typical real-time application. To make the discussion self-contained, some descriptive material will be presented by way of background.

Figure 6.14 is a representative functional block diagram for the DT2828 in single-conversion mode. The adapter accepts four channels of analog data, which are multiplexed through a programmable gain amplifier to the A/D converter, which yields a 12-bit digitized output. The dynamic range of the converter is ±10 volts spread across 4096 quanta (12-bit decades); hence each bit corresponds to a scale factor

$$\text{scale1} = 20./4096 \qquad (6.3)$$

where $20 = 10 - (-10)$. In the case of the DT2828, this 12-bit value is returned to the IBM I/O bus via a port (0×0244) register or DMA transfer. Thus, in

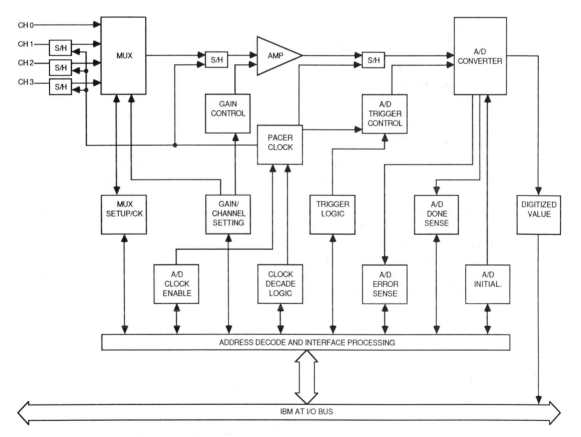

Figure 6.14 Representative functional block diagram for the Data Translation DT2828 A/D conversion module (single-conversion mode).

single-conversion mode the I/O port 0×0244 can be used to input the A/D value.

A pacer clock, with programmable frequency, can be used to control the sample rate of the A/D conversion process. Finally, the A/D process is initiated by suitable triggering. In the case of the single-conversion mode, this is achieved by setting a software trigger. The remaining blocks in the functional diagram specify various logic that must be set up to properly format the adapter for the A/D conversion. Appropriate address decode and interface processing logic are needed to translate the IBM AT port I/O into A/D adapter register format. Basically, the DT2828 has a number of control registers that must be properly specified to set up the A/D processing. In general, Data Translation indicates this control logic by specifying the adapter registers and register format. We will consider each later and apply the register format to a typical A/D conversion problem. Then code will be indicated for a workable driver. The correspondence between abstract register format and actual programming will become apparent. Finally, output for a typical A/D application will be presented.

Returning to Figure 6.14, it is clear that the following logic is needed to properly set up the board:

1. Multiplexer setup
2. A/D clock enable
3. Gain and channel selection
4. Clock divider logic (based on 4-MHz maximum)
5. Software trigger
6. Check for A/D error
7. Check for A/D done
8. Initialize the A/D

Central to any programming problem is a need to understand in what order to accomplish the above tasks. Obviously, this requires some understanding of the DT2828 operation. Some tasks are obvious: the gain and channel selection should be implemented early in the programming. As we will see, many of the tasks fall under the heading of initialization, and these tasks can be accomplished in semiindependent fashion prior to actual real-time execution. Before discussing this, however, we briefly examine the DT2828 A/D-related registers and their function. This information is presented in Table 6.6. The registers listed only indicate the needed ports for implementing the specification of the A/D conversion process. The actual informa-

TABLE 6.6 THE DT2828 A/D-RELATED REGISTERS

Register	Port Address	Comments
ADCSR	0×0240	A/D control status register
CHLCSR	0×0242	Channel-gain specification register
ADDAT	0×0244	Digital data output register from A/D process
SUPCSR	$0 \times 024C$	Supervisor control/status register
TMRCTR	$0 \times 024E$	Pacer clock register

tion output and input from these ports depends on the contents of these registers and the real-time processing dynamics.

Consider each of these registers in some detail with regard to the information content of words input and output from them. We will only consider the non-DMA single-conversion information bits that apply. For the ADCSR register, the single-conversion bits applicable are

ADCSR:

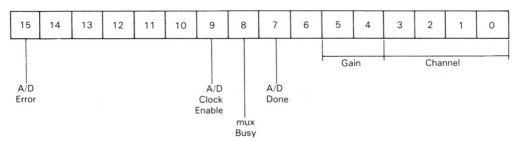

Clearly, when bit 15 is set, an error condition exists in the A/D conversion and data should be flagged. Bits 0 to 3 correspond to the channel designation. Since only channel 0 is to be considered, all these bits are set to zero. Similarly, for the DT2828, gain of unity in the programmable gain amplifier corresponds to bits 4 and 5 equal to zero. Bit 7 indicates that the A/D conversion is complete when set, and bit 8 indicates that the multiplexer is busy selecting an alternate channel when set. Bit 9 enables the A/D pacer clock, but does not trigger the A/D process. The sequence for considering these bits will become apparent in the following discussion.

The channel-gain register is defined as follows:

CHLCSR:

For purposes of establishing the single-conversion process, only bit 15 is of interest. When set, this bit allows the channel selection (bits 0 to 3) and gain setting (bits 4 and 5) of ADCSR to be defined. In the application to be illustrated in this section, this bit will be used to turn on a setting associated with these ADCSR bits.

The ADDAT register returns an A/D value that is scaled and normalized to the converter output. For the DT2828 A/D mode set at the factory, this value can be referenced to a voltage by the following formula:

$$V_{A/D} = \left[(ADDAT) \left(\frac{20}{4096} \right) \right] + 10 \tag{6.4}$$

This formula is accurate to within one least significant bit (LSB).

The supervisory and control register has the following format (applicable to non-DMA single-conversion mode):

SUPCSR:

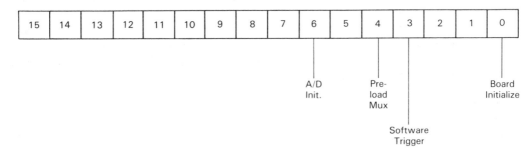

Here board initialization is bit 0 and A/D initialization is bit 6. Preloading the multiplexer (bit 4) ensures that the multiplexer sequence (channels 0 to 3) are properly ordered on each individual A/D conversion. Finally, bit 3 is the all-important software trigger that allows specification of an A/D conversion under program control.

Register TMRCTR has the form

TMRCTR:

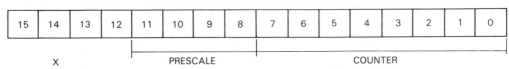

Here the prescale is a divider on the 4-MHz clock and the counter a subdivider. According to Data Translation tables, an A/D clock frequency of 3906.25 Hz is defined by a TMRCTR output value of $0 \times 06F0$. This clock value was used in all subsequent processing.

At this point we have seen how hardware setup values are specified for a typical real-time application in terms of register values. Much of the available hardware for microcomputer development is specified in a fashion similar to the methods illustrated here. The user can expect to receive hardware with register address and contents defined, and he or she is faced with the task of properly defining register contents to accomplish various hardware objectives. We have now seen how the Data Translation DT2828 A/D conversion adapter must be controlled in order to execute a single-conversion process based on register contents. The only remaining step is to specify the dynamics of that control: the order in which registers are set up and controlled.

Figure 6.15 is a flow chart that illustrates the dynamics of a single-conversion process in which the output is scaled and graphed. The first steps in this process set up the DT2828 for proper operation and preload the multiplexer. During this preload process, the real-time programming must wait to ensure that the multiplexer has settled and is ready to begin the A/D conversion cycle. This initialization phase must only be completed once, with the resulting input values representing the state of the adapter at the beginning of each subsequent A/D conversion operation.

Next the software trigger is implemented to accomplish the A/D conversion and both the A/D done status and A/D error status checked to ensure a valid conversion.

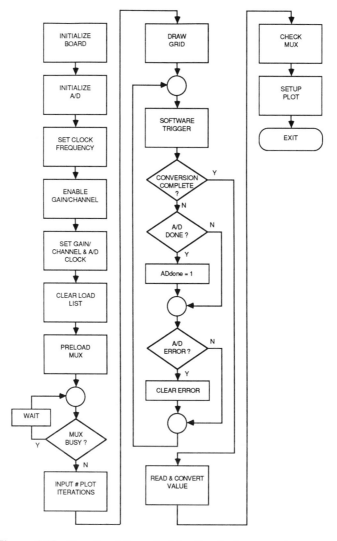

Figure 6.15 Functional flow chart for the single-conversion process.

Following a successful A/D conversion, the value is read from ADDAT, appropriately scaled, and plotted on the display.

Figure 6.16a illustrates the main calling program used to implement the single-conversion A/D process. Each register value used in setting up the board is initialized as an external variable in this routine. Two primary functions are called as part of main(): InitSC(), which initializes the single-conversion process, and Single Convert(), which actually implements the conversion. (The routine plotterm() terminates the plotting mode initiated within Single Convert().) Figure 6.16b presents the routine grid() that sets up the screen clear, 320 × 200 graphics mode, and draws a box.

```
/* Function to call single conversion routines */

int SUPCSR = 0x024C;                                    /* Supervisor */
int TMRCTR = 0x024E;                                    /* timer reg */
int CHLCSR = 0x0242;                                    /* chan-gain reg */
int ADCSR  = 0x0240;                                    /* AD ctrl-stat reg */
int ADDAT  = 0x0244;                                    /* AD data reg */
int ADClockSpeed = 0x06F0;                              /* 3906.25 Hz */

main()
        {
        InitSC();                                       /* Initialize S.C. */
        SingleConvert();                                /* Conversion */
        plotterm();                                     /* terminate plot */
        }
```

(a)

```
/* Function to generate grid */
grid()
        {
        SCRCL();                                        /* clear screen */
        SC320();                                        /* 320 x 200 mode */

        lineh(25,25,275);                               /* top line */
        lineh(175,25,275);                              /* bottom line */
        linev(25,25,175);                               /* left side */
        linev(275,25,175);                              /* right side */
        }
```

(b)

Figure 6.16 (a) Main calling program for the single conversion process and (b) the screen graphics function for displaying the grid and box.

Figure 6.17 contains the initialization function, InitSC(). This routine initializes the following values:

BDInit = 0 x 0001	Initializes the board with SUPCSR
ADInit = 0 x 0040	Initializes the A/D with SUPCSR
LLEnab = 0 x 8000	Turns on load list with CHLCSR
CLKEnb = 0 x 0200	Enables the A/D clock with ADCSR
CLEAR= 0 x 0000	Clears the load list with CHLCSR
PreLdMUX = 0 x 0010	Preloads the MUX with SUPCSR

In addition, the A/D clock speed is specified for the pacer clock. These values are all output via the function outw(), to be discussed shortly. A time-out condition on the MUX busy status is checked by reading ADCSR using inw() and checking bit 8.

Figure 6.18 contains the main processing module, Single Convert(). This routine reads the number of overall iterations of 50 points each to be input and plotted. A grid is set up in the graphics mode and the A/D triggered by setting bit 3 of the SUPCSR register. Both the done condition (bit 7 of ADCSR) and the error condition (bit 15 of ADCSR) are checked and a valid A/D conversion qualified. The array

```
/* Function to Initialize Single Conversion AD */

#include <stdio.h>

InitSC()
        {
        extern int SUPCSR,TMRCTR,CHLCSR,ADCSR;          /* AD reg */
        extern int ADClockSpeed;                        /* clock speed */
        int timer = 500,TOlow;                          /* timer parameters */

        int BDInit = 0x0001;                            /* Clear board reg */
        int ADInit = 0x0040;                            /* init AD value */
        int LLEnab = 0x8000;                            /* enable L.L. value */
        int CLKEnb = 0x0200;                            /* enable AD clk */
        int CLEAR  = 0x0000;                            /* clear L.L. value */
        int PreLdMUX = 0x0010;                          /* Preload Mux value */

        outw(SUPCSR,BDInit);                            /* init board */
        outw(SUPCSR,ADInit);                            /* init AD */
        outw(TMRCTR,ADClockSpeed);                      /* set clock */
        outw(CHLCSR,LLEnab);                            /* load list enable */
        outw(ADCSR,CLKEnb);                             /* AD clock */
        outw(CHLCSR,CLEAR);                             /* clear load list */
        outw(SUPCSR,PreLdMUX);                          /* Preload MUX */

        TOlow = inw(ADCSR);                             /* time-out */
        while((TOlow & 0x0100) != CLEAR)
            {
            timer--;
            if(timer < 5)
                {
                printf("Error on time-out -- MUX busy \n");
                exit(1);
                }
            TOlow = inw(ADCSR);
            }
        }
```

Figure 6.17 Function InitSC() used to initialize the DT2828.

yy1[] is next loaded with the A/D data and a MUX busy check performed. Once 50 values are obtained, scaling and plotting are performed. The plotting is accomplished via DMA techniques previously outlined in order to ensure rapid turnaround of the graphics output.

Figure 6.19a and b illustrates inw() and outw(), the port I/O assembly language routines. These routines were developed because C port I/O routines outp() and inp() are intended for byte I/O and the DT2828 uses word I/O. [In Chapter 7 we will see that Version 5.0 has two additional routines, inpw() and outpw(), that accomplish this function.]

Figure 6.20 illustrates the experimental setup employed to check the performance of the DT2828. A B and K Precision Model 3011 Function Generator was used to generate analog inputs to the board (DT2828) via the Data Translation DT707 Terminal Board. A B and K Precision Model 1541 40-MHz Dual Trace Oscilloscope was used to monitor the function generator output. The DT707 Terminal Board was connected to a DT2828 A/D adapter in an IBM AT microcomputer.

Figure 6.21a presents the output for no signal present. Figure 6.21b illustrates the response for a 100-Hz sine wave with peak-to-peak amplitude of 1.5 volts. Figures 6.21c and d illustrate the response of this sine wave with peak-to-peak amplitudes of 5.0 and 7.5 volts, respectively. Finally, Figures 6.21e and f illustrate

```
/* Function to perform conversion and plot*/

#include <stdio.h>

SingleConvert()
    {
    extern int SUPCSR,ADCSR,ADDAT;                  /* AD regs */
    int timer,n,N,RegCheck,ADdone,TOlow;            /* parameters */
    int m,l;                                        /* misc indexes */
    float xx1[51],xx2[51],yy1[51],yy2[51];          /* plot arrays */
    float scale1;                                   /* plot parameters */

    int SOFTTRIG = 0x0008;                          /* Soft trigger */
    int CLEARERR = 0x0040;                          /* Clear error flag */
    int CLEAR    = 0x0000;                          /* Clear */

    printf("Input number of iterations \n");
    scanf("%d",&N);
    scale1 = 20./4096.;                             /* AD scale */
    grid();                                         /* plot grid */
    for(n = 1;n <= 50;n++)
       xx1[n] = n*5. + 25.;                         /* x-axis points */
    for(n = 1;n <= N;n++)
        {
        for(m = 1;m <= 50;m++)
            {
            timer = 100;                            /* timer limit */
            RegCheck = 0x0000;                      /* clear reg var */
            ADdone = 0;                             /* AD done flag */
            outw(SUPCSR,SOFTTRIG);                  /* software trigger */
            while((ADdone == 0) && (timer >5))
                {
                RegCheck = inw(ADCSR);              /* ck AD done */
                if((RegCheck & 0x0080) != 0x0000)
                    ADdone = 1;                     /* AD done */
                if((RegCheck & 0x8000) != 0x0000)
                    outw(SUPCSR,CLEARERR);          /* Clear error bit */
                timer--;                            /* decrement timer */
                }
                                                    /* Process data */
            yy1[m] = inw(ADDAT);                    /* input AD */
                                                    /* Time-out */
            timer = 10000;                          /* MUX busy check */
            TOlow = inw(ADCSR);
            while((TOlow & 0x0100) != CLEAR)
                {
                timer--;
                if(timer < 5)
                    {
                    printf("Error on time-out -- Conversions \n");
                    exit(1);
                    }
                TOlow = inw(ADCSR);
                }
            }
        for(l = 1;l <= 50;l++)
            yy1[l] = 100. - 7.5*(yy1[l]*scale1-10.);
        if(n != 1)
            {
            for(l = 2;l <= 49;l++)
                uDMApoin(xx2[l-1],xx2[l],yy2[l-1],yy2[l]);   /* unplot */
            }
        for(l = 2;l <= 49;l++)
            DMApoint(xx1[l-1],xx1[l],yy1[l-1],yy1[l]);       /* plot */
        for(l = 1;l <= 50;l++)
            {
            xx2[l] = xx1[l];                        /* swap x-points */
            yy2[l] = yy1[l];                        /* swap y-points */
            }
        }
    }
```

Figure 6.18 Function SingleConvert(), which performs the A/D conversions and plots the results.

```
PAGE 40,132
TITLE INW - INPUT WORD QUANTITY FROM C PROGRAM (INW.ASM)
;
;         DESCRIPTION: Input word quantity from C calling program
;
;                          register - [BP + 4]
;                          value    - AX
;
_TEXT   SEGMENT BYTE PUBLIC 'CODE'
        ASSUME CS:_TEXT
        PUBLIC _inw
_inw    PROC    NEAR
                                        ;
        PUSH BP                         ;Save caller's frame ptr
        MOV BP,SP                       ;frame ptr to old BP
        SUB SP,8                        ;allocate lcl var. space
                                        ;
        MOV DX,WORD PTR[BP + 4]         ;input register
        IN AX,DX                        ;input word value in AX
                                        ;
        MOV SP,BP
        POP BP
        RET
_inw    ENDP
_TEXT   ENDS
        END
```

(a)

```
PAGE 40,132
TITLE OUTW - OUTPUT WORD QUANTITY (OUTW.ASM)
;
;         DESCRIPTION: Word output with
;
;                          register - [BP + 4]
;                          value    - [BP + 6]
;
_TEXT   SEGMENT BYTE PUBLIC 'CODE'
        ASSUME CS:_TEXT
        PUBLIC _outw
_outw   PROC    NEAR
                                        ;
        PUSH BP                         ;Save caller's frame ptr
        MOV BP,SP                       ;frame ptr to old BP
        SUB SP,8                        ;allocate lcl var. space
                                        ;
        MOV DX,WORD PTR[BP + 4]         ;output register
        MOV AX,WORD PTR[BP + 6]         ;word value for output
        OUT DX,AX
                                        ;
        MOV SP,BP
        POP BP
        RET
_outw   ENDP
_TEXT   ENDS
        END
```

(b)

Figure 6.19 (a) Word input function and (b) word output function in assembly language.

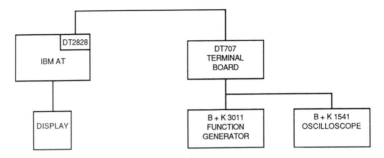

Figure 6.20 Experimental A/D setup.

the response for a 100-Hz triangular wave with amplitudes of 1.5 and 5.0 volts, respectively.

The routines used in this program are defined as follows:

`main()`	(Figure 6.16a)
`InitSC()`	(Figure 6.17)
`Single Convert()`	(Figure 6.18)
`plotterm()`	(Figure 2.8d)
`grid()`	(Figure 6.16b)
`SCRCL()`	(Figure 2.8b)
`SC320()`	(Figure 2.8b)
`lineh()`	(Figure 2.8e)
`linev()`	(Figure 2.8e)
`outw()`	(Figure 6.19b)
`inw()`	(Figure 6.19a)
`uDMApoin()`	(Figure 4.33b)
`DMApoint()`	(Figure 4.33a)

With regard to the scaling in Figures 6.21a through f, note that there are approximately 1.3 cycles of sine or triangular wave appearing in each figure. Since this corresponds to 50 samples of a frequency of 100 Hz, it follows that the apparent sample frequency satisfies

$$t_s = \frac{(1.3 \text{ cycles})(1/100 \text{ Hz})}{50 \text{ samples}} \qquad (6.5)$$

$$= 260 \text{ microseconds}$$

This translates to an approximate sampling frequency of

$$f_s = \frac{1}{t_s} \qquad (6.6)$$

$$= 3844 \text{ Hz}$$

This perceived value is approximate, based on the approximate number of cycles visible in 50 samples, and is very close to the actual 3906.25-Hz sample rate. Note that it is particularly critical that the real-time processing not introduce delays in the code in Single Convert(), which intervenes between samples.

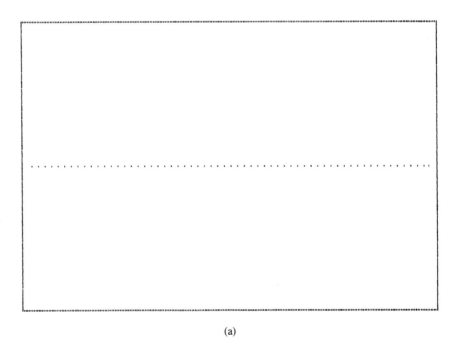

(a)

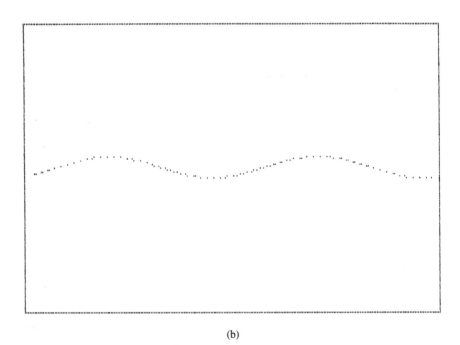

(b)

Figure 6.21 Output for the A/D converter: (a) no signal, (b) 1.5 volt, 100 Hz,

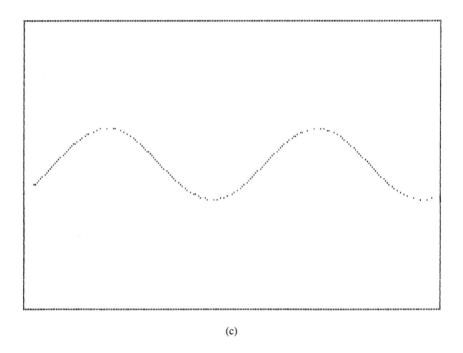

(c)

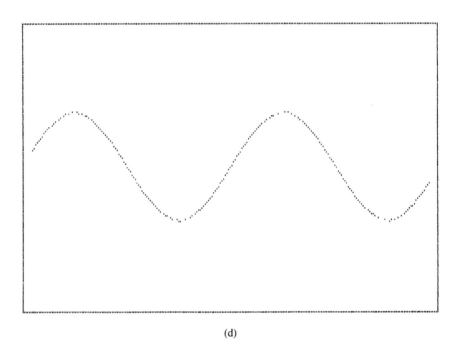

(d)

Figure 6.21 (*Continued*) (c) 5 volt, 100 Hz, (d) 7.5 volt, 100 Hz,

Real Time Programming with C   Chap. 6

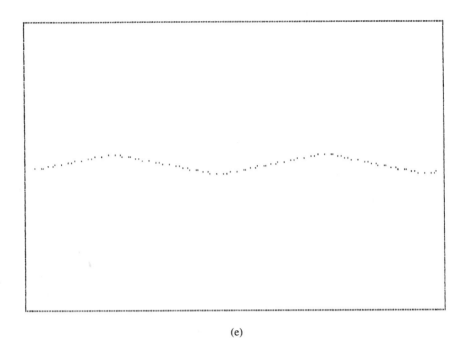

(e)

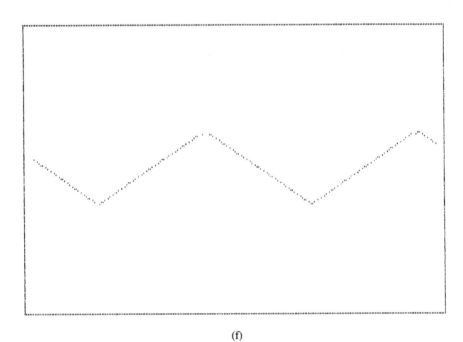

(f)

Figure 6.21 (*Concluded*) (e) 1.5 volt triangle, 100 Hz, and (f) 5 volt triangle, 100 Hz.

SUMMARY

This chapter has addressed the topic of real-time programming in the context of the C language. Generally, real-time programming tends to be time critical, and normal C optimization (compiler) is insufficient for such applications. At time-sensitive points in the program dynamics, the code is best generated using assembly language, where register arithmetic is enforced and the execution avoids memory-oriented instructions. Real-time programming is an important microcomputer application and can be expected to become even more so as the PS/2 computers, with their greater speed, come into wider acceptance. The issue of what operating system should be used for such applications is being resolved by IBM. It should be emphasized that DOS 3.x is adequate for many applications; however, OS/2 has the limitation that memory may not be directly accessed under program control because of the multitasking feature.

Two examples were presented: a serial port communications program, based on the Hayes Smartmodem 1200, and an A/D conversion program, using the Data Translation DT2828. The communications program runs successfully on the 80286 (or higher) machines under DOS 3.x. No run-time examples were presented because the screen print feature causes the communications program to misinterpret print commands. The actual operation was validated, however, and successful communications established. The A/D conversion program was successfully operated against input from a function generator and the results presented.

REFERENCES

1. Savitzky, S. R., *Real-Time Microprocessor Systems*, Van Nostrand Reinhold Co., New York, p. 4 (1985).

2. *Smartmodem 1200 Hardware Reference Manual*, Hayes Microcomputer Products, Inc., 5923 Peachtree Industrial Blvd., Norcross, GA (1983).

3. *DT2801 Series User Manual*, Data Translation, 100 Locke Dr., Marlborough, MA (1987).

4. McNamara, J. E., *Technical Aspects of Data Communications*, Digital Press, Digital Equipment Corp., Bedford, MA (1982).

5. Papoulis, A., *Probability, Random Variables, and Stochastic Processes*, McGraw-Hill Book Co., New York, NY, p. 362 (1965).

6. *iAPX 286 Programmer's Reference Manual*, Intel Corp., 3065 Bowers Ave., Santa Clara, CA (1985).

7. Rauch-Hindin, W., "OS/2: Not the only Road on IBM's PS/2 Map," *Mini-Micro Systems*, p. 35, July (1987).

8. "NS16450/INS8250A/NS16C450/INS82C50A Asynchronous Communications Element," National Semiconductor Corp., 2900 Semiconductor Dr., Santa Clara, CA (1985).

9. *Technical Reference Personal Computer*, Personal Computer Hardware Reference Library, IBM Corp., P. O. Box 1328, Boca Raton, FL (1981).

10. Lafore, R., *Microsoft C Programming for the IBM*, Howard W. Sams and Co., Indianapolis, IN (1987).

PROBLEMS

6.1. Which of the following applications represent examples of real-time software development:
  a. The game PacMan
  b. DBase III
  c. Data loggers
  d. Lotus 1-2-3 graphics
  e. ProComm
  f. PC Talk

6.2. Indicate the highest frequency resolvable in a sampled data system where the sample interval is 1 microsecond? 1 millisecond? 1 second?

6.3. Call instructions can take in excess of 177 clock cycles to execute. What are the implications for real-time modular programming on the IBM AT in view of this consideration?

6.4. A null modem configuration is one in which two devices (a computer and a plotter, for example) are directly connected. Assuming an RS-232C cable configuration is used, indicate what pins must be connected to what pins for the two devices to properly hand shake and pass data.

6.5. Describe how one would encode a quadrature phase shift keyed (QPSK) signal assuming an arbitrary reference bit grouping for the +45 degree state.

6.6. Indicate the port addresses for each 8250 register.

6.7. Indicate the AX register inputs for INT 14H for the following cases:
  a. 300 baud, even parity, 1 stop bit, 7 bit word
  b. 9600 baud, even parity, 1 stop bit, 7 bit word
  c. 1200 baud, no parity, 1 stop bit, 8 bit word
  d. 4800 baud, odd parity, 2 stop bits, 7 bit word

6.8. In Figure 6.5, why is it possible to reference __DATA1 and not __DATA? When is __DATA reloaded and what happens to segment __DATA1 at this point?

6.9. Instead of

```
LEA DX,_MES1
```

write an alternate set of instructions that accomplishes the same thing.

6.10. What would be the Hayes Smartmodem 1200 command to dial information using pulse dialing?

6.11. What is the command to change the wait time (following dialing) for a carrier to 60 seconds before hang-up?

6.12. In Figure 6.6, what happens if row and col are made local to main()?

6.13. In modck() (Figure 6.9), why isn't the test on the result code OK of the form

```
if(ch=='0')?
```

6.14. In Figure 6.10, the function charout() has three sets of screen output statements. These statements are grouped to output characters. What modifications must be made to reduce these statements from pairs to a single output in each of the three cases?

6.15. In a 12-bit A/D converter that spans a ±10-volt dynamic range, what is the resolution or quanta associated with this converter?

6.16. What register value should be loaded to specify setting the A/D initialization for the DT2828?

6.17. Why is it necessary in Figure 6.18 [in the function Single Convert()] to input the A/D value to yy1[] and not scale the data simultaneously?

PART III
Higher Levels of Abstraction

7

Compiler Enhancements and IBM Display Modes

Throughout the preceding discussion we emphasized that the programming techniques developed in this book up to this point are applicable to both Versions 4.0 [1] and 5.0 [2] of the Microsoft C Compiler. With regard to graphics programming, for example, we accessed the system software using interrupts and screen DMA. This programming is characteristically referred to as low-level programming. It requires specific knowledge about IBM microcomputer system firmware (the BIOS) and the operating system. A primary goal for the text is to provide the reader with this low-level knowledge in order that a solid base can be developed for understanding programming mechanisms in the IBM microcomputer context. Microsoft has included the facility for generating screen graphics, as an example, directly from the compiler support library in Version 5.0 [3]. These additions to the normal include file library (the files graph.h. and bios.h) are not portable and are specific to the Microsoft implementation. The naming convention is nonstandard.

In earlier discussion we focused on the IBM microcomputer text and Color Graphics Adapter (CGA) standards. Most readers have access to these display modes and are able to generate a hard-copy output for these modes. With the advent of the Enhanced Graphics Adapter (EGA) and Video Graphics Adapter (VGA) standards, other display modes with greater resolution are possible [4]. These two additional modes are addressed in this chapter.

The principal programming example used in this chapter involves an estimation of the correlation between two processes. Included with this example is a brief discussion of the mathematics behind this estimation procedure. This discussion is written for readers with little or no experience in understanding correlation. The reader will need, however, to use the FFT of Appendix A. An application of the correlation function is illustrated based on perceived trends in stock market activity. The initial programming examples, which include generation of EGA graphics display for the logarithm plot presented in Chapter 5, are intended to illustrate the primitives provided as part of the Version 5.0 compiler.

7.1 MICROSOFT C COMPILER VERSION 5.0 ENHANCEMENTS

Changes to the Version 5.0 compiler include a number of features that are all categorized as enhancements: internal compiler software changes, syntax changes, new options and methods for compiling, and additional library routines (see reference 2, for example). We briefly consider each of these enhancements in this section. Next, we will address the PS/2 displays (Section 7.2) and follow this discussion with several examples (Section 7.3).

7.1.1 Syntax Changes

As part of the Version 5.0 implementation, complete function prototyping (specification of the argument type for formal parameters) has led to the function type *void* for functions that do not use parameters. This function type has been recognized by earlier compiler additions but not formally implemented. Other types can be alternatively specified for functions that contain no parameters but return values.

A type specifier, *const*, is now allowed. This specifier indicates values that cannot be modified. It should be particularly useful when passing fixed parameters that are globally initialized, but used in separate linkable modules. In this case, the define directive cannot be easily used to categorize local variables. Use of the const type without additional modifiers assumes a basic int type for the variable (short). The type *volatile* has been introduced to allow a variable to be used that can be changed by events beyond the control of the immediate program (such as an asynchronous process). We do not recommend the use of this type unless absolutely needed, as in some low-level I/O applications.

An integer type, *enum*, has been included and has the general form

```
enum [tag] {list} [declarator1 [,,,,declaratorN]];
```

An example of this type would be

```
enum color
  {
  black,
  blue,
  purple,
  yellow = 0,
  white = 0,
  green,
  }dark;
```

In this example, the values assigned are black = 1, blue = 2, purple = 3, yellow = 0, white = 0, and green = 4. An enumeration type named color is defined, and a variable dark is declared to be of that type. A declaration of the form

```
enum color light = white;
```

assigns the value 0 to light. This type is of basic type integer and can be used to categorize members of a similar class that are conveniently ordered.

The Version 5.0 compiler has several string-handling features that enhance or facilitate string manipulation. One such feature is the concatenation of long strings enclosed in double quotation marks. Consider the printf output statement

```
printf ("Several lines of text can be connected,"
        "together using this feature,");
```

This yields the line

```
Several lines of text can be connected together using this feature,
```

The "stringizing" and "token-pasting" operators provide quite useful enhancements to the C macro capabilities. The token-pasting operator is the double pound sign, ##, and acts in similar fashion to the assembly language concatenation operation &. Consider a macro

```
# define sq_array(n)    array##n * array##n
```

When called as sq__array(7), this yields the replacement

```
array7 * array7
```

The stringizing operator is the single pound sign and when used passes the calling argument as a string literal. Consider the macro

```
# define   array_class(y)   printf(#y":\n")
```

When called as

```
array_class(arrayA)
```

this yields

```
arrayA:
```

Clearly, these preprocessor directives can be useful to introduce flexibility into C macros.

The use of + in front of a number (unary operator) to indicate justification is now permitted. Use of *long double* is allowed and specifies a *double* type. Use of *long float* is not permitted.

7.1.2 Invoking the Compiler and Linker

Version 5.0 of the Microsoft C compiler has modified the calls to the compiler from the earlier Version 4.0. Essentially, the use of the msc command has been replaced by the use of the command. The user can actually accomplish the compile and link operations using a single step. We continue to recommend that each module be separately compiled, because this helps isolate compilation errors. The user would then link these object modules in the usual fashion.

7.1.3 DOS and BIOS Additions

In Chapter 4, we considered the DOS and BIOS services, which called interrupts and functions, associated with INT 21H. The Version 5.0 compiler has an added set of functions that allows direct access to these services using manifest constants to specify service options. It is beyond the scope of this text to provide a detailed description for each added function (the reader is referred to reference 3), but Table 7.1 lists the added functions and associated service. Chapter 4 contains a more detailed description of the activities of each service associated with the corresponding interrupt.

It is important to recognize the low-level flexibility added to the Microsoft C compiler by the functions appearing in Table 7.1. Many of the operations that required accessing DOS and BIOS using int86() can now be accomplished using these functions. The programmer must still understand the purpose of the interrupt (as was always required), but a more abstract access technique has now been provided.

In addition to allowing high-level access of the BIOS and DOS services, several of the functions appearing in Table 7.1 provide means for avoiding assembly language mixed-programming interfaces when operations are not time sensitive. We recall that in Chapter 6 it was necessary to clear and enable interrupts for some of the real-time programming. Using __disable() and __enable() allows the programmer to implement the CLI and STI instructions for which no C counterpart has previously existed.

It is clear, then, that the Version 5.0 compiler includes a significant low-level capability for the C language when implemented with DOS, which could only be accessed using the int86() function earlier. The distinction here is that a more abstract high-level call to these DOS and BIOS services is now possible using the added Version 5.0 routines. These routines are still based on the same underlying DOS and BIOS services called using int86(), as discussed earlier in this text. The added BIOS and DOS functions are contained in bios.h and dos.h, respectively.

7.1.4 Graphic Primitives

It is probably clear that Microsoft has attempted to make its Version 5.0 compiler more user friendly. Throughout this book we have generated graphics output from programs using low-level calls to int86() with INT 10H specified. These calls were implemented in some basic routines: SCRCL(), SC320(), SC80(), and WRDOT(). Microsoft has added a number of high-level graphics routines that can be used for generating this type of output. Table 7.2 illustrates these routines and their associated function. The reader is again referred to reference 3 for a more detailed discussion. These functions are contained in graph.h. Most of the functions contained in Table

TABLE 7.1 BIOS AND DOS C COMPILER SERVICES

Service	INT/Function	Comment
_bios_disk	13H	Disk access
_bios_equiplist	11H	Specifies equipment
_bios_keybrd	16H	Keyboard service
_bios_memsize	12H	Memory size
_bios_printer	17H	Printer services
_bios_serialcom	14H	Serial communication services
_bios_timeofday	1AH	Current clock count
_dos_allocmem	48H	Memory allocation
_dos_close	3EH	Closes file (handle)
_dos_creat	3CH	Creates file (handle)
_dos_creatnew	5BH	Creates file (handle)
_dos_findfirst	4EH	Info about first instance at file
_dos_findnext	4FH	Next name that matches *path*
_dos_freemem	49H	Release block of memory
_dos_getdate	2AH	Obtains current date
_dos_getdiskfree	36H	Obtains info on disk drive
_dos_getdrive	19H	Obtains disk drive
_dos_getfileattr	43H	Obtains file attributes
_dos_getftime	57H	Obtains date/time of file (handle)
_dos_gettime	2CH	Obtains system time
_dos_getvect	35H	Obtains value of interrupt vector
_dos_keep	31H	Installs TSR programs
_dos_open	3DH	Opens file
_dos_read	3FH	Reads file
_dos_setblock	4AH	Changes segment size
_dos_setdate	2BH	Changes date
_dos_setdrive	0EH	Sets drive (A, B, . . .)
_dos_setfileattr	43H	Sets file attribute
_dos_setftime	57H	Sets date/time of file (handle)
_dos_settime	2DH	Sets system time
_dos_setvect	25H	Sets the interrupt vector
_dos_write	40H	Writes file
_chain_intr	—	Chains one interrupt handler to another
_disable	—	Executes a clear interrupts instruction
_enable	—	Executes a set interrupts instruction
_farjmp	—	Executes a jump beyond 128 bytes
_harderr	—	Establishes INT 24H invoked routine
_hardresume	—	Returns to DOS from INT 24H service call
_hardretn	—	Return to application from INT 24H service call

7.2 are self-explanatory, and we will illustrate several of these in Section 7.3 when the graphic examples for this chapter are presented.

7.1.5 Other Functions

Microsoft has added some additional function capability to the Version 5.0 compiler, and it will be convenient to merely refer the reader to reference 3 for a discussion of these functions. Basically, an enhanced capability for debugging heap-related

TABLE 7.2 VERSION 5.0 GRAPHICS ROUTINES

Function	Comment
_arc	Draws an elliptical arc
_clearscreen	Clears the screen
_displaycursor	Turns cursor on in graphics mode
_ellipse	Draws an allipse
_floodfill	Fills an area of display using the fill mask
_getbkcolor	Retrieves background pixel color
_getcolor	Returns pixel color
_getcurrentposition	Returns logical coordinate position
_getfillmask	Returns current fill mask
_getimage	Stores the bounded screen image
_getlinestyle	Returns current line style
_getlogcoord	Translates physical to logical coordinates
_getphyscoord	Translates logical to physical coordinates
_getpixel	Retrieves the pixel value at the logical point
_gettextcolor	Returns the pixel value of the text color
_gettextposition	Returns the current text position
_getvideoconfig	Returns the current graphics configuration
_imagesize	Returns the number of bytes needed to store the image
_lineto	Draws a line
_moveto	Moves the cursor to a logical position
_outtext	Outputs a string
_pie	Draws a wedge
_putimage	Transfers to the screen an image stored in a buffer
_rectangle	Draws a rectangle
_remapallpalette	Remaps all available pixels
_selectpalette	Selects palette in selected CGA or EGA modes
_setactivepage	Specifies screen buffer page locations
_setbkcolor	Sets the background color
_setcliprgn	Masks the screen
_setcolor	Sets color
_setfillmask	Sets the fill mask
_setlinestyle	Sets the line style
_setlogorg	Moves the logical origin to a physical point
_setpixel	Sets pixel color
_settextcolor	Sets the text color
_settextposition	Relocates current text position
_settextwindow	Defines a text window
_setvideomode	Fixes the video mode
_setviewport	Defines a screen mask and sets origin at upper left
_setvisualpage	Selects visual page for EGA mode
_wrapon	Controls wraparound of text

problems is included. Since we do not devote too much effort in this text to heap manipulation (this is primarily of interest to systems programmers), we will not consider these routines further. Two useful routines, however, are inpw( ) and outpw( ). These are the counterpart to the input and output port routines for word I/O that we developed in assembly language in Chapter 6, since Version 4.0 did not support these routines.

7.2 PS/2 DISPLAY SUPPORT

With the advent of the IBM PS/2 microcomputers, a new graphics standard, the Video Graphics Adapter (VGA), was developed. Table 7.3 lists the common IBM display modes, and the VGA modes are available to the IBM Personal Computer, IBM Personal Computer XT, and IBM Personal Computer AT (or Model 286) if the IBM Personal System/2 Display Adapter (reference 4) is installed. In this book we have emphasized the use of 320 × 200 graphics (with AL = 5) for use on a black and white graphics screen. In the Version 5.0 compiler, this would correspond to a setup command:

```
_setvideomode (_MRESNOCOLOR);
```

The manifest constants indicated in Table 7.3 represent the parameter setting required by the __setvideomode() function. Also indicated is the AL value corresponding to the mode in question. [We could set the mode in the usual fashion with int86().] A hard-copy output for this medium resolution CGA mode was achievable using the Prt-Sc command with GRAPHICS.COM resident. In the following section, programs to generate EGA and VGA output are developed. A resident program, egaepson.com, by Van Horn was used to generate hard-copy output for EGA screen graphics in a fashion similar to that for CGA [5] (where GRAPHICS.COM was used).

TABLE 7.3 DISPLAY MODE ALTENATIVES (AH = 0)

Raster	Type	Colors	Manifest Constant	AL	Comments
40 × 25	CGA	16	_TEXTBW40	00H	Requires graphics display
40 × 25	CGA	16	_TEXTC40	01H	Requires graphics display (color)
80 × 25	CGA	16	_TEXTBW80	02H	Requires graphics display
80 × 25	CGA	16	_TEXTC80	03H	Requires graphics display (color)
320 × 200	CGA	4	_MRES4COLOR	04H	Requires graphics display (color)
320 × 200	CGA	4	_MRESNOCOLOR	05H	Requires graphics display (color)
640 × 200	CGA	2	_HRESBW	06H	Requires graphics display
80 × 25	MONO	1	_TEXTMONO	07H	Requires monochrome display
320 × 200	EGA	16	_MRES16COLOR	0DH	Requires graphics display (color)
640 × 200	EGA	16	_HRES16COLOR	0EH	Requires graphics display (color)
640 × 350	EGA	1	_ERESNOCOLOR	0FH	Requires graphics display
640 × 350	EGA	64	_ERESCOLOR	10H	Requires graphics display (color)
640 × 480	VGA	2	_VRES2COLOR	11H	PS/2 adapter only (color)
640 × 480	VGA	16	_VRES16COLOR	12H	PS/2 adapter only (color)
320 × 200	VGA	256	_MRES250COLOR	13H	PS/2 adapter only (color)
—	—	—	_DEFAULTMODE	—	—

7.3 ADDITIONAL GRAPHIC EXAMPLES

The primary purpose of this section is to introduce the Version 5.0 compiler graphic enhancements. Also, we illustrate the correspondence between graphic functions developed earlier in the text and their implementation based on these enhancements.

We emphasize that use of int86() to accomplish such activities as setting the display mode is very similar to use of the more general __setvideomode() function with its array of manifest constants. The latter approach sets the CPU registers in an identical fashion to that used when calling int86(). The addition of primitives such as __lineto() facilitates drawing straight lines. The reader will note that the same number of parameters must be input to both processes: two points, (x_1, y_1) and (x_2, y_2). In the Version 5.0 case, for example, the function __moveto() must first be called to locate the starting point. Then the __lineto() function is called to draw a line to the second point.

From the viewpoint of programming, both approaches are useful. The low-level approach demonstrates how the assembly-level programming interface is accomplished, among other features. The high-level primitives facilitate a user-friendly environment. Since this is a book about how to program, understanding dictates that both approaches be developed.

A secondary purpose for this section is to introduce programming for the EGA and VGA modes. Table 7.3 illustrates how __setvideomode() can be used to change the display mode. It further presents the variety of modes available to the programmer (VGA can only be accessed with PS/2 hardware or a PS/2 Display Adapter in the PC, XT, XT286, and AT).

Finally, we examine the use of structures in a higher level of abstraction for data architectures. As this discussion points out, the emphasis on modularity developed in this text frequently requires that large amounts of data be passed from one module to another. In some respects this is counter to current approaches to programming, where the emphasis is on locally defined data structures. On the other hand, the trade-off is that complex calculations can be modularized and implemented a segment at a time. This topic is treated in Section 7.3.4.

7.3.1 EGA Mode

The Enhanced Graphics Adapter or EGA display mode has become an accepted IBM standard in the quest for increased screen raster resolution. This mode denotes a raster of 640×350 pixels, and it corresponds to an increase in vertical screen resolution by a factor of 1.75 over the earlier CGA graphics (where a maximum of 200 scan lines was possible).

In Chapter 5, we illustrated the results for a geometric sum in the semilog plot of Figure 5.13. This plot was set up using CGA graphics. Figure 7.1 illustrates a main calling program for accomplishing this plot and the graphics function SCEGA() used to set up the EGA mode. This latter function is based on setting the appropriate register value and calling int86().

Examination of Figure 7.1 demonstrates the expanded resolution of the EGA mode, where, for example, the y range for the containing box spans [25, 325] pixels. In Figure 7.1, the main() function calls a function log__plot__EGA(), which is illustrated in Figure 7.2. This routine first reads the data from a disk file, acquires new minimum and maximum values for plotting, calls box__log__EGA() to set up the EGA mode, and generates the log plot for the array x[] and y[] loaded from disk.

The function box__log__EGA() is illustrated in Figure 7.3. This routine is

```
/* Function to set EGA 640 x 350 mode */

#include <dos.h>

SCEGA()
        {
        union REGS regs;

        regs.h.ah = 0;                                  /* Set mode */
        regs.h.al = 0x10;                               /* EGA 640 x 350 clr*/

        int86(0x10,&regs,&regs);
        }
/* Function to drive log_plot() */

#include <stdio.h>
#include <dos.h>
#include <conio.h>

int xxbeg=25;                                           /* x box begin */
int xxend=525;                                          /* x box end */
int yybeg=25;                                           /* y box begin */
int yyend=325;                                          /* y box end */
int y_scale=150;                                        /* y scale factor */
int x_scale=500;                                        /* x scale factor */
float min=1.e14;                                        /* max limit */
float max=-1.e14;                                       /* min limit */
int x_grid1=125;                                        /* 1st vert grid */
int x_grid2=225;                                        /* 2nd vert grid */
int x_grid3=325;                                        /* 3rd vert grid */
int x_grid4=425;                                        /* 4th vert grid */
int grid_scale=100;                                     /* total scale */

float x[250],y[250],xx[250],yy[250];

main()
        {
        log_plot_EGA();
        plotterm();
        }
```

Figure 7.1 Functions to (a) specify EGA mode and (b) set up logarithm plot using EGA.

general purpose and only restricted to EGA mode because of the call to SCEGA(). We could have removed the two calls to SCRCL() and SCEGA() and the routine could then apply to any video mode selected (externally) because of the generalized nature of the variable references. The box and grid lines are drawn using bbox__ EGA(), lineh(), and linev(), which are all presented in Figure 7.4 [along with plotterm() and plotpoint()]. The primitives used in Figure 7.4 all correspond to Version 5.0 library functions; no reference to the int86() function has been made in Figure 7.4. The reader should note, for example, that the routine SCEGA() appearing in Figures 7.1 and 7.4 is functionally equivalent. This is also true of all the functions appearing in Figure 7.4 and their earlier counterparts. Similarly, Figure 7.5 presents the routines linev() and lineh(), which are functionally equivalent to their earlier counterparts but call the Version 5.0 primitives. The correspondence between Version 5.0 functions and earlier graphics routines should now be clear. Figure 7.6 illustrates the EGA annotated output for the semilog plot of the geometric sum appearing in Figure 5.13.

```
/* Function to create log plot */

#include <dos.h>
#include <math.h>
#include <stdio.h>
#include <conio.h>

log_plot_EGA()
        {
        extern float x[],y[],xx[],yy[];                /* Data arrays */
        extern float min,max;
        extern int grid_scale,x_scale,y_scale,yyend,xxbeg;
        int N,n,yy1;
        float yy11,scale;
        double x1,y1;

        N = diskrd();                                  /* Read data disk */

        for(n = 1;n <= N;n++)                          /* determine from y */
            {
            if(max < y[n])
                max = y[n];
            if(min > y[n])
                min = y[n];
            }

        printf("max = %f ,min = %f \n",max,min);
        printf("Input adjusted max\n");               /* input new max/min */
        scanf("%f",&max);
        printf("Input adjusted min\n");
        scanf("%f",&min);

        box_log_EGA();                                 /* Draw box-grids */
                                                       /* Scale [0,100] */
        scale = grid_scale/(max - min);
        for(n = 1;n <= N;n++)
            {
            x1 = (double)(scale*y[n]);                 /* start y log */
            if((y[n]>min) && (y[n]<max))
                {
                y1 = log10(x1);                        /* calculate y log */
                yy11 = (float)(y1);
                yy1 = (int)(yyend - yy11*y_scale);     /* scaled for graph */
                }
            else
                yy1 = 0.;                              /* out of range */
            xx[n] = xxbeg + (n - 1)*(x_scale/N);       /* x scale */
            yy[n] = yy1;
            }

        for(n = 1;n <= (N - 1);n++)                    /* plot in range pts */
            {
            if((y[n]>=min) && (y[n+1]>=min) && (y[n]<=max) && (y[n+1]<=max))
                plotpoint(xx[n],xx[n+1],yy[n],yy[n+1]);
            }
        }
```

Figure 7.2 Function to generate logarithm plot.

7.3.2 VGA Mode

IBM has developed an additional graphics standard, the Video Graphics Adapter
(VGA) mode, for use with the PS/2 computers and associated adapters. Figure 7.7
presents the main calling routine for a program that plots the geometric sum of
Figure 7.6 (and Figure 5.13) in VGA mode. Note in Figure 7.7 the range of *y*

```
/* Function to draw log box */

#include <math.h>
#include <dos.h>

box_log_EGA()
        {
        extern int xxbeg,xxend,yybeg,yyend;                /* box limits */
        extern int x_grid1,x_grid2,x_grid3,x_grid4,y_scale;
        int n,yy1;
        float yy11;
        double x1,y1;

        SCRCL();                                           /* clear screen */
        SCEGA();                                           /* 640 x 350 EGA clr */

        bbox_EGA(xxbeg,xxend,yybeg,yyend);                 /* standard box */

        linev(x_grid1,yybeg,yyend);                        /* Vertical grids */
        linev(x_grid2,yybeg,yyend);
        linev(x_grid3,yybeg,yyend);
        linev(x_grid4,yybeg,yyend);

                                                           /* 2 cycle log */
        for(n = 2;n <= 10;n++)
            {
            x1 = (double)(n);
            y1 = log10(x1);                                /* 1st y-grids */
            yy11 = (float)(y1);
            yy1 = (int)(yyend - yy11*y_scale);             /* scaled point */
            lineh(yy1,xxbeg,xxend);
            }

        for(n = 20;n <= 100;n = n + 10)
            {
            x1 = (double)(n);
            y1 = log10(x1);                                /* 2nd y-grids */
            yy11 = (float)(y1);
            yy1 = (int)(yyend - yy11*y_scale);             /* scaled point */
            lineh(yy1,xxbeg,xxend);
            }
        }
```

Figure 7.3 Function to generate logarithm grid in EGA mode.

values spans [25, 425] pixels. Also, a new VGA log plot routine, log__plot__ VGA(), has been called. This function is illustrated in Figure 7.8, and it, in turn, calls box__log__VGA(), which sets the display mode through a call to SCVGA(). Both of these latter routines are illustrated in Figure 7.9. The SCVGA() routine appearing in Figure 7.9 simply calls the Version 5.0 primitive __setvideomode() with the 16-color VGA manifest constant, __VRES16COLOR.

The VGA mode selected has a 640 × 480 raster and was successful in yielding the high-resolution VGA presentation. We do not illustrate the performance because no VGA terminate and stay resident (TSR) program was accessible to yield a hard copy of the screen. The programs illustrated in Figures 7.6 through 7.9 are basically the same as those counterparts for the EGA presentation. The only differences are in the graph limits appearing in the preprocessor definitions (Figure 7.6) and the actual __setvideomode() routine [SCVGA()]. We still call the general-purpose box routine bbox__EGA(), which is really independent of mode. Figure 7.10 illustrates

```
/* Function to terminate plot -- version 5.0 routines */

#include <stdio.h>
#include <graph.h>

plotterm()
        {
        while(!kbhit());                                /* wait keystroke */
        _setvideomode(_DEFAULTMODE);                    /* return 80 x 25 */
        }
/* Function to plot connecting line -- version 5.0 routines */

plotpoint(xx1,xx2,yy1,yy2)
        float xx1,xx2,yy1,yy2;
        {
        short x1,x2,y1,y2;
        short color_line = 0x07;                        /* white line */
        short style = 0xFFFF;                           /* solid line */

        x1 = (int)(xx1);                                /* type convert */
        x2 = (int)(xx2);
        y1 = (int)(yy1);
        y2 = (int)(yy2);

        _moveto(x1,y1);                                 /* locate start */
        _setcolor(color_line);                          /* set line color */
        _setlinestyle(style);                           /* set style */
        _lineto(x2,y2);                                 /* draw line */
        }
/* Function to draw box -- version 5.0 routines */

bbox_EGA(xbeg,xend,ybeg,yend)
        int xbeg,xend,ybeg,yend;
        {
        _rectangle(_GBORDER,xbeg,ybeg,xend,yend);
        }
/* Function to clear screen -- version 5.0 routines */

SCRCL()
        {
        _clearscreen(_GCLEARSCREEN);
        }
/* Function to set EGA mode -- version 5.0 routines */

SCEGA()
        {
        _setvideomode(_ERESCOLOR);
        }
```

Figure 7.4 Screen graphics functions using Version 5.0 primitives.

a library, egalib.lib, that is used to hold all the EGA and VGA display-related setup functions.

7.3.3 Structures Revisited

Data structures can be used to considerable advantage when clarifying the overall data architecture in a large program. We have not emphasized their use because the programs contained within this book all tend to be small in size and, hence, the advantages posed by using structures are not apparent. One problem associated with structures is that they cannot easily be defined in one module and used in

```
/* Function to plot horizontal line -- version 5.0 routines */

#include <graph.h>

lineh(y,x1,x2)
        int y,x1,x2;
        {
        if(x1 > x2)
            {
            _moveto(x2,y);
            _lineto(x1,y);
            }
        else
            {
            _moveto(x1,y);
            _lineto(x2,y);
            }
        }
/* This routine plots a vertical line -- version 5.0 routines */

#include <graph.h>

linev(x,y1,y2)
        int x,y1,y2;
        {
        if(y1 > y2)
            {
            _moveto(x,y2);
            _lineto(x,y1);
            }
        else
            {
            _moveto(x,y1);
            _lineto(x,y2);
            }
        }
```

Figure 7.5 Functions lineh() and linev() using Version 5.0 primitives.

another module because the compiler has no way to cross-reference the structure storage.

In this section, we present three different data architectures for a program that sets up and plots a sequence of grid lines and rectangles. These will eventually be used, with slight modification, for plotting results of a program that generates correlated output from two processes (more on correlation later). Figure 7.11a presents the main calling routine for a function corr__setup( ), which plots these correlation grids. Arrays containing the grid start positions (x or y) for EGA mode are illustrated in this figure and defined as global integer quantities in the preprocessor area. The actual plotting is accomplished with the function corr__setup( ) in Figure 7.11b. We emphasize that although this is an apparently small program it must call each grid variant individually and would become large if many operations were required. For example, the instructions calling __rectangle( ) were individually stated for each box: box1, box2, and box3.

In Figure 7.12, a structure, box, was created to act as a template for each set of box variables. Following this, three structures, b[], were set up with the same information as appeared in Figure 7.11. Again, a routine corr__setup( ) was used

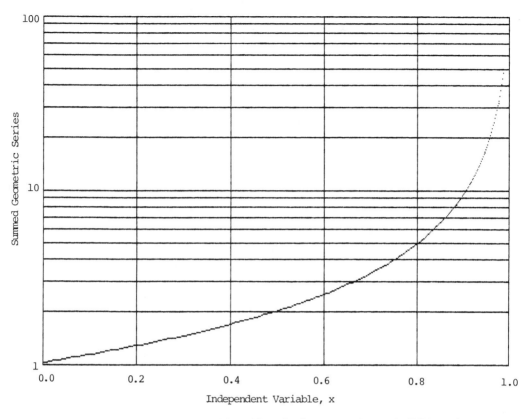

Figure 7.6   Annotated logarithm plot for geometric sum in EGA mode.

```
/* Function to drive log_plot() -- VGA mode */

#include <stdio.h>
#include <dos.h>
#include <conio.h>

int xxbeg=25;                                      /* x box begin */
int xxend=525;                                     /* x box end */
int yybeg=25;                                      /* y box begin */
int yyend=425;                                     /* y box end */
int y_scale=200;                                   /* y scale factor */
int x_scale=500;                                   /* x scale factor */
float min=1.e14;                                   /* max limit */
float max=-1.e14;                                  /* min limit */
int x_grid1=125;                                   /* 1st vert grid */
int x_grid2=225;                                   /* 2nd vert grid */
int x_grid3=325;                                   /* 3rd vert grid */
int x_grid4=425;                                   /* 4th vert grid */
int grid_scale=100;                                /* total scale */

float x[250],y[250],xx[250],yy[250];

main()
        {
        log_plot_VGA();
        plotterm();
        }
```

Figure 7.7   Function to set up logarithm plot using VGA.

```
/* Function to create log plot -- VGA mode */

#include <dos.h>
#include <math.h>
#include <stdio.h>
#include <conio.h>

log_plot_VGA()
    {
        extern float x[],y[],xx[],yy[];              /* Data arrays */
        extern float min,max;
        extern int grid_scale,x_scale,y_scale,yyend,xxbeg;
        int N,n,yy1;
        float yy11,scale;
        double x1,y1;

        N = diskrd();                                /* Read data disk */

        for(n = 1;n <= N;n++)                         /* determine from y */
            {
            if(max < y[n])
                max = y[n];
            if(min > y[n])
                min = y[n];
            }
        printf("max = %f ,min = %f \n",max,min);
        printf("Input adjusted max\n");              /* input new max/min */
        scanf("%f",&max);
        printf("Input adjusted min\n");
        scanf("%f",&min);

        box_log_VGA();                               /* Draw box-grids */
                                                     /* Scale [0,100] */
        scale = grid_scale/(max - min);
        for(n = 1;n <= N;n++)
            {
            x1 = (double)(scale*y[n]);               /* start y log */
            if((y[n]>min) && (y[n]<max))
                {
                y1 = log10(x1);                      /* calculate y log */
                yy11 = (float)(y1);
                yy1 = (int)(yyend - yy11*y_scale);   /* scaled for graph */
                }
            else
                yy1 = 0.;                            /* out of range */
            xx[n] = xxbeg + (n - 1)*(x_scale/N);     /* x scale */
            yy[n] = yy1;
            }

        for(n = 1;n <= (N - 1);n++)                   /* plot in range pts */
            {
            if((y[n]>=min) && (y[n+1]>=min) && (y[n]<=max) && (y[n+1]<=max))
                plotpoint(xx[n],xx[n+1],yy[n],yy[n+1]);
            }
    }
```

Figure 7.8 Function to generate logarithm plot that calls VGA routine.

for the actual plot. The structure box and the actual structure variables b[] were treated as global and called from corr__setup() using structure pointers. It was necessary to compile *both* main() and corr__setup() as part of the same module in order that corr__setup() would have information about box and b[]. Note the simpler form for the called routine, corr__setup().

Figure 7.13 illustrates a third alternative in which the structure definition is handled locally to corr__setup(). In this instance, the functions can be treated as

```
/* Function to draw log box -- VGA mode */

#include <math.h>
#include <dos.h>

box_log_VGA()
        {
        extern int xxbeg,xxend,yybeg,yyend;              /* box limits */
        extern int x_grid1,x_grid2,x_grid3,x_grid4,y_scale;
        int n,yy1;
        float yy11;
        double x1,y1;

        SCRCL();                                          /* clear screen */
        SCVGA();                                          /* 640 x 480 VGA clr */

        bbox_EGA(xxbeg,xxend,yybeg,yyend);                /* standard box */

        linev(x_grid1,yybeg,yyend);                       /* Vertical grids */
        linev(x_grid2,yybeg,yyend);
        linev(x_grid3,yybeg,yyend);
        linev(x_grid4,yybeg,yyend);

                                                          /* 2 cycle log */
        for(n = 2;n <= 10;n++)
            {
            x1 = (double)(n);
            y1 = log10(x1);                               /* 1st y-grids */
            yy11 = (float)(y1);
            yy1 = (int)(yyend - yy11*y_scale);            /* scaled point */
            lineh(yy1,xxbeg,xxend);
            }
        for(n = 20;n <= 100;n = n + 10)
            {
            x1 = (double)(n);
            y1 = log10(x1);                               /* 2nd y-grids */
            yy11 = (float)(y1);
            yy1 = (int)(yyend - yy11*y_scale);            /* scaled point */
            lineh(yy1,xxbeg,xxend);
            }
        }
```

(a)

```
/* Function to set VGA mode -- version 5.0 routines */

#include <graph.h>

SCVGA()
        {
        _setvideomode(_VRES16COLOR);
        }
```

(b)

Figure 7.9 Functions to (a) generate logarithm grid in VGA mode and (b) to set VGA mode.

separately compiled modules because all structure references are local. Figure 7.14 presents the output for each of the programs appearing in Figures 7.11, 7.12, and 7.13. In the following section, we briefly discuss the implications for the modularity of programs in light of the above considerations about structures and data architecture.

```
_bbox_EGA.........pltterm                _lineh...........lineh
_linev...........linev                   _plotpoint........pltterm
_plotterm........pltterm                  _SCEGA...........pltterm
_SCRCL...........pltterm                  _SCVGA...........scvga


linev              Offset: 00000010H  Code and data size: 40H
  _linev

lineh              Offset: 00000180H  Code and data size: 42H
  _lineh

pltterm            Offset: 000002f0H  Code and data size: ceH
  _bbox_EGA           _plotpoint        _plotterm          _SCEGA
  _SCRCL

scvga              Offset: 00000620H  Code and data size: 12H
  _SCVGA
```

Figure 7.10 Listing of library, egalib.lib.

7.3.4 More on Modularity

To design and debug large programs, modular construction is a key to success. Associated with this notion, however, are two conflicting requirements. First, it is desirable that variable definitions be treated as local whenever possible. Second, complex computations must be reduced to subunits during the calculation process for implementation and debugging purposes. This latter requirement suggests that variables must be passed among modules, frequently in global fashion because they represent large arrays of data. Clearly, the software design must represent a compromise between these two extremes.

How does one approach the resolution of designing large-scale systems within the above constraints? The following guidelines are suggested:

1. Modularize computational units of relative complexity into subunits that produce a single intermediate product where possible.
2. For complex computational modules, pass the same final input/output global arrays from module to module.
3. Use intermediate arrays in a local fashion (even though they are defined globally) where possible.
4. Use pointer arithmetic (or known index values) to address array elements when passing values among functions.

In this discussion, we have used intermediate to refer to dummy arrays, and it is assumed that all arrays are defined globally to avoid loading the stack. The emphasis above has been on arrays because it is assumed that large data blocks will be of interest. The manipulation of small amounts of variable data can easily be implemented within the confines of the normal formal parameter mechanism.

```
/* Main calling program to ck scorega.c */

short box12_xgrid[5] = {0,65,105,145,185};          /* box12 vert */
short box3_xgrid[5] = {0,365,405,445,485};          /* box3 vert */
short box1_ygrid[5] = {0,45,65,85,105};             /* box1 hor */
short box2_ygrid[5] = {0,220,240,260,280};          /* box2 hor */
short box3_ygrid[4] = {0,95,165,235};               /* box3 hor */

main()
      {
      corr_setup();
      plotterm();
      }
```

(a)

```
/* Function to setup correlation screens -- EGA */

#include <graph.h>
#include <stdio.h>

corr_setup()
      {
      short x1box1=25,x2box1=225,y1box1=25,y2box1=125;
      short x1box2=25,x2box2=225,y1box2=200,y2box2=300;
      short x1box3=325,x2box3=525,y1box3=25,y2box3=305;

      extern short box12_xgrid[];                    /* box12 vertical */
      extern short box3_xgrid[];                     /* box3 vertical */
      extern short box1_ygrid[];                     /* box1 horizontal */
      extern short box2_ygrid[];                     /* box2 horizontal */
      extern short box3_ygrid[];                     /* box3 horizontal */

      short color_line=0x07;
      int n;

      _setvideomode(_ERESCOLOR);                     /* 640 x 350 EGA */
      _clearscreen(_GCLEARSCREEN);
      _setcolor(color_line);
      _rectangle(_GBORDER,x1box1,y1box1,x2box1,y2box1);
      _rectangle(_GBORDER,x1box2,y1box2,x2box2,y2box2);
      _rectangle(_GBORDER,x1box3,y1box3,x2box3,y2box3);

      for(n = 1;n <= 3;n++)
         lineh(box3_ygrid[n],x1box3,x2box3);

      for(n = 1;n <=4;n++)
         {
         lineh(box1_ygrid[n],x1box1,x2box1);
         lineh(box2_ygrid[n],x1box2,x2box2);

         linev(box12_xgrid[n],y1box1,y2box1);
         linev(box12_xgrid[n],y1box2,y2box2);
         linev(box3_xgrid[n],y1box3,y2box3);
         }
      }
```

(b)

Figure 7.11 Functions to (a) call correlation grid setup and (b) generate grid. Illustrates conventional data architecture.

```
/* Main calling program to ck scoreg    */

#include <graph.h>
#include <stdio.h>

#define Y_GRID 5                                    /* maximum y-grid+1 */
#define X_GRID 5                                    /* maximum x-grid+1 */
#define Y_SHORT_GRID 4                              /* short y-grid+1 */

struct box
        {
        short x1,x2,y1,y2;                          /* box parameters */
        short x_grid[X_GRID];                       /* vert grid pos */
        short y_grid[Y_GRID];                       /* hor grid pos */
        };

                                                    /* Initialize boxes */
struct box b[3] =
        {{25,225,25,125,{0,65,105,145,185},{0,45,65,85,105}},
        {25,225,200,300,{0,65,105,145,185},{0,220,240,260,280}},
        {325,525,25,305,{0,365,405,445,485},{0,95,165,235,0}}};

main()
        {
        corr_setup(b,b);
        plotterm();
        }

/* Function to setup correlation screens -- EGA */

corr_setup(BI,M)
        struct box *BI,*M;                          /* box index ptr */
        {
        short color_line = 0x07;
        int n,m;

        _setvideomode(_ERESCOLOR);                  /* 640 x 350 EGA */
        _clearscreen(_GCLEARSCREEN);
        _setcolor(color_line);
        for(m = 0;m <= 2;m++,M++)
            _rectangle(_GBORDER,M->x1,M->y1,M->x2,M->y2);

        M = BI;
        for(m = 0;m <= 2;m++,M++)
            {
            for(n = 1; n<= 4;n++)
                {
                if(!((m==2) && (n==4)))
                    lineh(M->y_grid[n],M->x1,M->x2);
                }
            }
        M = BI;
        for(m = 0;m <= 2;m++,M++)
            {
            for(n = 1;n <= 4;n++)
                {
                linev(M->x_grid[n],M->y1,M->y2);
                }
            }
        }
```

Figure 7.12 Function to set up and generate correlation grid. Illustrates data structures globally defined.

```
                /* Main calling program to ck ckscor2.c */

        main()
                {
                corr_setup();
                plotterm();
                }
```

(a)

```
/* Function to setup correlation screens -- EGA */

#include<graph.h>

corr_setup()
        {
struct box
        {
        short x1,x2,y1,y2;                       /* box parameters */
        short x_grid[5];                         /* vert grid pos */
        short y_grid[5];                         /* hor grid pos */
        };
                                                 /* Initialize boxes */
static struct box b[3] =
        {
        {25,225,25,125,{0,65,105,145,185},{0,45,65,85,105}},
        {25,225,200,300,{0,65,105,145,185},{0,220,240,260,280}},
        {325,525,25,305,{0,365,405,445,485},{0,95,165,235,0}}
        };
        struct box *M;                           /* pointer to box */
        short color_line = 0x07;
        int n,m;

        _setvideomode(_ERESCOLOR);               /* 640 x 350 EGA */
        _clearscreen(_GCLEARSCREEN);
        _setcolor(color_line);
        M = b;
        for(m = 0;m <= 2;m++,M++)
            _rectangle(_GBORDER,M->x1,M->y1,M->x2,M->y2);
        M = b;
        for(m = 0;m <= 2;m++,M++)
            {
            for(n = 1; n<= 4;n++)
                {
                if(!((m==2) && (n==4)))
                    lineh(M->y_grid[n],M->x1,M->x2);
                }
            }
        M = b;
        for(m = 0;m <= 2;m++,M++)
            {
            for(n = 1;n <= 4;n++)
                {
                linev(M->x_grid[n],M->y1,M->y2);
                }
            }
        }
```

(b)

Figure 7.13 Function to (a) set up and (b) generate correlation grid. Illustrates data structures locally defined allowing modularity.

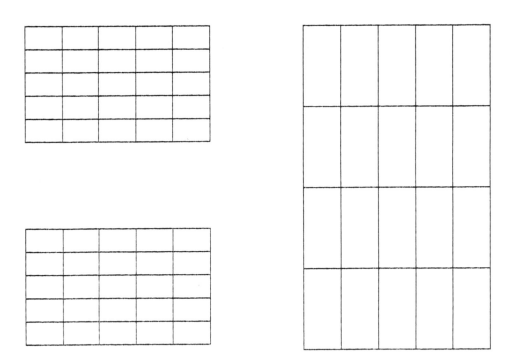

Figure 7.14   Output for Figures 7.11, 7.12, and 7.13.

7.3.5 Correlation Functions

The expectation value of the product of two real-valued quantities is defined to be the correlation of these quantities at lag T, where [6]

$$R_{xy}(T) = E\{x(t)y(t + T)\} \qquad (7.1)$$

Here the expectation value, $E\{. . .\}$, corresponds to the average of the product of these quantities when they are offset an amount T. Suppose, for example, we have the arrays $\{x(1), x(2), x(3), . . . , x(N - 3), x(N - 2), x(N - 1), x(N)\}$ and $\{y(1), y(2), y(3), . . . , y(N - 3), y(N - 2), y(N - 1), y(N)\}$. The cross-correlation $R_{xy}(2)$ would satisfy

$$R_{xy}(2)$$
$$= \frac{1}{N[x(1)y(3) + x(2)y(4) + \cdots + x(N - 2)y(N) + x(N - 1)y(1) + x(N)y(2)]} \qquad (7.2)$$

Here the series are said to wrap-around. If $y = x$, the resulting output is the auto-correlation function.

If we are given $\{x(n)\}$ and $\{y(n)\}$ as real-valued arrays, the complete correlation $\{R(n)\}$ can be defined for values of n from $-N/2$ to $N/2$ using the fast Fourier transform (FFT) of Appendix A. Specifically, assume

$$X(m) = \text{FFT}_m[x(n)] = X_R(m) + iX_I(m) \qquad (7.3a)$$

$$Y(m) = \text{FFT}_m[y(n)] = Y_R(m) + iY_I(m) \qquad (7.3b)$$

where $n = 1, 2, \ldots, N$ and $m = 1, 2, \ldots, N$. The results $X(m)$ and $Y(m)$ are frequency-domain results and can be multiplied together to yield the cross-spectrum

$$S_{xy}(m) = [X_R(m)Y_R(m) + X_I(m)Y_I(m)] + i[X_I(m)Y_R(m) - X_R(m)Y_I(m)] \quad (7.4)$$

where R and I denote real and complex components, respectively, of the frequency-domain transforms. The cross-spectrum above comes from

$$S_{xy}(m) = X(m)Y^*(m) \quad (7.5)$$

where the asterisk denotes complex conjugation [that is, $(x + iy)^* = (x - iy)$]. The output correlation function then satisfies

$$R_{xy}(n) = \text{FFT}_n^{-1}[S_{xy}(m)] \quad (7.6)$$

where the inverse FFT has been indicated. What is the significance of $R_{xy}(n)$? Clearly, this quantity is a measure of how closely two variables track each other. We will address a philosophical interpretation of correlation below, but first we consider the implementation of the above algorithm.

Correlation function program. Figure 7.15a illustrates a main calling module for a program designed to generate the correlation of two arrays (of equal length) of input data. This routines calls five functions:

load_arrays()	(Figure 7.16)
corr()	(Figure 7.17)
corr_setup()	(Figure 7.19)
plot_arrays()	(Figure 7.20)
plotterm()	(Figure 7.4)

```
/* Main calling routine for correlation program */

float areal[256],aimag[256],x1_real[256],x1_imag[256];
float x2_real[256],x2_imag[256],x[256],y[256],R[256],R1[256];
float xx1[256],xx3[256],yy1[256],yy2[256],yy3[256];      /* plot arrays */
float x1[256],x2[256];                                    /* initial values */

float x1_max=-1.e14,x1_min=1.e14,x2_max=-1.e14,x2_min=1.e14;
float x11_max,x22_max;                                    /* array scaling */
float Rmax=-1.e14,Rmin=1.e14;                             /* R graph scaling */
int NSTART,NEND,NTOTAL,m;

main()
        {
        int N,n,n1;                                       /* array count */

        load_arrays();                                    /* load 2 arrays */
        N = NTOTAL;                                        /* set count */
        corr(N);                                          /* calc correlation */

        corr_setup();                                     /* plot setup */
        plot_arrays(N);                                   /* plotting */
        plotterm();

        }
```

Figure 7.15a Main calling program for generating correlation function output.

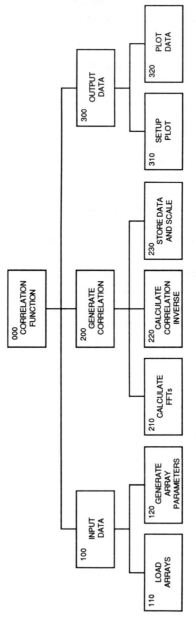

Figure 7.15b Structure chart for program to generate correlation.

```
/* Function to load arrays for correlation */

#include <stdio.h>

load_arrays()
        {
        extern float x[],y[],x1_real[],x1_imag[],x2_real[];
        extern float x2_imag[],x1[],x2[];
        extern int NSTART,NTOTAL,NEND,m;

        int n,N1,N2;

        N1 = diskrd();                                  /* 1st array */
        for(n = 1;n <= N1;n++)
            {
            x1_real[n] = y[n];                          /* initial values */
            x1[n] = y[n];
            x1_imag[n] = 0.;
            }
        N2 = diskrd();                                  /* 2nd array */
        for(n = 1;n <= N2;n++)
            {
            x2_real[n] = y[n];                          /* initial values */
            x2[n] = y[n];
            x2_imag[n] = 0.;
            }
        if(N1 != N2)
            {
            printf("Error on matching array lengths");
            exit(1);
            }
        printf("Array length = %d\n",N1);
        printf("Input start array index\n");
        scanf("%d",&NSTART);
        printf("Input total array length\n");
        scanf("%d",&NTOTAL);
        NEND = (NSTART + NTOTAL) - 1;
        printf("Input order of FFT\n");
        scanf("%d",&m);
        }
```

Figure 7.16 Function to load two arrays from disk and set up correlation function inputs.

The function load_arrays() places the two arrays to be correlated in memory; corr() computes the actual scaling and calls correlation() (Figure 7.18); corr_setup() is a modified version of Figure 7.13 in which only the outer box is plotted for box3; and plot_arrays() plots the actual correlated output. Note the modular method by which this computation is performed. This allowed easy debugging at each stage in the calculation. Figure 7.15b presents the overall structure chart for the program. This program is general purpose and can be used to correlate any two sequences of less than 256 points, but the sequences must be of equivalent length and this length an integer power of 2.

Figure 7.16 contains the module that loads the two arrays, and it calls the function diskrd() appearing in Figure 5.6. We have modified diskrd() slightly so that it no longer prints out the data read in. The two sets of arrays returned are x1_real[], x1_imag[], x2_real[], and x2_imag[]. A more desirable approach, but in this case conceptually difficult, would be to call load_arrays() twice, once each to load the x1 and x2 arrays. In small programs of this sort, the trade-off is about even. Figure 7.17 calculates the two transformed arrays (see Equations 7.3a

```
/* Function to setup correlation and scale */

#include <stdio.h>

corr(N)
        int N;                                          /* # pts */
        {
        extern float areal[],aimag[];
        extern float x1_real[],x1_imag[],x2_real[],x2_imag[];
        extern int NSTART,NEND,m;
        extern float x1_max,x2_max,x1_min,x2_min;
        extern float x11_max,x22_max;                   /* scaling */

        int n,n1;

        for(n = NSTART;n <= NEND;n++)
            {
            if(x1_real[n] > x1_max)                     /* min/max */
                x1_max = x1_real[n];
            if(x1_real[n] < x1_min)
                x1_min = x1_real[n];
            if(x2_real[n] > x2_max)
                x2_max = x2_real[n];
            if(x2_real[n] < x2_min)
                x2_min = x2_real[n];
            }
        new_scale();                                    /* complete scaling */

        n1 = NSTART;
        for(n = 1;n <= N;n++)                            /* load x1 */
            {
            areal[n] = x1_real[n1]/x11_max;
            aimag[n] = x1_imag[n1]/x11_max;
            n1++;
            }

        FFT(m,1);                                       /* Fast Fourier Tran */

        n1 = NSTART;
        for(n = 1;n <= N;n++)                            /* reload */
            {
            x1_real[n] = areal[n];
            x1_imag[n] = aimag[n];
            areal[n] = x2_real[n1]/x22_max;
            aimag[n] = x2_imag[n1]/x22_max;
            n1++;
            }

        FFT(m,1);                                       /* Fast Fourier Tran */

        for(n = 1;n <= N;n++)                            /* reload */
            {
            x2_real[n] = areal[n];
            x2_imag[n] = aimag[n];
            }

        correlation(N,m);                               /* Calc. correlation */
        }

/* Function to generate new scaling */

new_scale()
        {
        extern float x1_max,x1_min,x2_max,x2_min,x11_max,x22_max;

        printf("x1 (max,min) = %f %f\n",x1_max,x1_min);
        printf("Input new max for scaling array\n");
        scanf("%f",&x11_max);
```

Figure 7.17 Function to generate inputs to frequency-domain calculation of correlation. Scaling is also performed.

```
            printf("x2 (max,min) = %f %f\n",x2_max,x2_min);
            printf("Input new max for scaling array\n");
            scanf("%f",&x22_max);

            printf("x1 max = %f\n",x1_max);
            printf("Input new value for scaling graph\n");
            scanf("%f",&x1_max);

            printf("x1 min = %f\n",x1_min);
            printf("Input new value for scaling graph\n");
            scanf("%f",&x1_min);

            printf("x2 max = %f\n",x2_max);
            printf("Input new value for scaling graph\n");
            scanf("%f",&x2_max);

            printf("x2 min = %f\n",x2_min);
            printf("Input new value for scaling graph\n");
            scanf("%f",&x2_min);

            }
```

Figure 7.17 (*Concluded*)

```
/* Function to generate correlation values */

correlation(N,m)
        int m,N;
        {
        extern float areal[],aimag[],R[];
        extern float x1_real[],x1_imag[],x2_real[],x2_imag[];
        extern float Rmax,Rmin;                         /* R graph limits */
        int n;

        for(n = 1;n <= N;n++)                           /* cross-spectrum */
            {
            areal[n] = x1_real[n]*x2_real[n]+x1_imag[n]*x2_imag[n];
            aimag[n] = x2_real[n]*x1_imag[n]-x1_real[n]*x2_imag[n];
            }

        FFT(m,-1);                                      /* Fast Fourier Tran */

        for(n = 1;n <= N;n++)
            {
            R[n] = areal[n];                            /* correlation */
            if(R[n] > Rmax)
                Rmax = R[n];
            if(R[n] < Rmin)
                Rmin = R[n];
            }

        printf("Rmax = %f Rmin = %f\n",Rmax,Rmin);
        printf("Input new Rmax for graph scale\n");
        scanf("%f",&Rmax);
        printf("Input new Rmin for graph scale\n");
        scanf("%f",&Rmin);

        }
```

Figure 7.18 Function to perform frequency-domain correlation.

```
/* Function to setup correlation screens -- EGA */

#include<graph.h>

corr_setup()
    {
struct box
    {
    short x1,x2,y1,y2;                          /* box parameters */
    short x_grid[5];                            /* vert grid pos */
    short y_grid[5];                            /* hor grid pos */
    };
                                                /* Initialize boxes */
static struct box b[3] =
    {
    {25,225,25,125,{0,65,105,145,185},{0,45,65,85,105}},
    {25,225,200,300,{0,65,105,145,185},{0,220,240,260,280}},
    {325,525,25,305,{0,0,0,0,0},{0,0,0,0,0}}
    };
    struct box *M;                              /* pointer to box */
    short color_line = 0x07;
    int n,m;

    _setvideomode(_ERESCOLOR);                  /* 640 x 350 EGA */
    _clearscreen(_GCLEARSCREEN);
    _setcolor(color_line);
    M = b;
    for(m = 0;m <= 2;m++,M++)
        _rectangle(_GBORDER,M->x1,M->y1,M->x2,M->y2);
    M = b;
    for(m = 0;m <= 1;m++,M++)
        {
        for(n = 1; n<= 4;n++)
            lineh(M->y_grid[n],M->x1,M->x2);
        }
    M = b;
    for(m = 0;m <= 1;m++,M++)
        {
        for(n = 1;n <= 4;n++)
            linev(M->x_grid[n],M->y1,M->y2);
        }
    }
```

Figure 7.19 Modified function to set up grids for correlation screen.

and 7.3b). Some scaling is accomplished by this routine. Figure 7.18 yields the correlation function output itself. This consists of first taking the product of X(m) and Y(m) (in this case {x1_real[m]+i x1_imag[m]} and {x2_real[m]-i x2_imag[m]} and then calculating the inverse FFT. Only areal[] is used from the FFT (remember that the FFT function uses two general-purpose arrays, areal[] and aimag[]). Figure 7.19 sets up the correlation display screen and Figure 7.20 actually implements the output plot. The FFT program must be reordered when the inverse is calculated (as part of the butterfly operation, a reordering of the input occurs and upon calculating the inverse the user must reorder the outputs). The function plot_arrays() sets up the plot of the two input arrays and the correlated output data.

Correlating random sequences. To appreciate the significance of the correlation function, it is useful to consider the cross-correlation of two random sequences and the autocorrelation of the same sequence. For purposes of illustration the two sequences generated by the function grand() (Figure 2.15) will be used because they are independent.

```
/* Function to plot correlation arrays */

plot_arrays(N)
        int N;                                          /* array length */
        {
                                                        /* graph */
        extern float x1_max,x1_min,x2_max,x2_min,Rmax,Rmin;

struct bbox
        {
        float x1box1,x2box1,y1box1,y2box1;
        float x1box2,x2box2,y1box2,y2box2;
        float x1box3,x2box3,y1box3,y2box3;
        };
static struct bbox bb =
        {
        25.,225.,25.,125.,
        25.,225.,200.,300.,
        325.,525.,25.,305.,
        };

        extern float x1[],x2[],R[];
        extern int NSTART,NEND;
        extern float xx1[],xx3[],yy1[],yy2[],yy3[];

        float ybox1_scale,ybox2_scale,ybox3_scale;
        float xbox1_scale,xbox3_scale;
        int n;

        reorder_R(N);

                                                        /* calc "scales" */
        ybox1_scale = (bb.y2box1 - bb.y1box1)/(x1_max - x1_min);
        ybox2_scale = (bb.y2box2 - bb.y1box2)/(x2_max - x2_min);
        ybox3_scale = (bb.y2box3 - bb.y1box3)/(Rmax - Rmin);
        xbox1_scale = (bb.x2box1 - bb.x1box1)/(float)(N);
        xbox3_scale = (bb.x2box3 - bb.x1box3)/(float)(N);

        for(n = 1;n <= N;n++)
            {
            yy1[n] = bb.y1box1 + ybox1_scale * (x1_max - x1[n]);
            yy2[n] = bb.y1box2 + ybox2_scale * (x2_max - x2[n]);
            yy3[n] = bb.y1box3 + ybox3_scale * (Rmax - R[n]);

            xx1[n] = bb.x1box1 + (n-1) * xbox1_scale;
            xx3[n] = bb.x1box3 + (n-1) * xbox3_scale;
            }
        for(n = 1;n <= (N-1);n++)
            {
            plotpoint(xx1[n],xx1[n+1],yy1[n],yy1[n+1]);
            plotpoint(xx1[n],xx1[n+1],yy2[n],yy2[n+1]);
            plotpoint(xx3[n],xx3[n+1],yy3[n],yy3[n+1]);
            }
        }

/* Function to reorder R */

reorder_R(N)
        int N;
        {
        extern float R[],R1[];
        int N2,n1,n;

        N2 = N/2;
        n1 = 1 + N2;
        for(n = 1;n <= N2;n++)
            {
            R1[n1] = R[n];
            R1[n] = R[n1];
            n1++;
            }

        for(n = 1;n <= N;n++)
            R[n] = R1[n];

        }
```

Figure 7.20 Function to set up and plot correlation data.

```
/* Function to generate disk files */

#include <stdio.h>

float x[128],y[128];
float num1,num2;                                        /* random numbers */

main()
      {
      int n,N,NO;
      n = 1;
      printf("Input # pts \n");
      scanf("%d",&N);
      printf("Input rnd option: (1)-x1 (2)-x2\n");
      scanf("%d",&NO);

      for(n = 1;n <= N;n++)
         {
         grand();
         x[n] = (float)(n);
         if(NO != 2)
            y[n] = num1;
         else
            y[n] = num2;
         }

      N = n-1;
      diskwt(N);
      }
```

Figure 7.21 Main calling routine to generate random number disk files.

The sequences generated using grand() are uncorrelated, by definition, from point to point. Hence, the cross-correlation function output should show some nominal low-level value across the entire range of log values, [-N/2, N/2]. Figure 7.21 illustrates a program that sets up one of the two independent sequences output from grand(). This program calls diskwt() (Figure 5.3), which writes the array values to the specified disk. Figure 7.22a illustrates the correlated output when the two independent Gaussian random sequences are correlated across 64 points. Also illustrated in the figure are two input sequences. Note that the correlation function does not appear to display anything other than a random structure, with no pronounced peaks to indicate agreement between the two sequences. Figure 7.22b indicates the nature of the lag space for the correlated output. Basically, the FFT implementation assumes a periodicity in the input sequences and yields an output that is assumed to be periodically extended as indicated. We have illustrated a case similar to the cross-correlated output of Figure 7.22a. In Figure 7.23a the autocorrelation output is illustrated for one of the sequences discussed in Figure 7.22a. Here both inputs are the same, and a rather sharp peak occurs at zero lag, where both sequences are 100% correlated. Figure 7.23b presents the intrinsic periodic nature of this sequence (correlation) and demonstrates how the peak repeats itself at intervals of N points. We can only see 64 lag points centered at zero.

Examination of Figures 7.22a and 7.23a demonstrates that the correlation function can be expected to display peaks at points in the sequence where the two

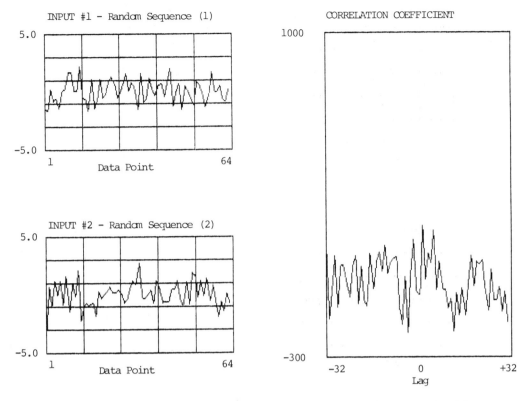

Figure 7.22a Output illustrating cross-correlation between two uncorrelated Gaussian random sequences (64 values).

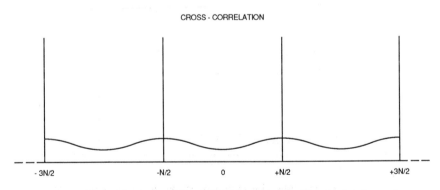

Figure 7.22b Illustration of periodicity associated with calculated correlation coefficient.

values correspond in a similar fashion. This implies that the underlying probability distributions are similar at the point where the peak occurs. In other words, the processes have similar statistics at these points.

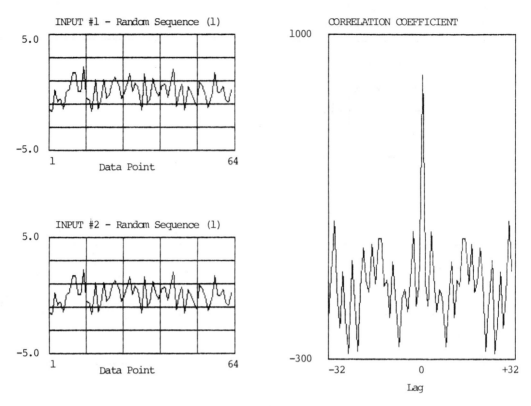

Figure 7.23a Output illustrating autocorrelation for a single Gaussian random sequence (64 values).

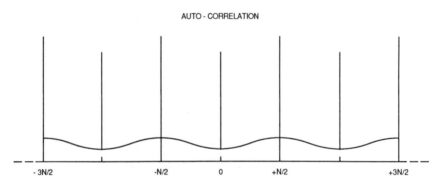

Figure 7.23b Illustration of periodicity associated with calculated correlation coefficient.

7.3.6 Stock Market Forecasting

The correlation function as we are using it still has contributions from the mean value. We will simply consider this to be a constant, and since we are only concerned with the behavior or dynamic variation of the function, the relative value for R_{xy} will not be considered important.

One candidate for examination using correlation functions is stock activity. It would be useful, for example, to know whether or not a given stock follows the behavior represented by the Dow Jones Average. Of particular interest would be whether or not a stock correlates with another stock or an index (such as the Dow Jones) at some lag value other than zero. In this case, the leading stock or index could be used to predict performance for the remaining stock or index, which follows with a similar behavior pattern. This approach intrinsically assumes several things:

1. The time histories for each stock are well known.

2. Each stock can be described statistically with some underlying distribution.

It is plausible, for example, that two stocks might agree for a period of time and then disagree (the processes are then said to differ in a nonstationary fashion).

Figure 7.24 illustrates a simple program that is used to create a database of x[] and y[] values. We used it to generate stock histories (32 values) from January 1983 to August 1985 for the following:

Dow Jones Average

International Business Machines

Digital Equipment Corporation

Hewlett-Packard Corporation

Sperry Corporation

The values used in this example are contained in Table 7.4. Figure 7.25 illustrates the correlation between IBM and the Dow Jones Average. The pronounced peak at zero lag indicates that both inputs are correlated at this lag value. Examination of the input functions demonstrates that the two sequences do, in fact, display a remark-

```
/* Function to generate disk files */

#include <stdio.h>

float x[128],y[128];

main()
        {
        int n,N;
        n = 1;
        printf("Input # pts \n");
        scanf("%d",&N);

        while(n <= N)
            {
            printf("Input x-value\n");
            scanf("%f",&x[n]);
            printf("Input y-value\n");
            scanf("%f",&y[n]);
            n++;
            }

        N = n-1;
        diskwt(N);
        }
```

Figure 7.24 Main calling routine to generate disk file for a sequence of paired values.

TABLE 7.4 STOCK AND INDEX HISTORIES
(JANUARY 1983 TO AUGUST 1985)

Dow Jones	IBM	DEC	HPC	SPC
1105.0	100.0	122.0	42.0	40.0
1135.0	100.0	127.0	44.0	40.0
1160.0	101.0	128.0	44.0	39.0
1225.0	115.0	127.0	41.0	39.0
1230.0	115.0	120.0	44.0	41.0
1265.0	120.0	121.0	46.0	42.0
1260.0	121.0	120.0	47.0	47.0
1210.0	120.0	110.0	44.0	48.0
1270.0	122.0	113.0	47.0	49.0
1290.0	127.0	109.0	46.0	50.0
1300.0	122.0	75.00	42.0	48.0
1270.0	120.0	76.00	44.0	50.0
1290.0	120.0	96.00	47.0	50.0
1200.0	110.0	91.00	42.0	50.0
1185.0	110.0	98.00	40.0	44.0
1190.0	110.0	99.00	39.0	43.0
1190.0	114.0	100.0	40.0	43.0
1130.0	105.0	94.00	40.0	40.0
1130.0	105.0	87.00	40.0	40.0
1215.0	120.0	100.0	46.0	46.0
1220.0	122.0	103.0	41.0	42.0
1215.0	121.0	106.0	41.0	39.0
1240.0	121.0	111.0	40.0	40.0
1205.0	120.0	120.0	38.0	43.0
1285.0	130.0	120.0	40.0	52.0
1295.0	140.0	122.0	40.0	54.0
1300.0	135.0	117.0	40.0	55.0
1280.0	130.0	107.0	37.0	52.0
1305.0	130.0	104.0	37.0	56.0
1310.0	130.0	104.0	36.0	58.0
1350.0	131.0	104.0	37.0	55.0
1340.0	130.0	105.0	38.0	54.0

able similarity in structure. While not necessarily a good predictive indicator, this correlation does suggest that IBM has a large agreement with other stocks typical of the Dow Jones composite.

The correlation function appearing in Figure 7.25 demonstrates a tendency toward peaking at the edges of the interval. This lesser peaking results from the half-interval symmetry that exists in the data: if the data are shifted one-half of the sample interval ($N/2$), a similarity in the slope of the data can be perceived. Figure 7.26 is the autocorrelation of the Dow Jones with itself, and it demonstrates a large peak at zero lag. Also, the half-interval symmetry is present, as might be expected, and this leads to peaking at the sequence edges ($N/2$ points).

Figure 7.27 is interesting in that there appears to be peaking at nonzero lag values, hence suggesting the possibility of predicting or forecasting. If the DEC sequence is shifted forward by about one-fifth the sample interval, a striking similarity

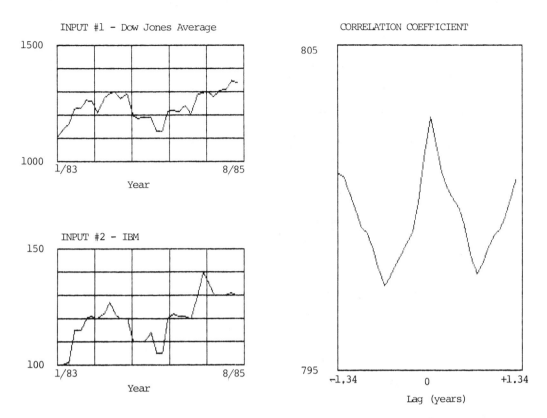

Figure 7.25 Output illustrating cross-correlation between the Dow Jones average and IBM stock prices from 1983 to 1986 (32 values).

exists between the Dow Jones Average and Digital's performance. This manifests itself in the correlated output at about the one-half year point. Based on this methodology, we could predict general changes in the Dow Jones approximately 6 months ahead by watching Digital Equipment Corporation's stock activity. Obviously, before we buy index futures, we need to process the entire history of each (the Dow Jones and DEC stock) and ascertain if this performance still holds. Figure 7.28 compares the Dow Jones Average and Hewlett-Packard stock for the years indicated. Clearly, the correlation is not good, with the trend in the Dow Jones being overall upward while Hewlett-Packard stock moved down in value. The correlation function bears this disagreement out with a complete absence of peaks. Finally, Figure 7.29 presents the agreement, as evidenced by the correlation function, between the Dow Jones Average and Sperry Corporation (now Unisys) stock. A pronounced peak occurs at zero lag, indicating general agreement. Again the half-interval symmetry suggests peaking at the edges of the time interval ($N/2$). All figures in this section have been annotated for clarity. This completes the discussion of correlation, and it has provided an opportunity to illustrate the use of the Version 5.0 graphic functions as well as output using EGA resolution.

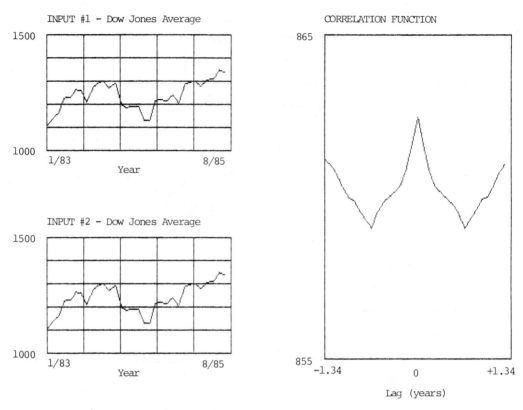

Figure 7.26 Output illustrating autocorrelation for the Dow Jones average from 1983 to 1986 (32 values).

7.4 THREE-DIMENSIONAL SURFACES

This subsection presents an analytical approach for describing three-dimensional surfaces within the framework of simple vector arithmetic. A technique for removing hidden lines is illustrated based on consideration of the rotating characteristics of facets. Here a facet is a member of a logical subdivision of the three-dimensional surface. We begin with a brief discussion of surface characterization.

7.4.1 Functions of Two Variables

It is convenient to denote a function of one variable using the notation

$$y = f(x) \tag{7.7}$$

Graphically, such a relationship is represented with a two-dimensional plot using the independent variable x along the horizontal axis and the dependent variable y along the vertical axis. When a function depends on two variables, it is representable in a three-dimensional space defined by

$$z = f(x, y) \tag{7.8}$$

In displaying such data, a third axis must somehow be represented on a two-dimensional surface, the display screen. We have seen that it is useful to assume three perpendicular (orthogonal) axes: an x-axis, a y-axis, and a z-axis. Points in this space are denoted by

$$(x, y, z) = (x, y, f(x, y)) \qquad (7.9)$$

Figure 7.30 illustrates the geometry for a three-dimensional surface. In the figure, a *grid* of x-y points has been illustrated.

$$\{(x_n, y_m, 0): n = 1, 2, \ldots, N; m = 1, 2, \ldots, M\}$$

Here the sets $\{x_n\}$ and $\{y_m\}$ have been chosen to span the space of interest. The three-dimensional surface is then determined relative to this grid using Equation (7.8). We further assume that an observer is located at the point (x_p, y_p, z_p), which is achieved by a rotation (alpha, beta, gamma) about the x, y, and z axes, respectively. (Note that this rotation is *not* composed of orthogonal components.) This rotation has been treated in some detail in Chapter 4, and the reader is referred to the routine rotmat() (Figure 4.31) and rotpt() (Figure 4.32) for a complete discussion.

With this formulation, then, we can generate an abstract three-dimensional space with the observer located at any point in this space. Following the rotation, a new set of coordinates is defined by

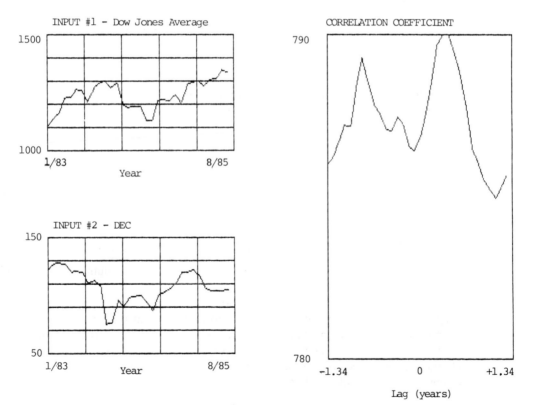

Figure 7.27 Output illustrating cross-correlation for the Dow Jones average and DEC stock prices from 1983 to 1986 (32 values).

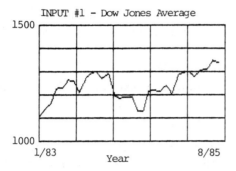

INPUT #1 - Dow Jones Average

1500

1000

1/83   Year   8/85

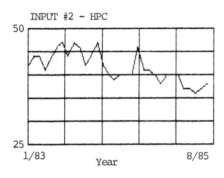

INPUT #2 - HPC

50

25

1/83   Year   8/85

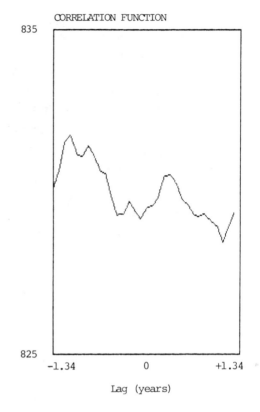

CORRELATION FUNCTION

835

825

-1.34   0   +1.34

Lag (years)

Figure 7.28 Output illustrating cross-correlation for the Dow Jones average and HPC stock prices from 1983 to 1986 (32 values).

$$\begin{pmatrix} x'_n \\ y'_m \\ f(x'_n, y'_m) \end{pmatrix} = R(\text{alpha, beta, gamma}) \begin{pmatrix} x_n \\ y_m \\ f(x_n, y_m) \end{pmatrix} \qquad (7.10)$$

R(alpha, beta, gamma) is given by Table 4.7. To display this space, it will be useful to collapse the x-axis once a suitable rotation has been achieved. The points plotted on this display will then be members of the set

$$\{(0, y'_m, f(x'_n, y'_m)): n = 1, 2, \ldots, N; m = 1, 2, \ldots, M\}$$

The order for the display will be to let $\{y'_m\}$ correspond to column positions and $\{f(x'_n, y'_m)\}$ correspond to row positions.

One final concept is needed: the notion of a facet. Basically, for plotting purposes it is useful to break the surface into facets (or small localized areas). The methodology for achieving this (used here) is to consider the grid structure of the x-y plane appearing in Figure 7.30 and assume a facet to be bounded by each set of grid lines projected onto the surface. For example, if we consider the grid appearing in Figure 7.31, it is clear that the four x-y plane grid points

1: $(x_n, y_m, 0)$

2: $(x_n, y_{m+1}, 0)$

$$3: \quad (x_{n+1}, y_{m+1}, 0)$$

$$4: \quad (x_{n+1}, y_m, 0)$$

define the locations of the vertices of the grid. Lines connecting 1 and 2, 2 and 3, 3 and 4, and 4 and 1, respectively, define the grid. Projecting these lines onto the surface yields the surface points

$$1: \quad (x_n, y_m, f(x_n, y_m))$$

$$2: \quad (x_n, y_{m+1}, f(x_n, y_{m+1}))$$

$$3: \quad (x_{n+1}, y_{m+1}, f(x_{n+1}, y_{m+1}))$$

$$4: \quad (x_{n+1}, y_m, f(x_{n+1}, y_m))$$

Connecting these points cyclically yields the surface facet. When collapsed along the x-axis, we have the final points:

$$1: \quad (0, y_m, f(x_n, y_m))$$

$$2: \quad (0, y_{m+1}, f(x_n, y_{m+1}))$$

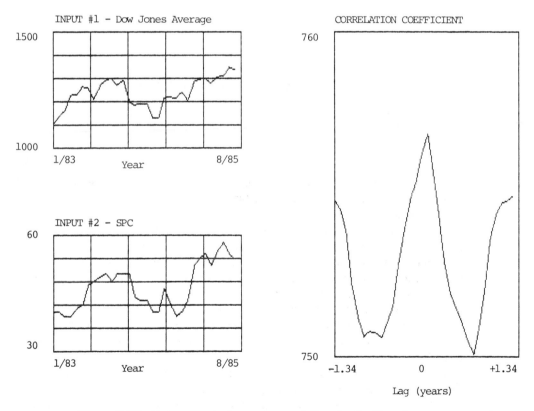

Figure 7.29 Output illustrating cross-correlation for the Dow Jones average and SPC stock prices from 1983 to 1986 (32 values).

Sec. 7.4   Three-Dimensional Surfaces

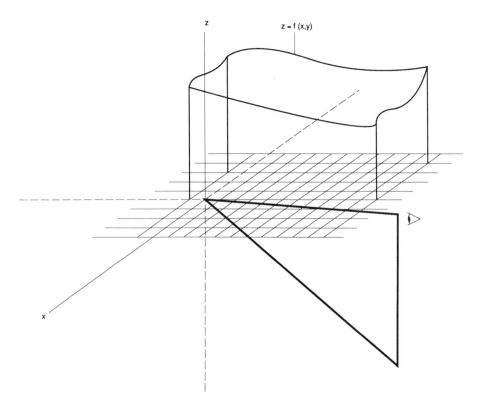

Figure 7.30 Three-dimensional surface with an observer.

$$3: \quad (0, y_{m+1}, f(x_{n+1}, y_{m+1}))$$

$$4: \quad (0, y_m, f(x_{n+1}, y_m))$$

If these points are plotted with the y-axis corresponding to column values and the z-axis corresponding to row values, a surface representation will be displayed with facets outlined.

It is important to recognize that the surface described above will display all lines appearing in the facets. This includes hidden lines, which are those lines appearing in facets whose view would normally be obstructed. This obstruction results from the fact that other facets are located in front of the facet in question when viewed in the chosen direction.

To avoid illustrating hidden lines, it is useful to delete plotting of facets containing these lines. While there are several ways to eliminate these hidden line facets, a very simple procedure is to create a vector normal to the facet and ignore the facet if this vector has a negative component pointing into the screen. Since the x-axis is normal to the screen, this implies that a negative x-component of this normal vector would denote a facet with hidden lines [8].

We can create this normal vector from any three points in the surface. Suppose we have the vertices defined by vectors from the origin:

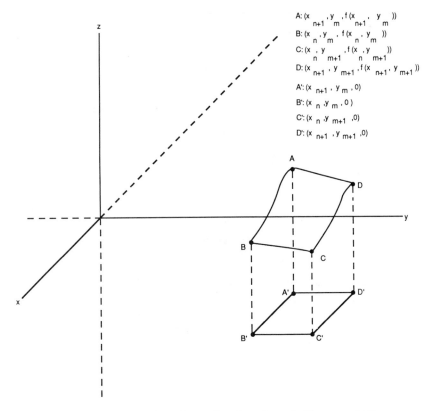

$A: (x_{n+1}, y_m, f(x_{n+1}, y_m))$

$B: (x_n, y_m, f(x_n, y_m))$

$C: (x_n, y_{m+1}, f(x_n, y_{m+1}))$

$D: (x_{n+1}, y_{m+1}, f(x_{n+1}, y_{m+1}))$

$A': (x_{n+1}, y_m, 0)$

$B': (x_n, y_m, 0)$

$C': (x_n, y_{m+1}, 0)$

$D': (x_{n+1}, y_{m+1}, 0)$

Figure 7.31 Illustration of a surface facet bounded by x-y grid lines.

$$\vec{p}_1 = (x_1, y_1, z_1) \tag{7.11a}$$

$$\vec{p}_2 = (x_2, y_2, z_2) \tag{7.11b}$$

$$\vec{p}_3 = (x_3, y_3, z_3) \tag{7.11c}$$

and cyclically define line segments

$$\vec{m}_1 = (\vec{p}_1 - \vec{p}_3) \tag{7.12a}$$

$$\vec{m}_2 = (\vec{p}_2 - \vec{p}_1) \tag{7.12b}$$

$$\vec{m}_3 = (\vec{p}_3 - \vec{p}_2) \tag{7.12c}$$

Then a normal to the surface subtended by these three line segments is given by

$$\vec{n} = \vec{m}_i \times \vec{m}_{i+1} \qquad (i = 1,2,3) \tag{7.13}$$

In this equation, i is cyclic(modulo 3). The vector product is defined by the determinant

$$\vec{n} = \begin{vmatrix} \hat{i} & \hat{j} & \hat{k} \\ m_{ix} & m_{iy} & m_{iz} \\ m_{(i+1)x} & m_{(i+1)y} & m_{(i+1)z} \end{vmatrix} \tag{7.14}$$

```
/* generate 3d surface */

#include <math.h>

float xarray[2000],x[500],y[500],z[500];

main()
        {
        int n,m,ncount = 21,mcount = 21,m1,m2,N,NN;
        float A= 10., error = 1.e-5;
        double PI = 3.141592654,u,v;

        printf("Input interval divider\n");
        scanf("%d",&NN);

        m2 = 1;
        m1 = 1;
        for(n = 1;n <= ncount;n++)
            {
            for(m = 1;m <= mcount;m++)
                {
                x[m2] = (float)(m - mcount + 10);
                y[m2] = (float)(n - ncount + 10);
                u = (double)(x[m2]);
                v = (double)(y[m2]);
                u = (double)((PI/NN)*sqrt(u*u + v*v));

                if((u < error) && (u > -error))
                    z[m2] = A;
                else
                    z[m2] = A*(sin(u)/u);

                z[m2] = z[m2]*z[m2];
                xarray[m1] = x[m2];
                xarray[m1+1] = y[m2];
                xarray[m1+2] = z[m2];
                m2++;
                m1 = m1 + 3;
                }
            }
            N = m1-1;
            xarray_diskwt(N);
        }


/* Main calling function for 3D plots */

float xarray[3072],scalex,scaley,scalez,x,y,z,a[10];
int ncount,mcount,count;

main()
        {
        printf("Input ncount\n");
        scanf("%d",&ncount);                    /* x-axis count */
        printf("\n Square array: ncount = mcount\n");

        mcount = ncount;                         /* y-axis count */
        count = ncount;                          /* grid shift */

        threeD_graph();                          /* plot 3D graph */
        plotterm();
        }
```

Figure 7.32 Main calling program (a) for generating a three-dimensional surface and (b) plotting a three-dimensional surface.

where the first row consists of Cartesian unit vectors. Since it is the x-axis term we are interested in, we examine

$$n_x = m_{iy}m_{(i+1)z} - m_{iz}m_{(i+1)y} \qquad (7.15)$$

Here

$$\overrightarrow{\mathbf{m}}_i = m_{ix}\hat{\mathbf{i}} + m_{iu}\hat{\mathbf{j}} + m_{iz}\hat{\mathbf{k}} \qquad (7.16)$$

If

$$n_x < 0 \qquad (7.17)$$

the facet contains hidden lines.

```
/* Function to load data */

#include <stdio.h>

threeD_graph()
        {
        extern int ncount,mcount;
        extern float xarray[],x,y,z;
        int n,m,m1,N,nm_count;
        float alpha0,beta0,gamma0;

        printf("Input x-rotation (rad)\n");
        scanf("%f",&alpha0);
        printf("Input y-rotation (rad)\n");
        scanf("%f",&beta0);
        printf("Input z-rotation (rad)\n");
        scanf("%f",&gamma0);

        rot_mat(alpha0,beta0,gamma0);               /* Loads global a[] */
        N = xarray_diskrd();                        /* Loads disk values */
        m1 = 1;
        for(n = 1;n <= ncount;n++)
           {
           for(m = 1;m <= mcount;m++)
              {
              x = xarray[m1];                       /* x,y,z values */
              y = xarray[m1+1];
              z = xarray[m1+2];
              rot_point();
              xarray[m1] = x;
              xarray[m1+1] = y;
              xarray[m1+2] = z;
              m1 = m1 + 3;                          /* point index inc. */
              }
           }
        scale();                                    /* x,y,z -> [-1,1] */
        SCRCL();                                    /* clear screen */
        SCEGA();                                    /* set EGA mode */
        m1 = 1;
        nm_count = 3*ncount*mcount-(ncount*3 + 6);  /* adj. limit */
        for(n = 1;n <= ncount;n++)                  /* plot facets */
           {
           for(m = 1;m <= mcount;m++)
              {
              if(m1 < nm_count)
                 threeD_facets(m1);
              m1 = m1 + 3;
              }
           }
        }
```

Figure 7.33 Function threeD_graph().

```
/* Function to scale xarray data */

scale()
        {
        extern int ncount,mcount;
        extern float xarray[],scalex,scaley,scalez;
        int n,m,m1;
        float max_x = -1.e14,max_y = -1.e14,max_z = -1.e14;
        float min_x = 1.e14,min_y = 1.e14,min_z = 1.e14;

        m1 = 1;
        for(n = 1;n <= ncount;n++)
            {
            for(m = 1;m <= mcount;m++)
                {
                if(max_x < xarray[m1])
                    max_x = xarray[m1];
                if(min_x > xarray[m1])
                    min_x = xarray[m1];
                if(max_y < xarray[m1+1])
                    max_y = xarray[m1+1];
                if(min_y > xarray[m1+1])
                    min_y = xarray[m1+1];
                if(max_z < xarray[m1+2])
                    max_z = xarray[m1+2];
                if(min_z > xarray[m1+2]);
                    min_z = xarray[m1+2];
                m1 = m1 + 3;                          /* next point set */
                }
            }
                                                      /* scale [-1,1] */
        scalex = 2./(max_x - min_x);
        scaley = 2./(max_y - min_y);
        scalez = 2./(max_z - min_z);
        m1 = 1;
        for(n = 1;n <= ncount;n++)
            {
            for(m = 1;m <= mcount;m++)
                {
                xarray[m1] = -1. + scalex*(xarray[m1] - min_x);
                xarray[m1+1] = -1. + scaley*(xarray[m1+1] - min_y);
                xarray[m1+2] = -1. + scalez*(xarray[m1+2] - min_z);
                m1 = m1 + 3;
                }
            }
        }
```

Figure 7.34 Function scale(), which scales the raw three-dimensional data to between -1 and $+1$.

7.4.2 A Simple Mathematical Example

It is useful to create a simple example to illustrate a three-dimensional surface. Consider the function

$$z = A^2 \frac{\sin^2[(\pi/N)\sqrt{x^2 + y^2}]}{[(\pi/N)\sqrt{x^2 + y^2}]^2} \tag{7.18}$$

This function has the familiar $(\sin x/x)^2$ behavior. We note that in the limit $(x, y) = (0, 0)$ the result is

$$z = A^2 \tag{7.19}$$

It is useful to generate values for x and y in the range $[-10, 10]$ with $N =$ an

```
/* Function to plot 3D facets: coordinates for EGA */

#include <graph.h>

threeD_facets(m1)
        int m1;                                         /* index */
        {
        extern int count;
        extern float xarray[],x,y,z,scaley = 250.,scalez = 150.;
        int n,z1,z2,y1,y2,nc;
        float z_start = 25.,y_start = 25.,z_mid = 150.,y_mid = 250.;
        float dy1,dy2,dz1,dz2,xa[5],ya[5],za[5];

        nc = 3*count;                                   /* next y-value */
        xa[1] = xarray[m1];                             /* 1st y-value grid */
        ya[1] = xarray[m1+1];
        za[1] = xarray[m1+2];
        xa[2] = xarray[m1+3];
        ya[2] = xarray[m1+4];
        za[2] = xarray[m1+5];

        xa[3] = xarray[m1+nc+3];                        /* 2nd y-value grid */
        ya[3] = xarray[m1+nc+4];
        za[3] = xarray[m1+nc+5];
        xa[4] = xarray[m1+nc];
        ya[4] = xarray[m1+nc+1];
        za[4] = xarray[m1+nc+2];

        dy1 = ya[2] - ya[1];                            /* ck rotation */
        dy2 = ya[3] - ya[2];
        dz1 = za[2] - za[1];
        dz2 = za[3] - za[2];
        if((dy1*dz2 - dz1*dy2) > 0)
            {
            for(n = 1;n <= 4;n++)                       /* scale facet */
                {
                za[n] = z_start + (z_mid - za[n]*scalez);
                ya[n] = y_start + (y_mid + ya[n]*scaley);
                }
            for(n = 1;n <= 3;n++)                       /* plot 3 of 4 */
                {
                y1 = (int)(ya[n]);
                y2 = (int)(ya[n+1]);
                z1 = (int)(za[n]);
                z2 = (int)(za[n+1]);
                _moveto(y1,z1);                         /* collapsed y-z */
                _lineto(y2,z2);
                }
            y1 = (int)(ya[4]);
            y2 = (int)(ya[1]);
            z1 = (int)(za[4]);
            z2 = (int)(za[1]);
            _moveto(y1,z1);                             /* 4th segment */
            _lineto(y2,z2);
            }
        }
```

Figure 7.35 Function threeD_facet(), which plots the faceted surface.

input value that is a measure of the range of z. Figure 7.32a illustrates a main calling program that generates these values and writes them to disk. Initially, the total number of values (x, y, z) for each point on an x-y grid spaced at unity intervals in the above range is written to disk, followed by the points themselves in x, y, and z order. The disk write function xarray__diskwt() is similar to the earlier diskwt() function, except a single array is output to disk. This array is defined as specified above and is the array xarray[] in Figure 7.32.

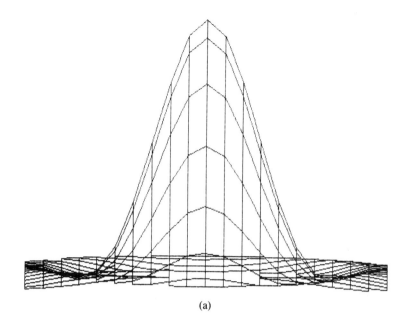

(a)

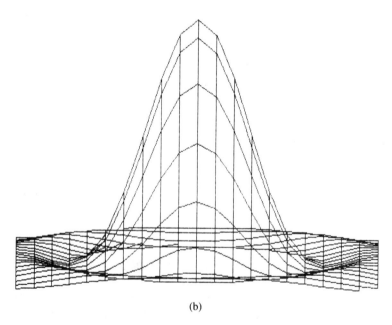

(b)

Figure 7.36 Three-dimensional surface of Figure 7.32a with alpha = gamma = 0 and beta (radians) = (a) 0.4, (b) 0.8,

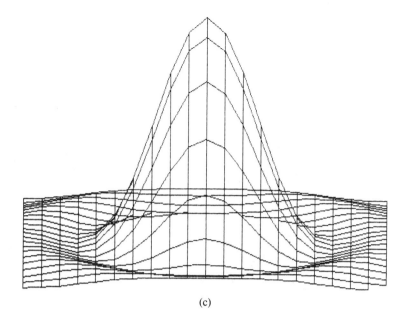

(c)

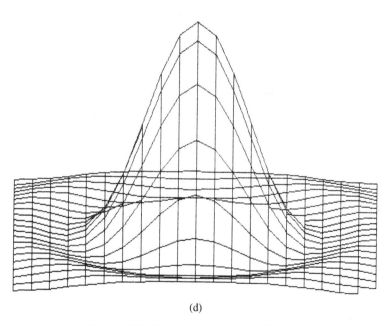

(d)

Figure 7.36 (*Continued*)   (c) 1.1, (d) 1.2,

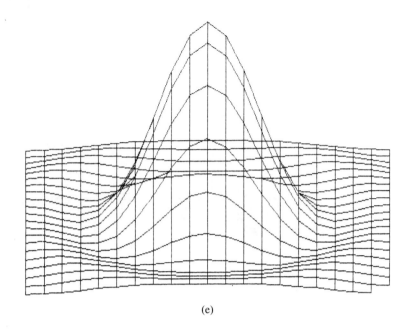

(e)

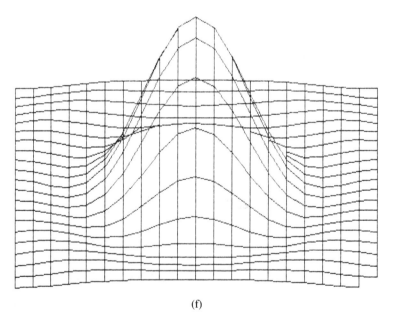

(f)

Figure 7.36 (*Concluded*)   (e) 1.3, and (f) 1.4.

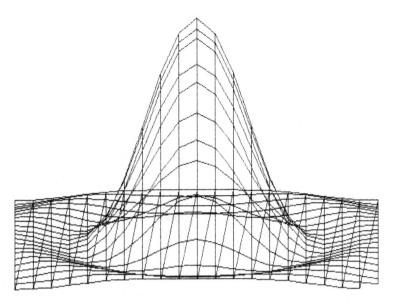

Figure 7.37 Three-dimensional surface of Figure 7.32a with alpha = gamma = 0 and beta (radians) = 1.1. Hidden lines are displayed.

Figure 7.32b presents a main calling function for the program that plots the three-dimensional surface input using xarray__diskrd(), which is contained in threeD__graph() appearing in Figure 7.33. The function threeD__graph() reads rotation angles for locating the observer and rotates the input points. These functions, rotmat() and rotpt(), have been previously mentioned. Next, the data are scaled using scale(), which appears in Figure 7.34. [The routine that reads the disk, xarray__diskrd(), is equivalent to diskrd() (Figure 2.4c), except a single array, xarray[], is loaded.] The function scale() simply ensures that all x, y, and z values lie within the interval $[-1, 1]$.

After scaling the data, threeD__graph() clears the screen, sets EGA display mode, and plots the facets using threeD__facet(). This function appears in Figure 7.35. The routine threeD__facet() first loads the arrays xa[], ya[], and za[] with each of the four vertex points on the facet. A check for a hidden line condition is made, and if the facet is to be plotted, further scaling from $[-1, 1]$ to screen coordinates is implemented. Here only the y-z plane is considered (the x-axis is collapsed). Actual plotting of the facet lines is accomplished using the Version 5.0 screen primitives __moveto() and __lineto().

Figure 7.36a illustrates the output with alpha = gamma = 0 (no rotation about the x- and z-axes). In this figure, beta = 0.4, which is a counterclockwise rotation of 0.4 radian about the y-axis. Effectively, this tilts the viewing angle upward so that the observer is looking down at an angle toward the image. Figures 7.36b through f maintain alpha and gamma at zero, but change beta to span 0.8, 1.1, 1.2, 1.3, and 1.4 radians, respectively. This progressively tilts the image toward the reader, as illustrated. Figure 7.37 presents the figure for alpha = gamma = 0 and beta = 1.1 with hidden lines retained. (Note that positive-slope hidden lines remain.)

SUMMARY

This chapter has presented several key improvements provided with the Version 5.0 C Optimizing Compiler developed by Microsoft (over the earlier Version 4.0 compiler). Both DOS and BIOS library functions have been added. In some cases, these functions provide routines that allow the programmer to avoid the need for tailored assembly language functions where such programming is not time critical. For example, the addition of word I/O functions circumvents the need for writing such functions in assembly language (these routines complement the earlier byte I/O routines).

Many graphics-oriented routines have been added. In this chapter we only considered a small subset of the available routines and illustrated the parallel between these routines and functions developed earlier in the text. The earlier development provides the programmer with a lower-level understanding of how these primitives work. Both EGA and VGA graphics were considered and example programs presented demonstrating these two display modes.

Although we did not discuss QuickC in this chapter, this user-friendly programming environment is part of the Version 5.0 software development kit provided by Microsoft [7]. QuickC is discussed in Chapter 1 as an environment that has considerable attraction for the beginning user and the programmer involved in small-scale prototyping.

Finally, several graphic applications were developed. Routines for examining correlated behavior between two different functional histories were presented. Also, display techniques for three-dimensional surfaces were illustrated [8].

REFERENCES

1. *Microsoft C Compiler User's Guide* (Version 4.0), Microsoft Corp., 16011 NE 36th Way, Box 97017, Redmond, WA (1984).

2. *Microsoft C Optimizing Compiler User's Guide and Mixed-Language Programming Guide*, Microsoft Corp., 16011 NE 36th Way, Box 97017, Redmond, WA (1987).

3. *Microsoft C Optimizing Compiler Run-time Library Reference*, 16011 NE 36th Way, Box 97017, Redmond, WA (1987).

4. *IBM Personal System/2 Display Adapter Technical Reference*, IBM Corporation, P. O. Box 1328, Boca Raton, FL (1987), 68X2251.

5. Van Horn, R. B., "egaepson.exe," 701 Fall Place, Herndon, VA 22070 (1987).

6. Bendat, J. S., and Piersol, A. G., *Engineering Applications of Correlation and Spectral Analysis*, John Wiley & Sons, Inc., New York, p. 47 (1980).

7. *Microsoft QuickC Compiler*, Microsoft Corp., 16011 NE 36th Way, Box 97017, Redmond, WA (1987).

8. Angell, I. O., *Advanced Graphics with the IBM Personal Computer*, Halsted Press, New York, (1986).

PROBLEMS

7.1. Define a routine that sets the video mode to monochrome EGA graphics mode.

7.2. Write a program that draws one-quarter of an ellipse.

7.3. Modify WRDOT() to use the Version 5.0 graphics functions.

7.4. Modify WRDOT0() to use the Version 5.0 graphics functions for normal background (BLACK).

7.5. Write a program that prints a set of coordinates diagonally down the screen in EGA mode. Space the coordinates at row + 50 and column + 100 intervals.

7.6. For the correlation sequence in Figure 7.22a, the random processes were taken to be independent and Gaussian. In the limit that an infinite sequence is assumed input to the FFT, what would the resulting transforms look like when presented as an auto-spectrum?

$$S_{xy}(m) = |X(m)X*(m)|$$

7.7. When examining the correlation of a sequence, the length of the sequence is referred to as the coherence interval. In terms of the Nyquist interval from earlier chapters, what would the expected coherence interval be?

7.8. What is the major feature of the Version 5.0 enhancements that facilitates more complex C programming?

7.9. When programming for OS/2, the initial compilers rely on specific calls to the API functions (see Chapter 10). How does this compare with the high-level abstractions used in this chapter?

7.10. When can high-level abstractions be undesirable?

8

Windows: An Integrated C Environment

Up to this point in the text, we have considered programming that is largely static (except for the bouncing ball and rotating cube) and only interactive in the sense that the program asks for specific input and waits for a specific response (or range of values, for example) from the user. Once the response is received, the program executes its task and either waits for additional input or terminates. With the development of more complex environments, where applications such as the static entities considered up to now are treated as objects and these objects are subject to time-dependent activity, dynamic programming is possible. One such environment is the C environment called Windows Presentation Manager [1] developed by Microsoft. Windows is a dynamic executive that allows programs written in C (using the Microsoft C 4.0 or 5.0 compilers, for example) to be developed in a highly visual and active mode. To achieve the needed interfacing between the Windows environment and conventional C programming, an entire class of special-purpose functions and data entities must be employed. These entities are available through the include file, windows.h, and associated libraries of the Microsoft Windows Software Development Kit (SDK) [2–4]. For much of the programming in this book, we use the Version 1.03 of the SDK.

8.1 INTRODUCTION TO THE WINDOWS SOFTWARE DEVELOPMENT KIT (SDK)

Why should a textbook on C applications focus on an implementation such as Windows? First, Windows is an applications programming environment that is programmed using the C language. Hence it is an extension of normal C programming that uses special libraries and defined functions. It yields high-level abstracted code that performs very elegant tasks. The Presentation Manager has a graphics display that is very structured and capable of interactive interfacing in a fashion similar to that made possible by the Apple MacIntosh operating system. This interface is complex and can be used with a mouse to achieve a dynamic flow of activity. It is the preferred interface format for such enhancements as the OS/2 Presentation Manager provided as part of the OS/2 Extended Edition. The Presentation Manager is an object-oriented executive capable of user-friendly implementations and represents an ideal methodology for developing C applications. Returning to the above question, no book on C applications can ignore such object-oriented techniques; hence, we now devote discussion to the Windows implementation.

8.1.1 The Windows Template

In the next section we consider several beginning Windows programs. The presentation there will be such that actual code is developed and explained in the context of the Windows required program structure. Essentially, Windows programs require a fixed framework or template around which the code is organized. In conventional C programs, the basic template might appear as

```
Preprocessor
main()
    {
    ...
    }
function1()
    {
    ...
    }
    ...
functionN()
    {
    ...
    }
```

Each function would be callable internal to either main() or another (group of) function(s). As we will see shortly, Windows programming has a structure that is considerably more complex because of the graphics presentation inherent to this executive. A simple Windows program with one window might have a template of the following form:

```
Preprocessor
WinMain()
    {
    -code to initialize window
    -loop to continuously read "messages" sent from the
     executive
    }
"window function"
    {
```

```
        -this function directs execution to appropriate Windows
         functions based on "message" input from Windows
         executive
        }
    "initialization functions"
        {
        -functions needed to initialize the first, additional,
        and every instance of a window
        }
    . . .
    other needed functions
    . . .
```

In this template, reference is made to an instance of a window. We will discuss this concept at a number of places in the subsequent text, but it basically refers to a single task corresponding to the window. As added tasks are established for the same window, Windows passes information developed for the initial instance to these later representations. Hence, the initialization functions must consider all possibilities for an instance of a window. (A window is a ''window'' through which to ''watch'' the execution of an application.)

Figure 8.1a is a structure chart for the upper hierarchical levels of a Windows application. This chart is generic in the sense that it only indicates entities that are common to all Windows programs. Figure 8.1b presents the dynamics of a Windows application in flow-chart format. The Windows library of functions is very extensive, and we will illustrate the use of several of these functions shortly. Each Windows application is compiled using standard Microsoft C compilers, as alluded to earlier, but several additional files are required or can be optional. A definitions file with extension .def is required to provide the linker with information about the candidate applications environment. Also, a special-purpose resources file with extension .rc

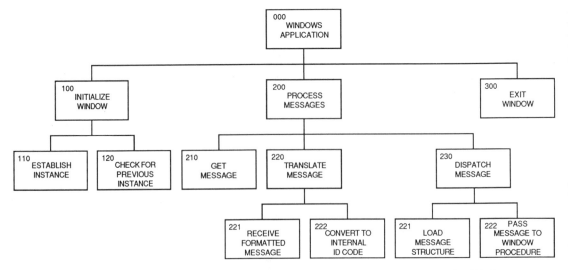

Figure 8.1a   Generic structure chart for the upper hierarchical levels of a Windows application.

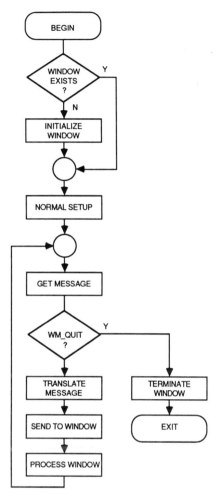

Figure 8.1b Dynamic picture of a Windows application.

can be used to support the application data structures. Clearly, these files call for a new linker, and Windows has such a linker as part of its system resources, the LINK4 linker.

8.1.2 Simple Beginning Examples

Windows is a complicated programming environment, and there is almost no simple beginning for learning how to use this very flexible and creative tool. We begin with two examples of the basic Windows program: first, a program that simply checks to make sure the compiling and linking steps are correct (similar to the nothing.c program by Petzold [5]) and, second, a program that establishes a simple blank window (with header line). It is a large step to go from one to the other, as we will see, and the second program illustrates several of the major features of Windows: a menu box in the upper-left corner (with a pull-down menu), arrows in the upper-right corner to expand or contract the displayed box, a title bar at the top of the window rectangular area, and a client area that can occupy the remainder of the screen. It is in this client area that actual Windows program output is displayed. Windows supplies all the interfacing used to generate this display based on dynamic calls to the appropriate Windows functions. The reader is cautioned to recognize that access of this code must proceed in the structured orderly manner alluded to in the previous section.

With these thoughts in mind, we examine Figure 8.2a, a simple Windows program that merely addresses the Windows executive. It is important to realize that this program, when executed, will not change the basic Windows display other than to momentarily cause the default mouse pointer (an arrow) to become an hourglass (Windows SDK 1.03 under Windows 2.03). We have included specific reference to the Microsoft versions implemented for this discussion to allow for differences in the Presentation Manager display as Windows evolves. Figure 8.2b presents the definition file associated with the program nodo appearing in Figure 8.2a, and Figure 8.2c contains the appropriate MAKE file for nodo.

```
/* "NO DO" test program for windows */

#include <windows.h>

int PASCAL WinMain(hInst,hPrev,CmdLine,cmdShow)
        HANDLE hInst,hPrev;
        LPSTR CmdLine;
        int cmdShow;
        {
        return FALSE;
        }
```

(a)

```
NAME            nodo

DESCRIPTION     'no do program'

EXETYPE         WINDOWS

STUB            'WINSTUB.EXE'

CODE            MOVEABLE
DATA            MOVEABLE MULTIPLE

HEAPSIZE        2048
STACKSIZE       4096
```

(b)

```
nodo.obj: nodo.c
        cl -c -D LINT_ARGS -Gsw -Od -W2 -Zp -FPa -AM nodo.c

nodo.exe: nodo.obj nodo.def
        link4 nodo,/align:16,/map,mlibw/NOE,nodo
```

(c)

Figure 8.2 (a) A simple do-nothing Windows program, (b) the associated definition file, and (c) the MAKE file.

Returning to Figure 8.2a, we see that the program has the form of a C function, WinMain(), and the include file, windows.h, has been added. WinMain() is the major calling module for execution under Windows and is similar to the main() function appearing in conventional C programs, as previously discussed. This function has been explicitly typed as int PASCAL. What does this mean? The integer portion is clear; however, PASCAL requires some explanation. Basically, PASCAL refers to the calling convention used in accessing the function. Remember that when a C function is called the formal parameters are loaded on the stack starting with the Nth parameter first. In the PASCAL convention, the Nth parameter is loaded last. Figure 8.3 illustrates the method used to load the stack for both conventions.

In the assembler instruction set, the PUSH instruction places its operand on the stack and *decrements* the stack pointer. Hence, the initiating assembly language code sequence (at the beginning of each function)

```
. . .
push bp
mov bp,sp
sub sp,N
. . .
```

causes the previous module's (or calling module's) base pointer, bp, to be saved on the stack and the current stack pointer value, sp, placed in bp. Prior to execution of this code, the *calling program* caused the called function (procedure) parameters to be placed on the stack along with a return address (invoked at the CALL) for the C convention. The *called program* places the parameters on the stack along with a return address for the PASCAL convention. This difference in parameter-

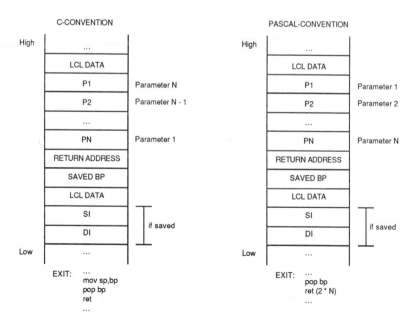

Figure 8.3 Comparison between the C-convention and PASCAL-convention stacks with return code indicated.

loading technique accounts for the different return calls at exit illustrated in Figure 8.3. Also, the parameter order is reversed on the stack. The sub sp,N instruction simply reserves *N* bytes of stack for local usage (*N* should be even).

In Figure 8.2a, four formal parameters are indicated for the function WinMain(): hInst and hPrev, both of type HANDLE; CmdLine, a long pointer to a string (LPSTR); and cmdShow, an integer. This parameter-passing technique is typical of Windows, and to appreciate its use we need to consider both the function definition and the new Windows-type definitions. The interested reader can list the include file windows.h to see the full Windows convention defined.

WinMain() has the following format:

```
WinMain (hInstance, hPrevInstance, lpCmdLine, nCmdShow): nExitCode
```

where

hInstance is the instance handle for the new instance.

hPrevInstance is the instance handle for the previous instance.

lpCmdLine is a long pointer to a command line.

nCmdShow is an integer specifying whether the window should be displayed, left iconic, or hidden.

nExitCode is a parameter value (wParam) from the last message received.

Clearly, this requires some explanation. First, an instance is a single occurrence of a window. As we saw earlier, Windows is dynamic, and the existing window is constantly subject to update based on messages sent to the application by Windows. Each occurrence of a window then represents an instance. Based on the nCmdShow value, which is generated by Windows, the window can be displayed or hidden (or left iconic). Iconic windows are active windows that are not displayed but exist as small icons in the lower-left corner. These icons represent the window entity and may be recalled, for example, by activation (clicking the mouse) with the mouse. The handles are simply integer values used to refer to logical entities created by the program. For example, when accessing a disk drive in assembly language, the associated device is assigned a handle. Here the memory representation for a window is treated as a logical entity with an assigned handle. All these parameters are defined internally by Windows. The programmer will usually not be required to specify these parameters with assignment statements.

Windows uses the typedef operation to define types for recognition purposes. We have seen that HANDLE is simply of integer type. The type LPSTR has the form

```
typedef char (FAR *LPSTR);
```

Thus, LPSTR is a FAR pointer of type char. Note that Windows frequently accesses routines from other code segments and, as a consequence, most Windows pointers are FAR pointers or LONG pointers. In Figure 8.2a, the only executable function code is to return a FALSE value. This causes Windows to terminate processing. No effort has been made to create, display, or destroy a window. This program would be incorrect if the return value were TRUE, because Windows would not have permission to terminate. (Actually, the Windows executive would note an error condition.)

There is an additional file needed with every Windows program, the definition file or .def file. Figure 8.2b contains this file for nodo. Windows uses a new linker, LINK4, to create the .exe file, as previously mentioned. The definition file indicates to the linker the contents and system requirements for each application. The following statements are needed (some or all depending on use):

NAME: a module name without extension, the .exe name

DESCRIPTION: text description inserted in module header

HEAPSIZE: number of bytes needed for local heap

STACKSIZE: number of bytes needed for local stack

CODE: three possible options in sequence

    1. memory-option: FIXED (no movement of code segment)
                           MOVABLE (memory manager can move segment)
                           DISCARDABLE (segment can be discarded)
    2. load-option: PRELOAD (segment loaded immediately)
                           LOADONCALL (loaded when called)
    3. pure-option: PURE (code only)
                           IMPURE (code and data)

DATA: two possible options in sequence

    1. memory-option: FIXED (no movement of data segment)
                           MOVABLE (memory manager can move segment)
                           DISCARDABLE (segment can be discarded)
    2. instance-option: NONE (no data segment)
                           SINGLE (one data segment)
                           MULTIPLE (one segment per instance)

EXPORTS: names and attributes of functions to be accessed by other applications such as Windows functions

EXETYPE: specifier for an application developed under WINDOWS (Windows 1.xx) or OS/2; used by Windows 2.xx when referring to earlier Windows SDK programs

IMPORTS: names and attributes of functions to be accessed by current application

STUB: an MSDOS executable file that defaults if an attempt is made to execute the module without first loading Windows (WINSTUB.EXE is a Windows SDK-supplied routine to be used as an example)

SEGMENT: defines an additional code segment

LIBRARY: defines the name of a library module

The reader should refer to the appropriate Microsoft manuals for a more complete description of each of these statements. We have provided sufficient discussion to enable the material in this text to be understood. In general, this caveat is intended to apply to all discussion where specific reference to format is made: the basic needed material is presented, with additional enhanced discussion obtainable from appropriate references.

Finally, the MAKE file appearing in Figure 8.2c compiles nodo.c using the Microsoft C compiler (in this case the Version 5.0 compiler is used) with the medium model (-AM) and conventional floating point package (-FPa) required by Windows. The reader is referred to the Windows SDK and C Optimizing Compiler [6] manuals for further explanation of the compiler options. The LINK4 execution follows with both nodo.obj and nodo.def linked. This linker has five command line fields: an object module field, the executable module field, a map option field, a library option field, and the define type file field, respectively. As we indicated, the nodo.exe program simply causes the mouse cursor to change momentarily from an arrow to an hourglass and back. This execution is an indicator that definition file format is correct and all versions of the appropriate system routines (compiler, linker, and Windows) are working correctly. If, for example, incorrect library usage occurs, it will be noted during execution of nodo.exe. It is recommended that the reader execute this or a similar program to verify that his or her software is correctly integrated.

Figure 8.4a illustrates a second Windows program that creates a window, as discussed above. This program represents a major increase in complexity over nodo.c and, yet, it simply establishes a blank window. At first glance this may appear incongruous; however, a little reflection with regard to what a window is and does puts everything in perspective. We should remember that the window is first a dynamic graphics object. It is continuously being updated via the Windows application executive and has a graphics presentation that includes text output. We recall from previous chapters how much code is required to generate even simple graphics examples with updating, and it follows that the program in Figure 8.4a suddenly does not seem too complicated. It has been mentioned that Windows defines a large number of general-purpose functions, and the development of a Windows program in most cases consists of calling these functions to display or exercise particular subsets of these functions. With these thoughts in mind, we now examine the beginw.c program appearing in Figure 8.4a (actual file reference to this program will be as beginw4.c in the MAKE file).

The preprocessor area for beginw.c includes a structure with typedef SETUP-DATA consisting of a single integer dummy. Next the SETUPDATA structure setupData is defined as static, the static handle hInst is declared, and two strings, begin and first, are loaded into arrays szName[] and szTitle[], respectively. The array szName[] will be used to reference the module and szTitle[], the window title. The next three statements are function prototypes and are required because the typedef BOOL has been used to describe these functions. While we have not used function prototypes, they are a recommended C convention for functions not of integer type. In the prototype, the function specification must include formal parameter-type specification. Here Window1Init() will be used to initialize the window, Window1InitEvery() provides information needed by every occurrence or instance of the window, and Window1InitAdd() provides information needed by each instance of the window after the initial instance. Finally, the window procedure Window1Proc()

```
/* Beginning Windows program: beginw.c */

#include <windows.h>

typedef struct
        {
        int dummy;
        }
        SETUPDATA;
static  SETUPDATA setupData;

static HANDLE hInst;
char szName[5] = {'b','e','g','i','n'};
char szTitle[5] = {'f','i','r','s','t'};

BOOL FAR PASCAL Window1Init(HANDLE);
BOOL FAR PASCAL Window1InitEvery(HANDLE,int);
BOOL FAR PASCAL Window1InitAdd(HANDLE,HANDLE);

long FAR PASCAL Window1Proc(HWND,unsigned,WORD,LONG);

int NEAR PASCAL WinMain(hInstance,hPrevInstance,lpszCmdLine,cmdShow)
        HANDLE hInstance,hPrevInstance;
        LPSTR lpszCmdLine;
        int cmdShow;
        {
        MSG msg;

        if(!hPrevInstance)
            Window1Init(hInstance);
        else
            Window1InitAdd(hInstance,hPrevInstance);
        Window1InitEvery(hInstance,cmdShow);

        while(GetMessage((LPMSG)&msg,NULL,0,0))
            {
            TranslateMessage((LPMSG)&msg);
            DispatchMessage((LPMSG)&msg);
            }
        exit(msg.wParam);
        }
/* Functions which make up Window1 class */

long FAR PASCAL Window1Proc(hWnd,message,wParam,lParam)
        HWND hWnd;
        unsigned message;
        WORD wParam;
        LONG lParam;
        {
        switch(message)
            {
            case WM_PAINT:
                PaintBeginWindow(hWnd);
                break;
            case WM_DESTROY:
                PostQuitMessage(0);
                break;
            default:
                return(DefWindowProc(hWnd,message,wParam,lParam));
                break;
            }
        return(0L);
        }

PaintBeginWindow(hWnd)
        HWND hWnd;
        {
        PAINTSTRUCT ps;
```

Figure 8.4a Windows program beginw.c, which creates a simple empty window.

```
            BeginPaint(hWnd,(LPPAINTSTRUCT)&ps);
            ValidateRect (hWnd,(LPRECT)NULL);
            EndPaint(hWnd,(LPPAINTSTRUCT)&ps);

            return TRUE;
            }

/* Initialization Module for beginw.c */
/* performed only once at inception */

BOOL FAR PASCAL Window1Init(hInstance)
            HANDLE hInstance;
            {
            WNDCLASS            Window1Class;

            Window1Class.hCursor = LoadCursor(NULL,IDC_ARROW);
            Window1Class.hIcon = LoadIcon(hInstance,(LPSTR)szName);
            Window1Class.lpszMenuName = (LPSTR)NULL;
            Window1Class.lpszClassName = (LPSTR)szName;
            Window1Class.hbrBackground = GetStockObject(WHITE_BRUSH);
            Window1Class.hInstance = hInstance;
            Window1Class.style = CS_HREDRAW | CS_VREDRAW;
            Window1Class.lpfnWndProc = Window1Proc;
            Window1Class.cbClsExtra = 0;
            Window1Class.cbWndExtra = 0;

            RegisterClass((LPWNDCLASS)&Window1Class);
            return TRUE;
            }

/* Performed for every instance of the window */

BOOL FAR PASCAL Window1InitEvery(hInstance,cmdShow)
            HANDLE hInstance;
            int cmdShow;
            {
            HWND hWnd;

            hWnd = CreateWindow((LPSTR)szName,
                                (LPSTR)szTitle,
                                WS_TILEDWINDOW,
                                0,0,0,0,
                                (HWND)NULL,
                                (HMENU)NULL,
                                (HANDLE)hInstance,
                                (LPSTR)NULL);
            ShowWindow(hWnd,cmdShow);
            UpdateWindow(hWnd);
            return TRUE;
            }

/* Performed for instances beyond initial */

BOOL FAR PASCAL Window1InitAdd(hInstance,hPrevInstance)
            HANDLE hInstance,hPrevInstance;
            {
            GetInstanceData(hPrevInstance,(PSTR)&setupData,sizeof(SETUPDATA));
            }
```

Figure 8.4a *(Concluded)*

is prototyped. The reader should observe that ample use is made of HANDLE and
HWND (window handles). These handle declarations will become clear when we
discuss the individual functions and how these handle parameters are passed to
Windows functions. The typedef WORD and LONG is self-explanatory and constitutes
an additional Windows declaration.

Following the preprocessor area, the required Windows main calling function WinMain() appears. WinMain() is a NEAR function of PASCAL type (all Windows functions are of PASCAL type). Again the four formal parameters corresponding to this function are declared. We have used the actual Windows default-naming convention for these parameters in Figure 8.4a. In the main body of the function, a structure msg is declared to be of type MSG. This structure is defined in windows.h as

```
typedef struct{
    HWND hwnd;
    WORD message;
    WORD wParam;
    LONG lParam;
    DWORD time;
    POINT pt;
}MSG;
```

with several associated typdef statements, including

```
typedef MSG FAR *LPMSG;
```

Here LPMSG is a FAR pointer to the MSG structure.
The first executable statement is

```
if(!hPrevInstance)
```

This causes

```
Window1Init(hInstance);
```

to execute when hPrevInstance is FALSE. WinMain() is the executive routine for the application. Since multitasking is allowed, WinMain() may be called for multiple instances. The first call has hPrevInstance FALSE and subsequent calls have this handle TRUE. If hPrevInstance is TRUE, then the function

```
Window1InitAdd(hInstance,hPrevInstance);
```

executes. Finally, the routine

```
Window1InitEvery(hInstance,cmdShow);
```

executes for each instance of the window.
We note that the key concept here is one of an instance. With multiple instances created, the same window can exist as more than one copy. This does not address the multiple calls to each instance of the windows by the Windows executive. Two executives exist in this hierarchy: WinMain() for the application code and Windows for the environment. Shortly, we will consider the functions indicated above in detail, and their structure will be clarified at that time.

The last portion of WinMain() concerns the dynamic updating needed to define a window. In practice, the window will contain devices such as pull-down menus that are accessible by the mouse. If, for example, the mouse cursor is placed over the window menu box in the upper-left corner (after the application is started), a menu box will appear on the screen with several options, such as

Restore	Alt + F5
Move	Alt − F7
Size	Alt − F8
Minimize	Alt + F9
Maximize	Alt + F10
Close	Alt + F4

The user can then move the mouse cursor to the beginning of the word Minimize and click to cause the window to be reduced to an icon in the lower-left corner. (Alternatively, the Alt + F9 keys accomplish the same effect.) The icon can be restored by placing the mouse cursor over the icon and clicking the mouse button. Similarly, the window can be destroyed by placing the mouse cursor over Close in the window menu and clicking the mouse button.

All this activity implies that Windows is continuously updating the applications and looking for user inputs in some form. This updating of the application takes the form of messages that are sent to the application from Windows. Now the purpose of the structure msg becomes clear: it is a vehicle for passing Windows-generated messages to the application. The last portion of the WinMain() code contains provision for dynamically processing these Windows messages. The first Windows function GetMessage() retrieves the next Windows message for the application from the application queue. This message is placed in the structure msg pointed to by (LPMSG)&msg. The handle for the window instance is the second parameter, and when NULL GetMessage() processes all messages as being associated with the application making the call. The last two parameters can be used to filter the messages processed and when both are set to 0 all messages are processed. Table 8.1 illustrates typical Windows messages that are sent to applications. Note that the return value for GetMessage() is nonzero unless the message WM__QUIT is sent. When this message is sent, the while loop terminates and the application ceases. While the while loop is active, the code

```
TranslateMessage((LPMSG)&msg);
DispatchMessage((LPMSG)&msg);
```

continues to execute in loop fashion each time a new message is obtained from Windows using the function call to GetMessage(). TranslateMessage() simply converts any virtual key-stroke messages into character messages (such as mouse input). DispatchMessage() passes the message in the Window structure of type MSG (in this case the structure msg) to the appropriate window function of the specified window. Here the window function is Window1Proc(), to be considered next. When GetMessage() returns a 0, the Windows executive has sent a WM__QUIT message.

TABLE 8.1 WINDOWS MESSAGES

Message	Description
Window management messages	
WM_CREATE	Create a window initialization
WM_SETVISIBLE	Sent before a window is made visible or hidden
WM_QUERYOPEN	Sent to an icon requesting it be opened to a window
WM_ENABLE	Occurs after a window has been enabled or disabled
WM_SETFOCUS	Sent after a window gets the input focus
WM_KILLFOCUS	Sent after a window loses the input focus
WM_ACTIVATE	Occurs after a window becomes active or inactive
WM_ACTIVEAPP	Sent when window being activated is from different window
WM_SHOWWINDOW	Sent when window is to be hidden or shown
WM_SIZE	Occurs after size of window is changed
WM_MOVE	Sent when window is moved
WM_ERASEBKGND	Occurs when window background needs erasing
WM_PAINT	Occurs when request to repaint portion of window
WM_CTLCOLOR	Sent to parent when control or message box is to be drawn
WM_GETTEXT	Copies text corresponding to a window
WM_GETTEXTLENGTH	Finds the length of the text associated with a window
WM_SETTEXT	Sets text of a window
WM_SETREDRAW	Sets text of a window
WM_GETDLGCODE	Allows an application to take control of an input
WM_CLOSE	Occurs when a window is closed
WM_DESTROY	Sent when DestroyWindow() is called
WM_QUERYENDSESSION	Occurs when "End Session" command invoked
WM_ENDSESSION	Sent in response to WM_QUERYENDSESSION
WM_QUIT	Indicates a request to terminate
Initialization messages	
WM_INITMENUPOPUP	Sent before pop-up menu displayed
WM_INITMENU	Request to initialize a menu
WM_INITDIALOG	Sent before dialog box displayed
Input messages	
WM_MOUSEMOVE	Occurs when mouse moves
WM_LBUTTONDOWN	Occurs when left mouse button pushed
WM_LBUTTONUP	Occurs when left mouse button released
WM_RBUTTONDOWN	Occurs when right mouse button pushed
WM_RBUTTONUP	Occurs when right mouse button released
WM_MBUTTONDOWN	Occurs when middle mouse button pushed
WM_MBUTTONUP	Occurs when middle mouse button released
WM_LBUTTONBLCLK	Occurs when left mouse button double-clicked
WM_RBUTTONBLCLK	Occurs when right mouse button double-clicked
WM_MBUTTONBLCLK	Occurs when middle mouse button double-clicked
WM_KEYDOWN	Sent when nonsystem key pressed
WM_KEYUP	Sent when nonsystem key released
WM_CHAR	Message contains ASCII value of key pressed
WM_DEADCHAR	Specifies the character value of a dead key
WM_TIMER	Occurs when time limit elapsed
WM_COMMAND	Occurs when item selected from menu, control passes message to parent, or accelerator input translated
WM_VSCROLL	Occurs when mouse clicked on vertical scroll bar
WM_HSCROLL	Occurs when mouse clicked on horizontal scroll bar

TABLE 8.1 *(Continued)*

System messages

WM_SYSKEYDOWN	Occurs when ALT key plus another pressed
WM_SYSKEYUP	Occurs when ALT key plus another released
WM_SYSCHAR	Specifies virtual key code of system menu
WM_SYSDEADCHAR	Specifies value of a dead key
WM_SYSCOMMAND	Occurs when command selected from system menu

Clipboard messages

WM_RENDERFORMAT	Requests clipboard owner to format last data
WM_RENDERALLFORMATS	Requests clipboard owner to render all formats
WM_DESTROYCLIPBOARD	Sent in response to EmptyClipboard()
WM_DRAWCLIPBOARD	Sent to first window in chain when clipboard changes
WM_CHANGECBCHAIN	Notifies a window is being removed from chain
WM_PAINTCLIPBOARD	Requests repainting of portion of clipboard
WM_SIZECLIPBOARD	Requests change in size of clipboard
WM_VSCROLLCLIPBOARD	Sent when clipboard event changes vertical scroll
WM_HSCROLLCLIPBOARD	Sent when clipboard event changes horizontal scroll
WM_ASKCBFORMATNAME	Requests a copy of the format name

System information messages

WM_SYSCOLORCHANGE	Sent to top-level windows in response to color change
WM_DEVMODECHANGE	Sent in response to changes in device mode
WM_FONTCHANGE	Sent when font resources change
WM_TIMECHANGE	Change to system time
WM_WININICHANGE	Change to initialization file
WM_SYSTEMERROR	Sent when out-of-memory system error

Button control messages

BM_GETCHECK	Indicates a radio button or check box is checked
BM_GETSTATE	Nonzero if cursor is over button and mouse pressed
BM_SETCHECK	Checks or unchecks radio button or check box
BM_SETSTATE	Highlights a button or check box

Edit control messages

EM_GETSEL	Returns starting/ending character positions
EM_SETSEL	Selects characters between starting/ending character positions
EM_GETRECT	Retrieves control formatting rectangle
EM_SETRECT	Sets control formatting rectangle
EM_SETRECTNP	Same as EM_SETRECT except control not painted
EM_SETHANDLE	Establishes buffer to hold contents of control
EM_GETHANDLE	Returns data handle of control buffer
EM_GETLINECOUNT	Returns number of lines of text in control
EM_LINEINDEX	Number of positions before first character in line
EM_LINESCROLL	Scrolls control by indicated lines
EM_SCROLL	Scrolls by full amount
EM_LINELENGTH	Length of line in control text buffer
EM_REPLACESEL	Replaces current selection with new text
EM_SETFONT	Sets the edit control font
EM_GETLINE	Copies a line from edit control
EM_LIMITTEXT	Limits length of user text
EM_UNDO	Undoes the last edit
EM_CANUNDO	Determines if EM_UNDO possible
EM_FMTLINES	Adds or removes end-of-line character
WM_CUT	Deletes a section of the control window
WM_COPY	Sends selection to the clipboard

TABLE 8.1 (*Concluded*)

WM_PASTE	Inserts data from the clipboard into control
WM_CLEAR	Deletes the current selection
List box messages	
LB_ADDSTRING	Adds a string to the list box
LB_INSERTSTRING	Inserts a string into the list box
LB_DELETESTRING	Deletes a string from the list box
LB_SETSEL	Sets the selection state of a string
LB_SETCURSEL	Selects a string and scrolls it into view
LB_GETSEL	Returns the selection state of an item
LB_GETCURSEL	Returns the index of the currently selected item
LB_GETTEXT	Copies a string from the list into a buffer
LB_GETTEXTLEN	Returns the length of a list box string
LB_GETCOUNT	Count of the number of items in the list box
LB_SELECTSTRING	Changes selection to string with specified prefix
LB_DIR	Adds a list of files to the list box

Notification messages

These messages notify the parent window of actions within the control. (The reader is referred to references 1 to 3.)

Nonclient area messages	
WM_NCCREATE	Sent before WM__CREATE
WM_NCDESTROY	Sent after WM__DESTROY
WM_NCCALCSIZE	Sent when size of client area needs to be calculated
WM_NCHITTEST	When mouse moved, sent to windows
WM_NCPAINT	Sent when frame needs painting
WM_NCACTIVATE	Sent when icon or caption changed to indicate active/ inactive
WM_NCMOUSEMOVE	Sent when mouse moved in nonclient area
WM_NCLBUTTONDOWN	Sent when left button pressed while mouse in nonclient area
WM_NCLBUTTONUP	Sent when left button released while mouse in nonclient area
WM_NCLBUTTONDBLCLK	Sent when left button double-clicked mouse in nonclient area
WM_NCRBUTTONDOWN	Sent when right button pressed mouse in nonclient area
WM_NCRBUTTONUP	Sent when right button released mouse in nonclient area
WM_NCRBUTTONDBLCLK	Sent when right button double-clicked mouse in nonclient area
WM_NCMBUTTONDOWN	Sent when middle button pressed mouse in nonclient area
WM_NCMBUTTONUP	Sent when middle button released mouse in nonclient area
WM_NCMBUTTONDBLCLK	Sent when middle button double-clicked mouse in non- client area

This message places a value in msg.wParam of the MSG-type structure, which corresponds to a value sent to a Windows routine PostQuitMessage(). Clearly, the function PostQuiteMessage() has had to previously execute in response to an earlier message sequence. As we will see, the wParam value is 0, and this is passed to exit() in WinMain(), where a full exit from the application takes place.

Table 8.1 is quite extensive and covers most of the message types generated by Windows. We have included this depth in the discussion in order to illustrate the sort of interchanges that take place in the Windows environment. A major difficulty with learning how to program for Windows is the sheer magnitude of functions, structures, and messages that the programmer must become aware of when implementing software in this framework. Part of the goal of this chapter is to present the reader with most of these Windows entities (including brief descriptions) so that an awareness can begin to develop for the Windows interface. Table 8.1 and the discussion surrounding Figure 8.4a are the beginning of this awareness process. In many cases the material in Table 8.1 references Windows components (such as dialog boxes) that are, as yet, unexplained. As the discussion unfolds in this chapter and Chapter 9, most of these references will be covered.

By now the reader is beginning to grasp the power of the Windows environment. We have seen a simple application executive, WinMain(), and developed a feel for how this executive dynamically acts to accomplish the window generation. What has not been clarified is how the routine DispatchMessage() sends the message to the window function [in this case Window1Proc()]. This is part of the job of Windows, and the initialization file has had to tell Windows about Window1Proc(). Also, another structure of type WNDCLASS, used when the window is initiated and the window class registered, is defined for the application.

Window1Proc() is the window function that appears as the second function in Figure 8.4a. This function has four parameters: hWnd, a handle of HWND type; message, an unsigned integer designating the message sent from Windows; wParam, a WORD-type parameter; and lParam, a LONG-type parameter. Both wParam and lParam are used to indicate various Windows conditions (such as the exit code indicated earlier), and these parameters act much like a flag. Upon entry to Window1Proc(), the window procedure for this instance, message is used in a switch statement to control the flow of Windows activity for the window. Only three indicated options are available: response to the messages WM_PAINT or WM_DESTROY or response to any other message (the default). Three additional functions are called in response to these messages, respectively:

```
PaintBeginWindow(nWnd);
PostQuitMessage(0);
DefWindowProc(hWnd,message,wParam,lParam);
```

What do these functions accomplish upon being called? The first function, PaintBegin-Window(), is contained in subsequent code and could be called by any name since it is user created. This routine actually "paints" the window and will be discussed shortly. The remaining two functions are Windows functions and act as follows:

```
PostQuitMessage(nExitCode);
```

This function informs Windows that the application wishes to terminate execution. It is sent (usually) in response to a Windows message WM_DESTROY. How does such a message ever get sent to the application? The third routine DefWindow-Proc() calls another Windows function, DestroyWindow(), when the mouse, for example, is clicked with the cursor position over Close. The DestroyWindow() function sends a WM_DESTROY message to the window specified by the handle hWnd contained in DefWindowProc(). Note that the user does not actually specify DestroyWindow() in a call in this program. It is left to Windows to make this call in response to a particular input message (such as clicking the Close option with the mouse). Returning to PostQuitMessage(), the exit code nExitCode is the wParam variable contained in the WM__QUIT message structure. In this application, we pass a 0 to this structure. In WinMain(), this parameter value is, in turn, passed back to the structure msg, where exit() uses it to specify the appropriate exit made from the application.

Clearly, a workhorse function in this application is DefWindowProc(). This Windows function carries out default processing of Windows messages sent to the application. Based on messages received by the application, translated using TranslateMessage(), and dispatched to Windows functions using DispatchMessage(), a sequence of messages is exchanged that is processed on the application side by DefWindowProc(). Only messages WM__PAINT and WM__DESTROY are separately processed by the application. Much of this procedure was alluded to in the earlier discussion of the previous section. We now see the dynamic mechanism by which messages are continuously created by Windows and responded to within the application. So far, however, we have not discussed the actual painting of the window. This occurs in response to the Windows message WM__PAINT. When this message is received from Windows (in response to a mouse cursor activity, for example), the user-generated routine PaintBeginWindow() is called. This routine has the handle hWnd passed to it by the call from the window procedure, Window1Proc(), and it, in turn, calls three Windows functions:

```
BeginPaint(hWnd, (LPPAINTSTRUCT)&ps);
ValidateRect(hWnd, (LPRECT)NULL);
EndPaint(hWnd, (LPPAINTSTRUCT)&ps);
```

We now consider these three Windows functions.

The function BeginPaint() prepares the window associated with the application instance for painting. A structure ps of type PAINTSTRUCT is loaded with correct parameter data for painting the screen. Since we are using default procedures, Windows sets up much of this structure based on minimal information supplied in the initialization routines (mentioned earlier and to be discussed below). The important aspect of this programming is to recognize that Windows actually creates the screen image (appropriately drawing lines, icons, text, shading, menu boxes, headers, and other features) with Windows code. It is this code that is transparent to the user. We have seen many features of this type of code in the earlier chapters with their lower-level focus. Now in Windows we move into a high-level environment that is object oriented, and we manipulate these objects without regard for their low-level origin.

In BeginPaint(), the second parameter is a pointer of type LPPAINTSTRUCT, which points to ps. The next function call is to the Windows function ValidateRect(). The form of the function call is

```
ValidateRect(hWnd, (LPRECT)NULL);
```

and the call releases the rectangular area of the screen associated with the handle hWnd following repainting. The second parameter is a long pointer to a data structure of type RECT. When the pointer is to NULL, this structure refers to coordinates corresponding to the whole screen. The structure has the form

```
typedef struct {
        int left;
        int top;
        int right;
        int bottom;
}RECT;
```

with associated typing (partial)

```
typedef RECT FAR *LPRECT;
```

Clearly, RECT must be specified for the WM__PAINT function calls. In this application, default values are generated as a result of the return from DefWindowProc() and the initialization routines.

Finally, the PaintBeginWindow() function calls a Windows routine

```
EndPaint(hWnd, (LPPAINTSTRUCT)&ps);
```

This call corresponds to ending the painting process and is needed for each call to BeginPaint(). The parameter specification is symmetrical with that for BeginPaint().

The remaining three functions in Figure 8.4a are the initialization routines. These routines are called when a window instance is created or updated. We begin with Window1Init(), a user-generated function. This function has a single parameter, the instance handle. It merely defines a window structure of type WNDCLASS and registers this window. The structure has the form

```
typedefstruct{
        WORD        style;
        long        (FAR PASCAL *lpfnWndProc);
        int         cbClsExtra;
        int         cbWndExtra;
        HANDLE      hInstance;
        HICON       hIcon;
        HCURSOR     hCursor;
        HBRUSH      hbrBackground;
        LPSTR       lpszMenuName;
        LPSTR       lpszClassName;
}WNDCLASS;
```

with associated pointers such as

```
typedef WNDCLASS FAR *LPWNDCLASS;
```

The routine Window1Init() sets up this structure (Window1Class) for the present application as follows:

```
Window1Class.hCursor = LoadCursor(NULL,IDC_ARROW);
```

This loads hCursor by calling the Windows routine LoadCursor() to return a handle for predefined cursors (NULL) of type standard arrow (IDC__ARROW).

```
Window1Class.hIcon = LoadIcon(hInstance,(LPSTR)szName);
```

This loads the icon resource named by the character string pointed to by the long pointer [(LPSTR)szName] for the instance with handle hInstance.

```
Window1Class.lpszMenuName = (LPSTR)NULL;
```

This points to the name of the class menu and, if NULL, indicates no default menu exists for this class.

```
Window1Class.lpszClassName = (LPSTR)szName;
```

This specifies a pointer to the name of the window class.

```
Window1Class.hbrBackground = GetStockObject(WHITE_BRUSH);
```

This is a handle to the physical brush used for painting the background color, and it is returned by GetStockObject() as a white pen background brush (stock Windows color).

```
Window1Class.hInstance = hInstance
```

This is the class module specification, an instance handle.

```
Window1Class.style = CS_HREDRAW | CS_VREDRAW;
```

This is the class style: in this case the entire window is redrawn if horizontal or vertical size changes.

```
Window1Class.lpfnWndProc = Window1Proc;
```

This is a pointer to the window function.

```
Window1Class.cbClsExtra = 0;
```

This is a buffer storage area after the class structure specified in bytes.

```
Window1Class.dbWndExtra = 0;
```

This is a buffer storage area after the window instance specified in bytes.

Following specification of the Window1Class structure of type WNDCLASS, the structure is registered with the call

```
RegisterClass((LPWNDCLASS)&Window1Class);
```

This function sets up the window class for use in calls to the CreateWindow() function. These calls occur for every instance of the window and in the application corresponding to Figure 8.4a are made from Window1InitEvery() (to be discussed next). In Window1Init(), the last statement is to return a TRUE value, which indicates that the window was registered. For this application, we do not actually use this return value.

The function Window1InitEvery() recevies two parameters: the window instance handle and an integer flag corresponding to a particular window condition. The window handle hWnd is created of type HWND and a call to CreateWindow() made. This function has the following form:

```
CreateWindow(lpClassName,lpWindowName,dwStyle,
             X,YnWidth,nHeight,hWndParent,
             hMenu,hInstance,lpParam)
```

It creates tiled, pop-up, and child windows for Windows Version 1.03 (an earlier version of the SDK). What are the parameters specified in Figure 8.4a? The correspondence is as follows:

`lpClassName = (LPSTR)szName:`	a long pointer to the ASCII string naming the window class
`lpWindowName = (LPSTR)szTitle:`	a long pointer to the ASCII string naming the window
`dwStyle = WS_TILEDWINDOW:`	a long unsigned integer indicating a key word designation for the window style (tiled windows here)
`X,Y = 0,0:`	short integer values specifying the initial position of the window; for tiled windows, X is ignored and Y is determined by Windows (hence 0,0 is meaningless)
`nWidth,nHeight = 0,0:`	ignored for tiled windows
`hWndParent = (HWMD)NULL:`	handle to a parent window must be NULL when creating a tiled window
`hMenu = (HMENU)NULL:`	handle to the menu to be used with the window; if NULL, the class menu is used
`hInstance = (HANDLE)hInstance:`	the instance handle for the associated instance

```
lpParam = (LPSTR)NULL:
```
long pointer to a value passed to the application by Windows through the lParam parameter of the WM_CRE-ATE message

Following the call to CreateWindow(), where hWnd is the returned handle to the new window, the ShowWindow() function is called. This function displays or removes the window with handle hWnd (the first parameter) according to the value of cmdShow, which was returned to WinMain() from Windows in response to the dynamic requirements indicated by the mouse or keyboard input. The function UpDateWindow() keeps track of changes in a window's characteristics and sends WM_PAINT messages directly to the window function [Window1Proc()] as updates are needed. Finally, a return value of TRUE is sent. This value is not used by the application.

The last function appearing in Figure 8.4a is a routine called for instances following the initial instance. This routine, Window1InitAdd(), simply calls GetInstanceData() to copy from the previous instance of an application to the current instance. In this application, the GetInstanceData() call takes the form

```
GetInstanceData(hPrevInstance,(PSTR)&setupData,sizeof(SETUPDATA));
```

Here the first parameter is the instance handle of a previous instance and will always be nonzero, since the function Window1InitAdd() is only called after the initial creation of the window. The pointer (PSTR)&setupData points to the buffer created by the structure setupData defined in the preprocessor area. This buffer is a single integer, and the third parameter merely specifies its size.

At this point we have examined the code needed to specify a beginning window program capable of displaying an empty client area with a default pull-down menu, icon capability, and header bar with title first. Figure 8.4b illustrates the definition file for this program, where the application is named beginw4. Figure 8.4c contains the MAKE file for this application.

This completes the discussion of the introductory programming examples using the Windows SDK. We have only attempted to provide a flavor of the techniques to be explored in subsequent discussion. These programs were generated within the framework of Windows 2.03, the Presentation Manager. Since the Windows SDK and the Windows Presentation Manager (the Windows executive) are two different software entities, we briefly discuss this latter program in the following subsection.

8.1.3 Executing with the MS-DOS Presentation Manager: Windows 2.0

The actual Presentation Manager version used in this chapter is 2.03 with programs developed using the SDK Version 1.03. The Presentation Manager must be installed in an appropriate directory and is invoked by issuing the command

```
win
```

```
NAME            beginw4

EXETYPE         WINDOWS

STUB            'WINSTUB.EXE'

DESCRIPTION     'Beginning Windows Program'

CODE            MOVEABLE
DATA            MOVEABLE MULTIPLE

HEAPSIZE        2048
STACKSIZE       4096

EXPORTS
        Window1Proc
```

(b)

```
# MAKE file for beginning Windows program

beginw4.obj: beginw4.c
        cl -c -d -AS -Os -Gsw -Zp -FPa beginw4.c

beginw4.exe: beginw4.obj beginw4.def
        link4 beginw4,/align:16,/map,slibw/NOE swinlibc/NOE,beginw4
```

(c)

Figure 8.4b, c   (b) Definition file associated with beginw.c and (c) corresponding MAKE file.

(for win.exe) to DOS or OS/2. Following initiation of the program the user is immediately placed under the MS-DOS Executive. The user can position the mouse arrow over a file name and double-click to initiate the program under Windows, provided it is a program written for the Windows environment. Clearly, all the MS-DOS and other non-Windows programs cannot be executed under Windows. When the user attempts to execute such a file, Windows creates a message box with a message indicating that the program in question cannot be executed under Windows.

8.2 WINDOWS SDK PROGRAM ARCHITECTURE

In Section 8.3, we will examine the Windows SDK routines and data structures in some detail. At that time, specific entities particular to Windows will be discussed. The purpose of this section is to consider some of the conceptual aspects of Windows as an environment for representing program output.

8.2.1 Windows as a Dynamic Framework

In many respects, Windows performs like an operating system within an operating system. It is a true executive capable of responding in real time to inputs from the user. We have seen that the heart of the Windows program is the message-polling loop characterized by the GetMessage(), TranslateMessage(), and Dispatch-

Message() functions. These functions allow the Windows Executive to interpret mouse or keyboard commands and issue messages to either an application or within the Executive itself. These messages serve as the basis for calling a variety of routines to perform various Windows and applications activities.

It is the use of this third dimension, time, that differentiates Windows from the static environment of the earlier programming considered in this book. Such earlier programming is at the heart of Windows, and it is only through the message-polling loop context that time becomes important. Finally, the message interchange itself must be considered. Since Windows is an example of object-oriented programming, it is clear that the message interchange is crucial to defining object selection. Fortunately, the Windows message hierarchy demonstrates a carefully thought out exchange mechanism for obtaining a continuous window update in response to user-initiated actions.

8.2.2 Windows SDK Defined Functions: An Operational Protocol

Having seen examples of the SDK programming in the code of Figure 8.4a, it is clear that these routines provide the capability to structurally organize program execution. A protocol is a means for systematically defining the interfaces among processes within the context of an overall methodology. The Windows functions define such a protocol in an operational sense. The activities associated with each function serve as processes, and the formal parameter architecture represents an interface mechanism (when coupled with the underlying message structure). Hence, the functions can be thought of as an operational protocol, which defines the interfaces in an operational sense. While this is somewhat of a hybrid definition, it places the Windows functions in a perspective that lends organization to their actual activity. This is important because, when reading a Windows program such as illustrated in Figure 8.4a, the high-level abstractions represented by such code take on added meaning if the Windows functions are considered from the viewpoint of how they define the interfacing within the overall program. It is this interfacing that is most difficult to understand about the Windows environment.

8.2.3 Implications of Multitasking

Windows is a multitasking environment. This implies that the processor can effect execution of multiple jobs by time sharing its services. This time sharing is controlled by the Windows Executive. A typical example of multitasking would be to generate several instances of first (Figure 8.4a) using the Minimize option of the first control menu to reduce each instance to an icon, reopen MS-DOS Executive, and create a new instance. Each of these instances represents a separate task and executes separately. During the establishment of the initial first instance, a number of data structures are developed. Subsequent instances keep track of the fact that they are not the original task through the parameter hPrevInstance. Using GetInstanceData(), for example, prior data are passed among these subsequent tasks.

Clearly, each instance of first, for example, must be self-contained. That is, it must be capable of re-creating itself from an icon. Thus, multitasking must partition each task into a separate memory area, and Windows does this. Also, each application must be programmed judiciously in order that it does not occupy an excessive portion of the operating time. In the multitasking environment provided by Windows, the programmer must respect the need of other applications for access to the CPU and program each application for minimum execution time. This will become clearer when we actually begin using the client area. This is basically similar to interleaving the reading of a communications port and simultaneous program execution: the program must shift back and forth between each task. A final area of consideration is the passing of data and simultaneous access of files among several instances (or tasks). All these factors must influence the design of Windows programs because of the intrinsic multitasking nature of this executive.

8.2.4 Initialization and Termination

Windows initializes an instance based on placing the mouse cursor over the .exe file under the MS-DOS Executive window and double-clicking. This creates the instance or task and causes the initialization routines, called by WinMain(), to be executed. For the Windows SDK Version 1.03 used in this chapter, only tiled windows (not overlapped windows) are used. In this situation, the appearance of the initialized window is controlled by Windows. With the minimize and maximize box, the user can cause the application window to occupy the entire screen or be reduced to an icon. At inception, however, this is controlled by Windows. The self-contained feature exhibited by each task ensures that full window capability is always intrinsic to each instance.

Termination of a window is accomplished by activating the Close or Exit options associated with an application control menu or the MS-DOS Executive menu, respectively. The issue of a termination instruction from the display (using the mouse, for example) causes the WM_DESTROY and WM-QUIT message sequence to be sent to the application, with subsequent action by appropriate Windows functions. In the code appearing in Figure 8.4a, we have seen an example of how this termination is accomplished when DispatchMessage() passes WM_DESTROY to Window1Proc(). This latter window function calls PostQuitMessage(0), which informs Windows that the application wishes to terminate execution. PostQuitMessage() passes WM_QUIT to the application window function [in this case Window1Proc()], where it is processed. For the window function, Window1Proc() WM_QUIT elicits the default switch case, and DefWindowProc() is called to process the message. This function takes appropriate internal action to terminate the window under default window conditions.

8.3 WINDOWS SDK PROGRAM COMPONENTS

Up to this point we have developed C code for a simple Windows program using the SDK libraries and include files (the beginw4.c program). During this development, a number of Windows entities were described and used. It is the purpose of this section to consider the general types of Windows entities available to the C programmer, with some indication of their usage. The reader is referred to the Microsoft documentation for a complete discussion of the use and syntax associated with these Windows elements.

8.3.1 Window Functions

Table 8.2 illustrates the various functions available to the user (which are classified as window functions in the references by Windows SDK literature). These functions have been explicitly referenced in Table 8.2 by a descriptor in order to provide the reader with a brief topical indication of the functions capability. We intend to provide this table as a vehicle for achieving a broad perspective on the Windows window-type functions. It is clear that this table is rather lengthy, indicating the variety and flexibility of Windows routines available for simply creating and modifying the window context.

For convenience, it is useful to cover briefly some of the Windows references made in this table. An accelerator is a combination of key strokes treated as a command. A class is a grouping of windows (all of the same type) corresponding to a fixed parent instance with similar attributes. A tiled window is nonoverlapped, a pop-up occurs as a pull-down feature within a window, and a child is a subwindow category referenced to a parent within a class. An icon is a symbol representative for a window file. A dialog box is used for obtaining additional user input beyond the menu format. It usually appears as a pop-up window with child window controls. There are two types: modal and modeless. Modal dialog boxes allow switching between the box and other programs, but the programmer cannot switch windows. Modeless dialog boxes, however, allow switching among dialog boxes, other windows, and other programs. A list box is a collection of text strings displayed as a scrollable columnar grouping within a rectangular space. Buttons can be filled with check marks or pushed, depending on type, and represent sensitized screen shapes useful for indicating a screen input. The clipboard is an entity that is used to pass data from one program to another. Any program notified of changes in the clipboard is a clipboard viewer, and the clipboard view chain consists of all those programs linked together to pass information regarding the changing status of the clipboard. A metric is an internal system standard used as a measure of physical information. As those elements are encountered in the ensuing descriptive material, their function will become more apparent.

TABLE 8.2 WINDOW FUNCTIONS

Function	Description
Main function	
WinMain()	Entry point for initialization and setup of the application program
Message functions	
PostQuitMessage()	Informs Windows an application wishes to terminate
GetMessage()	Retrieves a message from the application queue
PeekMessage()	Retrieves a message from the application queue with an immediate return independent of message availability
WaitMessage()	Yields control to other applications when no additional tasks exist for the present application

TABLE 8.2 (*Continued*)

GetMessagePos()	Returns a long value representing the mouse position in screen coordinates where the last message occurred [received by GetMessage()]
GetMessageTime()	Returns a long integer specifying the message time
GetCurrentTime()	Returns the current time
TranslateMessage()	Converts virtual keystroke messages (mouse input) to character messages
TranslateAccelerator()	Processes keyboard accelerators (keyboard input treated as a command not a keystroke combination) for menu commands
DispatchMessage()	Passes message in the MSG structure to the window function
SendMessage()	Sends a message to a window or Windows
PostMessage()	Places a message in a window's application queue
ReplyMessage()	Allows a routine responding to a message sent with SendMessage() to generate a reply without returning control to the function calling
PostAppMessage()	Posts a message to an application
RegisterWindowMessage()	Defines a new window message

Window function
WndProc()	Here, WndProc() is generic. The window function can have any name. It is an application-supplied function that processes the window messages.

Default window function
DefWindowProc()	Provides default processing for any Windows messages not processed by a given application

Window class functions
RegisterClass()	Registers a window class for subsequent use in calls to CreateWindow()
GetClassName	Retrieves the class name
GetClassWord()	Retrieves a WNDCLASS parameter value
GetClassLong()	Retrieves a long WNDCLASS parameter value
SetClassWord()	Replaces a WNDCLASS parameter value
SetClassLong()	Replaces a long WNDCLASS parameter value
CallWindowProc()	Passes message information to a previously defined Windows function

Windows creation functions
CreateWindow()	Creates a tiled, pop-up, or child window
IsWindow()	Returns value indicating window existence
DestroyWindow()	Sends a WM_DESTROY message to a window and frees the memory it occupied
GetWindowWord()	Retrieves window information
GetWindowLong()	Retrieves a long pointer to the window function or the style
SetWindowWord()	Sets window information
SetWindowLong()	Changes a window attribute

Window display/movement functions
ShowWindow()	Displays or removes a window
OpenIcon()	Opens a window from the icon area
CloseWindow()	Closes the specified window
MoveWindow()	Gives new size information to a window

TABLE 8.2 *(Continued)*

`BringWindowToTop()`	Brings a pop-up or child window to the top of a stack of windows
`SetActiveWindow()`	Makes a tiled or pop-up window the active window
`IsWindowVisible()`	Specifies whether window is visible
`AnyPopup()`	Specifies whether a pop-up window is visible
`IsIconic()`	Specifies whether a window is iconic
`EnumWindows()`	Enumerates windows on the screen
`EnumChildWindows()`	Enumerates child windows belonging to a specified parent

Dialog box functions

`CreateDialog()`	Creates a modeless dialog box
`IsDialogMessage()`	Determines whether a given message is intended for the specified modeless dialog box
`DialogBox()`	Creates a modal dialog box
`EndDialog()`	Frees resources and destroys windows associated with a modal dialog box
`DlgDirList()`	Fills a list box with file names specified by a path directory
`DlgDirSelect()`	Gets a selection from a list box
`GetDlgItem()`	Retrieves the handle of a dialog item
`SetDlgItemInt()`	Sets the text of a dialog item to the string representation of an integer value
`GetDlgItemInt()`	Translates the text of a dialog item into an integer value
`SetDlgItemText()`	Sets the caption of a dialog item
`GetDlgItemText()`	Retrieves the caption associated with a dialog item
`CheckDlgButton()`	Places or removes a check mark next to a button control
`IsDlgButtonChecked()`	Determines whether a button control has a check mark
`CheckRadioButton()`	Checks a radio button (same as a check box but circular)
`SendDlgItemMessage()`	Sends a message to the dialog item
`MapDialogRect()`	Converts dialog box coordinates to client coordinates

Clipboard functions

`OpenClipboard()`	Opens the clipboard for examination
`CloseClipboard()`	Closes the clipboard
`EmptyClipboard()`	Clears or empties the clipboard
`GetClipboardOwner()`	Retrieves handle of current clipboard owner
`SetClipboardData()`	Sets clipboard data
`GetClipboardData()`	Retrieves clipboard data
`RegisterClipboardFormat()`	Registers a new clipboard format
`CountClipboardFormats()`	Retrieves a count of the number of formats that the clipboard can render
`EnumClipboardFormats()`	Enumerates the clipboard formats
`GetClipboardFormatName()`	Retrieves the name of the clipboard's *registered* format
`SetClipboardViewer()`	Adds the window to a chain that is notified whenever the contents of the clipboard change
`GetClipboardViewer()`	Retrieves the handle of the first window in the clipboard viewer chain
`ChangeClipboardChain()`	Modifies the clipboard viewer chain

Input functions

`SetFocus()`	Assigns the input focus to the specified window
`GetFocus()`	Retrieves the current focus
`GetKeyState()`	Retrieves the state of a virtual key
`SetCapture()`	Sends all subsequent mouse input to the specified window
`ReleaseCapture()`	Releases mouse input from a SetCapture()
`SetTimer()`	Creates a system timer

TABLE 8.2 *(Continued)*

KillTimer()	Kills the timer event created by SetTimer()
EnableWindow()	Enables or disables mouse and keyboard input to the specified window
IsWindowEnabled()	Determines whether mouse or keyboard input is enabled for the specified window

Menu functions

SetMenu()	Sets a given window's menu
GetMenu()	Retrieves a window's menu handle
CreateMenu()	Creates a menu
DestroyMenu()	Destroys a menu
ChangeMenu()	Modifies a menu
DrawMenuBar()	Redraws the menu bar
CheckMenuItem()	Places or removes menu check marks
EnableMenuItem()	Enables or disables a menu item
HiliteMenuItem()	Highlights or removes highlighting from a menu-bar item
GetSubMenu()	Retrieves a pop-up menu handle
GetSystemMenu()	Allows access to the system menu
GetMenuString()	Copies the label of a specified menu item to a string buffer

Window painting functions

GetDC()	Retrieves the display context for a specified window's client area
GetWindowDC()	Retrieves the display context for an entire window
ReleaseDC()	Releases a display context when an application is finished with it
BeginPaint()	Prepares a window for painting
EndPaint()	Marks the end of repainting
UpdateWindow()	Ensures a window's appearance is up to date
GetUpdate Rect()	Returns the rectangle that bounds the region of the window that needs updating
InvalidateRect()	Marks a specified window rectangular area for repainting
ValidateRect()	Releases from repainting the InvalidateRect() area
ValidateRgn()	Releases from repainting the InvalidateRgn() region
InvalidateRgn()	Marks a specified window region for repainting

Scrolling functions

ScrollWindow()	Scrolls a window's client area
SetScrollPos()	Sets the current position of a scroll bar elevator
GetScrollPos()	Retrieves the current position of a scroll bar elevator
SetScrollRange()	Sets minimum/maximum positions for scroll bar
GetScrollRange()	Retrieves minimum/maximum for scroll bar

Property list functions

SetProp()	Copies a character string and data handle to the specified property list
GetProp()	Retrieves a property list's data handle
RemoveProp()	Removes the property list
EnumProps()	Enumerates all the properties of the specified window

Window attribute functions

SetWindowText()	Sets the given window's caption title
GetWindowText()	Copies the given window's caption title into the specified buffer
GetWindowTextLength()	Returns the length of a window's caption
FindWindow()	Returns the handle of window

TABLE 8.2 (*Concluded*)

GetParent()	Retrieves the handle of a window's parent
GetClientRect()	Copies the coordinates of a window's client area into a data structure
GetWindowRect()	Copies the coordinates of a window's bounding area into a data structure
GetSysModalWindow()	Returns the handle of a system modal window
SetSysModalWindow()	Makes the specified window a system modal window

Error functions

MessageBox()	Displays a window that contains application-supplied message, caption, icons, and push buttons
MessageBeep()	Generates a beep at the speaker when a message box is displayed
FlashWindow()	Flashes a window once to change its appearance

Cursor functions

SetCursor	Sets the cursor shape
SetCursorPos()	Sets the position of the mouse cursor
ClipCursor()	Restricts the cursor to the specified rectangle
GetCursorPos()	Gets the position of the mouse cursor
ShowCursor()	Displays or hides the cursor

Caret functions

CreateCaret()	Creates a caret
DestroyCaret()	Destroys a caret
HideCaret()	Removes the system caret from the display
ShowCaret()	Displays a caret created with CreateCaret()
SetCaretPos()	Moves the specified caret to the indicated location
SetCaretBlinkTime()	Establishes the caret flash rate
GetCaretBlinkTime()	Returns the caret flash rate

Coordinate functions

ClientToScreen()	Converts client to screen coordinates
ScreenToClient()	Converts screen to client coordinates
WindowFromPoint()	Identifies the window that contains a given point
ChildWindowFromPoint()	Identifies the child window that contains a given point

Rectangle functions

SetRect()	Fixes the specified rectangle
SetRectEmpty()	Clears the specified rectangle
CopyRect()	Makes a copy of an existing rectangle
InflateRect()	Expands the selected rectangle
IntersectRect()	Finds the intersection of two rectangles and copies it to a buffer
UnionRect()	Creates the union of two rectangles
OffsetRect()	Offsets the specified rectangle
IsRectEmpty()	Determines whether or not a specified rectangle is empty
PtInRect()	Indicates whether or not a point lies within a rectangle

System information functions

GetSystemMetrics()	Retrieves information about system metrics
GetSysColor()	Retrieves information about system colors
SetSysColors()	Changes system colors

Window hook function

SetWindowsHook()	Used to install system or application hook functions (message filter or keyboard filters)

8.3.2 Graphics Device Interface (GDI) Functions

The GDI functions are used to fill or paint the client area of a window. Associated with a given window is the device context, which is really a structure maintaining all environment data about a given window. The window handle HDC is a handle to this context. The values in the device context structure are known as the attributes of the context. Table 8.3 lists the majority of the GDI functions callable using Windows. A bitmap is a local mapping of client area or window area pixels in memory. Objects are items like pens and brushes. The extent of an object is the range of its dimension along a given direction. A viewpoint is the region mapped from a window to a set of device coordinates, suitable for display. The clipping region is a region in the client area that can be updated in response to user inputs.

TABLE 8.3 GRAPHICS DEVICE INTERFACE FUNCTIONS

Function	Description
Display context functions	
CreateDC()	Creates a display context for the specified device
CreateCompatibleDC()	Creates a memory display context compatible with the specified device
CreateIC()	Creates an information context for the specified device
DeleteDC()	Deletes the specified display context
SaveDC()	Saves the current state of the specified display context
RestoreDC()	Restores the specified display context
Output functions	
MoveTo()	Moves current position to specified position
GetCurrentPosition()	Retrieves the logical current position
LineTo()	Draws a line from the current to specified position
Polyline()	Draws a set of line segments connecting the specified points
Rectangle()	Draws the specified rectangle
RoundRect()	Draws the specified rectangle with rounded corners
Polygon()	Draws a polygon using the specified points
Ellipse()	Draws the specified ellipse
Arc()	Draws the specified elliptical arc
Pie()	Draws the specified pie-shaped wedge
PatBlt()	Creates the specified bit pattern
BitBlt()	Moves a bitmap from a source to destination device
StretchBlt()	Moves a bitmap from a source rectangle into a destination rectangle, stretching or compressing the bitmap
TextOut()	Writes a character string on the specified display
DrawText()	Draws formatted text in the specified rectangle
GrayString()	Writes and grays a character string
DrawIcon()	Draws the specified icon on a display

TABLE 8.3 (*Continued*)

SetPixel()	Sets a pixel at the specified point
GetPixel()	Retrieves the color of the specified pixel
FloodFill()	Fills an area with the current brush
LineDDA()	Computes all successive points in the specified line
FillRgn()	Fills the specified region with the indicated brush
FrameRgn()	Draws a border around the specified region
InvertRgn()	Inverts the colors in the specified region
PaintRgn()	Fills the specified region with the current brush
FillRect()	Fills a given rectangle using the specified brush
FrameRect()	Draws a border around the specified rectangle
InvertRect()	Inverts the colors in the specified rectangle

Drawing object functions

GetStockObject()	Retrieves a handle to a predefined object
CreatePen()	Creates a logical pen with specified characteristics
CreatePenIndirect()	Creates a logical pen with characteristics specified in the associated data structure
CreateSolidBrush()	Creates a logical brush with the specified solid color
CreateHatchBrush()	Creates a logical brush with the specified hatched color
CreatePatternBrush()	Creates a logical brush with the pattern specified by the associated bitmap
CreateBrushIndirect()	Creates a logical brush with characteristics specified in the associated data structure
CreateBitmap()	Creates a bitmap as specified
CreateBitmapIndirect()	Creates a bitmap as specified in the associated data structure
CreateCompatibleBitmap()	Creates a bitmap compatible with the specified device
SetBitmapBits()	Sets the bits in a bitmap
GetBitmapBits()	Gets the bits in a bitmap and copies them to the specified buffer
SetBitmapDimension()	Associates a width and height to a bitmap
GetBitmapDimension()	Returns the width and height of the specified bitmap
CreateFont()	Creates a logical font with specified characteristics
CreateFontIndirect()	Creates a logical font based on the associated data structure
DeleteObject()	Deletes a logical object from memory

Selection functions

SelectObject()	Selects the specified logical object
SelectClipRgn()	Selects the given region as the current clipping region
GetObject()	Fills a buffer with data from the specified logical object

Display context attribute functions

SetRelAbs()	Specifies whether relative or absolute coordinates are used

TABLE 8.3 *(Continued)*

`GetRelAbs()`	Retrieves whether relative or absolute coordinates are used
`SetBkColor()`	Sets the background color
`GetBkColor()`	Returns the background color
`SetBkMode()`	Sets the background mode
`GetBkMode()`	Returns the background mode
`SetTextColor()`	Sets the text color
`GetTextColor()`	Retrieves the current text color
`SetROP2()`	Sets the drawing mode on raster devices
`GetROP2()`	Retrieves the drawing mode for raster devices
`SetStretchBltMode()`	Sets the StretchBlt() stretching mode
`GetStretchBltMode()`	Retrieves the StretchBlt() stretching mode
`SetPolyFillMode()`	Sets the polygon-filling mode
`GetPolyFillMode()`	Retrieves the polygon-filling mode
`SetMapMode()`	Sets the unit of measure used for transforming logical units to device units
`GetMapMode()`	Retrieves the SetMapMode() mapping measure
`SetWindowOrg()`	Sets the window origin
`GetWindowOrg()`	Retrieves the window origin
`SetWindowExt()`	Sets the x and y extents of the window
`GetWindowExt()`	Retrieves the x and y extents of the window
`SetViewportOrg()`	Sets the viewport origin
`GetViewportOrg()`	Retrieves the viewport origin
`ScaleWindowExt()`	Modifies the window extents
`ScaleViewportExt()`	Modifies the viewport extents
`OffsetWindowOrg()`	Modifies the window origin
`OffsetViewportOrg()`	Modifies the viewport origin
`SetViewportExt()`	Sets the viewport extents
`GetViewportExt()`	Retrieves the viewport extent
`GetBrushOrg()`	Retrieves the current brush origin
`SetBrushOrg()`	Sets the origin of the selected brushes
`UnrealizeObject()`	Resets the origin of the given brush

Clipping region functions

`GetClipBox()`	Retrieves the rectangle around the current clipping boundary
`IntersectClipRect()`	Creates a new specified clipping region
`OffsetClipRgn()`	Moves the specified clipping region a given offset
`ExcludeClipRect()`	Creates a new clipping region less the specified rectangle
`PtVisible()`	Indicates whether point is inside clipping region
`RectVisible()`	Indicates whether any part of the given rectangle is within the clipping region

Region functions

`CombineRgn()`	Combines two existing regions
`EqualRgn()`	Checks two regions to see if they are identical
`OffsetRgn()`	Moves a given region by specified offsets
`CreateRectRgn()`	Creates a rectangular region
`CreateRectRgnIndirect()`	Creates a rectangular region based on the associated data structure
`CreateEllipticRgn()`	Creates an elliptical region

TABLE 8.3 (*Concluded*)

CreateEllipticRgnIndirect()	Creates an elliptical region based on the associated data structure
Create PolygonRgn()	Creates a polygon region
PtInRegion()	Specifies whether or not the given point is in the specified region

Text justification functions

SetTextJustification()	Prepares the GDI to justify a line of text
GetTextExtent()	Computes the width and height of a line of text
SetTextCharacterExtra()	Sets the intercharacter spacing
GetTextCharacterExtra()	Retrieves the intercharacter spacing

Metafile functions

CreateMetaFile()	Creates a metafile display context
CloseMetaFile()	Closes the metafile and creates a handle
GetMetaFile()	Creates a metafile handle
CopyMetaFile()	Copies the metafile to a new file and returns a handle
PlayMetaFile()	Plays the contents of the specified metafile on the given device context
DeleteMetaFile()	Deletes a metafile
GetMetaFileBits()	Returns a handle to a global memory block containing the specified metafile bits
SetMetaFileBits()	Creates a global memory block from the specified metafile

Control functions
The Escape() functions specified in this category are all variants on each other that allow an application to access facilities of a device not directly available through the GDI.

GDI information functions

EnumFonts()	Enumerates the fonts available on a given device
EnumObjects()	Enumerates the objects available on a device
GetTextFace()	Copies the facename of the currently selected font into the specified buffer
GetTextMetrics()	Fills the specified buffer with the metrics for the currently selected font
GetDeviceCaps()	Retrieves device-specific information about a given display device
SetEnvironment()	Copies the contents of the specified buffer into the environment associated with the named port
GetEnvironment()	Copies the contents of the environment associated with a named port into the specified buffer
GetDCOrg()	Returns the final translation origin for the screen display context
GetNearestColor()	Returns the closest color a device can represent to a given logical color

Conversion functions

DPtoLP()	Converts device points to logical points
LDtoDP()	Converts logical points to device points

This area is usually a bounded subset of the window and represents an invalidate condition during repainting.

A metafile is a memory entity consisting of a collection of GDI functions, logically connected, with its own device context and in binary form. Basically, a metafile would be used as a GDI element to, for example, create a given window object and is callable or can be played on a real device context. This discussion, then, completes the description of GDI functions with Table 8.3. We anticipate that the reader will be able to infer the behavior of most of the GDI functions appearing in Table 8.3, and this should serve as a basis for further understanding of the Windows interface. It is through this gradual exposure and assimilation that the power of Windows can be grasped, and eventual application examples will become clearer once this groundwork is established.

8.3.3 Windows Data Types and Structures

Table 8.4 illustrates the majority of Windows data types. Similarly, Table 8.5 contains the majority of callable Windows data structures. Both of these tables are self-

TABLE 8.4 WINDOWS-DERIVED TYPES

Type	Description
Value types	
BYTE	Unsigned 8-bit integer
WORD	Unsigned 16-bit integer
LONG	Unsigned 32-bit integer
DWORD	Unsigned 32-bit integer
BOOL	16-bit Boolean
VOID	An empty value
Pointer types	
PSTR	Pointer to character string
PINT	Pointer to signed 16-bit integer
LPSTR	Long pointer to character string
LPINT	Long pointer to signed 16-bit integer
LPRECT	Long pointer to RECT data structure
LPMSG	Long pointer to MSG data structure
FARPROC	Long pointer to a function
FAR	FAR data-type attribute
NEAR	NEAR data-type attribute
Handles	
HANDLE	General handle
HSTR	Handle to string resource
HCURSOR	Handle to cursor resource
HICON	Handle to icon resource
HMENU	Handle to menu resource
HDC	Handle to display context
HPEN	Handle to physical pen
HFONT	Handle to physical font
HBRUSH	Handle to physical brush
HBITMAP	Handle to physical bitmap
HRGN	Handle to physical region
GLOBALHANDLE	Handle to global memory
LOCALHANDLE	Handle to local memory
HWND	Handle to window

Windows: An Integrated C Environment   Chap. 8

TABLE 8.5 WINDOWS DATA STRUCTURES

Structure	Description

Window structures

WNDCLASS — This structure is used for window class registration. It contains the fields:

WORD	style	Class style
FARPROC	lpfnWndProc	Window function (long pointer)
int	cbClsExtra	Bytes allocated after WNDCLASS
int	cbWndExtra	Bytes allocated after window
HANDLE	hInstance	Handle for window instance
HICON	hIcon	Handle for icon
HCURSOR	hCursor	Handle for cursor
HBRUSH	hbrBackground	Handle for background color
LPSTR	lpszMenuName	Long pointer to menu name
LPSTR	lpszClassName	Long pointer to class name

MSG — This structure is used to pass messages from the application queue and it contains the fields:

HWND	hWnd	Handle to receiving window
WORD	message	Message number
WORD	wParam	Message information
LONG	lParam	Additional message information
DWORD	time	Time message posted
POINT	pt	Mouse position when posted

PAINTSTRUCT — This structure contains information that can be used to paint the client area. It contains the fields:

HDC	hDC	Painting display context handle
BOOL	fErase	Specifies whether background redrawn
RECT	rcPaint	Specifies rectangle coordinates
BOOL	fRestore	Used internally
BOOL	fIncUpdate	Used internally
BYTE	rgbReserved[16]	Used internally

CREATESTRUCT — Defines the initialization parameters passed to a window and it contains the fields:

LPSTR	lpCreateParams	Window creation parameters
HANDLE	hInstance	Window instance handle
HANDLE	hMenu	Handle to menu
HWND	hwndParent	Handle of window owning new window

TABLE 8.5 *(Continued)*

int	cy	Height
int	cx	Width
int	y	Upper-left corner y-coordinate
int	x	Upper-left corner x-coordinate
long	style	Window style
LPSTR	lpszName	Window name
LPSTR	lpszClass	Window class name

GDI data structures

LOGPEN   Defines the style, width, and color of a pen. It contains the fields:

WORD	lopenStyle	Specifies the pen type
POINT	lopenWidth	Pen width in logical units
DWORD	lopenColor	Pen color

LOGBRUSH   Defines the style, color, and pattern of a physical brush. It contains the fields:

WORD	lbStyle	Brush style
DWORD	lbColor	Brush color
short	lbHatch	Hatch style

LOGFONT   Defines the attributes of a font. It contains the fields:

short	lfHeight	Font height
short	lfWidth	Font width
short	lfEscapement	Font angle of escapement vector
short	lfOrientation	Font angle to baseline
short	lfWeight	Weight
BYTE	lfItalic	Italic
BYTE	lfUnderline	Underline
BYTE	lfStrikeOut	Strikeout
BYTE	lfCharSet	Character type
BYTE	lfOutPrecision	Match between request and output
BYTE	lfClipPrecision	How to clip characters partial outside clip
BYTE	lfQuality	Match of output to logical attributes
BYTE	lfPitchAndFamily	Pitch and family
BYTE	lfFaceName [LF_FACESIZE]	Typeface

BITMAP   Defines a logical bitmap. It contains:

short	bmType	Bitmap type
short	bmWidth	Width in pixels
short	bmHeight	Height in pixels
short	bmWidthBytes	Number bytes per raster line
BYTE	bmPlanes	Number of color planes
BYTE	bmBitsPixel	Number of adjacent bits needed to define a color

TABLE 8.5 *(Continued)*

	LPSTR	bmBits	Location of the bit values
POINT	Defines the *x*- and *y*-coordinates of a point.		
	int x		*x*-coordinate
	int y		*y*-coordinate
RECT	Defines a rectangle.		
	int	left	*x*-coordinate upper-left corner
	int	top	*y*-coordinate upper-left corner
	int	right	*x*-coordinate lower-right corner
	int	bottom	*y*-coordinate lower-right corner
RGB	A long integer specifying color fields and intensity.		
TEXTMETRIC	Structure containing basic metrics of a physical font.		
	short	tmHeight	Character height
	short	tmAscent	Units above baseline
	short	tmDescent	Units below baseline
	short	tmIntervalLeading	Amount of leading inside char box
	short	tmExternalLeading	Extra leading between rows
	short	tmAveCharWidth	Average character width
	short	tmWeight	Weight of font
	BYTE	tmItalic	Italic font
	BYTE	tmStruckOut	Struck-out font
	BYTE	tmUnderlined	Underlined font
	BYTE	tmFirstChar	Value of first character
	BYTE	tmLastChar	Value of last character
	BYTE	tmDefaultChar	Value of substitute character
	BYTE	tmBreakChar	Value of character for word breaks
	BYTE	tmPitchAndFamily	Pitch and family of selected font
	BYTE	tmCharSet	Character set of font
	short	tmOverhand	Per string extra width
	short	tmDigitizedAspectX	Aspect ratio *X* value
	short	tmDigitizedAspectY	Aspect ratio *Y* value
METAFILEPICT	Defines the metafile picture format.		
	int	mm	Mapping mode
	int	xExt	*x* extent of picture
	int	yExt	*y* extent of picture
	HANDLE	hMF	Handle to memory metafile

TABLE 8.5 *(Concluded)*

Communication data structures			
DCB	Defines the control setting for the serial communications device. (This structure will not be used in this text and the reader is referred to the Microsoft documentation, references 1, 2, and 3.)		
COMSTAT	Contains information about a communications device. (See references 1, 2, and 3.)		
Open file structure			
OFSTRUCT	Opens a file.		
	BYTE	cBytes	Length of structure
	BYTE	fFixedDisk	Byte specifying file or fixed disk
	WORD	nEwCode	DOS error code if file failure
	BYTE	reserved[4]	Internal usage
	BYTE	szPathName[128]	Path name of file

explanatory. We have seen examples of the use of elements from these tables in the earlier programming (see, for example, use of the structure WNDCLASS).

8.3.4 Messages

Table 8.1 contained a fairly complete description of the Windows messages available under Version 1.03 of the SDK. This table clearly illustrates the richness and wide variety of transactions carried out within a Windows session. It is clear that the dynamic nature of Windows is attributable to this message hierarchy, and this key feature of the environment provides the update mechanism used by the program. The message-polling loop in WinMain() represents the interface between the application and Windows, and these messages set the stage for subsequent Windows activity (which is usually quite complex).

8.3.5 The Remaining Components

Windows has a number of components that we have not yet touched upon. Specifically, the following areas represent additional Windows elements:

1. File structures
2. File formats
3. System resources (additional functions)
4. Macros

We have seen examples of some of these components in the programs. For example, the function

```
GetInstanceData();
```

is a system resource of the module manager type. In general, we will not elucidate these components in any great depth. The reader, however, is cautioned to become familiar with these elements because they will be used throughout the programming of Windows applications. The Microsoft documentation (references 2, 3, and 4) should be referenced. The reason we have chosen not to explicitly discuss these elements is that such discussion does not particularly enhance the baseline already established for programming (based on the other components discussed). As applications require these elements, we will discuss them.

8.4 ADDITIONAL WINDOWS EXAMPLES

This section moves beyond introductory examples: following a simple illustration of a program that generates the Windows pop-up menu and message boxes. We combine the three-dimensional surface illustrated in Chapter 7 with the Windows environment in order to demonstrate some of the flexibility of the Presentation Manager. The goal of illustrating these examples is to demonstrate to the reader how to implement Windows code that integrates C programming in the Windows environment. Also, modular techniques are employed in the three-dimensional surface example. It is highly desirable to implement this approach rapidly in light of the generally massive programming requirements that exist for using this environment.

8.4.1 A Menu Program

Figure 8.5 presents the main program menu1.c. The principal difference between this program and those illustrated earlier is the processing indicated for the WM_ COMMAND message and the pointer to a menu name in WNDCLASS. The message WM_COMMAND is sent to the application by Windows when the user selects an item from a menu (we will discuss generation of the menu shortly), when an accelerator key stroke is translated, or when a control passes a message to its parent window. When WM_COMMAND is sent, the parameter wParam contains either the menu item, the control ID, or the accelerator ID. In the case of the program appearing in Figure 8.5, the following menu items exist and their corresponding activities:

Item	Activity
One	Beeps the speaker once
Two	Beeps the speaker twice
Four	Beeps the speaker four times
Six	Beeps the speaker six times
Eight	Beeps the speaker eight times
ExitMsg	Exits the window
About	Explains "Menu1Demo" in a message box

The second switch statement, subordinate to the WM_COMMAND case, selects the appropriate menu activity and calls MessageBeep(0), SendMessage(), or Message-

```
/* Windows program to test menu: menu1.c */

#include <windows.h>
#include <menu1.h>

typedef struct
        {
        int dummy;
        }
        SETUPDATA;
static  SETUPDATA setupData;

static HANDLE hInst;
char szName[5] = {'m','e','n','u','1'};
char szTitle[11] = {'m','e','n','u','p','r','o','g','r','a','m'};

BOOL FAR PASCAL Window1Init(HANDLE);
BOOL FAR PASCAL Window1InitEvery(HANDLE,int);
BOOL FAR PASCAL Window1InitAdd(HANDLE,HANDLE);

long FAR PASCAL Window1Proc(HWND,unsigned,WORD,LONG);

int NEAR PASCAL WinMain(hInstance,hPrevInstance,lpszCmdLine,cmdShow)
        HANDLE hInstance,hPrevInstance;
        LPSTR lpszCmdLine;
        int cmdShow;
        {
        MSG msg;

        if(!hPrevInstance)
            Window1Init(hInstance);
        else
            Window1InitAdd(hInstance,hPrevInstance);
        Window1InitEvery(hInstance,cmdShow);

        while(GetMessage((LPMSG)&msg,NULL,0,0))
            {
            TranslateMessage((LPMSG)&msg);
            DispatchMessage((LPMSG)&msg);
            }
        exit(msg.wParam);
        }
/* Functions which make up Window1 class */

long FAR PASCAL Window1Proc(hWnd,message,wParam,lParam)
        HWND hWnd;
        unsigned message;
        WORD wParam;
        LONG lParam;
        {
        int n1;

        switch(message)
            {
            case WM_COMMAND:
              switch(wParam)
                {
                case One:
                    MessageBeep(0);
                    break;
                case Two:
                    for(n1 = 1;n1 <= 2;n1++)
                        MessageBeep(0);
                    break;
                case Four:
                    for(n1 = 1;n1 <= 4;n1++)
                        MessageBeep(0);
                    break;
```

Figure 8.5 Windows program to test the menu features.

```
                case Six:
                    for(n1 = 1;n1 <= 6;n1++)
                        MessageBeep(0);
                    break;
                case Eight:
                    for(n1 = 1;n1 <= 8;n1++)
                        MessageBeep(0);
                    break;
                case ExitMsg:
                    SendMessage(hWnd,WM_CLOSE,0,0L);
                    break;
                case About:
                    MessageBox(hWnd,"Menu1 Demo",szName,MB_OKCANCEL);
                    break;
                default:
                    break;
            }
            break;
        case WM_DESTROY:
            PostQuitMessage(0);
            break;
        default:
            return(DefWindowProc(hWnd,message,wParam,lParam));
            break;
        }
    return(0L);
    }

/* Initialization Module for beginw.c */
/* performed only once at inception */



BOOL FAR PASCAL Window1Init(hInstance)
    HANDLE hInstance;
    {
    WNDCLASS        Window1Class;

    Window1Class.hCursor = LoadCursor(NULL,IDC_ARROW);
    Window1Class.hIcon = LoadIcon(hInstance,(LPSTR)szName);
    Window1Class.lpszMenuName = (LPSTR)szName;
    Window1Class.lpszClassName = (LPSTR)szName;
    Window1Class.hbrBackground = GetStockObject(WHITE_BRUSH);
    Window1Class.hInstance = hInstance;
    Window1Class.style = CS_HREDRAW | CS_VREDRAW;
    Window1Class.lpfnWndProc = Window1Proc;
    Window1Class.cbClsExtra = 0;
    Window1Class.cbWndExtra = 0;

    RegisterClass((LPWNDCLASS)&Window1Class);
    return TRUE;
    }

/* Performed for every instance of the window */

BOOL FAR PASCAL Window1InitEvery(hInstance,cmdShow)
    HANDLE hInstance;
    int cmdShow;
    {
    HWND hWnd;

    hWnd = CreateWindow((LPSTR)szName,
                        (LPSTR)szTitle,
                        WS_TILEDWINDOW,
                        0,0,0,0,
                        (HWND)NULL,
                        (HMENU)NULL,
                        (HANDLE)hInstance,
                        (LPSTR)NULL);
```

Figure 8.5 *(Continued)*

```
        ShowWindow(hWnd,cmdShow);
        UpdateWindow(hWnd);
        return TRUE;
        }

/* Performed for instances beyond initial */

BOOL FAR PASCAL Window1InitAdd(hInstance,hPrevInstance)
        HANDLE hInstance,hPrevInstance;
        {
        GetInstanceData(hPrevInstance,(PSTR)&setupData,sizeof(SETUPDATA));
        }
```

Figure 8.5 *(Concluded)*

Box(). MessageBeep(0) simply generates a beep at the system speaker, and 0 is a convenient parameter value. SendMessage() has the format

```
SendMessage(hWnd,wMsg,wParam,lParam)
```

hWnd	Window handle
wMsg	Message to be sent
wParam	Additional message information
lParam	Additional message information

In

```
SendMessage(jWnd,WM_CLOSE,0,0L);
```

a message to close the window is sent. Windows subsequently sends WM_DE-STROY. Finally,

```
MessageBox(hWnd,"MenulDemo",szName,MB_OKCANCEL);
```

creates a message-type box with the message "MenulDemo" and caption pointed to by szName. The message box contains OK and CANCEL push buttons.

The important aspects of the program appearing in Figure 8.5 are the method by which menu items are specified, using the switch (wParam) statement, and the recognition that Windows automatically sends a WM_COMMAND message when a menu item is activated. Now we need to consider how the menu is actually created in the window. Figure 8.6a illustrates the usual definition file associated with the program menu1.c, and Figure 8.6b presents the resource file for menu1.c. This file is a new entity with extension .rc and is compiled with the resource compiler invoked with a command

```
rc [-r] filename [executable-file]
```

Here rc invokes the compiler, -r directs rc to compile the resource file and save the result as a special binary resource file with extension .res, and executable-file

```
NAME            menu1

DESCRIPTION     'Demonstrate Menu'

EXETYPE         WINDOWS

STUB            'WINSTUB.EXE'

CODE            MOVEABLE
DATA            MOVEABLE MULTIPLE

HEAPSIZE        2048
STACKSIZE       4096

EXPORTS         Window1Proc
```

(a)

```
#include <menu1.h>

menu1   MENU
        BEGIN
            POPUP "Beep"
                BEGIN
                    MENUITEM "&One",        One,CHECKED
                    MENUITEM "&Two",        Two
                    MENUITEM "&Four",       Four
                    MENUITEM SEPARATOR
                    MENUITEM "&Exit",       ExitMsg
                    MENUITEM "&About",      About
                END
            POPUP "Cont"
                BEGIN
                    MENUITEM "&Six",        Six,CHECKED
                    MENUITEM "E&ight",      Eight
                END
        END
```

(b)

```
menu1.obj: menu1.c
        cl -c -D LINT_ARGS -Gsw _Os _W2 _Zp menu1.c

menu1.res: menu1.rc
        rc -r menu1.rc

menu1.exe: menu1.obj menu1.def menu1.res
        link4 menu1,/align:16,/map,slibw/NOE swinlibc/NOE,menu1
        rc menu1.res
```

(c)

Figure 8.6 Definition file for the menu program, (b) resource file containing
the menu parameters, and (c) corresponding MAKE file.

is a file specified in which to put the resources. We will return to Figure 8.6b in a
moment, but it is useful to consider briefly the MAKE file appearing in Figure
8.6c.

The second sequence of statements appearing in Figure 8.6c invokes the resource
compiler and specifies that the resource script file menu1.rc be compiled and the

binary output saved as menu1.res. Following the link4 execution, the resource compiler is again invoked to put menu1.res in menu1.exe (note that the absence of specifying menu1.exe is permissible because this executable file has the same filename as the resource file, menu1).

Returning to Figure 8.6b, we see that a complete menu framework is established in the structured specification of the form

```
filename MENU
         BEGIN
            POPUP...
               BEGIN
                  MENUITEM...
                  ...
                  MENUITEM...
               END
            ...
            POPUP...
            ...
         END
```

Each pop-up menu is introduced with the keyword POPUP, followed by a string caption in quotation marks. The menu items are specified as a string in quotation marks, followed by the ID variable offset with a comma. The menu item string has an underlined character specified by the ampersand, which corresponds to a keyboard selection, and a straight line menu separator can be included using MENUITEM SEPARATOR. One aspect of the program appearing in Figure 8.5 and the script in Figure 8.6b is the question as to how the IDs are defined for menu items. These ID values are specified in an include file, menu1.h, of the form

```
#define  One      1
#define  Two      2
#define  Four     4
#define  Six      6
#define  Eight    8
#define  ExitMsg  16
#define  About    32
```

Here the numerical significance of each designator is unimportant and simply differentiates the ID from other values.

8.4.2 Three-D Graphics

Figure 8.7 illustrates the program win3.c used to set up and plot the surface (sinx/x figure) appearing in Chapter 7. To avoid confusion, this program is designated win3D for "window three-dimensional," but referred to as win3.c in the MAKE file. Some parts of it are referenced to the beginw.c file. This figure develops the manner in which modular code is established for Windows programs. Clearly, modular techniques can prove very valuable in the complex Windows environment when general-purpose functions can be developed. The program in Figure 8.7 prototypes

```
/* Windows 3D graph program: win3D.c */

#include <windows.h>

typedef struct
        {
        int dummy;
        }
        SETUPDATA;
static  SETUPDATA setupData;

static HANDLE hInst;
char szName[5] = {'w','i','n','3','D'};
char szTitle[6] = {'t','h','r','e','e','D'};

BOOL FAR PASCAL Window1Init(HANDLE);
BOOL FAR PASCAL Window1InitEvery(HANDLE,int);
BOOL FAR PASCAL Window1InitAdd(HANDLE,HANDLE);
int FAR PASCAL ArrayGen();
int FAR PASCAL threeD_graph();
int FAR PASCAL rot_mat();

long FAR PASCAL Window1Proc(HWND,unsigned,WORD,LONG);

float xarray[3072],xx,yy,zz,scalex,scaley,scalez,a[10];
int ncount = 21,mcount = 21,count = 21;
float alpha = 0.0,beta = 1.1,gamma = 0.0;
int yy1,yy2,zz1,zz2;

int NEAR PASCAL WinMain(hInstance,hPrevInstance,lpszCmdLine,cmdShow)
        HANDLE hInstance,hPrevInstance;
        LPSTR lpszCmdLine;
        int cmdShow;
        {
        MSG msg;

        if(!hPrevInstance)
            Window1Init(hInstance);
        else
            Window1InitAdd(hInstance,hPrevInstance);
        Window1InitEvery(hInstance,cmdShow);

        while(GetMessage((LPMSG)&msg,NULL,0,0))
            {
            TranslateMessage((LPMSG)&msg);
            DispatchMessage((LPMSG)&msg);
            }
        exit(msg.wParam);
        }
/* Functions which make up Window1 class */



long FAR PASCAL Window1Proc(hWnd,message,wParam,lParam)
        HWND hWnd;
        unsigned message;
        WORD wParam;
        LONG lParam;
        {
        switch(message)
            {
            case WM_PAINT:
                PaintBeginWindow(hWnd);
                break;
            case WM_DESTROY:
                PostQuitMessage(0);
                break;
```

Figure 8.7 Program that generates the (sin(x)/x)**2 function within Windows in modular form.

```
                default:
                    return(DefWindowProc(hWnd,message,wParam,lParam));
                    break;
            }
        return(0L);
        }

PaintBeginWindow(hWnd)
        HWND hWnd;
        {
        extern float xarray[],scaley,scalez;
        int n,nc,nm_count,m1,m;
        extern int yy1,yy2,zz1,zz2;
        float z_start = 25.,y_start = 25.,z_mid = 150. y_mid = 250.;
        float dy1,dy2,dz1,dz2,xa[5],ya[5],za[5];
        float half_yscale = 250.,half_zscale = 150.;

        HDC hDC;
        PAINTSTRUCT ps;

        ArrayGen();
        rot_mat();
        threeD_graph();

        hDC = BeginPaint(hWnd,(LPPAINTSTRUCT)&ps);

        m1 = 1;
        scaley = half_yscale;
        scalez = half_zscale;
        nm_count = 3*ncount*mcount - (ncount*3 +6);
        for(n = 1;n <= ncount;n++)
            {
            for(m = 1;m <= mcount;m++)
                {
                if(m1 < nm_count)
                    {
                    nc = 3*count;                          /* next y-value */
                    xa[1] = xarray[m1];                    /* 1st y-value grid */
                    ya[1] = xarray[m1+1];
                    za[1] = xarray[m1+2];
                    xa[2] = xarray[m1+3];
                    ya[2] = xarray[m1+4];
                    za[2] = xarray[m1+5];

                    xa[3] = xarray[m1+nc+3];               /* 2nd y-value grid */
                    ya[3] = xarray[m1+nc+4];
                    za[3] = xarray[m1+nc+5];
                    xa[4] = xarray[m1+nc];
                    ya[4] = xarray[m1+nc+1];
                    za[4] = xarray[m1+nc+2];

                    dy1 = ya[2] - ya[1];                   /* ck rotation */
                    dy2 = ya[3] - ya[2];
                    dz1 = za[2] - za[1];
                    dz2 = za[3] - za[2];
                    if((dy1*dz2 - dz1*dy2) > 0)
                        {
                        for(n = 1;n <= 4;n++)              /* scale facet */
                            {
                            za[n] = z_start + (z_mid - za[n]*scalez);
                            ya[n] = y_start + (y_mid + ya[n]*scaley);
                            }
                        for(n = 1;n <= 3;n++)              /* plot 3 of 4 */
                            {
                            yy1 = (int)(ya[n]);
                            yy2 = (int)(ya[n+1]);
                            zz1 = (int)(za[n]);
                            zz2 = (int)(za[n+1]);
                            MoveTo(hDC,yy1,zz1);            /* collapsed y-z */
                            LineTo(hDC,yy2,zz2);
                            }
```

Figure 8.7 (*Continued*)

```
                              yy1 = (int)(ya[4]);
                              yy2 = (int)(ya[1]);
                              zz1 = (int)(za[4]);
                              zz2 = (int)(za[1]);
                              MoveTo(hDC,yy1,zz1);                  /* 4th segment */
                              LineTo(hDC,yy2,zz2);
                              }
                        }
                  m1 = m1 + 3;
                  }
            }

         EndPaint(hWnd,(LPPAINTSTRUCT)&ps);

         return TRUE;
         }

/* Initialization Module for beginw.c */
/* performed only once at inception */

BOOL FAR PASCAL Window1Init(hInstance)
         HANDLE hInstance;
         {
         WNDCLASS            Window1Class;

         Window1Class.hCursor = LoadCursor(NULL,IDC_ARROW);
         Window1Class.hIcon = LoadIcon(hInstance,(LPSTR)szName);
         Window1Class.lpszMenuName = (LPSTR)NULL;
         Window1Class.lpszClassName = (LPSTR)szName;
         Window1Class.hbrBackground = GetStockObject(WHITE_BRUSH);
         Window1Class.hInstance = hInstance;
         Window1Class.style = CS_HREDRAW | CS_VREDRAW;
         Window1Class.lpfnWndProc = Window1Proc;
         Window1Class.cbClsExtra = 0;
         Window1Class.cbWndExtra = 0;

         RegisterClass((LPWNDCLASS)&Window1Class);
         return TRUE;
         }

/* Performed for every instance of the window */

BOOL FAR PASCAL Window1InitEvery(hInstance,cmdShow)
         HANDLE hInstance;
         int cmdShow;
         {
         HWND hWnd;

         hWnd = CreateWindow((LPSTR)szName,
                             (LPSTR)szTitle,
                             WS_TILEDWINDOW,
                             0,0,0,0,
                             (HWND)NULL,
                             (HMENU)NULL,
                             (HANDLE)hInstance,
                             (LPSTR)NULL);
         ShowWindow(hWnd,cmdShow);
         UpdateWindow(hWnd);
         return TRUE;
         }

/* Performed for instances beyond initial */

BOOL FAR PASCAL Window1InitAdd(hInstance,hPrevInstance)
         HANDLE hInstance,hPrevInstance;
         {
         GetInstanceData(hPrevInstance,(PSTR)&setupData,sizeof(SETUPDATA));
         }
```

Figure 8.7 (*Concluded*)

three new FAR PASCAL integer-type functions: ArrayGen(), threeD__graph(), and rot__mat(). All the initial function calls and program logic are similar to that developed earlier in template form. When the WM__PAINT message is received, however, a new PaintBeginWindow() function is called. This routine calls the three new integer-type functions, and a number of global variables (also specified in the preprocessor) are accessed. These are returned to PaintBeginWindow(), and the main variable item consists of the familiar array xarray[], which contains the packed format three-dimensional plotting information in scaled form.

PaintBeginWindow() sets up each facet for plotting and calls the Windows GDI functions

```
MoveTo(hDC,x,y);
LineTo(hDC,x',y');
```

which move the cursor to (x, y) and draws a line from this point to (x', y'). The earlier call to the Windows function

```
hDC = BeginPaint(hWnd,(LPPAINTSTRUCT)&ps)
```

returns a device context handle, hDC, for the structure ps. This specifies a default device context for use in the GDI function calls. Note, for example, that this device context defaults to a white background color and a black pen. These two options are not particularly useful, although very esthetic, when attempting to print a screen dump of the window (as we will see following the next example).

The PaintBeginWindow() function appearing in Figure 8.7 is largely ordinary C code with a few special calls to Windows functions, data items, and structures. The three added functions are illustrated in Figures 8.8a and b, and 8.9a. Figure 8.9b illustrates the function rot__point() called by rot__mat(), and Figure 8.10 contains scale(), which is called by rot__mat() also. These routines are very similar to their counterparts in Chapter 7, except they are configured using the PASCAL calling convention.

Figure 8.11a illustrates the definition file associated with win3.c. The modules are specified as follows in Figure 8.11b:

```
win3.c                          (Figure 8.7)
wingrp.c    (threeD_graph())     (Figure 8.8a)
wingen.c    (ArrayGen())         (Figure 8.8b)
winrot.c    (rot_mat())          (Figure 8.9a)
winpt.c     (rot_point())        (Figure 8.9b)
winsca.c    (scale())            (Figure 8.10)
```

The purpose of this chapter has been to introduce gradually the nature of Windows programming and, at the same time, to provide enough advanced technique to allow the reader a meaningful exposure to this environment. The next example combines all the features of the previous examples to demonstrate the power of Windows programming. Note that many features must still await further exploration (such as text I/O), but a rather sophisticated capability has already been established.

```
/* Function to setup data plot */

#include <windows.h>

int FAR PASCAL rot_mat(float,float,float);
int FAR PASCAL rot_point();
int FAR PASCAL scale();

int FAR PASCAL threeD_graph()
        {
        extern int ncount,mcount;
        extern float xarray[],xx,yy,zz;
        int n,m,m1,N,nm_count;

        m1 = 1;
        for(n = 1;n <= ncount;n++)
            {
            for(m = 1;m <= mcount;m++)
                {
                xx = xarray[m1];                        /* x,y,z values */
                yy = xarray[m1+1];
                zz = xarray[m1+2];
                rot_point();
                xarray[m1] = xx;
                xarray[m1+1] = yy;
                xarray[m1+2] = zz;
                m1 = m1 + 3;                            /* point index inc. */
                }
            }
        scale();                                        /* x,y,z -> [-1,1] */
        }
```

(a)

```
/* function to generate 3d surface */

#include <windows.h>
#include <math.h>

int FAR PASCAL ArrayGen()
        {
        extern float xarray[];
        extern int mcount = 21,ncount = 21,count = 21;
        int n,m,m1,NN = 2;
        float A= 10., error = 1.e-5;
        double PI = 3.141592654,u,v;

        m1 = 1;
        for(n = 1;n <= ncount;n++)
            {
            for(m = 1;m <= mcount;m++)
                {
                xarray[m1] = (float)(m - mcount + 10);
                xarray[m1+1] = (float)(n - ncount + 10);
                u = (double)(xarray[m1]);
                v = (double)(xarray[m1+1]);
                u = (double)((PI/NN)*sqrt(u*u + v*v));

                if((u < error) && (u > -error))
                    xarray[m1+2] = A;
                else
                    xarray[m1+2] = A*(sin(u)/u);

                xarray[m1+2] = xarray[m1+2]*xarray[m1+2];
                m1 = m1 + 3;
                }
            }
        }
```

(b)

Figure 8.8 (a) Windows callable function threeD_graph( ) and (b) Windows callable function used to generate the (sin(x)/x)**2 data array.

```
/* Function to calculate rotation matrix */

#include <windows.h>
#include <math.h>

int FAR PASCAL rot_mat()
        {
        extern float a[],alpha,beta,gamma;                /* rotation matrix */
        double a1,CA,CB,CG,SA,SB,SG;

        a1 = (double)(alpha);                             /* Sines & cosines */
        CA = cos(a1);
        SA = sin(a1);
        a1 = (double)(beta);
        CB = cos(a1);
        SB = sin(a1);
        a1 = (double)(gamma);
        CG = cos(a1);
        SG = sin(a1);

        a[1] = (float)(CB*CG);                            /* Matrix elements */
        a[2] = (float)(SA*SB*CG - CA*SG);
        a[3] = (float)(CA*SB*CG + SA*SG);
        a[4] = (float)(CB*SG);
        a[5] = (float)(SA*SB*SG + CA*CG);
        a[6] = (float)(CA*SB*SG - SA*CG);
        a[7] = (float)(-SB);
        a[8] = (float)(SA*CB);
        a[9] = (float)(CA*CB);
        }
```

(a)

```
/* Function to generate rotated point */

#include <windows.h>

int FAR PASCAL rot_point()
        {
        extern float xx,yy,zz;                            /* point */
        extern float a[];                                 /* rotation matrix */
        float x1,y1,z1;                                   /* intermediate */

        x1 = a[1]*xx + a[2]*yy + a[3]*zz;
        y1 = a[4]*xx + a[5]*yy + a[6]*zz;
        z1 = a[7]*xx + a[8]*yy + a[9]*zz;

        xx = x1;
        yy = y1;
        zz = z1;
        }
```

(b)

Figure 8.9 (a) Windows callable rotation matrix function and (b) routine that rotates a given point.

Figure 8.12 illustrates the program win4.c based on upgrading win3D code to include menu flexibility. The called functions are similar to those for win3.c in Figure 8.7, except the window procedure, Window1Proc(), now has provision for many selectable menu options. The angles alpha = gamma = 0 are fixed for the surface viewing orientation, but beta is allowed to vary across a range of values. Also, the range of surface values is variable depending on what divisor appears in

```
/* Function to scale xarray data */

#include <windows.h>

int FAR PASCAL scale()
    {
    extern int ncount,mcount;
    extern float xarray[],scalex,scaley,scalez;
    int n,m,m1;
    float max_x = -1.e14,max_y = -1.e14,max_z = -1.e14;
    float min_x = 1.e14,min_y = 1.e14,min_z = 1.e14;

    m1 = 1;
    for(n = 1;n <= ncount;n++)
        {
        for(m = 1;m <= mcount;m++)
            {
            if(max_x < xarray[m1])
                max_x = xarray[m1];
            if(min_x > xarray[m1])
                min_x = xarray[m1];
            if(max_y < xarray[m1+1])
                max_y = xarray[m1+1];
            if(min_y > xarray[m1+1])
                min_y = xarray[m1+1];
            if(max_z < xarray[m1+2])
                max_z = xarray[m1+2];
            if(min_z > xarray[m1+2]);
                min_z = xarray[m1+2];
            m1 = m1 + 3;                        /* next point set */
            }
        }
                                               /* scale [-1,1] */
    scalex = 2./(max_x - min_x);
    scaley = 2./(max_y - min_y);
    scalez = 2./(max_z - min_z);
    m1 = 1;
    for(n = 1;n <= ncount;n++)
        {
        for(m = 1;m <= mcount;m++)
            {
            xarray[m1] = -1. + scalex*(xarray[m1] - min_x);
            xarray[m1+1] = -1. + scaley*(xarray[m1+1] - min_y);
            xarray[m1+2] = -1. + scalez*(xarray[m1+2] - min_z);
            m1 = m1 + 3;
            }
        }
    }
```

Figure 8.10 Windows callable function used to scale the (sin(x)/x)**2 data into [−1, 1].

the $\sin(x)/x$ function of ArrayGen() (the parameter value NN, equal to 2 or 7). In addition, message box output can be called up in real time to familiarize the reader with what he or she is viewing. For example, selection of About3 from the About menu displays

```
0/.8/0 : N=7
```

which means that alpha = 0, beta = 0.8 radian, and gamma = 0 with the $\sin(x)/x$ divisor equal to 7. The menu ''PPP'' (see Figure 8.13a) has an ID item PP that is used to invalidate the window, or release it for updating, and then update it. This is necessary when a surface parameter changes in order to initiate that change as a Windows display.

```
NAME            win3

EXETYPE         WINDOWS

STUB            'WINSTUB.EXE'

DESCRIPTION     'Windows 3D Surface Plot'

CODE            MOVEABLE
DATA            MOVEABLE MULTIPLE

HEAPSIZE        2048
STACKSIZE       4096

EXPORTS
        Window1Proc
```

(a)

```
# MAKE file for 3D Windows program

win3.obj: win3.c
        cl -c -d -Os -Gsw -Zp -FPa win3.c

wingrp.obj: wingrp.c
        cl -c -d -Os -Gsw -Zp -FPa wingrp.c

wingen.obj: wingen.c
        cl -c -d -Os -Gsw -Zp -FPa wingen.c

winrot.obj: winrot.c
        cl -c -d -Os -Gsw -Zp -FPa winrot.c

winpt.obj: winpt.c
        cl -c -d -Os -Gsw -Zp -FPa winpt.c

winsca.obj: winsca.c
        cl -c -d -Os -Gsw -Zp -FPa winsca.c

win3.exe: win3.obj win3.def wingrp.obj wingen.obj winrot.obj\
        winpt.obj winsca.obj
        link4 win3+wingen+wingrp+winrot+winpt+winsca,\
        /align:16,/map,slibw/NOE swinlibc/NOE,win3
```

(b)

Figure 8.11 (a) Associated definition file for the Windows program that generates the $(sin(x)/x)**2$ output and (b) corresponding MAKE file.

The function PaintBeginWindow() has several changes to allow a hard copy of the resulting screen. Essentially, we are using egaepson.com to copy the EGA screen with PrtSc. Since the default background is white, any attempt to copy the screen will result in print output for the background. The program egaepson.com does not print, however, when a black background is used. Hence, code has been inserted into PaintBeginWindow() to reverse the client area display and illustrate white on black (which will print as black on white). This code takes the form

```
hPen = GetStockObject(WHITE_PEN);
SelectObject(hDC,hPen);
```

```
/* Windows 3D graph program: win3D.c */

#include <windows.h>
#include <win4.h>

typedef struct
        {
        int dummy;
        }
        SETUPDATA;
static   SETUPDATA setupData;

static HANDLE hInst;
char szMenuNm[5] = {'m','e','n','u','4'};
char szName[4] = {'w','i','n','4'};
char szTitle[6] = {'t','h','r','e','e','D'};

BOOL FAR PASCAL Window1Init(HANDLE);
BOOL FAR PASCAL Window1InitEvery(HANDLE,int);
BOOL FAR PASCAL Window1InitAdd(HANDLE,HANDLE);
int FAR PASCAL ArrayGen();
int FAR PASCAL threeD_graph();
int FAR PASCAL rot_mat();

long FAR PASCAL Window1Proc(HWND,unsigned,WORD,LONG);

float xarray[3072],xx,yy,zz,scalex,scaley,scalez,a[10];
int ncount = 21,mcount = 21,count = 21;
float alpha = 0.0,beta = 1.1,gamma = 0.0;
int yy1,yy2,zz1,zz2,NN = 2;

int NEAR PASCAL WinMain(hInstance,hPrevInstance,lpszCmdLine,cmdShow)
        HANDLE hInstance,hPrevInstance;
        LPSTR lpszCmdLine;
        int cmdShow;
        {
        MSG msg;

        if(!hPrevInstance)
            Window1Init(hInstance);
        else
            Window1InitAdd(hInstance,hPrevInstance);
        Window1InitEvery(hInstance,cmdShow);

        while(GetMessage((LPMSG)&msg,NULL,0,0))
            {
            TranslateMessage((LPMSG)&msg);
            DispatchMessage((LPMSG)&msg);
            }
        exit(msg.wParam);
        }
/* Functions which make up Window1 class */

long FAR PASCAL Window1Proc(hWnd,message,wParam,lParam)
        HWND hWnd;
        unsigned message;
        WORD wParam;
        LONG lParam;
        {
        switch(message)
            {
            case WM_COMMAND:
                switch(wParam)
                    {
                    case One:
                        beta = .4;
                        NN = 7;
                        break;
```

Figure 8.12 A more complex program that displays multiple versions of (sin(x)/x)**2 corresponding to different parameter values and menu selectable.

```
                case Two:
                   beta = .6;
                   NN = 7;
                   break;
                case Three:
                   beta = .8;
                   NN = 7;
                   break;
                case Four:
                   beta = 1.1;
                   NN = 7;
                   break;
                case Five:
                   beta = 1.4;
                   NN = 7;
                   break;
                case Six:
                   beta = .8;
                   NN = 2;
                   break;
                case Seven:
                   beta = 1.1;
                   NN = 2;
                   break;
                case Eight:
                   beta = 1.4;
                   NN = 2;
                   break;
                case ExitMsg:
                   SendMessage(hWnd,WM_CLOSE,0,0L);
                   break;
                case About1:
                   MessageBox(hWnd,"0/.4/0 : N=7",szName,MB_OK);
                   break;
                case About2:
                   MessageBox(hWnd,"0/.6/0 : N=7",szName,MB_OK);
                   break;
                case About3:
                   MessageBox(hWnd,"0/.8/0 : N=7",szName,MB_OK);
                   break;
                case About4:
                   MessageBox(hWnd,"0/1.1/0 : N=7",szName,MB_OK);
                   break;
                case About5:
                   MessageBox(hWnd,"0/1.4/0 : N=7",szName,MB_OK);
                   break;
                case About6:
                   MessageBox(hWnd,"0/.8/0 : N=2",szName,MB_OK);
                   break;
                case About7:
                   MessageBox(hWnd,"0/1.1/0 : N=2",szName,MB_OK);
                   break;
                case About8:
                   MessageBox(hWnd,"0/1.4/0 : N=2",szName,MB_OK);
                   break;
                case PP:
                   InvalidateRect(hWnd,(LPRECT)NULL,TRUE);
                   UpdateWindow(hWnd);
                   break;
                default:
                   break;
                   }
                break;
             case WM_PAINT:
                PaintBeginWindow(hWnd);
                break;
             case WM_DESTROY:
                PostQuitMessage(0);
                break;
```

Figure 8.12   (*Continued*)

```
                default:
                    return(DefWindowProc(hWnd,message,wParam,lParam));
                    break;
            }
        return(0L);
        }

PaintBeginWindow(hWnd)
        HWND hWnd;
        {
        extern float xarray[],scaley,scalez;
        int n,nc,nm_count,m1,m;
        extern int yy1,yy2,zz1,zz2;
        float z_start = 25.,y_start = 25.,z_mid = 150.,y_mid = 250.;
        float dy1,dy2,dz1,dz2,xa[5],ya[5],za[5];
        float half_yscale = 250.,half_zscale = 150.;

        HDC hDC;
        HPEN hPen;
        PAINTSTRUCT ps;

        ArrayGen();
        rot_mat();
        threeD_graph();

        hDC = BeginPaint(hWnd,(LPPAINTSTRUCT)&ps);
        hPen = GetStockObject(WHITE_PEN);
        SelectObject(hDC,hPen);

        m1 = 1;
        scaley = half_yscale;
        scalez = half_zscale;
        nm_count = 3*ncount*mcount - (ncount*3 +6);
        for(n = 1;n <= ncount;n++)
            {
            for(m = 1;m <= mcount;m++)
                {
                if(m1 < nm_count)
                    {
                    nc = 3*count;                          /* next y-value */
                    xa[1] = xarray[m1];                    /* 1st y-value grid */
                    ya[1] = xarray[m1+1];
                    za[1] = xarray[m1+2];
                    xa[2] = xarray[m1+3];
                    ya[2] = xarray[m1+4];
                    za[2] = xarray[m1+5];

                    xa[3] = xarray[m1+nc+3];               /* 2nd y-value grid */
                    ya[3] = xarray[m1+nc+4];
                    za[3] = xarray[m1+nc+5];
                    xa[4] = xarray[m1+nc];
                    ya[4] = xarray[m1+nc+1];
                    za[4] = xarray[m1+nc+2];
                    dy1 = ya[2] - ya[1];                   /* ck rotation */
                    dy2 = ya[3] - ya[2];
                    dz1 = za[2] - za[1];
                    dz2 = za[3] - za[2];
                    if((dy1*dz2 - dz1*dy2) > 0)
                        {
                        for(n = 1;n <= 4;n++)              /* scale facet */
                            {
                            za[n] = z_start + (z_mid - za[n]*scalez);
                            ya[n] = y_start + (y_mid + ya[n]*scaley);
                            }
                        for(n = 1;n <= 3;n++)              /* plot 3 of 4 */
                            {
                            yy1 = (int)(ya[n]);
                            yy2 = (int)(ya[n+1]);
                            zz1 = (int)(za[n]);
```

Figure 8.12 (*Continued*)

```
                                zz2 = (int)(za[n+1]);
                                MoveTo(hDC,yy1,zz1);            /* collapsed y-z */
                                LineTo(hDC,yy2,zz2);
                                }
                          yy1 = (int)(ya[4]);
                          yy2 = (int)(ya[1]);
                          zz1 = (int)(za[4]);
                          zz2 = (int)(za[1]);
                          MoveTo(hDC,yy1,zz1);                  /* 4th segment */
                          LineTo(hDC,yy2,zz2);
                          }
                    }
              m1 = m1 + 3;
              }
        }
      ValidateRect(hWnd,(LPRECT)NULL);

      EndPaint(hWnd,(LPPAINTSTRUCT)&ps);

      return TRUE;
      }

/* Initialization Module for beginw.c */
/* performed only once at inception */

BOOL FAR PASCAL Window1Init(hInstance)
      HANDLE hInstance;
      {
      WNDCLASS           Window1Class;

      Window1Class.hCursor = LoadCursor(NULL,IDC_ARROW);
      Window1Class.hIcon = LoadIcon(hInstance,(LPSTR)szName);
      Window1Class.lpszMenuName = (LPSTR)szMenuNm;
      Window1Class.lpszClassName = (LPSTR)szName;
      Window1Class.hbrBackground = GetStockObject(BLACK_BRUSH);
      Window1Class.hInstance = hInstance;
      Window1Class.style = CS_HREDRAW | CS_VREDRAW;
      Window1Class.lpfnWndProc = Window1Proc;
      Window1Class.cbClsExtra = 0;
      Window1Class.cbWndExtra = 0;

      RegisterClass((LPWNDCLASS)&Window1Class);
      return TRUE;
      }

/* Performed for every instance of the window */

BOOL FAR PASCAL Window1InitEvery(hInstance,cmdShow)
      HANDLE hInstance;
      int cmdShow;
      {
      HWND hWnd;

      hWnd = CreateWindow((LPSTR)szName,
                          (LPSTR)szTitle,
                          WS_TILEDWINDOW,
                          0,0,0,0,
                          (HWND)NULL,
                          (HMENU)NULL,
                          (HANDLE)hInstance,
                          (LPSTR)NULL);
      ShowWindow(hWnd,cmdShow);
      UpdateWindow(hWnd);
      return TRUE;
      }

/* Performed for instances beyond initial */

BOOL FAR PASCAL Window1InitAdd(hInstance,hPrevInstance)
      HANDLE hInstance,hPrevInstance;
      {
      GetInstanceData(hPrevInstance,(PSTR)&setupData,sizeof(SETUPDATA));
      }
```

Figure 8.12 (*Concluded*)

```
#include <win4.h>

menu4    MENU
           BEGIN
             POPUP "Selection"
               BEGIN
                 MENUITEM "&One",        One,CHECKED
                 MENUITEM "&Two",        Two
                 MENUITEM "T&hree",      Three
                 MENUITEM "&Four",       Four
                 MENUITEM "Fi&ve",       Five
                 MENUITEM "&Six",        Six
                 MENUITEM "Seve&n",      Seven
                 MENUITEM "Ei&ght",      Eight
                 MENUITEM SEPARATOR
                 MENUITEM "&Exit",       ExitMsg
               END
             POPUP "About"
               BEGIN
                 MENUITEM "About&1",     About1
                 MENUITEM "About&2",     About2
                 MENUITEM "About&3",     About3
                 MENUITEM "About&4",     About4
                 MENUITEM "About&5",     About5
                 MENUITEM "About&6",     About6
                 MENUITEM "About&7",     About7
                 MENUITEM "About&8",     About8
               END
             POPUP "PPP"
               BEGIN
                 MENUITEM "&Paint",      PP
                 MENUITEM SEPARATOR
                 MENUITEM "&Exit",       ExitMsg
               END
           END
```

(a)

```
#define One      1
#define Two      2
#define Three    3
#define Four     4
#define Five     5
#define Six      6
#define Seven    7
#define Eight    8
#define ExitMsg  16
#define About1   17
#define About2   18
#define About3   19
#define About4   20
#define About5   21
#define About6   22
#define About7   23
#define About8   24
#define PP       30
```

(b)

Figure 8.13 Menu resource file associated with the multiple $(\sin(x)/x)^{**2}$
program and (b) include file defining the resource file parameters.

coupled with a specification for BLACK__BRUSH in the Window1Class.hbrBackground association (routine Window1Init()).

Figure 8.13a illustrates the .rc file, which contains the three menus, and Figure 8.13b illustrates the include file win4.h used to identify the resource script file parameters. The resource script file is indicated as menu4.rc and will be compiled to menu4.res using rc. Figure 8.14a presents the definition file and Figure 8.14b the MAKE file. Note that following link4 execution the rc invocation requires both the resource filename and the executable-file filename be specified because they are different.

```
NAME            win4

DESCRIPTION     'Windows 3D Surface Plots'

EXETYPE         WINDOWS

STUB            'WINSTUB.EXE'

CODE            MOVEABLE
DATA            MOVEABLE MULTIPLE

HEAPSIZE        4096
STACKSIZE       4096

EXPORTS
                Window1Proc
```

(a)

```
# MAKE file for 3D Windows program

win4.obj: win4.c
        cl -c -d -Os -Gsw -Zp -FPa win4.c

wingrp.obj: wingrp.c
        cl -c -d -Os -Gsw -Zp -FPa wingrp.c

winggen.obj: winggen.c
        cl -c -d -Os -Gsw -Zp -FPa winggen.c

winrot.obj: winrot.c
        cl -c -d -Os -Gsw -Zp -FPa winrot.c

winpt.obj: winpt.c
        cl -c -d -Os -Gsw -Zp -FPa winpt.c

winsca.obj: winsca.c
        cl -c -d -Os -Gsw -Zp -FPa winsca.c

menu4.res: menu4.rc
        rc -r menu4.rc

win4.exe: win4.obj win4.def wingrp.obj winggen.obj winrot.obj\
        winpt.obj winsca.obj menu4.res
        link4 win4+winggen+wingrp+winrot+winpt+winsca,\
        /align:16,/map,slibw/NOE swinlibc/NOE,win4
        rc menu4.res win4.exe
```

(b)

Figure 8.14 Definition file for Figure 8.12 and (b) corresponding MAKE file.

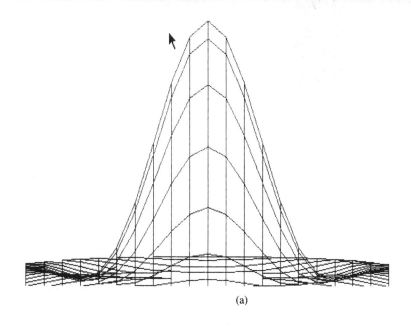

(a)

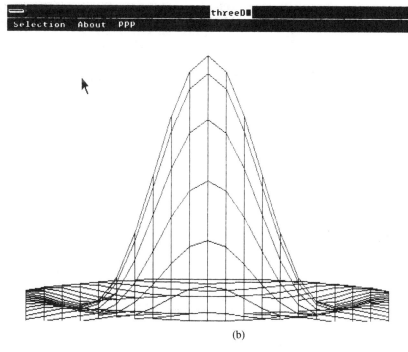

(b)

Figure 8.15 Windows output for the (sin(x)/x)**2 program with (a) beta = 0.4 and NN = 7 and (b) beta = 0.6 and NN = 7.

Sec. 8.4   Additional Windows Examples

415

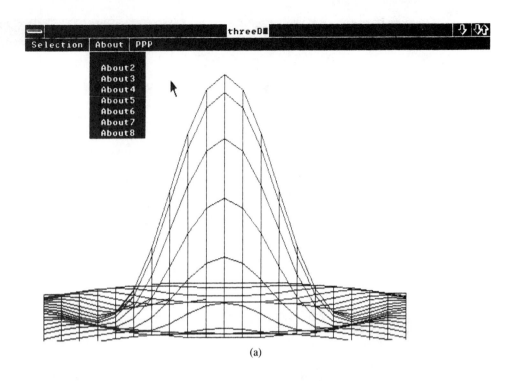

(a)

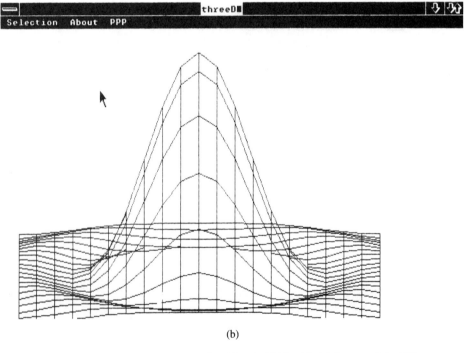

(b)

Figure 8.16 Windows output for $(\sin(x)/x)^{**}2$ with (a) beta = 0.8, NN = 7 and a menu box displayed and (b) beta = 1.1 and NN = 7.

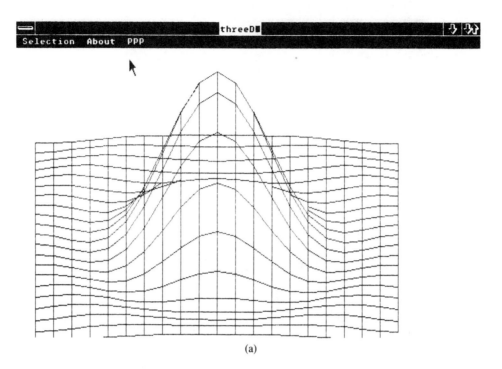

(a)

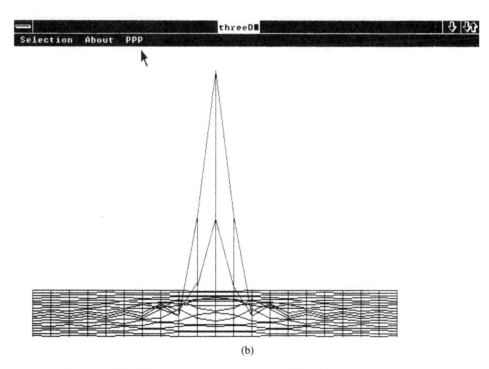

(b)

Figure 8.17 Windows output for $(\sin(x)/x)^{**}2$ with (a) beta $= 1.4$ and NN $= 7$, and (b) beta $= 0.8$ and NN $= 2$.

Sec. 8.4   Additional Windows Examples

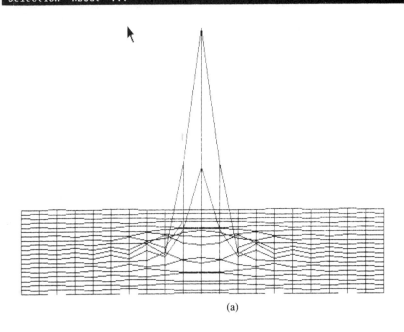

(a)

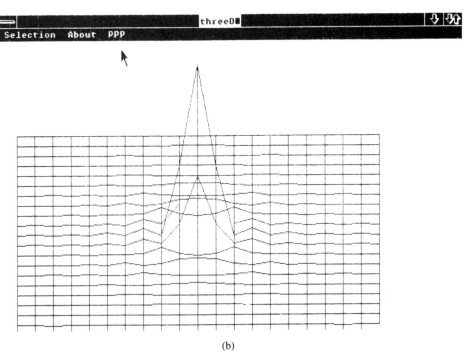

(b)

Figure 8.18 Windows output for $(\sin(x)/x)^{**}2$ with (a) beta $= 1.1$ and NN $= 2$ and (b) beta $= 1.4$ and NN $= 2$.

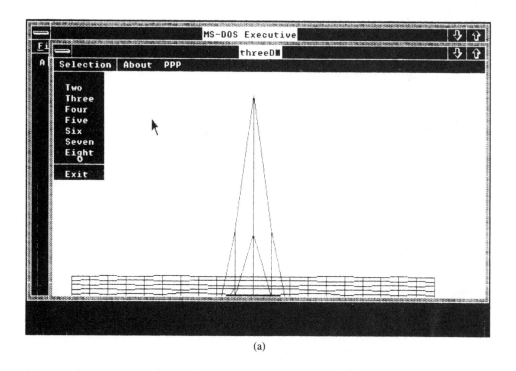

(a)

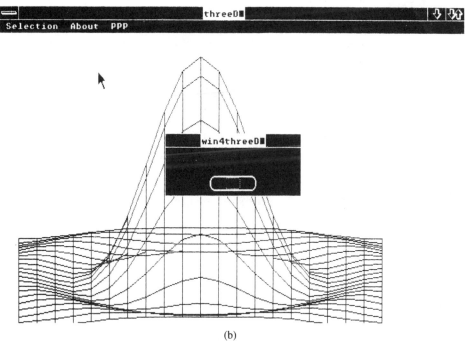

(b)

Figure 8.19 Windows output illustrating (a) tiled windows with the MS-DOS Executive and a pop-up menu for parameter selection and (b) a dialog box (partially obscured by the print routine).

Figure 8.15a and 8.15b contain the output for beta = 0.4 and 0.6, respectively, with NN = 7. Figure 8.16a and 8.16b present similar output, with beta = 0.8 and 1.1. In Figure 8.16a, the About menu box is displayed (note that "About1" does not appear because it is obscured in the printout since it is actually colored red on the display). Figure 8.17a contains the output for beta = 1.4 and NN = 7, and Figure 8.17b the output for beta = 0.8 with NN = 2. Figure 8.18a and 8.18b are the same output with beta = 1.1 and 1.4, respectively. Finally, Figure 8.19a and 8.19b show partial representations of Windows output with some of the features obscured in the printout due to coloring. Figure 8.19a is a reproduction of the initial call to win4.exe with the Selection menu displayed. Note that the MS-DOS Executive window is partially eclipsed by threeD. Everywhere a nonblack or clear color appears in these examples, the print routine returns "black"; hence these are not exact facsimiles. Figure 8.19a illustrates a typical message box format with the contents obscured because of color. Nonetheless, both of these examples are useful in understanding the power of Windows.

SUMMARY

This chapter has introduced the programming environment Windows. We have been exposed to the Windows Software Development Kit (SDK) Version 1.03 and the Windows Presentation Manager 2.03. This is a complex programming framework from which dynamic access to data and execution is possible. The underlying architecture is based on C and requires that all program code for use with the SDK be compiled as C code interfaced to the Windows routines and structures. Windows is an impressive C approach to object-oriented, device-independent programming. This type of program executive and development is certainly to be desired as more intricate interfaces between hardware and software evolve. Windows truly marks an evolutionary step in system programming development.

As an example of object-oriented design, it is clear that Windows achieves abstraction, information hiding, and modularity. Clearly, the message handling in Windows accomplishes a great deal of hiding, as does the unspecified use of Windows data structures. The program conceptually abstracts everything to a window viewport, which also introduces a dynamic dimension to execution. Finally, the code is very modular when interpreted in light of the many easy to use, yet unspecified, Windows functions. This code is very structured, as evidenced by the template approach to programming.

We saw examples intended to introduce the Windows environment, illustrate the programming complexity (also clarified through the tables), and provide motivation for using Windows as a C development tool. Each application must weigh the merits of Windows. The benefit of added programming complexity is an object-oriented display capable of enhanced user-friendly execution.

REFERENCES

1. *Microsoft Windows User's Guide Version 2.0*, Microsoft Corporation, P. O. Box 97017, Redmond, WA (1987).

2. *Microsoft Windows Software Development Kit Programmer's Reference*, Microsoft Corporation, P. O. Box 97017, Redmond, WA (1986).

3. *Microsoft Windows Software Development Kit Update/Programmer's Utility Guide*, Microsoft Corporation, P. O. Box 97017, Redmond, WA (1986).

4. *Microsoft Windows Software Development Kit QR/Programming Guide/Applications Style Guide*, Microsoft Corporation, P. O. Box 97017, Redmond, WA (1986).

5. Petzold, C., *Programming Windows*, Microsoft Press, 16011 NE 36th Way, Box 97017, Redmond, WA (1988).

6. *Microsoft C 5.0 Optimizing Compiler User's Guide and Mixed-Language Programming Guide*, Microsoft Corporation, P. O. Box 97017, Redmond, WA (1987).

PROBLEMS

8.1. Define in what sense Windows software represents an object-oriented architecture? Could it be construed as data structure oriented? Why?

8.2. Given a call to the function

```
int FAR PASCAL func(x1,x2,beta,target1,target2)
```

identify the byte location of target1 on the stack relative to the calling function's base pointer. Assume no local data are saved. Assume all parameters are of word length.

8.3. If a program needs to change the brush color from the default value to gray, define the needed modifications in template fashion starting with the window procedure.

8.4. Define a resource script file for a menu box that returns three messages indicating "angle" equals 120 degrees, 180 degrees, and 240 degrees. Indicate in template fashion the window procedure code corresponding to the processing of these messages.

8.5. Define the MAKE file that generates object code for a program win10.c with a resource file menu.rc and a definitions file win10.def. Assume the usual small C compiler options.

8.6. Define the resource script file and any associated files and templates for a set of menus that changes the background color to span white, black, or gray.

8.7. If a call to GetBkColor(hDC) returns a value equivalent to the long integer 8,355,711, what does this mean? A value of 0? A value of 16,777,215?

8.8. What code fragment is needed to acquire a gray brush? Where would such a fragment be located in the template?

8.9. How are colors specified in the Windows environment?

8.10. What is wrong with the following sequence of operations designed to handle the message transactions:

```
...
switch(message)
   {
   case WM_COMMAND:
   switch(wParam)
      {
```

```
    case one:
     MessageBeep(0);
     break;
    case two:
      MessageBeep(0);
      MessageBeep(0);
      break;
    default:
      break;
    }
  case WM_PAINT:
    PaintBeginWindow(hWnd);
  caseWM_DESTROY:
    PostQuitMessage(0);
  default:
    return(DefWindowProc(hWnd,message,wParam,lParam));
    break;
  }
  ...
```

8.11. Write a paint procedure to be called from the window procedure that draws a white line on a gray background at $y = 150$ from $x = 25$ to $x = 525$. How was the graphics mode specified?

8.12. Write a paint procedure to be called from the window procedure that draws a bar (white) on a gray background at $x = 150$ (to $x = 170$) of height corresponding to the second largest value of xarray[]. The plot is to span y-coordinates [25,325], where this range corresponds to the maximum and minimum xarray[] value. Assume xarray[] is all positive values.

8.13. Under the Windows SDK Version 2.03 and higher, overlapped windows are possible. What modification(s) are needed to use these windows?

8.14. What is the Windows call to open a disk file with path b:\win1\filenm.ext for reading?

8.15. In Problem 8.14, a file, b:\win1\filenm.ext, was opened for reading. Indicate the needed code to close this file under Windows.

8.16. In the programs presented in this chapter, the window name and title, for example, were initialized in the preprocessor to equal specific character string values. Illustrate a more general technique whereby these string values can be defined externally.

8.17. In the program presenting GDI interfacing, we used the MM_TEXT mapping mode that addresses screen points in pixels (640×350 for EGA mode). Using this mapping mode, write the word MIDDLE starting at the center of the window with the default font.

8.18. Windows communicates with applications through formatted messages. A message has three parts: a message number or predefined message name, a word parameter, and a long parameter. The names begin WM_. . . . The word and long parameters, named wParam and lParam contain values that depend on the message number. In Figure 8.5, explain the processing for wParam.

8.19. Using the message parts message number or predefined message name, word parameter (wParam), and long parameter (lParam), explain what would happen to the program in Figure 8.5 if no ExitMsg value were passed using the message word parameters wParam.

9

Windows: A Structured Methodology

Chapter 8 introduced Windows and provided examples of how the Windows environment can be dynamically interfaced to the user. In addition to the basic Windows template and some simple examples of Windows usage, the GDI environment was presented with the three-dimensional surface from Chapter 7. This chapter focuses on I/O between Windows and the user in order to develop an interactive Windows environment. We would like to establish a dynamic interchange between the user and the program that allows intelligent I/O. For example, in Chapter 8 the three-dimensional surface could be viewed from one of several perspectives, depending on a menu-selected orientation. An alternative to this would be input of arbitrarily selected angles and generation of the corresponding three-dimensional surface. This is what we mean by intelligent I/O; the user actually affects program execution in the Windows environment (which is dynamic in and of itself). How is this accomplished? That is the subject of Section 9.1, where dialog boxes are introduced. We should note that earlier reference to dialog material in box form actually applies to the message box and menu box concepts. True dialog boxes are now treated in this chapter and can be differentiated from menu boxes by the form of the .rc file and the creation statements in the .c file.

9.1 WINDOWS I/O

Figure 9.1a illustrates the .c file used to create a simple example of a dialog box. Figure 9.1b presents the associated .rc file, which contains a menu and dialog box specification. This resource file initiates the creation of a menu bar with a pull-down menu, "CallD." The menu has two fields: "Angles" and "Exit." Angles is associated with the ID EDIT__B and Exit has the ID ExitMsg.

```
/* Windows program to test dialog box I/O: menu3.c */

#include <windows.h>
#include <menu3.h>

typedef struct
        {
        int dummy;
        }
        SETUPDATA;
static   SETUPDATA setupData;

static HANDLE hInst;
char szName[5] = {'m','e','n','u','3'};
char szTitle[11] = {'m','e','n','u','p','r','o','g','r','a','m'};
char TText[7] = {'x','x','x','x','x','x','x'};
int MAXLENGTH = 7;

BOOL FAR PASCAL Window1Init(HANDLE);
BOOL FAR PASCAL Window1InitEvery(HANDLE,int);
BOOL FAR PASCAL Window1InitAdd(HANDLE,HANDLE);

long FAR PASCAL Window1Proc(HWND,unsigned,WORD,LONG);
BOOL FAR PASCAL IOBox(HWND,unsigned,WORD,LONG);
BOOL FAR PASCAL PaintBeginWindow(HWND);

int NEAR PASCAL WinMain(hInstance,hPrevInstance,lpszCmdLine,cmdShow)
        HANDLE hInstance,hPrevInstance;
        LPSTR lpszCmdLine;
        int cmdShow;
        {
        MSG msg;

        if(!hPrevInstance)
            Window1Init(hInstance);
        else
            Window1InitAdd(hInstance,hPrevInstance);
        Window1InitEvery(hInstance,cmdShow);

        while(GetMessage((LPMSG)&msg,NULL,0,0))
            {
            TranslateMessage((LPMSG)&msg);
            DispatchMessage((LPMSG)&msg);
            }
        exit(msg.wParam);
        }
/* Functions which make up Window1 class */

long FAR PASCAL Window1Proc(hWnd,message,wParam,lParam)
        HWND hWnd;
        unsigned message;
        WORD wParam;
        LONG lParam;
        {
        static HWND      hInstance;
        static FARPROC   lpDlgProcedure;

        switch(message)
            {
            case WM_COMMAND:
                switch(wParam)
                    {
                    case EDIT_B:
                        DialogBox(hInstance,"EDITBOX",hWnd,lpDlgProcedure);
                        InvalidateRect(hWnd,(LPRECT)NULL,TRUE);
                        PostMessage(hWnd,WM_PAINT,0,0L);
                        break;
```

Figure 9.1a Windows source code for menu3.c program, which develops dialog box text I/O.

```
                    case ExitMsg:
                        SendMessage(hWnd,WM_CLOSE,0,0L);
                        break;
                    default:
                        break;
                }
                break;
        case WM_PAINT:
            PaintBeginWindow(hWnd);
            break;
        case WM_DESTROY:
            PostQuitMessage(0);
            break;
        case WM_CREATE:
            hInstance = ((LPCREATESTRUCT)lParam)->hInstance;
            lpDlgProcedure = MakeProcInstance(IOBox,hInstance);
            break;
        default:
            return(DefWindowProc(hWnd,message,wParam,lParam));
            break;
        }
    return(0L);
    }

BOOL FAR PASCAL IOBox(hBox,message,wParam,lParam)
    HWND     hBox;
    unsigned        message;
    WORD     wParam;
    LONG     lParam;
    {
    switch(message)
        {
        case WM_INITDIALOG:
            SetFocus(GetDlgItem(hBox,ID_ANGLE));
            break;
        case WM_COMMAND:
            switch(wParam)
                {
                case ID_OK:
                    GetDlgItemText(hBox,ID_ANGLE,(LPSTR)TText,MAXLENGTH);
                    EndDialog(hBox,0);
                    break;
                case ID_CANCEL:
                    EndDialog(hBox,0);
                    break;
                default:
                    return FALSE;
                }
        default:
            return FALSE;
        }
    }


BOOL FAR PASCAL PaintBeginWindow(hWnd)
        HWND     hWnd;
        {
        HDC hDC;
        PAINTSTRUCT     ps;

        hDC = BeginPaint(hWnd,(LPPAINTSTRUCT)&ps);
        TextOut(hDC,100,100,(LPSTR)TText,MAXLENGTH-1);
        ValidateRect(hWnd,(LPRECT)NULL);
        EndPaint(hWnd,(LPPAINTSTRUCT)&ps);
        return TRUE;
        }

/* Initialization Module for beginw.c */
/* performed only once at inception */
```

Figure 9.1a *(Continued)*

```
BOOL FAR PASCAL Window1Init(hInstance)
        HANDLE hInstance;
        {
        WNDCLASS            Window1Class;

        Window1Class.hCursor = LoadCursor(NULL,IDC_ARROW);
        Window1Class.hIcon = LoadIcon(hInstance,(LPSTR)szName);
        Window1Class.lpszMenuName = (LPSTR)szName;
        Window1Class.lpszClassName = (LPSTR)szName;
        Window1Class.hbrBackground = GetStockObject(WHITE_BRUSH);
        Window1Class.hInstance = hInstance;
        Window1Class.style = CS_HREDRAW | CS_VREDRAW;
        Window1Class.lpfnWndProc = Window1Proc;
        Window1Class.cbClsExtra = 0;
        Window1Class.cbWndExtra = 0;

        RegisterClass((LPWNDCLASS)&Window1Class);
        return TRUE;
        }

/* Performed for every instance of the window */

BOOL FAR PASCAL Window1InitEvery(hInstance,cmdShow)
        HANDLE hInstance;
        int cmdShow;
        {
        HWND hWnd;

        hWnd = CreateWindow((LPSTR)szName,
                            (LPSTR)szTitle,
                            WS_TILEDWINDOW,
                            0,0,0,0,
                            (HWND)NULL,
                            (HMENU)NULL,
                            (HANDLE)hInstance,
                            (LPSTR)NULL);
        ShowWindow(hWnd,cmdShow);
        UpdateWindow(hWnd);
        return TRUE;
        }

/* Performed for instances beyond initial */

BOOL FAR PASCAL Window1InitAdd(hInstance,hPrevInstance)
        HANDLE hInstance,hPrevInstance;
        {
        GetInstanceData(hPrevInstance,(PSTR)&setupData,sizeof(SETUPDATA));
        }
```

Figure 9.1a (*Concluded*)

Returning to the C program menu3.c, we see that the window procedure
Window1Proc() selects cases based on the wParam value in response to the WM_
COMMAND message. When wParam equals EDIT__B, a call to the dialog box
function is made with the form

```
DialogBox(hInstance, "EDITBOX", hWnd, lpDlgProcedure)
```

It is this call that creates a modal dialog box based on the EDITBOX reference to
the resource file in Figure 9.1b.

The dialog box call has four formal parameters:

```
#include <windows.h>
#include <menu3.h>

menu3    MENU
         BEGIN
             POPUP "CallD"
                 BEGIN
                     MENUITEM "&Angles",      EDIT_B
                     MENUITEM SEPARATOR
                     MENUITEM "&Exit",        ExitMsg
                 END
         END

EDITBOX DIALOG PRELOAD MOVEABLE DISCARDABLE 25,25,100,75
STYLE   WS_POPUP | WS_DLGFRAME
         BEGIN
                 CONTROL "OK" ID_OK,BUTTON,
                     BS_PUSHBUTTON | WS_TABSTOP | WS_GROUP, 30,50,25,14
                 CONTROL "CANCEL" ID_CANCEL,BUTTON,
                     BS_PUSHBUTTON | WS_TABSTOP | WS_GROUP, 60,50,25,14
                 CONTROL "Enter 6 characters:",-1,"static",
                     SS_LEFT | WS_GROUP, 20,6,80,12
                 CONTROL "" ID_ANGLE,EDIT,
                     ES_LEFT | WS_BORDER | WS_TABSTOP | WS_GROUP, 30,20,40,14
         END
```

Figure 9.1b   Resource file for dialog box text I/O.

hInstance	Instance handle of the structure containing the dialog template
"EDITBOX"	Long pointer to a character string naming the dialog template (in the .rc file)
hWnd	Handle to the window owning the dialog box
lpDlgProcedure	Long pointer to the dialog box function

Note that a modal dialog box retains the focus until it is destroyed.

In Figure 9.1a, it is clear that EDITBOX refers to the template of Figure 9.1b, and hWnd is the window handle passed to Window1Proc() by Windows. What about hInstance and lpDlgProcedure? Where did these parameters get identified? The answer to these questions is that the dialog box instance was created in response to a WM_CREATE message sent by Windows to Window1Proc(). When this message was sent, the lParam value was used to identify the structure with instance handle hInstance. Next a call

```
lpDlgProcedure = MakeProcInstance(IOBox,hInstance);
```

is made to define the dialog box function. Here, lpDlgProcedure is a long pointer to the function IOBox() after IOBox() is associated with the data structure, which is identified by hInstance, to yield the dialog box instance.

So far we have said nothing about the dialog box itself. Returning to Figure 9.1b, we see it has the name EDITBOX and is loaded starting with upper-left corner at the row and column coordinates 25 and 25, respectively. The length of the box in the *x*-direction is 100 pixels and it is 75 pixels high (*y*-direction). Remember

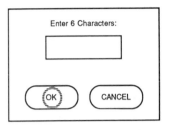

Figure 9.2 Facsimile dialog box used for text I/O.

that this is imposed on an EGA field that is 640 pixels wide (*x*-direction) by 350 pixels high (*y*-direction). The style of the box is a pop-up menu style with the default dialog box frame. Inside the box are four controls defined as follows:

1. OK pushbutton: with ID ID__OK at relative location (30, 50) of length 25 and height 14
2. CANCEL pushbutton: with ID ID__CANCEL at relative location (60, 50) of length 25 and height 14
3. "Enter 6 characters:": message displayed at (20, 6) of length 80 and height 12 with ID -1
4. editbox: input box with ID ID__ANGLE at (30, 20) of width 40 and height 14.

Figure 9.2 illustrates a representative facsimile for the dialog box, which appears in response to the mouse pointer on "Angles" (followed by clicking the mouse button) in the menu. The actions taken by the dialog box in response to internal mouse activity are predicated on the contents of the dialog box function IOBox().

In Figure 9.1a the routine IOBox() contains the code that is executed in response to activity in the dialog box. Once the box is created, the dialog box function takes control. This function responds to three classes of Windows messages: WM__INITDIALOG, WM__COMMAND, and all others. The default return value is FALSE, which tells Windows that the dialog box has not been updated. The response to WM__INITDIALOG is a call of the form

```
SetFocus(GetDlgItem(hBox,ID_ANGLE));
```

This call simply sets the focus of the window on the dialog box containing ID__ANGLE. If the mouse cursor is moved about and clicked over a control, the control is activated. For example, when the cursor is moved to the editbox below the string "Enter 6 characters:" and clicked, a vertical bar appears and the editbox is ready to accept input. The user can then input values from the keyboard. Whether or not these values are treated as a number (integer) or text depends on the function that eventually accepts this input.

The second delineated message is WM__COMMAND. When this message is sent in response to a mouse click, for example, the above action takes place if the cursor is over the editbox. If the cursor is over the OK box, however, case ID__OK executes. Here the function

```
GetDlgItemText(hBox,ID_ANGLE,(LPSTR)TText,MAXLENGTH);
```

followed by

```
EndDialog(hBox,0);
```

executes. The first function reads text of length MAXLENGTH into the string TText[]. This text is contained in the editbox associated with the ID ID_ANGLE. At this point, the contents of the editbox are interpreted as characters not integers. Next, the dialog is terminated. If the CANCEL button were clicked, no input of values from the editbox would occur. The outcome of all this activity is to either load text (up to six characters) from the editbox or leave the input unchanged. The string TText[] is changed if text is input.

Returning to the window procedure, we see that following the DialogBox() function call is a call to InvalidateRect(). This causes a WM_PAINT message that, in turn, calls PaintBeginWindow(). In the program menu3.exe, PaintBeginWindow() is used to output text from the string TText[] at position (100, 100). Earlier this string had been initialized with all x values. The output is sent with the function

```
TextOut(hDC,100,100,(LPSTR)TText,MAXLENGTH-1);
```

Here MAXLENGTH = 7, so six characters are output for each call to TextOut(). The display context handle hDC is obtained by a call to BeginPaint(). Once the text is output, the client area (display context) is validated and the EndPaint() function called. Control then returns to the polling loop. Figure 9.3a contains the definition file for menu3.exe, and the dialog box function has been exported as well as the window function. Figures 9.3b and 9.3c contain the menu3.h file and the MAKE file, respectively.

The dialog box illustration we have just seen loads a text string, TText[]. An alternative and desirable I/O capability is the input of numerical values to Windows. Integer input can be easily accommodated using dialog boxes with the function GetDlgItemInt(). To see the implementation for integer input, consider the function menu4.c illustrated in Figure 9.4a. This program is essentially the program menu3.c with several key modifications to allow for integer input.

First, the global variables TText[] and MAXLENGTH have been replaced with integers: scale, xx0, xx1, yy0, and yy1. The integer scale is the value to be input using the editbox control in the dialog box. All dialog box setup code is the same as Figure 9.1a except

```
scale = GetDlgItemInt(hBox,ID_ANGLE,(LPSTR)NULL,1);
```

Here the third parameter is a Boolean variable that returns a nonzero value for correct translation of the input integer value. We use NULL, so the translation errors are ignored. The fourth parameter indicates the input integer can be signed if this value is nonzero. The function returns the translated integer in scale.

In Figure 9.4a, the window paint routine has been written so that it displays a white rectangle starting at (100, 100) on a black field with the length of the

```
```

```
NAME              menu3

DESCRIPTION       'Demonstrate Menu'

EXETYPE           WINDOWS

STUB              'WINSTUB.EXE'

CODE              MOVEABLE
DATA              MOVEABLE MULTIPLE

HEAPSIZE          4096
STACKSIZE         4096

EXPORTS           Window1Proc
                  IOBox
```

(a)

```
#define ExitMsg 16
#define EDIT_B  64
#define ID_OK     66
#define ID_CANCEL 68
#define ID_ANGLE 70
```

(b)

```
menu3.obj: menu3.c
        cl -c -D LINT_ARGS -Gsw _Os _W2 _Zp -W3 menu3.c

menu3.res: menu3.rc
        rc -r menu3.rc

menu3.exe: menu3.obj menu3.def menu3.res
        link4 menu3,/align:16,/map,slibw/NOE swinlibc/NOE,menu3
        rc menu3.res
```

(c)

Figure 9.3 (a) Definition file, menu3.def, (b) include file, menu3.h, and (c) MAKE file, menu3.mak.

rectangle sides equal to the integer value of scale in pixels. This provides an easily observed indicator of the correctness of the input translated value for the integer. Figure 9.4b contains the resource file menu4.rc, and the text control outputs the message "Integer less than 100:". Note that with the exception of this control all other features of the .rc file are identical to Figure 9.1b (except the file-naming convention).

Figure 9.5a illustrates the definition file menu4.def, and Figure 9.5b the MAKE file. The file menu4.h is identical to menu3.h appearing in Figure 9.3b. Figure 9.6a and b present facsimile Windows output for the cases where scale equals 25 and 75, respectively.

The sequence of programs illustrated in these figures provides for text and integer I/O to Windows. We now have a reasonably sophisticated interactive set of Windows tools. Using the dialog box with editbox features, it is possible to input

```
/* Windows program to test dialog box I/O-integer: menu4.c */
```

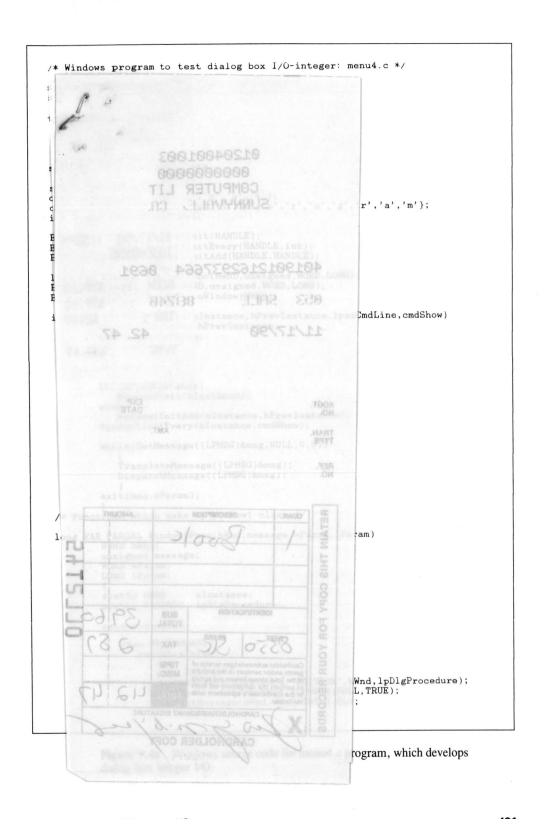

`r','a','m'};`

`CmdLine,cmdShow)`

`long FAR PASCAL` ... `ram)`

`Wnd,lpDlgProcedure);`
`L,TRUE);`

rogram, which develops

```
                    case ExitMsg:
                        SendMessage(hWnd,WM_CLOSE,0,0L);
                        break;
                    default:
                        break;
                }
                break;
            case WM_PAINT:
                PaintBeginWindow(hWnd);
                break;
            case WM_DESTROY:
                PostQuitMessage(0);
                break;
            case WM_CREATE:
                hInstance = ((LPCREATESTRUCT)lParam)->hInstance;
                lpDlgProcedure = MakeProcInstance(IOBox,hInstance);
                break;
            default:
                return(DefWindowProc(hWnd,message,wParam,lParam));
                break;
        }
        return(0L);
    }

BOOL FAR PASCAL IOBox(hBox,message,wParam,lParam)
    HWND     hBox;
    unsigned         message;
    WORD     wParam;
    LONG     lParam;
    {
    switch(message)
        {
        case WM_INITDIALOG:
            SetFocus(GetDlgItem(hBox,ID_ANGLE));
            break;
        case WM_COMMAND:
            switch(wParam)
                {
                case ID_OK:
                    scale = GetDlgItemInt(hBox,ID_ANGLE,(LPSTR)NULL,1);
                    EndDialog(hBox,0);
                    break;
                case ID_CANCEL:
                    EndDialog(hBox,0);
                    break;
                default:
                    return FALSE;
                }
        default:
            return FALSE;
        }
    }



BOOL FAR PASCAL PaintBeginWindow(hWnd)
    HWND     hWnd;
    {
    HDC hDC;
    HPEN     hPen;
    PAINTSTRUCT     ps;

    hDC = BeginPaint(hWnd,(LPPAINTSTRUCT)&ps);
    hPen = GetStockObject(WHITE_PEN);
    SelectObject(hDC,hPen);

    xx0 = 100;
    yy0 = 100;
```

Figure 9.4a   *(Continued)*

```
            xx1 =xx0 + scale;
            yy1 = yy0 + scale;

            MoveTo(hDC,xx0,yy0);                        /* Draw scaled rect */
            LineTo(hDC,xx0,yy1);
            LineTo(hDC,xx1,yy1);
            LineTo(hDC,xx1,yy0);
            LineTo(hDC,xx0,yy0);

            ValidateRect(hWnd,(LPRECT)NULL);
            EndPaint(hWnd,(LPPAINTSTRUCT)&ps);
            return TRUE;
            }
/* Initialization Module for beginw.c */
/* performed only once at inception */

BOOL FAR PASCAL Window1Init(hInstance)
        HANDLE hInstance;
        {
        WNDCLASS             Window1Class;

        Window1Class.hCursor = LoadCursor(NULL,IDC_ARROW);
        Window1Class.hIcon = LoadIcon(hInstance,(LPSTR)szName);
        Window1Class.lpszMenuName = (LPSTR)szName;
        Window1Class.lpszClassName = (LPSTR)szName;
        Window1Class.hbrBackground = GetStockObject(BLACK_BRUSH);
        Window1Class.hInstance = hInstance;
        Window1Class.style = CS_HREDRAW | CS_VREDRAW;
        Window1Class.lpfnWndProc = Window1Proc;
        Window1Class.cbClsExtra = 0;
        Window1Class.cbWndExtra = 0;

        RegisterClass((LPWNDCLASS)&Window1Class);
        return TRUE;
        }

/* Performed for every instance of the window */

BOOL FAR PASCAL Window1InitEvery(hInstance,cmdShow)
        HANDLE hInstance;
        int cmdShow;
        {
        HWND hWnd;

        hWnd = CreateWindow((LPSTR)szName,
                            (LPSTR)szTitle,
                            WS_TILEDWINDOW,
                            0,0,0,0,
                            (HWND)NULL,
                            (HMENU)NULL,
                            (HANDLE)hInstance,
                            (LPSTR)NULL);
        ShowWindow(hWnd,cmdShow);
        UpdateWindow(hWnd);
        return TRUE;
        }

/* Performed for instances beyond initial */

BOOL FAR PASCAL Window1InitAdd(hInstance,hPrevInstance)
        HANDLE hInstance,hPrevInstance;
        {
        GetInstanceData(hPrevInstance,(PSTR)&setupData,sizeof(SETUPDATA));
        }
```

Figure 9.4a   *(Concluded)*

```
#include <windows.h>
#include <menu4.h>

menu4    MENU
         BEGIN
             POPUP "CallD"
                 BEGIN
                     MENUITEM "&Angles",        EDIT_B
                     MENUITEM SEPARATOR
                     MENUITEM "&Exit",          ExitMsg
                 END
         END

EDITBOX DIALOG PRELOAD MOVEABLE DISCARDABLE 25,25,100,75
STYLE   WS_POPUP | WS_DLGFRAME
        BEGIN
                CONTROL "OK" ID_OK,BUTTON,
                    BS_PUSHBUTTON | WS_TABSTOP | WS_GROUP, 30,50,25,14
                CONTROL "CANCEL" ID_CANCEL,BUTTON,
                    BS_PUSHBUTTON | WS_TABSTOP | WS_GROUP, 60,50,25,14
                CONTROL "Integer less than 100:",-1,"static",
                    SS_LEFT | WS_GROUP, 5,6,90,12
                CONTROL "" ID_ANGLE,EDIT,
                    ES_LEFT | WS_BORDER | WS_TABSTOP | WS_GROUP, 30,20,40,14
        END
```

Figure 9.4b Resource file for dialog box integer I/O.

```
NAME            menu4

DESCRIPTION     'Demonstrate Dialog Integer'

EXETYPE         WINDOWS

STUB            'WINSTUB.EXE'

CODE            MOVEABLE
DATA            MOVEABLE MULTIPLE

HEAPSIZE        4096
STACKSIZE       4096

EXPORTS         Window1Proc
                IOBox
```

(a)

```
menu4.obj: menu4.c
        cl -c -D LINT_ARGS -Gsw _Os _W2 _Zp -W3 menu4.c

menu4.res: menu4.rc
        rc -r menu4.rc

menu4.exe: menu4.obj menu4.def menu4.res
        link4 menu4,/align:16,/map,slibw/NOE swinlibc/NOE,menu4
        rc menu4.res
```

(b)

Figure 9.5 (a) Definition file, menu4.def, and (b) MAKE file, menu4.mak.

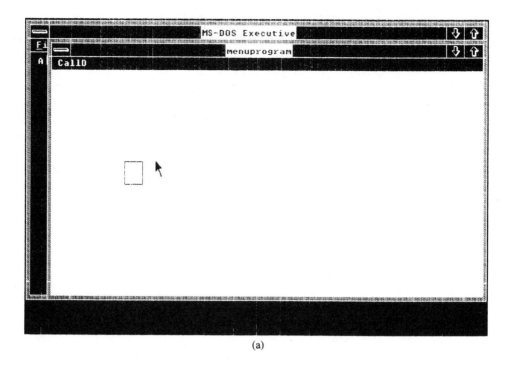

(a)

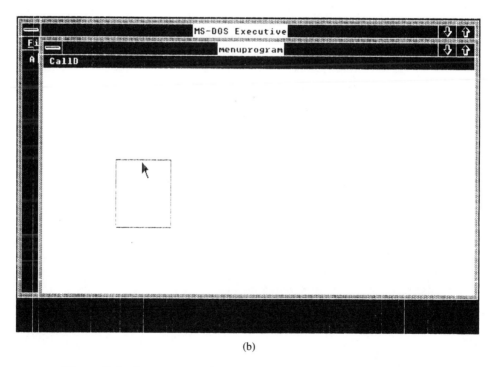

(b)

Figure 9.6 Output screen from menu4 illustrating input value (a) 25 and (b) 75 used to scale rectangle.

data to Windows programs. The integer input mechanism GetDlgItemInt() will be used with scaling for subsequent examples. We could, alternatively, generate an intermediate routine that converts floating point text input to internal integer values in order to allow for floating point I/O.

Figure 9.7 contains an updated version of the $\sin(x)/x$ (squared) code in which a dialog box is used to input the rotation angle values. This represents a reasonably common application for a Windows program. Note that in the dialog box procedure IOBox() three integer values receive the input: scale1, scale2, and scale3. The associated dialog box IDs are ID__ANGLE1, ID__ANGLE2, and ID__ANGLE3. The values scale1, scale2, and scale3 are converted to floating point numbers (alpha,

```
/* Windows 3D graph program: win3D.c */

#include <windows.h>
#include <menu10.h>

typedef struct
        {
        int dummy;
        }
        SETUPDATA;
static   SETUPDATA setupData;

static HANDLE hInst;
char szMenuNm[5] = {'w','i','n','1','0'};
char szName[5] = {'w','i','n','1','0'};
char szTitle[6] = {'t','h','r','e','e','D'};

BOOL FAR PASCAL Window1Init(HANDLE);
BOOL FAR PASCAL Window1InitEvery(HANDLE,int);
BOOL FAR PASCAL Window1InitAdd(HANDLE,HANDLE);
int FAR PASCAL ArrayGen();
int FAR PASCAL threeD_graph();
int FAR PASCAL rot_mat();

long FAR PASCAL Window1Proc(HWND,unsigned,WORD,LONG);
BOOL FAR PASCAL IOBox(HWND,unsigned,WORD,LONG);
BOOL FAR PASCAL PaintBeginWindow(HWND);

float xarray[3072],xx,yy,zz,scalex,scaley,scalez,a[10];
int ncount = 21,mcount = 21,count = 21;
float alpha = 0.0,beta = 1.1,gamma = 0.0;
int yy1,yy2,zz1,zz2,NN = 7;
int scale1,scale2,scale3;

int NEAR PASCAL WinMain(hInstance,hPrevInstance,lpszCmdLine,cmdShow)
        HANDLE hInstance,hPrevInstance;
        LPSTR lpszCmdLine;
        int cmdShow;
        {
        MSG msg;

        if(!hPrevInstance)
           Window1Init(hInstance);
        else
           Window1InitAdd(hInstance,hPrevInstance);
        Window1InitEvery(hInstance,cmdShow);
```

Figure 9.7 Windows source code for sin(x)/x surface plot employing dialog box input for rotation angles.

```
            while(GetMessage((LPMSG)&msg,NULL,0,0))
                {
                TranslateMessage((LPMSG)&msg);
                DispatchMessage((LPMSG)&msg);
                }
            exit(msg.wParam);
            }
/* Functions which make up Window1 class */

long FAR PASCAL Window1Proc(hWnd,message,wParam,lParam)
        HWND hWnd;
        unsigned message;
        WORD wParam;
        LONG lParam;
        {
        static HWND     hInstance;
        static FARPROC  lpDlgProcedure;

        switch(message)
            {
            case WM_COMMAND:
                switch(wParam)
                    {
                    case ExitMsg:
                        SendMessage(hWnd,WM_CLOSE,0,0L);
                        break;
                    case EDIT_B:
                        DialogBox(hInstance,"EDITBOX",hWnd,lpDlgProcedure);
                        InvalidateRect(hWnd,(LPRECT)NULL,TRUE);
                        PostMessage(hWnd,WM_PAINT,0,0L);
                    default:
                        break;
                    }
                break;
            case WM_PAINT:
                PaintBeginWindow(hWnd);
                break;
            case WM_DESTROY:
                PostQuitMessage(0);
                break;
            case WM_CREATE:
                hInstance = ((LPCREATESTRUCT)lParam) -> hInstance;
                lpDlgProcedure = MakeProcInstance(IOBox,hInstance);
                break;
            default:
                return(DefWindowProc(hWnd,message,wParam,lParam));
                break;
            ;
        return(0L);
        }
BOOL FAR PASCAL IOBox(hBox,message,wParam,lParam)
        HWND        hBox;
        unsigned         message;
        WORD     wParam;
        LONG     lParam;
        {

        switch(message)
            {
            case WM_INITDIALOG:
                SetFocus(GetDlgItem(hBox,ID_ANGLE1));
                break;
            case WM_COMMAND:
                switch(wParam)
                    {
                    case ID_OK:
                        scale1 = GetDlgItemInt(hBox,ID_ANGLE1,(LPSTR)NULL,1);
                        scale2 = GetDlgItemInt(hBox,ID_ANGLE2,(LPSTR)NULL,1);
                        scale3 = GetDlgItemInt(hBox,ID_ANGLE3,(LPSTR)NULL,1);
```

Figure 9.7 (*Continued*)

```
                   alpha = (float)(scale1)/1000.;
                   beta = (float)(scale2)/1000.;
                   gamma = (float)(scale3)/1000.;
                EndDialog(hBox,0);
                break;
               case ID_CANCEL:
                EndDialog(hBox,0);
                break;
              default:
                 return FALSE;
              }
         default:
             return FALSE;
          }

      }
BOOL FAR PASCAL PaintBeginWindow(hWnd)
      HWND hWnd;
      {
      extern float xarray[],scaley,scalez;
      int n,nc,nm_count,m1,m;
      extern int yy1,yy2,zz1,zz2;
      float z_start = 25.,y_start = 25.,z_mid = 150.,y_mid = 250.;
      float dy1,dy2,dz1,dz2,xa[5],ya[5],za[5];
      float half_yscale = 250.,half_zscale = 150.;

      HDC hDC;
      HPEN hPen;
      PAINTSTRUCT ps;

      ArrayGen();
      rot_mat();
      threeD_graph();

      hDC = BeginPaint(hWnd,(LPPAINTSTRUCT)&ps);
      hPen = GetStockObject(WHITE_PEN);
      SelectObject(hDC,hPen);

      m1 = 1;
      scaley = half_yscale;
      scalez = half_zscale;
      nm_count = 3*ncount*mcount - (ncount*3 +6);
      for(n = 1;n <= ncount;n++)
         {
         for(m = 1;m <= mcount;m++)
            {
            if(m1 < nm_count)
               {
               nc = 3*count;                          /* next y-value */
               xa[1] = xarray[m1];                    /* 1st y-value grid */
               ya[1] = xarray[m1+1];
               za[1] = xarray[m1+2];
               xa[2] = xarray[m1+3];
               ya[2] = xarray[m1+4];
               za[2] = xarray[m1+5];

               xa[3] = xarray[m1+nc+3];               /* 2nd y-value grid */
               ya[3] = xarray[m1+nc+4];
               za[3] = xarray[m1+nc+5];
               xa[4] = xarray[m1+nc];
               ya[4] = xarray[m1+nc+1];
               za[4] = xarray[m1+nc+2];

               dy1 = ya[2] - ya[1];                   /* ck rotation */
               dy2 = ya[3] - ya[2];
               dz1 = za[2] - za[1];
               dz2 = za[3] - za[2];
               if((dy1*dz2 - dz1*dy2) > 0)
                  {
```

Figure 9.7 *(Continued)*

```
                        for(n = 1;n <= 4;n++)                    /* scale facet */
                            {
                            za[n] = z_start + (z_mid - za[n]*scalez);
                            ya[n] = y_start + (y_mid + ya[n]*scaley);
                            }
                        for(n = 1;n <= 3;n++)                    /* plot 3 of 4 */
                            {
                            yy1 = (int)(ya[n]);
                            yy2 = (int)(ya[n+1]);
                            zz1 = (int)(za[n]);
                            zz2 = (int)(za[n+1]);
                            MoveTo(hDC,yy1,zz1);                 /* collapsed y-z */
                            LineTo(hDC,yy2,zz2);
                            }
                        yy1 = (int)(ya[4]);
                        yy2 = (int)(ya[1]);
                        zz1 = (int)(za[4]);
                        zz2 = (int)(za[1]);
                        MoveTo(hDC,yy1,zz1);                     /* 4th segment */
                        LineTo(hDC,yy2,zz2);
                        }
                    }
                m1 = m1 + 3;
                }
            }
        ValidateRect(hWnd,(LPRECT)NULL);

        EndPaint(hWnd,(LPPAINTSTRUCT)&ps);

        return TRUE;
        }

/* Initialization Module for beginw.c */
/* performed only once at inception */

BOOL FAR PASCAL Window1Init(hInstance)
        HANDLE hInstance;
        {
        WNDCLASS            Window1Class;

        Window1Class.hCursor = LoadCursor(NULL,IDC_ARROW);
        Window1Class.hIcon = LoadIcon(hInstance,(LPSTR)szName);
        Window1Class.lpszMenuName = (LPSTR)szMenuNm;
        Window1Class.lpszClassName = (LPSTR)szName;
        Window1Class.hbrBackground = GetStockObject(BLACK_BRUSH);
        Window1Class.hInstance = hInstance;
        Window1Class.style = CS_HREDRAW | CS_VREDRAW;
        Window1Class.lpfnWndProc = Window1Proc;
        Window1Class.cbClsExtra = 0;
        Window1Class.cbWndExtra = 0;

        RegisterClass((LPWNDCLASS)&Window1Class);
        return TRUE;
        }

/* Performed for every instance of the window */

BOOL FAR PASCAL Window1InitEvery(hInstance,cmdShow)
        HANDLE hInstance;
        int cmdShow;
        {
        HWND hWnd;

        hWnd = CreateWindow((LPSTR)szName,
                            (LPSTR)szTitle,
                            WS_TILEDWINDOW,
                            0,0,0,0,
                            (HWND)NULL,
```

Figure 9.7   *(Continued)*

```
                          (HMENU)NULL,
                          (HANDLE)hInstance,
                          (LPSTR)NULL);
          ShowWindow(hWnd,cmdShow);
          UpdateWindow(hWnd);
          return TRUE;
          }

/* Performed for instances beyond initial */

BOOL FAR PASCAL Window1InitAdd(hInstance,hPrevInstance)
          HANDLE hInstance,hPrevInstance;
          {
          GetInstanceData(hPrevInstance,(PSTR)&setupData,sizeof(SETUPDATA));
          }
```

Figure 9.7 (*Concluded*)

beta, and gamma) for use by the surface drawing functions after being appropriately scaled by 1000.

Figure 9.8a illustrates the resource file for the code appearing in Figure 9.7. Observe that the three IDs indicated above correspond to edit controls and are used as the input mechanism for data that are interpreted as integer [here the GetDlg-ItemInt() function call is used].

Figure 9.8b presents the definition file for the program of Figure 9.7. Figure 9.9a and b contain the associated MAKE file and include file for the program appearing in Figure 9.7. This program represents a simple application of intelligent I/O to the Windows environment. The dynamic Windows features are easily seen in this example. It is through the use of dialog boxes with the edit control that this intelligent I/O is most easily implemented.

9.2 DATA PASSING: THE CLIPBOARD

Windows possesses a mechanism for easily passing formatted data from one window to another. This mechanism is known as the clipboard, and it allows the typing and localizing of formatted data for such transfer. Figure 9.10 is another example of Windows source code used to implement the $\sin(x)/x$ (squared) surface in which the clipboard is used to transfer a blow-up of a rectangular region from one display context to another.

The Windows procedure Window1Proc() employs several new data types as structures, variables, and handles: POINT, BITMAP, and HBITMAP. Here POINT is a structure type of the form

```
typedef struct
   {
   int x;
   int y;
   } POINT;
```

```
#include <windows.h>
#include <menu10.h>

win10    MENU
         BEGIN
            POPUP "edit3D"
               BEGIN
                  MENUITEM "&Angles",        EDIT_B
                  MENUITEM SEPARATOR
                  MENUITEM "&Exit",          ExitMsg
               END
         END

EDITBOX DIALOG  PRELOAD MOVEABLE DISCARDABLE 25,25,300,225
STYLE   WS_POPUP | WS_DLGFRAME
BEGIN
        CONTROL "Alpha (x 1000):",-1,"static",
                SS_LEFT | WS_GROUP, 50,50,100,10
        CONTROL "Beta (x 1000):",-1,"static",
                SS_LEFT | WS_GROUP, 50,80,100,10
        CONTROL "Gamma (x 1000):",-1,"static",
                SS_LEFT | WS_GROUP, 50,110,100,10
        CONTROL "OK" ID_OK,BUTTON,
                BS_PUSHBUTTON | WS_TABSTOP | WS_GROUP, 90,140,45,14
        CONTROL "Cancel" ID_CANCEL,BUTTON,
                BS_PUSHBUTTON | WS_TABSTOP | WS_GROUP, 144,140,45,14
        CONTROL "" ID_ANGLE1,EDIT,
                ES_LEFT | WS_BORDER | WS_TABSTOP | WS_GROUP, 50,61,180,12
        CONTROL "" ID_ANGLE2,EDIT,
                ES_LEFT | WS_BORDER | WS_TABSTOP | WS_GROUP, 50,91,180,12
        CONTROL "" ID_ANGLE3,EDIT,
                ES_LEFT | WS_BORDER | WS_TABSTOP | WS_GROUP, 50,121,180,12
END
```

(a)

```
NAME            win10

DESCRIPTION     'Windows 3D Surface Plots'

EXETYPE         WINDOWS

STUB            'WINSTUB.EXE'

CODE            MOVEABLE
DATA            MOVEABLE MULTIPLE

HEAPSIZE        8192
STACKSIZE       4096

EXPORTS
        Window1Proc
        IOBox
```

(b)

Figure 9.8 (a) Resource file for surface plot program and (b) associated definition file.

```
# MAKE file for 3D Windows program

win10.obj: win10.c
        cl -c -d -Os -Gsw -Zp -FPa -W3 win10.c

wingrp.obj: wingrp.c
        cl -c -d -Os -Gsw -Zp -FPa -W3 wingrp.c

winggen.obj: winggen.c
        cl -c -d -Os -Gsw -Zp -FPa -W3 winggen.c

winrot.obj: winrot.c
        cl -c -d -Os -Gsw -Zp -FPa -W3 winrot.c

winpt.obj: winpt.c
        cl -c -d -Os -Gsw -Zp -FPa -W3 winpt.c

winsca.obj: winsca.c
        cl -c -d -Os -Gsw -Zp -FPa -W3 winsca.c

win10.res: win10.rc
        rc -r win10.rc

win10.exe: win10.obj win10.def wingrp.obj winggen.obj winrot.obj\
        winpt.obj winsca.obj win10.res
        link4 win10+winggen+wingrp+winrot+winpt+winsca,\
        /align:16,/map,slibw/NOE swinlibc/NOE,win10
        rc win10.res
```

(a)

```
#define ExitMsg 16
#define EDIT_B  40
#define ID_ANGLE1    50
#define ID_ANGLE2    60
#define ID_ANGLE3    70
#define ID_OK        80
#define ID_CANCEL    90
```

(b)

Figure 9.9 (a) MAKE file for surface plot program and (b) associated include file.

This structure type defines two integers, x and y. The handle HBITMAP is used to declare a handle to a bitmap, which is a subgroup of formatted screen data. The structure type BITMAP has the following form:

```
typedef struct
   {
   short bmType;
   short bmWidth;
   short bmHeight;
   short bmWidthBytes;
   BYTE  bmPlanes;
   BYTE  bmBitsPixel;
   1PSTR bmBits;
   } BITMAP;
```

```
/* Windows 3D graph program: win3D.c */

#include <windows.h>
#include <menu10.h>

typedef struct
        {
        int dummy;
        }
        SETUPDATA;
static   SETUPDATA setupData;

static HANDLE hInst;
char szMenuNm[5] = {'w','i','n','1','1'};
char szName[5] = {'w','i','n','1','1'};
char szTitle[6] = {'t','h','r','e','e','D'};
short xClient,yClient;

BOOL FAR PASCAL Window1Init(HANDLE);
BOOL FAR PASCAL Window1InitEvery(HANDLE,int);
BOOL FAR PASCAL Window1InitAdd(HANDLE,HANDLE);
int FAR PASCAL ArrayGen();
int FAR PASCAL threeD_graph();
int FAR PASCAL rot_mat();

long FAR PASCAL Window1Proc(HWND,unsigned,WORD,LONG);
BOOL FAR PASCAL IOBox(HWND,unsigned,WORD,LONG);
BOOL FAR PASCAL PaintBeginWindow(HWND);

float xarray[3072],xx,yy,zz,scalex,scaley,scalez,a[10];
int ncount = 21,mcount = 21,count = 21;
float alpha = 0.0,beta = 1.1,gamma = 0.0;
int yy1,yy2,zz1,zz2,NN = 7;
int scale1,scale2,scale3;

int NEAR PASCAL WinMain(hInstance,hPrevInstance,lpszCmdLine,cmdShow)
        HANDLE hInstance,hPrevInstance;
        LPSTR lpszCmdLine;
        int cmdShow;
        {
        MSG msg;

        if(!hPrevInstance)
            Window1Init(hInstance);
        else
            Window1InitAdd(hInstance,hPrevInstance);
        Window1InitEvery(hInstance,cmdShow);

        while(GetMessage((LPMSG)&msg,NULL,0,0))
            {
            TranslateMessage((LPMSG)&msg);
            DispatchMessage((LPMSG)&msg);
            }
        exit(msg.wParam);
        }
/* Functions which make up Window1 class */

long FAR PASCAL Window1Proc(hWnd,message,wParam,lParam)
        HWND hWnd;
        unsigned message;
        WORD wParam;
        LONG lParam;
        {
        static HWND      hInstance;
        static FARPROC   lpDlgProcedure;
        static POINT beg,leng;
        static BOOL capture,block;
```

Figure 9.10 Windows source code for sin(x)/x program to illustrate StretchBlt( ) operation to enlarge portion of picture.

```
BITMAP bm;
HDC hDC,hMDC;
HBITMAP hBitm;

switch(message)
    {
    case WM_COMMAND:
        switch(wParam)
            {
            case ExitMsg:
                SendMessage(hWnd,WM_CLOSE,0,0L);
                break;
            case EDIT_B:
                DialogBox(hInstance,"EDITBOX",hWnd,lpDlgProcedure);
                InvalidateRect(hWnd,(LPRECT)NULL,TRUE);
                PostMessage(hWnd,WM_PAINT,0,0L);
            default:
                break;
            }
        break;
    case WM_PAINT:
        PaintBeginWindow(hWnd);
        break;
    case WM_DESTROY:
        PostQuitMessage(0);
        break;
    case WM_CREATE:
        hInstance = ((LPCREATESTRUCT)lParam) -> hInstance;
        lpDlgProcedure = MakeProcInstance(IOBox,hInstance);
        break;
    case WM_SIZE:
        xClient = LOWORD(lParam);
        yClient = HIWORD(lParam);
        break;
    case WM_RBUTTONDOWN:
        if(!capture)
            {
            capture = TRUE;
            SetCapture(hWnd);
            SetCursor(LoadCursor(NULL,IDC_CROSS));
            }
        else if(!block)
            {
            block = TRUE;
            beg = MAKEPOINT(lParam);
            }
        break;

    case WM_MOUSEMOVE:
        if(capture)
            SetCursor(LoadCursor(NULL,IDC_CROSS));
        if(block)
            {
            leng = MAKEPOINT(lParam);
            leng.x = leng.x - beg.x;
            leng.y = leng.y - beg.y;
            IInvert(hWnd,beg,leng);
            IInvert(hWnd,beg,leng);
            }
        break;
    case WM_RBUTTONUP:
        if(!block)
            break;
        capture = FALSE;
        block = FALSE;
        SetCursor(LoadCursor(NULL,IDC_ARROW));
        ReleaseCapture();
        if((leng.x==0) || (leng.y==0))
            break;
```

Figure 9.10 (*Continued*)

```
                        hDC = GetDC(hWnd);
                        hMDC = CreateCompatibleDC(hDC);
                        hBitm = CreateCompatibleBitmap(hDC,abs(leng.x),abs(leng.y));
                        if(hBitm)
                            {
                            SelectObject(hMDC,hBitm);
                            StretchBlt(hMDC,0,0,abs(leng.x),abs(leng.y),\
                                hDC,beg.x,beg.y,leng.x,leng.y,SRCCOPY);
                            OpenClipboard(hWnd);
                            EmptyClipboard();
                            SetClipboardData(CF_BITMAP,hBitm);
                            CloseClipboard();
                            InvalidateRect(hWnd,(LPRECT)NULL,TRUE);
                            }
                        else
                            MessageBeep(0);
                        DeleteDC(hMDC);
                        ReleaseDC(hWnd,hDC);
                        break;
                    default:
                        return(DefWindowProc(hWnd,message,wParam,lParam));
                        break;
                    }
            return(0L);
            }
int IInvert(hWnd,beg,leng)
        HWND hWnd;
        POINT beg,leng;
        {
        HDC hDC;
        hDC = CreateDC("DISPLAY",NULL,NULL,NULL);
        ClientToScreen(hWnd,&beg);
        PatBlt(hDC,beg.x,beg.y,leng.x,leng.y,DSTINVERT);
        DeleteDC(hDC);
        }

BOOL FAR PASCAL IOBox(hBox,message,wParam,lParam)
        HWND        hBox;
        unsigned        message;
        WORD        wParam;
        LONG        lParam;
        {

        switch(message)
            {
            case WM_INITDIALOG:
                SetFocus(GetDlgItem(hBox,ID_ANGLE1));
                break;
            case WM_COMMAND:
                switch(wParam)
                    {
                    case ID_OK:
                        scale1 = GetDlgItemInt(hBox,ID_ANGLE1,(LPSTR)NULL,1);
                        scale2 = GetDlgItemInt(hBox,ID_ANGLE2,(LPSTR)NULL,1);
                        scale3 = GetDlgItemInt(hBox,ID_ANGLE3,(LPSTR)NULL,1);
                        alpha = (float)(scale1)/1000.;
                        beta  = (float)(scale2)/1000.;
                        gamma = (float)(scale3)/1000.;
                        EndDialog(hBox,0);
                        break;
                    case ID_CANCEL:
                        EndDialog(hBox,0);
                        break;
                    default:
                        return FALSE;
                    }
            default:
                return FALSE;
            }
        }
```

Figure 9.10   (*Continued*)

```
BOOL FAR PASCAL PaintBeginWindow(hWnd)
      HWND hWnd;
      {
      HDC hDC,hMDC;
      HPEN hPen;
      HBITMAP hBitm;
      BITMAP bm;
      PAINTSTRUCT ps;

      InvalidateRect(hWnd,(LPRECT)NULL,TRUE);
      hDC = BeginPaint(hWnd,(LPPAINTSTRUCT)&ps);
      hPen = GetStockObject(WHITE_PEN);
      SelectObject(hDC,hPen);

      OpenClipboard(hWnd);
      if(hBitm = GetClipboardData(CF_BITMAP))
          {
          SetCursor(LoadCursor(NULL,IDC_WAIT));
          hMDC = CreateCompatibleDC(hDC);
          SelectObject(hMDC,hBitm);
          GetObject(hBitm,sizeof(BITMAP),(LPSTR)&bm);
          SetStretchBltMode(hDC,COLORONCOLOR);
          StretchBlt(hDC,0,0,xClient,yClient,\
              hMDC,0,0,bm.bmWidth,bm.bmHeight,SRCCOPY);
          SetCursor(LoadCursor(NULL,IDC_ARROW));
          DeleteDC(hMDC);
          }
      else
          SurfacePlot(hDC);                           /* 3D surface plot */
      EmptyClipboard();
      CloseClipboard();
      ValidateRect(hWnd,(LPRECT)NULL);
      EndPaint(hWnd,(LPPAINTSTRUCT)&ps);
      }


int SurfacePlot(hDC)
      HDC hDC;
      {
      extern float xarray[],scaley,scalez;
      int n,nc,nm_count,m1,m;
      extern int yy1,yy2,zz1,zz2;
      float z_start = 25.,y_start = 25.,z_mid = 150.,y_mid = 250.;
      float dy1,dy2,dz1,dz2,xa[5],ya[5],za[5];
      float half_yscale = 250.,half_zscale = 150.;

      ArrayGen();
      rot_mat();
      threeD_graph();

      m1 = 1;
      scaley = half_yscale;
      scalez = half_zscale;
      nm_count = 3*ncount*mcount - (ncount*3 +6);
      for(n = 1;n <= ncount;n++)
          {
          for(m = 1;m <= mcount;m++)
              {
              if(m1 < nm_count)
                  {
                  nc = 3*count;                       /* next y-value */
                  xa[1] = xarray[m1];                 /* 1st y-value grid */
                  ya[1] = xarray[m1+1];
                  za[1] = xarray[m1+2];
                  xa[2] = xarray[m1+3];
                  ya[2] = xarray[m1+4];
                  za[2] = xarray[m1+5];
```

Figure 9.10 (*Continued*)

```
                xa[3] = xarray[m1+nc+3];              /* 2nd y-value grid */
                ya[3] = xarray[m1+nc+4];
                za[3] = xarray[m1+nc+5];
                xa[4] = xarray[m1+nc];
                ya[4] = xarray[m1+nc+1];
                za[4] = xarray[m1+nc+2];

                dy1 = ya[2] - ya[1];                  /* ck rotation */
                dy2 = ya[3] - ya[2];
                dz1 = za[2] - za[1];
                dz2 = za[3] - za[2];
                if((dy1*dz2 - dz1*dy2) > 0)
                    {
                    for(n = 1;n <= 4;n++)             /* scale facet */
                        {
                        za[n] = z_start + (z_mid - za[n]*scalez);
                        ya[n] = y_start + (y_mid + ya[n]*scaley);
                        }
                    for(n = 1;n <= 3;n++)            /* plot 3 of 4 */
                        {
                        yy1 = (int)(ya[n]);
                        yy2 = (int)(ya[n+1]);
                        zz1 = (int)(za[n]);
                        zz2 = (int)(za[n+1]);
                        MoveTo(hDC,yy1,zz1);             /* collapsed y-z */
                        LineTo(hDC,yy2,zz2);
                        }
                    yy1 = (int)(ya[4]);
                    yy2 = (int)(ya[1]);
                    zz1 = (int)(za[4]);
                    zz2 = (int)(za[1]);
                    MoveTo(hDC,yy1,zz1);                 /* 4th segment */
                    LineTo(hDC,yy2,zz2);
                    }
                }
            m1 = m1 + 3;
            }
        }
    }

/* Initialization Module for beginw.c */
/* performed only once at inception */

BOOL FAR PASCAL Window1Init(hInstance)
        HANDLE hInstance;
        {
        WNDCLASS          Window1Class;

        Window1Class.hCursor = LoadCursor(NULL,IDC_ARROW);
        Window1Class.hIcon = LoadIcon(hInstance,(LPSTR)szName);
        Window1Class.lpszMenuName = (LPSTR)szMenuNm;
        Window1Class.lpszClassName = (LPSTR)szName;
        Window1Class.hbrBackground = GetStockObject(BLACK_BRUSH);
        Window1Class.hInstance = hInstance;
        Window1Class.style = CS_HREDRAW | CS_VREDRAW;
        Window1Class.lpfnWndProc = Window1Proc;
        Window1Class.cbClsExtra = 0;
        Window1Class.cbWndExtra = 0;

        RegisterClass((LPWNDCLASS)&Window1Class);
        return TRUE;
        }

/* Performed for every instance of the window */

BOOL FAR PASCAL Window1InitEvery(hInstance,cmdShow)
        HANDLE hInstance;
        int cmdShow;
        {
```

Figure 9.10   (*Continued*)

```
            HWND hWnd;

            hWnd = CreateWindow((LPSTR)szName,
                                (LPSTR)szTitle,
                                WS_TILEDWINDOW,
                                0,0,0,0,
                                (HWND)NULL,
                                (HMENU)NULL,
                                (HANDLE)hInstance,
                                (LPSTR)NULL);
            ShowWindow(hWnd,cmdShow);
            UpdateWindow(hWnd);
            return TRUE;
            }

/* Performed for instances beyond initial */

BOOL FAR PASCAL Window1InitAdd(hInstance,hPrevInstance)
        HANDLE hInstance,hPrevInstance;
        {
        GetInstanceData(hPrevInstance,(PSTR)&setupData,sizeof(SETUPDATA));
        }
```

Figure 9.10 *(Concluded)*

Here

bmType	Specifies type, where for logical bitmaps this must be 0
bmWidth	Width of bitmap in pixels
bmHeight	Height of bitmap in raster lines
bmWidthBytes	Number of bytes in each raster line (must be even)
bmPlanes	Number of color planes
bmBitsPixel	Number of bits to define a pixel
bmBits	Long pointer to array containing bitmap values

In addition to responding to the messages from earlier examples, this program has added responses to

```
WM_SIZE
WM_RBUTTONDOWN
WM_MOUSEMOVE
WM_RBUTTONUP
```

The first of these messages, WM_SIZE, is simply used to store the size of the client area in xClient and yClient. These values will eventually be used to create a blow-up of a selected rectangular area where the contents of the area are stretched to fit the rectangle defined by this client area.

The message WM_RBUTTONDOWN is sent when the right-hand mouse button is pressed. A variable, capture, is checked to see if it is FALSE. If FALSE, this variable is set to TRUE, and the functions SetCapture() and SetCursor() are called. SetCursor() is simply called to change the cursor to a cross. SetCapture() has the form

```
SetCapture(hWnd);
```

where hWnd is a handle to the current window. With this function, all subsequent mouse input [until a ReleaseCapture() is executed] is sent to the window specified by hWnd. If capture is TRUE and block FALSE, the POINT type structure beg is used to load the beginning coordinate values (for the rectangle to be captured) based on MAKEPOINT(). MAKEPOINT() converts a long value into a structure of type POINT.

The next message, WM_MOUSEMOVE, is used to process messages sent to the application during mouse movement. In this case, either captive equal to TRUE or block equal to TRUE results in processing. In the former case, the cursor continues to be specified as a cross. In the latter case, the captured rectangle is dynamically defined as the cursor moves across the client area. Again, MAKEPOINT() is used to define the POINT structure specifying the cursor location, and this is translated into a length value in the x- and y-directions.

When WM_MOUSEMOVE is sent and the window function executes, the function IInvert() is called twice. This function allows the user to glimpse briefly the rectangular area that is being captured. How is this accomplished? IInvert() creates a display context that is the entire display window. Next, the coordinates specified by the structure beg are converted to screen coordinates and PatBlt() called. PatBlt() takes the bit pattern spanning the subtended rectangle specified starting at (beg.x, beg.y) and of length x pixels, leng.x, and y pixels, leng.y, and creates an inverted display image in the overall display context. This appears as a flickering reverse image on the normal context. Since IInvert() is called twice, the normal image is always restored.

Finally, processing for WM_RBUTTONUP completes the execution in response to release of the right-hand mouse button. If block is FALSE, no capture is in process and the button movement is ignored. If block is TRUE, however, it is set to FALSE, the cursor loaded with an arrow, and ReleaseCapture() called. Next, a bitmap is created for the rectangular area subtended by the mouse movement. At this point, the clipboard is loaded with a bitmap of the subtended rectangle starting at absolute coordinates (0, 0). The clipboard has the bitmap stretched if needed. The clipboard is closed and the client rectangle released. Finally, the display context used to create the bitmap for loading into the clipboard is released. The next processing that must take place is an update of the client area in response to the WM_PAINT message.

When the WM_PAINT message is sent, PaintBeginWindow() is called. We have seen the initial features of this function in earlier examples. The call to OpenClipboard(), however, is new. Here the program attempts to open the clipboard and then get clipboard data of type BITMAP. If a bitmap type exists in the clipboard, a handle, hBitm, is created, the cursor set to an effective NULL (wait) mode, and a new display context created with handle hMDC. The bitmap is then stretched to fit the client area from the context pointed to by hMDC to that with handle hDC (the paint context). The call to StretchBlt() accomplishes the stretching and screen painting. The cursor is returned to an arrow and the compatible display context deleted. Finally, the clipboard is emptied and closed. The screen is validated and EndPaint() called. If no bitmap exists in the clipboard, the normal surface plot is displayed and screen capture is allowed. The remaining source code is the same as found in some of the earlier examples. Figure 9.11a illustrates a typical display

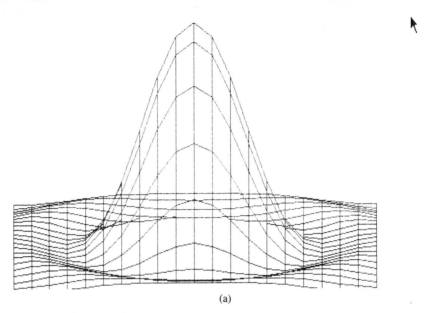

(a)

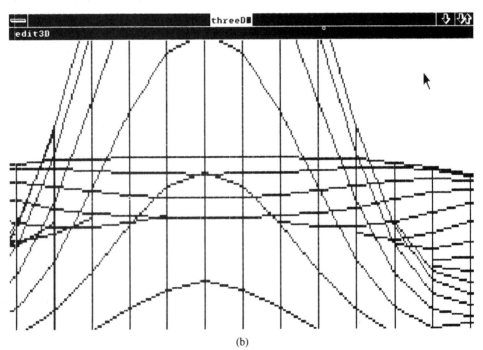

(b)

Figure 9.11 (a) Typical sin(x)/x (squared) output and (b) enlarged portion of surface.

with alpha = gamma = 0 and beta = 1.1 radians (with NN = 7). Figure 9.11b shows a representative blow-up of portions of this surface plot based on the program in Figure 9.10.

The program appearing in Figure 9.10 presents the source code for illustrating various orientations of the $\sin(x)/x$ (squared) surface and subsequent blow-ups of portions of this surface. This code has the portions used for enlarging the displayed image based on similar programming by Petzold [1]. Such universal code is a good illustration of clipboard use (particularly involving bitmaps) and StretchBlt(). In this program, the dialog box represented by IOBox() is called to change the orientation angle values as was done in the previous example. This example is again representative of the flexibility of the Windows environment.

9.3 TEXT I/O

We have already seen the use of text with the Windows function call TextOut(). In general, the subject of text I/O is very complex in the Windows environment. A variety of types, styles, fonts, pitches, and other assorted characterizations are possible with the Windows display capability. We will not delve into text characterization and the interested reader is referred to Petzold [1] for a complete discussion of the Windows text features. We will, however, address one aspect of text I/O: the need to annotate graphical output.

The program appearing in Figure 9.10, which plots and enlarges the $\sin(x)/x$ graphic display, serves as a useful model for implementation of a simple text description. Figure 9.12 illustrates the Windows C code for the program win12.C. This program generates simple text in a box associated with the $\sin(x)/x$ output. The annotation defines the display

```
"sin(x)/x  N=7"
```

and lists the rotation angle values (times 1000) based on user text values corresponding to the ASCII input values for the angles. This is in addition to integer values for the angles, which are used by the program to calculate the rotation in the usual fashion.

In Figure 9.12, the four arrays (TText1[], TText2[], TText3[], and TText4[]) contain written text to be output as descriptive material. The length of these arrays is specified with the variables MAXLENGTH1, . . . , MAXLENGTH4. Three character arrays (INT1[], INT2[], and INT3[]) are used to contain the value of the angles (alpha, beta, and gamma) in ASCII form. These arrays are initialized with "0," "1100," and "0," respectively. (*Note*: All values are multiplied by 1000.) Finally, two arrays (xxa[] and yya[]) have been added. These contain information about the vertices of a box that is to enclose the descriptive material when output to the display. The integers ML2, ML3, and ML4 contain a count of the applicable string length for INT1[], INT2[], and INT3[], respectively. This string length is important because output to the GDI interface results in a blocking character for each nonprintable ASCII character. Hence, only the actual string characters are

```
/* Windows 3D graph program: win3D.c */

#include <windows.h>
#include <menu12.h>

typedef struct
        {
        int dummy;
        }
        SETUPDATA;
static  SETUPDATA setupData;

static HANDLE hInst;
char szMenuNm[5] = {'w','i','n','1','2'};
char szName[5] = {'w','i','n','1','2'};
char szTitle[6] = {'t','h','r','e','e','D'};

char TText1[14] = {'s','i','n','(','x',')','/','x',' ',' ','N','=','7',' '};
char TText2[13] = {'a','l','p','h','a','(','x','1','0','0','0',')','='};
char TText3[12] = {'b','e','t','a','(','x','1','0','0','0',')','='};
char TText4[13] = {'g','a','m','m','a','(','x','1','0','0','0',')','='};

short xClient,yClient;

int MAXLENGTH1 = 14;                                    /* length TTexts */
int MAXLENGTH2 = 13;
int MAXLENGTH3 = 12;
int MAXLENGTH4 = 13;
int ML2=1,ML3=5,ML4=1,MAXLENGTH=6;

char INT1[6] = {'0',' ',' ',' ',' ',' '};
        /* integer text */
char INT2[6] = {'1','1','0','0','0',' '};
char INT3[6] = {'0',' ',' ',' ',' ',' '};

int xxa[5] = {0,50,50,180,180},yya[5] = {0,50,130,130,50};

BOOL FAR PASCAL Window1Init(HANDLE);
BOOL FAR PASCAL Window1InitEvery(HANDLE,int);
BOOL FAR PASCAL Window1InitAdd(HANDLE,HANDLE);
int FAR PASCAL ArrayGen();
int FAR PASCAL threeD_graph();
int FAR PASCAL rot_mat();

long FAR PASCAL Window1Proc(HWND,unsigned,WORD,LONG);
BOOL FAR PASCAL IOBox(HWND,unsigned,WORD,LONG);
BOOL FAR PASCAL PaintBeginWindow(HWND);

float xarray[3072],xx,yy,zz,scalex,scaley,scalez,a[10];
int ncount = 21,mcount = 21,count = 21;
float alpha = 0.0,beta = 1.1,gamma = 0.0;
int yy1,yy2,zz1,zz2,NN = 7;
int scale1,scale2,scale3;

int NEAR PASCAL WinMain(hInstance,hPrevInstance,lpszCmdLine,cmdShow)
        HANDLE hInstance,hPrevInstance;
        LPSTR lpszCmdLine;
        int cmdShow;
        {
        MSG msg;

        if(!hPrevInstance)
            Window1Init(hInstance);
        else
            Window1InitAdd(hInstance,hPrevInstance);
        Window1InitEvery(hInstance,cmdShow);
```

Figure 9.12 Windows source code for sin(x)/x (squared) program, which includes text I/O for parameter box.

```
        while(GetMessage((LPMSG)&msg,NULL,0,0))
            {
            TranslateMessage((LPMSG)&msg);
            DispatchMessage((LPMSG)&msg);
            }
        exit(msg.wParam);
        }
/* Functions which make up Window1 class */

long FAR PASCAL Window1Proc(hWnd,message,wParam,lParam)
        HWND hWnd;
        unsigned message;
        WORD wParam;
        LONG lParam;
        {
        static HWND     hInstance;
        static FARPROC  lpDlgProcedure;
        static POINT beg,leng;
        static BOOL capture,block;
        BITMAP bm;
        HDC hDC,hMDC;
        HBITMAP hBitm;

        switch(message)
            {
            case WM_COMMAND:
                switch(wParam)
                    {
                    case ExitMsg:
                        SendMessage(hWnd,WM_CLOSE,0,0L);
                        break;
                    case EDIT_B:
                        DialogBox(hInstance,"EDITBOX",hWnd,lpDlgProcedure);
                        InvalidateRect(hWnd,(LPRECT)NULL,TRUE);
                        PostMessage(hWnd,WM_PAINT,0,0L);
                    default:
                        break;
                    }
                break;
            case WM_PAINT:
                PaintBeginWindow(hWnd);
                break;
            case WM_DESTROY:
                PostQuitMessage(0);
                break;
            case WM_CREATE:
                hInstance = ((LPCREATESTRUCT)lParam) -> hInstance;
                lpDlgProcedure = MakeProcInstance(IOBox,hInstance);
                break;
            case WM_SIZE:
                xClient = LOWORD(lParam);
                yClient = HIWORD(lParam);
                break;
            case WM_RBUTTONDOWN:
                if(!capture)
                    {
                    capture = TRUE;
                    SetCapture(hWnd);
                    SetCursor(LoadCursor(NULL,IDC_CROSS));
                    }
                else if(!block)
                    {
                    block = TRUE;
                    beg = MAKEPOINT(lParam);
                    }
                break;
```

Figure 9.12 (*Continued*)

```
                        case WM_MOUSEMOVE:
                            if(capture)
                                SetCursor(LoadCursor(NULL,IDC_CROSS));
                            if(block)
                                {
                                leng = MAKEPOINT(lParam);
                                leng.x = leng.x - beg.x;
                                leng.y = leng.y - beg.y;
                                IInvert(hWnd,beg,leng);
                                IInvert(hWnd,beg,leng);
                                }
                            break;
                        case WM_RBUTTONUP:
                            if(!block)
                                break;
                            capture = FALSE;
                            block = FALSE;
                            SetCursor(LoadCursor(NULL,IDC_ARROW));
                            ReleaseCapture();
                            if((leng.x==0) || (leng.y==0))
                                break;
                            hDC = GetDC(hWnd);
                            hMDC = CreateCompatibleDC(hDC);
                            hBitm = CreateCompatibleBitmap(hDC,abs(leng.x),abs(leng.y));
                            if(hBitm)
                                {
                                SelectObject(hMDC,hBitm);
                                StretchBlt(hMDC,0,0,abs(leng.x),abs(leng.y),\
                                    hDC,beg.x,beg.y,leng.x,leng.y,SRCCOPY);
                                OpenClipboard(hWnd);
                                EmptyClipboard();
                                SetClipboardData(CF_BITMAP,hBitm);
                                CloseClipboard();
                                InvalidateRect(hWnd,(LPRECT)NULL,TRUE);
                                }
                            else
                                MessageBeep(0);
                            DeleteDC(hMDC);
                            ReleaseDC(hWnd,hDC);
                            break;
                        default:
                            return(DefWindowProc(hWnd,message,wParam,lParam));
                            break;
                }
            return(0L);
            }
int IInvert(hWnd,beg,leng)
        HWND hWnd;
        POINT beg,leng;
        {
        HDC hDC;
        hDC = CreateDC("DISPLAY",NULL,NULL,NULL);
        ClientToScreen(hWnd,&beg);
        PatBlt(hDC,beg.x,beg.y,leng.x,leng.y,DSTINVERT);
        DeleteDC(hDC);
        }

BOOL FAR PASCAL IOBox(hBox,message,wParam,lParam)
        HWND        hBox;
        unsigned        message;
        WORD        wParam;
        LONG        lParam;
        {

        switch(message)
            {
            case WM_INITDIALOG:
                SetFocus(GetDlgItem(hBox,ID_ANGLE1));
                break;
```

Figure 9.12 (*Continued*)

```
            case WM_COMMAND:
                switch(wParam)
                    {
                    case ID_OK:
                        scale1 = GetDlgItemInt(hBox,ID_ANGLE1,(LPSTR)NULL,1);
                        scale2 = GetDlgItemInt(hBox,ID_ANGLE2,(LPSTR)NULL,1);
                        scale3 = GetDlgItemInt(hBox,ID_ANGLE3,(LPSTR)NULL,1);
                        ML2=GetDlgItemText(hBox,ID_ANGLE11,(LPSTR)INT1,MAXLENGTH);
                        ML3=GetDlgItemText(hBox,ID_ANGLE22,(LPSTR)INT2,MAXLENGTH);
                        ML4=GetDlgItemText(hBox,ID_ANGLE33,(LPSTR)INT3,MAXLENGTH);
                        alpha = (float)(scale1)/1000.;
                        beta = (float)(scale2)/1000.;
                        gamma = (float)(scale3)/1000.;
                        EndDialog(hBox,0);
                        break;
                    case ID_CANCEL:
                        EndDialog(hBox,0);
                        break;
                    default:
                        return FALSE;
                    }
            default:
                return FALSE;
            }
        }


BOOL FAR PASCAL PaintBeginWindow(hWnd)
        HWND hWnd;
        {
        HDC hDC,hMDC;
        HBITMAP hBitm;
        BITMAP bm;
        PAINTSTRUCT ps;

        InvalidateRect(hWnd,(LPRECT)NULL,TRUE);
        hDC = BeginPaint(hWnd,(LPPAINTSTRUCT)&ps);

        OpenClipboard(hWnd);
        if(hBitm = GetClipboardData(CF_BITMAP))
            {
            SetCursor(LoadCursor(NULL,IDC_WAIT));
            hMDC = CreateCompatibleDC(hDC);
            SelectObject(hMDC,hBitm);
            GetObject(hBitm,sizeof(BITMAP),(LPSTR)&bm);
            SetStretchBltMode(hDC,COLORONCOLOR);
            StretchBlt(hDC,0,0,xClient,yClient,\
                hMDC,0,0,bm.bmWidth,bm.bmHeight,SRCCOPY);
            SetCursor(LoadCursor(NULL,IDC_ARROW));
            DeleteDC(hMDC);
            }
        else
            {
            SurfacePlot(hDC);                                    /* 3D surface plot */
            TextOut(hDC,60,60,(LPSTR)TText1,MAXLENGTH1);
            TextOut(hDC,55,70,(LPSTR)TText2,MAXLENGTH2);
            TextOut(hDC,55,90,(LPSTR)TText3,MAXLENGTH3);
            TextOut(hDC,55,110,(LPSTR)TText4,MAXLENGTH4);
            TextOut(hDC,75,80,(LPSTR)INT1,ML2);
            TextOut(hDC,75,100,(LPSTR)INT2,ML3);
            TextOut(hDC,75,120,(LPSTR)INT3,ML4);
            }
        EmptyClipboard();
        CloseClipboard();
        ValidateRect(hWnd,(LPRECT)NULL);
        EndPaint(hWnd,(LPPAINTSTRUCT)&ps);
        }
```

Figure 9.12 (*Continued*)

```
int SurfacePlot(hDC)
    HDC hDC;
    {
    extern float xarray[],scaley,scalez;
    int n,nc,nm_count,m1,m;
    extern int yy1,yy2,zz1,zz2,xxa[],yya[];
    float z_start = 25.,y_start = 25.,z_mid = 150.,y_mid = 250.;
    float dy1,dy2,dz1,dz2,xa[5],ya[5],za[5];
    float half_yscale = 250.,half_zscale = 150.;

    ArrayGen();
    rot_mat();
    threeD_graph();

    m1 = 1;
    scaley = half_yscale;
    scalez = half_zscale;
    nm_count = 3*ncount*mcount - (ncount*3 +6);

    MoveTo(hDC,xxa[1],yya[1]);                          /* label box */
    for(n = 2;n <= 4;n++)
        LineTo(hDC,xxa[n],yya[n]);
    LineTo(hDC,xxa[1],yya[1]);

    for(n = 1;n <= ncount;n++)
        {
        for(m = 1;m <= mcount;m++)
            {
            if(m1 < nm_count)
                {
                nc = 3*count;                           /* next y-value */
                xa[1] = xarray[m1];                     /* 1st y-value grid */
                ya[1] = xarray[m1+1];
                za[1] = xarray[m1+2];
                xa[2] = xarray[m1+3];
                ya[2] = xarray[m1+4];
                za[2] = xarray[m1+5];

                xa[3] = xarray[m1+nc+3];                /* 2nd y-value grid */
                ya[3] = xarray[m1+nc+4];
                za[3] = xarray[m1+nc+5];
                xa[4] = xarray[m1+nc];
                ya[4] = xarray[m1+nc+1];
                za[4] = xarray[m1+nc+2];

                dy1 = ya[2] - ya[1];                    /* ck rotation */
                dy2 = ya[3] - ya[2];
                dz1 = za[2] - za[1];
                dz2 = za[3] - za[2];
                if((dy1*dz2 - dz1*dy2) > 0)
                    {
                    for(n = 1;n <= 4;n++)               /* scale facet */
                        {
                        za[n] = z_start + (z_mid - za[n]*scalez);
                        ya[n] = y_start + (y_mid + ya[n]*scaley);
                        }
                    for(n = 1;n <= 3;n++)               /* plot 3 of 4 */
                        {
                        yy1 = (int)(ya[n]);
                        yy2 = (int)(ya[n+1]):
                        zz1 = (int)(za[n]);
                        zz2 = (int)(za[n+1]);
                        MoveTo(hDC,yy1,zz1);            /* collapsed y-z */
                        LineTo(hDC,yy2,zz2);
                        }
                    yy1 = (int)(ya[4]);
                    yy2 = (int)(ya[1]);
                    zz1 = (int)(za[4]);
                    zz2 = (int)(za[1]);
```

Figure 9.12   (*Continued*)

```
                        MoveTo(hDC,yy1,zz1);              /* 4th segment */
                        LineTo(hDC,yy2,zz2);
                        }
                  }
            m1 = m1 + 3;
            }
      }
}

/* Initialization Module for beginw.c */
/* performed only once at inception */

/* Initialization Module for beginw.c */
/* performed only once at inception */

BOOL FAR PASCAL Window1Init(hInstance)
      HANDLE hInstance;
      {
      WNDCLASS        Window1Class;

      Window1Class.hCursor = LoadCursor(NULL,IDC_ARROW);
      Window1Class.hIcon = LoadIcon(hInstance,(LPSTR)szName);
      Window1Class.lpszMenuName = (LPSTR)szMenuNm;
      Window1Class.lpszClassName = (LPSTR)szName;
      Window1Class.hbrBackground = GetStockObject(WHITE_BRUSH);
      Window1Class.hInstance = hInstance;
      Window1Class.style = CS_HREDRAW | CS_VREDRAW;
      Window1Class.lpfnWndProc = Window1Proc;
      Window1Class.cbClsExtra = 0;
      Window1Class.cbWndExtra = 0;

      RegisterClass((LPWNDCLASS)&Window1Class);
      return TRUE;
      }

/* Performed for every instance of the window */

BOOL FAR PASCAL Window1InitEvery(hInstance,cmdShow)
      HANDLE hInstance;
      int cmdShow;
      {
      HWND hWnd;

      hWnd = CreateWindow((LPSTR)szName,
                        (LPSTR)szTitle,
                        WS_TILEDWINDOW,
                        0,0,0,0,
                        (HWND)NULL,
                        (HMENU)NULL,
                        (HANDLE)hInstance,
                        (LPSTR)NULL);
      ShowWindow(hWnd,cmdShow);
      UpdateWindow(hWnd);
      return TRUE;
      }

/* Performed for instances beyond initial */

BOOL FAR PASCAL Window1InitAdd(hInstance,hPrevInstance)
      HANDLE hInstance,hPrevInstance;
      {
      GetInstanceData(hPrevInstance,(PSTR)&setupData,sizeof(SETUPDATA));
      }
```

Figure 9.12   (*Concluded*)

desired upon output. MAXLENGTH specifies the maximum allowed number of characters in these strings and has been set at 6.

The first modification to the actual executable code appears in the ID__OK switch for IOBox(), the dialog box function used to input angular data. Here, both integer and text I/O takes place. The ID references ID__ANGLE11, ID__ANGLE22, and ID__ANGLE33 have been added, and calls to GetDlgItemText() are used to load the arrays INT1[], INT2[], and INT3[]. Note that the dialog box contains positions for this text to be input, as we will see when the resource file is discussed.

The function PaintBeginWindow() outputs the descriptive text following generation of the plot using SurfacePlot(). The calls to TextOut() reflect the output of this information. We have simplified the operation of this feature by requiring that the user input each angular value twice: once as an integer input and once as text input. This avoids the need to do an open-ended, integer-to-ASCII conversion [2]. We could have added code to convert the initial integer values (scale1, scale2, and scale3) to ASCII strings, but in the interest of simplicity a second text read was installed.

In SurfacePlot(), four lines of code have been inserted to accomplish the drawing of the box around the text material in the GDI environment. This code is

```
...
MoveTo(hDC,xxa[1],yya[1]);
for(n=2;n<=4;n++)
    LineTo(hDC,xxa[n],yya[n]);
LineTo(hDC,xxa[1],yya[1]),
...
```

Figure 9.13a contains the resource file and Figure 9.13b contains the include file menu12.h. We have modified the edit boxes to occupy less space and added three boxes to contain the new angular data in text format. The include file was modified to reflect the new edit box IDs: ID__ANGLE11, ID__ANGLE22, and ID__ANGLE33. Finally, Figure 9.14a contains the MAKE file for win12.exe and Figure 9.14b the definition file win12.def. These files are basically the same as earlier versions, except the new file designations are presented.

9.4 PRINTING WITH WINDOWS

Accessing the printer from Windows is reasonably complex. In this section we treat an example in which a screen image is created. The user then has an option of implementing a screen dump (PrtSc-type operation) that uses StretchBlt() to adjust the screen image size to that of the printer device context (based on a menu selection), if desired. The goal of the discussion is to provide the reader with a knowledge of printer access techniques. This includes the use of banding for partial access of a display context (in this case the screen) using the printer interface. Basically, banding is employed when the printer display context buffer is smaller than the buffer of the display context being output.

Figure 9.15 illustrates the routines PrintPage(), GetPrnDC(), and AbortProc(),

```
#include <windows.h>
#include <menu12.h>

win12    MENU
         BEGIN
            POPUP "edit3D"
                BEGIN
                    MENUITEM "&Angles",        EDIT_B
                    MENUITEM SEPARATOR
                    MENUITEM "&Exit",         ExitMsg
                END
         END

EDITBOX DIALOG  PRELOAD MOVEABLE DISCARDABLE 25,25,300,225
STYLE   WS_POPUP | WS_DLGFRAME
BEGIN
        CONTROL "Alpha (x 1000):",-1,"static",
            SS_LEFT | WS_GROUP, 50,50,60,10
        CONTROL "Beta (x 1000):",-1,"static",
            SS_LEFT | WS_GROUP, 50,80,60,10
        CONTROL "Gamma (x 1000):",-1,"static",
            SS_LEFT | WS_GROUP, 50,110,60,10
        CONTROL "OK" ID_OK,BUTTON,
            BS_PUSHBUTTON | WS_TABSTOP | WS_GROUP, 90,140,45,14
        CONTROL "Cancel" ID_CANCEL,BUTTON,
            BS_PUSHBUTTON | WS_TABSTOP | WS_GROUP, 144,140,45,14
        CONTROL "" ID_ANGLE1,EDIT,
            ES_LEFT | WS_BORDER | WS_TABSTOP | WS_GROUP, 50,61,60,12
        CONTROL "" ID_ANGLE2,EDIT,
            ES_LEFT | WS_BORDER | WS_TABSTOP | WS_GROUP, 50,91,60,12
        CONTROL "" ID_ANGLE3,EDIT,
            ES_LEFT | WS_BORDER | WS_TABSTOP | WS_GROUP, 50,121,60,12
        CONTROL "" ID_ANGLE11,EDIT,
            ES_LEFT | WS_BORDER | WS_TABSTOP | WS_GROUP, 135,61,60,12
        CONTROL "" ID_ANGLE22,EDIT,
            ES_LEFT | WS_BORDER | WS_TABSTOP | WS_GROUP, 135,91,60,12
        CONTROL "" ID_ANGLE33,EDIT,
            ES_LEFT | WS_BORDER | WS_TABSTOP | WS_GROUP, 135,121,60,12
        CONTROL "Text:",-1,"static",
            SS_LEFT | WS_GROUP, 120,50,60,10
        CONTROL "Text:",-1,"static",
            SS_LEFT | WS_GROUP, 120,80,60,10
        CONTROL "Text:",-1,"static",
            SS_LEFT | WS_GROUP, 120,110,60,10
END
```

(a)

```
#define ExitMsg 16
#define PP      30
#define EDIT_B  40
#define ID_ANGLE1       50
#define ID_ANGLE2       60
#define ID_ANGLE3       70
#define ID_OK           80
#define ID_CANCEL       90
#define ID_ANGLE11      110
#define ID_ANGLE22      120
#define ID_ANGLE33      130
```

(b)

Figure 9.13 (a) Resource file illustrating improved controls for text I/O and (b) menu12.h include file.

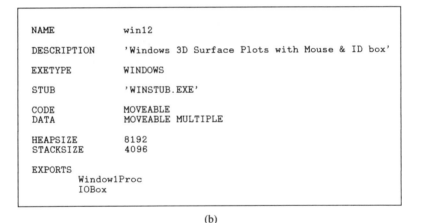

```
# MAKE file for 3D Windows program

win12.obj: win12.c
        cl -c -d -Os -Gsw -Zp -FPa -W3 win12.c

wingrp.obj: wingrp.c
        cl -c -d -Os -Gsw -Zp -FPa -W3 wingrp.c

winggen.obj: winggen.c
        cl -c -d -Os -Gsw -Zp -FPa -W3 winggen.c

winrot.obj: winrot.c
        cl -c -d -Os -Gsw -Zp -FPa -W3 winrot.c

winpt.obj: winpt.c
        cl -c -d -Os -Gsw -Zp -FPa -W3 winpt.c

winsca.obj: winsca.c
        cl -c -d -Os -Gsw -Zp -FPa -W3 winsca.c

win12.res: win12.rc
        rc -r win12.rc

win12.exe: win12.obj win12.def wingrp.obj winggen.obj winrot.obj\
        winpt.obj winsca.obj win12.res
        link4 win12+winggen+wingrp+winrot+winpt+winsca,\
        /align:16,/map,slibw/NOE swinlibc/NOE,win12
        rc win12.res
```

(a)

```
NAME            win12

DESCRIPTION     'Windows 3D Surface Plots with Mouse & ID box'

EXETYPE         WINDOWS

STUB            'WINSTUB.EXE'

CODE            MOVEABLE
DATA            MOVEABLE MULTIPLE

HEAPSIZE        8192
STACKSIZE       4096

EXPORTS
        Window1Proc
        IOBox
```

(b)

Figure 9.14 (a) The MAKE file for win12.exe and (b) the .def file, win12.def.

which are used to output information to a printer device context. Since no specific Windows function addresses printer device contexts, how is a printer device context created? The answer to this question lies in GetPrnDC(), where the Windows function CreateDC() is used to create a device context for the printer based on printer device information obtained from a special Windows initialization file, WIN.INI. The structure of this file follows normal programming practice (see references 1 and 3, for example).

```
/* Function to print page -- Windows */

#include <windows.h>
#include <string.h>

HDC GetPrnDC(void);
BOOL FAR PASCAL AbortProc(HDC,short);

BOOL FAR PASCAL PrintPage(hWnd,hInst)
        HANDLE  hInst;
        HWND    hWnd;
        {
        HDC     hPrnDC,hScDC,hMemDC;
        static char msg[8] = "Printing";
        BOOL EError = FALSE;
        short xP,yP,xS,yS,xB,yB;
        FARPROC lpfnAbortProc;
        RECT    rect;
        HBITMAP hBitmp;

        if((hPrnDC = GetPrnDC()) == NULL)
            return TRUE;
        if(!(RC_BITBLT & GetDeviceCaps(hPrnDC,RASTERCAPS)))
            {
            DeleteDC(hPrnDC);
            return TRUE;
            }
        xP = GetDeviceCaps(hPrnDC,HORZRES);
        yP = GetDeviceCaps(hPrnDC,VERTRES);
        hScDC = CreateDC("DISPLAY",NULL,NULL,NULL);
        xS = GetDeviceCaps(hScDC,HORZRES);
        yS = GetDeviceCaps(hScDC,VERTRES);
        if(!(hBitmp = CreateBitmap(xS,yS,1,1,NULL)))
            {
            DeleteDC(hPrnDC);
            DeleteDC(hScDC);
            return TRUE;
            }

        hMemDC = CreateCompatibleDC(hScDC);
        SelectObject(hMemDC,hBitmp);
        BitBlt(hMemDC,0,0,xS,yS,hScDC,0,0,SRCCOPY);
        DeleteDC(hScDC);

        EnableWindow(hWnd,FALSE);
        lpfnAbortProc = MakeProcInstance(AbortProc,hInst);
        Escape(hPrnDC,SETABORTPROC,0,(LPSTR)lpfnAbortProc,NULL);

        if(Escape(hPrnDC,STARTDOC,strlen(msg),msg,NULL) > 0 &&
            Escape(hPrnDC,NEXTBAND,0,NULL,(LPSTR)&rect))
            {
            while(!IsRectEmpty(&rect))
                {
                (*lpfnAbortProc) (hPrnDC,0);
                xB = rect.right - rect.left;
                yB = rect.bottom - rect.top;

                StretchBlt(hPrnDC,rect.left,rect.top,xB,yB,hMemDC,
                (short)((long)rect.left*xS/xP),(short)((long)rect.top*yS/yP),
                 (short)((long)xB*xS/xP),(short)((long)yB*yS/yP),SRCCOPY);
                (*lpfnAbortProc) (hPrnDC,0);
                if(Escape(hPrnDC,NEXTBAND,0,NULL,(LPSTR)&rect) < 0)
                    {
                    EError = TRUE;
                    return TRUE;
                    }
                }
            }
```

Figure 9.15 Windows print routines for screen bitmaps.

```
            else
                EError = TRUE;
            if(!EError)
                Escape(hPrnDC,ENDDOC,0,NULL,NULL);

            FreeProcInstance(lpfnAbortProc);
            EnableWindow(hWnd,TRUE);
            DeleteDC(hMemDC);
            DeleteDC(hPrnDC);
            DeleteObject(hBitmp);
            return EError;
            }

/* Function to parse WIN.INI for printer DC */

HDC GetPrnDC()
        {
        char    PPrinter[64];
        char *DDevice,*DDriver,*OOutput;

        GetProfileString("windows","device",NULL,PPrinter,64);
        if((DDevice=strtok(PPrinter,","))&&
            (DDriver=strtok(NULL,","))&&
            (OOutput=strtok(NULL,",")))
          return (CreateDC(DDriver,DDevice,OOutput,NULL));
        return FALSE;
        }

/* Function "abort procedure" */

BOOL FAR PASCAL AbortProc(hPrnDC,nCode)
        HDC     hPrnDC;
        short   nCode;
        {
        MSG     msg;

        while(PeekMessage(&msg,NULL,0,0,1))
            DispatchMessage(&msg);
        return TRUE;
        }
```

Figure 9.15 (*Concluded*)

The heart of GetPrnDC() is a call to

```
GetProfileString("windows", "device", NULL, PPrinter, 64);
```

where PPrinter is a pointer to a 64-character buffer, PPrinter[]. The function GetProfileString() has the form

```
GetProfileString(lpAppl, lpKey, lpDefault, lpReturn, nSize)
```

where

lpAppl	= long pointer to a character string naming the application
lpKey	= long pointer to a character string naming the key
lpDefault	= long pointer to a character string to be used if key does not exist
lpReturn	= long pointer to the buffer to receive the string
nSize	= maximum number of bytes to be copied to the buffer

All these definitions are assumed to apply to the WIN.INI structure since this is the file searched by a call to GetProfileString(). The typical format of a WIN.INI entry is

```
[App1]
    ...
    key = string
```

In the printer application, the following entry in the Windows WIN.INI file exists (for the author's system):

```
...
[windows]
; ...
; ...
; ...
DEVICE = Epson FX-80, EPSON, LPT1:
spooler = yes
...
```

Here the semicolons set off comment lines. The call to GetProfileString() indicated above searches for an application named windows and a key named DEVICE (case is important). The string

```
Epson FX-80, EPSON, LPT1:
```

is loaded into PPrinter[].

The creation of the display context requires CreatePC(), which has been discussed somewhat. To reiterate, however, CreateDC() has a format

```
CreateDC(lpDriver, lpDevice, lpOutput, lpInit)
```

where

    lpDriver = long pointer to MS-DOS filename for device driver
    lpDevice = long pointer to ASCII string specifying name of specific device
    lpOutput = long pointer to MS-DOS file or port name
    lpInit   = NULL if device driver requires no initialization

In the case of the printer used in this application,

    lpDriver = EPSON
    lpDevice = Epson FX-80
    lpOutput = LPT1:

The C library function strtok() is used to fragment the string in PPrinter[] into these components and assign them for subsequent use where the CreateDC() call is employed. The return value for CreateDC() is a handle to the created display context (in this case a display context for the printer). Note that a display context is a set of data, maintained by GDI, that describes a graphics device and its driver. This, then, is the procedure used to create a display context for the printer. This is the first active call by PrintPage() when a dump of the screen is to be accomplished (to the printer).

PrintPage() next calls GetDeviceCaps() to check whether the printer device context is suitable for transferring bitmaps. This capability is intrinsically a function of the user's printer and the associated drivers. Assuming the capability for handling bitmaps exists on the resident printer, PrintPage() sets up the horizontal and vertical (*x* and *y* axes) resolution for the printer device context (hPrnDC) and the display device context (hScDC).

Next, a device context compatible with the screen device context is selected and a bitmap associated with this new context (hMemDC). This bitmap is hBitmp. The display bitmap, associated with hScDC, is moved into the bitmap (hBitmp) associated with the compatible display context (hMemDC). The actual printing is accomplished based on the use of Escape() calls. Before considering the structure of these calls, however, we need to introduce the notion of banding. Banding is preferred or needed when the print buffer is insufficient to hold an entire bitmap of the context to be printed. The printer output is then segmented into bands, and printer action occurs until an output band is determined to be empty. Each band must occupy an adjacent bitmap region (to the previously output region). To achieve this, a structure of type RECT must be associated with the banding so that this structure updates its parameters to reflect the new band, following a band output.

How is this banding accomplished for the printer display context? The following structure is employed:

```
...
if(Escape(hPrnDC,STARTDOC,strlen(msg),msg,NULL)>0&&
   Escape(hPrnDC,NEXTBAND,0,NULL,(LPSTR)&rect)
   {
   while(!IsRectEmpty(&rect))
      {
      ... [GDI commands]
      if(Escape(hPrnDC,NEXTBAND,0,NULL,(LPSTR)&rect)<0)
      }
   }
...
```

The first Escape() call informs the device driver for the printer device context (hPrnDC) that a new print job is beginning. This also indicates that all subsequent calls to Escape() with the NEXTBAND option, for example, should be spooled under the same job until an ENDDOC option is encountered. A job name (msg) is required with this call. Note that Windows spools printer output in order to efficiently implement multitasking. (Spooling is the off-line buffering of printer output.)

The call

```
Escape(hPrnDC,NEXTBAND,0,NULL,(LPSTR)&rect)
```

at the end of the while loop processing follows GDI commands in which a band is presumably output to the printer. This call informs the device driver that the I/O is complete and rect (the structure of type RECT) must be updated with the new coordinates of the next band. The while loop conditional checks to see whether or not rect is empty (all structure values equal to 0). If this condition holds, the processing falls through the loop.

In Figure 9.15 the actual output to the screen occurs with the GDI command

```
StretchBlt()(hPrnDC,rect.left,rect.top,xB,yb,hMemDC,
   (short)((long)rect.left*xS/xP),(short)((long)rect.top*ys/
yP),
   (short)((long)xB*xS/xP),(short)((long)yB*yS/yP),SRCCOPY);
```

Note that the parameter values for rect are used in both cases (the printer hPrnDC and the compatible screen image hMemDC). The values xB and yB, for the band, satisfy

$$xB = \text{rect.right-rect.left;}$$
$$yB = \text{rect.bottom-rect.top;}$$

These values specify the extent of the rectangular band. The scaling performed by xS/xP and yS/yP adjusts the screen image dimensions to fit the printer image within the rect band. To see how this is accomplished, consider the x-dimension. Here the screen image is mapped from xB*xS/xP to xB. Assume for simplicity that the rectangle has an x-axis start value of 0. Then StretchBlt() will map the entire screen axis extent into xB, which really spans xP in device coordinates. Thus, we must recognize that xB is defined within the printer display context constraints. (xB is the device equivalent of xP, the printer context limit.)

When StretchBlt() executes, Windows outputs the screen-compatible bitmap for the band to the printer. Following execution of the banding logic, PrintPage() executes a final Escape(), which terminates the document output to the printer. Finally, the display contexts are deleted and the bitmap destroyed prior to returning from PrintPage().

One aspect of the code appearing in PrintPage(), which has not been delineated, is the reference to AbortProc(), the abort function. One problem with the GDI output to the printer is that if this output is large it must be written to disk prior to eventual output to the printer. Remember, we used banding because the print buffer was too small to hold the bitmap. Sometimes the disk can fill up before the spooler has time to dump all a context's print output to the printer. When Windows senses this condition, it looks for an abort function, which can be executed while the spooler continues to output data, hence freeing needed disk space. Windows is informed of the abort function name with the SETABORTPROC Escape() call.

How does this abort function execute? The routine AbortProc() in Figure 9.15 is the abort function for PrintPage(). In the call to AbortProc(), the second formal parameter passes a value 0 if all is going well or an indication of out of disk space if problems arise. This is the nCode value and is used by Windows. The actual code that executes simply mirrors the loop in WinMain(), except a PeekMessage()

call is made rather than a GetMessage(). All messages are then dispatched to Windows. Note that no translation is used. This is because the sequence

```
...
EnableWindow(hWnd,FALSE);
...
EnableWindow(hWnd,TRUE);
...
```

executes in PrintPage(). This sequence disables input from the keyboard and mouse; hence no translations are needed.

Figure 9.16 illustrates the associated resource file (note the file designation

```
#include <windows.h>
#include <menu13.h>

win13   MENU
        BEGIN
            POPUP "Print1"
                BEGIN
                    MENUITEM "P&rint1",      PPrint
                END
            POPUP "edit3D"
                BEGIN
                    MENUITEM "&Angles",      EDIT_B
                    MENUITEM SEPARATOR
                    MENUITEM "&Exit",        ExitMsg
                END
        END

EDITBOX DIALOG  PRELOAD MOVEABLE DISCARDABLE 25,25,300,225
STYLE   WS_POPUP | WS_DLGFRAME
BEGIN
        CONTROL "Alpha (x 1000):",-1,"static",
                SS_LEFT | WS_GROUP, 50,50,60,10
        CONTROL "Beta (x 1000):",-1,"static",
                SS_LEFT | WS_GROUP, 50,80,60,10
        CONTROL "Gamma (x 1000):",-1,"static",
                SS_LEFT | WS_GROUP, 50,110,60,10
        CONTROL "OK" ID_OK,BUTTON,
                BS_PUSHBUTTON | WS_TABSTOP | WS_GROUP, 90,140,45,14
        CONTROL "Cancel" ID_CANCEL,BUTTON,
                BS_PUSHBUTTON | WS_TABSTOP | WS_GROUP, 144,140,45,14
        CONTROL "" ID_ANGLE1,EDIT,
                ES_LEFT | WS_BORDER | WS_TABSTOP | WS_GROUP, 50,61,60,12
        CONTROL "" ID_ANGLE2,EDIT,
                ES_LEFT | WS_BORDER | WS_TABSTOP | WS_GROUP, 50,91,60,12
        CONTROL "" ID_ANGLE3,EDIT,
                ES_LEFT | WS_BORDER | WS_TABSTOP | WS_GROUP, 50,121,60,12
        CONTROL "" ID_ANGLE11,EDIT,
                ES_LEFT | WS_BORDER | WS_TABSTOP | WS_GROUP, 135,61,60,12
        CONTROL "" ID_ANGLE22,EDIT,
                ES_LEFT | WS_BORDER | WS_TABSTOP | WS_GROUP, 135,91,60,12
        CONTROL "" ID_ANGLE33,EDIT,
                ES_LEFT | WS_BORDER | WS_TABSTOP | WS_GROUP, 135,121,60,12
        CONTROL "Text:",-1,"static",
                SS_LEFT | WS_GROUP, 120,50,60,10
        CONTROL "Text:",-1,"static",
                SS_LEFT | WS_GROUP, 120,80,60,10
        CONTROL "Text:",-1,"static",
                SS_LEFT | WS_GROUP, 120,110,60,10
END
```

Figure 9.16   Resource file for win13.exe, illustrating the print menu.

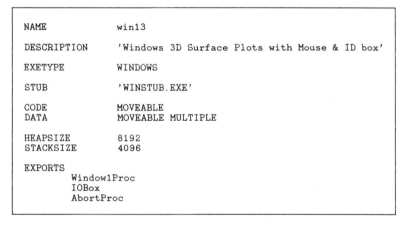

```
# MAKE file for 3D Windows program
win13.obj: win13.c
        cl -c -d -Os -Gsw -Zp -FPa -W3 win13.c

winprt.obj: winprt.c
        cl -c -d -Os -Gsw -Zp -FPa -W3 winprt.c

wingrp.obj: wingrp.c
        cl -c -d -Os -Gsw -Zp -FPa -W3 wingrp.c

winggen.obj: winggen.c
        cl -c -d -Os -Gsw -Zp -FPa -W3 winggen.c

winrot.obj: winrot.c
        cl -c -d -Os -Gsw -Zp -FPa -W3 winrot.c

winpt.obj: winpt.c
        cl -c -d -Os -Gsw -Zp -FPa -W3 winpt.c

winsca.obj: winsca.c
        cl -c -d -Os -Gsw -Zp -FPa -W3 winsca.c

win13.res: win13.rc
        rc -r win13.rc

win13.exe: win13.obj win13.def wingrp.obj winggen.obj winrot.obj\
        winpt.obj winsca.obj winprt.obj win13.res
        link4 win13+winggen+wingrp+winrot+winpt+winprt+winsca,\
        /align:16,/map,slibw/NOE swinlibc/NOE,win13
        rc win13.res
```

(a)

```
NAME            win13

DESCRIPTION     'Windows 3D Surface Plots with Mouse & ID box'

EXETYPE         WINDOWS

STUB            'WINSTUB.EXE'

CODE            MOVEABLE
DATA            MOVEABLE MULTIPLE

HEAPSIZE        8192
STACKSIZE       4096

EXPORTS
        Window1Proc
        IOBox
        AbortProc
```

(b)

Figure 9.17 MAKE file, win13.mak, and (b) the definition file illustrating the exported abort procedure.

win13 for win13.rc). This is the same resource file as appears in Figure 9.13a, except a pop-up menu has been added. This menu displays the designation "Print1" and has an associated ID, PPrint, which appears in menu13.h. Also, this ID corresponds to wParam option in the switch command used to select cases for the WM_ COMMAND message. We have not included win13.c, the main Windows program

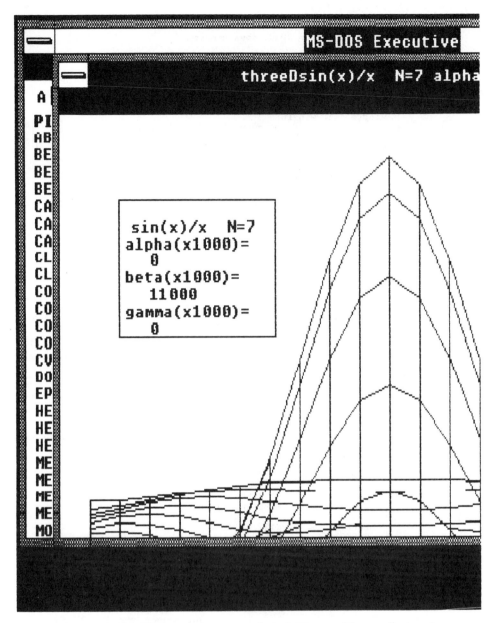

Figure 9.18 Windows print output for win13.exe with no adjustment for 132-character printer width.

for this example, because it is the same as win12.c (Figure 9.12), except for the following code:

```
...
switch (wParam)
    {
    ...
```

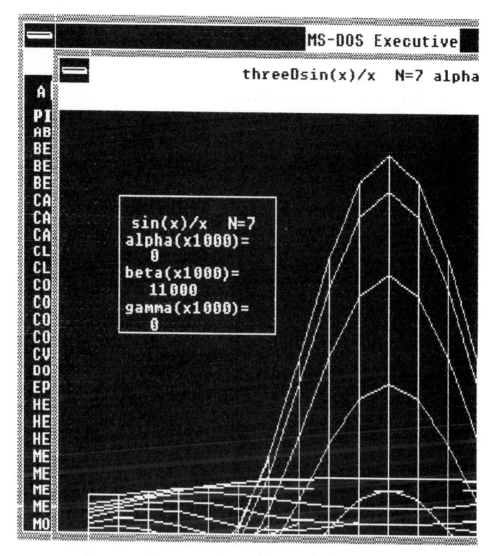

Figure 9.19 Output for Figure 9.18 with SRCINVERT option.

```
case PPrint:
    PrintPage(hWnd,hInst);
    break;
...
```

Here hWnd is the window handle and hInst the instance handle.

Figure 9.17a contains the MAKE file that adds winprt.c (the file appearing in Figure 9.15) to the processing. Figure 9.17b is the associated definition file, which exports the abort function AbortProc(). Figure 9.18 illustrates the printer output for win13.exe when the print menu is executed with a mouse. Figure 9.19 illustrates the same output when the StretchBlt() raster operation is SRCINVERT instead of

```
/* Function to print page -- Windows */

#include <windows.h>
#include <string.h>

HDC GetPrnDC(void);
BOOL FAR PASCAL AbortProc(HDC,short);

BOOL FAR PASCAL PrintPage(hWnd,hInst)
        HANDLE   hInst;
        HWND     hWnd;
        {
        HDC      hPrnDC,hScDC,hMemDC;
        static char msg[8] = "Printing";
        BOOL EError = FALSE;
        short xP,yP,xS,yS,xB,yB;
        FARPROC lpfnAbortProc;
        RECT     rect;
        HBITMAP hBitmp;
        float PrintConv = 80./132.;                    /* 132 char line */

        if((hPrnDC = GetPrnDC()) == NULL)
            return TRUE;
        if(!(RC_BITBLT & GetDeviceCaps(hPrnDC,RASTERCAPS)))
            {
            DeleteDC(hPrnDC);
            return TRUE;
            }
        xP = GetDeviceCaps(hPrnDC,HORZRES);
        xP = (short)((float)(xP)*PrintConv);
        yP = GetDeviceCaps(hPrnDC,VERTRES);
        hScDC = CreateDC("DISPLAY",NULL,NULL,NULL);
        xS = GetDeviceCaps(hScDC,HORZRES);
        yS = GetDeviceCaps(hScDC,VERTRES);

        if(!(hBitmp = CreateBitmap(xS,yS,1,1,NULL)))
            {
            DeleteDC(hPrnDC);
            DeleteDC(hScDC);
            return TRUE;
            }

        hMemDC = CreateCompatibleDC(hScDC);
        SelectObject(hMemDC,hBitmp);
        BitBlt(hMemDC,0,0,xS,yS,hScDC,0,0,SRCCOPY);
        DeleteDC(hScDC);

        EnableWindow(hWnd,FALSE);
        lpfnAbortProc = MakeProcInstance(AbortProc,hInst);
        Escape(hPrnDC,SETABORTPROC,0,(LPSTR)lpfnAbortProc,NULL);

        if(Escape(hPrnDC,STARTDOC,strlen(msg),msg,NULL) > 0 &&
            Escape(hPrnDC,NEXTBAND,0,NULL,(LPSTR)&rect))
            {
            while(!IsRectEmpty(&rect))
                {
                (*lpfnAbortProc) (hPrnDC,0);
                xB = rect.right - rect.left;
                yB = rect.bottom - rect.top;

                StretchBlt(hPrnDC,rect.left,rect.top,xB,yB,hMemDC,
                    (short)((long)rect.left*xS/xP),
                    (short)((long)rect.top*yS/yP),
                    (short)((long)xB*xS/xP),
                    (short)((long)yB*yS/yP),
                    SRCCOPY);
                (*lpfnAbortProc) (hPrnDC,0);
```

Figure 9.20 Windows print routines for screen bitmaps with 132-character printer width adjustment.

```
                    if(Escape(hPrnDC,NEXTBAND,0,NULL,(LPSTR)&rect) < 0)
                        {
                        EError = TRUE;
                        return TRUE;
                        }
                    }
                }
            else
                EError = TRUE;
            if(!EError)
                Escape(hPrnDC,ENDDOC,0,NULL,NULL);

            FreeProcInstance(lpfnAbortProc);
            EnableWindow(hWnd,TRUE);
            DeleteDC(hMemDC);
            DeleteDC(hPrnDC);
            DeleteObject(hBitmp);
            return EError;
            }

/* Function to parse WIN.INI for printer DC */

HDC GetPrnDC()
        {
        char    PPrinter[64];
        char *DDevice,*DDriver,*OOutput;

        GetProfileString("windows","device",NULL,PPrinter,64);
        if((DDevice=strtok(PPrinter,","))&&
            (DDriver=strtok(NULL,","))&&
            (OOutput=strtok(NULL,",")))
            return (CreateDC(DDriver,DDevice,OOutput,NULL));
        return FALSE;
        }

/* Function "abort procedure" */

BOOL FAR PASCAL AbortProc(hPrnDC,nCode)
        HDC     hPrnDC;
        short   nCode;
        {
        MSG     msg;

        while(PeekMessage(&msg,NULL,0,0,1))
            DispatchMessage(&msg);
        return TRUE;
        }
```

Figure 9.20   *(Concluded)*

SRCCOPY. Note that the figure displayed corresponds to the program default figure that displays at the initial execution.

In Figures 9.18 and 9.19, only the left-hand portion of the screen display context actually prints out on the printer. It is clear, however, that the vertical resolution of the display context is correctly imaged on the printer display context. What is the cause of this? The problem lies in the Windows interpretation of the printer display context for an Epson FX-80 printer using the Windows SDK Version 1.03 (which was employed in generating these figures). Essentially, Windows assumes that the printer used with this display context has a 132-character width. This would, for example, be appropriate for generating a reasonable aspect ratio on the printer when compared with the screen.

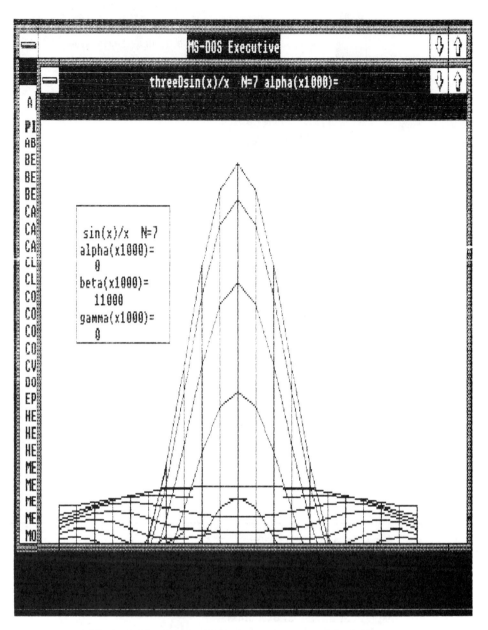

Figure 9.21 Corrected Windows print output for win13.exe.

Figure 9.20 contains a PrintPage() routine modified to scale the printer display context *x*-resolution from 132 to 80 characters. Basically, xP is multiplied by 80/ 132. Figure 9.21 illustrates the resulting output, which now perfectly maps the screen display context into the printer display context. Note that the representation distorts the screen display appearance but is complete; this is a property of the StretchBlt() operation.

SUMMARY

In this chapter we have continued to explore the structured approach to programming represented by Windows [3]. The programming examples presented were compiled and linked under both Versions 1.0 and 2.0 of the SDK. The Windows Executive is a very flexible operating environment and provides the user with a great deal of latitude in program presentation. This chapter highlighted a number of features:

1. User input/output of text
2. User input/output of numerical values
3. Mouse control
4. Passing data among program entities in real time: the clipboard
5. Refocusing the screen image [StretchBlt()]
6. Printing under Windows program control
7. True dialog boxes
8. Menus

The material covered in Chapters 8 and 9 is a suitable introduction to Windows and provides the user with a basis for appreciating the object-oriented approach to achieving user-friendly C programs. One area that was omitted is dynamic library linking, and this is left as an exercise to the reader. It should be emphasized, however, that the dynamic library linking constitutes an advanced feature beyond the introductory topics covered in these chapters. It adds a degree of modularity to Windows programs that enhances ease of programming.

What are some of the disadvantages of Windows? By now it should be apparent that Windows presents the programmer with a significant amount of overhead in order to achieve the user-friendly operating environment. Although not touched upon, Windows provides the programmer with a symbolic debugger, Symdeb. This debugger requires a standard terminal interface over a communications port. Symdeb must be run in this mode because Windows itself requires the complete screen for program I/O. This debugging interface is somewhat cumbersome and could be replaced by a context-switching arrangement for debugging purposes. Windows is a large-scale programming framework and, consequently, the programmer is faced with a substantial amount of material to absorb. This takes time and the user should be prepared to devote this time if he or she hopes to reap the rewards of this rich environment.

REFERENCES

1. Petzold, C., *Programming Windows*, Microsoft Press, Microsoft Corporation, 16011 NE 36th Way, Box 97017, Redmond, WA (1988).
2. Godfrey, J. T., *IBM Microcomputer Assembly Language*: *Beginning to Advanced*, Prentice Hall, Inc., Englewood Cliffs, NJ (1989).

3. Durant, D., G. Carlson, and P. Yao, *Programmer's Guide to Windows*, Sybex, Inc., San Francisco (1987).

PROBLEMS

9.1. What is the difference between a mode and a modeless dialog box?

9.2. In the following control (Figure 9.1b) explain each field:

```
CONTROL "Enter 6 characters:", -1, "static",
    SS_LEFT | WS_GROUP, 20, 6, 80, 12
```

9.3. What is wrong with the following text:

```
...
hDC = BeginPaint(hWnd,(LPPAINTSTRUCT)ps);
TextOut(hDC,932,931,(LPSTR)TText,MAXLENGTH-1);
ValidateRect(hWnd,(LPRECT)NULL);
EndPoint(hWnd,(LPPAINTSTRUCT)ps);
...
```

9.4. What is wrong with the control

```
CONTROL " " ID_ANGLE EDIT,
    ES_LEFT | WS_BORDER | WS_TABSTOP | WS_GROUP 30, 20, 40, 14
```

9.5. What happens in the resource file appearing in Figure 9.1b if menu3.h is omitted? If windows.h is omitted?

9.6. What is wrong with the statement

```
hInstance = (*(LPCREATESTRUCT)lParam).hInstance;
```

instead of

```
hInstance = ((LPCREATESTRUCT)lParam) -> hInstance;
```

9.7. If the Windows programs in this chapter were running under OS/2, what change(s) would need to be made to the definition file?

9.8. For a modal dialog box, how is the linkage established between the dialog box procedure and the call to create the dialog box?

9.9. Suppose the programmer desired to input floating point numbers to a dialog box routine. How could this be accomplished?

9.10. In Figure 9.1a, what is wrong with the following sequence of code:

```
...
case WM_PAINT:
    ValidateRect(hWnd,(LPRECT)NULL);
    PaintBeginWindow(hWnd);
    break;
...
BOOL FAR PASCAL PaintBeginWindow(hWnd)
    HWND hWnd;
    {
    HDC hDC;
    PAINT STRUCT ps;
```

```
hDC = BeginPaint(hWnd,(LPPAINTSTRUCT)&ps);
TextOut(hDC,100,100,(LPSTR)TTextMAXLENGTH-1);
EndPaint(hWnd,(LPPAINTSTRUCT)&ps);
return TRUE;
}
...
```

9.11. In the dialog box routine for Figure 9.7, what would be the effect of using

```
...
alpha = (float)(scale1/1000);
beta = (float)(scale2/1000);
gamma = (float)(scale3/1000);
...
```

9.12. In Figure 9.7, hBox is the handle to a modal dialog box. Where does this handle get defined?

9.13. Why is IOBox exported in Figure 9.8?

9.14. In Figure 9.9a, the link statement of the MAKE file is followed by

```
rc win10.res
```

Why wasn't this specified as

```
rc win10.exe win10.res
```

9.15. In Figure 9.10 what does the function IInvert() accomplish?

9.16. Why isn't the MAKEPOINT operation called under the WM__RBUTTONUP message processing in Figure 9.10?

9.17. What is wrong with the sequence of code

```
...
EmptyClipboard();
OpenClipboard(hWnd);
SetClipboardData(CF_BITMAP,hBitm);
CloseClipboard();
...
```

9.18. In Figure 9.10, what happens if the bitmap of the stretched image cannot be created?

9.19. Why is the function OpenClipboard() called twice in Figure 9.10?

9.20. In Figure 9.12, does the label box get drawn before it is filled with text, or vice versa?

9.21. In Figure 9.15, how is the display context for the printer created?

PART IV
Operating System 2

10

The OS/2 Environment

DOS is a single-user operating system. While it has many advanced features, it fails to take advantage of the multitasking capability offered by the more recent members of the Intel 8086 family of integrated circuits: the 80286 and 80386. As CPU clock rates increase, multitasking becomes a viable candidate for improving system performance. A number of executives have been written to implement multitasking, and Windows, for example, provides the user with the ability to execute multiple instances of programs under the Windows executive. Windows, however, does not use the Protected Mode in its early implementations.

10.1 ARCHITECTURE CONSIDERATIONS

IBM has created Operating System 2 as its first example of a microcomputer operating system that utilizes the Protected Mode capability of the Intel chips. In Section 10.1.2, we discuss the hardware features of the 80286 and 80386 that permit Protected Mode operation. Basically, Protected Mode facilitates isolation of individual processes, thereby allowing multitasking. A major contribution to this multitasking environment is common sharing of system resources. Microsoft developed, in parallel, a version of OS/2, which was released a number of months prior to the IBM version. (The IBM version, known as Standard Edition 1.0, came out in December 1987.) This version employed a DOS-like user interface that allows Protected Mode multitasking and context switching between OS/2 Protected Mode and the OS/2 DOS Compatibility Mode.

Standard Edition 1.0 is IBM's first version of OS/2. The Version 1.1 represents an upgraded operating system that uses the Presentation Manager, a Windows-like user interface. The reader is cautioned, however, to be aware of the greatly expanded capabilities of the Version 1.1 both in user-friendly interface and multitasking. Because of the addressing scheme used to implement Protected Mode, it is necessary to develop special-purpose routines to achieve a proper interface between the relocatable applications code and physical addresses (to be discussed shortly). OS/2 provides these routines through the Applications Program Interface (API), which is discussed in Section 10.1.4. The important point to remember is that these OS/2 Protected Mode service routines allow resource sharing in a multitasking environment. A virtual display, for example, is maintained for each program requiring graphics output. Access of this display is under program control, with the focus shifting depending on the task that exists in the foreground (visible context).

10.1.1 DOS Compatibility Mode and Protected Mode

A prerequisite for using the OS/2 Protected Mode is that application software exists that runs under this mode. In this book, programs are developed for OS/2 Protected Mode using the IBM Macro Assembler/2 [1] and the Microsoft Optimizing C Compiler Version 5.1 [2]. These two system routines permit development of OS/2 Protected Mode software, when coupled with the needed system libraries, application libraries, and linkers. Program development, however, was conducted under DOS since the editors employed were written for this operating system (EDLIN and VEDIT PLUS). This was possible because of the OS/2 DOS Compatibility Mode, which allows most DOS software to be executed in the OS/2 environment. It should be emphasized that the DOS Compatibility Mode and the Protected Mode each constitute different hardware modes for the Intel chips. Within Protected Mode, for example, multiple tasks can execute. Under DOS Compatibility Mode, only a single DOS task is permitted.

Software written for DOS will generally run under OS/2 DOS Compatibility Mode except where the following conditions exist:

1. The software contains specific references to actual memory locations (known as physical memory).
2. The software contains specific references to actual register or port addresses (in a physical sense).

As an example, it is permissible to reference certain interrupts in DOS Compatibility Mode, but direct reference to screen buffer addresses such as BA000H is not allowed. This means that earlier programs developed using screen buffer DMA will not execute within the DOS Compatibility Mode.

In the above discussion, the terminology physical memory and physical (address) were used. This refers to the actual address range that is physically accessible at any point in time. Since there are 24 address pins on the 80286 chip, there exist 2^{24} possible physical locations that can be accessed at any given time. This leads to a physical memory size of 16 Mbyte [3]. An alternate memory, virtual memory, which involves the swapping of program segments to and from external storage, has a limit of 2^{30} or 1 gigabyte with the 80286 architecture.

OS/2 permits rapid context switching between the OS/2 Protected Mode and DOS Compatibility Mode. Hence, program development is not hindered when using

DOS editors. The programmer should think of the two OS/2 modes (Protected Mode and DOS Compatibility Mode) as distinct entities that can easily be invoked under OS/2 and that maintain context, whether running as the primary task (foreground) or switched into a secondary task where they continue to exist but are not visible on the display (background). It should be emphasized that the DOS task is suspended when running in the background. All Protected Mode tasks continue to run regardless of where they are located (foreground or background).

10.1.2 Hardware Characteristics

Multitasking is permitted with the Intel CPU chips (later versions) because a rather stringent protection mechanism exists in the hardware implementation. By invoking this mechanism, the system programmer creates an environment in which each task's context can be preserved and memory partitioned to eliminate overwrites and subsequent destruction of needed information. It is useful to consider the 80286 and 80386 implementation in order to understand the hardware basis for Protected Mode.

The 80286 is a 16-bit microprocessor that has 19 registers, 14 of which are of interest to the general applications programmer. These 14 registers consist of AX, BX, CX, DX, BP, SP, DI, SI, CS, DS, ES, SS, IP, and the flags register, which is clearly the set of registers available for 8088 and 8086 programming. These registers behave in identical fashion to their counterparts in the 8088 and 8086. The remaining five 80286 registers, used with the Protected Mode and multitasking, are as follows:

1. Global descriptor table register (GDTR)
2. Interrupt descriptor table register (IDTR)
3. Local descriptor table register (LDTR)
4. Task register (TR)
5. Machine status word register (MSW)

These Protected Mode registers are used by the operating system to differentiate Real Address Mode (used with the DOS, for example) from Protected Mode operation (the MSW register), to specify the segment address for the task or program currently executing (the TR register), and to specify the location and size of the table defining a local task (LDTR), interrupt routines (IDTR), and the overall system programs (GDTR).

It is important to recognize that we are talking about the Intel 80286 and 80386 when considering OS/2 and Protected Mode. Earlier chips (the 8086 and 8088) do not possess the capability for Protected Mode operation. Hence, only the PC, AT, and PS/2 Models 50, 60, and 80 (as well as the later PS/2 Protected Mode systems) are capable of running under OS/2.

Using memory management, the 80286 can access up to 1 gigabyte. How is this accomplished? The 80286 memory management instructions must be used to set up virtual addressing. In normal 8088 or 8088 addressing, a 16-bit offset is added to a shifted 16-bit segment address to get a 20-bit physical address. In Protected Mode, the segment *selector* has the form

INDEX   TI   RPL

The table indicator bit (TI) defines two separate address spaces,

0 = global addresses
1 = local addresses

The global addresses are used by all tasks in a multitasking environment. Local addresses are only accessible within a single task. Since the INDEX is 13 bits, each address space may subdivide into 2^{13} segments at most. This 13-bit quantity effectively indexes a memory-resident table called a descriptor table. This descriptor table contains the mapping between a segment address and the physical locations. There is a single global descriptor table (GDT) and one or more local descriptor tables (LDT). Each descriptor table entry consists of an 8-byte value where these values are defined as follows:

Byte	Function
0, 1	Limit: Specifies the size of the segment up to 64K
2, 3, 4	Base: Specifies a 24-bit physical base address for the start of the segment
5	Access rights byte: Bit 7: protection present Bits 5–6: descriptor privilege level (0 is most trusted, 3 is least trusted) Bit 4: segment descriptor (1, applications and 0, system) Bit 3: 1, code and 0, data Bit 0–2: protection access
6, 7	These bytes are set equal to 0 to ensure compatibility with 80386-based systems

To generate the physical address from a 32-bit virtual address, the processor selects the GDT or one of the LDTs based on the TI bit and multiplies the INDEX field by 8 to get the descriptor table location. The 24-bit segment base (bytes 2, 3, and 4) is then summed with the 16-bit offset to yield the 24-bit physical address. Clearly, the operating system software must ensure that addressing is properly set up in order to take advantage of a 24-bit segment base and 16-bit offset.

It is important to recognize that segments are still restricted to 64K-size maximums, but movement across 64K boundaries is easily possible using independent modules. The 80286 has protection features using bits 0 through 2 of byte 5 in the descriptor tables, as well as bits 0 and 1 in the segment selector. This protection is necessary in a multitasking environment and ensures isolation of system software from users, isolation of users from each other, and data access by privilege level. Finally, the Protected Mode provides for intersegment calls and a class of control descriptors (8-byte) that facilitates transfer of program execution from one segment to another.

The 80386 is a full 32-bit microprocessor and distinctly different from its earlier 16-bit counterparts (the 8086, 8088, and 80286). The 80386 has separate 32-bit address and data buses and registers. It also incorporates the memory management function as part of its internal architecture. OS/2 is written to maximize efficiency for the 80286 chip architecture. Hence, while the 80386 performs well in the OS/2 environment, it is not optimized for this operating system. To truly take advantage of the 32-bit capability inherent in the 80386, a new operating system candidate must eventually evolve. In the 80386 the segment address calculation is performed, for example, using on-chip address-translation buffer memory (or caches).

Whereas the 80286 employs word arithmetic, the 80386 uses double-word arithmetic. There are eight general registers: EAX, EBX, ECX, EDX, EBP, ESP, ESI, and EDI. Here the prefix E indicates that the familiar 16-bit general registers (AX, BX, . . .) have simply been extended to 32 bits. In fact, the low-order word of each of these eight registers can be treated as the equivalent 16-bit register, with all the reserved name definitions applied to these 16-bit quantities. (They further subdivide, for example, into 8-bit halves, AH, AL, BH, BL, . . .). Clearly, this implies a downward compatibility for running 16-bit microprocessor code.

The instruction pointer (EIP) and flags register (EFLAGS) have similar downward compatibility features. Finally, there are six segment registers: CS, DS, SS, ES, FS, and GS. The last two are new and provide for additional independent data segment access using overrides. These segment registers are each of word length. As with the 80286, many of the architectural features of the 80386 are only used by systems programmers. In addition to the registers specified above, the 80386 has the following:

1. Memory management registers (4): GDTR, LDTR, IDTR, TR (also found in the 80286)
2. Control registers (4): CR0, CR1, CR2, CR3
3. Debug and test registers (8): DR0, DR1, DR2, DR3, DR4, DR5, DR6, DR7

Aside from additional system functions based on new instructions, the 80386 has a significantly improved applications capability over the 80286. This improved capability is due to the presence of the 32-bit architecture, which doubles the significance with which computations can be performed.

The 80386 Protected Mode is conceptually similar to its 80286 counterpart: both perform memory management, enforce protection mechanisms, and provide for multitasking. These are all basically systems programming functions, and the programmer should not expect to use instructions related to the application of these concepts. In defining the 80386 Protected Mode environment, however, we briefly consider these functions from an architectural viewpoint.

80386 memory management has perhaps the most striking Protected Mode modifications from the earlier 80286 architecture. In the 80386 the notions of linear address and paging are introduced. Paging occurs during the second phase of address transformation when a linear address is changed into a physical address. The linear address is obtained from a segment selector and a segment offset. A 16-bit segment selector is used to obtain the 32-bit segment base from a descriptor table. When this 32-bit segment base is added to an offset in an allowed way, the 32-bit linear address is created. A linear address has the form

31	22	12	0
Directory	Page	Offset	

Here OFFSET specifies an offset within a page frame (4096), which is pointed to by PAGE. The page table is, in turn, pointed to by DIRECTORY. Clearly, since each OFFSET is 12 bits long, pages can have at most 4K-byte entries. The page table, however, references an entry that is uniquely specified over a 32-bit field. This entry includes a page frame address, a read–write bit, and other system-oriented bits. Since the PAGE entry consists of a 10-bit field, 1K entries can be specified, but these entries correspond to 32-bit elements. Hence the page table is also a page frame. Finally, the DIRECTORY field can specify up to 1K page table locations. (In Real Address Mode the 80386 has a 21-bit address, not the full 32-bit mapping illustrated here for the Protected Mode.)

In addition to the descriptor table entries used to define FAR addresses, the segmented architecture of the Intel chips provides for a four-word control descriptor. This descriptor is used to redirect a control transfer to different code segments. There are four types of control descriptors, called gates: call, trap, interrupt, and task gates. These gates are distinguished by the form of the access rights byte. Specifically, bits 0 to 2 indicate protection access and are 0, 1, 2, or 3 for normal descriptors. For gates, these bits assume the values

4 Call gate
5 Task gate
6 Interrupt gate
7 Trap gate

The remaining descriptor bytes assume different meanings (when compared with the conventional descriptor). Specifically these bytes take the following forms:

Byte	Function
0, 1	Destination offset
2, 3	Destruction selector
4	Word count to copy from caller's stack
5	Access rights byte
6, 7	Reserved

This completes an examination of the basic Intel chip architectures for Protected Mode. The emphasis has been on register definition and address formation. The 80386 was included because both the 80286 and 80386 run under OS/2, although

OS/2 is optimized for the 80286. The descriptor table provides for the Protected Mode architecture (through appropriate specification in the 8-byte entries).

10.1.3 Threads, Processes, and Protection

The basis unit of reference in OS/2 (or any multitasking system) is a *dispatchable unit*. Associated with each dispatchable unit is a collection of program elements that can execute in self-contained fashion. A *thread* identifies a dispatchable unit of work, and it provides program code with an *execution instance* that differentiates this code from other threads in the system. If a thread is preempted and redispatched, it has precisely the same register and stack data it had before preemption. A *process* is a collection of one or more threads and the needed associated system resources. A characteristic of processes and threads is that, while they frequently have synchronous properties when interfaced, they can be considered as asynchronous during execution. Each process has at least one thread.

OS/2 achieves multitasking by switching the CPU context among the various threads. This sharing of the CPU extends to system resources. OS/2 ensures each process has its own resource parameters preserved during the context switching among threads. Processes are created in a hierarchical structure with a parent able to initialize execution of one or more child processes. Each child can, in turn, extend the process. Synchronous execution suspends the parent, while asynchronous execution allows the parent to continue tasking. OS/2 implements a multilevel priority scheme with dynamic variation and round-robin dispatching. All threads have an assigned priority with those at a similar level equally dispatched. Priority can be changed under program control. The dispatcher is a preemptive time slicer, with each thread getting a fixed period of time during a given dispatch cycle. A rigorous methodology for sharing resources is implemented so that program performance is optimized. Semaphores, pipes, queues, and shared memory are all used to regulate access of data entities among processes and threads in a multitasking environment such as OS/2. We will see some examples of these features in the subsequent program illustrations in the Sections 10.2 and 10.3.

As we have seen, OS/2 is an 80286 multitasking, protection-oriented operating system. Essential to this operating system is the ability to isolate programs from each other and ensure that during execution one task does not overwrite another task's address space (see references 3 and 4). This feature is primarily implemented by the 80286 (and 80386) through Protected Mode operation. Table 10.1 summarizes the protection provided by the 80286.

10.1.4 The Application Program Interface (API)

We have seen how a multitude of system services are accessible under DOS through interrupt service calls. These calls result in the execution of hardware instructions that vector the execution path to appropriate service code. In DOS this was possible by fixing a vector table in memory at the initiation of the boot sequence. OS/2 does not provide for user access to this mechanism and, consequently, a complete new set of OS/2 function calls exists. This set of calls is known as the Application Programming Interface (API).

TABLE 10.1 80286 PROTECTED MODE FEATURES

Feature	Discussion
I/O protection	To help manage I/O activities such as setting/clearing interrupts and port read/writes, the 80286 implements an I/O protection level (IOPL). This flag defines the minimum protection level at which a program must execute to perform I/O. This provides operating system control of the hardware.
Privilege levels	The 80286 provides for four levels of protection: 1. PLO (privilege 0): most trusted, can access data at levels 0, 1, 2, and 3 2. PL1 (privilege 1): can access data at levels 1, 2, and 3 3. PL2 (privilege 2): can access data at levels 2 and 3 4. PL3 (privilege 3): least trusted, can access data at 3
Address protection	Through use of LDTs, each application program is allocated a private memory space. No other tasks are allowed to enter or use a given task's LDT area. Any common memory elements must be shared using the GDT.
Memory attributes	These attributes are specified in the descriptor table access byte. They include such features as read/write access and descriptor privilege level, as well as a flag to indicate execution only (versus addresses associated with variable allocation).

Function calls generally execute code in the system kernel (ring 0 or level 0 of the privilege hierarchy). When OS/2 calls a device driver, for example, it does so with the thread that was executing OS/2. This is the thread that belongs to the client process that made the original service call, the task-time thread. The task-time part of the device driver is then running at ring 0 in the client's context. The client's LDT is active, the addresses are active, and the device driver cannot be preempted by other task-time threads (excluding interrupt service) until it returns to OS/2 or blocks until the device is available [5].

In OS/2, a system service is accessed using the API function calls, which constitute FAR calls to the system. These function calls presuppose that the needed parameters are loaded on the local stack, rather than placed in registers, which is the usual convention for assembler interrupt calls. If OS/2 code using API calls is to be run under DOS Compatibility Mode, the program must be bound using BIND so that API call parameter values are loaded in the appropriate registers before interrupts are executed. The API call format is ideally suited for high-level language (HLL) operation. Table 10.2 illustrates the API functions. Also indicated in this table are the family API functions, which run as a proper subset of API under the DOS Compatibility Mode. These functions basically reflect the properties of INT 21H, INT 10H, and INT 16H.

10.1.5 Dynamic Linking

OS/2 has the feature that applications may be developed and linked without actually having each external reference satisfied by relocation of the entire module (code) associated with the reference. At execution the requisite code is then loaded to

TABLE 10.2 APPLICATION PROGRAMMING INTERFACE ROUTINES

Name	API	FAPI	Description
Tasking			
DosCreateThread	×		Creates asynchronous thread
DosCWait	×		Places current thread in wait state
DosEnterCritSec	×		Disables thread switching
DosExecPgm		×	Allows another program to execute a child
DosExit		×	Issued at completion of execution
DosExitCritSec	×		Reenables thread switching
DosExitList	×		Maintains an exit list for routines
DosGetInfoSeg	×		Returns the address of a data segment
DosGetPrty	×		Gets the priority of the current thread
DosKillProcess	×		Terminates a process
DosPtrace	×		Interface to kernel for debugging
DosSetPrty	×		Changes priority of child process
Asynchronous notification			
DosHoldSignal		×	Changes signal processing
DosSetSigHandler		×	Notifies OS/2 of a handler for a signal
Interprocess communication			
DosCloseQueue	×		Closes a queue
DosCloseSem	×		Closes a semaphore
DosCreateQueue	×		Creates a queue
DosCreateSem	×		Creates a semaphore
DosFlagProcess	×		Allows a process to set an event flag
DosMakePipe	×		Creates a pipe
DosMaxSemWait	×		Blocks until semaphore clears
DosOpenQueue	×		Opens queue
DosOpenSem	×		Opens semaphore
DosPeekQueue	×		Examines element in queue
DosPurgeQueue	×		Purges a queue
DosQueryQueue	×		Finds the size of a queue
DosReadQueue	×		Reads an element from a queue
DosResumeThread	×		Restarts a thread
DosSemClear	×		Clears a semaphore
DosSemRequest	×		Obtains a semaphore
DosSemSet	×		Sets a semaphore
DosSemSetWait	×		Blocks a thread until a semaphore
DosSemWait	×		Waits for a semaphore to clear
DosSuspendThread	×		Temporarily suspends thread execution
DosWriteQueue	×		Adds an element to a queue
Timer			
DosGetDateTime		×	Gets the current date/time
DosSetDateTime		×	Sets the date/time
DosSleep		×	Suspends the current thread
Memory management			
DosAllocSeg		×	Allocates a segment of memory
DosAllocShrSeg	×		Allocates a shared segment
DosAllocHuge		×	Allocates multiple memory segments
DosCreateCSAlias		×	Creates a code segment descriptor
DosFreeSeg		×	Reallocates a memory segment
DosGetHugeShift		×	Returns a shift count for deriving selectors
DosGetShrSeg	×		Accesses shared memory
DosGetSeg	×		Accesses shared memory
DosGiveSeg	×		Yields shared access to another process

TABLE 10.2 (*Continued*)

Name	API	FAPI	Description
DosLockSeg	×		Locks a discardable segment
DosMemAvail	×		Returns size of largest free block
DosReallocHuge		×	Changes huge memory size
DosReallocSeg		×	Changes segment size
DosSubAlloc		×	Allocates from a previous allocated segment
DosSubFree		×	Frees from a previous allocated memory
DosSubSet		×	Initializes a segment
DosUnlockSeg	×		Unlocks a discardable segment
Dynamic linking			
DosFreeModule	×		Frees a dynamic link module
DosGetModHandle	×		Returns handle for dynamic link module
DosGetModName	×		Returns path name for dynamic link module
DosGetProcAddr	×		Returns FAR procedure address
DosLoadModule	×		Loads a dynamic link module
DosGetMachineMode		×	Returns current CPU mode
BadDynLink		×	Error on dynamic link
Device monitors			
DosMonClose	×		Terminates character device monitoring
DosMonOpen	×		Accesses a character device
DosMonRead	×		Moves data
DosMonReg	×		Establishes I/O buffer
DosMonWrite	×		Writes to the monitor's buffer
Session management			
DosStartSession	×		Starts a session
DosStopSession	×		Stops a session
DosSelectSession	×		Allows a parent to switch to a child
DosSetSession	×		Sets child session status
Device I/O services			
DosBeep		×	Beeps speaker
DosCLIAccess	×		Requests privilege for enabling/disabling interrupts
DosDevConfig		×	Gets information about attached devices
DosDevIOCtl		×	Sets up control functions for a specified device
DosGetPID		×	Returns current process ID
DosPFSActivate	×		Specifies the code page and foot to make active
DosPFSCloseUser	×		Indicates the spool file is closed
DosPFSInit	×		Allows initialization of the code page and font
DosPFSQueryAct	×		Queries the active code page and font
DosPFSVerifyFont	×		Indicates validity for the specified code page and font
DosPhysicalDisk	×		Obtains disk information
DosPortAccess	×		Requests or releases port I/O privilege
DosSendSignal	×		Sends a Ctl/c or control-break to process
KbdDeRegister	×		Deregisters a keyboard
KbdCharIn		×	Reads a character
KbdClose	×		Ends the existing logical keyboard
KbdFlushBuffer		×	Clears the keyboard buffer
KbdFreeFocus	×		Frees the logical to physical keyboard bond
KbdGetCp	×		Allows access to the current code page

TABLE 10.2 (*Continued*)

Name	API	FAPI	Description
KbdGetFocus	×		Binds the logical to physical keyboard
KbdGetStatus		×	Gets the state of the keyboard
KbdOpen		×	Creates a new logical keyboard
KbdPeek		×	Returns the last character without clearing the keyboard buffer
KbdRegister	×		Registers a keyboard
KbdSetCp	×		Sets the code page
KbdSetCustXt	×		Installs a code page and calling handle
KbdSetFgnd	×		Raises the priority of the foreground keyboard's thread
KbdSetStatus		×	Sets the keyboard characteristics
KbdStringIn		×	Reads a character string
KbdSynch	×		Synchronizes access for a keyboard to device driver
KbdXlate	×		Translates scan codes to ASCII
MouClose	×		Closes the mouse driver
MouDeRegister	×		Deregisters a mouse device
MouDrawPtr	×		Opens a mouse pointer image to the mouse
MouFlushQue	×		Empties the mouse queue
MouGetDevStatus	×		Returns status flags for the mouse driver
MouGetEvenMask	×		Returns event mask for mouse
MouGetNumButtons	×		Returns number mouse buttons supported
MouGetNumMickeys	×		Returns number of mouse movement units per centimeter
MouGetNumQueEl	×		Returns status for mouse device drive event queue
MouGetPtrPos	×		Gets row and column position of mouse
MouGetPtrShape	×		Gets the pointer shape
MouGetScaleFact	×		Gets the scaling factors for the mouse
MouInitReal	×		Initializes the DOS mode mouse
MouOpen	×		Opens the mouse device
MouReadEventQue	×		Reads an event from the mouse device event queue
MouRegister	×		Registers a mouse
MouRemovesPtr	×		Clears a pointer area from mouse use
MouSetDevStatus	×		Sets mouse status
MouSetEventMask	×		Assigns a new event mask
MouSetPtrPos	×		Resets the row and column position for the mouse
MouSetPtrShape	×		Sets the mouse shape
MouSetScaleFact	×		Assigns the mouse a new pair of scaling factors
MouSynch	×		Synchronizes the mouse
VioDeRegister	×		Deregisters a video subsystem
VioEndPopUp	×		Closes a temporary screen
VioGetAnsi	×		Returns the current ANSI ON/OFF state
VioGetBuf	×		Returns the address of the logical video buffer
VioGetCp	×		Allows a query of the code page
VioGetConfig		×	Returns the display configuration
VioGetCurPos		×	Returns the cursor position
VioGetCurType		×	Returns the cursor type

TABLE 10.2 (*Continued*)

Name	API	FAPI	Description
VioGetFont		×	Returns font
VioGetMode		×	Returns display mode
VioGetPhysBuf		×	Gets addressability to physical display buffer
VioGetState		×	Gets display state
VioModeUndo	×		Changes mode
VioModeWait	×		Allows notification when display must be restored
VioPopUp	×		Allocates a temporary screen
VioPrtSc	×		Copies the screen to printer
VioPrtScToggle	×		Called when Ctrd-PrtSc is entered
VioReadCellStr		×	Reads character-attribute pairs (cells) from screen
VioReadCharStr		×	Reads a character string from the display
VioRegister	×		Registers an alternate video subsystem
VioSaveRedrawUndo	×		Cancels a VioSavRedrawWait
VioSavRedrawWait	×		Notifies a redraw must be performed
VioScrLock		×	Locks the physical display
VioScrollDn		×	Scrolls down
VioScrollUp		×	Scrolls up
VioScrollLf		×	Scrolls left
VioScrollRt		×	Scrolls right
VioScrUnLock		×	Unlocks the physical display
VioSetAnsi	×		Activates or deactivates ANSI support
VioSetCp	×		Sets the code page
VioSetCurPos		×	Sets the cursory position
VioSetCurType		×	Sets the cursor type
VioSetFont		×	Downloads a display font
VioSetMode		×	Sets display mode
VioSetState		×	Sets the display state
VioShowBuf	×		Updates the physical display with the logical
VioWrtCellStr		×	Writes a string of character-attribute cells to display
VioWrtCharStr		×	Writes a character string to display
VioWrtCharStrAtt		×	Writes a repeated attribute string to display
VioWrtNAtt		×	Writes an attribute M times to display
VioWrtNCell		×	Writes a cell M times to the display
VioWrtNChar		×	Writes a character M times to the display
VioWrtTTY		×	Writes a character string to the display
File I/O			
DosBufReset		×	Flushes a requesting process cache buffer
DosChDir		×	Defines the current directory
DosChgFilePtr		×	Moves the read/write pointer
DosClose		×	Closes a file handle
DosDelete		×	Removes a directory entry
DosDupHandle		×	Returns a new file handle for an open file
DosFileLocks		×	Locks and unlocks a range in an open file
DosFindClose		×	Closes the association between directory handles and search functions
DosFindFirst		×	Find the first set of names that match a directory specification
DosFindNext		×	Locates the next set of matching directory entries

TABLE 10.2 *(Concluded)*

Name	API	FAPI	Description
DosMkDir		×	Creates specific directory
DosMove		×	Moves a file
DosNewSize		×	Changes a file size
DosOpen		×	Opens a file
DosQCurDir		×	Gets full path name for current directory
DosQCurDisk		×	Gets the current default drive
DosQFHandState		×	Queries the state of the specified file
DosQFileInfo		×	Returns information for a specific file
DosQFileMode		×	Returns the attributes of a file
DosQFsInfo		×	Queries information from a file system device
DosQHandType		×	Determines whether a handle references file/device
DosQVerify		×	Returns the value of the verify flag
DosRead		×	Reads from a file to a buffer
DosReadAsync	×		Transfers from a file to a buffer asynchronously
DosRunDir		×	Removes a subdirectory
DosScanEnv	×		Searches an environment for a value
DosSearchPath	×		Searches a path for a file name
DosSelectDisk		×	Specifies the default drive
DosSetFHandState		×	Sets the state of a file
DosSetFileInfo		×	Specifies information for a file
DosSetFileMode		×	Changes the attributes of a file
DosSetFsInfo		×	Specifies information for a file system device
DosSetMaxFH	×		Defines a maximum number of file handles
DosSetVerify		×	Sets a verify switch
DosWrite		×	Transfers from a buffer to a file
DosWriteAsync	×		Transfers from a buffer to a file asynchronously
Errors and exceptions			
DosErrClass		×	Returns error code options
DosError		×	Allows the disabling or user notification on errors
DosSetVac		×	Allows address registration for machine exceptions
Messages			
DosGetMessage		×	Retrieves a message from a message file
DosInsMessage		×	Inserts text into message body
DosPutMessage		×	Outputs a message
Trace/program start-up			
DosGetEnv		×	Returns a pointer to the environment string
DosGetVersion		×	Returns the OS/2 version number
Code page support			
DosGetCp		×	Gets the current code page
DosSetCp		×	Sets the current code page
DosSetProcCp	×		Sets the current code page
Country support			
DosCaseMap		×	Case maps country codes to a binary string
DosGetCollate		×	Obtains country information
DosGetCtryInfo		×	Obtains country information
DosGetDBCSEv		×	Obtains country environment vector

satisfy the full external reference. How does OS/2 accomplish this feat? The answer lies in the use of dynamic linking. Dynamic linking requires two types of files:

1. Dynamic-link definition library files (.LIB)
2. Dynamic-link library (.DLL)

The contents of these files contain the names of external references and their associated reference points. The second class of files is the actual modules installed by the loader during the execution sequence. Basically, the source code is assembled or compiled to generate an object module with FAR external references for dynamic-link routines. Similarly, a dynamic-link definition library file is generated similar to the definition file format used with Windows. This is input to the linker and external references satisfied. Once executed, the loader calls the dynamic-link library (.DLL) routines as they are needed in real time.

Load-time dynamic linking requires that all external references be known and specified during program development. A second type of dynamic linking, run-time dynamic linking, is built around several DOS function calls and simply requires reference by name with no definition file specification.

10.1.6 Debugging: CodeView

The CodeView debugger has been modified to run under the Protected Mode of OS/2. Both DOS and OS/2 Protected Mode versions of CodeView are supplied with the IBM Macro Assembler/2 and Microsoft C Optimizing Compiler Version 5.1 used with OS/2 in developing this book. Assuming a file named first.exe exists and has been linked with the OS/2 linker, the Protected Mode CodeView (with no options) call is

```
cvp first.exe
```

The usual DOS Compatibility Mode employs an OS/2 DOS Compatibility Mode version of CodeView with the following call:

```
cv first.exe
```

Both OS/2 CodeView routines are substantially larger than their DOS counterparts, but provide excellent debugging aids both in the OS/2 DOS Compatibility Mode and Protected Mode.

10.2 INTRODUCTORY ASSEMBLY LANGUAGE PROGRAMMING FOR OS/2

This book is about the implementation of a programming language (the C language), rather than about the theory of the language. With this in mind, the current section has been included in the book because of the way in which assembly language reveals the operation of basic program structure. This, also, was the justification for the earlier treatment of assembly language and C prior to examining higher levels of abstraction within the C context. We were exposed earlier to the semantic and programming characteristics of the IBM Macro Assembler. It is now convenient to extend this assembly language treatment into the realm of OS/2 as a precursor to examining C in this environment. The IBM Macro Assembler/2 (reference 1) will be used to accomplish this transition with the illustration of some rather basic Protected Mode assembly language programs.

10.2.1 Creating, Assembling, and Linking

Program creation must be accomplished using a suitable editor. Both EDLIN and VEDIT PLUS were used throughout this book, with most emphasis on the screen editor. The version of VEDIT PLUS used runs under DOS, and context switching between the DOS Compatibility Mode and the Protected Mode was employed following the creation step. The programs were assembled in Protected Mode using the usual responses to assembler interrogatives (see Chapter 5, for example). Next the OS/2 linker was invoked to link the program modules as required. This step involves accessing the Protected Mode library DOSCALLS.LIB, which contains all the entry point references to API routines. The DOSCALLS.LIB library must be entered at link time.

10.2.2 Function-calling Conventions

The OS/2 Technical Reference manuals [6] describe the calling convention for the API and FAPI functions. Typically, these functions are accessed by placing parameter values on the stack, executing the function, and recalling any return value.

A sequence of instructions, for example, that closes a logical keyboard within an OS/2 task might look like

```
...
mov ax, handle          ; load handle in ax
push ax                 ; place handle offset on stack
call far ptr KBDCLOSE   ; call API routine
...
```

Here KBDCLOSE is assumed to represent a far pointer to a dynamic-link routine previously declared with an extrn declaration:

```
extrn KBDCLOSE: FAR
```

IBM has simplified the calling procedure for API and FAPI functions through the use of an include file, subcalls.inc, and another called doscalls.inc. These two files set up the function calls as macros in transparent function form. For example, the above call to KBDCLOSE would appear as

```
...
@kbdClose handle
...
```

where the subcalls.inc macro definition is as follows:

```
;
;
; * KbdClose - Close a logical keyboard
;
;*@KbdClose KbdHandle
;
@KbdClose        macro          handle
                 @define KBDCLOSE
                 @pushw handle
                 call    far ptr   KBDCLOSE
                 endm
```

The two required general-purpose macros are further defined according to

```
;
                      ifndef        @pushw
@pushw                macro         parm
                      mov           ax,parm
                      push          ax
                      endm
                      endif
```

and

```
;
                      ifndef        @define
@define               macro         call name
                      ifndef        call name
                      extrn         callname:far
                      endif
                      endm
                      endif
```

It is clear that these macros, set up within subcalls.inc, will create the needed references to the API and FAPI (doscalls.inc). A third include file comes with the Macro Assembler/2. This file is sysmac.inc and is a master file that sets up both subcalls.inc and doscalls.inc. In program references, only sysmac.inc will be used.

At entry to an initial assembly language module, the following code will be used to load the function call references:

```
        ...
        .sall                     ; suppresses macro printing
IF1
        include   sysmac.inc      ; include API/FAPI files
EMDIF
        ....
```

10.2.3 Getting Started

Figure 10.1 illustrates a very simple Protected Mode program, which merely writes the message

```
This is OS/2 protected mode
```

to the screen in 80 × 25 alphanumeric mode, the default screen mode. The program calls two API/FAPI functions, VioWrtTTY and DosExit. The first of these functions employs three input parameters: a pointer to the message, the length of the message, and the video subsystem handle. For video calls, we always use a handle of zero. The second call terminates OS/2 Protected Mode threads. It is used in place of the RET instruction (note that OS21 is a FAR procedure) and takes as input a completion code for error vectoring and a termination option value.

In this program three segments are defined: STACK, DATA, and CSEG. Figure 10.2 illustrates a slightly expanded version of the program appearing in Figure 10.1. In this latter program, a call to cls takes place so that the screen is

```
PAGE 55,132
TITLE OS2ONE - This is the initial OS/2 program (OS2ONE.ASM)
;
;          DESCRIPTION: This program simply prints a message to the
;          display in protected mode.
;
IF1
           include sysmac.inc
ENDIF
;
           .sall                          ;Suppresses macro lists
dgroup  GROUP   data
;
STACK   SEGMENT PARA STACK 'STACK'
        db      256 dup('STACK    ')
STACK   ENDS
;
DATA    SEGMENT PARA PUBLIC 'DATA'
;
msg_p   db      'This is OS/2 protected mode'
        db      0DH                        ;Carriage return
        db      0AH                        ;Line feed
lmsg_p  equ     $-msg_p
viohdl  equ     0                          ;Required video handle
result  dw      0                          ;Completion code
action  equ     0                          ;Terminates current thread
;
DATA    ENDS
;
CSEG    SEGMENT PARA PUBLIC 'CODE'
        assume cs:cseg,ds:dgroup
OS21    PROC    FAR
;
        @VioWrtTTY msg_p,lmsg_p,viohdl   ;Write msg to screen
        @DosExit action,result           ;Terminate process
;
OS21    ENDP
CSEG    ENDS
        END     OS21
```

Figure 10.1 Simple Protected Mode assembly language program that writes a message to the screen (OS2ONE.ASM).

```
PAGE 55,132
TITLE OS2TWO - This is the initial OS/2 program (OS2TWO.ASM)
;
;          DESCRIPTION: This program simply prints a message to the
;          display in protected mode.
;
IF1
          include sysmac.inc
ENDIF
;
          .sall                              ;Suppresses macro lists
dgroup   GROUP    data
;
STACK    SEGMENT PARA STACK 'STACK'
         db       256 dup('STACK      ')
STACK    ENDS
;
DATA     SEGMENT PARA PUBLIC 'DATA'
;
msg_p    db       'This is OS/2 protected mode'
         db       0DH                        ;Carriage return
         db       0AH                        ;Line feed
lmsg_p   equ      $-msg_p
viohdl   equ      0                          ;Required video handle
result   dw       0                          ;Completion code
action   equ      0                          ;Terminates current thread
tr       dw       0                          ;Top row screen clear
lc       dw       0                          ;Left column screen clear
br       dw       23                         ;Bottom row screen clear
rc       dw       79                         ;Right column screen clear
no_line  dw       25                         ;Number lines scrolled
blank    dw       0007H                      ;Blank character pair
;
DATA     ENDS
;
CSEG     SEGMENT PARA PUBLIC 'CODE'
         assume cs:cseg,ds:dgroup
OS21     PROC     FAR
;
         call cls                            ;Clear screen
         @VioWrtTTY msg_p,lmsg_p,viohdl      ;Write msg to screen
         @DosExit action,result             ;Terminate process
;
OS21     ENDP
;
cls      PROC     NEAR
;
         @VioScrollUp tr,lc,br,rc,no_line,blank,viohdl
                                             ;Call to clear screen
         ret
;
cls      ENDP
;
CSEG     ENDS
         END      OS21
```

Figure 10.2 Slightly more complex version of the program appearing in Figure 10.1. In this example, Protected Mode is illustrated with a screen clear (OS2TWO.ASM).

first cleared before the message is output. The routine cls is defined as a NEAR procedure within CSEG and simply uses the API function VioScrollUp to accomplish the clear operation. Basically, this call scrolls the screen up and writes a screen blank (0007H) out to the display. The scrolling operation occurs from the top row (0) and left column (0) to the bottom row (23) and right column (79). A total of

25 lines is scrolled. In this procedure, a NEAR return must be specified at termination of the procedure and prior to returning to the calling module.

In these two figures we have seen simple examples of the basic Protected Mode programming for OS/2. Instead of the usual calls to interrupts, OS/2 loads a set of references to dynamic-linked library routines. These are accessible through the include file sysmac.inc, which is called at the beginning of each Macro Assembler/2 module during assembly.

10.2.4 Protected Mode Screen Graphics

Figure 10.3 is a somewhat expanded Protected Mode program that places the screen in CGA mode and displays a box on the screen. The same main calling FAR procedure name, OS21, is employed; however, the routine is substantially different from the earlier examples. Initially, a call to cls is performed. Next the VioSetMode function is invoked to place the screen for the current task in CGA mode. The parameters on this call consist of a structure containing the CGA information and a handle. The structure is 12 bytes long with the form

```
        * * *
lmodeE    dw    12
typeCGA   db    00000111B
colCGA    db    2
txtcCGA   dw    40
txtrCGA   dw    25
hrCGA     dw    720
vrCGA     dw    400
        * * *
```

This structure specifies the mode parameters: lmodeE (length of structure block), typeCGA (a special internal mode field), colCGA (color option), txtcCGA (ignore), txtrCGA (ignore), hrCGA (horizontal resolution), and vrCGA (vertical resolution).

Next the routine clsCGA is called. This procedure is NEAR and clears the screen buffer by writing zero attributes to this buffer. First, however, the screen context is locked so that the display buffer may not be written to until all physical transformations are complete. This is done with VioScrLock. Next the *physical* buffer pointer is returned in the structure PVBPtr1; this is called with VioGetPhysBuf. The structure has the following form

```
        * * *
bufst1    dd    0B8000H      ;start address
buflen1   dd    8000H        ;buffer length
physel1   dw    0            ;initial screen selector
```

The resulting screen selector value is placed in the extra segment register to be used to reference the physical screen. This step is distinctly different from running under DOS, where screen DMA would normally be permitted. In the call to VioGet-PhysBuf, the start address was specified as B8000H. The even scan line buffer ends at B9F3FH; hence, zeros are loaded until 1F3FH zeros have been placed in

```
PAGE 55,132
TITLE OS2THREE - This is the third OS/2 program (OS24.ASM)
;
;           DESCRIPTION: This program plots a box in protected
;           mode and hesitates using a keyboard delay. Graphics
;           mode 05H is used to display the box.
;
.8087
PUBLIC  xx,xxx                              ;CodeView symbol map
IF1
        include sysmac.inc
ENDIF
;
        .sall                              ;Suppresses macro lists
dgroup  GROUP   data

STACK   SEGMENT PARA STACK 'STACK'
        db      256 dup('STACK   ')
STACK   ENDS
;
DATA    SEGMENT PARA PUBLIC 'DATA'
;
viohdl  equ     0                          ;Required video handle
result  dw      0                          ;Completion code
action  equ     0                          ;Terminates current thread
tr      dw      0                          ;Top row screen clear
lc      dw      0                          ;Left column screen clear
br      dw      23                         ;Bottom row screen clear
rc      dw      79                         ;Right column screen clear
no_line dw      25                         ;Number lines scrolled
blank   dw      0007H                      ;Blank character pair

CGAm    label   FAR                        ;Video mode structure-CGA
lmodeE  dw      12                         ;Structure length
typeCGA db      00000111B                  ;Mode identifier
colCGA  db      2                          ;Color option-Mode 5
txtcCGA dw      40                         ;text characters/line-ignore
txtrCGA dw      25                         ;text lines-ignore
hrCGA   dw      320                        ;horizontal resolution
vrCGA   dw      200                        ;vertical resolution
;
STDm    label   FAR                        ;Video mode structure-80x25
lmode80 dw      12                         ;Structure length
type80  db      00000001B                  ;Mode identifier-Mode 3+
col80   db      4                          ;Color option
txtc80  dw      80                         ;text characters/line
txtr80  dw      25                         ;text lines
hr80    dw      720                        ;horizontal resolution
vr80    dw      400                        ;vertical resolution
;
kbd_buf db      80                         ;Keyboard buffer
lkbd_buf dw     $-kbd_buf                  ;Length keyboard buffer
iowait  dw      0                          ;Wait for CR
kbdhdl  equ     0                          ;Keyboard handle
;
waitf   equ     1                          ;Screen waiting status
dstat   db      ?                          ;Returned status
;
PVBPtr1 label   FAR                        ;Video buffer structure
bufst1  dd      0B8000H                    ;Start physical address
buflen1 dd      8000H                      ;Buffer length
physel1 dw      0                          ;OS/2 screen buffer selector

MASK1   db      01H                        ;PEL byte mask
MASK11  dw      0001H                      ;Odd/even row mask
OFFSET1 dw      2000H                      ;Odd row buffer offset
four    dw      4
```

Figure 10.3 This Protected Mode assembly language program invokes CGA graphics to display a box on the screen (OS24.ASM).

```
xx          dw      ?                   ;PEL modulo parameter
dummy       dw      ?                   ;80287 dummy "pop"
two         db      2
xxx         db      ?                   ;Output value
eighty      dw      80
row         dw      ?                   ;row
col         dw      ?                   ;column
address     dw      ?                   ;Address screen dot
;
x           dw      ?                   ;Box col parameter
y           dw      ?                   ;Box row parameter
xb          dw      75                  ;Start column
xe          dw      150                 ;End column
yb          dw      25                  ;Start row
ye          dw      175                 ;End row
;
DATA        ENDS
;
CSEG        SEGMENT PARA PUBLIC 'CODE'
            assume cs:cseg,ds:dgroup
OS21        PROC    FAR
;
            call cls                    ;Clear screen
            @VioSetMode CGAm,viohdl     ;Set CGA Graphics mode
            call clsCGA                 ;Clear CGA screen

            @VioScrLock waitf,dstat,viohdl   ;Lock screen context
            @VioGetPhysBuf PVBPtr1,viohdl    ;Get physical buffer selector
            push physel1                ;Save selector
            pop es                      ;Load selector into extra segment
;
            call boxx                   ;Draw box
;
            @VioScrUnLock    viohdl     ;Unlock screen context
;
            @KbdStringIn kbd_buf,lkbd_buf,iowait,kbdhdl    ;hesitate
;
            @VioSetMode STDm,viohdl     ;80 x 25 alpha mode
            @DosExit action,result      ;Terminate process
;
OS21        ENDP
;
boxx        PROC    NEAR
;
;           xb = x-begin,xe = x-end,yb = y-begin,ye = y-end
            mov ax,yb                   ;Top box line
            mov y,ax
            call lineh                  ;Draw top horizontal line
            mov ax,ye                   ;Bottom box line
            mov y,ax
            call lineh                  ;Draw bottom horizontal line
            mov ax,xb                   ;Left box line
            mov x,ax
            call linev                  ;Draw left vertical line
            mov ax,xe                   ;Right box line
            mov x,ax
            call linev                  ;Draw right vertical line
;
            ret
boxx        ENDP
;
cls         PROC    NEAR
;
            @VioScrollUp tr,lc,br,rc,no_line,blank,viohdl
            ret
;
cls         ENDP
;
```

Figure 10.3 (*Continued*)

```
clsCGA    PROC     NEAR
;
          @VioScrLock waitf,dstat,viohdl     ;Lock screen context
          @VioGetPhysBuf PVBPtr1,viohdl      ;Get physical buffer
          push physel1                       ;Screen selector
          pop es                             ;Load extra segment
;
          mov bp,0                           ;Start offset zero
          mov al,0                           ;Zero attribute-clear
DO1:
          mov es:[bp],al                     ;Clear byte
          inc bp
          cmp bp,1F3FH                        ;Check end 1st buffer
          jle DO1
;
          mov bp,2000H                       ;Offset 2nd buffer-odd
          mov al,0                           ;Zero attribute-clear
DO2:
          mov es:[bp],al                     ;Clear byte
          inc bp
          cmp bp,3F3FH                        ;Check end 2nd buffer
          jle DO2
;
          @VioScrUnLock viohdl               ;Unlock screen context
;
          ret
clsCGA    ENDP
;
wdot      PROC     NEAR
;
          (col,row) = (x,y)
;
          fild four                          ;Load stack with 4
          fild col                           ;ST = col, ST(1) = 4
          fprem                              ;Modulo
          fistp xx                           ;Store remainder in xx
          fistp dummy                        ;Pop stack
          mov al,3
          mov bl,byte ptr xx
          sub al,bl                          ;(3 - col % 4)
          mov ah,0                           ;Clear upper multiplicand
          mul two
          mov cl,al                          ;Shift value for PEL
          mov al,MASK1                       ;PEL color mask
          shl al,cl                          ;Shift to correct PEL
          mov xxx,al                         ;Store buffer value

          mov ax,row                         ;Begin address calculation
          shr ax,1                           ;Divide row by 2
          mov dx,0                           ;Clear upper multiplicand
          mul eighty
          mov bx,col                         ;Convert column value to bytes
          shr bx,1
          shr bx,1
          add ax,bx                          ;offset in ax
          mov address,ax                     ;Save offset base
          mov ax,row                         ;Check even/odd row
          and ax,MASK11                      ;Look for bit 0 set
          cmp ax,0
          jle ELSE1
              mov ax,address
              add ax,OFFSET1                 ;add odd buffer offset
              jmp IF11
ELSE1:
          mov ax,address
IF11:
          mov bp,ax                          ;screen buffer address
          mov al,xxx                         ;Attribute value for dot
;
```

Figure 10.3 (*Continued*)

```
                or es:[bp],al                   ;Write dot
        ;
                ret
        wdot    ENDP
        ;
        lineh   PROC    NEAR
        ;
        ;       y = row position, xb = begin, xe = end
        ;
                mov ax,y                         ;Establish row for wdot
                mov row,ax
                                                 ;
                mov ax,xb                        ;Establish start column
        DO10:
                mov col,ax
                push ax                          ;Save column value
                call wdot                        ;Write dot (col,row)
                pop ax                           ;Recall column
                inc ax                           ;Increment column
                cmp ax,xe                        ;Check end horizontal line
                jle DO10
                                                 ;
                ret
        lineh   ENDP
        ;
        linev   PROC    NEAR
        ;
        ;       x = col position, yb = begin, ye = end
        ;
                mov ax,x                         ;Establish column for wdot
                mov col,ax
                                                 ;
                mov ax,yb                        ;Establish start row
        DO20:
                mov row,ax
                push ax                          ;Save row value
                call wdot                        ;Write dot (col,row)
                pop ax                           ;Recall row
                inc ax                           ;Increment row
                cmp ax,ye                        ;Check end vertical line
                jle DO20
                                                 ;
                ret
        linev   ENDP
        ;
        CSEG    ENDS
                END
```

Figure 10.3 *(Concluded)*

the buffer. Next the address is incremented by 2000H, and an additional 1F3FH buffer locations are cleared for the added scan lines. At this point the screen is unlocked, and a return is made to the main calling routine.

The main calling program again locks the screen and gets the physical buffer address. A simple box is drawn with corners at (x, y): {(75, 25), (75, 175), (150, 25), (150, 175)}. The actual lines are drawn with calls to local routines lineh (horizontal line) and linev (vertical line). Each of these procedures sets up the pixel calls to create the lines and calls the procedure wdot. This latter procedure performs the usual vector correlation for the screen write (this is the same as the earlier screen DMA) and writes a byte to the screen. The screen buffer segment address exists in es from the earlier VioGetPhysBuf call.

Once the screen write is complete, the program calls KbdStringIn, looking for keyboard input. This has the effect of causing the system to hesitate while the display is active in CGA mode. Following the striking of any key combination except Ctd-PrtSc, the program resumes execution, the mode of the display is returned to 80 × 25 alpha, and the program is terminated.

Figure 10.4 contains the same set of programs except in modular form. Here OS251.ASM is the main calling module with associated data area and OS252.ASM the supplemental routines. Note that OS252.ASM uses extra declarations to reference the undefined variables, and procedures referenced in OS251.ASM exist as FAR entities. A new procedure, boxx, is defined for creating the box. In both Figures 10.3 and 10.4, the coprocessor is directly called by wdot. Routines needed by the other module are declared PUBLIC in the defining module. OS252.ASM is in Figure 10.5.

This set of programs completes the definition of simple Macro Assembler/2 examples that perform normal Protected Mode functions. We have seen how the API/FAPI calls are used in the OS/2 environment and how program modularity is employed with module OS252.ASM. In the next section, OS252.ASM is linked with another module to create an additional screen graphics example.

10.2.5 Multitasking

OS/2 is intended to be used as a multitasking operating system. The purpose of this section is to illustrate an example of this multitasking based on shared memory [7]. There are other forms of implementing multitasking using semaphores, queues, and pipes. Shared memory, however, is simple to illustrate and easy to understand.

Figure 10.6 is the main calling module for a program that plots 100 boxes in a square on the screen 200 × 200 pixels. The sizes of the boxes are randomly determined based on values placed in shared memory by another task, OS261.ASM. The first task has essentially the same data segment as earlier programs, except for a set of parameters referencing the task to be turned on to generate the random boxes (in this case OS261.ASM). This module will be accessed using the prgm_ nm parameter.

The first statement of the opening procedure is a call to DosAllocShrSeg, which creates a shared segment (global) area of length 404 bytes and returns a selector to this segment, shrsel. Also, a return value of zero in ax indicates successful completion of this operation. The selector address is placed in es. The first two words in the shared memory are loaded with the buffer size (404) and a creation flag (1), respectively. Next the buffer is cleared. Following this step, the program task OS261.ASM is turned on and the two tasks run concurrently. This is accomplished with the function call to DosExecPgm. The creation flag is checked to see if it is zero, and a wait ensues until this takes place. If the program had other parallel activity, it could have been performed at this time.

Once the task OS261.ASM (Figure 10.7) is complete and the random boxes generated, the task appearing in Figure 10.6 loads a local buffer, ESDI, with the shared memory data points. Next the data values are used in pairs to load xb(x-begin), xe(x-end), yb(y-begin), and ye(y-end). Since the values are random, we act to ensure that

$$xb < xe$$

$$xb < ye$$

```
PAGE 55,132
TITLE OS251 - This is the calling OS/2 program (OS251.ASM)
;
;          DESCRIPTION: This program plots a box in protected
;          mode and hesitates using a keyboard delay. Graphics
;          mode 05H is used to display the box. It is the same
;          as OS24 except it uses external modules.
;
.8087
;
EXTRN      boxx:FAR,cls:FAR,clsCGA:FAR
;
PUBLIC     viohdl,tr,lc,br,rc,no_line,blank,CGAm,lmodeE,typeCGA,colCGA
PUBLIC     txtcCGA,txtrCGA,hrCGA,vrCGA,STDm,lmode80,type80,col80
PUBLIC     txtc80,txtr80,hr80,vr80,waitf,dstat,PVBPtr1,bufst1,buflen1,physel1
PUBLIC     MASK1,MASK11,OFFSET1,four,xx,dummy,two,xxx,eighty,row,col
PUBLIC     address,x,y,xb,xe,ye,yb
;
IF1
           include sysmac.inc
ENDIF
;
           .sall                              ;Suppresses macro lists
dgroup     GROUP     data
;
STACK      SEGMENT PARA STACK 'STACK'
           db        256 dup('STACK    ')
STACK      ENDS
;
DATA       SEGMENT PARA PUBLIC 'DATA'
;
viohdl     equ       0                        ;Required video handle
result     dw        0                        ;Completion code
action     equ       0                        ;Terminates current thread
tr         dw        0                        ;Top row screen clear
lc         dw        0                        ;Left column screen clear
br         dw        23                       ;Bottom row screen clear
rc         dw        79                       ;Right column screen clear
no_line    dw        25                       ;Number lines scrolled
blank      dw        0007H                    ;Blank character pair
;
CGAm       label     FAR                      ;Video mode structure-CGA
lmodeE     dw        12                       ;Structure length
typeCGA    db        00000111B                ;Mode identifier
colCGA     db        2                        ;Color option-Mode 5
txtcCGA    dw        40                       ;text characters/line-ignore
txtrCGA    dw        25                       ;text lines-ignore
hrCGA      dw        320                      ;horizontal resolution
vrCGA      dw        200                      ;vertical resolution
;
STDm       label     FAR                      ;Video mode structure-80x25
lmode80    dw        12                       ;Structure length
type80     db        00000001B                ;Mode identifier-Mode 3+
col80      db        4                        ;Color option
txtc80     dw        80                       ;text characters/line
txtr80     dw        25                       ;text lines
hr80       dw        720                      ;horizontal resolution
vr80       dw        400                      ;vertical resolution
;
kbd_buf    db        80                       ;Keyboard buffer
lkbd_buf   dw        $-kbd_buf                ;Length keyboard buffer
iowait     dw        0                        ;Wait for CR
kbdhdl     equ       0                        ;Keyboard handle
;
waitf      equ       1                        ;Screen waiting status
dstat      db        ?                        ;Returned status
;
```

Figure 10.4 This Protected Mode assembly language program is the same as the program appearing in Figure 10.3, except the supporting procedures are called as a separate module (OS251.ASM).

```
PVBPtr1  label  FAR                     ;Video buffer structure
bufst1   dd     0B8000H                 ;Start physical address
buflen1  dd     8000H                   ;Buffer length
physel1  dw     0                       ;OS/2 screen buffer selector
;
MASK1    db     01H                     ;PEL byte mask
MASK11   dw     0001H                   ;Odd/even row mask
OFFSET1  dw     2000H                   ;Odd row buffer offset
four     dw     4
xx       dw     ?                       ;PEL modulo parameter
dummy    dw     ?                       ;80287 dummy "pop"
two      db     2
xxx      db     ?                       ;Output value
eighty   dw     80
row      dw     ?                       ;row
col      dw     ?                       ;column
address  dw     ?                       ;Address screen dot
;
x        dw     ?                       ;Box col parameter
y        dw     ?                       ;Box row parameter
xb       dw     75                      ;Start column
xe       dw     150                     ;End column
yb       dw     25                      ;Start row
ye       dw     175                     ;End row
;
DATA     ENDS
;
CSEG     SEGMENT PARA PUBLIC 'CODE'
         assume cs:cseg,ds:dgroup
OS21     PROC   FAR
;
         call cls                       ;Clear screen
         @VioSetMode CGAm,viohdl        ;Set CGA Graphics mode
         call clsCGA                    ;Clear CGA screen
;
         @VioScrLock waitf,dstat,viohdl ;Lock screen context
         @VioGetPhysBuf PVBPtr1,viohdl  ;Get physical buffer selector
         push physel1                   ;Save selector
         pop es                         ;Load selector into extra segment
;
         call boxx                      ;Draw box
;
         @VioScrUnLock   viohdl         ;Unlock screen context
;
         @KbdStringIn kbd_buf,lkbd_buf,iowait,kbdhdl      ;hesitate
;
         @VioSetMode STDm,viohdl        ;80 x 25 alpha mode
         @DosExit action,result         ;Terminate process
;
OS21     ENDP
;
CSEG     ENDS
         END    OS21
```

Figure 10.4 (*Concluded*)

This loading is accomplished using two new NEAR routines xload and yload. The display then is updated using the 100 random boxes, and the process started to create the random box data is terminated. The shared data segment is released and the program terminated.

Figure 10.7 contains the child process module OS261.ASM. This program simply gets the shared segment (already created by OS2512.ASM, appearing in Figure 10.6), calls a procedure ldmem to load memory with the random data, clears

```
PAGE 55,132
TITLE OS252 - Supplemental routines for box plotting (OS252.ASM)
;
;          DESCRIPTION: These routines set up box plots in CGA
;          mode and hesitate using a keyboard delay. Graphics
;          mode 05H is used to display the box. This set of routines
;          is called by box plotting main routine.
;
.8087
IF1
          include sysmac.inc
ENDIF
;
          .sall                         ;Suppresses macro lists
;
EXTRN     viohdl:WORD,tr:WORD,lc:WORD,br:WORD,rc:WORD
EXTRN     no_line:WORD,blank:WORD,CGAm:FAR,lmodeE:WORD,typeCGA:BYTE
EXTRN     colCGA:BYTE,txtcCGA:WORD,txtrCGA:WORD,hrCGA:WORD,vrCGA:WORD
EXTRN     STDm:FAR,lmode80:WORD,type80:BYTE,col80:BYTE,txtc80:WORD,txtr80:WORD
EXTRN     hr80:WORD,vr80:WORD
EXTRN     waitf:WORD,dstat:BYTE,PVBPtr1:FAR,bufst1:DWORD
EXTRN     buflen1:DWORD,physel1:WORD,MASK1:BYTE,MASK11:WORD,OFFSET1:WORD
EXTRN     four:WORD,xx:WORD,dummy:WORD,two:BYTE,xxx:BYTE,eighty:WORD
EXTRN     row:WORD,col:WORD,address:WORD,x:WORD,y:WORD,xb:WORD,xe:WORD
EXTRN     yb:WORD,ye:WORD
;
CSEG      SEGMENT PARA PUBLIC 'CODE'
PUBLIC    cls,boxx,clsCGA
          assume cs:cseg
boxx      PROC    FAR
;
;         xb = x-begin,xe = x-end,yb = y-begin,ye = y-end
;
          mov ax,xb                     ;Check xb l.t. xe
          cmp ax,xe
          jl ELSE10
              xchg ax,xe                ;Swap xb and xe
              mov xb,ax
ELSE10:
          mov ax,yb                     ;Check yb l.t. ye
          cmp ax,ye
          jl ELSE11
              xchg ax,ye                ;Swap yb and ye
              mov yb,ax
ELSE11:
          mov ax,yb                     ;Top box line
          mov y,ax
          call lineh                    ;Draw top horizontal line
          mov ax,ye                     ;Bottom box line
          mov y,ax
          call lineh                    ;Draw bottom horizontal line
          mov ax,xb                     ;Left box line
          mov x,ax
          call linev                    ;Draw left vertical line
          mov ax,xe                     ;Right box line
          mov x,ax
          call linev                    ;Draw right vertical line
;
          ret
boxx      ENDP
;
cls       PROC    FAR
;
          @VioScrollUp tr,lc,br,rc,no_line,blank,viohdl
          ret
```

Figure 10.5 These Protected Mode assembly language routines are assembled as a separate module and support screen graphics (OS252.ASM).

```
;
cls     ENDP
;
clsCGA  PROC    NEAR
;
        @VioScrLock waitf,dstat,viohdl      ;Lock screen context
        @VioGetPhysBuf PVBPtr1,viohdl       ;Get physical buffer
        push physel1                        ;Screen selector
        pop es                              ;Load extra segment
;
        mov bp,0                            ;Start offset zero
        mov al,0                            ;Zero attribute-clear
DO1:
        mov es:[bp],al                      ;Clear byte
        inc bp
        cmp bp,1F3FH                        ;Check end 1st buffer
        jle DO1
;
        mov bp,2000H                        ;Offset 2nd buffer-odd
        mov al,0                            ;Zero attribute-clear
DO2:
        mov es:[bp],al                      ;Clear byte
        inc bp
        cmp bp,3F3FH                        ;Check end 2nd buffer
        jle DO2
;
        @VioScrUnLock viohdl                ;Unlock screen context
;
        ret
clsCGA  ENDP
;
wdot    PROC    NEAR
;
;       (col,row) = (x,y)
;
        fild four                           ;Load stack with 4
        fild col                            ;ST = col, ST(1) = 4
        fprem                               ;Modulo
        fistp xx                            ;Store remainder in xx
        fistp dummy                         ;Pop stack
        mov al,3
        mov bl,byte ptr xx
        sub al,bl                           ;(3 - col % 4)
        mov ah,0                            ;Clear upper multiplicand
        mul two
        mov cl,al                           ;Shift value for PEL
        mov al,MASK1                        ;PEL color mask
        shl al,cl                           ;Shift to correct PEL
        mov xxx,al                          ;Store buffer value
                                            ;
        mov ax,row                          ;Begin address calculation
        shr ax,1                            ;Divide row by 2
        mov dx,0                            ;Clear upper multiplicand
        mul eighty
        mov bx,col                          ;Convert column value to bytes
        shr bx,1
        shr bx,1
        add ax,bx                           ;offset in ax
        mov address,ax                      ;Save offset base
        mov ax,row                          ;Check even/odd row
        and ax,MASK11                       ;Look for bit 0 set
        cmp ax,0
        jle ELSE1
            mov ax,address
            add ax,OFFSET1                  ;add odd buffer offset
            jmp IF11
ELSE1:
        mov ax,address
```

```
IF11:
            mov bp,ax                        ;screen buffer address
            mov al,xxx                       ;Attribute value for dot
    ;
            or es:[bp],al                    ;Write dot
    ;
            ret
wdot        ENDP
    ;
lineh       PROC    NEAR
    ;
    ;       y = row position, xb = begin, xe = end
    ;
            mov ax,y                         ;Establish row for wdot
            mov row,ax
                                             ;
            mov ax,xb                        ;Establish start column
DO10:
            mov col,ax
            push ax                          ;Save column value
            call wdot                        ;Write dot (col,row)
            pop ax                           ;Recall column
            inc ax                           ;Increment column
            cmp ax,xe                        ;Check end horizontal line
            jle DO10
                                             ;
            ret
lineh       ENDP
    ;
linev       PROC    NEAR
    ;
    ;       x = col position, yb = begin, ye = end
    ;
            mov ax,x                         ;Establish column for wdot
            mov col,ax
                                             ;
            mov ax,yb                        ;Establish start row
DO20:
            mov row,ax
            push ax                          ;Save row value
            call wdot                        ;Write dot (col,row)
            pop ax                           ;Recall row
            inc ax                           ;Increment row
            cmp ax,ye                        ;Check end vertical line
            jle DO20
                                             ;
            ret
linev       ENDP
    ;
CSEG        ENDS
            END     OS21
```

Figure 10.5 (*Concluded*)

the shared memory flag, frees the shared memory segment, and terminates. The routines ldmem is based on the algorithm defined by McCracken [8]:

$$x_{n+1} = (2053x_n + 13,849)\mod 2^{16}$$

This then completes the discussion of Macro Assembler programming in the OS/2 context. We have a basis for comparison of low-level operation under OS/2 with the higher-level C programming. The purpose of the remaining chapter discussion is to address this higher-level C programming in the OS/2 environment.

```
PAGE 55,132
TITLE OS2512 - This is the calling OS/2 program (OS2512.ASM)
;
;          DESCRIPTION: This program plots boxes in protected
;          mode and hesitates using a keyboard delay. Graphics
;          mode 05H is used to display the boxes. It is the same
;          as OS24 except it uses external modules.  This routine
;          employs multitasking to access the input box parameters,
;          which are generated randomly (100 boxes in square 200 x 200).
;
.8087
;
EXTRN    boxx:FAR,cls:FAR,clsCGA:FAR
;
PUBLIC   viohdl,tr,lc,br,rc,no_line,blank,CGAm,lmodeE,typeCGA,colCGA
PUBLIC   txtcCGA,txtrCGA,hrCGA,vrCGA,STDm,lmode80,type80,col80
PUBLIC   txtc80,txtr80,hr80,vr80,waitf,dstat,PVBPtr1,bufst1,buflen1,physel1
PUBLIC   MASK1,MASK11,OFFSET1,four,xx,dummy,two,xxx,eighty,row,col
PUBLIC   address,x,y,xb,xe,ye,yb
;
IF1
         include sysmac.inc
ENDIF
;
         .sall                           ;Suppresses macro lists
dgroup   GROUP   data
;
STACK    SEGMENT PARA STACK 'STACK'
         db      256 dup('STACK    ')
STACK    ENDS
;
DATA     SEGMENT PARA PUBLIC 'DATA'
;
viohdl   equ     0                       ;Required video handle
result   dw      0                       ;Completion code
action   equ     0                       ;Terminates current thread
tr       dw      0                       ;Top row screen clear
lc       dw      0                       ;Left column screen clear
br       dw      23                      ;Bottom row screen clear
rc       dw      79                      ;Right column screen clear
no_line  dw      25                      ;Number lines scrolled
blank    dw      0007H                   ;Blank character pair
;
CGAm     label   FAR                     ;Video mode structure-CGA
lmodeE   dw      12                      ;Structure length
typeCGA  db      00000111B               ;Mode identifier
colCGA   db      2                       ;Color option-Mode 5
txtcCGA  dw      40                      ;text characters/line-ignore
txtrCGA  dw      25                      ;text lines-ignore
hrCGA    dw      320                     ;horizontal resolution
vrCGA    dw      200                     ;vertical resolution
;
STDm     label   FAR                     ;Video mode structure-80x25
lmode80  dw      12                      ;Structure length
type80   db      00000001B               ;Mode identifier-Mode 3+
col80    db      4                       ;Color option
txtc80   dw      80                      ;text characters/line
txtr80   dw      25                      ;text lines
hr80     dw      720                     ;horizontal resolution
vr80     dw      400                     ;vertical resolution
;
kbd_buf  db      80                      ;Keyboard buffer
lkbd_buf dw      $-kbd_buf               ;Length keyboard buffer
iowait   dw      0                       ;Wait for CR
kbdhdl   equ     0                       ;Keyboard handle
;
```

Figure 10.6 This Protected Mode assembly language program employs
multitasking and shared memory to pass 100 random box coordinates from
a generating process. The resulting boxes are displayed (OS2512.ASM).

```
waitf      equ     1                        ;Screen waiting status
dstat      db      ?                        ;Returned status
;
PVBPtr1 label      FAR                       ;Video buffer structure
bufst1  dd         0B8000H                   ;Start physical address
buflen1 dd         8000H                     ;Buffer length
physel1 dw         0                         ;OS/2 screen buffer selector
;
MASK1      db      01H                       ;PEL byte mask
MASK11     dw      0001H                     ;Odd/even row mask
OFFSET1 dw         2000H                     ;Odd row buffer offset
four       dw      4
xx         dw      ?                         ;PEL modulo parameter
dummy      dw      ?                         ;80287 dummy "pop"
two        db      2
xxx        db      ?                         ;Output value
eighty     dw      80
zero       dw      0
one        dw      1
row        dw      ?                         ;row
col        dw      ?                         ;column
address dw         ?                         ;Address screen dot
;
x          dw      ?                         ;Box col parameter
y          dw      ?                         ;Box row parameter
xb         dw      ?                         ;Start column
xe         dw      ?                         ;End column
yb         dw      ?                         ;Start row
ye         dw      ?                         ;End row
;
obj_name_buf    dd     10 dup(0)             ;object name buffer
lobj_name_buf   dw     $-obj_name_buf        ;buffer length
async      dw      1                         ;Flag indicates async
argptr     dw      0                         ;0 for argument ptr
envptr     dw      0                         ;0 for environment ptr
pid        dw      ?                         ;Process ID result code
           dw      ?
prgm_nm db         'OS261.EXE',0             ;program name & parameter
;
shared_length   dw     404                   ;Length shared buffer
shrname db         '\SHAREMEM\SDAT.DAT',0
shrsel  dw         ?                         ;selector
;
ESDI       db      400 dup(?)                ;Buffer for shared data
count      dw      ?                         ;Buffer size in bytes
;
DATA       ENDS
;
CSEG       SEGMENT PARA PUBLIC 'CODE'
           assume cs:cseg,ds:dgroup
OS21       PROC    FAR
;
           @DosAllocShrSeg shared_length,shrname,shrsel
           cmp ax,0                          ;Check on successful creation
           jz NO_ERROR1                      ;Successful
           jmp ERROR1                        ;Error
                                             ;
NO_ERROR1:
;
           push shrsel                       ;Save selector
           pop es                            ;Selector in extra segment
                                             ;
           mov ax,one
           mov es:[2],ax                     ;Flag indicating creation
                                             ;
           mov ax,shared_length              ;Length shared buffer
           mov es:[0],ax                     ;Length parameter passed-multitask
                                             ;
```

Figure 10.6 (*Continued*)

```
            mov di,four                    ;Data record offset in buffer
            mov cx,shared_length           ;Data buffer length + 4
            sub cx,four                    ;Data buffer length
            mov ax,zero                    ;Clear character
lloop:
            mov es:[di],al                 ;Clear buffer
            inc di                         ;Next buffer point
            loop lloop
;
            @DosExecPgm obj_name_buf,lobj_name_buf,async,argptr,envptr,pid,prgm_nm
            cmp ax,0                       ;Check error condition
            jz NO_ERROR2                   ;Jump no error
            jmp ERROR2                     ;Jump error
;
NO_ERROR2:
;
            mov ax,zero                    ;Indicates buffer write complete
;
NO_ERROR22:
;
            cmp es:[2],ax                  ;Check buffer write
            jz MEM_CL                      ;Jump if buffer write complete
            jmp NO_ERROR22                 ;Otherwise wait
;
MEM_CL:
;
            mov si,zero                    ;Offset in intermediate buffer
            mov di,four                    ;Offset in shared buffer
            mov cx,shared_length           ;Length data buffer + 4
            sub cx,four                    ;Length data buffer
            mov count,cx                   ;Data buffer size in bytes
loop22:
            mov al,es:[di]                 ;Obtain shared buffer value
            mov ESDI[si],al                ;Load shared memory buffer
            inc di                         ;Increment shared buffer ptr
            inc si                         ;Increment intermediate buffer ptr
            loop loop22
;
            call cls                       ;Clear screen
            @VioSetMode CGAm,viohdl        ;Set CGA graphics mode
            call clsCGA                    ;Clear CGA screen
            @VioScrLock waitf,dstat,viohdl ;Lock screen context
            @VioGetPhysBuf PVBPtr1,viohdl  ;Get physical buffer selector
            push physel1                   ;Save selector
            pop es                         ;Load selector into extra segment
;
            mov di,0                       ;Intermediate buffer offset
            mov dx,0                       ;Clear upper dividand
            mov ax,count                   ;Data buffer byte count
            div four                       ;Reduce to sets of four
            mov cx,ax                      ;Loop count
loop2:
            push cx                        ;Save loop count
            mov al,ESDI[di]                ;Obtain 1st buffer value-set
            mov ah,ESDI[di+1]              ;Obtain 2nd buffer value-set
            cmp ah,al                      ;Check values equal
            jne EELSE1
                mov al,170                 ;Arbitrarily set 1st equal value
                mov ah,180                 ;Arbitrarily set 2nd equal value
                call xload                 ;Load xb and xe
                jmp IIF1
EELSE1:
            cmp ah,al                      ;Check ah g.t. al
            jle ELSE1
                call xload                 ;Load xb and xe
                jmp IIF1
ELSE1:
            mov bl,al                      ;Swap ah and al
            mov al,ah
```

Figure 10.6   *(Continued)*

Sec. 10.2   Introductory Assembly Language Programming for OS/2   507

```
                mov   ah,bl
                call  xload                    ;Load xb and xe
IIF1:
                mov   al,ESDI[di+2]             ;Obtain 3rd buffer value-set
                mov   ah,ESDI[di+3]             ;Obtain 4th buffer value-set
                cmp   ah,al                     ;Check values equal
                jne   EELSE2
                    mov   al,170                ;Arbitrarily set 1st equal value
                    mov   ah,180                ;Arbitrarily set 2nd equal value
                    call  yload                 ;Load yb and ye
                    jmp   IIF2
EELSE2:
                cmp   ah,al                     ;Check ah g.t. al
                jle   ELSE2
                    call  yload                 ;Load yb and ye
                    jmp   IIF2
ELSE2:
                    mov   bl,al                 ;Swap ah and al
                    mov   al,ah
                    mov   ah,bl
                    call  yload                 ;Load yb and ye
IIF2:
                push  di                        ;Save buffer offset
                call  boxx                      ;Draw box
                pop   di                        ;Recall buffer offset
                add   di,four                   ;Increment data ptr 4 bytes
;
                pop   cx                        ;Recall loop count
                loop  loop2
                @VioScrUnLock   viohdl          ;Unlock screen context
                @KbdStringIn kbd_buf,lkbd_buf,iowait,kbdhdl      ;hesitate
                @VioSetMode STDm,viohdl         ;80 x 25 alpha mode
;
                @DosKillProcess 1,pid           ;Terminate child process
ERROR2:
                @DosFreeSeg shrsel              ;Free shared memory
ERROR1:
                @DosExit action,result          ;Terminate process
;
OS21    ENDP
;
xload   PROC    NEAR
                mov   bh,0                      ;Clear upper register half
                mov   bl,al                     ;al = start
                mov   xb,bx                     ;Load xb less than 199
                mov   bh,0                       ;Clear upper register half
                mov   bl,ah                     ;ah = end
                mov   xe,bx                     ;Load xe less than 199
                ret
xload   ENDP
;
yload   PROC    NEAR
                mov   bh,0                      ;Clear upper register half
                mov   bl,al                     ;al = start
                mov   yb,bx                     ;Load yb less than 199
                mov   bh,0                       ;Clear upper register half
                mov   bl,ah                     ;ah = end
                mov   ye,bx                     ;Load ye less than 199
                ret
yload   ENDP
;
CSEG    ENDS
        END     OS21
```

Figure 10.6 (*Concluded*)

```
PAGE 55,132
TITLE OS261 - Generates multitask r.n. (OS261.ASM)
;
;          DESCRIPTION: This process generates the multitasked
;          random numbers.  It is called by the plot process.
;
.8087
;
IF1
          include sysmac.inc
ENDIF
;
          .sall                                    ;Suppresses macro lists
dgroup  GROUP    data1
;
STACK1   SEGMENT PARA STACK 'STACK'
          db        256 dup('STACK1  ')
STACK1   ENDS
;
DATA1    SEGMENT PARA PUBLIC 'DATA'
;
rnd1     dw       ?                                ;seed value
;
one      dw       1
action   equ      0
result   dw       0
ssize    dw       ?                                ;Buffer size + 4
shrsel   dw       ?                                ;Selector
shrname  db       '\SHAREMEM\SDAT.DAT',0           ;Shared memory name
zero     dw       0
;
DATA1    ENDS
;
CSEG1    SEGMENT PARA PUBLIC 'CODE'
          assume   cs:cseg1,ds:dgroup
OS261    PROC     FAR
;
          mov ax,one                               ;Load initial seed value
          mov rnd1,ax
          @DosGetShrSeg shrname,shrsel             ;Get shared segment
          push shrsel                              ;Save selector
          pop es                                   ;Selector to extra segment
;
          mov ax,es:[0]                            ;Establish shared buffer size
          mov ssize,ax                             ;Define buffer size + 4
;
          mov di,4                                 ;Pointer to data buffer
          mov cx,ssize                             ;Loop byte count + 4
          sub cx,4                                 ;Loop byte count
loop1:
          mov al,0                                 ;Clear buffer
          mov es:[di],al                           ;Buffer write
          inc di                                   ;Increment offset
          loop loop1
                                                   ;
          mov di,4                                 ;Pointer to data buffer
          mov cx,ssize                             ;Loop byte count + 4
          sub cx,4                                 ;Loop byte count
loop2:
          call ldmem                               ;Generate random value
          mov es:[di],al                           ;Load shared buffer (byte)
          inc di                                   ;Increment byte offset
          loop loop2
                                                   ;
          mov ax,zero                              ;Flag indicating write complete
```

Figure 10.7 This Protected Mode assembly language program generates
100 random box coordinates. It passes these coordinates to a multitasked
parent process using shared memory (OS261.ASM).

```
              mov es:[2],ax                    ;Flag loaded
                                               ;
       ;
              @DosFreeSeg shrsel
              @DosExit action,result
                                               ;
       OS261  ENDP
       ;
       ldmem  PROC    NEAR
       ;                                       ;Generate r.n.
              mov dx,0                         ;Load upper multiplicand zero
              mov ax,rnd1                      ;Load previous r.n.
              mov bx,2053                      ;Multiplier
              mul bx
              mov bx,13849                     ;Load additative constant
              clc
              add ax,bx                        ;Add low order result
              adc dx,0                         ;Add carry if needed
              mov bx,0FFFFH                    ;Load 2(16) - 1
              div bx                           ;Calculate modulo
              mov ax,dx                        ;Move remainder into ax
              mov rnd1,ax                      ;Save r.n.
              mov bx,350                       ;Scale r.n. to less than 200
              mov dx,0                         ;Clear upper dividand
              div bx                           ;Scale
              mov ah,0                         ;Save al
              ret
       ldmem  ENDP
       ;
       CSEG1  ENDS
              END     OS261
```

Figure 10.7 (*Concluded*)

10.3 PROTECTED MODE AND C PROGRAMMING

The Microsoft C Optimizing Compiler Version 5.1 allows C programmers to write code that will run under OS/2 Protected Mode. In this book we are specifically concerned with the Standard Edition Version 1.0 of IBM's OS/2. Throughout the book we have emphasized a mix of both low- and high-level implementations for the C programming examples and techniques illustrated. For example, when using the Microsoft C Compiler Version 4.0, low-level graphics techniques were needed to provide the interface between C and the IBM hardware capability. Later, when the Microsoft C Optimizing Compiler Version 5.0 was introduced, higher-level graphic primitives became available, which facilitated using the graphics mode. This was based on using the DOS environment. With OS/2 and the Protected Mode, the techniques of the previous section on assembly language, for example, apply and hardware access requiring the use of physical buffers must now be accomplished through the API functional interface. Hence, we will use the earlier low-level techniques combined with the more abstract Protected Mode API functions [when compared with int86()] to achieve the same sorts of hardware access achieved in the earlier chapters.

The Version 5.1 neglects to provide the high-level reentrant graphics primitives that we found so useful for the earlier examples. Thus, we resort to the lower-level techniques of the Version 4.0 compiler (used in the earlier chapters), except

TABLE 10.3 FUNCTIONS SUPPORTED IN REAL MODE ONLY

bdos	_dos_creat	_dos_getvect	_enable
_bios_disk	_dos_creatnew	_dos_keep	_harderr
_bios_equiplist	dosexterr	_dos_open	_hardresume
_bios_keybrd	_dos_findfirst	_dos_read	_hardretn
_bios_memsize	_dos_findnext	_dos_setblock	inp
_bios_printer	_dos_freemem	_dos_setdate	inpw
_bios_serialcom	_dos_getdate	_dos_setdrive	int86
_bios_timeofday	_dos_getdiskfree	_dos_setfileattr	int86x
_chain_intr	_dos_getdrive	_dos_setftime	intdos
_disable	_dos_getfileattr	_dos_settime	intdosx
_dos_allocmem	_dos_getftime	_dos_setvect	outp
_dos_close	_dos_gettime	_dos_write	outpw

we use them with the OS/2 Protected Mode API reference calls. This allows graphics manipulation using OS/2.

Table 10.3 illustrates the conventional Microsoft C Compiler Real-Time Library functions supported only in Real Mode. The majority of the Microsoft C Optimizing Compiler Version 5.1 Real-Time Library functions that are supported are not reentrant and can only be used with one thread at a time. Table 10.4 presents those functions that are reentrant and can be called by multiple threads. This yields a slightly cumbersome operating environment when contrasted with the DOS Version 5.0 compiler: the price, however, provides full Protected Mode capability. As with our earlier emphasis, we will focus on the graphics interface because this is a highly visual and intuitive set of hardware access modes. It fully demonstrates the needed technique for accessing the system hardware in Protected Mode and serves as a model for understanding how to use the API function calls in the C environment.

10.3.1 Protected Mode C Compiler

This section briefly discusses the Microsoft C Optimizing Compiler Version 5.1 system software. The compiler is invoked in a fashion similar to the Version 5.0 compiler. For example, to get a compiled version of a C program, clss.c, the following command would suffice:

```
cl /c    /Faclss.lst \os2c\clss.c
```

TABLE 10.4 REENTRANT FUNCTIONS

abs	labs	memset	strcmpi	strnset
atoi	lfind	mkdir	strcpy	strrchr
atol	lsearch	movedata	stricmp	strrev
bsearch	memccpy	putch	strlen	strset
chdir	memchr	rmdir	strlwr	strstr
getpid	memcmp	segread	strncat	strupr
halloc	memcpy	strcat	strncmp	swab
hfree	memicmp	strchr	strncpy	tolower
itoa	memmove	strcmp	strnicmp	toupper

Here the switch /Fa causes a list file in assembly language format to be generated and clss.c resides in the subdirectory os2c.

The compiler comes with all the needed include files, linkers, and two copies of CodeView: one for Real Mode and one for Protected Mode. Both the Protected Mode linker and the Real Mode linker can be installed jointly or either one installed individually. Microsoft recommends two executable file directories, BIN and BINP, to differentiate the two software packages. The include file graph.h does not operate under Protected Mode as discussed earlier. Two new include files, doscalls.h. and subcalls.h, are provided with the access to the API functions (and FAPI functions). An additional global include file, doscall.h, loads both of these files.

Microsoft does not provide the API libraries needed to access the Protected Mode functions. In this book we use the libraries that come with the IBM Programmer's Toolkit, which were used earlier with the IBM Macro Assembler/2. The doscall.h include file sets up the linkages for proper calling of the API routines from C programs. It is necessary to list the include files, doscalls.h and subcalls.h, to see how Microsoft has implemented the parameters used with each API call. Note that this convention is similar to the macro calls used with the sysmac.inc in the assembler implementation. The user must implement the correct association for each parameter when calling API functions from the Version 5.1 C code. An additional caveat is needed regarding the form of the calls: the Microsoft C is case sensitive, but the IBM Programmer Toolkit implementation uses uppercase. Hence, reference to the Toolkit routines should be uppercase.

The following reference illustrates the Microsoft include declaration for DOS exit:

```
extern void far pascal DOSEXIT (unsigned, unsigned);
```

where the first unsigned parameter is 0 to end the current thread and 1 to end all threads. Similarly, the second unsigned parameter is a Result Code to save for final exit. As indicated, the programmer will need to set up each function call in accordance with these Microsoft declarations. The declarations will be standardized on the OS/2 calling format for the API (which is indicated in the *OS/2 Technical Reference* manuals, volumes 1 and 2).

10.3.2 Simple Protected Mode C Programs

Figure 10.8a presents a very simple Protected Mode program (os21.c). This program runs under OS/2 Protected Mode, yet looks like an ordinary C coding example of printf(). In fact, it is. The Protected Mode implementation establishes three of the five standard I/O streams and yields default I/O for these streams. When calling from a single thread, these I/O routines will appear to execute as though in Real Mode. Unfortunately, the power of OS/2 lies in multitasked Protected Mode, and here we must resort to the API calls. Figure 10.8b illustrates C programming based on API calls to print a similar message to the screen.

To understand the function calls in Figure 10.8b, consider the Microsoft include file declaration for VioWrtTTY:

```
extern unsigned far pascal VIOWRTTTY(
char far *,
unsigned,
unsigned);
```

Here the pointer (FAR) is to the string to be written, the second parameter is the length of the string, and the third parameter is the video handle (=0). In Figure 10.8b, msg__p is a pointer to the message and lmsg__p the string length obtained using strlen(). The reader should contrast these programs with the code appearing in Figure 10.1. Clearly, some understanding of the assembler calling convention will be useful when programming the OS/2 Protected Mode API functions. During the presentation of this section, we will develop programming examples that somewhat parallel the earlier examples for the Macro Assembler/2. Hence, we will concentrate on CGA graphics and the drawing of boxes to illustrate the C Compiler interface to the API calls.

Figure 10.9 illustrates an additional Protected Mode program that has a screen clear in the standard 80 × 25 alphanumeric mode. This program should be contrasted

```
/* This program checks default Protected Mode -- os21.c*/

#include <stdio.h>

main()
        {
        printf("This is Protected Mode");
        }
```

Figure 10.8a Simple Protected Mode C program that writes a message to the screen with standard I/O (os21.c).

```
/* This program tests API calls in Protected Mode -- os211.c*/
#include <doscall.h>
#include <error.h>
#include <string.h>

main()
        {
        unsigned vio_hdl = 0;                           /* video handle */
        unsigned action = 0;                            /* end thread */
        unsigned error_code = 0;                        /* result code */
        char *msg_p = "This is OS/2 Protected Mode";
        unsigned lmsg_p = 0;                            /* string length */

        lmsg_p = strlen(msg_p);
        VIOWRTTTY((char far *)msg_p,lmsg_p,vio_hdl);
        DOSEXIT(action,error_code);                     /* termination */
        }
```

Figure 10.8b Simple Protected Mode C program that writes a message to the screen with API calls (os211.c).

```
/* This program tests API calls in Protected Mode -- os212c.c
 * It has a screen clear
 */

#include <doscall.h>
#include <error.h>
#include <string.h>

unsigned vio_hdl = 0;                                    /* video handle */
blank[2];                                                /* blank cell */

main()
        {
        unsigned action = 0;                             /* end thread */
        unsigned error_code = 0;                         /* result code */
        char *msg_p = "This is OS/2 Protected Mode";
        unsigned lmsg_p = 0;                             /* string length */

        lmsg_p = strlen(msg_p);

        ccls();                                          /* clear screen */

        VIOWRTTTY((char far *)msg_p,lmsg_p,vio_hdl);
        DOSEXIT(action,error_code);                      /* termination */
        }

ccls()
        {
        unsigned tr = 0;                                 /* top row */
        unsigned lc = 0;                                 /* left column */
        unsigned br = 23;                                /* bottom row */
        unsigned rc = 79;                                /* right column */
        unsigned no_lines = 25;                          /* number lines */

        blank[0] = 0x00;                                 /* blank attribute */
        blank[1] = 0x07;                                 /* blank attribute */

        VIOSCROLLUP(tr,lc,br,rc,no_lines,(char far *)blank,vio_hdl);
        }
```

Figure 10.9 Slightly more complex version of the C program appearing in Figure 10.8b. In this example, the Protected Mode is illustrated with a screen clear (os212c.c).

with the code appearing in Figure 10.2. We note that the pointer to the blank character pair is of character type (FAR) and

```
char far *
```

would normally operate on an address. Here blank is the same as blank [0], which is the same as &blank. Again the API call to VIOSCROLLUP() scrolls the screen with blank characters.

Figure 10.10 should be examined relative to portions of the code in Figure 10.3. In this example the program simply enters CGA mode, waits for a key stroke, and then returns to standard mode. The call to VIOSETMODE() uses two structures, CGAm and STDm, to contain the needed mode parameters for the API call. These structures are identical to those set up in the Macro Assembler/2 program. Actual execution of the linked version of this program results in a set of multicolored parallel lines appearing on the screen in CGA mode. As in the assembly language example, this screen must be cleared by the programmer.

```
/* This routine sets and clears CGA mode--os22c.c */

#include <doscall.h>
#include <error.h>

struct KbdStringInLength lkbd_buf;                      /* keyboard buf len */
char kbd_buf[80];                                       /* keyboard buffer */

unsigned action = 0;                                    /* end thread */
unsigned error_code = 0;                                /* result code */
unsigned wait = 1;                                      /* reserved word */

main()
        {
        unsigned vio_hdl = 0;                           /* video handle */
        unsigned kbd_hdl = 0;                           /* keyboard handle */

        struct ModeData CGAm;                           /* CGA structure */
        struct ModeData STDm;                           /* 80 x 25 struct */

        CGAm.length = 12;                               /* struct length */
        CGAm.type = 7;                                  /* CGA mode */
        CGAm.color = 2;                                 /* CGA color */
        CGAm.col = 40;                                  /* text columns */
        CGAm.row = 25;                                  /* text rows */
        CGAm.hres = 320;                                /* CGA hor res */
        CGAm.vres = 200;                                /* CGA vert res */

        STDm.length = 12;                               /* struct length */
        STDm.type = 1;                                  /* 80 x 25 mode */
        STDm.color = 4;                                 /* STD color */
        STDm.col = 80;                                  /* text columns */
        STDm.row = 25;                                  /* text rows */
        STDm.hres = 720;                                /* STD hor res */
        STDm.vres = 400;                                /* STD vert res */

        lkbd_buf.Length = 80;                           /* buffer size */

        VIOSETMODE(((struct ModeData far *)&CGAm),vio_hdl);
        KBDSTRINGIN(((char far *)kbd_buf,
                ((struct KbdStringInLength far *)&lkbd_buf),
                wait,kbd_hdl);
        VIOSETMODE(((struct ModeData far *)&STDm),vio_hdl);
        DOSEXIT(action,error_code);
        }
```

Figure 10.10   This Protected Mode C program simply invokes CGA mode (os22c.c).

Figure 10.11 contains a function set cclsCGA() and clrCGA(), which implements this screen clear. Note that an include macro, MAKEP(), is used to create a
FAR pointer from selector and offset value. This macro is part of the routines
found in an additional library include file, os2.h. In Figure 10.11, it was necessary
to lock the screen and access the physical buffer to accomplish the screen clear.
Again, the parallel between the code of Figure 10.11 and Figure 10.3 is remarkable
and expected. The reader should pay particular attention to the form of the C code
API function references. This form can be appreciated by listing the function prototypes appearing in the doscalls.h and subcalls.h files, as indicated earlier, and examining the OS/2 API function references in the *OS/2 Technical Reference* manuals. In
Figure 10.11, only 12 bytes are used in the VIOSETMODE() structures, but in
the Microsoft structures two additional reserved word characters exist. These should
be ignored in the reference. Figure 10.12 is the same program as Figure 10.11,

```
/* This routine sets & clears CGA mode with screen clear--os23c.c */

#include <doscall.h>
#include <error.h>
#include <os2.h>

struct KbdStringInLength lkbd_buf;                    /* keyboard buf len */
char kbd_buf[80];                                      /* keyboard buffer */

unsigned action = 0;                                   /* end thread */
unsigned error_code = 0;                               /* result code */
unsigned wait = 1;                                     /* reserved word */

char dstat[1];

main()
        {
        unsigned vio_hdl = 0;                          /* video handle */
        unsigned kbd_hdl = 0;                          /* keyboard handle */

        struct ModeData CGAm;                          /* CGA structure */
        struct ModeData STDm;                          /* 80 x 25 struct */

        CGAm.length = 12;                              /* struct length */
        CGAm.type = 7;                                 /* CGA mode */
        CGAm.color = 2;                                /* CGA color */
        CGAm.col = 40;                                 /* text columns */
        CGAm.row = 25;                                 /* text rows */
        CGAm.hres = 320;                               /* CGA hor res */
        CGAm.vres = 200;                               /* CGA vert res */

        STDm.length = 12;                              /* struct length */
        STDm.type = 1;                                 /* 80 x 25 mode */
        STDm.color = 4;                                /* STD color */
        STDm.col = 80;                                 /* text columns */
        STDm.row = 25;                                 /* text rows */
        STDm.hres = 720;                               /* STD hor res */
        STDm.vres = 400;                               /* STD vert res */

        lkbd_buf.Length = 80;                          /* buffer size */

        VIOSETMODE(((struct ModeData far *)&CGAm),vio_hdl);

        cclsCGA(vio_hdl);                              /* clear CGA screen */

        KBDSTRINGIN((char far *)kbd_buf,
                    ((struct KbdStringInLength far *)&lkbd_buf),
                    wait,kbd_hdl);
        VIOSETMODE(((struct ModeData far *)&STDm),vio_hdl);
        DOSEXIT(action,error_code);
        }

cclsCGA(vio_hdl1)
        unsigned vio_hdl1;
        {
        unsigned int MM;
        unsigned wait1 = 1;
        struct PhysBufData PVBPrt1;

        PVBPrt1.buf_start = 0xB8000;                   /* phys buf start */
        PVBPrt1.buf_length = 0x8000;                   /* buffer length */

        VIOSCRLOCK(wait1,(char far *)dstat,vio_hdl1);
        VIOGETPHYSBUF((struct PhysBufData far *)&PVBPrt1,vio_hdl1);
        MM = PVBPrt1.selectors[0];
        clrCGA(MM);
        VIOSCRUNLOCK(vio_hdl1);
        }
```

Figure 10.11 This Protected Mode C program simply invokes CGA mode and clears the screen (os23c.c).

```
clrCGA(MM)
        unsigned int MM;
        {
        int n;
        int N1 = 0x1F3F;                             /* end odd buffer */
        int DM = 0x2000;                             /* even offset */
        char far *ptr;                               /* pointer scr buf */

        for(n = 0;n <= N1;n++)
            {
            ptr = MAKEP(MM,n);                       /* odd far pointer */
            *ptr = 0;                                /* clear odd buffer */
            }
        for(n = 0;n <= N1;n++)
            {
            ptr = MAKEP(MM,DM+n);                    /* even far pointer */
            *ptr = 0;                                /* clear even buffer */
            }
        }
```

Figure 10.11 (*Concluded*)

```
/* This routine sets & clears CGA mode with screen clear--os24c.c
 * The generalized nomenclature is used.
 */

#include <doscall.h>
#include <error.h>
#include <os2.h>

struct KbdStringInLength lkbd_buf;                   /* keyboard buf len */
CHAR kbd_buf[80];                                    /* keyboard buffer */

UINT action = 0;                                     /* end thread */
UINT error_code = 0;                                 /* result code */
UINT wait = 1;                                       /* reserved word */

CHAR dstat[1];

main()
        {
        SHANDLE vio_hdl = 0;                         /* video handle */
        SHANDLE kbd_hdl = 0;                         /* keyboard handle */

        struct ModeData CGAm;                        /* CGA structure */
        struct ModeData STDm;                        /* 80 x 25 struct */

        CGAm.length = 12;                            /* struct length */
        CGAm.type = 7;                               /* CGA mode */
        CGAm.color = 2;                              /* CGA color */
        CGAm.col = 40;                               /* text columns */
        CGAm.row = 25;                               /* text rows */
        CGAm.hres = 320;                             /* CGA hor res */
        CGAm.vres = 200;                             /* CGA vert res */

        STDm.length = 12;                            /* struct length */
        STDm.type = 1;                               /* 80 x 25 mode */
        STDm.color = 4;                              /* STD color */
        STDm.col = 80;                               /* text columns */
        STDm.row = 25;                               /* text rows */
```

Figure 10.12 This Protected Mode C program invokes CGA mode and clears the screen. It is similar to the program in Figure 10.11, except it uses generalized OS/2 nomenclature (os24c.c).

```
          STDm.hres = 720;                          /* STD hor res */
          STDm.vres = 400;                          /* STD vert res */

          lkbd_buf.Length = 80;                     /* buffer size */

          VIOSETMODE(((struct ModeData far *)&CGAm),vio_hdl);

          cclsCGA(vio_hdl);                         /* clear CGA screen */

          KBDSTRINGIN((char far *)kbd_buf,
                      ((struct KbdStringInLength far *)&lkbd_buf),
                      wait,kbd_hdl);
          VIOSETMODE(((struct ModeData far *)&STDm),vio_hdl);
          DOSEXIT(action,error_code);
          }
cclsCGA(vio_hdl1)
          SHANDLE vio_hdl1;
          {
          UINT MM;
          UINT wait1 = 1;
          struct PhysBufData PVBPrt1;

          PVBPrt1.buf_start = 0xB8000;              /* phys buf start */
          PVBPrt1.buf_length = 0x8000;              /* buffer length */

          VIOSCRLOCK(wait1,(char far *)dstat,vio_hdl1);
          VIOGETPHYSBUF((struct PhysBufData far *)&PVBPrt1,vio_hdl1);
          MM = PVBPrt1.selectors[0];
          clrCGA(MM);
          VIOSCRUNLOCK(vio_hdl1);
          }

clrCGA(MM)
          UINT MM;
          {
          INT n;
          INT N1 = 0x1F3F;                          /* end odd buffer */
          INT DM = 0x2000;                          /* even offset */
          PCHAR ptr;                                /* pointer scr buf */

          for(n = 0;n <= N1;n++)
             {
             ptr = MAKEP(MM,n);                     /* odd far pointer */
             *ptr = 0;                              /* clear odd buffer */
             }
          for(n = 0;n <= N1;n++)
             {
             ptr = MAKEP(MM,DM+n);                  /* even far pointer */
             *ptr = 0;                              /* clear even buffer */
             }
          }
```

Figure 10.12 (*Concluded*)

except some new nomenclature is used to reference types, for example, as defined
with typedef in os2.h. This new use of descriptive terminology has the advantage
of customizing the OS/2 C references.

Figure 10.13 adds the routine

```
bboxx(xb,xe,yb,ye,mm1)
```

to the programs of the earlier example. This routine draws a box in CGA mode
with column values 75 to 150 and row values 25 to 175. The programming is

```
/* This routine sets & clears CGA mode with screen clear--os25c.c
 *  The generalized nomenclature is used.
 *  A box has been added to the CGA mode output. This is called externally
 *  from the routine os251c.c.
 */

#include <doscall.h>
#include <error.h>
#include <os2.h>

struct KbdStringInLength lkbd_buf;                    /* keyboard buf len */
CHAR kbd_buf[80];                                     /* keyboard buffer */

UINT action = 0;                                      /* end thread */
UINT error_code = 0;                                  /* result code */
UINT wait = 1;                                        /* reserved word */

CHAR dstat[1];
CHAR dstat1[1];

main()
        {
        SHANDLE vio_hdl = 0;                          /* video handle */
        SHANDLE kbd_hdl = 0;                          /* keyboard handle */
        UINT wait2 = 1;                               /* reserved */
        UINT xb = 75,xe = 150,yb = 25,ye = 175;       /* box points */
        UINT MM1;                                     /* selector */
        extern bboxx();

        struct PhysBufData PVBPrt2;                   /* physical buffer */
        struct ModeData CGAm;                         /* CGA structure */
        struct ModeData STDm;                         /* 80 x 25 struct */

        PVBPrt2.buf_start = 0xB8000;                  /* buffer start */
        PVBPrt2.buf_length = 0x8000;                  /* buffer size */

        CGAm.length = 12;                             /* struct length */
        CGAm.type = 7;                                /* CGA mode */
        CGAm.color = 2;                               /* CGA color */
        CGAm.col = 40;                                /* text columns */
        CGAm.row = 25;                                /* text rows */
        CGAm.hres = 320;                              /* CGA hor res */
        CGAm.vres = 200;                              /* CGA vert res */

        STDm.length = 12;                             /* struct length */
        STDm.type = 1;                                /* 80 x 25 mode */
        STDm.color = 4;                               /* STD color */
        STDm.col = 80;                                /* text columns */
        STDm.row = 25;                                /* text rows */
        STDm.hres = 720;                              /* STD hor res */
        STDm.vres = 400;                              /* STD vert res */

        lkbd_buf.Length = 80;                         /* buffer size */

        VIOSETMODE(((struct ModeData far *)&CGAm),vio_hdl);

        cclsCGA(vio_hdl);                             /* clear CGA screen */
        VIOSCRLOCK(wait2,(char far *)dstat1,vio_hdl);
        VIOGETPHYSBUF((struct PhysBufData far *)&PVBPrt2,vio_hdl);
        MM1 = PVBPrt2.selectors[0];

        bboxx(xb,xe,yb,ye,MM1);                       /* draw box */

        VIOSCRUNLOCK(vio_hdl);
        KBDSTRINGIN((char far *)kbd_buf,
                ((struct KbdStringInLength far *)&lkbd_buf),
                wait,kbd_hdl);
```

Figure 10.13 This Protected Mode C program draws a box in CGA mode (os25c.c).

```
            VIOSETMODE(((struct ModeData far *)&STDm),vio_hdl);
            DOSEXIT(action,error_code);
            }
cclsCGA(vio_hdl1)
        SHANDLE vio_hdl1;
        {
        UINT MM;
        UINT wait1 = 1;
        struct PhysBufData PVBPrt1;

        PVBPrt1.buf_start = 0xB8000;                    /* phys buf start */
        PVBPrt1.buf_length = 0x8000;                    /* buffer length */

        VIOSCRLOCK(wait1,(char far *)dstat,vio_hdl1);
        VIOGETPHYSBUF((struct PhysBufData far *)&PVBPrt1,vio_hdl1);
        MM = PVBPrt1.selectors[0];
        clrCGA(MM);
        VIOSCRUNLOCK(vio_hdl1);
        }
clrCGA(MM)
        UINT MM;
        {
        INT n;
        INT N1 = 0x1F3F;                                /* end odd buffer */
        INT DM = 0x2000;                                /* even offset */
        PCHAR ptr;                                      /* pointer scr buf */

        for(n = 0;n <= N1;n++)
            {
            ptr = MAKEP(MM,n);                          /* odd far pointer */
            *ptr = 0;                                   /* clear odd buffer */
            }
        for(n = 0;n <= N1;n++)
            {
            ptr = MAKEP(MM,DM+n);                       /* even far pointer */
            *ptr = 0;                                   /* clear even buffer */
            }
        }
```

Figure 10.13 *(Concluded)*

modular, with the actual box-drawing routine appearing in Figure 10.14. Note that all structure members are identified according to their Microsoft API reference designation. For example, the statement

```
MM1 = PVBPrt2.selectors[0];
```

loads the first selectors integer from the physical buffer structure PVBPrt2 into MM1. This is the selector value returned by VIOGETPHYSBUF(), and the Microsoft prototype definition for this structure is

```
struct PhysBufData{
    unsigned long buf_start;
    unsigned long buf_length;
    unsigned selectors[2];
    };
```

Hence, the correspondence between PVBPrt2 and its elements is clear.

```
/* Box generator routines Protected Mode--os251c.c */

#include <os2.h>
#include <doscall.h>
#include <error.h>

bboxx(xb,xe,yb,ye,MM1)
        UINT xb,xe,yb,ye,MM1;
        {
        lineh(yb,xb,xe,MM1);                              /* top line */
        lineh(ye,xb,xe,MM1);                              /* bottom line */
        linev(xb,yb,ye,MM1);                              /* right line */
        linev(xe,yb,ye,MM1);                              /* left line */
        }
lineh(y,x1,x2,MM1)
        UINT y,x1,x2,MM1;
        {
        UINT n;
        for(n = x1;n <= x2;n++)
            wdot(n,y,MM1);                                /* hor line */
        }
linev(x,y1,y2,MM1)
        UINT x,y1,y2,MM1;
        {
        UINT n;
        for(n = y1;n <= y2;n++)
            wdot(x,n,MM1);                                /* vertical line */
        }
wdot(x,y,MM1)
        UINT x,y,MM1;
        {
        PCHAR ptr;
        UINT DM = 0x0000;
        CHAR MASK1 = 0x01;

        if(y & 0x01)
            DM = 0x2000;                                 /* even buffer */
        ptr = MAKEP(MM1,DM+(80*(y >> 1) + (x >> 2)));     /* dot location */
        *ptr =(*ptr | (MASK1 << (2*(3 - x % 4))));        /* write dot */
        }
```

Figure 10.14 This Protected Mode C routine creates the box for Figure 10.13 (os251c.c).

The function wdot() appearing in Figure 10.14 actually writes the dot on the screen in the usual fashion. Note that this is basically a FAR screen DMA write to the physical buffer using MAKEP() to set up the physical pointer.

Having spent considerable time looking at the CGA box-generating example, it is useful to contrast this example with the assembly language code appearing in Figures 10.4 and 10.5. Again, the remarkable similarity of the code is evident. Basically, the Protected Mode C code implementation is very low level when the API functions are needed. The great deal of effort spent in this book examining low-level references from C, when handling hardware for example, is now of benefit when implementing these same sorts of references under OS/2 Protected Mode.

Figures 10.15 and 10.16 constitute the final examples of this chapter. Again, they represent the C code for a parallel example from the previous section: drawing 100 random boxes in a multitasked environment. In Figure 10.15, a shared data segment named \SHAREMEM\SDAT.DAT is created with 402 integer values in it. The first two integers are the length of the memory, 402, and a flag indicating access. This buffer is cleared to zero and a child task started using DOSEXECPGM().

```
/* The program is labeled os26c.c.
 * This routine starts a child process that generates random corners--os261c.c
 *  The generalized nomenclature is used.
 *  The box routine is called externally from os251c.c
 *  It plots 100 random boxes on the CGA screen.
 */

#include <stdio.h>
#include <doscall.h>
#include <error.h>
#include <os2.h>
#include <bsesub.h>

struct KbdStringInLength lkbd_buf;                  /* keyboard buf len */
CHAR kbd_buf[80];                                   /* keyboard buffer */
CHAR argst[1];                                      /* argument pointer */
CHAR envst[1];                                      /* environ. pointer */

struct ResultCodes PIDD;                            /* result codes */

ULONG obj_nm_buf[30];                               /* buffer name */
UINT array[402];                                    /* intermediate buf */

CHAR shrname[19]={'\\','S','H','A','R','E','M','E','M','\\','S','D','A','T',
        '.','D','A','T','\0'};
CHAR prgm_nm[11]={'O','S','2','6','1','c','.','E','X','E','\0'};

UINT action = 0;                                    /* end thread */
UINT error_code = 0;                                /* result code */
UINT wait = 1;                                      /* reserved word */
UINT count = 400;                                   /* shr buf length */
UINT lobj_nm_buf = 120;                             /* length name buf */
UINT async = 0;                                     /* wait on child */


CHAR dstat[1];
CHAR dstat1[1];

main()
        {
        SHANDLE vio_hdl = 0;                        /* video handle */
        SHANDLE kbd_hdl = 0;                        /* keyboard handle */
        UINT wait2 = 1;                             /* reserved */
        UINT xb,xe,yb,ye;                           /* box points */
        UINT shared_length = 804;                   /* shr length(bytes) */
        UINT MM3;                                   /* shr buf intm sel */
        UINT error2;                                /* error flag */
        UINT shrsel;                                /* shr buf selector */
        UINT one = 1;
        UINT MM1;                                   /* selector */
        UINT zero = 0;
        INT n;
        INT count1;                                 /* reduced count */
        PUINT ptr1;                                 /* pointer shr mem */
        extern bboxx();

        struct PhysBufData PVBPrt2;                 /* physical buffer */
        struct ModeData CGAm;                       /* CGA structure */
        struct ModeData STDm;                       /* 80 x 25 struct */

        PVBPrt2.buf_start = 0xB8000;                /* buffer start */
        PVBPrt2.buf_length = 0x8000;                /* buffer size */

        CGAm.length = 12;                           /* struct length */
        CGAm.type = 7;                              /* CGA mode */
        CGAm.color = 2;                             /* CGA color */
        CGAm.col = 40;                              /* text columns */
        CGAm.row = 25;                              /* text rows */
        CGAm.hres = 320;                            /* CGA hor res */
        CGAm.vres = 200;                            /* CGA vert res */
```

Figure 10.15 This Protected Mode C program employs multitasking and shared memory to pass 100 random box coordinate sets from a generating process. The resulting boxes are displayed (os26c.c).

```
STDm.length = 12;                                    /* struct length */
STDm.type = 1;                                       /* 80 x 25 mode */
STDm.color = 4;                                      /* STD color */
STDm.col = 80;                                       /* text columns */
STDm.row = 25;                                       /* text rows */
STDm.hres = 720;                                     /* STD hor res */
STDm.vres = 400;                                     /* STD vert res */

error2 = DOSALLOCSHRSEG(shared_length,(PCH)shrname,(PUINT)&shrsel);
if(error2 != 0)
    {
    printf("Error in shared memory allocation");
    exit(1);
    }
MM3 = shrsel;                                        /* memory selector */
ptr1 = MAKEP(MM3,2);                                 /* 2nd buffer wd */
*ptr1 = one;                                         /* set create flag */
ptr1 = MAKEP(MM3,0);                                 /* 1st buffer wd */
*ptr1 = shared_length;                               /* length buffer */

for(n = 2;n <= (shared_length/2) - 1;n++)
    {
    ptr1 = MAKEP(MM3,2*n);                           /* point to buffer */
    *ptr1 = zero;                                    /* clear buffer */
    }

argst[0] = 0;                                        /* argument */
envst[0] = 0;                                        /* environment */

error2 = DOSEXECPGM((PCH)obj_nm_buf,
                    lobj_nm_buf,
                    async,
                    (PCH)argst,(PCH)envst,
                    (struct ResultCodes far *)&PIDD,
                    (PCH)prgm_nm);
if(error2 != 0)
    {
    printf("Error on child start");
    exit(1);
    }

ptr1 = MAKEP(MM3,2);                                 /* flag--complete */
*ptr1 = zero;

for(n = 2;n <= (shared_length/2) - 1;n++)
    {
    ptr1 = MAKEP(MM3,2*n);
    array[n-2] = *ptr1;                              /* load intm buffer */
    }

lkbd_buf.Length = 80;                                /* buffer size */

VIOSETMODE(((struct ModeData far *)&CGAm),vio_hdl);

cclsCGA(vio_hdl);                                    /* clear CGA screen */
VIOSCRLOCK(wait2,(char far *)dstat1,vio_hdl);
VIOGETPHYSBUF((struct PhysBufData far *)&PVBPrt2,vio_hdl);
MM1 = PVBPrt2.selectors[0];

count1 = count/4;                                    /* corner grouping */
for(n = 0;n <= count1;n++)
    {
    if(array[n] == array[2*n])
        {
        xb = 170;                                    /* arbitrary corner */
        xe = 180;                                    /* arbitrary corner */
        }
    else
        {
        if(array[n] < array[2*n])
            {
            xb = array[n];
            xe = array[2*n];
            }
```

Figure 10.15 (*Continued*)

523

```
                         else
                            {
                            xb = array[2*n];
                            xe = array[n];
                            }
                         }
                    if(array[3*n] == array[4*n])
                         {
                         yb = 170;                              /* arbitrary corner */
                         ye = 180;                              /* arbitrary corner */
                         }
                    else
                         {
                         if(array[3*n] < array[4*n])
                              {
                              yb = array[3*n];
                              ye = array[4*n];
                              }
                         else
                              {
                              yb = array[4*n];
                              ye = array[3*n];
                              }
                         }

                    bboxx(xb,xe,yb,ye,MM1);                     /* draw box */
                    }

          VIOSCRUNLOCK(vio_hdl);
          DOSKILLPROCESS(1,PIDD.TermCode_PID);
          DOSFREESEG(shrsel);
          KBDSTRINGIN((char far *)kbd_buf,
                      ((struct KbdStringInLength far *)&lkbd_buf),
                      wait,kbd_hdl);
          VIOSETMODE(((struct ModeData far *)&STDm),vio_hdl);
          DOSEXIT(action,error_code);
          }

cclsCGA(vio_hdl1)
          SHANDLE vio_hdl1;
          {
          UINT MM;
          UINT wait1 = 1;
          struct PhysBufData PVBPrt1;

          PVBPrt1.buf_start = 0xB8000;                          /* phys buf start */
          PVBPrt1.buf_length = 0x8000;                          /* buffer length */
          VIOSCRLOCK(wait1,(char far *)dstat,vio_hdl1);
          VIOGETPHYSBUF((struct PhysBufData far *)&PVBPrt1,vio_hdl1);
          MM = PVBPrt1.selectors[0];
          clrCGA(MM);
          VIOSCRUNLOCK(vio_hdl1);
          }

clrCGA(MM)
          UINT MM;
          {
          INT n;
          INT N1 = 0x1F3F;                                     /* end odd buffer */
          INT DM = 0x2000;                                     /* even offset */
          PCHAR ptr;                                           /* pointer scr buf */

          for(n = 0;n <= N1;n++)
             {
             ptr = MAKEP(MM,n);                                /* odd far pointer */
             *ptr = 0;                                         /* clear odd buffer */
             }
          for(n = 0;n <= N1;n++)
             {
             ptr = MAKEP(MM,DM+n);                             /* even far pointer */
             *ptr = 0;                                         /* clear even buffer */
             }
          }
```

Figure 10.15 *(Concluded)*

```
/* Program to generate child process for random corners--os261c.c */

#include <stdio.h>
#include <doscall.h>
#include <error.h>
#include <os2.h>
#include <bsesub.h>
#include <stdlib.h>

UINT array[400];                                    /* intermediate buf */
UINT shared_length;                                 /* shr buf length */

CHAR shrname[19]={'\\','S','H','A','R','E','M','E','M','\\','S','D','A','T',
     '.','D','A','T','\0'};
main()
        {
        UINT zero = 0;
        UINT one = 1;
        UINT shrsel;                                /* selector */
        UINT MM1;                                   /* pointer selector */
        UINT error2;                                /* return value */
        UINT action = 0;                            /* end thread */
        UINT error_code = 0;                        /* result code */
        INT n;                                      /* index */
        PUINT ptr1;                                 /* memory pointer */

        error2 = DOSGETSHRSEG((PCH)shrname,(PUINT)&shrsel);
        if(error2 != 0)
            {
            printf("Error on acquiring shared memory");
            exit(1);
            }
        MM1 = shrsel;                               /* reassign */

        ptr1 = MAKEP(MM1,0);                        /* pointer to buf */
        shared_length = *ptr1;                      /* length buf */

        lmem();                                     /* random numbers */

        for(n = 2;n <= (shared_length/2) - 1;n++)
            {
            ptr1 = MAKEP(MM1,2*n);                   /* pointer buf */
            *ptr1 = array[n-2];
            }

        DOSFREESEG(shrsel);
        DOSEXIT(action,error_code);
        }
lmem()
        {
        INT n;
        UINT x;                                     /* random value */

        for(n = 2;n <= (shared_length/2) - 1;n++)
            {
            x = rand()/175;                          /* value < 200 */
            array[n-2] = x;
            }
        }
```

Figure 10.16 This Protected Mode C program generates 100 random box coordinate sets. It passes these coordinates to a multitasked parent process using shared memory (os261c.c).

Figure 10.16 contains the child task which simply generates 400 random corner values (100 sets of box coordinates). The 100 random boxes are then written to the screen in CGA mode in an area 200 × 200. This multitasking example parallels the assembler code for Figures 10.6 and 10.7.

SUMMARY

This chapter has examined in a brief but in-depth set of examples the assembler and C programming for OS/2 Protected Mode. The examples stressed the use of API calls as a means of illustrating Protected Mode OS/2 services. When faced with programming under OS/2, the designer will need to use the API calls to implement manipulation of the system hardware. In many respects, these function references take the place of the earlier DOS interrupt services, except the API functions are more extensive.

Considerable emphasis should be placed on using the Protected Mode of OS/2. This is IBM's version of a multitasking operating system, which is designed to run using the full features of the Intel 80286 hardware protection. OS/2 is a true multitasking operating system that accommodates multiple tasks executing simultaneously and exchanging information dynamically. Clearly, rather complex dynamic program structures can evolve in this environment. It would not be unusual, for example, to have multiple reentrant code calling back upon itself many times as complexity increases. OS/2 has significant potential for advanced program development. It is to be expected that OS/2 will result in a new dimension of programming capability.

REFERENCES

1. *IBM Macro Assembler/2*, Language Reference and Fundamentals, International Business Machines, Inc., P.O. Box 1328-W, Boca Raton, FL 33429-1328 (1987).

2. *Microsoft Optimizing C Compiler Version 5.1*, Microsoft Corporation, P. O. Box 97017, Redmond, WA (1988).

3. *iAPX 286 Programmer's Reference Manual*, Intel Corporation, Literature Distribution, 3065 Bowers Avenue, Santa Clara, CA 95051 (1985).

4. Iacobucci, E., *OS/2 Programmer's Guide*, Osborne McGraw-Hill, Berkeley, CA (1988).

5. Letwin, G., *Inside OS/2*, Microsoft Press, 16011 NE 36th Way, Box 97017, Redmond, WA (1988).

6. *Operating System/2 Technical Reference*, Vols. 1 and 2, International Business Machines, Inc., P. O. Box 1328-W, Boca Raton, FL 33429-1328 (1988).

7. *Operating System/2 Programmer's Toolkit*, Programmer's Guide, International Business Machines, Inc., P. O. Box 1328-W, Boca Raton, FL 33429-1328 (1987).

8. McCracken, D., *A Guide to PL/M Programming for Microcomputer Applications*, Addison-Wesley Publishing Co., Reading, MA (1978).

PROBLEMS

10.1. In Figure 10.1, what would happen if the msg__p variable was defined without the last two bytes (0DH and 0AH)?

10.2. Explain the OS/2 calling convention for Macro Assembler/2 API calls using subcalls.inc.

10.3. In many of the API assembly language calls, pointers to buffers must be pushed on the stack as part of the required parameters. Define a macro for doing this such that the address saved is a far address.

10.4. Why are all procedures within the same code segment terminated using ret except the main calling procedure for a Protected Mode program?

10.5. In assembly language execution, how is the starting routine (procedure) designated as an entry point?

10.6. In the @VioSetMode data structures appearing in Figure 10.3, what is the meaning of the first word (set equal to 12)?

10.7. What is the second executable instruction of the @VioSetMode macro and what are its implications for the associated data structures?

10.8. What is the purpose of the FAR label PVBPrt1 appearing in Figure 10.3?

10.9. What is the horizontal resolution for the standard 80 × 25 alphanumeric mode? The vertical resolution for this mode?

10.10. When must the screen be locked, and what is the sequence of calls used to access the screen buffer in assembly language?

10.11. What do the assembly language instructions

```
. . .
fild four
fild col
fprem
fistp xx
fistp dummy
. . .
```

accomplish in Figure 10.3?

10.12. How is the allocated shared segment uniquely defined when using @DosAllocShrSeg in assembly language? When using DOSALLOCSHRSEG() in C?

10.13. At what address does the shared memory buffer begin loading in Figure 10.7?

10.14. In Figure 10.8b, why doesn't the first field of the V10WRTTTY() call read

```
(char far *)&msg-p
```

10.15. In Figure 10.9, why isn't the sixth field in the V10SCROLLUP() call given by

```
(char far *)&blank
```

10.16. In Figure 10.10, the structure lkbd__buf was defined in the preprocessor. Why isn't this defined in the body of main()?

10.17. In cclsCGA() appearing in Figure 10.11, a structure PVBPrt1 is defined as of type PhysBufData. What are the third and fourth elements in this structure? The fifth element?

10.18. What is the form of the MAKEP macro used to create a FAR pointer?

10.19. In the buffer clear in Figure 10.11, what is the significance of the value 1F3FH?

10.20. In Figure 10.14, what would happen if the wdot() pointer definition was

```
*ptr = (MASK1 << (2*(3-x%4)));
```

10.21. In Figure 10.14, what does

```
y & 0x01
```

return?

10.22. In Figure 10.15, why isn't the sixth field of the call to DOSEXECPGM() of the form

```
(struct ResultCodes far *)PIDD
```

10.23. What is the structure of the buffer created in Figure 10.16?

APPENDIX

A

The Fast Fourier Transform and Spectral Analysis

Many processes display characteristics with a periodic nature. In the presence of noisy background fluctuations, however, it can be difficult to discern the underlying periodicity inherent in these processes. The Fourier transform [1] developed as a method for generating a *spectrum* associated with any given process. Essentially, the process is presumed describable across an epoch (which usually has the independent variable time), and the transform of this process yields the spectrum with independent variable *frequency*. Here, frequency is used in a complementary sense (to the independent variable describing the process). For a process defined as a time series (where the epoch is based on a description over time), the independent variable appearing as complement in the transform is the usual frequency definition measured in units of inverse time. In the following section, we discuss the Fourier transform and the discrete Fourier transform (DFT).

A.1 THE DISCRETE FOURIER TRANSFORM (DFT)

When describing processes that are aperiodic, the Fourier transform is defined by an integral of the form

$$X(f) = \frac{1}{\sqrt{2\pi}} \int_{-\infty}^{\infty} x(t) e^{-j2\pi ft} \, dt \tag{A.1}$$

Here the magnitude squared of $X(f)$ is the familiar power spectrum, and the complex phasor satisfies

$$e^{-j2\pi ft} = \cos(2\pi ft) - j \sin(2\pi ft) \tag{A.2}$$

with $j = \sqrt{-1}$. For processes that display a periodic behavior of time interval T, it follows that

$$x(t) = x(t + nT) \tag{A.3}$$

Substituting Equation (A.3) in Equation (A.2) yields the result

$$e^{-j2\pi nfT} = 1 \tag{A.4}$$

or $f = 1/T$. With these relationships, it is possible to reduce Equation (A.1) to

$$X(f) = \frac{1}{\sqrt{2\pi}} \sum_{n \, -\infty}^{\infty} \int_{-nT/2}^{nT/2} x(t)e^{-j2\pi ft} \, dt \tag{A.5}$$

Obviously, the transform calculated in Equation (A.5) is infinite except for a certain class of functions. In practice, the time-domain function $x(t)$, is either unknown outside some interval or becomes vanishingly small outside some interval (for a large group of functions of interest). We will restrict the discussion to this class of functions. It then becomes permissible to multiply $x(t)$ by a *weighting function*, $w(t)$, which is zero outside this interval, and if we choose the interval to be of length T, centered at t_0,

$$X(f) = \frac{1}{\sqrt{2\pi}} \sum_{n \, -\infty}^{\infty} \int_{-nT/2}^{nT/2} x(t)w(t)e^{-j2\pi ft} \, dt$$

$$= \frac{1}{\sqrt{2\pi}} \int_{t_0 - T'/2}^{t_0 + T'/2} x(t)w(t)e^{-j2\pi ft} \, dt \tag{A.6}$$

Many examples of weighting functions exist, and each has a characteristic behavior with regard to its impact on such parameters as feature resolution and *sidelobe* reduction. In this appendix, we will use Hanning weighting [2], which has the form

$$w_H(t) = \begin{cases} \frac{1}{2} \; 1 - \cos(2\pi(t - t_0)/T'), & \dfrac{t_0 - T'}{2} \le t \le \dfrac{t_0 + T'}{2} \\ 0, & \text{elsewhere} \end{cases} \tag{A.7}$$

Equation (A.6) then reduces to

$$X(f) = \int_{t_0 - T'/2}^{t_0 + T'/2} x_H(t)e^{-j2\pi ft} \, dt \tag{A.8}$$

where $x_H(t) = x(t)w_H(t)/\sqrt{2\pi}$. Rewriting this expression yields

$$X(f) = e^{j2\pi ft_0} \int_{-T'/2}^{T'/2} x_H(t + t_0)e^{-j2\pi ft} \, dt \tag{A.9}$$

where the quantity $e^{-j2\pi ft_0}$ is an arbitrary phase factor of magnitude unity.

Centering x_H at t_0 and defining $t = n \, \Delta t$, where Δt is some discrete time interval, it becomes possible to approximate Equation (A.9) by

$$X(f) = \sum_{n \, -N/2}^{N/2} x_H(n \, \Delta t)e^{-j2\pi fn \, \Delta t} \tag{A.10}$$

Here the multiplying phasor has been suppressed. [We will eventually calculate the magnitude squared of $X(f)$ and, hence, this phasor will be irrelevant.] The quantity N is defined by $T' = N \Delta t$. The key factor needed to link the time and frequency domains is the uncertainty relationship, which yields

$$\Delta f = \frac{1}{N \Delta t} \tag{A.11}$$

In Equation (A.11), the left side is taken as an equality and constitutes the resolution achievable in the frequency domain. Equation (A.11) was obtained from

$$\Delta f \Delta t \geq \frac{1}{N} \tag{A.12}$$

Examination of these latter two equations implies that it is possible to discretely quantize frequency. Using $f = m \Delta f$, Equation (A.10) becomes

$$X(m \Delta f) = \sum_{n \, -N/2}^{N/2} x_H(n \Delta t)e^{-j2\pi mn/N} \tag{A.13a}$$

Suppressing dependence on Δf and Δt,

$$X(m) = \sum_{n \, -N/2}^{N/2} x_H(n)e^{-j2\pi mn/N} \tag{A.13b}$$

Equation (A.13b) is the usual form for the discrete Fourier transform (DFT). There are N values for $X(m)$, $m = -N/2, -N/2 + 1, -N/2 + 2, \ldots, N/2$. Each of these terms is defined by a sum of N multiples. Since one of these multiples has unity phasor, the calculation of Equation (A.13b) requires

$$[N - 1]^2$$

multiples (complex). Suppose the sequence was broken into two smaller sequences of length $N/2$. Then for large N the number of needed multiples is approximately

$$\left[\frac{N}{2}\right]^2 2 = \frac{N^2}{2}$$

This reduces the number of multiples needed to calculate the transform by a factor of 2. Hence a strategy is possible to generate the transform with a smaller number of multiples than is called for by the DFT. One such strategy is known as the fast Fourier transform (FFT), and this is the subject of the next section.

A.2 THE FAST FOURIER TRANSFORM (FFT)

The FFT is a method or strategy for calculating the *frequency-domain* transform of a *time-domain* function using a smaller number of mathematical operations than would normally be called for with the DFT. Rewriting Equation (A.13b) as

$$X(m) = \sum_{n \, -N/2}^{N/2} x_H(n)W^{mn} \tag{A.14}$$

it follows that $W_N = e^{-j2\pi/N}$ (not to be confused with the lowercase w corresponding to the weighting function). Based on Equation (A.2), it is clear that W is periodic and

$$W_N^{(m+m'N)(n+n'N)} = W_N^{mn}, \qquad m', n' = 0, \pm 1, \pm 2, \ldots \qquad \text{(A.15)}$$

For purposes of understanding the FFT structure, it is useful to slightly modify the summation appearing in Equation (A.14), rewriting

$$X(m) = \sum_{n\,0}^{N-1} x_H(n) W^{mn} \qquad \text{(A.16)}$$

Equation (A.15) is identical to Equation (A.14) under the assumption that $x_H(n)$ can be periodically extended to within a constant phase factor. Since we are only interested in magnitude and magnitude-squared values for $X(m)$, the arbitrary phase factor is irrelevant.

Dividing the sum appearing in Equation (A.16) into even and odd components,

$$X(m) = \sum_{n\,0}^{N/2-1} x_e(2n) W_N^{(2n)m} + W_N^m \sum_{n\,0}^{N/2-1} x_0(2n+1) W_N^{(2n)m} \qquad \text{(A.17a)}$$

$$= X_e(m) + W_N^m X_0(m)$$

Here $x_e(2n) = \{x(n): n = 0, 2, 4, \ldots, \frac{N}{2} - 1\}$ and $x_0(2n+1) = \{x(n): n = 1, 3, 5, \ldots, \frac{N}{2} + 1\}$. The expression for $X(m)$ in Equation (A.17a) must be extended for $m > \frac{N}{2} - 1$:

$$X(m) = X_e\left(m - \frac{N}{2}\right) + W_N^m X_0\left(m - \frac{N}{2}\right); \qquad \left(\frac{N}{2} \le m \le N - 1\right) \qquad \text{(A.17b)}$$

Figure A.1 illustrates the steps needed to evaluate Equations (A.17a) and (A.17b) for $N = 4$. It is clear that the problem can always be reduced to an initial coefficient realignment, followed by a *set* of two-point DFTs, and then appropriate combinatorial realignment of the coefficients with "butterflies."

Normal FFT usage employs the notion of bit reversal to define the shuffled data needed at the input. This concept simply states that if M bits are used to define the count index for the FFT (M = order of the FFT) then each input must be entered in the bit-reversed order of its index for normal order output. For example, if $M = 4$ (4 bits), then index number 10 would be (binary form)

1010 .

In bit-reversed form, this would be

0101 ,

which is 5. Hence, the point with index 10 must be input to the DFT process as though it was indexed as 5. We leave it to the reader to convince himself or herself

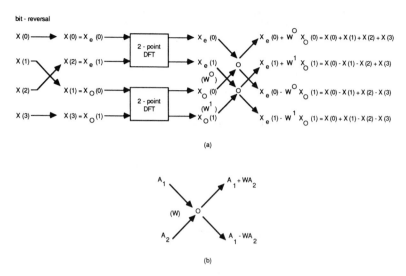

bit - reversal

$X(0) \longrightarrow X(0) = X_e(0) \longrightarrow$ [2 - point DFT] $\longrightarrow X_e(0)$

$X_e(0) + W^0 X_O(0) = X(0) + X(1) + X(2) + X(3)$

$X(1) \longrightarrow X(2) = X_e(1) \longrightarrow$

$X_e(1) + W^1 X_O(1) = X(0) - X(1) - X(2) + X(3)$

$X(2) \longrightarrow X(1) = X_O(0) \longrightarrow$ [2 - point DFT] $\longrightarrow X_O(0)$

$X_e(0) - W^0 X_O(1) = X(0) - X(1) + X(2) - X(3)$

$X(3) \longrightarrow X(3) = X_O(1) \longrightarrow$

$X_e(1) - W^1 X_O(1) = X(0) + X(1) - X(2) - X(3)$

(a)

$A_1 \searrow \qquad \nearrow A_1 + WA_2$

$(W) \quad O$

$A_2 \nearrow \qquad \searrow A_1 - WA_2$

(b)

Figure A.1 Steps needed to evaluate the fast Fourier transform for (a) N = 4 and (b) the multiplying "butterfly."

that bit reversal achieves the ordering illustrated by Figure A.1 and needed, in general, by FFTs.

Figure A.2a presents the flow chart for a C function that calculates a general order (defined by the formal parameter m) FFT for complex input. Figure A.2b is the function. The parameter $m1$ is chosen equal to $+1$ for the FFT and -1 for the inverse FFT (to go back, for example, from the frequency domain to the time domain). The two arrays areal and aimag contain the input time functions for real and imaginary values, respectively. Also appearing in the figure is the function hanwt. This function simply allows the user to preweight the input time series with Hanning weighting (Hanning weighting was selected because it has some desirable properties such as good resolution; however, many other weighting schemes exist).

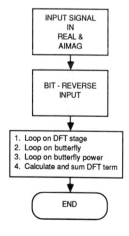

INPUT SIGNAL
IN
REAL &
AIMAG

BIT - REVERSE
INPUT

1. Loop on DFT stage
2. Loop on butterfly
3. Loop on butterfly power
4. Calculate and sum DFT term

END

Figure A.2a Flow chart for a function FFT, which calculates the fast Fourier transform.

```
/* This function generates the FFT output
** The FFT is complex with m = order and m1 = 1 (FFT), -1 (inverse) */

#include <math.h>

FFT(m,m1)
        int m,m1;
        {
        double x,y,z;
        int N,N1,N2,i,j,k,l,l0,l1,i1;
        float r1,r2,u1,u2,w1,w2,u9,pi = 3.141592654;
        extern float areal[],aimag[];

        x = 2.;
        y = m;
        z = pow(x,y);
        N = z;

        N1 = N - 1;
        N2 = N/2;

        j = 1;
        for(i = 1;i <= N1;i++)
            {
            if(i <= j)
                {
                r1 = areal[j];                          /* Bit reversal */
                r2 = aimag[j];
                areal[j] = areal[i];
                aimag[j] = aimag[i];
                areal[i] = r1;
                aimag[i] = r2;
                }
            k = N2;
            while(k < j)
                {
                j = j - k;
                k = k/2;
                }
            j = j + k;
            }
        for(l = 1;l <= m;l++)
            {
            x = 2.;
            y = l;
            z = pow(x,y);
            l0 = z;

            l1 = l0/2;
            u1 = 1;
            u2 = 0;

            w1 = cos(pi/l1);
            w2 = -m1*sin(pi/l1);

            for(j = 1;j <= l1;j++)
                {
                for(i = j;i <= N;i = i + l0)
                    {
                    i1 = i + l1;
                    r1 = areal[i1]*u1 - aimag[i1]*u2;
                    r2 = areal[i1]*u2 + aimag[i1]*u1;
                    areal[i1] = areal[i] - r1;
                    aimag[i1] = aimag[i] - r2;
                    areal[i] = areal[i] + r1;
                    aimag[i] = aimag[i] + r2;
                    }
                u9 = u1;
                u1 = u1*w1 - u2*w2;
                u2 = u9*w2 + u2*w1;
                }
            }
        }
```

Figure A.2b Function FFT, which calculates the fast Fourier transform.

```
/* Hanning weighting */

hanwt(m)
        int m;
        {
        double x,y,z;
        int i,N;
        extern float areal[],aimag[];
        float pi = 3.141592654,b;

        x = 2.;
        y = m;
        z = pow(x,y);
        N = z;

        for(i = 1;i <= N;i++)
            {
            b = .5*(1. - cos(2.*pi*i/N));
            areal[i] = areal[i] * b;
            aimag[i] = aimag[i] * b;
            }
        }
```

Figure A.2b *(Concluded)*

Figure A.3a illustrates a typical driver for the FFT function FFT. In this
program, a unit impulse is loaded into the real array areal. The imaginary array
aimag is set equal to zero. Execution of ckfft yields the output listed in Figure
A.3b. As might be expected, this output is constant or "white" for all output

```
/* Program to check FFT with impulse */

#include <stdio.h>
#include <math.h>

float areal[9],aimag[9],ssignal[9];

main()
        {
        int m,n,m1;

        for(n = 1;n <=8;n++)
            {
            aimag[n] = 0.0;
            ssignal[n] = aimag[n];                    /* Input values */

            areal[n] = 0.0;
            }
        aimag[1] = 1.0;                               /* Impulse */
        ssignal[1] = aimag[1];

        m = 3;                                        /* Order */
        m1 = 1;                                       /* Forward FFT */

        hanwt(m);                                     /* Hanning wt */
        FFT(m,m1);

        printf(" n    Input   Out-real  Out-imag \n");
        for (n = 1;n <= 8;n++)
            printf(" %d   %f   %f   %f \n",n,ssignal[n],areal[n],aimag[n]);
        }
```

Figure A.3a Driver ckfft used to calculate the transform of a real unit
impulse (N = 8).

```
<C:\>ckfft
  n  Input     Out-real  Out-imag
  1  1.000000  0.146447  0.000000
  2  0.000000  0.146447  0.000000
  3  0.000000  0.146447  0.000000
  4  0.000000  0.146447  0.000000
  5  0.000000  0.146447  0.000000
  6  0.000000  0.146447  0.000000
  7  0.000000  0.146447  0.000000
  8  0.000000  0.146447  0.000000

<C:\>
```

Figure A.3b Output of ckfft illustrating the "white" response.

```
/* Program to check FFT with impulse */

#include <stdio.h>
#include <math.h>

float areal[9],aimag[9],ssignal[9];

main()
        {
        int m,n,m1;

        for(n = 1;n <=8;n++)
            {
            areal[n] = 0.0;
            ssignal[n] = areal[n];                    /* Input values */

            aimag[n] = 0.0;
            }
        areal[1] = 1.0;                               /* Impulse */
        ssignal[1] = areal[1];

        m = 3;                                        /* Order */
        m1 = 1;                                       /* Forward FFT */

        hanwt(m);                                     /* Hanning wt */
        FFT(m,m1);

        printf(" n  Input  Out-real  Out-imag \n");
        for (n = 1;n <= 8;n++)
            printf(" %d   %f   %f   %f \n",n,ssignal[n],areal[n],aimag[n]);
```

Figure A.3c Driver ckffti used to calculate the transform of an imaginary unit impulse (N = 8).

```
<C:\>ckffti
  n   Input     Out-real  Out-imag
  1  1.000000  0.000000  0.146447
  2  0.000000  0.000000  0.146447
  3  0.000000  0.000000  0.146447
  4  0.000000  0.000000  0.146447
  5  0.000000  0.000000  0.146447
  6  0.000000  0.000000  0.146447
  7  0.000000  0.000000  0.146447
  8  0.000000  0.000000  0.146447

<C:\>
```

Figure A.3d Output of ckffti illustrating the "white" response.

frequencies. Figures A.3c and d present similar output for ckffti, which checks the operation of the imaginary portion of the function FFT. Again a "white" output is obtained. These tests are a good measure of the performance of the FFT and can be used as an independent method for verifying operation of the algorithm appearing in Figure A.2.

A.3 POWER SPECTRUM

Given a complex signal, $x(n)$, it can be written in terms of its real and imaginary components as follows:

$$x(n) = x_R(n) + jx_I(n) \tag{A.18}$$

The transform of this signal satisfies

$$X(m) = X_R(m) + jX_I(m) \tag{A.19}$$

A quantity defined as the power spectrum is given by

$$S(m) = |X(m)|^2 \tag{A.20}$$

and is phase independent. This spectral output illustrates the degree to which various frequency components are present in the underlying process.

By way of example, it is useful to consider a program that generates a combination of sinusoidal inputs combined with an underlying noise process. This is the familiar problem of narrowband tonals corrupted with background noise. Figure A.4a illustrates the flow chart for a function, wavefm, that asks for the number of

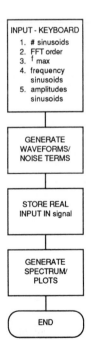

Figure A.4a Flow chart for a function that calculates a time-domain signal consisting of sinusoids and noise.

```
/* This routine generates a power spectrum */

#include <stdio.h>
#include <math.h>
#include <stdlib.h>

wavefm()
        {
        extern float areal[],aimag[],num1,num2,ssignal[];

        double x,y,z;
        float fmax,f0,pi = 3.141592654,snr,b;
        int nums,m,N,n,i;

        printf("Input number of sinusoids\n");         /* Input data */
        scanf("%d",&nums);
        printf("Input order of FFT\n");
        scanf("%d",&m);
        printf("Input max frequency\n");
        scanf("%f",&fmax);

        x = 2.;
        y = m;
        z = pow(x,y);
        N = z;

        for(i = 1;i <= N;i++)                           /* Clear arrays */
            {
            areal[i] = 0.0;
            aimag[i] = 0.0;
            }
        for(n = 1;n <= nums;n++)                        /* Load sinusoids */
            {
            printf("Input frequency (Hz)\n");
            scanf("%f",&f0);
            f0 = f0/fmax;
            printf("Input SNR for sinusoid (dB)\n");
            scanf("%f",&snr);

            x = 10.;
            y = snr/20.;
            z = pow(x,y);
            snr = z;

            for(i = 1;i <= N;i++)                       /* Generate waveform*/
                {
                areal[i] = areal[i] + snr*cos(2.*pi*i*f0);
                aimag[i] = aimag[i] + snr*sin(2.*pi*i*f0);
                }
            }
        b = sqrt(nums+1.);                              /* Adder */
        for(i = 1;i <= N;i++)
            {
            grand();                                    /* Additative noise*/
            areal[i] = areal[i] + num1;
            areal[i] = areal[i]/b;
            aimag[i] = aimag[i] + num2;
            aimag[i] = aimag[i]/b;
            }
                                                        /* Save real sig. */
        for(i = 1;i <= N;i++)
            ssignal[i] = areal[i];

        spectrum(m);                                    /* Power spectrum */

        }

<C:\>
```

Figure A.4b   Function wavefm that generates the signals in noise.

sinusoids, their frequencies, and the signal-to-noise ratio. Figure A.4b presents the associated code. The signal-to-noise ratio is asked for in decibels, where y_0 in decibels is related to y_0 in amplitude by

$$y_0 \text{ (dB)} = 20 \log_{10} y_0 \text{ (amplitude)} \qquad (A.21)$$

Also, the user is prompted for the order of the FFT and the maximum frequency to be considered. The summed noise plus sinusoids is then normalized and input to a function spectrum. Both real and imaginary inputs are assumed, where

$$x_R(n) = \cos 2\pi f \frac{n}{f_{\max}} \qquad (A.22a)$$

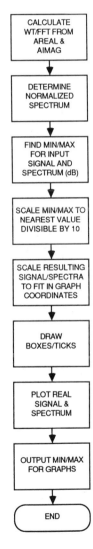

Figure A.5a Flow chart for the function spectrum that generates the power spectrum for an input time series.

```
/* This routine generates a power spectrum and plots it */

#include <stdio.h>
#include <math.h>
#include <stdlib.h>

spectrum(m)
        int m;                                          /* FFT order */
        {
        extern float areal[],aimag[],ssignal[],xx[];
        extern buffer[],buffer1[],buffer2[];

        double x,y,z;
        float maxt,mint,maxs,mins,b,b1;
        int N,n,i;
        int delta,nmaxs,nmins;


        x = 2.;
        y = m;
        z = pow(x,y);
        N = z;



        hanwt(m);                                       /* Hanning wt */
        FFT(m,1);                                       /* FFT */

                                                        /* Calc spectra */
        for(i = 1;i <= N;i++)
            {
            areal[i] = areal[i]*areal[i]+aimag[i]*aimag[i];
            areal[i] = .5*sqrt(areal[i]);
            }

        mins = 1.e4;
        maxs = 0.0;
        mint = 1.e4;
        maxt = 0.0;

        for(i = 1;i <= N;i++)                           /* max/min */
            {
            if(maxt < ssignal[i])
                maxt = ssignal[i];
            if(mint > ssignal[i])
                mint = ssignal[i];
            if(maxs < areal[i])
                maxs = areal[i];
            if(mins > areal[i])
                mins = areal[i];
            }
                                                        /* Log plot */
        for(i = 1;i <= N;i++)
            {
            aimag[i] = areal[i]/maxs;
            x = areal[i];
            y = log10(x);
            areal[i] = 20. * y;
            }

                                                        /* Rescale */
        maxs = 0.0;
        mins = 1.e4;
```

Figure A.5b Code for spectrum.

```
        for(n = 1;n <= N;n++)
            {
            if(maxs < areal[n])
                maxs = areal[n];
            if(mins > areal[n])
                mins = areal[n];
            }

        delta = maxs - mins;
        delta = delta/10;
        if(delta < 10)
            delta = 10;
        if(delta > 10 && delta < 20)
            delta = 20;
        if(delta > 20 && delta < 50)
            delta = 50;
        if(delta > 50 && delta < 100)
            delta = 100;
        if(delta > 100 && delta < 500)
            delta = 500;
        if(delta > 500 && delta < 1000)
            delta = 1000;
        if(delta > 1000)
            exit(1);
        nmaxs = maxs/delta+1;
        nmins = mins/delta;
        maxs = delta*nmaxs;
        mins = delta*nmins;
        if(mins <= 0)
            mins = mins - delta;

        delta = maxt - mint;
        delta = delta/10;
        if(delta < 1)
            delta = 1;
        if(delta > 1 && delta < 5)
            delta = 5;
        if(delta > 5 && delta < 10)
            delta = 10;
        if(delta > 10 && delta < 50)
            delta = 50;
        if(delta > 50 && delta < 100)
            delta = 100;
        if(delta > 100 && delta < 500)
            delta = 500;
        if(delta > 500)
            exit(1);
        nmaxs = maxt/delta+1;
        nmins = mint/delta;
        maxt = delta*nmaxs;
        mint = delta*nmins;
        if(mint <= 0)
            mint = mint - delta;
        x = mint;
        y = fabs(x);
        z = (float)(y);
        b1 = (z)/((float)(x));
        if(maxt > z && b1 < 0)
            mint = - maxt;
        else
            {
            if(maxt < z && b1 < 0)
                maxt = z;
            }
/* Scale -- time domain fit between 75 and 25 on CRT and spectra fit
** between 175 and 95 on CRT */
        b = 50./(maxt - mint);
```

Figure A.5b (*Continued*)

```
        b1 = 80./(maxs - mins);
        for(i = 1;i <= N;i++)
            {
            ssignal[i] = 25 + (50 - b*(ssignal[i] - mint));
            areal[i] = 95 + (80 - b1*(areal[i] - mins));
            xx[i] = 25 +(i - 1)* (256/N);
            }

                                                    /* Plot */
        box_spect();
                                                    /* Labels */

        for(n = 0;n <= 89;n++)
            buffer[n] = buffer1[n];
        PLTBUF(0,0);

        for(n = 1;n <= (N-1);n++)
            linev1(xx[n],xx[n+1],ssignal[n],ssignal[n+1]);
        for(n = 1;n <= (N-1);n++)
            plotpoint(xx[n],xx[n+1],areal[n],areal[n+1]);

        plotterm();

        printf(" maxs = %f\n",maxs);
        printf(" mins = %f\n",mins);
        printf(" maxt = %f\n",maxt);
        printf(" mint = %f\n",mint);
        }
```

Figure A.5b   *(Concluded)*

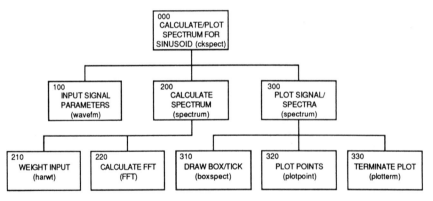

Figure A.6a   Structure chart for the program that generates sinusoids in noise and calculates their spectrum.

```
/* This routine checks the spectrum */

#include <stdio.h>
#include <math.h>
#include <dos.h>
#include <stdlib.h>

float areal[1024],aimag[1024],ssignal[1024],num1,num2,xx[1024],yy[1024];
char buffer[90],buffer1[90];

main()
        {
        read_title();
        wavefm();
        }
```

Figure A.6b   Calling program for the sinusoids in noise spectral analysis.

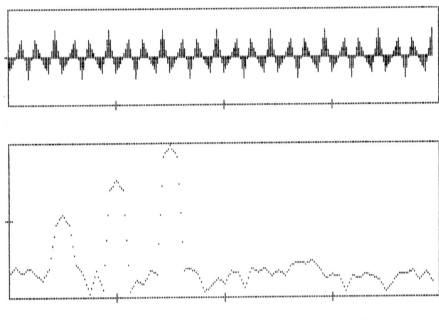

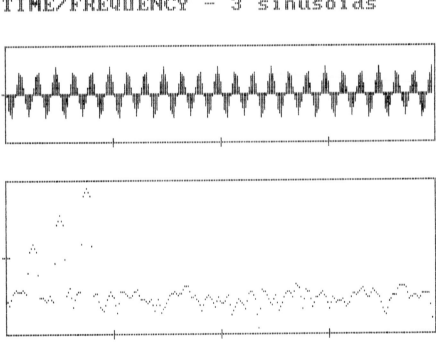

Figure A.7 Output plots for sinusoids in noise (real input) and resulting spectrums: (a) 200 Hz(20-dB SNR), 400 Hz(40 dB), and 600 Hz(60 dB), $N = 6$ and $f_{max} = 1600$ Hz; (b) same as (a) with $N = 7$ and $f_{max} = 3200$ Hz; and (c) 200 Hz (20-dB SNR) with $N = 6$ and $f_{max} = 1600$ Hz.

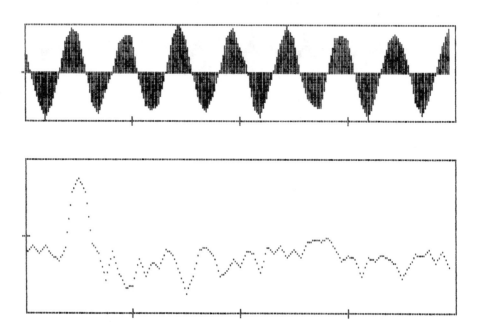

```
<C:\>ckspect
Input title -- max 80 char      TIME/FREQUENCY - 3 sinusoids
Input number of sinusoids
3
Input order of FFT
6
Input max frequency
1600
Input frequency (Hz)
200
Input SNR for sinusoid (dB)
20
Input frequency (Hz)
400
Input SNR for sinusoid (dB)
40
Input frequency (Hz)
600
Input SNR for sinusoid (dB)
60
Input 1-grid or 0-no grid0


  maxs =   80.000000
  mins =  -10.000000
  maxt = 1000.000000
  mint = -1000.000000

<C:\>
```

Figure A.8a Input and maximums for Figure A.7a.

```
<C:\>ckspect
Input title -- max 80 char        TIME/FREQUENCY - 3 sinusoids
Input number of sinusoids
3
Input order of FFT
7
Input max frequency
3200
Input frequency (Hz)
200
Input SNR for sinusoid (dB)
20
Input frequency (Hz)
400
Input SNR for sinusoid (dB)
40
Input frequency (Hz)
600
Input SNR for sinusoid (dB)
60
Input 1-grid or 0-no grid0


 maxs = 90.000000
 mins = -20.000000
 maxt = 1000.000000
 mint = -1000.000000

<C:\>
```

Figure A.8b Input and maximums for Figure A.7b.

```
<C:\>ckspect
Input title -- max 80 char        TIME/FREQUENCY - sinusoid
Input number of sinusoids
1
Input order of FFT
6
Input max frequency
1600
Input frequency (Hz)
200
Input SNR for sinusoid (dB)
20
Input 1-grid or 0-no grid0


 maxs = 50.000000
 mins = -20.000000
 maxt = 8.000000
 mint = -8.000000

<C:\>
```

Figure A.8c Input and maximums for Figure A.7c.

Sec. A.3   Power Spectrum

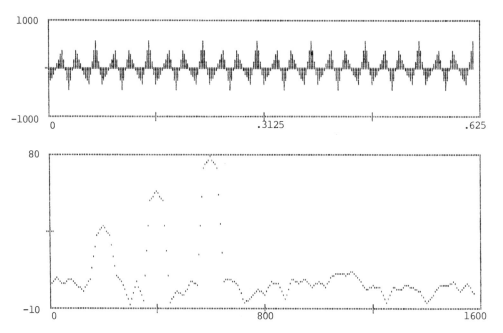

Figure A.9   Plot for Figure A.7a with all labeling present.

$$x_I(n) = \sin 2\pi f \frac{n}{f_{max}} \qquad \text{(A.22b)}$$

Here $T = 1/f_{max}$.

Figure A.5a is the flow-chart for the function spectrum and Figure A.5b the associated code. This routine calculates the weighted FFT, for areal and aimag, determines the resulting power spectrum, normalizes and scales the spectrum based on minimum and maximum values, and plots the result along with appropriate labeling and the initial real input. Figure A.6a is the structure chart for the program to calculate the spectrum of sinusoids in noise. Figure A.6b is the calling program, and Figures A.7a, b, and c illustrate representative output. In these figures no scale information has been plotted because of the undue complexity it would add to the function spectrum. Figure A.7a presents the output for three sinusoids: 200 hertz (Hz) [20-dB signal-to-noise ratio (SNR)], 400 Hz (40-dB SNR), and 600 Hz (60-dB SNR). The order of the FFT was $N = 6$. In the figure, the time-domain plot (upper plot) is scaled between [-1000, 1000] and has a horizontal range of 0 to .625 milliseconds (ms). The maximum frequency is 1600 Hz. The vertical spectrum scale in decibels is [-10, 80]. Figure A.7b is the same output for $N = 7$ with the maximum frequency of 3200 Hz, time-domain scale [-1000, 1000], time range [0, 0.625 ms], and vertical spectrum scale [-20, 90]. Finally, Figure A.7c is the output for a single 200 Hz sinusoid with 20-dB SNR. Here $N = 6$ and the time-domain scale is [-8, 8], spanning [0, 0.625 ms]. The spectral output scales across [-20,

```
/* Function to draw boxes for spectral plots */

#include <stdio.h>

box_spect()
        {
        int xxbeg,xxend,yybeg,yyend;
        int row,col,grid,xxtick,yytick,n;
        int ssxtick,ssytick,eextick,eeytick;

        printf("Input 1-grid or 0-no grid");
        scanf("%d",&grid);

                                                /* Plot upper box */
        xxbeg = 25;                             /* Box parameters */
        xxend = 281;
        yybeg = 25;
        yyend = 75;

        SCRCL();                                /* Clear screen */
        SC320();                                /* 320 x 200 mode */

        bbox(xxbeg,xxend,yybeg,yyend);          /* Plot box */

        xxtick = 89;                            /* Draw x-ticks */
        ssxtick = 73;
        eextick = 77;
        for(n = 1;n <= 3;n++)
            {
            xtick(xxtick,ssxtick,eextick);
            xxtick = xxtick + 64;
            }

        yytick = 50;                            /* Draw y-tick */
        ssytick = 23;
        eeytick = 27;
        ytick(yytick,ssytick,eeytick);

                                                /* 2nd box */
        yybeg = 95;
        yyend = 175;
        bbox(xxbeg,xxend,yybeg,yyend);

                                                /* Draw x-ticks */
        xxtick = 89;
        ssxtick = 173;
        eextick = 177;
        for(n = 1;n <= 3;n++)
            {
            xtick(xxtick,ssxtick,eextick);
            xxtick = xxtick + 64;
            }
                                                /* Draw y-tick */
        yytick = 135;
        ytick(yytick,ssytick,eeytick);

        if(grid == 1)
            {                                   /* Draw grids */
            linev(89,25,75);
            linev(153,25,75);
            linev(217,25,75);

            linev(89,95,175);
            linev(153,95,175);
            linev(217,95,175);

                                                /* Hor. lines */
            lineh(50,25,281);
            lineh(135,25,281);
            }
```

Figure A.10 Code for the associated functions box_spect, bbox, xtick, and ytick.

```
        }
/* Function bbox */

bbox(xxbeg,xxend,yybeg,yyend)
        int xxbeg,xxend,yybeg,yyend;
        {
        int row,col;

        row = yybeg;
        col = xxbeg;

        for(row = yybeg;row <= yyend;row++)
            WRDOT(row,col);
        row--;
        for(col = xxbeg;col <= xxend;col++)
            WRDOT(row,col);
        col--;
        for(row = yyend;row >= yybeg;row--)
            WRDOT(row,col);
        row++;
        for(col = xxend;col >= xxbeg;col--)
            WRDOT(row,col);
        col++;
        }

/* x-tick function */

xtick(xpos,ssxtick,eextick)
        int xpos,ssxtick,eextick;
        {
        int row,col;

        col = xpos;
        for(row = ssxtick;row <=eextick;row++)
            WRDOT(row,col);
        }

/* y-tick function */

ytick(ypos,ssytick,eeytick)
        int ypos,ssytick,eeytick;
        {
        int row,col;

        row = ypos;
        for(col = ssytick;col <= eeytick;col++)
            WRDOT(row,col);
        }
```

Figure A.10 (*Concluded*)

50], decibels, and the upper frequency maximum is 1600 Hz. As part of the program output, however, maximum and minimum values for the time-domain performance and spectrum are printed out and have been indicated in Figures A.8a, b, and c. (The horizontal scale for the time domain is $[0, N/f_{max}]$ and for the spectrum is $[0, f_{max}]$.) Figures A.8a, b, and c also illustrate the input data to the function waveform. In the case of the three sinusoids, the effects of increasing FFT resolution are readily apparent. Figure A.9 illustrates a typical plot with all labeling present.

A number of functions are called to generate Figures A.8a, b, and c. Figure A.10 illustrates the functions box__spect, bbox, xtick and ytick. These functions set up and plot the boxes and tick marks. The routine linevl plots the linearly interpolated vertical lines appearing in the time-domain graph. It is necessary to

```
/* This routine is special purpose for spectrum()
** It plots the signal profile in the time-domain */

linev1(x1,x2,y1,y2)
        float x1,x2,y1,y2;
        {
        float m;
        int xx1,ss1;

        if(x1 == x2)
                m = 1000;
        else
                m = (y2 - y1)/(x2 - x1);
        for(xx1 = x1;xx1 <= x2;xx1++)
                {
                ss1 = y1 + m * (xx1 - x1);
                linev(xx1,50,ss1);
                }
        }


/* Function to plot horizontal line */

lineh(y,x1,x2)
        int y,x1,x2;
        {
        int ncount,col,row,n;

        if(x1 > x2)
                {
                ncount = x1 - x2;
                row = y;
                col = x2;
                for(n = 0;n <= ncount;n++)
                        {
                        WRDOT(row,col);
                        col++;
                        }
                }
        else
                {
                ncount = x2 - x1;
                row = y;
                col = x1;
                for(n = 0;n <= ncount;n++)
                        {
                        WRDOT(row,col);
                        col++;
                        }
                }
        }
```

Figure A.11 Routines linevl and lineh.

interpolate between output spectral values, since a total of 256 x-axis points are graphed, while the spectral output may be some smaller subset of points, depending on the selected FFT order. The routine lineh is used to generate horizontal grid lines, if called for. The routines linevl and lineh are illustrated in Figure A.11. The function PLTBUF writes a single character to the screen in graphics mode and is used for labeling (as illustrated in Figures A.8a, b, and c). The routine read_ title is used to input the title. These functions are illustrated in Figure A.12. Finally, Figure A.13 illustrates the contents of the library cplotlib.lib, which contains all the remaining needed routines that are discussed in the text.

```
/* Plot graphics char buffer in "buffer". */

#include <dos.h>

PLTBUF(x1,y1)
        int x1,y1;
        {
        extern char buffer[];
        int n;
        union REGS regs;

        regs.h.dh = y1;                                 /* Initialize regs */
        regs.h.dl = x1;
        regs.h.bh = 0;

        for(n = 2;n < (buffer[1]+2);n++)
            {
            regs.h.ah = 2;                              /* position cursor */
            int86(0x10,&regs,&regs);

            regs.x.cx = 1;                              /* Single char */
            regs.h.ah = 10;                             /* Write char */
            regs.h.al = buffer[n];
            regs.h.bl = 1;                              /* Attribute */
            int86(0x10,&regs,&regs);
            regs.h.dl++;                                /* Inc x-pos */
            }
        }




/* This routine captures title */

# include <stdio.h>

read_title()
        {
        extern char buffer1[];
        int n,ch;

        buffer1[0] = 80;                                /* Buffer max */
        buffer1[81] = '$';                              /* End delimiter */
        printf("Input title -- max 80 char ");
        for(n = 2;(n < 80) && ((ch = getchar()) != '\n');n++)
            buffer1[n] = ch;
        buffer1[1] = n - 2;                             /* Buffer count */
        }
```

Figure A.12 Routines PLTBUF and read_title.

```
lib

Microsoft (R) Library Manager   Version 3.04
Copyright (C) Microsoft Corp 1983, 1984, 1985, 1986.  All rights reserved.

Library name: cplotlib
Operations: +title+pltbuf
List file: cplotlib.dir
Output library:

<C:\>type cplotlib.dir
_bbox.............bbox              _box..............box
_box_spect.......bbox              _KEYDEL..........cplot
_lineh...........lineh             _linev...........linev
_linev1..........linev1            _plotpoint.......ppoint
_plotterm........plotterm          _PLTBUF..........pltbuf
_read_title......title             _SC320...........cplot
_SC80............cplot             _SCRCL...........cplot
_tick............tick              _WRDOT...........cplot
_xtick...........bbox              _ytick...........bbox


cplot            Offset: 00000010H  Code and data size: 3d0H
   _KEYDEL          _SC320           _SC80              _SCRCL
   _WRDOT

linev            Offset: 00000840H  Code and data size: 14bH
   _linev

ppoint           Offset: 00000c50H  Code and data size: 78H
   _plotpoint

plotterm         Offset: 00000e90H  Code and data size: 12H
   _plotterm

box              Offset: 00000fd0H  Code and data size: aaH
   _box

tick             Offset: 00001200H  Code and data size: 194H
   _tick

lineh            Offset: 00001680H  Code and data size: 81H
   _lineh

linev1           Offset: 00001820H  Code and data size: 7cH
   _linev1

bbox             Offset: 00001a60H  Code and data size: 2c0H
   _bbox            _box_spect       _xtick             _ytick

title            Offset: 00001f20H  Code and data size: 1c1H
   _read_title

pltbuf           Offset: 00002330H  Code and data size: 2b7H
   _PLTBUF

<C:\>
```

Figure A.13 Library contents for cplotlib.lib.

REFERENCES

1. Rabiner, L. R., and R. Gold, *Theory and Application of Digital Signal Processing*, Prentice-Hall, Inc., Englewood Cliffs, NJ, pp. 356–368 (1975).
2. Harris, F. J., "On the Use of Windows for Harmonic Analysis with the Discrete Fourier Transform," *IEEE Proceedings*, Vol. 66, No. 1, p. 51 (1978).

APPENDIX

B
A Summary of C Language Syntax

This appendix summarizes the syntax used by the C language. We cover the following topical categories:

1. Control structures
2. Operators
3. Data types and storage classes
4. Other syntax

B.1 CONTROL STRUCTURES

Control structures fall into three groups:

1. Loops
2. Decision structures
3. Jumps

Loops consist of the for, while, and do while syntax. Examples of these constructs are as follows:

for

```
for(n=1; n<=N; n++)
    {
    ...
    }
```

Here the code represented by the ellipsis executes N times as n increments.

while

```
. . .
n=N-M;
while(n!=N)
   {
   . . .
   n++;
   }
. . .
```

This code fragment causes the code contained in the braces to execute iteratively M times.

do

```
. . .
n=N;
do
   {
   . . .
   n++;
   }
while(n<M)
. . .
```

Again the code contained in the braces executes iteratively until n = M.

The decision structures are represented by if, else, case, switch, and default. Consider

if

```
. . .
if(n==M)
   {
   . . .
   n++;
   }
```

Here the code in the braces executes when n = M.

if-else

```
. . .
if(n==M)
   {
   . . .
   n++;
   }
```

```
else
  {
                   . . .
  n++;
  }
```

Again the code following the if (contained in braces) executes when n = M. Otherwise, the code in the braces following the else executes.

The case and switch (and default) decision elements work together. Consider the following:

```
. . .
switch (A)
  {
  case B:
    statement1;
    break;
  case C:
    statement2;
    break;
  . . .
  case Z:
    statementN;
    break;
  default:
    statement N+1;
    break;
  }
  . . .
```

This sequence of statements permits selection of an execution path depending on multiple decision making. With the switch statement, the expression A is examined and compared with B, C, . . . , Z to check for a match. Any match results in the subsequent execution of the following statement (this could be multiple statements contained in braces). The break statement then causes execution to jump out of the switch processing. If the break were omitted, all subsequent code within the switch processing would execute consecutively. Note that the default processing executes only when no match occurs.

As part of the switch processing, we saw the break syntax used. This is a typical jump implementation. The continue command is another jump command. It is used in a loop and causes the execution to jump to the end of the loop. Consider

```
. . .
for (n=1; n<N; n+1)
  {
  if (n<M)
    {
    a=B;
    continue;
    }
```

```
if((n>M)&&(n<MM))
   {
   a=C;
   continue;
   }
a=D;
   }
```

This code accomplishes selective assignment. When n is less than M, a is set equal to B. When n is greater than M but less than MM, a is set equal to C. Otherwise, a is set equal to D.

The goto syntax is a direct jump of the form

```
. . .
goto number;
. . .
number:
   {
   . . .
   }
. . .
```

This syntax is not recommended because it leads to unstructured programs.

B.2 OPERATORS

Table B.1 illustrates the operators found in the C language. Table B.2 contains additional C operators that are lesser used.

B.3 DATA TYPES AND STORAGE CLASSES

The basic data types are as follows:

int   integer (2 bytes); signed
long   integer (4 bytes); signed
short   integer (2 bytes); signed
unsigned   integer; zero or positive
   unsigned int (2 bytes)
   unsigned long (4 bytes)
   unsigned short (2 bytes)
char   character (1 byte)
float   floating point (4 bytes)
double   floating point (8 bytes)

TABLE B.1 C OPERATORS

Operator	Discussion
( )	Grouping
{ }	Executes all contained syntax
++	Increment
--	Decrement
*	Multiply
/	Divide
+	Add
-	Subtract
<	Less than
>	Greater than
<=	Less than or equal
>=	Greater than or equal
&&	AND: logical
||	OR: logical
=	Equal: assignment
+=	Adds right-hand quantity to left hand
-=	Subtracts right-hand quantity from left hand
*=	Multiplies left hand by right hand
/=	Divides left hand by right hand
==	Equal to: relational
!=	Not equal to: relational
%	Modulus
%=	Modulus after dividing left hand by right hand
*	Pointer: gives the value at the pointed address
&	Pointer: gives the address of the variable

TABLE B.2 ADDITIONAL C OPERATORS

Operator	Discussion
(type)	Changes the type of a variable
sizeof	Returns the size in bytes of the variable
->	Assigns a structure member
.	Assigns a structure member
!	NOT: bitwise
~	Takes one's complement: bitwise
&	AND: bitwise
^	EXCLUSIVE OR: bitwise
|	OR: bitwise
?:	Conditional operator
<<	Left shift: bitwise
>>	Right shift: bitwise

Storage classes exist as four kinds: auto, external, static, and register.

auto: Generated with temporary duration within a module as local

external: Generated for all time as a global

static: Generated for all time but local in scope

register: Generated with temporary duration within a module as local and, if possible, associated with a CPU register

B.4 OTHER SYNTAX

The syntax

```
function ()
  {
  ...
  return(d)
  }
```

returns the value d from the function

A C structure can be defined as the following, for example:

```
struct
  {
  int a
  float b
  } name;
```

Reference to structure members is by variable name:

```
name.a = 10;
```

or

```
name.b = 1.473;
```

Using pointers, it follows

```
struct
  {
  int c;
  int d;
  float e;
  } name1,*ptrname1;
```

can be referenced using the $->$ operator. The following expressions are equivalent:

```
name.c
ptrname1 -> c
```

and

```
(*Ptrname1).c
```

A union of the form

```
union
    {
    intc;
    intd;
    floate;
    } name1,*Ptrname1;
```

is referenced the same as a structure, but room for the largest variable only is saved and shared across the other types. For example, in name1 above as a union only 8 bytes of storage are reserved. If e is saved in the common union storage, the remaining types cannot be saved until c is released. The structure name1 indicated earlier saves storage for each type specified. Hence, while the structure occupies more storage, the memory is not treated as common.

APPENDIX

C

Programs Used in This Text

In this appendix, we list the programs found throughout the book. Table C.1 indicates each program with a brief description and page number. Table C.2 contains the MAKE files used in creating the .EXE files for the first seven chapters. The programs contained in Chapters 8 and 9 are illustrated with an associated MAKE file in each chapter. The programs contained in Chapter 10 were compiled or assembled and linked separately.

Figure C.1 illustrates the contents of cplotlib.lib and Figure C.2 contains the contents of commlib.lib. Similarly, Figure C.3 presents the contents of egalib.lib and Figure C.4 the contents of asmlib.lib. All the referenced functions or procedures are contained in the book in the chapter where the library is first referenced.

TABLE C.1 PROGRAMS CONTAINED IN THIS TEXT

Program	Discussion	Page
firstc.c	Beginning program that prints message to display	12
timhist.c	Creates a time history and value database	53
thistin.c	Reads a time history and value database	57
mortgage.c	Calculates monthly mortgage payment	59
savings.c	Calculates constant dollar appreciation	62
llcr.c	Creates a file using low-level I/O	64
llrd.c	Reads a file using low-level I/O	65
dja.c	Reads Dow Jones history and plots graph	67
box2nor.c	Draws a box for normal plot	69
cplot.c	Coutines for plotting, which partially encompass cplotlib.lib [cplotlib.lib also includes PLTBUF() on page 72, plotpoint() on page 72, and linev() and lineh() on page 73]	71

TABLE C.1 (*Continued*)

fmwave.c	Creates FM spectrum data	80
spectra2.c	Calculates spectrum and plots points	82
gaussck.c	Sets up and plots Gaussian random numbers	88
grand.c	Generates Gaussian random numbers	90
gauhist.c	Generates and plots Gaussian random number histogram	92
bracket.c	Allocates time history into brackets	114
diskrd1.c	Reads month, year, and value arrays from disk	115
bball.c	Generates bouncing ball setup and output	153
xmot.c	Generates *x* and *y* motion for bouncing ball	154
balshp1.c	Creates ball shape on screen using BIOS interrupt calls	155
setup.c	Sets up bouncing ball screen	156
beep.c	Generates output beep based on register calls	164
wrdot0.c	Clears dot (this appears as a function in Figure 4.7, but was generated as a separate C program)	156
bbball.c	Generates bouncing ball setup and output for DMA version	165
(xmot.c)	Modified to include BEEP()	166
bbalsp1.c	Ball shape using DMA	167
bbalsp0.c	Ball erase using DMA	168
delay.c	Arbitrary delay	168
timer.c	Generates time interval	169
rdtm.c	Program to read time based on function rd__tm() in Figure 4.16	170
zerotm.c	Program to zero out time based on function	170
tone.c	Generates extended tone	171
ttime.c	Read-set time	172
settm.c	Function module to set time	172
ddate.c	Set date	173
setdate.c	Function module to set date	174
memory.c	Reads memory size	175
rotate.c	Program to set up and generate rotating cube	189
rotcube.c	Function to rotate cube with DMA	190
rotmat.c	Generates rotation matrix	191
rotpt.c	Rotates point	191
dmapoint.c	Creates connecting line using DMA	192
udmapoin.c	Removes connecting line using DMA	193
geomser.c	Geometric series	241
diskwt.c	General disk write routine	241
drlp.c	Logarithmic plotting function	242
logplt.c	Logarithmic plot driver	243
diskrd.c	General disk read routine	244
logbox.c	Generates box and grid lines for logarithmic plot	245
(lineh.c, lineu.c, ppoint.c, pltbuf.c, plotterm.c, and bbox.c)	All these routines correspond to their functional equivalent as appearing in the cplotlib.lib library	
barck.c	Calling program for bar graph	251
bargrp.c	Function to create bar graph	252
bar.asm	Assembler routine to generate bar	253

TABLE C.1 *(Continued)*

comp.c	Compound interest setup and plot	255
poww.asm	Calculates compound interest using coprocessor calls	256
modemck.c	Calling routine for RS232 modem communications	282
modct1.c	Modem control functions	284
modchar.c	Function to output character	285
(modchar.c)	Function to output character modified for DMA	286
loopio.c	Operational loop function for communications processing	287
(commlib.lib)	Communications library routines	288
mainsc.c	Calling program for single-conversion A/D	296
grid.c	Generates grid for A/D plot	296
initsc.c	Initializes the DT2828	297
sconv.c	Performs conversion and plots	298
inw.asm	Input word at port	299
outw.asm	Output word at port	299
drlpega.c	Calling program for log plot EGA mode	314
lpega.c	Function to create log plot, EGA	315
lboxega.c	Function to draw log box, EGA	316
drlpvga.c	Calling program for log plot VGA mode	319
lpvga.c	Function to create log plot, VGA	320
lboxvga.c	Function to draw log box, VGA	321
ckscor.c	Main calling program to check correlation grid	323
scorega.c	Set up correlation, EGA	323
ckscor1.c	Second example of correlation grid	324
ckscor3.c	Third example of correlation grid	325
ckcorr1.c	Main correlation function calling program	327
ldarry.c	Function to load correlation arrays	329
corr.c	Function to set up and scale correlation	330
corfun.c	Function to generate correlation values	331
ckscor2.c	Function to set up correlation screens, EGA	332
pltarry.c	Function to plot correlation arrays	333
rndgen.c	Random number disk file generator	334
diskgen.c	Program to generate arbitrary disk write	337
main3d.c	Main calling program for 3D plot	346
gen3D.c	Main calling program for 3D plot generator	346
graph3D.c	Function to load 3D data	347
xscale.c	Function to scale 3D data	348
facet3D.c	Function to plot 3D facets	349
xadiskr.c	Function same as diskrd.c (Figure 2.4c) except reads single array xarray [ ]	
xadiskw.c	Function same as diskwt.c except writes single array xarray [ ]	
nodo.c	Creates and destroys a window	360
beginw.c	Beginning Windows program: creates window	365
menu1.c	Windows program to test menus	396
win3.c	Sin$(x)/x$ Windows program	401
wingrp.c	Sets up Windows 30 graph	405
wingen.c	Generates 3D surface, Windows	405
winrot.c	Rotates plot, Windows	406
winpt.c	Defines rotated point, Windows	406
winsca.c	Scales 3D plot, Windows	407
win4.c	Modified win3.c, which is continuous in angle	409

TABLE C.1 *(Concluded)*

menu4.rc	Resource file for win4.c menu	413
win4.def	Definition file for win4.c	414
menu3.c	Program to test dialog box	424
menu3.rc	Resource file for menu3.c	427
menu4.c	Program to test dialog box I/O	431
win10.c	Sin(x)/x program with dialog box	436
win10.rc	Resource file for win10.c	441
win10.def	Definition file for win10.c	441
win11.c	Clipboard: stretch blt sin(x)/x	443
win12.c	clip3D.c with parameter box	452
win12.def	Definition file for win12.c	460
win12.rc	Resource file for win12.c	459
win13.c	Calling program to print sin(x)/x	461
win13.rc	Resource file for win13.c	466
win13.def	Definition file for win13.c	467
win14.c	Modified win13.c for correct page width	470
OS2ONE.ASM	Starter Protected Mode.ASM program	492
OS2TWO.ASM	Protected Mode .ASM screen clear	493
OS24.ASM	CGA screen clear Protected Mode (.ASM) displays a box	495
OS251.ASM	Modular calling routine (.ASM) for creating Protected Mode box	500
OS252.ASM	Box generator for OS251.ASM	502
OS2512.ASM	Multitasked Protected Mode random box routine	505
OS261.ASM	Box generator for OS2512.ASM multitasked	509
os21.c	Simple Protected Mode C program	513
os211.c	API version of os21.c-C	513
os212c.c	Screen clear and write Protected Mode C program	514
os22c.c	Set and clear CGA mode in Protected Mode, C	515
os23c.c	Set and clear CGA mode with a screen clear in Protected Mode, C	516
os24c.c	Same as os23c.c with generated nomenclature, C	517
os25c.c	Draws Protected Mode CGA box, C	519
os251c.c	Box routine for os25c.c, C	521
os26c.c	Multitasked Protected Mode random box routine, C	522
os261c.c	Multitasked box generator for os26c.c	525
fft.c	Fast Fourier transform calculation	534
ckfft.c	Check real FFT output	535
ckffti.c	Check imaginary FFT output	536
(wavefm.c)	FM waveform generator	538
spectrum.c	Power spectrum and plot routine	540
ckspect.c	Sinusoids in noise calling program	542
(boxspect.c)	Routines for generating graphics boxes and tick marks	547
(linev1() and lineh())	Vertical and horizontal line routines	549
(read_title())	Routine to input title for graph zero__tm() in Figure 4.16	550

TABLE C.2 MAKE FILES APPROPRIATE TO THE PROGRAMS IN THIS BOOK

```
#MAKE file to generate firstc.exe
firstc.obj: \c\firstc.c
         cl/c \c\firstc.c
firstc.exe: firstc.obj
         link firstc
#MAKE file to create time history program
timhist.obj: \c\timhist.c
         cl/c \c\timhist.c
timhist.exe: timhist.obj
         link timhist,,,,
#MAKE file to create time history input program
thistin.obj: \c\thistin.c
         cl/c \c\thistin.c
thistin.exe: thistin.obj
         link thistin,,,,
#MAKE file to create mortgage calculation program
mortgage.obj: \c\mortgage.c
         cl/c \c\mortgage.c
mortgage.exe: mortgage.obj
         link mortgage,,,,
#MAKE file for savings calculation
savings.obj: \c\savings.c
         cl/c \c\savings.c
savings.exe: savings.obj
         link savings,,,,
#MAKe file to create low-level file creation program
llcr.obj: \c\llcr.c
         cl/c \c\llcr.c
llcr.exe: llcr.obj
         link llcr,,,,
#MAKE file to create low-level file read program
llrd. obj: \c\llrd.c
         cl/c \c\llrd.c
llrd.exe: llrd.obj
         link llrd,,,,
#MAKE file for Dow Jones Average plot
dja.obj: \c\dja.c
         cl/c \c\dja.c
box2nor.obj: \c\box2nor.c
         cl/c \c\box2nor.c
dja.exe: dja.obj box2nor.obj cplotlib.lib
         link dja+box2nor,,,,cplotlib
#MAKE file for FM waveform program
fmwave.obj: \c\fmwave.c
         cl/c \c\fmwave.c
spectra2.obj: \c\spectra2.c
         cl/c spectra2.c
fmwave.exe: fmwave.obj spectra2.obj fft.obj cplotlib.lib
         link fmwave+spectra2+fft,,,,cplotlib
```

App. C   Programs Used in This Text   **563**

TABLE C.2 *(Continued)*

```
#MAKE file for random number plot
gaussck.exe: gaussck.obj grand.obj cplotlib.lib
        link gaussck+grand,,,cplotlib
#MAKE file for Gaussian r.n. histogram plot
gauhist.obj: \c\gauhist.c
        cl/c \c\gauhist.c
gauhist.exe: gauhist.obj grand.obj cplotlib.lib
        link gauhist+grand,,,cplotlib
#MAKE file to generate bracket intervals on input file
#   diskrd1( diskrd with value, month, and years specified)
bracket.exe: bracket.obj diskrd1.obj cplotlib.lib
        link bracket+diskrd1,,,cplotlib
#MAKE file for bouncing ball __ interrupts
#   balshp1(balshp1, balshp0); xmot(xmotion, ymotion)
bball.exe: bball.obj balshp1.obj xmot.obj setup.obj wrdot0.obj\
                beep.obj cplotlib.lib
        link bball+balshp1+xmot+setup+wrdot0+beep,,,cplotlib
#MAKE file for bouncing ball with screen DMA
bbball.exe: bbball.obj bbalsp1.obj bbalsp0.obj delay.obj beep.obj\
                xmot.obj setup.obj cplotlib.lib
        link bbball+bbalsp1+bbalsp0+delay+beep+xmot+setup,,,\
                cplotlib
#MAKE file for timer
timer.exe: timer.obj tone.obj rdtm.obj zerotm.obj cplotlib.lib
        link timer+tone+rdtm+zerotm,,,cplotlib
#MAKE file for set/read time
ttime.exe: ttime.obj settm.obj rdtm.obj
        link ttime+rdtm+settm
#MAKE file for checking and setting date
ddate.exe: ddate.obj setdate.obj
        link ddate+setdate
#MAKE file for memory read
memory.obj: \c\memory.c
        cl/c \c\memory.c
memory.exe: memory.obj
        link memory,,,,
#MAKE file to generate rotating cube program
rotate.exe: rotate.obj delay.obj rotcube.obj rotmat.obj rotpt.obj\
                dmapoint.obj udmapoin.obj cplotlib.lib
        link rotate+delay+rotcube+rotmat+rotpt+dmapoint+udmapoin,,,\
                cplotlib
#MAKE file to generate geometric sum and disk write
geomser.exe: geomser.obj diskwt.obj
        link geomser+diskwt,,,,
#MAKE file for program to generate log plot of geom series
drlp.exe: drlp.obj logplot.obj logbox.obj diskrd.obj \
                lineh.obj linev.obj ppoint.obj \
                pltbuf.obj plotterm.obj bbox.obj asmlib.lib
        link drlp+logplot+logbox+diskrd+linev+lineh+ppoint+\
                pltbuf+plotterm+bbox,,,asmlib
#MAKE file to check bar graph generator
barck.exe: barck.obj bargrp.obj bar.obj cplotlib.lib
        link barck+bargrp+bar,,,cplotlib
```

TABLE C.2   (Concluded)

```
#MAKE file for compound interest
comp.exe: comp.obj bargrp.obj bar.obj poww.obj cplotlib.lib
          link comp+bargrp+bar+poww,,,,cplotlib
#MAKE file for modem program
#   modemck(main); modctl(modout...);modchar(charout...)
modemck.exe: modemck.obj modctl.obj modchar.obj loopio.obj \
                commlib.lib cplotlib.lib
          link modemck+modctl+modchar+loopio,,,comblib+cplotlib
#MAKE file for AD converter
#   mainsc(main); initsc(InitSC); sconv(SingleConvert)
mainsc.exe: mainsc.obj initsc.obj sconv.obj inw.obj outw.obj \
                grid.obj dmapoint.obj udmapoint.obj cplotlib.lib
          link mainsc+initsc+sconv+inw+outw+grid+dmapoint+udampoint,,,\
                cplotlib
#MAKE file for log plot EGA mode
drlpega.exe: drlpega.obj lpega.obj lboxega.obj diskrd.obj egalib.lib
          link drlpega+lpega+lboxega+diskrd,,,egalib
#MAKE file for log plot VGA mode
drlpvga.exe: drlpvga.obj lpvga.obj lboxvga.obj diskrd.obj egalib.lib
          link drlpvga+lpvga+lboxvga+diskrd,,,egalib
#MAKe file to check grid data structures #1
ckscor.exe: ckscor.obj scorega.obj egalib.lib
          link ckscor+scorega,,,egalib
#MAKe file to generate intermediate structures correlation grid
#   ckscor1(main, corr_setup)
ckscor1.exe: ckscor1.obj egalib.lib
          link ckscor1,,,,egalib
#MAKe file for 3rd structure oriented grid program
ckscor3.exe: ckscor3.obj ckscor2.obj egalib.lib
          link ckscor3+ckscor2,,,egalib
#MAKE file to generate correlation function
#   ckscor1(main); ldarry(load_arrays); corr(corr); corfun(correlation)
#   ckscor2(corr_setup); pltarry(plot_arrays); fft(fft); diskrd(diskrd)
ckcorr1.obj: \eega\ckcorr1.c
          cl/c \eega\ckcorr1.c
ckscor.exe: ckcorr1.obj ldarry.obj corfun.obj diskrd.obj fft.obj\
          corr.obj pltarry.obj ckscor2.obj egalib.lib
          link ckcorr1+ldarry+corr+corfun+diskrd+fft+pltarry+ckscor2\
                ,,,egalib
#MAKE file to generate random input for disk write
rndgen.exe: rndgen.obj grand.obj diskwt.obj
          link rndgen+grand+diskwt,,,,
#MAKE file for arbitrary disk file generation
dskgen.exe: dskgen.obj diskwt.obj
          link dskgen+diskwt,,,,
#MAKE file for 3D plot
main3d.exe: main3d.obj graph3d.obj xscale.obj facet3d.obj\
                rotmat.obj rotpt.obj xadiskr.obj egalib.lib
          link main3d+graph3d+xscale+facet3d+rotmat+rotpt+\
                xadiskr,,,egalib
#MAKE file for sin2 3D plot
gen3D.exe: gen3D.obj xadiskw.obj
          link gen3D+xadiskw,,,,
```

```
_bbox............bbox          _box.............box
_box_spect........bbox         _KEYDEL...........cplot
_lineh............lineh        _linev............linev
_linev1...........linev1       _plotpoint........ppoint
_plotterm.........plotterm     _PLTBUF...........pltbuf
_read_title.......title        _SC320............cplot
_SC80.............cplot        _SCRCL............cplot
_tick.............tick         _WRDOT............cplot
_xtick............bbox         _ytick............bbox


cplot          Offset: 00000010H  Code and data size: 3d0H
  _KEYDEL          _SC320             _SC80              _SCRCL
  _WRDOT

linev          Offset: 00000840H  Code and data size: 14bH
  _linev

ppoint         Offset: 00000c50H  Code and data size: 78H
  _plotpoint

plotterm       Offset: 00000e90H  Code and data size: 12H
  _plotterm

box            Offset: 00000fd0H  Code and data size: aaH
  _box

tick           Offset: 00001200H  Code and data size: 194H
  _tick

lineh          Offset: 00001680H  Code and data size: 81H
  _lineh

linev1         Offset: 00001820H  Code and data size: 7cH
  _linev1

bbox           Offset: 00001a60H  Code and data size: 2c0H
  _bbox            _box_spect         _xtick             _ytick

title          Offset: 00001f20H  Code and data size: 1c1H
  _read_title

pltbuf         Offset: 00002330H  Code and data size: 2b7H
  _PLTBUF
```

Figure C.1   Contents of the library cplotlib.lib.

```
_INITSP...........commlib        _RCVR.............commlib
_STATUS...........commlib        _XMIT.............commlib

commlib        Offset: 00000010H  Code and data size: b4H
  _INITSP          _RCVR              _STATUS            _XMIT
```

Figure C.2   Contents of the library commlib.lib.

```
_bbox_EGA.........pltterm          _lineh............lineh
_linev............linev            _plotpoint.......pltterm
_plotterm.........pltterm          _SCEGA............pltterm
_SCRCL............pltterm          _SCVGA............scvga


linev             Offset: 00000010H  Code and data size: 40H
  _linev

lineh             Offset: 00000180H  Code and data size: 42H
  _lineh

pltterm           Offset: 000002f0H  Code and data size: ceH
  _bbox_EGA           _plotpoint       _plotterm          _SCEGA
  _SCRCL

scvga             Offset: 00000620H  Code and data size: 12H
  _SCVGA
```

Figure C.3 Contents of the library egalib.lib.

```
_KEYDEL...........keydel           _SC320............sc320
_SC80.............sc80             _SCRCL............scrcl
_WRDOT............wrdot

keydel            Offset: 00000010H  Code and data size: 1aH
  _KEYDEL

scrcl             Offset: 00000070H  Code and data size: 25H
  _SCRCL

sc320             Offset: 000000e0H  Code and data size: 1cH
  _SC320

sc80              Offset: 00000140H  Code and data size: 1cH
  _SC80

wrdot             Offset: 000001a0H  Code and data size: 22H
  _WRDOT
```

Figure C.4 Contents of the library asmlib.lib.

APPENDIX

D

Systems Programming and C

The UNIX operating system was written in C, and this served to establish a precedent for the language. Essentially, C has become recognized as a user-friendly implementation that can be used to facilitate the development of systems software, in addition to the usual applications requirements. We could spend some time simply defining systems software, but it is convenient to assume that it includes the following categories [1, 2]:

1. Assemblers
2. Linkers
3. Loaders
4. Compilers
5. Operating systems
6. Editors
7. Debuggers

In addition to these programs, macro processors and database management systems (DBMS) are also considered systems programs, but these tend to be more specialized and applications oriented; hence, we separate them from the above list.

D.1 WHAT IS SYSTEMS PROGRAMMING?

As the above list indicates, a great deal of system software consists of programs that act on more familiar applications. For example, in this book we develop numerous applications that are written in the C language using an editor. This C source code is, in turn, compiled using the Microsoft C Compiler. Subsequent run-time development encompasses a debugging phase using CodeView, a symbolic debugger. Prior to execution in the run-time environment, the compiler output (object code) is input to the Microsoft Linker, which links all the references from different modules and locates the program in memory. Alternatively, if the source code had been written in assembly language, an assembler would be used to generate the object code. Finally, everything resides under the control of the operating system, which manages the computer system interfaces. It is clear, then, that system software displays a degree of machine dependency that is not found at the applications level of programming.

Applications programming can be thought of as programming concerned with accomplishing a specific (focused) task, while systems programming is intended to support the computer implementation. That is not to say that some conceptual aspects of systems programming are not machine independent; they are. It is a characteristic, however, that a large percentage of systems software is by definition machine dependent. One attribute of the C language is that such programming can be accomplished with only occasional resort to assembly language in time-critical applications. In the following discussion, we touch briefly on the above categories of systems programs.

D.2 SYSTEMS PROGRAMMING TECHNIQUES

Systems programs tend to be reasonably complex because of the large variety of contingencies they must be prepared to handle. Aside from accomplishing a fixed task, the system program module must act in a user-friendly fashion. The user should not be allowed to crash the system with erroneous or out-of-bound input. Furthermore, enough flexibility must be designed into such software that the user can always recover from situations of uncertainty.

Editors allow users to create and update files. In this book we restrict the discussion to text editors where the files consist of lines of text. (A specific example is the VEDIT PLUS program used to generate C source code for this book [3] and EDLIN, the IBM line editor [4].) From a purely mechanical viewpoint, editors display a block of text within a document and allow this block to be modified via input instructions. The major tools for inputting such changes are a keyboard or a mouse. Current editors are moving in the direction of mouse-type interfaces because of the ease and efficiency of using such software.

Figure D.1 illustrates a representative functional block diagram for a text editor. This figure represents a modified interpretation of text editors as viewed by Meyrowitz [5]. It is clear that edited material is obtained and returned to memory via DMA transfer, and input commands are entered using a keyboard or mouse, and intermediate buffered sections of memory are displayed using the display component. The traveling component fixes the editing and viewing pointers, which locate the text being modified and the text being viewed, respectively. The filters buffer segments of text to be either edited or viewed and use the appropriate pointers to locate this text.

Why is Figure D.1 important other than as a functional representation for text editors? It serves as a basis for defining what sections of code can be written

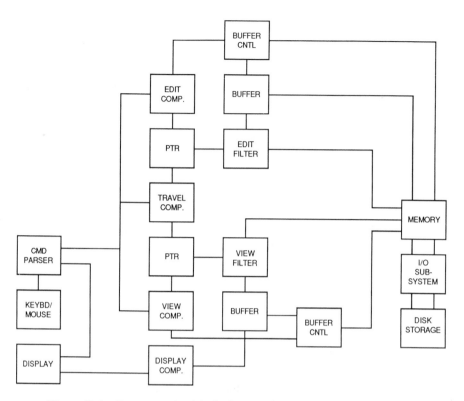

Figure D.1 Representative block diagram for text editor programming.

in C and what must be written in assembly language. We will not spend time on defining routines for text editors because this is beyond the scope of the present text, but it is useful to examine how C can play a role in the architecture of a text editor.

Clearly, all the memory-to-memory (buffer) data transfers are best written to execute as rapidly as possible; hence, the filters (editing and viewing) and buffer control code should be assembly language (the I/O processing). The remaining code, however, can easily be implemented in the C language. It is understood that the text editor will act as an application under the operating system. Thus, all the operating system service routines (such as disk I/O routines) are accessible to the text editor in whatever form they have been created. (The display processing, also, can be written in assembler because of the need to update the screen rapidly. This, however, will yield only slight improvements in speed and would only exist in this form in optimized editors.)

Figure D.2 illustrates a simplified functional block diagram for a debugging program that has both symbolic and assembly language debugging features. Again, the input command string is parsed and processed with modifications occurring only in a single buffer area.

Compilers and assemblers are somewhat more complex than debuggers and editors. Compilers are programs designed to recognize and process specific high-level languages called grammars. Typical of these are FORTRAN, COBOL, ALGOL,

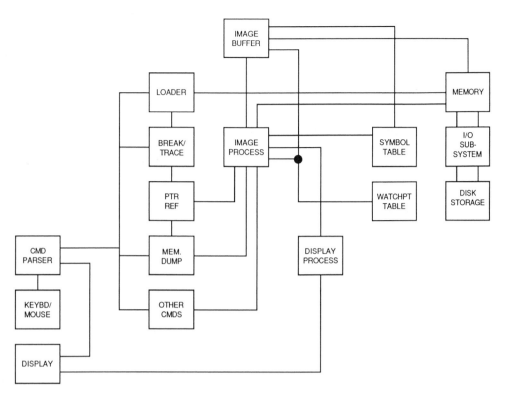

Figure D.2 Representative functional block diagram for a debugging program.

and C. The grammar defines the syntax of the language, and any sequence of source code input to the compiler must undergo a lexical analysis to separate each syntactical element. This is accomplished by the *scanner*, which is then followed by a syntactical analysis or parsing by the *parser*. Finally, the compiler creates *machine instructions* (assembly language equivalences may also be generated if requested as a compiler option). These three phases of compiling can usually be accomplished on two or more passes of the compiler for the C language.

Assemblers are conceptually similar to compilers but rely on a simpler process for accomplishing object code generation. Each mnemonic must be converted to machine code based on the equivalent operation code (op-code) for the mnemonic. Symbolic operands must be converted to their equivalent machine addresses and machine instructions must be generated in the proper format. Finally, data constants must be converted to their proper internal format. Again, one or two pass assemblers are normally used at the microcomputer level of program interfacing.

Loaders bring the object program into memory for execution and linkers combine two or more separate object programs to yield a run-time module. Loading is a nontrivial step in which linked object code is actually brought into memory and loaded on correct byte boundaries. Linking acts to ensure that cross references among various object modules are satisfied, as we have seen. Essentially, each external reference must be searched to find a corresponding public declaration and associated declaration.

The remaining category of systems program, operating systems, is the subject of the next section. It is the operating system that we will focus on predominantly in the rest of this appendix.

D.3 OPERATING SYSTEMS: DOS EMPHASIS

No software design reflects the designer's thinking more than an operating system. Such a program is the embodiment of a unique approach to a plan for managing the system resources. Basically, the essential components needed to describe system programming in general and operating systems in particular are as follows: (1) processes, (2) input/output, (3) memory management, and (4) file systems. Figure D.3 presents a high-level block structure for the IBM microcomputer software system environment. Clearly illustrated are the four components delineated above. Each of these components is discussed in the following subsections.

D.3.1 Processes

To paraphrase Tanenbaum [6], a process is a block of code executing in a program environment. It includes the linked object code, data and stack area, all CPU registers, and any additional hardware/software needed to execute the program. The DOS software (through Version 3.3) is a single-task operating system. Hence, DOS can only service one process at a time. The familiar *roll-out* that occurs on multitasking systems is not applicable in the DOS environment. Figure D.3 has no provision for multitasking (no process table or preserved core image). The function of process management, however, does take place. Once executing, each process continues to completion under DOS. The category of operations falling under the Command Processor constitutes process management in DOS. Three process categories can be implemented (individually) under the command processor shell: resident processor actions (including selected interrupt service and external command execution such as formatting disks), internal command processes (such as locating a file on disk under program control or assigning a time to a file creation by maintaining a count with the system timer), and the initialization processes (implemented when the system boots).

It does not take a great deal of imagination to envision how disk I/O processes, for example, might be handled in the DOS environment. A rather interesting example of a process, however, is the initialization process, which takes place upon power-up. It will be instructive to consider this process in some detail, and the *child* activities illustrated in Figure D.3 will then become clearer. Figure D.4 illustrates schematically the initialization process for the IBM PC. How does initialization work? Obviously, the processor must jump to a known address at some point in the initialization process. Intel has designed the 8088 and the 8086 to initialize the CS register and IP to FFFFH and 0, respectively. The code that resides at this location must then begin the rest of the initialization process. In the IBM PC, the power-on reset starts the 8088 (or 8086) at the above address; the instruction residing at FFFF:0000 is input to the CPU for execution. This instruction, in the case of the IBM PC, is a jump to the entry point RESET (which resides at address F0000:E05B) in the BIOS code. Following the jump, the code executes to check for error conditions,

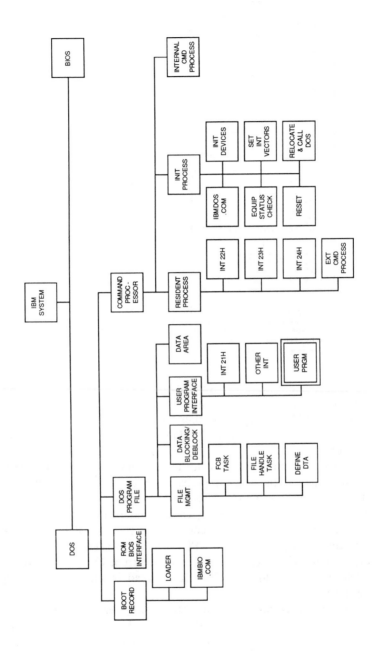

Figure D.3 IBM DOS operating system environment.

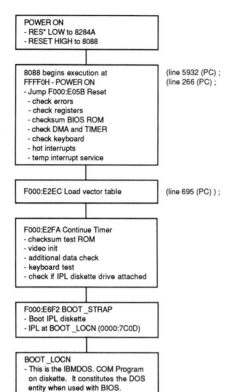

```
POWER ON
 - RES* LOW to 8284A
 - RESET HIGH to 8088
```

```
8088 begins execution at          (line 5932 (PC) ;
FFFF0H - POWER ON                 (line 266 (PC) ;
 - Jump F000:E05B Reset
   - check errors
   - check registers
   - checksum BIOS ROM
   - check DMA and TIMER
   - check keyboard
   - hot interrupts
   - temp interrupt service
```

```
F000:E2EC Load vector table       (line 695 (PC) ) ;
```

```
F000:E2FA Continue Timer
 - checksum test ROM
 - video init
 - additional data check
 - keyboard test
 - check if IPL diskette drive attached
```

```
F000:E6F2 BOOT _STRAP
 - Boot IPL diskette
 - IPL at BOOT _LOCN (0000:7C0D)
```

```
BOOT _LOCN
 - This is the IBMDOS. COM Program
   on diskette. It constitutes the DOS
   entity when used with BIOS.
```

Figure D.4 IBM PC initialization process.

check reading and writing registers, perform check sum error checks on the ROM code, test the 8237A DMA initialization, initialize the 8259A (with interrupts enabled), perform an 8259A interrupt controller test, check the timer, and install a temporary interrupt service routine. Then, at address F000:E2EC, code to load the interrupt vector table is executed.

Following loading of the vector table, some additional housekeeping functions are performed and the system prepares to initiate the system boot. At address F000:E620, a jump to BOOT__STRAP takes place and the bootstrap process begins. At this point, the equipment status check, initialization of devices, interrupt vector table load, and reset have all executed. The process BOOT__STRAP prepares to perform an initial program load (IPL) from the diskette in drive A (or fixed disk). A single section (512 bytes) is read using interrupt 13H. If the read is unsuccessful, INT 18H is used to load BASIC. If the read is successful, a jump to BOOT__LOCN takes place.

The INT 13H call essentially starts the process for loading IBMDOS.COM and the boot record (with IBMBIO.COM). The routine pointed to by BOOT__LOCN has been loaded as part of DOS (the code is unavailable for comment since it is proprietary). We can make several remarks about this code based on general inferences about how such code (in many cases) functions. First, as the tasks appearing in Figure D.3 indicate, DOS is eventually called as the final initialization process. The core of this process is a loop, which could have the form

```
DOSCALL:
        NOP
        JMP DOSCALL
```

This infinite loop ensures that the processor continues to function at all times and does not hang. How then do we enter the system? The only way to do so is via hardware interrupts using the resident process. Typically, the user might type in

```
PRGM.EXE    (example)
```

at the keyboard and, when the ENTER key is struck, an interrupt is generated to the 8259A (INT 9) to cause the loop to stop executing, and control then transfers to a DOS entry point in the DOS program file. The transfer would be based on the execution of an external command process that determined the input was a run-time file and not some special reserved word that denoted another DOS command.

As part of the relocation and call to DOS during initialization, working tables and the program segment prefix (PSP) area are set up. Once the DOS program file begins execution, a user program interface is defined for the example above. Also, file management begins to occur with the file management subfunction. This latter activity includes setting up the appropriate data areas for file handles or the file control block (FCB) to access the executable file (in this case PRGM.EXE, which resides on the default drive). Following completion of the program, the DOS program file returns control to DOS (the above-mentioned loop executes), and DOS waits for another hardware interrupt to signal entry to another task.

It is probably clear that a substantial amount of operating system activity involves input/output. We have seen how initialization takes place. The only ambiguous portion of this process is the actual relocation and call to DOS. The first two PSP bytes are a call to INT 20H, the DOS program terminate. The remaining PSP areas are delineated in the *DOS Technical Reference* (see reference 4) and illustrate the needed DOS parameters for setting up the DOS program file and resident process. When a .EXE program is defined by the linker, DS and ES are set to point to the PSP start address. CS, IP, SS, and SP are set to values passed by the linker. Hence, the DOS program file receives executable instructions and data that reside at known addresses. The entire system process can thus be thought of as a continuous program (moving from module to module), with an infinite loop at the core of DOS that can be interrupted by a hardware action.

Obviously, we do not know exactly how DOS operates because IBM has not released the code. The above procedure is exact until the entry to DOS. At this point it becomes facsimile, but is reasonable. The functions described have a core NOP loop, and DOS can be expected to implement this artifact. It is the recommended approach in the Intel literature.

D.3.2 I/O

As we have seen, there are two considerations to be applied to I/O: the interpretation of how the hardware functions and the structure of the software drivers. Both are essential to an understanding of how to handle I/O. There are two categories of I/

O devices in DOS: block devices, which pass and store data in groups of bytes, and character devices, which accept input from or output to a stream of characters (single-byte entities). Each I/O device consists of the mechanical peripheral hardware (a disk drive, for example) and the electronic controller or adapter that interfaces to the remaining system. The controller has intelligent integrated circuits that receive and return data via an internal I/O bus. The processing of these data in response to more global instructions is the function of the service routine, and this service is usually initiated via an interrupt call.

In the IBM microcomputer software, most of the I/O service routines reside in the ROM BIOS code. DOS provides the interface to this code via a ROM BIOS interface routine. Under the user program interface the INT 21H function calls (many of which accomplish I/O operations) and remaining interrupt processing jump via the vector table addresses to the appropriate service functions. The INT 21H routines, however, are resident in DOS, and these service functions, in turn, call BIOS routines as needed. The later versions of DOS provide for a device-independent format to access peripherals. This format sets up and calls function 44H; however, a device handler is still needed to service the peripheral. This handler must be in the device-independent format required by function 44H.

D.3.3 Memory Management

The idea of memory management with the IBM microcomputers has evolved considerably with the PS/2 models. Basically, the 8088 and 8086 had a limited capability for implementing sophisticated memory management schemes. When programs were linked, enough overhead code (pipes) was defined to allow the PSP area to connect to the user code, which in turn had access to the ROM service routines. This linking was defined by the linker based on segment and offset addresses. The offset addresses are determined by the assembler (or compiler) and passed to the linker via known locations. The linker generates the appropriate relocated address with correct segment allocation. The 8088 and 8086 CPU processes these addresses in program fashion to fetch the correct instruction sequence. To do this it must generate a correct 20-bit address. Clearly, the linker must be aware of the memory limitations of the system when generating run-time code. Thus, DOS has a minimal memory management function and this is reflected in Figure D.3.

The 80286 (AT, XT286, and PS/2 Models 50 and 60) have a substantial capability for multitasking and virtual memory use. DOS 3.3 does not provide for these capabilities, however, and it is only with the advent of OS/2 that the Protected Mode software takes advantage of this memory management feature. The Protected Mode architecture for the 80286 and 80386 provides descriptions used in the definition of global and local program areas. These areas can be used as the basis for multitasking, with memory management at the core of this activity. The global descriptor table (GDT) contains global descriptors that correspond to virtual segment addresses (24-bit) with other housekeeping and protection information. This table must be set up at link time and accessed by OS/2 at run time. Similarly, the local descriptor table(s) (LDT) contains local segment address information. There is a single GDT, but possibly more than one LDT (multitasking).

In Protected Mode, as in conventional 8088 or 8086 addressing, there is a 32-bit address consisting of a 16-bit offset and a segment selector (also, 16-bit). The upper 13 bits of the selector correspond to an INDEX that, when multiplied by 8 and added to the base address of the descriptor table, points to the correct segment descriptor entry. The segment descriptor contains the 24-bit segment base (physical base address) that, when added to the 16-bit offset, generates a 24-bit physical address (corresponding to a possible $2^{24} = 16$-megabyte memory access). Before concluding this section, it is useful to consider the final systems programming area: file systems.

D.3.4 File Systems

We have seen how files are created, stored, and retrieved (from disk or diskette, for example) in the IBM microcomputer environment. Naming convention includes a file name and extension. DOS is not particularly device independent because, other than the default drive, drive location must be specified. DOS has data files, directories, and block/character files. The latter are used to model I/O-type devices. Since files are stored on disk or diskette, the management of disk space is a major DOS concern. Access of files is through the DOS function calls, which, in turn, call the disk I/O service routines.

The DOS file management scheme uses the file allocation table (FAT). This approach is suboptimal because the file pointers in the FAT are randomly located and, hence, the entire FAT must be used for every file access, up to the sequential location of the file pointer desired. Clearly, as disk space increases, as it has in the PS/2 Models 60 and 80, FATs get larger and more difficult to access.

The DOS directory contains entries of the following form:

8	3	1	10	2	2	2	4
File Name	Ext	Attributes		Time	Date	First Block	Size

Each directory entry is used to chain to the next entry. A block is nominally 512 bytes. We will not consider the implications of multitasking, because DOS does not support this feature. Under OS/2, however, shared files can require special management. The protection mechanisms intrinsic to the 80286 and 80386 allow the sharing of files during run time. In section D.3.5, we will consider an additional feature provided for the 80386 CPU, a cache memory that allows faster access for such things as data items.

Within the IBM microcomputer environment, the normal file system provided as part of DOS functions in a straightforward fashion because it is single-threaded (only one user). As OS/2 becomes more well known, concurrency and multitasking will be dominant themes and system design techniques such as atomic updates, concurrency control, serializability, and locking will become major considerations (see reference 6, pp. 274–277). Protection and security are readily implemented in the PS/2 computers (80286 and 80386), and even the Model 30 has a password checking feature.

D.3.5 Systems Programming for 80386-based Computers

When programming microprocessors in an implementation such as the IBM microcomputer family, a major systems programming consideration is the flexibility of the microprocessor instruction set. Both the Intel 80286 and 80386 possess substantial systems capability through special registers and special-purpose assembler instructions. These instructions are not part of the normal IBM application instruction set, but exist in the newer Macro Assembler versions.

For the 80286- and 80386-based microcomputers, memory management and file protection are accomplished using the registers and selectors discussed in Chapter 6. One aspect of the 80386 that is new and interesting is the notion of a cache subsystem. The 80386 can operate at 16 MHz and has a 32-bit word and bus cycle of 125 nanoseconds (ns). This yields a maximum bandwidth of 32 megabytes per second (125 ns corresponds to an 8-MHz rate for bus cycles, and there are 4 bytes per word; hence $4 \times 8 \times 10^6 = 32$ megabytes per second). Clearly, memory access rates must match these speeds if the processor is not to slow down. Since most memory is of the slower dynamic RAM (DRAM) type, a technique for matching the processor to this DRAM must be developed. Since static RAM (SRAM) is capable of high-speed accesses, it becomes reasonable to think about using small amounts of SRAM as an intermediate buffer between the 80386 and DRAM. (SRAM is too costly to be considered for large-scale memory applications.) Such an intermediate buffer is called a cache and requires an additional controller to manage the cache. Some of the data in DRAM are duplicated in the cache with the hope that it will contain sequentially called code sequences, thereby allowing blocks of executable code or data to be moved into high-speed memory. The success with which these blocks are chosen to contain the needed code sequences is referred to as the "hit rate," and this is a measure of how efficiently the cache has been designed.

While the cache is not intrinsic to the 80386, this particular microprocessor can make efficient use of such a subsystem because of its high speed. As SRAM costs drop and DRAM speeds increase, the notion of cache memory management can be expected to evolve.

The PS/2 Model 80 is IBM's 80386 candidate for the personal computer family. From a process viewpoint, the OS/2 software serves primarily to support the 80286 systems capabilities; hence, it will continue to run as a subset of the Model 80 potential. I/O can be mapped into either a 64K address space, with the usual port mapping, or a full 4-gigabyte physical memory address space. In the latter case, devices are treated as though they are normal memory locations, while in the former case I/O-mapped devices can be accessed only through IN, OUT, INS, and OUTS instructions. The address bus consists of 30 address lines (A2 to A31) and four byte-enable lines (BEO# to BE3#). The address pins identify a 4-byte location (one of the 32-bit 80386 words), and each byte-enable pin selects a different byte within this word. For I/O purposes, address decoding can be simplified by staggering the addresses of I/O devices so that, for example, these devices are assigned values at every fourth address. Then the byte-enable outputs can be ignored for I/O accesses.

Memory management for the 80386-based computers can emulate the 16-bit members of this family or can use the newer 32-bit management scheme. As we have indicated, OS/2 uses the earlier scheme.

D.4 A SYSTEMS PROGRAMMING OVERVIEW WITH C

So far we have said little about C programming in the systems (and particularly operating systems) environment. The focus of the discussion has been to provide general background on systems programming with regard to type of programs and content. The section on operating systems emphasized DOS as an example and presented functional aspects of the DOS program. Where does C come into play?

As we have seen throughout this book, C is a versatile language capable of being implemented in applications spanning the range from high-level abstract computation to variable manipulation at the bit level. Hence, C intrinsically has the capability for managing computer resources as required by systems programming. The major issue is how rapidly can C implementations carry out the necessary operations in order to enable systems techniques in an orderly and timely fashion. Generally, the answer to this question is rather complex. First, an optimized C compiler is required. As we saw in Chapter 6, such a compiler can be expected to emphasize register usage as opposed to memory accesses. This means that the C code must be modular to allow isolated task execution with a small number of global variable accesses. The system designer must be prepared to develop time-critical routines in assembly language, but the bulk of the software in a systems application can usually be written in a higher-level language such as C. Clearly, C is somewhat ideally suited for this task. As programming languages have evolved, there is a general tendency toward higher levels of abstraction in modern high-level language definition (Ada, for example, is a good indicator [7]). These languages are symbolic and avoid manipulation of memory at the bit level. Hence, C provides an excellent bridge between the low-level requirements of register manipulation and the more abstract need, for example, to parse a command input from the operator.

REFERENCES

1. Beck, L. L., *System Software*: *An Introduction to Systems Programming*, Addison-Wesley Publishing Company, Reading, MA, p. 392 (1985).
2. Davis, W. S., *Operating Systems*: *A Systematic View*, Addison-Wesley Publishing Company, Reading, MA (1987).
3. *VEDIT Plus*: *Multiple File Editor/Word Processor*, CompuView Products, Inc., 1955 Pauline Blvd., Ann Arbor, MI (1986).
4. *Disk Operating System Technical Reference*, IBM Personal Computer Software, IBM Corp., P.O. Box 1328, Boca Raton, FL (1984).
5. Meyrowitz, N. and Andries van Dam, "Interactive Editing Systems: Part I and Part II, Association for Computing Machinery Computing Surveys, Vol. 14, pp. 321–416 (1982).
6. Tanenbaum, A. S., *Operating Systems*: *Design and Implementation*, Prentice-Hall, Inc., Englewood Cliffs, NJ (1987).
7. Booch, G., *Software Engineering with Ada*, Benjamin/Cummings Publishing Company, Inc., Menlo Park, CA (1987).

Answers to Selected Odd-Numbered Problems

Chapter 1

1.1 A6CA and 10FF9F (unallowed).

1.3 (a) A8CH
   (b) FFFDH
   (c) 16C8H
   (d) 13D89H
   (e) 210H

1.5 (a) FC21H
   (b) F762H
   (c) 481H
   (d) FFF6H
   (e) F831H

1.7 Because the data bus is an 8-bit bus with a 16-bit address bus.

1.9 Communications is generally considered a form of real-time processing. This can be accomplished in one of two ways: either polling the device in question or letting the device be driven by interrupts. The IBM microcomputer approach has been to poll the asynchronous communications adapter, rather than build a hardware interrupt capability into this adapter. This approach requires that the adapter be frequently polled so that any incoming traffic not be missed. In a multitasking environment, the CPU allocates time to each task on a priority basis. If another task has control of the CPU when a message is incoming, the message will be lost. Hence, polling will not work in the Protected Mode environment. The hardware must be modified to accept an interrupt-driven scheme for communications.

1.11 The file conio.h.

1.13 The index, n, assumes values from [0, 100]. This corresponds to 101 values. The declaration for array, however, only dimensions this array to 100 values: [0, 99]. Hence, the program overwrites memory at array [100].

1.15 **(a)** The initialized value of the loop (10) is greater than the end value (9) that is tested for.

(b) The argument of scanf must be a pointer: &alpha, not alpha.

(c) The pointer input must be so indicated in the FILE declaration: "FILE *input;". Also, the argument for fscanf, int1, must be a pointer: &int1, not int1.

(d) The contents of the while loop do not change the loop index n. This is a consequence of the failure to use brackets correctly. Consider the following correct fragment:

```
...
int n;
...
n=5;
while (n<7)
    {
    printf("%d=",n);
    n++;
    }
...
```

(e) Here, n is declared as a character and used as an integer.

1.17
```
#include <stdio.h>
...
FILE *input;
char array[81];
int n;
...
n=1
do
 {
fscanf(input,"%c", &array[n]);
n++;
}while (array[n]!='\n')
...
```

1.19
```
...
if (a<b)
    statement2;
else
    statement1;
statement4;
...
```
In the original code, *no* path exists to get to statement 3.

1.21
```
/*Calculates square root to nearest integer*/
#include <studio.h>
main()
    {
    int ,DIFF,x,y;

    printf("Input integer no.to be square root\n");
    scanf ("%d",&x);
    DIFF=100;
    y-x;                                /*Initiative*/
    y = y/2;
```

```
        while ((DIFF>1)||(DIFF<-1))
           {
        x = x/y;
        x = x + y;
        x = x/2;
        DIFF = x - y;
        y = x;
           }
     printf ("Square root = %d",y)
     }
```

1.23 ...
```
     #include<math.h>
     ...
     main()
         {
         double x,y;
         float v,P;
         ...
         x = (double)(v);                          /*Extend*/
         y = 20.*log10(x);
         P = (float)(y);                            /*Type convert*/
     ...
```

1.25 We need to calculate the square root of distance squared. This can be accomplished using the fragment in Problem 1.24 with x = distance squared.

1.27 One simply needs to affect a type conversion from int to float.

1.29 The program is
```
     # include <conio.h>
     main()
          {
          cprintf ("\x1B[2J"";
          cprintf ("\x07");
          }
```

1.31
```
     # include <conio.h>
     main()
          {
          int n;
          for (n = 1; n <= 1000; n++)
              cprintf("\x07");
          }
```

1.33 ...
```
     main()
         {
     float x,y;
     ...
     y=square(x);
     printf("square=%f",y);
     ...
     }
     float square(x1)
         float x1;
```

```
          {
          float y1;
          y1=x1*x1;
          return(y1);
          }
          . . .
```

1.35 **(a)** The formal parameter must be immediately declared with a "float x" following print1(x).

   (b) In the scanf function, x should be specified as an integer output with %d.

   (c) There is no way to return the value of x squared.

   (d) The value x input to the square operation must appear as an extern declaration or as a formal parameter. Also, square must be declared of type float.

1.37 The equal sign in the definition of pi is incorrect. A define declaration assumes that the delimiter should be a blank.

1.39 The union has two elements: an integer and an array of three bytes(char). Hence, it is three bytes in length. In the main() code fragment, the character array is treated as an integer array of 3, which requires 6 bytes. Thus, the union overflows when called by main().

Chapter 2

2.1
```
SCRCL()
    {
    union REGS regs;
    regs.h.ah=7;              /*Scroll active page down*/
    regs.h.al=0;              /*Blanks entire page*/
    regs.h.ch=0;              /*row=0*/
    regs.h.cl=0;              /*col=0*/
    regs.h.dh=23;             /*row lower right*/
    regs.h.al=79;             /*col lower right*/
    regs.h.bh=7;              /*blank attribute*/

    int86(0x10,&regs,&regs);
    }
```

2.3
```
#include <stdio.h>
diskwt(NCOUNT)
    int NCOUNT;                /*array length*/
    {
    int n,check;
    FILE *outfile;
    char FN1[81];
    extern float x[],y[];      /*external*/

    printf("Input database filename\n");
    gets(FN1);

    if((outfile=fopen(FN1,"w"))==NULL)
        {
        printf("Output file failure")
        exit(1);
        }
    fprintf(outfile,"%d",NCOUNT);
```

```
for (n=1; n<=NCOUNT;n++) /*array start=1*/
    fprintf(outfile,"%f %f", x[n],y[n]);

if((check=fclose(outfile))!=0)
    {
    printf("Error on output file close");
    exit(1);
    }
}
```

2.5 The spacing across the *x*-axis is

$$281 - 25 = 256$$

Dividing this into four intervals yields 64 units per interval. Thus

$$25 + 64 = 89$$
$$89 + 64 = 153$$
$$153 + 64 = 217$$
$$217 + 64 = 281$$

2.7 The Gaussian random numbers can assume values between $\pm\infty$. Roughly, 68% lie between $+1$ and -1. Similarly, about 98% lie between $+3$ and -3. The range of allowed number values in Figure 2.13 is $+75$ to -75, with the Gaussian number values scaled by 7.5. At the $+3$ to -3 ranges (98%), the scaled Gaussian random numbers will span $+22.5$ to -22.5 on the plotted output. The odds that values greater than $+3$ or less than -3 will arise are less than 2%.

Chapter 3

3.1
```
rread(x,y)
    float *x, *y;
    {
    scanf("%f %f",x,y);
    }
```

3.3 The stack is guaranteed to overflow.

3.5
```
/*Routine to convert ASCII to decimal */
    ASCII_decimal()
        {
        extern int array[];       /*Contains ASCII */
        int scratch,mul=10,a=1,n;

        for (n=1;n<=5;n++)
        {
        scratch=scratch+a*(array[n]-30.);
        a=a*mul;
        return(a);
        }
```

3.7
```
/* Function to ck screen memory addressing */

#include <dos.h>
#include <memory.h>
#include <string.h>

unsigned int array[1000];
int far *scr;
```

```
main()
        {
        array[0] = 0x55;
        src = array;
        SCRCL();
        SC320();
        movedata(FP_SEG(src),FP_OFF(src),0xB800,0x0000,1);

        KEYDEL();
        SC80();
        }
```

3.9 **(a)** $0 \times AA$
   (b) 0×55
   (c) 0×11
   (d) 0×44

3.11 ...
```
for(n=1;n<=NTOTAL;n++)
    {
    for(m=0;m<=3;m++)
      {
      if((value[n]>bbrak[m])&&(value[n]<=bbrak[m+1]))
          talley[m]++;
      }
    if(value[n]>bbrak[4])
    }
}
SCRCL();

for(n=0;n<=4;n++)
...
```

3.13

OPERATOR	COUNT	OPERAND	COUNT
=	3	x[]	3
<	1	y[]	3
++	1	z[]	2
*	2	n	8
for	1		
	8		16

Hence N = 8 + 16 = 24.

Chapter 4

4.1 The AL register must satisfy

$$1 \quad 0 \quad 0 \quad 0 \quad 0 \quad 0 \quad 1 \quad 1 \quad \text{(binary)}$$

$$8 \qquad\qquad 3 \qquad \text{(hex)}$$

Hence

```
...
union REGS regs;
...
regs.h.al = 0x83;
```

```
regs.h.ah = 0x00;

int86(0x14,&regs,&regs);
...
```

will initialize the port. Alternatively, using the specified port address, the following fragment will also work:

```
...
unsigned int port;
unsigned char value;
...
port = 0x3FB;
value = 0x83;
outp(port,value);
...
```

4.3
```
...
union REGS regs;
...
regs.h.ah = 0x00;
regs.h.al = 0x0B;

int86(0x10,&regs,&regs);
...
```

4.5 Since

G1	G2A	G2B	A	B	C
AEN*	XA9	XA8	XA5	XA6	XA7

it follows that

$$XA9 = 0$$
$$XA8 = 0$$
$$XA7 = 1$$
$$XA6 = 0$$
$$XA5 = 0$$

and

XA7	XA6	XA5	XA4	XA3	XA2	XA1	XA0
1	0	0	X_1	x	x	x	x
		Y				X	

Assuming $X_1 = 0$, this would correspond to an address $0 \times 8X$.

4.7
```
...
#include <stdlib.h>
...
double value;
int ndigits,n;
char buffer[81], ssign
int precision = (10), decimal,ssign = 0x20, ddecimal=0x2E;
...
buffer = ecvt(value,precision,&decimal,&sign);
```

```
if (sign == 0)
    putchar(ssign);
for (n = 1; n <= decimal; n++)
    putchar(buffer[n]);
putchar(ddecimal);
for (n = decimal + 1; n <= 10; n++)
    putchar(buffer [n]);
...
```

In a routine such as this, the programmer must know ahead of time the maximum number of ASCII digits that can be encountered in the numbers being converted. All digits should be initialized to blanks:

```
for (n = 1; n<= precision; n++)
    buffer[n] = 0x20;
```

4.9 The function DELAY() could be removed. Because the 8088(80286) is slow enough, a delay of one loop iteration must be used if reasonable motion is to be observed. Any greater delay further slows the motion. On the Model 80, however, DELAY() can serve a useful purpose.

4.11 ...

```
float a[11][11],b[11][11],c[11][11];
...
mat_mul1(N)
    intN;                               /*order*/
    {
    extern float a[],b[],c[];
    int j,K,l,offset1,offset2;

    for (j = 1;j <= N; j++)
        {
        offset1 = j * 11;
        for (K = 1;K <= N; K++)
            {
            for (1 = 1;1 <= N; 1++)
                {
                offset2 = 1 * 11;
                a[offset1+K]=a[offset1+K]+b[offset1+1]*c[offset2+K];
                }
            }
        }
    }
...
```

4.13 The associated figure illustrates dot() and udot() with FAR pointers. An increase in screen buffer DMA does take place over the versions in Figures 4.33a and b.

Chapter 5

5.1 The call to code segment __TEXT1, with __CCC, is a FAR call from __TEXT, with __DDD. Hence, the procedure __CCC must be defined as FAR.

5.3 (a) An infinite loop results because of the unconditional jump instruction.
(b) The JNE ELSE1 exit is not preceded by a test that examines a condition (within the loop).
(c) The repeat limit is 72,000, which places part of the searched array TABLE1 beyond the 64K segment boundary.

5.5 The macro source code should be placed outside the code segment and before the needed text. Alternatively, if it exists as a .ASM file named MAC1LIB.LIB, for example, it can be automatically included using

```
. . .
IF1
  INCLUDE MAC1LIB.LIB
ENDIF
. . .
```

as the first statements following the header information.

5.7
```
CHECK        MACRO N1,N
             LOCAL ELSE1
             PUSH AX
             PUSH BP
             MOV BP,N                ;;N=table index
             MOV AX,TABLE&N1[BP]     ;;N1=table indicator
             CMP AX,20H
             JNE ELSE1
                 CALL ERROR
ELSE1:
             ENDM
```

5.9
```
PIO          MACRO X
;
;       X is the printer number, Character in AX
;
             PUSH AX
             PUSH BX
             PUSH CX
             PUSH DX
             PUSH AX
             MOV DX,X               ;initialization
             MOV AH,1
             INT 17H
DO1:                                ;Check for busy
             MOV AH,2
             INT 17H
             AND AH,80H             ;Mask for busy
             CMP AH,0
             JE DO1
             POP AX
             MOV AH,0
             INT 17H               ;Output character
             POP DX
             POP CX
             POP BX
             POP AX
PIO          ENDM
```

5.11 Line feed:

```
LF           MACRO
             MOV AH,6
             MOV DL,0AH
```

```
                INT 21H
LF              ENDM
```

Carriage return:

```
CR              MACRO
                MOV AH,6
                MOV DL,0DH
                INT 21H
CR              ENDM
```

Both line feed and carriage return:

```
NLINE           MACRO
                MOV AH,6
                MOV DL,0AH
                INT 21H
                MOV AH,6
                MOV DL,0DH
                INT 21H
NLINE           ENDM
```

5.13 ...
```
FLD X
FMUL X
FST X
```
...

5.15 ...
```
FLD A                      ;Load radius
FLD A                      ;Radius in ST,ST(1)
FMULP ST(1),ST             ;Radius square in ST
FLDPI                      ;PI in ST
FMULP ST(1),ST             ;Answer in ST
FST A                      ;Area in A
```
...

Chapter 6

6.1 (a) Real time
   (b) Conventional
   (c) Real time
   (d) Conventional
   (e) Real time
   (f) Real time

6.3 Clearly, modular code using many function calls will result in high overhead and this leads to poor performance in real-time applications. Basic real-time applications should minimize functional boundaries for the critical time-sensitive portions of the code and reserve modular definition for the higher-level applications portion of the programming.

6.5 Typically, one could encode

BIT 1	BIT 2	OPSK MODULATION
1	1	$+315°$
1	0	$+225°$
0	1	$+135°$
0	0	$+45°$

6.7 (a) $0 \times 00AA$

(b) $0 \times 00FA$

(c) 0×0083

(d) $0 \times 00CE$

6.9
```
        MOV AX,OFFSET _MES1
        MOV DX,AX
```

6.11 `AT S7=60\r`

6.13 Only 1 byte is returned in ch, and a proper equivalence for '0' consists of a 2-byte equivalence. Hence the test on ch will never be valid in this form. The 1-byte test must compare ch and '\x30'.

6.15 12 bit = 4096 quantization levels

Thus

$$1 \text{ quanta} = \frac{20 \text{ volts}}{4096}$$
$$= 4.89 \text{ millivolts}$$

6.17 The added scaling operation would involve floating point operations, which would slow the processing down to the point that sample points would be lost.

Chapter 7

7.1
```
/*Function to set monochrome EGA graphics mode*/
#include <graph.h>
SCNOEGA()
    {
    _setvideomode (_ERESNCOLOR);
    }
```

7.3
```
/*Function WRDOT with version 5.0 primitives*/

#include<graph.h>

WRDOT(row,col)
    int row,col;
    {
    _setpixel(row,col);
    }
```

7.5
```
/*Function to print coordinates in EGA*/
#include<graph.h>
char buffer [256];

main(0
    {
    int n;
    struct rccoord rcoord;
    SCRCL();
    SCEGA();
    _settextposition(0,0)
    for(n=1; n<=b; n++)
        {
        rcoord = _gettextposition();
        sprintf(buffer,"(%d,%d)",rcoord.row, rcoord.col);
        _outtext(buffer);
```

```
rcoord.row = rcoord.row + 50;
rcoord.col = rcoord.col + 100;
_settextposition(rcoord.row,rcoord.col);
}
plotterm();
}
```

7.7 The bandwidth of a process contains all the spectral information of interest for the process. If this bandwidth is B, then the requisite coherence interval T must satisfy

$$T > 1/(2B)$$

7.9 The API calls are essentially low level. They represent initial Protected Mode access to the system services and are not abstraction. In this sense, they are a level below the primitives of this chapter. Undoubtedly, as compilers evolve for OS/2, these low-level Protected Mode functions will be replaced with more abstract entities comparable to the high-level Version 5.0 DOS function primitives.

Chapter 8

8.1 The Windows interface to an application is based on messages passed from Windows to the program in question. These messages are interpreted and appropriate responses generated. In this fashion, much of the underlying program structure is hidden from the developer. Activities performed by the window are highly abstracted using the associated Windows functions and corresponding data structures. Essentially, the program developer embeds his or her C code in an environment which performs user-friendly interfacing. The window, then, can be thought of as an object that interacts with other objects in the sense described above. Some aspects of Windows programming appear as data structure oriented. Windows does focus on a logical manipulation of data, but it significantly exceeds pure data structure-oriented programming. The motion of manipulating objects (devices, windows, data structures, and so on) clearly establishes Windows as object oriented.

8.3
```
...
long FAR PASCAL WindowProc(hWnd,message,wParam,lParam)
...
{
switch(message)
  {
  ...
  case WM_PAINT
    PaintBeginWindow(hWnd);
    break;
  ...
  }
  return(OL);
}
PaintBeginWindow(hWnd)
  HWND hWnd;
  {
  ...
  HDC           hDC;
  HBRUSH        hBrush;
  PAINTSTRUCT   ps;
  ...
```

```
hDC = BeginPaint(hWnd,(LPPAINTSTRUCT)&Ps);
hBrush = GetStockObject(GRAY_BRUSH);
SelectObject(hDC,hBrush);
...
```

8.5
```
win10.obj: win10.c
    cl -c -d LINT_ARGS -GSW -Od -W2 -ZP -FPa\
        win10.c

menu.res: menu.rc
    rc -r menu.rc

win10.exe: win10.obj win10.def menu.res
    link4 win10,/align:16,/map,slibw/NOE\
        swinlibc/NOE,win10
    rc menu.res win10.exe
```

8.7 8,355,711 = 7F7F7FH, which corresponds to a gray background color.

0 corresponds to a black background color

16,777,215 = FFFFFFH, which corresponds to all colors or a white background.

8.9 The color value is specified as an RGB option contained in a long integer. The values are packed in the three low-order bytes of the long integer according to

```
r+(2**8)g + (2**16)b
```

where r = red
      g = green
      b = blue

Here r is an intensity for red between 000H and 0FFH, g is an intensity for green between 000H and 0FFH, and b is an intensity for blue between the same limits. The system resource functions

```
GetRValue(rgbColor)
GetGValue(rgbColor)
GetBValue(rgbColor)
```

can be used to return these intensities. A value of 000000FFH would return red, for example.

8.11 ...
```
PaintBeginWindow(hWnd)
  HWND hWnd;
  {
  int xstart=25,xend=525,y=150

  HDC hDC;
  HPEN hPen;
  PAINTSTRUCT ps;

  hDC=BeginPaint(hWnd,(LPAINTSTRUCT)&ps);
  hPen=GetStockObject(WHITE_PEN);
  SelectObject(hDC,hPen);
  MoveTo(hDC,xstart,y);
  LineTo(hDC,xend,y);
```

```
ValidateRect(hWnd,(LPRECT)NULL);
EndPaint(hWnd,(LPPAINTSTRUCT)&ps);
return TRUE;
}
```
⋆ ⋆ ⋆

(Here GRAY__BRUSH has been selected as the background color in the window initialization routine that sets up WNDCLASS:

```
WindowClass.hbrBackground = GetStockObject(GRAY_BRUSH);
```

where WindowClass is the WNDCLASS structure.) The selection of mode is accomplished by Windows during initialization. Essentially, the user is prompted for the display mode to be used during setup of Windows. In this text, this mode was selected to be EGA (even though a VGA hardware capability exists) so that hard copy was possible using "egaepson.com". Had a range of y values been input that exceeded the EGA range for the Windows y-coordinates, an error would result.

8.13 The CreateWindow() function must have the third field specified as

```
WS_OVERLAPPEDWINDOW
```

Also, scaling and origin definition of child and parent client areas can now correspond to rectangles that overlap.

8.15 ⋆ ⋆ ⋆
```
#include<io.h>
⋆ ⋆ ⋆
HANDLE hFile;
char fname = "b\win1\filenm.ext";
OFSTRUCT opfile;
int result;
⋆ ⋆ ⋆
hFile = OpenFile((LPSTR)fname,(LPOFSTRUCT)&opfile,OF_READ);
⋆ ⋆ ⋆
result = close(hFile);
if (result)
    ⋆ ⋆ ⋆
else
    ⋆ ⋆ ⋆
⋆ ⋆ ⋆
```

8.17 ⋆ ⋆ ⋆
```
HDC hDC;
int X=320, Y=175;
char FAR *middle = "middle";
⋆ ⋆ ⋆
TextOut(hDC,X,Y,middle,strlen(middle));
⋆ ⋆ ⋆
```

Chapter 9

9.1 A modal dialog box does not allow the user to switch between the dialog box and another window in the program. An explicit termination must occur, usually by pushing a button marked OK or Cancel. Modal dialog boxes are created using DialogBox(). Modeless dialog boxes are created with CreateDialog() and act like a normal window. The user can shift into or out of a modeless dialog box. This adds I/O flexibility.

9.3 The pointer to the PAINTSTRUCT must point to an address for the structure. Also, the TextOut() coordinates are too large for the display.

9.5 When menu3.h is omitted, the references to EDIT__B and ExitMsg are not satisfied. If windows.h is omitted, all key words (such as MENU, BEGIN, END, CONTROL, and so on) are undefined.

9.7 ...

```
EXETYPE OS2
```
...

9.9 The programmer would need a call of the form (for example)

```
nC=GetDlgItemText(hBox,ID_ANGLE,(LPSTR)TText,MAXLENGTH);
```

followed by a call to a routine that converts ASCII formatted numbers to decimal values:

```
...
float number
...
number = ASCIItoDec(TText,nC);
```

Here nC is the number of characters, TText the ASCII floating point string, and the function ASCII to Dec() is assumed to return a floating point decimal value.

9.11 The angular values would be calculated incorrectly because they would truncate. For example, 400 would become 0.0 not 0.4. Similarly, 1100 would become 1.0 not 1.1.

9.13 IOBox() is exported because it is called by Windows internally, just as Window1Proc() is called internally by Windows.

9.15 This function processes a rectangular area subtended by the mouse increment. The function inverts the color bitmap for this area and then it inverts it back. This creates a momentary distortion of the screen corresponding to the area in question, thereby allowing the user to glimpse the affected part of the screen.

9.17 The clipboard cannot be 'emptied' or cleared until it is "opened."

9.19 Once to load the clipboard and once to paint the screen from its contents.

9.21 With a call to GetPrnDC(), which eventually calls CreateDC().

Chapter 10

10.1 The print to the screen would simply not include a carriage return and line feed.

10.3
```
        ifndef      @Pushs
@Pushs  macro       Parm
        mov         ax,SEG Parm
        push        ax
        lea         ax,Parm
        push        ax
        endm
        endif
```

10.5 This entry point is referenced in the final END statement for the calling module. Consider

```
END OS21
```

Here OS21 would be the entry point at which execution starts.

10.7 The second executable statement is

```
@pushs Mode
```

where the call is

```
@VioSetMode        /Mode,VioHandle
```

Note that @pushs loads an address (FAR) for Mode on the stack. This is treated as a pointer to the data structure in a call such as

```
@VioSetMode        STDm,vio_hdl
```

10.9 The horizontal number of points across a single line is 720 pixels and 400 lines is the vertical resolution. This reflects the VGA text modes.

10.11 They calculate

```
col % 4
```

and store the value in xx.

10.13 The address is based on a selector value returned by @DosGetShrSeg. This 16-bit quantity is placed in the ES register to define the extra segment address. Next the buffer is assumed to start at offset 0. Hence

```
. . .
push shrsel
pop es
mov ax, es:[0]
. . .
```

loads the first byte of the buffer into ax.

10.15 It could have been designated this way; however, blank=blank[0]=&blank is an address by array convention.

10.17 The third and fourth elements are the two possible selector values Microsoft allows the user to have returned from VIOGETPHYSBUF(). There is no fifth element in this structure.

10.19 This specifies the upper count value for each of the interleaved buffers [0, 1999] or 2000-byte buffers, where 1F3FH is the hexadecimal value for the upper count value.

10.21 The value is TRUE if odd buffer locations are specified. Otherwise, even scan lines are specified.

10.23 The buffer consists of 402 unsigned integer entries. The first integer is the buffer length and the second integer is a flag denoting activity (when used). The remaining 400 integers occupy integer positions [2, 402] and are called at byte locations with MAKEP().

Index

32-bit descriptor, 481
8250 ACE, 109
8253 Timer, 134
8253 Control Word Register, 162
8255A PPI, 147
8288 Bus Controller, 161

A

AbortProc(), 469
Abstraction, 127
Accelerator, 395
ACE addresses, 276
A/D adapters, manufacturers, 290
A/D response to sinusoid, 301
Addressing, assembler, 208
Address operator, 13
Address space, 7
Algorithm development, 123
Alpha 80 × 25 mode, assembler, 250
Amplitude modulation, 77
Analog-to-digital conversion (A/D), 266
ANSI.SYS file, 46
Appreciated savings, 58
Architecture structures:
   do while, 102
   for, 102
   if, 102
   while, 102
Arithmetic:
   binary, 5
   floating-point, 5
   hexadecimal, 5
Array, 22
ASCII, 20
ASCII characters, 32
Assembler listing, 19
Assembler/2 references, API, 490
Assembly language, 201
Asynchronous Communications Adapter
      Port Registers, 276
Asynchronous execution, 482
Auto-correlation, 332

B

Ball image:
   clear, 155
   write, 155
Ball shape, bouncing ball, 155
Banding, 458
Bandwidth, 79
Bar(), 245
Bar chart, assembler, 240
bbox(), 68

BCPL, 99
BEEP(), 164
BeginPaint(), 373
beginw.c, 365
Bell-shaped distribution, 91
BIOS, 39
bios.h, 309
Bitmap, 386
BITMAP, structure, 442
Bit reversal, 14
Bitwise operators, 61, 107
Bouncing ball, program, 147
Box, screen, 65
box(), 91
box_norm(), 68
Braces, 13
Bracket program, 114
Brushes, 386
Buffer, 53
Bus, 6
Buttons, 381
Byte, 5
Byte-oriented I/O, 60

C

Calling sequence, Windows, 361
Carriage control, printer, 139
CGA mode, assembler, 247
CGA mode, OS/2, 495
cgets(), 61
Channel selection (A/D), 292
Child, OS/2, 482
Chip selection, 161
Clear screen, assembler, 246
Clipboard, 381
cmdLine, 362
cmdShow, 362
CodeView, OS/2, 489
CodeView debugger:
    dialog window, 16
    display window, 16
    line pointer, 16
Color Graphics Adapter (CGA), 306
Comments, 11
Communications, 266
Communications Adapter:
    check status, 276
    initialization, 276
    receive a character, 276
    send a character, 276
Communications loop, 287
Communications timing, 287

Compiler, 7
Compiler optimization, 238
Compiler options, 14
Complexity:
    metric, 103
    module, 104
Complex number, 77
Compound interest, 249
Conditional execution, 118
Connecting line, 75
Constant dollar value, 59
Control logic, C, 34
Control registers (A/D):
    ADDAT, 292, 293
    ADSCR, 292, 293
    CHLCSR, 292, 293
    SUPCSR, 292, 294
    TMRCTR, 292, 294
Control Sequences, 47
Coprocessor, Intel:
    8087, 2, 226
    80287, 2, 226
    80387, 2, 226
corr(), 330
Correlated output, 326
Correlation functions, 326
Correlation lag, 326
corr_setup(), 323
cplotlib.lib, 70
C physical buffer structure, OS/2, 520
C Protected Mode CGA, OS/2, 514
C Protected Mode I/O, OS/2, 513
CPU speed, 268
CreateDC(), 463
CreateWindow(), 376
Creating dialog box, 426
Cross-correlation, 327
Cross-spectrum, 327

D

_DATA (data segment), 18
Data flow-oriented design, 128
Data passing, Windows, 440
Data structure-oriented design, 128
Data structures, 124
Data Translation A/D board:
    DT2828, 266
    DT707, 297
Date program, 174
debug.exe, 8
Decibel, 84
Define, 11

Definition file, Windows, 363
Definition files, OS/2, 489
DefWindowProc(), 372
Delimiters, 33
Descriptor tables, 7
Device context, Windows, 404
DGROUP, 20
Dialing, Hayes modem, 280
Dialog box, 381
Digital-to-Analog, 5
Digitized output, 289
Directed lines, surface facet, 342
Direct Memory Access (DMA), 7, 147
Discrete Fourier Transform, 79
diskrd(), 115
Disk read routine, C, 244
Disk write procedure, C, 241
Dispatchable unit, 482
DispatchMessage(), 368
Dispersion, 84
Display Modes:
    320 × 200 graphics (CGA), 4
    640 × 200 graphics (CGA), 4
    25 × 80 alpha, 4
    640 × 350 graphics (EGA), 4
    720 × 400 graphics (VGA), 4
dja.c, 67
DOS, 4
doscall.h, 512
doscalls.h, 512
DOSCALLS.LIB, 490
dos.h, 309
DOS Service Routines:
    BIOS, 136
    DOS, 136
    Intel, 136
Dow Jones Average, data, 97
Drawing lines, version 5.0, 313
DT2828, 291
Dynamic-linking, OS/2, 483
Dynamic-link library, 489
Dynamic random access memory (DRAM),
    268
Dynamic range (A/D), 291

E

Editbox, 427
Editor:
    line, 8
    screen, 8
egalib.lib, 322
EndDialog(), 429

EndPaint(), 373
Enhanced Graphics Adapter (EGA), 306
enum, integer type, 307
Environment, OS/2, 476
Equation of motion:
    friction component, 150
    horizontal, 150
    vertical, 150
Escape sequence, 13
Exception control, 119
Executive, Windows, 360
exit (), 54
Exit conditions, 119
External variables, 99
Extern declaration, 36

F

Facet, 342
FAR reference, 204
Fast Fourier Transform, 81
FFT(), 80
Figure annotation, 77
File handle, 62
FILE structure pointer, 53
Floating-point format:
    Intel coprocessor, 229
    Microsoft binary, 228
Flowchart, 66, 111
Form, program, 122
Formal parameter pointer arguments, 99
Formal parameter variable arguments, 99
Fourier Transform, 77
fprintf(), 53
Frequency modulation, 77
Function, 13
Function, two variables, 340
Function prototyping, 364
Function return:
    multiple-values passed, 116
    one-value returned, 115

G

Gain selection (A/D), 292
Game adapter operation, 290
Gaussian random numbers, 84
GDI functions, 386
Geometric sum, 240
GetDlgItemText(), 429

GetInstanceData(), 377
GetMessage(), 368
gets(), 53
Global variables, 99
grand(), 90
Graphics calls, high-level version 5.0, 309
GRAPHICS.COM, 312
Graphics dot location, 75
Graphics primitive, 21, 309

H

Halstead metric, 126
Handle, Windows, 362
Hanning weight, 533
hanwt(), 80
Hardware interface, assembler, 201
Hayes Smartmodem 1200, 266
Hidden lines, 344
Hierarchical description, 118, 127
High-level functions, version 5.0, 310
hInst, 362
Histogram, 93
hPrev, 362

I

IBM Asynchronous Communications
        Adapter, 271
IBM Hardware interfaces, 98
IBM Macro Assembler/2, 490
IBM Programmer's Toolkit, 512
Icon, 368
Iconic windows, 362
In-Circuit Emulator (ICE), 269
Include files, 9, 10, 175
Inflation, 58
Information:
    hiding, 127
    visibility, 128
Initialization, array, 51
Initialization values, A/D registers, 296
Instance, Windows programs, 358
Instructions, assembler, 20, 205, 208
Instruction times, 80286, 268
int86(), 39, 72
Integrated Circuits:
    8259A, 2,3
    8255A, 2,3
    8237A, 2,3

8253, 2,3
6845, 5
Interfacing, C and assembler, 235
Interrupts, 39, 136
I/O:
    console/port, 27, 163
    low-level, 27, 60
    standard, 51
    stream, 27
I/O, include files:
    conio.h, 102
    io.h, 102
    stdio.h, 102
I/O functions:
    close(), 61
    open(), 61
    read(), 61
    write(), 61
io.h, 60
Iterative programming, 106

K

Keyboard interrupt:
    INT 9H, 138
    INT 16H, 139
KEYDEL():
    assembler, 249
    C, 69

L

Label, 18
Least significant bit or quanta (A/D), 293
LIB, 14
Library files, 10, 177
LIFO buffer, 100
Line feed, 20
lineh(), 69
Line Status Register, 278
linev, 69
LINK4, 363
Linker, 8
Linker options, 14
Listbox, 381
llcr.c., 64
llrd.c, 65
Load__arrays(), 329
Local command functions, Hayes modem,
        284

Local command state, Hayes modem, 280
Local variables, 99
Lock screen, OS/2, 498
Log plot, assembler, 240
log_plot_EGA(), 315
log_plot_VGA(), 320
Long double, variable type, 309

M

Macro (assembler), 226, 227
Macro (C), 13
main(), 11
MAKEP(), 521
MAKE utility, 20
Manifest constants, 61
MARK, tone, 271
Mask, 108
math.h, 57
Maximum, 65
Memory map, C linker, 100
Memory model parameters, 261
Memory models, 11
Memory size, program, 175
menu1.c, 395
MessageBeep(), 395
MessageBox(), 396
Messages, Windows, 394
Metafile, 390
Metric, 381
Microcomputer, IBM:
    AT, 2, 3
    Jr, 2
    PC, 2, 3
    Portable, 2
    PS/2 Model 25, 2
    PS/2 Model 30, 2, 4
    PS/2 Model 50, 2, 4
    PS/2 Model 60, 2, 4
    PS/2 Model 80, 2, 5
    XT, 2, 3
    XT286, 2, 4
Microprocessor, Intel:
    8088, 1
    8086, 1
    80286, 1
    80386, 1
Microsoft Compiler:
    Version 4.0, 98
    Version 5.0, 306
    Version 5.1, 476

Minimum, 65
Modal dialog box, 381
Modeless dialog box, 381
Modem Control Register, 278
Modem escape code, Hayes, 280
Modem Status Register, 278
Modularity, strategy for, 322
Modular programming, 114
Module:
    guidelines, 117
    size, 126
mortgage.c, 59
Mortgage payment, 55
Motion:
    global, 148
    local, 148
Mouse button, 368
Mouse messages, Windows, 448
movedata(), 166
MSG, Windows structure, 371
Multiplexed I/O, 291
Multitasking, OS/2, 499
Multitasking, Windows, 367
Multitasking systems, 270

N

Natural language syntax, 111
NEAR reference, 204
Nested functions, 52
Newton-Raphson estimator, 45
Nibble, 7
nodo.c, 360
Normal distribution, 91
NUL, 12
Nyquist criterion, 267
Nyquist value, 81

O

Object-oriented design, 128
On-board real-time clock, 267
On-line state, Hayes modem, 280
OpenClipboard(), 449
Operators, assembler, 217
Operators, C, 22
Optimizing C code, assembler, 201
OS/2, 8
OS/2 Compatibility Mode, 134

P

Pacer clock (A/D), 292
Parameter input, Windows, 423
PASCAL, type, 361
Passing parameters, C and assembler, 235
Passing pointers, 36
Pens, 386
Phase, 77
Phone hang-up, Hayes modem, 280
Physical address, 6
Physical memory, 477
Physical pointer, 521
Pipe, 499
Pipeline processing, 268
plotpoint(), 69
plotterm(), 69
PLTBUF(), 69
Pointers, 24
Pop, off stack, 100
Popup, 381
Portability, 6
Port definition, IBM, 144
PostQuitMessage(), 371
pow(), 57
poww.ASM, 250
Preprocessor, 10
Presentation Manger, Windows, 360
Printer I/O, Windows, 458
printf(), 12
Process, 482
Program design languages (PDL), 118
Programmable clock frequency (A/D), 292
Programmable gain amplifier, 291
Protected Mode C, OS/2, 510
Protected Virtual Address Mode (Protected Mode), 2
Pseudo code, 111
Pseudo-op, 18, 203
PS/2 Interrupts, 135
Pull-down menu, 368
Pulse, linear FM, 77
Push, on stack, 210

Q

Queue, 499
QuickC, 20

R

Raster operations, Windows, 471
Read I/O option, 54
read__title(), 65
Read/write permission, 62
Real Address Mode, 2
Real-time debugging, 269
Real-time dynamics (A/D), 292
Real-time hardware, 268
Real-time operating systems, 269
Real-time programming, 266
RECT, structure, 374
Recursive programming, 106
Re-entrant functions, OS/2, 511
Registers:
    8088 family, 1
    8250, 273
REGS, union, 40
Resource file, 398
Returned variables, 99
Roll-out, 270
rotate.c, 189
Rotate point, 191
Rotating cube, 185
Rotation matrices, 187
Round-robin dispatching, 483
RS-232C serial adapter, 267

S

Sampling, 289
savings.c, 62
SC80():
    assembler, 250
    C, 71
SC320():
    assembler, 247
    C, 71
scale(), 353
Scaled A/D output, 293
Scaling print, Windows, 424
scanf(), 12
SCEGA(), 313
SCRCL():
    assembler, 246
    C language, 71
Screen buffer addressing (CGA), 105
Screen buffer algorithm:
    column byte value, 194
    even rows, 194
    odd rows, 194

Screen buffer DMA, 160
Screen clear, OS/2, 493
Screen control functions, 71
Scrolling vs. screen top buffering, 287
SCVGA(), 316
SDK, Windows, 360
SDK program architecture, 379
Segment address, 7
Segments:
    code, 7
    data, 7
    extra, 7
    stack, 7
Segment selector, 478
Selector index, 479
Semaphore, 499
SendMessage(), 398
SetFocus(), 428
setup(), global motion, 150
Shared memory, 499
ShowWindow(), 377
Significand, 228
Single conversion mode (A/D), 291
Sinusoidal wave, 77
Size, module, 126
Slope quantization, 75
Software drivers, 127
Software testing:
    debugging, 125
    testing, 125
Software trigger (A/D), 292
Source code, 14
SPACE, tone, 271
Speaker, BIOS reference, 163
Speaker, sound, 161
Special instructions, 80286 & 80386, 217
Spectra, 77
Stack, 99
Standard Edition 1.0, 476
Standard I/O, 10
Standard streams, 51
Static random access memory (SRAM), 268
Status, A/D operation, 294
Stock histories:
    DEC, 337
    DJA, 337
    HP, 337
    IBM, 337
    Sperry, 337
Stock market forecasting, 336
Stream, 27
StretchBlt(), 449
Stringizing operator, 308
Structure Chart, 63, 111
Structured code, 117

Structures, 34
Style, program, 120
subcalls.h, 512
Symbolic debugging, 14
Synchronous execution, 482
Syntax, C, 22
sysmac.inc, 491

T

Table indicator bit, 479
Tag, 37
Task-time thread, 483
Telephone line interface, 271
Template, C in assembler, 236
Termination code, Windows, 362
__TEXT (Code segment), 18
Text I/O, OS/2, 492
TextOut(), 429
Text output, Windows, 451
Theoretical program design, 114
thistin.c, 55, 57
Threads, 482
threeD__facet(), 349
threeD__graph(), 353
Three dimensional surfaces, 340
Tick marks, screen, 69
Tiled window, 381
Time-of-day, 170
Time series, 81
timhist.c, 51, 53
Token-pasting operator, 308
TONE(), 170
Top-down design, 110
TranslateMessage(), 368
triggering (A/D), 292
Types:
    C, 22
    definitions, 104

U

UART data register, 268
UART reference oscillator, 273
Unions, 34
Uniprocessor systems, 270
Universal Asynchronous Receiver
    Transmitter, 267
UpDateWindow(), 377

V

ValidateRect(), 373
Value Line reports, 65
Value/time-history database, 51
VEDIT, 8
Vertex points, facet, 353
Video graphics adapter (VGA), 306
Video interrupt, 138
Video register settings, 74
Video graphics adapter (VGA), 306
Viewpoint, Windows, 386
Virtual 8086 Mode, 2
Void, function type, 307
Volatile, variable type, 307

W

WAIT states, 268
Window functions, 381
Windows, 128
Windows function prototypes, 364

windows.h, 361
Windows initialization, 358
Windows parameters, 372
Windows template, 357
WIN.IN1, 463
WinMain(), 357
WinMain parameters, 362
WM_DESTROY, 380
WM_PAINT, 372
WM_QUIT, 368
WNDCLASS, structure, 375
Word, 5
WRDOT():
   assembler, 248
   C, 69
Write I/O option, 54

X

xarray—diskrd(), 353
xarray—diskwt(), 349